Bishops under Threat

Arbeiten zur Kirchengeschichte

Founded by
Karl Holl † and Hans Lietzmann †

Edited by
Christian Albrecht, Christoph Markschies
and Christopher Ocker

Volume 150

Bishops under Threat

Contexts and Episcopal Strategies in the
Late Antique and Early Medieval West

Edited by
Sabine Panzram and Pablo Poveda Arias

DE GRUYTER

ISBN 978-3-11-162241-5
e-ISBN (PDF) 978-3-11-077864-9
e-ISBN (EPUB) 978-3-11-077872-4
ISSN 1861-5996

Library of Congress Control Number: 2022950786

Bibliographic information published by the Deutsche Nationalbibliothek
The Deutsche Nationalbibliothek lists this publication in the Deutsche Nationalbibliografie; detailed bibliographic data are available on the Internet at http://dnb.dnb.de.

© 2024 Walter de Gruyter GmbH, Berlin/Boston
This volume is text- and page-identical with the hardback published in 2023.

www.degruyter.com

Preface and Acknowledgements

The murder of sovereigns and secular aristocrats, conspiracies or revolts that challenge the existing world order, have long been identified as general factors of political instability in the centuries between Late Antiquity and the Early Middle Ages. Yet it is only in recent years that researchers have begun to focus on the fact that bishops were exposed to structurally similar threats, because the institutionalisation and expansion of ecclesiastical power threatened the interests of others. These threats against ecclesiastical office holders were in fact – dependent on context – multifaceted and could lead in extremity to murder, at times so common that Paul Fouracre, in his pivotal 2003 study, asked "Why were so many bishops killed in Merovingian Francia?"

The idea of using the form of an international conference to systematically study the phenomenon of "threatened bishops" in successor states that established themselves after the respective regions' separation from the imperial federation in Gaul and Hispania, but also in the Alp regions, Britannia, and the Apennin Peninsula, can be attributed to Pablo Poveda Arias (Univ. Valladolid), who worked from April 2020 to September 2021 at the Center for Advanced Studies "RomanIslam – Center for Comparative Empire and Transcultural Studies" as a research associate. I took up his suggestion with pleasure, and we attempted not just to present the current state of research, but also to highlight the new knowledge that social-scientific studies – on topics such as conflict and competition – could provide. We aimed, on the one hand, to fathom the sphere for agency and the limits to episcopal power; on the other, we wanted to capture more precisely the individuality of specific bishops, whose actions were guided not just by the good of their parish but also by personal and family interests.

Because of the Coronavirus pandemic, the conference – which was originally supposed to have been held in Hamburg's Warburg House from 25 to 27 July 2020 – had to be postponed until 24 to 26 June 2021 and to take place virtually. Despite this less-than-ideal format for academic exchange, colleagues from ancient and medieval history, as well as philology – from Germany, Italy, France, Poland, Spain, the UK and the USA – vigorously discussed case studies from the 4th to the 9th century. These were only rarely concerned with episcopal murder as an extreme tool of conflict resolution and more often addressing subjects such as: the precarious position of metropolitan bishops in Gaul and Hispania, threatened by their colleagues, the *dux* or the king; the fashion in which the Carolingian bishops of Verona and Milan instrumentalised saints, relics and hagiographies as threats to enhance their competing claims to ecclesiastical precedence; or one of the deepest consequences, the threat to one's personal existence – exile, as the epigraphic monuments of the Appenin Peninsula from the 3rd to the early 7th century document in this case.

The present volume combines the contributions from the Hamburg conference in a revised version. The texts, which reflect the diversity of research questions and the different scholarly approaches, have been editorially revised; the responsibility for their content remains with the authors. The editors have the pleasant duty of thanking: the Fritz Thyssen Stiftung for its financing; the conference participants for their lively and provocative discussions; Kevin Grotherr (Hamburg) for his careful and tireless help in preparing the manuscript for print and for creating the register; Florian Klein (Hamburg), who has once again offered constructive criticism; Timothy Wardell (Hopewell, New Jersey) for additional language assistance; the anonymous reviewers for their constructive criticism, which has doubtlessly improved both the individual contributions and this volume as a whole; and last, but not least, Dr. Albrecht Döhnert (Berlin) at De Gruyter for including this work in the series of *Arbeiten zur Kirchengeschichte*.

Sabine Panzram
Hamburg, Autumn 2022

Table of Contents

Abbreviations —— IX

Sabine Panzram
Bishops Under Threat – Between Ascetics and "Combative Creatures" —— 1

Part One: **Threatening Episcopal Authority: Jurisdiction and Territory**

Pablo Poveda Arias
Threatening Metropolitan Authority in Fifth-Century Gaul —— 27

Kevin Grotherr
Between Royal Power and Legitimacy – The Bishops of Mérida (6th–7th c.) —— 55

Charles Mériaux
Bishops under Pressure: Priests and Episcopal Authority in Carolingian Francia —— 81

Katy Cubitt
Episcopal Authority and Diocesan Structure in England (c. 650–1050) —— 95

Katharina Winckler
Suspicious Minds: Bishops without Seat and Canonical Bishops in Eighth-Century Bavaria —— 115

Julio Escalona
The Tenth-Century Castilian Church in the Wider Iberian Context: The Large Gap between Ideal and Reality —— 139

Part Two: **Bishops and Politics**

Ian Wood
Burgundians and Bishops —— 167

Marco Cristini
Sailing to Byzantium: Sixth-Century Popes under Threat in Constantinople —— 183

Bruno Dumézil
Victims, Actors or Spectators? The Bishops of the Merovingian Kingdom during the Civil War of 575–613 —— 205

Francesco Veronese
Bishops, Relics and Multi-Directional Pressures in Carolingian Northern Italy: The Cases of Verona and Milan —— 217

Part Three: **Individualising Threats and Strategies**

Isabelle Mossong
Italy's Late Antique Bishops in Exile (3rd–Beginning of 7th c.): The Epigraphic Point of View —— 247

Martin Horst
Bishops between Reform and Heresy: Priscillian, Martin of Tours and Magnus Maximus —— 267

Margarita Vallejo Girvés
Bishop Licinianus of Carthago Spartaria, The Monastery of Asán and the Struggle between Visigoths and Byzantines —— 285

Pablo C. Díaz
Dumio-Braga. A Functional Duality, a Legal Anomaly —— 301

List of Contributors —— 329

Index of Places, Names and Subjects —— 333

Abbreviations

CIL	*Corpus Inscriptionum Latinarum.* Berlin 1863–.
ICI	*Inscriptiones Christianae Italiae.* Bari 1985–.
ICUR n.s.	*Inscriptiones Christianae Urbis Romae,* novae series. Rome 1922–.
ILCV	*Inscriptiones Latinae Christianae Veteres:* Ernst Diehl, ed. 1925–1931. Berlin: Weidmann.
Lib. pontif.	*Liber pontificalis:* Louis Duchesne, ed. 1886–1892. Paris: Thorin.
PLRE	Jones, Arnold Hugh Martin, John Robert Martindale, and John Morris. 1971–1992. *The Prosopography of the Later Roman Empire: Volume I–III.* Cambridge: Cambridge University Press.
PCBE 1	Mandouze, André, and Anne Marie LaBonnardière, eds. 1982. *Prosopographie chrétienne du Bas-Empire (PCBE).* Vol. 1, *Prosopographie de l'Afrique chrétienne (303–533).* Paris: Éd. du Centre National de la Recherche Scientifique.
PCBE 2	Pietri, Charles, and Luce Pietri, eds. 1999–2000. *Prosopographie chrétienne du Bas-Empire (PCBE).* Vol. 2, *Prosopographie de l'Italie chrétienne (313–604).* 2 Vols. Rome: Association des amis du Centre d'histoire et civilisation de Byzance.
PCBE 4	Pietri, Luce, and Marc Heijmans, eds. 2013. *Prosopographie chrétienne du Bas-Empire (PCBE).* Vol. 4, *Prosopographie de la Gaule chrétienne (314–614).* Paris: Association des amis du Centre d'histoire et civilisation de Byzance.

Sabine Panzram
Bishops Under Threat – Between Ascetics and "Combative Creatures"

The idea of an episcopal office was ambiguous from early on. Epitaphs celebrate office holders such as Hilarius of Arles (~429/430~449) in hexameters as someone whose every action was guided by Christ, who relinquished his property out of a love of poverty and toiled with his own hands to support the unfortunate.[1] They praise him as the magister not just of his parish, but of Christianity as a whole, and underline the obedience and especially the humility with which he conducted his office. Thanks to his manifold merits, they claim that he had earned entry to paradise, which he could enjoy in its full glory. Nicetius of Lyon's (~552/553~573) epitaph, too, casts him as an ascetic who lived a life for God alone: exemplary in his adherence to his *castitas*, his practice of *caritas* towards the people and clergy, as well as his fatherly care towards his parish and all those in need.[2] He also excelled in ecclesiastical music and acted as a judge who sought

---

[1] Le Blant 1865, no. 516/pp. 253–254; CIL XII 949b; ILCV 1062b: *Antistes domini, qui p[aupertatis] amorem / praeponens auro rapuit c[aelesti]a regna, / Hilarius, cui palma o[b]itus e[t viv]ere Xps, / contemnens fragilem ter[ren]i corporis usum / hic carnis spolium liquit a[d] astra volans. / sprevit opes, dum quaerit opes mortalia mu[t]ans / perpetuis, caelum donis terrestribus emit. / gemma sacerdotum plebisque orbisque magister, / rustica quin etiam pro Xpo [mu]nia sumens, / servile obsequium [non] dedignatus adire / officio vixit minimus et culmine summus. / nec mirum si post haec meruit tua limina, Xpe, / angelicasque domos intravit et aurea regna / divitias, paradise, tuas, flagrantia semper / gramina et halantes divinis floribus hortos / subiectasque videt nubes et sidera caeli.* See also the image in Biarne 2013. – This contribution evolved in the framework of the Center for Advanced Study "RomanIslam – Center for Comparative Empire and Transcultural Studies", funded by the German Research Foundation (Deutsche Forschungsgemeinschaft, DFG), at Universität Hamburg.

[2] Le Blant 1856, no. 25/pp. 57–60; CIL XIII 2400; ILCV 1073: *ecce Sacerdotis tenuit qui iura sacerdus, / quo recubat tumulo nomine Nicecius. / urbs Lugdune, tuum rexit per tempora clerum / ecclesiamque dei cordis amore colens / quique Sacerdotis f(a)ctus bis proximus eris / sanguine coniunctu(s), culmine, sede simul, / vir bonus, indultus cunctis famulisque benignus / [...] verbere quisque suo, / mansuetus patiens mitis venerabilis aptus, / pauperibus promptus simplicibusque pius. / psallere precipue normamque tenere canendi / primus et alterutrum (t)e(n)dere voce chorum, / noxia te(m)nendi vitans discrimina mundi, / inque dei solum vivere nuvit opus. / sic vigil ac sobrius, sic castus carnis ubique, / quo nichil in clero dulcius esse potest, / causarum sprevit strepitus vanosque furores / et simplex mundo, sed sapiens domino / iura potestatum verbi terrore cohercens, iurgia despiciens sus(p)i(c)iensque deum, / sic erectus simul mitis pietate serenus / transiit innocuus, regna superna tenet. / huc iam prima patet calcatis +pores dimittis, / iam paradisiacas possidet aptus opes. / obiit IIII non. Aprilis (anno) XXXIII post Iustinum et indict. sexta.*

to avoid trials. In short he was a man marked by mildness, goodness, *pietas* and serenity. John of Tarragona (~469/470~519/520), who held his office for 50 years, was defined by both his humility and his brilliant eloquence, by the *pietas* that complimented his care for the poor, had lived the life of a saint, leader and teacher to monks and to people alike.[3] His successor Sergius (~519/520~554/555) served as bishop of Tarragona for 35 years, restored the church roof and built a monastery close to the city.[4] Epitaphs describe him as a father to the poor and a guardian to those in need of protection. He gave comfort to the widowed, freed the imprisoned and provided the hungry with food. Loved by all, the epitome of benevolence, he is held as giving succour to the needy.

Hagiographic transmissions – Honoratus of Marseille concretely in the case of Hilarius of Arles (401–449) – paint a picture of a vigorous shepherd who knew how to combine both his monastic and ascetic tendencies with the requirements of the episcopal office: who founded a monastery in the episcopal centre of the city and ordered the construction of churches; who lived as a model of poverty and chastity; who worked with his own hands; someone who knotted nets and gave dictations while reading.[5] His biographer claims that he championed the poor, the sick and the orphaned, and sold expensive altarpieces to buy the freedom of prisoners. A tireless and verbally adept preacher, he knew both how to capture and reprimand his audience; when needed, he would place himself before his parish, a guardian, and once even expelled the praetorian prefect from church for refusing to rescind an exceptional tax. Meanwhile, in the case of Masona of Merida (~573~606), we are presented with the image of a bishop who acted as the spiritual leader and worldly patron of his parish members – who forgave debts, gifted wine, oil and honey and

---

[3] CIL II²/14, 2086: *Te Ioanne(m) Tarraco coluit mirificu(m) vatem / tuosq(ue) in hoc loco in pace co(n)didit artus. / In te libra mor(u)m, in te modestia tenuit regnum, / nitens eloquio mitissimus pollebas in corde, / gerens curam pauper(um) pietate pr(a)editus ampla. / S(an)c(tu)s namq(ue) vita, fide magnificent<i>us ipse / <ap>paruisti cunctis per{a}gens ad pr(a)emia Xp(ist)i. / Tuum nempe nomen tuamq(ue) dulcissima(m) mente(m) / laudabunt posteri, nu(m)quam abolenda p(er) (a)evu(m) / merita, pr(a)econiis adtollunt facta p(er) s(ae)clis (!). / denis (a)equo libram<ine minuan>tibus (?) lustris / rector doctorq(ue) pr(a)efuisti monacis et populis, / octiens denos vita p(er)agens feliciter annos.*
[4] CIL II²/14, 2087: *Sollers magnanimus pius ingenio cato / hic quiescit in tumulo Sergi(u)s pontifex s(an)c(tu)s, / qui sacri labentia restaurans culmina templi / haud procul ab urbe construxit cenobium s(an)c(t)is. / Pauperes patrem hunc tutore(m) hab<u>ere pupilli. / Viduas (!) solamen captibis (!) pretium, / esuriens repperit alimentum. / Profluus in acrimis depulit contagia carnis, / cunctis carissimus, exuberanti gratia polle(n)s, / parcus in abundantia, locuplex (!) egentibus, vixit / septies denos pr(a)esentis (a)evi peragens annos. / Tria sacer pontifex pariterq(ue) septena / religiosae vit(a)e explevit tempor{a}<e> lustra.*
[5] Jacob and Cavallin 1995.

built churches and monasteries.⁶ The *Vitas Sanctorum Patrum Emeretensium*, by an anonymous author, relates the celebration of the Holy Mass, the Easter processions, the adventus of the bishop; it tells of believers who pray, sing and acclaim; of the poor and the sick, of widows and orphans and pilgrims who are healed and cared for; of a bishop who with varying success rushes into conflicts about his bistum's reliquaries and, thanks to St. Eulalia's support, ultimately triumphs against the secular power.

These snapshots from grave inscriptions and hagiographic transmissions in Gaul and Hispania, among other regions of the former Roman Empire, evoke an image of the bishop of Late Antiquity and the Early Middle Ages that paints the episcopal office as powerful, ranking alongside the rulers and secular aristocrats.⁷ At first glance, the bishops seem far from *under threat*. They act as ascetics who pass up the temptations of the material world – riches and positions of honour – and centre their lives around a rigid, absolute emulation of Christ. As their accomplishments and merits determine the degree of their *sanctitas*, they can rest secure in the certainty of paradise if they distinguish themselves accordingly: in the early 5th century principally by giving up property and performing demeaning physical labour, as characterises the *homo pauper* who must earn his daily bread; to this is added charity to the poor, through the officially mandated duty of care towards all in need but also through voluntary donation of own's personal riches.⁸ Obedience, possibly as a tenet of a previously monastic life, and humility in conducting the episcopal office count as relevant criteria as well. By the late 6th century, the radical abdication of property is no longer necessary, with bishops allowed to preserve private title to their assets; *humilitas*, too, is no longer accounted a core virtue, with repercussions for aspects such as clothing and dining, previously marked by plainness and simplicity. Office holders acted as building contractors, served as judges and stood up to secular powers when they deemed their communities in danger. In any case, following an ascetic ideal (which transformed over time), exercising a duty of care towards the clergy and *plebs* (modelled on the *caritas* of Christ) and showing devotion to those under the *pater ecclesiae*'s charge remained decisive spheres of activity.

The epitaphs thus offer a one-sided depiction of the respective bishop as an ascetic of his time, unrelated to the sometimes senatorial origins of the office holder. They refrain from biographic schemes and name neither the ancestry nor family relationships, official functions or political activities. And even when they do –

---

6 Maya Sánchez 1992.
7 See e.g., Beaujard 1996; Jussen 1998. – Pérez Martínez 2012; Muñoz Melgar 2022 and the respective compendium depictions of both regions: Pietri 2001; Fontaine 2001.
8 On this, see Heinzelmann 1976, esp. 73–94. 152–174; Krön 1997; Hartmann 2006.

listing virtues and titles, with the highest ecclesiastical office topping off a *cursus honorum* – as in the case of Sacerdos of Lyon (~541~551/552), who surely came from a patrician family and probably served as *consilarius* to the Burgundian kings, perhaps even leading the king's council before he became bishop of Lyon[9] – they do not mention direct connections to fundamental deeds, office and honours.[10] Recipients had to draw this connection themselves – an easily accomplishable task, however, thanks to the equivalencies between virtues and characteristics with specific activities and dignities. Indeed, the context in which epigraphic monuments were erected – as a tablet attached above the burial site or very close to the sarcophagus if it rested in the church itself or in its crypts (in the case of Hilarius in those of the crypta of the *basilica sancti Genesii* in the Arlesian necropolis Aliscamps) – meant that it would be understood principally by those already aware of its existence. Yet both the epitaphs and the hagiographic transmissions are incredibly subtle literary accounts that presupposed a high level of literary understanding. For although the episcopal vita offers a time-bound relation of a bishop's stages of life, it links these with a temporally independent description of his characteristics.[11] By interweaving historically verifiable and theologically believed truth, the author could use his vita to offer seeming proof that both were in accord. Sometimes, the epitaph and episcopal vita complemented each other. Apart from the fact that the respective author must have been aware of the bishop's grave inscription, one can assume that the vita would have been read aloud during mass – e.g., on the bishop's death day – in the respective church. Monks, too, may have given readings during meal times and assemblies in chapter houses, thus spreading them amongst laypeople and clerics alike: just about anyone must have been able to appreciate significant quotes from the Bible and the Apocrypha, but clever references would have reached only those who had gone through a comparative spiritual education.[12]

At any rate, the humility and disdain for the secular world these two genres propagated came at no cost to the bishops' official functions and political activities.

---

9 Le Blant 1856, no. 24/pp. 55–57; CIL XIII 2398; ILCV 1072: *Nomine mente fide meritis pietate Sacerdus / officio cultu precio corde gradu / dogmate consilio sensu probitate vigore / stemate censura religione cluens, / gaudia cunctorum rapiens, lamenta reliquens / arcobus hic clausus laudibus ampla tenens, / patriciumque decus erexit culmine morum: / sic partos fasces fortia corda levant. / magnum namque bonum caelesti munire perstat: / corpora cum desint, inclita gesta manent. / pignoris annixus latiri: huc sorte suprema, / sanguine quos vita, sumire iuncxit amor. / cuius quanta viri mundo sapientia fulsit, / venturi saecli gloria testis erit. / qui vixit in amore et temore di annis LXV, obiit III idus Septembris / [XII] post consol(a)tum Iustini viri clarrisimi consolis indic. Prima.*
10 On this see Heinzelmann 1976, esp. 73–94. 152–174; Scherließ 2000, esp. 99–110.
11 Coué 1997; Haarländer 2000, esp. 1–28; Berschin ²2020, 241–266.
12 On this see Van Uytfanghe 2001.

These come into play when one takes into account their supra-regional agency and its consequences, which can be parsed from texts such as correspondence with Rome or with fellow brothers, as well as in the acts of diverse councils. Herein, Hilarius of Arles shines as a self-confident successor of his office's predecessor Patroclus: Zosimus of Rome not only granted him metropolitan rights over other provinces, but also appointed him the papal vicar for all of Gaul.[13] Hilarius convened and chaired councils – 439 in Riez, 441 in Orange and 442 in Vaison[14] – whose professed aim was to strengthen the general ecclesiastical discipline. The circle of participants grew each time, thus demonstrating his growing influence, but Hilarius's rigorous approach to implementing his reform programmes and to dismissing bishops – and his willingness to resort to violence – accrued him opposition: those in other parts of Gaul viewed his actions as excessive;[15] in Rome, Zosimus's successors – Bonifacius and Coelestin – had already revoked the bishop of Arles's authority as vicar of the apostolic chair for Gaul.[16] Scandal erupted when Hilarius joined with Germanus of Auxerre to take on the case of Chelidonius, the bishop of Besançon,[17] who had been accused of marriage to a widow – bishops were only allowed to wed virgins – and of passing death sentences and thus intervening in secular jurisdiction.[18] The council Hilarius convened concluded that the accusations were justified, stripping Chelidonius of his office, who immediately set out for Rome and in 445 registered his objection with Leo the Great. Hilarius, expecting an endorsement of his decision, made the journey as well, but was disappointed: Leo found that the proceedings had been conducted without sufficient evidence and with the use of armed force, concluding that the accusations were untenable, rehabilitated Chelidonius and certified his official appointment.[19] He also accused Hilarius of displaying insufficient humility and blatant disobedience in his behaviour in Rome. This case repeated itself: Bishop Proiectus,[20] stripped of his office by Hilarius for reasons of infirmity, also registered an objection with Leo.

---

13 *PCBE* 4, s.v. Patroclus 2, 1437–1440; *JK* 328 = *J³* 732 (22 March 417, *Placuit apostolicae sedi*); *MGH Ep.* 3, *Collectio Arelatensis* 1, 5–6.
14 *PCBE* 4, s.v. Hilarius 3, 998–1007; Munier 1963, *Concilium Regense* (Riez), 18 November 439, 61–75, subscriptions: 71–72; *Concilium Arausicanum* (Orange), 8 November 441, 76–93, subscriptions: 87–90; *Concilium Vasense* (Vaison), 23 November 442, 94–104, subscriptions: 102.
15 *Vitae Patrum Iurensium* 18.
16 *JK* 349 = *J³* 783 (13 June 419, *Valentinae nos clerici*); *JK* 362 = *J³* 790 (9 February 422, *Difficile quidem fidem*); *JK* 369 = *J³* 821 (26 July 428, *Cuperemus quidem de*).
17 *PCBE* 4, s.v. Germanus 1, 878–883; *PCBE* 4, s.v. Chelidonius, 464–465.
18 Honoratus Massiliensis, *Vita s. Hilarii Arelatensis* 21–22; *JK* 407 = *J³* 911 (445 in.-aet., *Divinae cultum religionis*) = Leo M. epist. 10, PL 54, 628–636, cf. *J³* *910.
19 Langgärtner 1964, 61–79; Mathisen 1989, 145–172; Heinzelmann 1992; Heijmans and Pietri 2009.
20 *PCBE* 4, s.v. Proiectus 1, 1548.

He, too, was vindicated. After all, the episcopal chair was only considered vacant upon its occupant's death. The pope's judgement of Hilarius was severe: He was forbidden from convening councils and undertaking episcopal consecrations. He did not lose his office, but his status as a metropolitan was revoked and his influence restricted to Arles. Pope Leo also sought imperial support of his decision. Valentinian III accordingly sent an edict not just to the *magister militum* Aëtius, but also to the Gallic bishops,[21] many of whom continued to hold Hilarius in high esteem despite recent events. After fleeing home from Rome, Hilarius's attempts to right things with Leo failed; even the intervention of Gaul's former prefect Auxilarius bore no fruit. Leo proved implacable, and Hilarius died only four years later. His was not an unique case. Rusticus, too, who held the episcopal office of Narbonne for three decades (427–458) and was responsible for various ecclesiastical constructions in the city and its surroundings,[22] went to Rome for advice – that is, approval of his decisions. He asked Leo about a conflict with two of his priests: striving to preserve the virtue of chastity, these men, Sabinianus and Leo, had inflicted what he considered excessive punishment on a believer who had committed adultery.[23] In any case, Rusticus used this event to consult the pope in a total of 19 cases and received answers marked by leniency. Yet he apparently could not resist the temptation to look out for the interests of those close to him, and influenced the episcopal election in Béziers by suggesting that the local clergy and parish choose his own archdeacon Hermes.[24] The parish rejected the new bishop and when Rusticus wanted to lay down his episcopal office and pass it to Hermes, Leo rejected the plan. After Rusticus's death, Hermes seized the episcopal chair of Narbonne by his own initiative (between 462 and 466?), driving the Gallic bishops to turn to Pope Hilarius,[25] who condemned this procedure as *iniquissima usurpatio*.[26] A council decision ultimately allowed Hermes to remain in office,[27] yet stripped him of the right to ordain bishops. Only after his death would the Church of Narbonne regain this privilege.

---

[21] *Constitutio Valentini Augusti*, apud Leo M. epist. 11, PL 54, 636–640.
[22] *PCBE* 4, s.v. Rusticus 3, 1657–1663. – Marrou 1970, here 332–340; Dellong 2002, 423–424; Riess 2016, 80–129.
[23] *JK* 544 = *J*³ 1098 (458–459, *Epistolas fraternitatis tuae*); ep. 167 = PL 54, 1199–1209.
[24] *PCBE* 4, s.v. Hermes, 980–981. *JK* 555 = *J*³ 1128 (3 December 462, *Quamquam notitiam dilectonis*); *MGH Ep.* 3, Collectio Arelatensis 18, 24–25.
[25] *JK* 559 = *J*³ 1135 (after 25 February 464, *Etsi meminerimus fraternitatem*); *MGH Ep.* 3, Collectio Arelatensis 20, 29–30.
[26] *JK* 554 = *J*³ 1126 (3 November 462, *Miramur fraternitatem tuam*); *MGH Ep.* 3, Collectio Arelatensis 15, 22–23.
[27] *JK* 555 = *J*³ 1128 (3 December 462, *Quamquam notitiam dilectonis*); *MGH Ep.* 3, Collectio Arelatensis 18, 25–28.

When it came to the use of Rome as a court of appeal, the bishops of the Iberian Peninsula in no way lagged behind their Gallic colleagues. Ascanius, the metropolitan of Tarraconensis,[28] had turned to Hilarius of Rome (461–468) claiming that the bishop of Calagurris (Calahorra), a certain Silvanus, had performed ordinations in violation of the fathers' guidelines and papal policies.[29] Upon receiving no answer, he wrote again and at the same time asked Hilarius to confirm the succession of Iraeneus to the episcopal chair of Barcino (Barcelona); his predecessor Nundiarius had appointed him in his will and also bequeathed him his entire fortune.[30] The pope, who had also received letters from a string of landowners,[31] addressed these (undated) concerns on 19 November 465 at a synode in Santa Maria Maggiore in Rome.[32] In the end, he decided to show leniency on the matter of the ordinations – the illegitimately consecrated bishops were allowed to stay in office – but insisted that in future no one should be ordained bishop without the metropolitan's knowledge and permission. Yet he also railed that the episcopal office was a god-given gift and not property to be willed away: he thus ordered that Irenaeus return from his episcopal see and that Barcino was to select a bishop from the local clergy. Ascanius was to bear full responsibility for the selection and consecration of a new candidate. The pope had his subdeacon Traianus deliver these decretals and one more, directed to Ascanius alone,[33] so that – as he stresses – everything he had set out might be implemented.[34] It is exceedingly dubious whether his efforts were successful and that he could actually control the realisation of his demands, for neither the number of letters sent to Rome nor the number of decretals sent from Rome decreased. Alongside these, it is especially council records that offer insight into the agency of both threatened and threatening bishops. The councils' strict organisation and sacral-liturgical character could not always prevent procedural errors and corruption that let the Holy Ghost himself seem

---

[28] Panzram 2020; cf. Pérez Martínez 2012, esp. 439–445.
[29] Knie, Panzram, et al. 2022, no. 42 = J^3 1136; Thiel 1867–1868, no. 13; Martín-Iglesias, Díaz, and Vallejo Girvés 2020, 261–262.
[30] Knie and Panzram 2022, no. 43 = J^3 1137; Thiel 1867–1868, no. 14; Martín-Iglesias, Díaz, and Vallejo Girvés 2020, 263–264.
[31] Knie and Panzram 2022, no. *45.
[32] Knie and Panzram 2022, no. 44 = JK I 76 = J^3 1138; Thiel 1867–1868, no. 15; Martín-Iglesias, Díaz, and Vallejo Girvés 2020, 264–270. – *Acta Concilii Romani* a. 465, 7, 959–965 (= Mansi ²1901).
[33] Knie and Panzram 2022, no. 46 = JK 560 = J^3 1139 (30 December 465, *Postquam litteras vestrae*); Thiel 1867–1868, no. 16; Martín-Iglesias, Díaz, and Vallejo Girvés 2020, 270–273. – Knie and Panzram 2022, no. 47 = JK 561 = J^3 1140 (465, *Divinae circa nos*); Thiel 1867–1868, no. 17; Martín-Iglesias, Díaz, and Vallejo Girvés 2020, 273–275.
[34] *PCBE* 2, s.v. Traianus 2, 2209–2210; *Epistulae pontificis Hilari* 2.3; 2.5. Larranaga Elorza 1989; Panzram 2018; Ferreiro 2020, 117–125.

under undue influence; this can be seen in the case in piont of Martianus of Écija, whose series of missteps at the third provincial council of Seville (between 622 and 624), chaired by Isidore, cost him his office.[35] The episcopal chair passed to Aventius, his accuser – yet the decision was not unanimous. When Martianus appealed for reexamination of the case at the Fourth Council of Toledo (633), Isidore rejected his demand for want of time. It was only after Isidore's death that Martianius's renewed appeal at the Sixth Council of Toledo (638) met with success: Aventius' accusations proved false, having even induced witnesses to give false testimony. Martianus, who had obviously fallen victim to factional struggles in Écija, could return to his office. Isidore's role, whose intervention changed a factional episode into a matter of Church government, becomes even more dubious in light of the preservation of the records of the Third Council of Seville: when the bishops in Toledo wanted to consult the documents in 636, they had disappeared.

Once they had dared to enter the field of politics, bishops clearly became "combative creatures".[36] Hilarius offers the clearest example of both facets – that of ascetic bishop and of combative creature – as he appears in all genres of transmitted texts, from the epitaph and hagiography to letters and council records, as well as in sermons he composed. This Gallic-Roman aristocrat, whose background had afforded him a classical, literary education but who had renounced a secular career after his conversion, moved into the monastery of Lérins. He does not seem to have sought the office of a metropolitan of Arles from any power-political ambitions – it apparently requires a miracle to convince the fleeing man to accept episcopal honours.[37] His ascetic way of life, which he preserved in this new function through waking, fasting, praying and exercising penance and humility, as well as his physical labour, were held to be extraordinary.[38] The reputation he gained through this conscious denial of his originally high social status was enhanced by his vigorous sermon work, which his biographer praises more highly than that of Augustinus.[39] Analysing the *Sermo de vita Honorati*, Carsten Scherließ has recently shown just how adept Hilarius was at creatively using his classical education to give "eine überaus sorgfältig gestaltete panegyrische Rede mit exhortativ-paränetischen, au-

---

35 Martín-Iglesias 2018 has now presented an edition of this text; on this, see Stocking 1997; Martin 2003, here 124–125 and 200; Castillo Maldonado 2007.
36 Natal Villazala and Wood 2016.
37 Honoratus Massiliensis, *Vita s. Hilarii Arelatensis* 9. On how strongly this flight should be considered a literary trope, see König 2008, 206; Scherließ 2000, 100–101.
38 Honoratus Massiliensis, *Vita s. Hilarii Arelatensis:* waking, fasting, praying and exercising penance and humility 7,5–14; 10,21–25; 11,2–9; 18,10–14; 19,1–7; 25–26; simple clothing (Tunika and *cilicium*) 11; 18; physical labour 11; 15, so also Gennadius, *De viris illustribus* 70.
39 Honoratus Massiliensis, *Vita s. Hilarii Arelatensis* 14.1–39; esp. 14.24–28.

tobiographischen und apologetischen Zügen", thus understanding how to use his rhetorical skills to realise political goals.[40] Indeed, he was a bishop deeply and ambitiously engaged with Church politics, one who enjoyed a high esteem and nurtured good relationships with the leading personalities of his time (such as the praetorian prefect[41]). This is shown by the synodal activities required after 439, the discussion and regulation of problems spanning Church provinces at the councils of Riez, Orange and Vaison. And it is shown in his disputes with Leo, which resulted from his demand to hold a position of authority in southeastern Gaul and the reactions of the pope, who not only sought to win the Gallic bishops to his side but also secured imperial support. While research traditionally postulates that Hilarius' of Arles office all but forced him into the "politische Kräftespiel", yet that his behaviour showed no trace of "eine grobe Entgleisung oder schlankwegs Verweltlichung",[42] more recent research has shifted to claiming that he was concerned with consolidating his position and realising his own goals.[43]

The contributions gathered in this volume intend to show that the bishops of Late Antiquity and the Early Middle Ages were genuinely "combative creatures". Indeed, they broke the peace as often as they attempted to keep it. As they sought at first to strategically position themselves and then improve that position, they found themselves in permanent competition: quarrels and conflict were their daily fare, and threats were thus bound to follow. Choosing to enter into conflict carried risks: they could always spin out of control, as the case of Hilarius so vividly demonstrates. Yet this in no way held the bishops back – "to play with fire" was their modus operandi.[44]

1 Historiographical Background, Current Perspectives

Previous researches of antique and early medieval provenance, which can be addressed only cursorily here, have primarily focused on the bishops as exponents of a new form of sovereignty, one that in a time of political-social realignment and disorientation, lacking an efficient supra-local power, established itself as a politi-

---

40 Scherließ 2000, 111–165, here 165.
41 Leo M. epist. 10, PL 54, 633.
42 Prinz 1974, here 15.
43 Scherließ 2000, 165.
44 Thus the fitting title of Natal Villazala and Wood's article 2016: "Playing with Fire. Conflicting Bishops in Late Roman Spain and Gaul".

cal-religious local rule, the so-called episcopal rule.⁴⁵ On the one hand, they argue that the bishops attained secular sovereignty by taking influential roles in politics, being active in the judiciary, and even engaging in the military defense of their cities – that is, filling the vacuum of an increasingly brittle civil administration and adopting basic protective functions.⁴⁶ On the other hand, they postulate that the bishops exercised these sovereign rights more or less on behalf of the central political power, and had been doing so since the Constantinian shift.⁴⁷ A series of regional⁴⁸ and local studies⁴⁹ allow a comparison between the form of the episcopal office and the profile of its office holders in the former imperial territories, with clearly defined case studies allowing similarities and differences to appear as a first step. In a second step, they allow researchers to reject generalising explanations – that is, ones rooted in analogous reasoning. Over the past 50 years, this has produced a wealth of studies on varying topics: on the social function of the martyr and reliquary cult, which the bishop could use to widen his authority,⁵⁰ but also on the question of the financial arrangements of the episcopal sees, which in turn implies the topic of the bishop's personal riches and how much the one can be untangled from the other.⁵¹ The bishop took on other civil functions alongside his role in the judiciary,⁵² in fields such as municipal administration and accounting.⁵³ Episcopal patronage could also extend to the surroundings or backcountry of one's episcopal see⁵⁴ to forge far-reaching social networks.⁵⁵ These relationships prove significant for episcopal elections on the one hand⁵⁶ and relations with secular power on the other.⁵⁷

Since the 1990s, when a young and dynamic research field established itself at the junction of Late Antiquity and the Early Middle Ages, open to new develop-

---

45 A detailed overview of previous research is given by Diefenbach 2013; see also Brown 1992; Rapp 2005.
46 So e.g. Prinz 1988, here 5–7; Anton 1996, esp. 463–464; Liebeschuetz 2001, 137–168.
47 Representatively Heinzelmann 1988, 23–82; Brown 1992, 71–117; Durliat 1996, 273–286.
48 Magnou-Nortier 1974; Gauthier 1980; Bührer-Thierry 1997; Jorge 2002; Ubric Rabaneda 2004; Nimmegeers 2014.
49 Pietri 1983; Anton 1987; Pérez Martínez 2012.
50 Brown 1981; Castellanos García 1998; Beaujard 2000.
51 Díaz 1995; Brown 2012; Destefanis 2013.
52 Cimma 1989; Fernández Ortiz de Guinea 1996.
53 Durliat 1979; Mor 1979; Pérez Martínez 2000.
54 Wood 1983; Lepelley 1998; Esders 2010; Halfond 2019.
55 Gauthier 2000; Cvetkovic, Gemeinhardt, and Bodin 2019.
56 Norton 2007; Leemans, Van Nuffelen, Keough, and Nicolaye 2011, 127–143.
57 Claude 1971; Prinz 1971; Collins 1980; Hagen 1995; Moore 2011; Halfond 2012; Chavarría Arnau 2018.

ments internationally in which ancient historians and medievalists cooperate fruitfully with representatives of other subjects – such as archaeologies and classical philologies, patristics and ecclesiastical history, Byzantine or Islamic studies, also social sciences and anthropology – thereby adopting a rigorously interdisciplinary approach, the classical studies debate has likewise profited from new approaches, questions and methods. On the one hand, this has allowed voices prominence to critically question aspects of the conception of episcopal rule, or even the concept itself, arguing for example that the power-political monopoly of bishops in the Gallic *civitates* was an illusion, that the majority was not prosopographically recruited from the aristocracy and that the emperor and empire – as Mischa Meier resolutely claims – continued to wield influence.[58] On the other hand, the topic of violence took on a central role, manifesting since the Early Middle Ages in the form of feuds, rebellions and resistance to the monarchy. Inspired by Anglo-American researches, the medievalist Gerd Althoff in particular argued that the underlying conflicts cannot be adequately judged with approaches from judicial history, but require social-scientific and cultural historical questions.[59] On this basis, conflicts could be understood as changes to a mesh of social relationships; from a cultural historical perspective, rituals, gestures and ceremonies gained significance.[60] This perspective was first applied to topics around statehood, and with time the bishops, episcopal office and the Church as an institution also became the subject of conflict research. The themes encompassed "episcopal murder",[61] the arrest and exile of bishops[62] and their function as city defenders, but also the violently tinged role they adopted within ecclesiastical disputes.[63] Due to the allocation and assignment of territory to the individual episcopal sees, the dioceses' genesis also turned out to be a permanent latent source of conflict.[64] The lists of bishops proved to be a means of competition between individual cities; the older and more intact they were – some could be traced back to the apostles themselves – the more symbolic capital the respective episcopal sees had at their disposal.[65] In any case, the idea of rivalry and competition under Christian portents subsequently proved fundamental: their exposed positions placed the bishops into constant competition – assuming office brought power, but it also brought

---

58 Patzold 2010; Meier 2019, esp. 640–645.
59 Althoff 1989, 265–290; Patzold 1999.
60 Halsall 1998; Hillgarth 2004; Reuter 2006.
61 Fryde and Reitz 2003.
62 Vallejo Girvés 2003; Fournier 2016.
63 Bührer-Thierry 2017; Kulikowski 2002.
64 Lauwers 2008; Mazel 2016; Poveda Arias 2019.
65 Panzram 2010; Wood 2012.

rivalry, conflict, danger and violence. This does not conversely imply that they acted in isolation: Regine Le Jan especially has shifted focus to their interactions and context. In her research project "Compétition dans les sociétés du haut Moyen Âge" (2010–2014), the medievalist makes use of game theory,[66] as its analytical instruments allow her to deduce decision-making behaviour in social conflict situations in which the success of an individual's actions depends not just on their own behaviour, but also on the actions of others who may be working in their own interest. After all, this was not inevitable since it is in the general interest to not upset the balance of the overall situation. Her systematic ordering of different analytical perspectives sparked numerous individual studies,[67] yet without leading to the articulation of a complete theory. In classical studies, too, these innovative approaches have shifted the focus to processes of state formation in the post-imperial *regna* in the western part of the Roman Empire, highlighting mechanisms utilising conflicts as a source of social stability or as a vehicle for transformation and ultimately enabling the creation of a new social order and new structures of belonging in so-called failed states.[68] Researchers also paid attention to the genesis of the institutions of the Church and papacy, especially the threats to which this process of institutionalisation and its protagonists were exposed.[69] Indeed, the making of the institutional Church was not a top-down process, but the result of local and regional conflicts and threatening scenarios, in which bishops asked their colleagues in Rome for intervention and thereby often consciously circumvented the metropolitan's authority – "scale jumping" that at first preserved their autonomy, but ultimately helped create a primacy. The present contributions dedicate themselves to analysing these threatening scenarios by focusing on bishops as threatened subjects in varying contexts in the West in both Late Antiquity and the Early Middle Ages.

2 Scholarly Goals

This volume seeks to contribute to the productively expanding research field of the long Late Antiquity by offering case studies that enable a comparative perspective of different regions when one systematically places them into relation. The Late

---

[66] Dépreux, Bougard, and Le Jan 2015; Loré, Bührer-Thierry, and Le Jan 2017; Joye and Le Jan 2018; Le Jan, Bührer-Thierry, and Gasparri 2018, 61–76.
[67] DesRosiers, Rosenblum, and Vuong 2014; Van Nuffelen 2014.
[68] See the contributions in Meier and Patzold 2014; Cooper and Leyser 2016.
[69] Fear, Ubiña, and Marcos Sánchez 2013; Panzram 2015 (revised Spanish version: Panzram 2018); Natal Villazala and Wood 2016.

Antique and Early Medieval West experienced the same processes of the disintegration of imperial structures, the making of new political realities and the rise of ecclesiastical structures as vital articulators of social life. As such, this geographic sphere offers itself in contrast to the eastern imperial territory, which remained under imperial control. However, such phenomena occurred at different rates and according to the particularities of each territory on different scales, from regional to local. These are determined, on the one hand, by the varying intensity of Romanisation that a region had experienced and, on the other hand, by the respective status quo of land acquisitions, which were of different durations and could have corresponding consequences – such as the establishment of Umayyad rule on the Iberian Peninsula. This brings to the fore differences and similarities that delineate a differentiated picture of this transformation process. The period of study has been consciously defined broadly – between the early 5th and the start of the 11th century – to allow the roots of the threats in the Late Antique Roman Empire to emerge just as clearly as the persistence of Late Antique interpretive patterns of social reality, which lasted far into the Early Middle Ages. The decidedly classical perspective adopted by two thirds of all international contributions is supplemented and expanded by the researches of the last years, which have been primarily shaped by medievalists; the interdisciplinary approach offers no mere additive assemblage of individual aspects, but rather studies the phenomenon of the threatened bishops from various perspectives at once.

The approach is fundamentally social historical: following the tradition of previous research, the focus clearly lies on the social factors as well as, especially, on individual relationships[70] – bishops are understood as social agents interacting with other actors, with everyone pursuing their own interests. This volume's aim is to present different threatening scenarios that bishops faced while exercising their office, to sketch out the influence of the social, political or religious context, and finally to analyse the varying strategies bishops developed to assert themselves in this situation. At what moment did courses of action become uncertain, were behaviours and routines called into question and when does it become necessary to establish a "threat communication"? What, exactly, did actors perceive not as the constancy and variation of order but as a danger to the fundamental model of social order? What molded the open-ended process – the re-ordering – over whose course an order that had gone off the rails was re-shaped and which followed a successful "Selbstalarmierung", to use the term Tübingen's Collaborative Research Center "Threatened Orders" (2011–2023) is currently develop-

---

70 See Innes 2000.

ing.[71] Three subject areas are central: first, the challenging of episcopal authority, which affected the administration of justice and the territory. Such challenges could come from the secular power, but also from colleagues, abbots and eremites, that is, members of the ecclesiastical hierarchy. Second, threats to the bishops through genuine political interests, advanced by an aristocratic magnate or the king himself. And finally, the individual threats to which a bishop was exposed because he acted not just in the interests of his parish, but in those of his own family and, not least, himself.

Part One – "Threatening Episcopal Authority: Jurisdiction and Territory" – first focuses on the legitimacy of episcopal power on the basis of two classical case studies from ancient history. Their authors analyse the threatened authority of the metropolitans of Arles and Mérida. Whereas Pablo Poveda Arias (Threatening Metropolitan Authority in Fifth-Century Gaul) can show that Arles' bishop asked Rome to grant him extraordinary powers to assert himself against his colleagues in the region – a status that, once reached, would prove very fragile – Kevin Grotherr (Between Royal Power and Legitimacy – The Bishops of Mérida [6th–7th c.]) specifically explores the threat the Visigothic king Liuvigild posed to Masona of Mérida. The bishop's situation required the intervention of St. Eulalia, whose miraculous aid ultimately allowed the pious bishop to triumph over his Arian opponents. After this, four medievalist contributions tackle this problem from the perspective of both another group of clergy and with a focus on the dioceses' structures: Charles Mériaux (Bishops under Pressure: Priests and Episcopal Authority in Carolingian Francia) draws attention to the local clergy in the diocese of Reims, which in the 9th century realised its power to exert pressure on its bishop precisely because of their Carolingian reform of the dioceses, which had aimed at inflicting stronger discipline on the surrounding clergy. Incubating in this clergy a new, confident awareness of itself as a pressure group had been by no means its intention. Katy Cubitt (Episcopal Authority and Diocesan Structure in England [c. 650–1066]) turns her attention to the territorial size of the English dioceses, which far exceeded those on the continent. This presented the bishops with a challenge tied to pastoral care and the general exercise of their office, for pastoral failings signified a threat to eternal salvation. The attempt to shrink these dioceses was thus logical, but proved difficult to implement due to religious, political and economic interests. Katharina Winckler (Suspicious Minds: Bishops without Seat and Canonical Bishops in Eighth-Century Bavaria) concentrates on bishops who cannot be ascribed a permanent see (wandering bishops, choir bishops, monastic bishops/abbots?) and thus acted in contravention of the rules stipulated by the

---

71 See https://bedrohte-ordnungen.de/ (accessed 30.10.2022).

Council of Nicaea. The pope viewed them as equal to their counterparts with seat, an attitude the canonical bishops could not accept. The implementation of the Carolingian Reforms forced these bishops to subordinate themselves to the archbishop of Salzburg, and their independence evidently came to an end in the early 9th century: from this point onwards, the sources fall quiet. By tackling the Church of Castille, Julio Escalona (The Tenth-Century Castilian Church in the Wider Iberian Context: The Large Gap between Ideal and Reality) examines an institution that frees itself from its own past: although a return to the powerful church of the Visigothic kingdom was propagated in the 10th century, reality diverged. The bishops lacked urban networks, and the porousness between secular and monastic interests also proved problematic. The Gregorian Reform – which allowed the Church to establish itself as more independent and strongly formalised – proved unsuccessful in Castille.

Part Two on "Bishops and Politics" studies conflicts carried out with both weapons and diplomatic means: Ian Wood (Burgundians and Bishops) postulates that the persecutions of Catholic bishops in the 5th and 6th centuries were seldom sparked by differences of faith, but rather appeared in the context of altercations with Franks and Visigoths over territorial control, while Marco Cristini (Sailing to Byzantium: Sixth-Century Popes under Threat in Constantinople) studies papal trips to Byzantium in the period between 525 and 545 – John I and Agapitus on behalf of the Ostrogothic kings, Vigilius for Emperor Justinian – that point to the equal weight of political and theological motivations. Meanwhile, Bruno Dumézil (Victims, Actors or Spectators? The Bishops of the Merovingian Kingdom during the Civil War of 575–613) shows that the so-called royal bloodfeud, often described as the most violent part of the Merowingian period, does not fundamentally differ from others if one studies the biographies of bishops like Aetherius of Lisieux, Egidius of Reims or Desiderius of Vienne. And Francesco Veronese (Bishops, Relics and Multi-Directional Pressures in Carolingian Northern Italy: The Cases of Verona and Milan) turns his attention to measures adopted after Carl the Great's conquest of Lombardy (774) that were aimed i.a., at promoting the integration of the social elites into the Carolingian system and appointing bishops. These bishops encouraged the worship of saints and veneration of relics, thus seeking to channel conflicts arising from their unstable position.

Finally, Part Three addresses "Individualising Threats and Strategies" in their most extreme forms of exile or the death sentence: Isabelle Mossong (Italy's Late Antique Bishops in Exile [3rd–Beginning of 7th c.]: The Epigraphic Point of View) studies epigraphic monuments in Italy – primarily in Rome – that supplement the transmitted literary texts dedicated to bishops in exile. They date from after their deaths and were set out by the state in the form of honorary inscriptions. Their sparse number suggests that not many existed. Martin Horst (Bishops between Reform and Heresy: Priscillian, Martin of Tours and Magnus Maximus), meanwhile, applies himself to Priscillian of Ávila, one of the most famous heretics of the Iberian Peninsula: the distribution of his teachings, banned by the councils of Zaragoza (380) and Bordeaux (384), culminated in his death in Trier. The state-enacted death penalty allowed Martin of Tours and others to question and successfully condemn the proceedings, as the networks of both parties were large and sustained by influential individuals. Focusing on the bishops from the period of the Byzantine capture of Hispania, Margarita Vallejo Girvés (Bishop Licinianus of Carthago Spartaria, the Monastery of Asán and the Struggle between Visigoths and Byzantines) studies an as yet all but unknown group of clergy. Using the examples of Licinianus of Cartagena, Ianuarius of Malaga and Stephen of Assidona, she shows the threats – such as the confiscation of their properties etc. – to which the bishops were subjected. They tried to enter into direct contact with the Visigoths, which Constantinople did not view kindly and, in the case of Licinianus, led to his death under unclear circumstances. Pablo C. Díaz (Dumio-Braga. A Functional Duality, A Legal Anomaly) closes the circle with a legal anomaly: a monastery that was also an episcopal see. Only one case is known from the Iberian Peninsula, namely the monastery of Dumio, located near Braga. This was under the authority of Martin, a native of Pannonia, who was elected Metropolitan of Braga after ten years. This practice – although not always in the form of a personal union – persisted until the Umayyad's land seizure, although the Council of Huesca (589) was not alone in condemning it.

By directing attention to the "combative creatures"[72] that the ambiguity of their offices forced the bishops to become, they enable us to analyse both the scenarios of competition and threat to which their status as agents of power exposed them as well as the motivations behind their supposedly religious, but in truth fundamentally political decisions. Comparing their varying reactions at different times would allow us to gain a deeper understanding of the years between Late Antiquity and the Early Middle Ages, years that were so crucial to the institutionalisation of the Church[73] – yet this is a step that must be left to further interdisciplinary studies, as it does not fit the framework of a volume published by ancient historians alone.

---

72 Natal Villazala and Wood 2016.
73 Bihrer and Röckelein 2022.

Bibliography

Primary Sources

Gennadius. *De viris illustribus:* Carl Albrecht Bernoulli, ed. 1968. *Hieronymus und Gennadius: De viris illustribus.* Sammlung ausgewählter kirchen- und dogmengeschichtlicher Quellenschriften 11. Freiburg/Leipzig: Mohr [Repr. 1968. Frankfurt]

Gundlach, Wilhelm, ed. 1892. *Monumenta Germaniae Historica. Epistolae (MGH EE).* III, *Epistolae Merowingici et Karolini aevi.* Vol. 1, *Inest tabula.* Berlin: Weidmann.

Jacob, Paul-André, and Samuel Cavallin. 1995. *La vie d'Hilaire d'Arles – Honorat de Marseille.* Sources chrétiennes 404. Paris: Éditions du Cerf.

Jaffé, Philipp, ed. ²1885. *Regesta Pontificum Romanorum ab condita ecclesia ad annum post Christum natum MCXCVIII.* Vol. 1, *A S. Petro ad a. MCXLIII (JK). Curavit Samuel Lowenfeld, Ferdinand Kaltenbrunner, Paul Ewald.* Leipzig [Repr. 1956. Graz].

Jaffé, Philipp, ed. 2016. *Regesta Pontificum Romanorum ab condita ecclesia ad annum post Christum natum MCXCVIII. Editionem tertiam emendatam et auctam iubente Academia Gottingensi sub auspiciis N. Herbers.* Vol. 1, *A S. Petro ad a. DCIV* (J³). *Curavit M. Schütz.* Göttingen.

Knie, Katharina, Sabine Panzram, Lorenzo Livorsi, and Rocco Selvaggi, eds. 2022. *Regesta Pontificum Romanorum. Iberia Pontificia.* Vol. VII, *Hispania Romana et Visigothica.* Göttingen: Vandenhoeck & Ruprecht.

Le Blant, Edmond Frédéric, ed. 1856. *Inscriptions chrétiennes de la Gaule antérieures au VIIIᵉ siècle.* Vol. I, *Provinces Gallicanes.* Paris : Impr. Impériale [Repr. 1999. Hildesheim et al.].

Le Blant, Edmond Frédéric, ed. 1865. *Inscriptions chrétiennes de la Gaule antérieures au VIIIᵉ siècle.* Vol. II, *Les Sept Provinces.* Paris : Impr. Impériale [Repr. 1999. Hildesheim et al.].

Mansi, Johannes D., ed. ²1901. *Sacrorum conciliorum nova et amplissima collectio.* Vol. 7. Paris [Repr. 1960. Graz].

Martín-Iglesias, José Carlos, Pablo C. Díaz, and Margarita Vallejo Girvés. 2020. *La Hispania Tardoantigua en las fuentes epistolares. Antología y comentario.* Nueva Roma 52. Madrid: Consejo Superior de Investigaciones Científicas.

Munier, Charles, ed. 1963. *Concilia Galliae. A. 314 – A. 506.* Corpus Christianorum, Series Latina 148. Turnhout: Brepols.

Thiel, Andreas, ed. 1867–1868. *Epistolae Romanorum Pontificum genuinae et quae ad eos scriptae sunt a S. Hilaro usque ad Pelagium II. Fasc. 1.* Braunsberg [Repr. 1974. Hildesheim/New York: Georg Olms].

Vitae patrum Iurensium: François Martine, ed. 2004. *Vie des Pères du Jura.* Sources chrétiennes 142. Paris: Éditions du Cerf.

Vitas Sanctorum Patrum Emeretensium: Antonio Maya Sánchez, ed. 1992. Corpus Christianorum. Series Latina 116. Turnhout: Brepols.

Secondary Sources

Althoff, Gerd. 1989. "Königsherrschaft und Konfliktbewältigung im 10. und 11. Jahrhundert." *Frühmittelalterliche Studien* 23:265–290.

Anton, Hans Hubert. 1987. *Trier im frühen Mittelalter.* Paderborn: Schöningh.

Anton, Hans Hubert. 1996. "'Bischofsherrschaften' und 'Bischofsstaaten' in Spätantike und Frühmittelalter. Reflexionen zu ihrer Genese, Struktur und Typologie." In *Liber amicorum necnon et amicarum für Alfred Heit. Beiträge zur mittelalterlichen Geschichte und geschichtlichen Landeskunde*. Trierer Historische Forschungen 28, edited by Friedhelm Burgard, Christoph Cluse, and Alfred Haverkamp, 461–473. Trier: Verlag Trierer Historische Forschungen.

Beaujard, Brigitte. 1996. "L'évêque dans la cité en Gaule aux Ve et VIe." In *La fin de la cité antique et le début de la cité médiévale: de la fin du IIIe siècle à l'avènement de Charlemagne*. Munera 8, edited by Claude Lepelley, 127–145. Bari: Edipuglia.

Beaujard, Brigitte. 2000. *Le culte des saints en Gaule: les premiers temps, d'Hilaire de Poitiers à la fin du VIe siècle*. Paris : Éditions du Cerf.

Berschin, Walter. ^{2}2020. *Biographie und Epochenstil im lateinischen Mittelalter.* Vol. I, *Von der Passio Perpetuae zu den Dialogi Gregors des Großen*. Stuttgart: Hiersemann.

Biarne, Jacques. 2013. "Honorat, Hilaire, Fauste, Maxime et les autres: les «moins-évêques» de Provence." In *L'Antiquité tardive en Provence (IVe–VIe siècle). Naissance d'une chrétienté*. BiAMA Hors Collection, edited by Marc Heijmans and Jean Guyon, 152–153. Marseille : Centre Camille-Jullian.

Bihrer, Andreas, and Hedwig Röckelein, eds. 2022. *Die "Episkopalisierung der Kirche" im europäischen Vergleich*. Studien zur Germania Sacra. Neue Folge 13. Berlin/Boston: De Gruyter.

Bleckmann, Bruno. 2002. "Arelate metropolis. Überlegungen zur Datierung des Konzils von Turin und zur Geschichte Galliens im 5. Jahrhundert." *Römische Quartalschrift für Christliche Altertumskunde und Kirchengeschichte* 97:162–173.

Brown, Peter. 1981. *The Cult of Saints. Its Rise and Function in Latin Christianity*. Chicago/London: University of Chicago Press-SCM Press.

Brown, Peter. 1992. *Power and Persuasion in Late Antiquity. Towards a Christian Empire*. Madison/London: The University of Wisconsin Press.

Brown, Peter. 2012. *Through the Eye of a Needle: Wealth, the Fall of Rome, and the Making of Christianity in the West, 350–550 AD*. Princeton: Princeton University Press.

Bührer-Thierry, Geneviève. 1997. *Évêques et pouvoir dans le royaume de Germanie : les églises de Bavière et de Souabe 876–973*. Paris : Picard.

Bührer-Thierry, Geneviève. 2017. "Bishops as City Defenders in Early Medieval Gaul and Germany." In *Between Sword and Prayer: Warfare and Medieval Clergy in Cultural Perspective*, edited by Radosław Kotecki, Jacek Maciejewski, and John S. Ott, 24–45. Leiden: Brill.

Castellanos García, Santiago. 1998. "Las reliquias de santos y su papel social: cohesión comunitaria y control episcopal en Hispania (ss. V–VII)." *Polis* 8:5–21.

Castillo Maldonado, Pedro. 2007. "In ecclesia contra ecclesiam: algunos ejemplos de disputas, violencias y facciones clericales en las iglesias tardoantiguas hispanas." *Antiquité Tardive* 15:263–276.

Chavarría Arnau, Alexandra. 2018. *A la sombra de un imperio: iglesias, obispos y reyes en la Hispania tardoantigua (siglos V–VIII)*. Bari: Edipuglia.

Cimma, Maria Rosa. 1989. *L'episcopalis audientia nelle costituzioni imperiali da Costantino a Giustiniano*. Turin: Giappichelli.

Claude, Dietrich. 1971. *Adel, Kirche und Königtum im Westgotenreich*. Stuttgart: Jan Thorbecke Verlag.

Collins, Roger. 1980. "Mérida and Toledo: 550–585." In *Visigothic Spain. New Approaches*, edited by Edward James, 189–210. Oxford: Clarendon Press.

Cooper, Kate, and Conrad Leyser, eds. 2016. *Making Early Medieval Societies. Conflict and Belonging in the Latin West, 300–1200*. Cambridge: Cambridge University Press.

Coué, Stephanie. 1997. *Hagiographie im Kontext. Schreibanlass und Funktion von Bischofsviten aus dem 11. und vom Anfang des 12. Jahrhunderts*. Arbeiten zur Frühmittelalterforschung 24. Berlin/New York: De Gruyter.

Cvetković, Carmen Angela, Peter Gemeinhardt, and Ariane Bodin, eds. 2019. *Episcopal Networks in Late Antiquity: Connection and Communication across Boundaries*. Berlin: De Gruyter.

Dellong, Eric. 2002. *Narbonne et le Narbonnais*. Carte Archéologique de la Gaule 11.1. Paris: Académie des Inscriptions et Belles-Lettres et al.

Dépreux, Philippe, François Bougard, and Régine Le Jan, eds. 2015. *Compétition et sacré au haut Moyen Âge. Entre médiation et exclusion*. Collection Haut Moyen Âge 21. Turnhout: Brepols.

DesRosiers, Nathaniel, Jordan Rosenblum, and Lily Vuong, eds. 2014. *Religious Competition in the Third Century CE: Jews, Christians, and the Greco-Roman World*. Göttingen: Vandenhoeck and Ruprecht.

Destefanis, Eleonora. 2013. "Episcopato e proprietà ecclesiastica. Il ruolo del vescovo nella gestione delle risorse tra città e territorio (IV–VII secolo)." In *'Episcopus, civitas, territorium', Atti del XV Congresso Internazionale di Archeologia Cristiana*, edited by Olof Brandt, Silvia Cresci, Jorge López Quiroga, and Carmelo Pappalardo, 483–498. Vatican City: Pontificio Istituto di Archeologia Cristiana.

Díaz, Pablo C. 1995. "Propiedad y poder: la Iglesia lusitana en el siglo VII." In *Los últimos romanos en Lusitania*, 51–72. Mérida: Museo Nacional de Arte Romano.

Diefenbach, Steffen. 2013. "'Bischofsherrschaft'. Zur Transformation der politischen Kultur im spätantiken und frühmittelalterlichen Gallien." In *Gallien in Antike und Frühmittelalter. Kulturgeschichte einer Region*. Millenium-Studien. Zu Kultur und Geschichte des ersten Jahrtausends n. Chr. 43, edited by Steffen Diefenbach and Gernot Michael Müller, 91–149. Berlin/New York: De Gruyter.

Durliat, Jean. 1979. "Les attributions civiles des évêques mérovingiens : l'exemple de Didier, évêque de Cahors (630–655)." *Annales du midi* 93:237–254.

Durliat, Jean. 1996. "Évêque et administration municipale au VIIe siècle." In *La fin de la cité antique et le début de la cité médiévale : de la fin du IIIe siècle à l'avènement de Charlemagne*. Munera 8, edited by Claude Lepelley, 273–286. Bari: Edipuglia.

Esders, Stefan. 2010. *Die Formierung der Zensualität. Zur kirchlichen Transformation des spätrömischen Patronatswesens im früheren Mittelalter*. Ostfildern: Jan Thorbecke Verlag.

Fear, Andrew, José Fernández Ubiña, and Mar Marcos Sánchez, eds. 2013. *The Role of the Bishop in Late Antiquity. Conflict and Compromise*. London: Bloomsbury.

Fernández Ortiz de Guinea, Lina. 1996. "Funciones sociales del cuerpo episcopal en el reino visigodo hispano: administración de justicia y protección de la comunidad cristiana." *Hispania Antiqva* 20:451–463.

Ferreiro, Alberto. 2020. *Epistolae Plenae. The Correspondence of the Bishops of Hispania with the Bishops of Rome (Third through Seventh Centuries)*. The Medieval and Early Modern Iberian World 74. Leiden/Boston: Brill.

Fontaine, Jacques. 2001. "Spanien zwischen Barbaren und Häretikern." In *Geschichte des Christentums. Religion – Politik – Kultur*. Vol. 3, *Der lateinische Westen und der byzantinische Osten (431–642)*, edited by Luce Pietri, 213–221. Freiburg et al.: Herder.

Fournier, Éric. 2016. "Constantine and Episcopal Banishment: Continuity and Change in the Settlement of Christian Disputes." In *Clerical Exile in Late Antiquity*, edited by Julia Hillner, 47–66. Frankfurt am Main et al.: Peter Lang.

Fryde, Natalie, and Dirk Reitz, eds. 2003. *Bischofsmord im Mittelalter.* Göttingen: Vandenhoeck & Ruprecht.
Gauthier, Nancy. 1980. *L'évangélisation des pays de la Moselle. La province romaine de Première Belgique entre Antiquité et Moyen Âge (IIIe-VIIIe siècles).* Paris : De Boccard.
Gauthier, Nancy. 2000. "Le réseau de pouvoirs de l'évêque dans la gaule du haut Moyen Âge." In *Towns and their Territories between Late Antiquity and the Early Middle Ages.* Transformation of the Roman World 9, edited by Gian P. Brogiolo, Nancy Gauthier, and Neil Christie, 173–207. Leiden: Brill.
Haarländer, Stephanie. 2000. *Vitae episcoporum. Eine Quellengattung zwischen Hagiographie und Historiographie, untersucht an Lebensbeschreibungen von Bischöfen des Regnum Teutonicum im Zeitalter der Ottonen und Salier.* Monographien zur Geschichte des Mittelalters 47. Stuttgart.
Hagen, Doris. 1995. *Herrschaftsbildung zwischen Königtum und Adel. Die Bischöfe von Freising in salischer und frühstaufischer Zeit.* Frankfurt am Main: Peter Lang.
Halfond, Gregory I. 2012. "All the King's Men: Episcopal Political Loyalties in the Merovingian Kingdoms." *Medieval Prosopography. History and Collective Bibliography* 27:76–96.
Halfond, Gregory I. 2019. *Bishops and the Politics of Patronage in Merovingian Gaul.* Ithaca/London: Cornell University Press.
Halsall, Guy, ed. 1998. *Violence and Society in the Early Medieval West.* Woodbridge: Boydell Press.
Hartmann, Götz. 2006. *Selbststigmatisierung und Charisma christlicher Heiliger der Spätantike.* Studien und Texte zu Antike und Christentum 38. Tübingen: Mohr Siebeck.
Heijmans, Marc, and Luce Pietri. 2009. "Le 'lobby' lérinien: le rayonnement du monastère insulaire du Ve siècle au début du VIIe siècle." In *Lérins, une île sainte de l'Antiquité au Moyen Âge.* Collection d'études médiévales de Nice 9. edited by Yann Codou and Michel Lauwers, 35–61. Turnhout: Brepols.
Heinzelmann, Martin. 1976. *Bischofsherrschaft in Gallien. Zur Kontinuität römischer Führungsschichten vom 4. bis 7. Jahrhundert. Soziale, prosopographische und bildungsgeschichtliche Aspekte.* Beihefte der Francia 5. Stuttgart: Jan Thorbecke Verlag.
Heinzelmann, Martin. 1988. "Bischof und Herrschaft vom spätantiken Gallien bis zu den karolingischen Hausmeiern. Die institutionellen Grundlagen." In *Herrschaft und Kirche. Beiträge zur Entstehung und Wirkungsweise episkopaler und monastischer Organisationsformen.* Monographien zur Geschichte des Mittelalters 33, edited by Friedrich Prinz, 23–82. Stuttgart: Hiersemann.
Heinzelmann, Martin. 1992. "The 'affair' of Hilary of Arles (445) and Gallo-Roman identity in the fifth century." In *Fifth-century Gaul: a crisis of identity?*, edited by John Drinkwater and Hugh Elton, 19–27. Cambridge: Cambridge University Press.
Hillgarth, Jocelyn N. 2004. "Murder and monarchy in the Visigothic kingdoms." In *Murder and monarchy: Regicide in European history, 1300–1800*, edited by Robert von Friedburg, 75–82. Basingstoke: Palgrave Macmillan.
Innes, Matthew. 2000. *State and Society in the Early Middle Ages: The Middle Rhine Valley, 400–1000.* Cambridge Studies in Medieval Life and Thought: Fourth Series 47. Cambridge: Cambridge University Press.
Jorge, Ana M.C.M. 2002. *L'épiscopat de Lusitanie pendant l'Antiquité tardive (IIIe-VIIe siècle).* Lisbon: Instituto Portuguôes de Arqueologia.
Joye, Sylvie, and Régine Le Jan, eds. 2018. *Genre et compétition dans les sociétés occidentales du haut Moyen Âge (IVe-XIe siècle).* Collection Haut Moyen Âge 29. Turnhout: Brepols.

Jussen, Bernhard. 1998. "Liturgie und Legitimation, oder: Wie die Gallo-Romanen das Römische Reich beendeten." In *Institutionen und Ereignis. Über historische Praktiken und Vorstellungen gesellschaftlichen Ordnens*, edited by Reinhard Blänkner and Bernhard Jussen, 75–136. Göttingen: Vandenhoeck & Ruprecht.

König, Daniel. 2008. *Bekehrungsmotive. Untersuchungen zum Christianisierungsprozess im römischen Weltreich und seinen romanisch-germanischen Nachfolgern (4.-8. Jh.)*. Historische Studien 493. Husum: Matthiesen Verlag.

Krön, Martin. 1997. *Das Mönchtum und die kulturelle Tradition des lateinischen Westens. Formen der Askese, Autorität und Organisation im frühen westlichen Zönobitentum*. Quellen und Forschungen zur antiken Welt 29. Munich: Tuduv Verlag.

Kulikowski, Michael. 2002. "Fronto, the Bishops, and the Crowd: Episcopal Justice and Communal Violence in Fifth-Century Tarraconensis." *Early Medieval Europe* 11.4:295–320.

Langgärtner, Georg. 1964. *Die Gallienpolitik der Päpste im 5. und 6. Jahrhundert. Eine Studie über den apostolischen Vikariat von Arles*. Theophaneia. Beiträge zur Religions- und Kirchengeschichte des Altertums 16. Bonn: Hanstein.

Larrañaga Elorza, Koldo. 1989. "En torno al caso del obispo Silvano de Calagurris: consideraciones sobre el estado de la Iglesia del Alto al Medio Ebro a fines del Imperio." *Veleia. Revista de Prehistoria, Historia Antigua, Arqueología y Filología Clásicas* 6:171–191.

Lauwers, Michel. 2008. "*Territorium non facere diocesim*. Conflits, limites et représentation territorial du diocese (V^e-Xe siècle)." In *L'espace du diocèse. Genèse d'un territoire dans l'Occident médiéval (Ve-XIIIe siècle)*, edited by Florian Mazel, 23–68. Rennes: Presses Universitaires de Rennes.

Le Jan, Régine, Geneviève Bührer-Thierry, and Stefano Gasparri, eds. 2018. *Coopétition. Rivaliser, coopérer dans les sociétés du haut Moyen Âge (500-1000)*. Collection Haut Moyen Âge 31. Turnhout: Brepols.

Leemans, Johan, Peter Van Nuffelen, Shawn W.J. Keough, and Carla Nicolaye, eds. 2011. *Episcopal Elections in Late Antiquity*. Berlin/Boston: De Gruyter.

Lepelley, Claude. 1998. "Le patronat épiscopal aux IVe et Ve siècles: continuités et ruptures avec le patronat classique." In *L'évêque dans la cité du IVe au Ve siècle. Image et autorité*, edited by Éric Rebillard and Claire Sotinel, 17–33. Rome: École Française de Rome.

Liebeschuetz, John H.W.G. 2001. *Decline and Fall of the Roman City*. Oxford: Oxford University Press.

Loré, Vito, Geneviève Bührer-Thierry, and Régine Le Jan, eds. 2017. *Acquérir, prélever, contrôler : les ressources en compétition (400-1100)*. Collection Haut Moyen Âge 25. Turnhout: Brepols.

Magnou-Nortier, Elisabeth. 1974. *La société laïque et l'Église dans la province ecclésiastique de Narbonne (zone cispyrénéenne) de la fin du VIIIe à la fin du Xie siècle*. Toulouse : Association des Publications de l'Université de Toulouse-Le Mirail.

Marcos Sánchez, Mar. 2013. "Papal Authority, Local Autonomy and Imperial Control. Pope Zosimus and the Western Churches (a. 417-18)." In *The Role of the Bishop in Late Antiquity. Conflict and Compromise*, edited by Andrew Fear, José Fernández Ubiña, and Mar Marcos Sánchez, 145–166. London: Bloomsbury.

Marrou, Henri-Irénée. 1970. "Le dossier épigraphique de l'évêque Rusticus de Narbonne." *Rivista di Archeologia Cristiana* 46.3-4:331–349.

Martín-Iglesias, José Carlos. 2018. "El 'Iudicium inter Marcianum et Habentium episcopos' (A. 638): estudio, edición y traducción." *Habis* 49:203–231.

Martin, Céline. 2003. *La géographie du pouvoir dans l'Espagne visigothique*. Lille: Presses Universitaires du Septentrion.

Mathisen, Ralph W. 1989. *Ecclesiastical Factionalism and Religious Controversy in Fifth-Century Gaul*. Washington D.C.: The Catholic University of America Press.

Mazel, Florian. *L'évêque et le territoire. L'invention de l'espace*. Paris : Éditions du Seuil.

Meier, Mischa. 2019. *Geschichte der Völkerwanderung. Europa, Asien und Afrika vom 3. bis zum 8. Jh. n. Chr.* Munich: C.H. Beck.

Meier, Mischa, and Steffen Patzold, eds. 2014. *Chlodwigs Welt. Organisation von Herrschaft um 500. Internationale Tagung. Weingarten 2011*. Roma Aeterna. Beiträge zu Spätantike und Frühmittelalter 3. Stuttgart: Franz Steiner Verlag.

Moore, Michael Edward. 2011. *A Sacred Kingdom: Bishops and the Rise of Frankish Kingship, 300–850*. Washington D. C.: Catholic University of America Press.

Mor, Carlo Guido. 1979. "Sui poteri civili del vescovi dal IV al secolo VIII." In *I poteri temporali dei vescovi in Italia e in Germania nel Medioevo*, edited by Carlo Guido Mor and Heinrich Schmidinger, 7–33. Bologna: Il Mulino.

Muñoz Melgar, Andreu. 2022. *Sant Fructuós de Tarragona. Aspectes històrics i arqueològics del seu culte, des de l'antiguitat fins a l'actualitat*. Collecció Studia Archaeologiae Christianae 4. Barcelona: ICAC.

Natal Villazala, David, and Jaime Wood. 2016. "Playing with Fire. Conflicting Bishops in Late Roman Spain and Gaul." In *Making Early Medieval Societies. Conflict and Belonging in the Latin West, 300–1200*, edited by Kate Cooper and Conrad Leyser, 33–57. Cambridge: Cambridge University Press.

Nimmegeers, Nathanaël. 2014. *Évêques entre Bourgogne et Provence (V^e–XIe). La province ecclésiastique de Vienne au haut Moyen Âge*. Rennes : Presses Universitaires de Rennes.

Norton, Peter. 2007. *Episcopal Elections AD 250–600: Hierarchy and popular will in late Antiquity*. Oxford: Oxford University Press.

Panzram, Sabine. 2010. "Mérida contra Toledo, Eulalia contra Leocadia: listados 'falsificados' de obispos como medio de autorepresentación municipal." In *Espacios urbanos en el occidente mediterráneo (s. VI–VIII)*, edited by Alfonso García, 123–130. Toledo: Toletum Visigodo.

Panzram, Sabine. 2015. "‚Hilferufe' aus Hispaniens Städten – Zur Ausbildung einer Metropolitanordnung auf der Iberischen Halbinsel (4.–6. Jahrhundert)." *Historische Zeitschrift* 301:626–661.

Panzram, Sabine. 2018. "La formación del orden metropolitano en la Península Ibérica (siglos IV a VI)." *Pyrenae* 49:125–154.

Panzram, Sabine. 2020. "¿*Tarraco* tardorromana sigue siendo *Tarraco*? A propósito de continuidad o discontinuidad de una capital de provincia." In *Academica Libertas. Essais en l'honneur du professeur Javier Arce*. Bibliothèque de l'Antiquité Tardive 39, edited by Dominic Moreau and Raul González Salinero, 193–209. Paris: Turnhout.

Patzold, Steffen. 1999. "Konflikte als Thema in der modernen Mediävistik." In *Moderne Mediävistik. Stand und Perspektiven der Mittelalterforschung*, edited by Hans-Werner Goetz, 198–205. Darmstadt 1999.

Patzold, Steffen. 2010. "Zur Sozialstruktur des Episkopats und zur Ausbildung bischöflicher Herrschaft in Gallien zwischen Spätantike und Frühmittelalter." In *Völker, Reiche und Namen im frühen Mittelalter*. MittelalterStudien 22, edited by Matthias Becher and Stefanie Dick, 121–140. Munich: Fink.

Pérez Martínez, Meritxell. 2000. "La burocracia episcopal en la Hispania tardorromana y visigótica (siglos IV–VII)." *Studia Historica. Historia medieval* 18/19:17–40.

Pérez Martínez, Meritxell. 2012. *Tarraco en la antigüedad tardía. Cristianización y organización eclesiástica (siglos III a VIII)*. Tarragona: Arola Editors.

Pietri, Luce. 1983. *La ville de Tours du IVe au VIe siècle : naissance d'une cité chrétienne*. Rome : École Française de Rome.

Pietri, Luce. 2001. "Gallien." In *Geschichte des Christentums. Religion – Politik – Kultur.* Vol. 3, *Der lateinische Westen und der byzantinische Osten (431–642)*, edited by Norbert Brox et al., 222–263. Freiburg et al.

Poveda Arias, Pablo. 2019. "La diócesis episcopal en la Hispania visigoda: concepción, construcción y disputas por su territorio." *Hispania Sacra* 71/143:9–24.

Prinz, Friedrich. 1971. *Klerus und Krieg im früheren Mittelalter: Untersuchungen zur Rolle der Kirche beim Aufbau der Königsherrschaft.* Stuttgart: Hiersemann.

Prinz, Friedrich. 1974. "Die bischöfliche Stadtherrschaft im Frankenreich vom 5. bis zum 7. Jahrhundert." *Historische Zeitschrift* 217:1–35.

Prinz, Friedrich. 1988. "Herrschaftsformen der Kirche vom Ausgang der Spätantike bis zum Ende der Karolingerzeit. Zur Einführung ins Thema." In *Herrschaft und Kirche. Beiträge zur Entstehung und Beiträge zur Entstehung und Wirkungsweise episkopaler und monastischer Organisationsformen.* Monographien zur Geschichte des Mittelalters 33, edited by Friedrich Prinz, 1–21. Stuttgart: Hiersemann.

Rapp, Claudia. 2005. *Holy Bishops in Late Antiquity. The Nature of Christian Leadership in an Age of Transition.* Transformation of the Classical Heritage 37. Berkeley/Los Angeles: University of California Press.

Reuter, Timothy. 2006. "Peace-breaking, Feud, Rebellion, Resistance: Violence and Peace in the Politics of the Salian Era." In *Medieval Polities*, edited by Janet L. Nelson, 355–387. Cambridge: Cambridge University Press.

Riess, Frank. 2016. *Narbonne and its Territory in Late Antiquity. From the Visigoths to the Arabs.* New York: Routledge.

Scherließ, Carsten. 2000. *Literatur und "conversio". Literarische Formen im monastischen Umkreis des Klosters von Lérins*. Europäische Hochschulschriften. Reihe 15; 82. Frankfurt am Main et al: Peter Lang Verlag.

Stocking, Rachel. 1997. "Martianus, Aventius and Isidore: provincial councils in seventh-century Spain." *Early Medieval Europe* 6.2:168–188.

Ubric Rabaneda, Purificación. 2004. *La Iglesia en la Hispania del siglo V.* Granada: Ediciones Universidad de Granada.

Vallejo Girvés, Margarita. 2003. "Los exilios de católicos y arrianos bajo Leovigildo y Recaredo." *Hispania sacra* 55:35–48.

Van Nuffelen, Peter. 2014. "The End of Open Competition? Religious Disputations in Late Antiquity." In *Religion and Competition in Antiquity*, edited by David Engels and Peter Van Nuffelen, 149–172. Brussels: Éditions Latomus.

Van Uytfanghe, Marc. 2001. "L'hagiographie de l'Antiquité tardive: une littérature populaire?" *Antiquité Tardive* 9:201–218.

Villegas Marín, Raúl. 2017. "La primacía de Arlés en las Iglesias galas durante el episcopado de Patroclo (411/413–426)." In *Costellazioni geo-ecclesiali da Costantino a Giustiniano: Dalle chiese 'principali' alle chiese patriarcali*, 307–317. Rome: Institutum Patristicum Augustinianum.

Wood, Ian N. 1983. "The Ecclesiastical Politics of Merovingian Clermont." In *Ideal and Reality in Frankish and Anglo-Saxon Society. Studies presented to J. M. Wallace-Hadrill*, edited by Patrick C. Wormald, Donald A. Bullough, and Roger Collins, 34–57. Oxford: B. Blackwell.

Wood, Jaime. 2012. "Playing the Fame Game: Bibliography, Celebrity, and Primacy in Late Antique Spain." *Journal of Early Christian Studies* 20:613–640.

Part One: **Threatening Episcopal Authority: Jurisdiction and Territory**

Pablo Poveda Arias
Threatening Metropolitan Authority in Fifth-Century Gaul

Abstract: Metropolitan bishops were exposed to the same threats as their suffragans but, because of their superior rank, they faced particular challenges to their office. This paper aims to highlight the different contexts of adversity faced by metropolitan bishops in 5th century Gaul. On the one hand, we intend to re-evaluate the real incidence of those disputes between metropolitans over questions of jurisdiction with the greatest resonance in the sources, as well as the role of the bishop of Rome in their resolution. On the other hand, we will also analyse the concrete impact that the political vicissitudes had on the metropolitan bishops, especially in the wake of the rise of the new barbarian kingdoms.

1 Introduction

Despite their superior rank, the metropolitan bishops of the fifth century were not immune to threats from their suffragans. Their power, position – and even sometimes life – could be imperiled or challenged at any time. Like any other prelate, the metropolitans were also exposed – perhaps even more so than others – to *razzias* by the barbarians,[1] to internal factionalisms that weakened their internal authority[2] when they failed to depose them and replace them with a new bishop,[3] or

---

[1] Such as the martyrdom the Bishop Nicasius of Reims was subjected to during one of these raids. *PCBE* 4, 1363. – This contribution evolved in the framework of the Center for Advanced Study "RomanIslam – Center for Comparative Empire and Transcultural Studies", funded by the German Research Foundation (Deutsche Forschungsgemeinschaft, DFG), at Universität Hamburg.

[2] Honoratus and Hilary of Arles were two of the bishops who made an internal opposition. Regarding Honoratus, Hil. Arel. Vita Honorat. 28, 1. Heinzelmann 1992, 246. In the case of Hilary, Honoratus of Marseille, Vita Hil. Arel. 10. Müller 2003, 219. On the internal problems in the Arles see at the time of both bishops, see also Natal 2015a. Better known is the existence of the confronted ecclesiastical factions during the time of Bishop Caesarius. Delaplace 2012. Rusticus of Narbonne also had to face the opposition of two priests, Sabinianus and Leo. Leo M. epist. 167. Griffe 1966, 196. On ecclesiastical factionalisms in fifth-century Gaul, and collecting all the cited casuistry, see Mathisen 1989.

[3] This fate was also suffered, for example, by Brice of Tours. Greg. Tur. Franc. II, 1; X, 31. Pietri 1983, 103–118.

to exile.[4] Nor would they have been immune to political vicissitudes, sometimes with quite dramatic results, as occurred with the execution of Bishop Patroclus of Arles by order of the *magister militum* Flavius Felix.[5] Additionally, there were other specific threats to the metropolitan, particularly ones that implied a direct attack on their privileges and scope of jurisdiction. This study will explore these issues and the strategies deployed by the bishops to manage them. To do this, we will limit the study to the fifth century and the situation that began with the Council of Turin (398/399),[6] which laid the foundations for the metropolitan order that prevailed during the two subsequent centuries, and many of the challenges the metropolitan bishops would have to address during that period.

Generally, the historiographic focus is usually placed on the party that is doing the threatening, as a transgressor of the prevailing *status quo*, while the equally interesting actions carried out by the aggrieved parties go unnoticed. A detailed analysis of these actions, together with a prioritisation of social factors over institutional ones, particularly the role of personal networks,[7] can facilitate a reassessment of the real impact some of the more significant threats had. What might have posed a serious threat to certain metropolitans could actually have been relative in view of the actions carried out by the aggrieved parties. As we will see, this perspective will be especially interesting when analysing territorial disputes between metropolitans in south-eastern Gaul. Focusing on the threatened parties will also allow us to re-evaluate the role of the papacy in fifth-century Gaul. When we know that the authority of a metropolitan was threatened, it is because we have documentary records left by the various papal interventions on those occasions. The richness of these records is often interpreted as reinforcing papal authority in Gaul during the fifth century.[8] But the purpose of this study is to question this idea, generally assumed by historiography.

---

[4] Episcopal exiles among metropolitans occurred especially in the Visigothic kingdom of Tolosa, particularly during the reigns of Euric (466–484) and Alaric II (584–507). See Stüber 2020.
[5] On the circumstances that led to his execution, Natal 2012, 114; Dunn 2014, 11.
[6] We take this date from the Mathisen 2013 study.
[7] As recently stated by Wood 2019, 229, in the Hispanic case, "by unpicking cycles of dispute and resolution, it is possible to observe the important role that social, political, and ecclesiastical networks played in the establishment and maintenance of the bishop's position in his city in relation to his peers at the provincial level".
[8] Griffe 1964, 351; Mathisen 1989, 205; Natal and Wood 2016. Conversely, given the dependence of our knowledge on the information sourced from the papal chancellery, a substantial informational imbalance occurs, since we have a good understanding of the vicissitudes of the metropolitan sees of the Gallic southeast, but know almost nothing about other areas such as Bordeaux, Trier or Reims. Griffe 1966, 141.

2 Victricius of Rouen, Brice of Tours and the First Interferences of the bishop of Rome in Gaul

In contrast to the previous period, interference by the bishop of Rome in the affairs of Gaul was common during the fifth century. It is true that papal intervention was never arbitrary, as it was always preceded by appeals from bishops, frequently of metropolitan rank. Deposed prelates – who sought replacement through the papal route – appealing to the pope was especially common.[9] In other cases, the extreme action of deposing was not necessary, as the mere threat was sufficient for the aggrieved bishop to resort to Rome. This was the case with Victricius of Rouen,[10] who was accused of heterodoxy by the bishops of his surrounding areas;[11] accusations that, beyond doctrinal questions, could underlie other types of motivations.[12] We know that during his episcopate, Victricius carried out intense evangelising activity beyond the space of his diocese.[13] Given this extradiocesan activity, it would seem logical that Victricius might have tried to assert his metropolitan authority over the dioceses of his surrounding areas, and that the neighbouring bishops would not have lent themselves to allowing him to take parts of their autonomy. This might have been why Pope Innocent I (401–417) issued that subsequent decree, addressed to the bishops in Victricius' province regarding the accusations levelled against him and in which he insists on the metropolitan rights of Rouen. In it he makes it clear that no single bishop can ordain another prelate, much less without the approval of the metropolitan, who is granted the right of veto. Along the lines proposed by Geoffrey D. Dunn, it is possible that the pope was making amends for the situation that prevailed until then in some parts of Gaul, with bishops denying their superior theorists.[14] After all, at this time the met-

---

[9] Mathisen 1989, 22. As an example, already at the end of the fourth century we have the case of Martin's successor at the Tours see, Brice, who appealed to Rome after being deposed. Pietri 1983, 103–111; Müller 2003.
[10] On Victricius, Andrieu-Guitrancourt 1970; Hunter 1999; *PCBE* 4, 1960–1964; Natal 2018.
[11] Dunn 2011, 153. Paulinus of Nola refers to the existence of internal opponents in Rouen. Paul. Nol. epist. 37, 4. Victricius himself alludes to such internal opposition. Victric. 11, 17. Natal 2018, 308. If the accusations had only come from his community, the appeal to Rome for a matter of exclusive internal resonance would not have been understood. However, the decree issued by Pope Innocent following this episode was also addressed to the suffragan bishops of Victricius. Innocentius papa v. Epist. pontif. 2.
[12] See Mathisen 1989, 46; Dunn 2011, 153–154, who is inclined to think that he might have been accused of Priscillianism.
[13] Paul. Nol. epist. 18, 4.
[14] Innocentius papa v. Epist. pontif. 2, 1; Dunn 2011, 156–159. 165.

ropolitan order was not yet consolidated, so it is not clear whether all the metropolitan bishops would have served as such. Within this scheme, it is possible to hypothesise that the accusations against Victricius had been a response by his suffragans to the attempts of the bishop of Rouen to exercise his metropolitan functions.

Whatever the reasons, the truth is that Victricius, seeing his position threatened, chose to turn to Pope Innocent, personally travelling to Rome between the end of 403 and the beginning of 404 to obtain his support. Such a move denotes a lack of internal support for Victricius that would have made an appeal to Rome unnecessary.[15] At the same time, appealing is a sign of the bishop of Rouen's helplessness, who finds himself unable to reverse the situation internally. His eagerness to accumulate relics during the previous years may have been part of a strategy aimed at reversing his precarious situation, but it certainly did not have the desired effects.[16] We must also remember that appealing to Rome was not a normalised practice at this time. Innocent I responded with the aforementioned decree, emphasising papal support for Victricius and his theses.[17] The mandate given by Innocent to Victricius to disseminate the decree also showed support for his authority in the region and his role as a direct intermediary between the pope and the bishops around him.

Unfortunately, the death of Victricius shortly after the papal decree was issued means we cannot know whether it had any effect, although we are inclined to think that its incidence was quite relative, if not null. This is the impression that we also get from the case of Brice of Tours, who at a fairly late time in his episcopate was accused by the people of Tours of fornication and deposed accordingly. Brice would go to the bishop of Rome, Celestine (422–432), who hosted him for seven years, until he was restored to his episcopal see.[18] The fact that, despite having papal support, he spent so much time in exile is an indication of the little influence the bishop of Rome had in the Gallic metropolitan churches. In fact, it seems that his restitution was due more to a change in the relationship of powers within the city of Tours and not so much to papal support. In short, the cases of Victricius and Brice shed light on how metropolitan bishops' need for external support made Rome an intermediary for appeals when it came to settling conflicts within the Gallic episcopate.[19]

---

15 Also highlighting this lack of internal support, Natal 2018, 326.
16 On the arrival and role of these relics, Van Dam 1985, 59–60; Natal 2018.
17 On this letter, Andrieu-Guitrancourt 1970; Dunn 2011.
18 Greg. Tur. Franc. II, 1; X, 31.
19 Natal and Wood 2016, 54.

3 Patroclus' Fight for Primacy: A Real Threat?

It is no surprise that the bishops who were more firmly established internally did not turn to the pope to address antagonistic situations. This is the situation that arose from an interference from the see of Arles during the episcopate of Patroclus, who tried to impose his ecclesiastical primacy by using the homologation of his ecclesiastical rank as a pretext over the recent civil title acquired by the city of Arles as see of the prefecture of the praetorium, first, and subsequently, the governorate of the province Viennensis.[20] This, however, meant breaking the order defined in the Council of Turin, where metropolitan jurisdiction was distributed over the various episcopal dioceses of the Viennensis between Vienne and Arles. According to this synod, both metropolitan sees would only have jurisdiction over the nearest dioceses.[21] In this author's opinion, more than the cause,[22] this homologation served as a pretext for an ambitious bishop who saw the opportunity to claim, with intense parallel activity, a position of primacy to the detriment of his metropolitan counterparts.[23] In particular, Patroclus claimed supreme authority in the episcopal ordination of the surrounding provinces (Viennensis, Narbonensis Prima and Narbonensis Secunda). Likewise, he also demanded that all communication to Rome be previously ratified by him.[24] This situation supposed a dilution of the other metropolitans' authority, who in practice became mere suffragans of Patroclus.[25] To carry out his aspirations, the ambitious bishop of Arles enlisted the support of Pope Zosimus (417–418),[26] who confirmed his rights over the neighbouring provinces, which would rectify and delegitimise the resolutions of the Council of Turin.[27] In return, Zosimus was able to ensure his influence over Gaul as an arbitration authority.[28] Nevertheless, papal support was not enough to accomplish his aspirations. In fact, Zosimus himself acknowledged that his au-

---

[20] On the chronological problem that revolves around the civil promotion of Arles, Dunn 2013, 170–171.
[21] Council of Turin (398/9) c. 2.
[22] Cf. Dunn 2013, 172.
[23] Neil 2018, 97: "Deep self-interest also played a part, then as now, with bishops seeking to promote their own diocese at the expense of others".
[24] Zosimus, *Epistolae Arelatenses genuinae* 1.
[25] Dunn 2015a, 45; 2016, 26–28.
[26] It has been suggested that in reality the powerful figure of Flavius Constancius was behind the promotion of Arles and the attacks on the other metropolitan sees, but this is a difficult assumption to confirm: Frye 1991; Heinzelmann 1992, 245; Villegas 2017.
[27] Zosimus, *Epistolae Arelatenses genuinae* 1; 4–5.
[28] Natal and Wood 2016, 49–50.

thority alone was not sufficient, which is why he legitimised the new order based on the tradition of Trophimus, of which he was guarantor.[29] It is perhaps also for this reason that he settled these matters in a council in Rome in 417, in which Patroclus also participated.[30]

Faced with Patroclus and Zosimus' attempts to pervert the order created in Turin, the aggrieved bishops responded in different ways, although with points in common. For example, none of them attended the Roman council of 417, despite having been summoned.[31] Perhaps they were aware that they would achieve nothing by attending the council, beyond being humiliated. However, in general, we notice a differential attitude towards the threat embodied by Patroclus, perhaps due to the personality or ambitions of the actors involved. Some specialists group the aggrieved bishops within the same faction, attributing to them a capacity for coordination and a willingness to join forces.[32] However, the evidence does not allow us to reach such conclusions.[33] For example, some assume that Proculus of Marseille and Simplicius of Vienne acted in collusion. Furthermore, a letter from Zosimus shows that Simplicius protested directly to the pope at the request of Proculus.[34] However, the letter only denounces the permissiveness of the bishop of Vienne to Proculus' action,[35] but there is no record of any collaboration between the two. Simplicius' general attitude thus seemed to be passive in this matter, perhaps knowing that the papal resolution by itself had no influence. We observe the same attitude in Hilary of Narbonne,[36] who would have only limited himself to replying with a letter to Zosimus.[37] It has been argued that Hilary's lack of response stemmed from being intimidated by Zosimus, who in his letter threatened the bishop of Narbonne with excommunication and even accused him of having obtained the

---

[29] According to Zosimus, the privileges granted to Arles derived from the greater antiquity of this metropolitan see, supposedly founded by Trophimus in the third century by mandate of the bishop of Rome. Zosimus, *Epistolae Arelatenses genuinae* 1; 3; 5. Dunn 2015b. However, as Mar Marcos 2013, 147, stated, the pope did not offer irrefutable proof of such ancient rights, nor does he give the impression that they had been previously used by the Arlesian see.

[30] On this council, Dunn 2015c.

[31] Zosimus, *Epistolae Arelatenses genuinae* 5. Mathisen 1989, 51–52; Dunn 2015a, 52.

[32] Mathisen 1989, 60; Riess 2013, 81.

[33] Supporting this perspective, the lack of unity of the Western churches has recently been highlighted: Schulz 2019.

[34] Zosimus, *Epistolae Arelatenses genuinae* 5. Mathisen 1989, 58; Dunn 2013, 179–180; Dunn 2016, 29–30. In a similar vein, Griffe 1966, 187.

[35] *PCBE* 4, 1815.

[36] Dunn 2015a, 47–48.

[37] This is deduced from reading the first lines of: Zosimus, *Epistolae Arelatenses genuinae* 3.

episcopate surreptitiously.[38] However, it is possible that, like Simplicius, in reality Hilary would not have felt very threatened by the papal resolution and would have continued to exercise his metropolitan rights over the region, at least over the areas of interest to him.[39] Proof of his rejection of the papal resolution is the fact that he addressed himself directly to Zosimus, and ignored the procedure set by Zosimus of referring first to Patroclus.[40]

There was also no reaction in the case of Remigius of Aix. It is possible that in this case his passivity was due to a possible alignment with Patroclus, with the aim of obtaining territories controlled by Proculus of Marseille,[41] or simply as revenge against the person who, years ago, promoted his episcopal deposition during the usurpation of Constantine III.[42] It would be the bishop of Marseille who would show a more bellicose attitude towards Patroclus and Zosimus, or this is the impression we get from the letters written by the bishop of Rome, who concentrates most of his criticism on Proculus. Although in theory, Marseille did not have the rank of metropolitan, Aix did, by virtue of the resolutions of the Council of Turin, when the exceptional commitment of allowing Proculus to maintain metropolitan rights in the Narbonensis Secunda was made, but only in a personal capacity. Only at his death would the metropolitan rank pass to the bishop of Aix.[43] However, Pope Zosimus delegitimised the Turin resolutions and accused Proculus of usurping metropolitan rights.[44] By extension, he also accused him of having illegitimately ordained Tuentius and Ursus as bishops in Citharista and Gargaria, enclaves situated in the vicinity of Marseille and which, we must assume, had

---

38 Zosimus, *Epistolae Arelatenses genuinae* 3. See Dunn 2015a. It has even been suggested that Hilary complied with Zosimus' orders even after his death. *PCBE* 4, 1008.
39 We do not rule out, as Dunn 2015a, 51–52, does, that this would have allowed Patroclus to act in a certain way.
40 See other readings in: Griffe 1966, 149–151; Natal 2012, 113.
41 Dunn 2013, 181.
42 Proculus of Marseille saw a risk in the usurper to consolidate his metropolitan rights, obtaining his support to depose the bishop of Aix, occupied at that moment by Remigius, and Arles. He would subsequently encourage the episcopal promotion of its own candidates, Lazarus, for the Aix see and Heros for the Arlesian one. However, making the episcopal chair dependent on political circumstances would result in the change of context and putting such chairs at risk. This is what happened when the ruling party recovered Gaul. Patroclus of Arles replaced Heros, Lazarus of Aix was deposed, and Remigius consequently returned. See Mathisen 1989, 30–36; Frye 1991; *PCBE* 4, 1599.
43 Council of Turin (398/9) c. 1. Alluding to these extraordinary rights, Zosimus, *Epistolae Arelatenses genuinae* 5.
44 Zosimus, *Epistolae Arelatenses genuinae* 4–5.

until then been integrated into the diocese of Marseille itself.⁴⁵ We thus observe how Proculus would establish new dioceses and ordain bishops directly dependent on him to reaffirm his metropolitan jurisdiction against the claims of Patroclus and Remigius.⁴⁶

To settle the matter, Zosimus would celebrate the aforementioned council of Rome in 417, where Proculus was dismissed and the bishops of Citharista and Gargaria excommunicated.⁴⁷ However, the bishop of Marseille defied the papal orders and continued his activity. With regard to Tuentius and Ursus, it is more difficult to know their fate, but it is possible that they managed to maintain their episcopal position, at least during Proculus' life. That is, the bishop of Marseille limited himself to ignoring the papal precepts, knowing the internal strength of his position.⁴⁸ Such that, it may be that Tuentius was the bishop with whom Pope Celestine corresponded years later.⁴⁹ Faced with his defiant attitude, Zosimus tried to undermine Proculus' internal support by addressing the clergy and the people of Marseille directly to let them know first-hand about the dismissal of their bishop. However, his appeals were completely unsuccessful.⁵⁰

Zosimus' movements had absolutely no effect whatsoever in asserting Patroclus' supra-provincial aspirations. The pope himself was ineffective in the face of the other bishops' apathy.⁵¹ It is true that Zosimus expressed greater concern for Proculus, which could serve as an indirect indication of Hilary of Narbonne and Simplicius of Vienne's submission to papal orders, but it is also true that he only removed the bishop of Marseille, which meant a greater humiliation.

Zosimus abandoned his attempts to promote the bishop of Arles and to impose his authority over Gaul, but Patroclus did not and instead remained obstinate in asserting his theoretical primacy by deploying new strategies. On one hand, he would choose to use religious arguments to revile and weaken his enemies.⁵² He specifically accused them of Priscillianism; an accusation that, beyond having a real basis, functioned as a pretext in his campaign to achieve supra-provincial ju-

---

45 Zosimus, *Epistolae Arelatenses genuinae* 2. Unfortunately, we do not know what see each of these characters occupied. Regarding Ursus, it has been suggested that he was the same person with whom Proculus had a dispute long ago: Natal 2012, 114.
46 Natal and Wood 2016, 52. On the importance of this episcopal ordination by the metropolitan, Müller 2003, 235–236.
47 Zosimus, *Epistolae Arelatenses genuinae* 2; 4.
48 Revealing the ineffectiveness of the papal decrees towards Proculus: Mathisen 1989, 59.
49 *PCBE* 4, 1898.
50 Zosimus, *Epistolae Arelatenses genuinae* 7.
51 Zosimus, *Epistolae Arelatenses genuinae* 6.
52 Fryc 1991, 360.

risdiction.[53] Having made such accusations, Patroclus tried to gain Augustine of Hippo's moral support by using Consencius as an intermediary, but the African bishop was uncommitted. He also tried to attract episcopal support in Tarragona, but was unsuccessful there too.[54] As these manoeuvres bore no fruit, Patroclus chose to appeal to the highest instances of secular power. In 425, he succeeded in having Emperor Valentinian III – perhaps through the intermediation of his mother Gala Placidia – grant him the power to judge the orthodoxy of Gallic bishops, ability to depose and replace those he considered heretical, and convene councils for the entire episcopate of Gaul.[55] However, the decree did not come to have any effect, since Patroclus was assassinated the following year.

Within Patroclus' campaign, there was an interesting occurrence that is worth noting. In the year 421/2 Patroclus ordained a new bishop for the see of Lodève, integrated into Narbonensis I. Faced with this interference, Boniface, the bishop of Rome (418–422), much less inclined to grant privileges to Patroclus, denounced the ordainment, doubtless using the occurrence as an excuse to rectify his predecessor's actions and deprive Arles of its supra-metropolitan rights.[56] The curious thing about this is that it was the people of Lodève who denounced Patroclus' invasion to the pope, not the metropolitan bishop, Hilary, proof that it was often much more effective to remain passive in the face of threats than to act. The papal resolution demanded the bishop of Narbonne to leave for Lodève to take charge of the situation as a competent authority.[57] Such behaviour could be understood as a submission to Patroclus,[58] which contrasts with the complaints sent to Rome by Hilary years ago. For this reason, we prefer to see a certain indifference from the bishop of Narbonne when it comes to exercising his metropolitan rights over this region. Moreover, it gave the impression that the Diocese of Lodève had acted outside any metropolitan jurisdiction, perhaps due to its own peripheral situation,[59] and that the bishop of Narbonne himself had not bothered to reverse the situation.

---

[53] As Bronwen Neil 2018, 94, recently noted, "religious conflict may mask other root causes of conflict, whether over politics, material conditions, institutional or social status, or a combination of these factors".
[54] On these movements, Ubric Rabaneda 2013; Villegas 2017, 313.
[55] Mathisen 1989, 72; Frye 1991, 359–360.
[56] Villegas 2017, 314. On the bellicose attitude of Pope Boniface and his successor Celestine towards Patroclus and his aspirations, Mathisen 1989, 69–71. 74. 98–99.
[57] Bonifatius I. papa v. Epist. pontif. 12.
[58] Mathisen 1989, 58, intuits a pact between Patroclus and Hilary.
[59] This is what Boniface himself noted in his letter. Bonifatius I. papa v. Epist. pontif. 12.

4 The Incidence of the Social Factor: The Case of Hilary and Ravenius of Arles' Supra-Metropolitan Aspirations

The tables will turn with Patroclus' successors in the Arles sees. Honoratus and, above all, Hilary of Arles will learn from the mistakes of their predecessor and will try to extend a supra-metropolitan authority for Arles through their direct intervention in areas of jurisdiction that theoretically depended on another metropolitan bishop. We can attribute such actions to the ambition of their promoters, but also to a certain need to assert themselves against rival internal factions.[60] The majority of the aggrieved bishops will turn to Rome during the first decades of the fifth century, and the pope will generally speak in favour of the appellant. This was the case of Celestine, who in a decree addressed to the bishops of the Viennensis and the Narbonensis ordered them not to occupy the jurisdiction of other dioceses and ecclesiastical provinces other than their own, and not to ordain foreign or individuals of a secular condition to the implicated see.[61] We know that Honoratus, in a violation of his jurisdiction, had appointed the bishop of Tarentaise as the metropolitan head of the Alps Graiae province, so it is more than likely that the decree had been addressed to him.[62] The mere fact that Pope Celestine did not dare to directly accuse Honoratus is an indication of the papal inability to enforce his orders.

This papal impotence will also be evident in later moments, particularly in the times of Pope Leo (440–461) and Bishop Hilary of Arles, who will try to impose ecclesiastical primacy over a large part of the Gallic territory.[63] Regarding his actions, in approximately 439 he presided over the Council of Riez, where bishops from the Viennensis, Narbonensis Secunda and Alpes Maritimae provinces met under the pretext of judging the irregular ordainment of Bishop Armentarius of Embrun. The council is resolved by dismissing the ordination and defending the exclusive authority of the bishop of Arles to ordain a new prelate here and in all these three provinces.[64] In this way Hilary was taking advantage of the support offered by the bishops in this council to do away with the metropolitan of Embrun. Hilary would celebrate a new synod in Orange in 441, where he again received the sup-

---

60 See n. 2.
61 Caelestinus papa v. Epist. pontif. 4, 4–6.
62 Mathisen 1989, 99–100.
63 Heinzelmann 1992.
64 Council of Riez (a. 439), cc. 3–4, 6. See De Leo 1983, 23–24.

port of the bishops of these provinces, and also of Eucherius of Lyons, to assume the power to summon all the Gallic episcopate to a council.⁶⁵ Making a show of his prerogatives, he did so again one year later also in Vaison, summoning the bishops of these provinces, including one of the Narbonensis Prima, Constantius of Uzès.⁶⁶

While legitimising his supra-provincial aspirations through the council, Hilary intervened directly in the dioceses of other provinces, including some of metropolitan rank, deposing and ordaining bishops at will. This occurred in the aforementioned case of Embrun, where he deposed Armentarius and subsequently promoted Ingenuus. A similar interventionism was carried out in Besançon, the metropolitan see of the Sequanensis, in which he promoted the deposition of his bishop Celidonius in a new council, as a result of harsh accusations made against him.⁶⁷ He would subsequently promote a candidate he trusted as a substitute for Celidonius, without attending to the canonical norms.⁶⁸ Furthermore, Hilary was especially adept at mobilising internal ecclesiastical factions against Celidonius. The ambitious bishop of Arles did not limit himself only to acting on metropolitan sees, but also promoted similar actions in dioceses of lesser rank. We know, for example, that he promoted the dismissal of a certain Projectus, whose see was unknown. In this case, he even resorted to intimidation, being accompanied by an armed entourage.⁶⁹ We also know that he ordained Constantius of Uzès, who theoretically depended on Narbonne.⁷⁰ Interestingly, we have no documents recording how Armentarius reacted, who perhaps resigned himself to accepting the resolution taken at Riez; and there also is no indication of how the bishop of Narbonne reacted to the ordination of Constantius. We do, however, know that Celidonius and Projectus ended up turning to Pope Leo, who aligned himself in favour of the appellants and thus against Hilary's supra-provincial aspirations.⁷¹ In a harsh resolution dated 445, Leo deprived Hilary of his metropolitan rank, and forbade him from convening councils and participating in episcopal tribunals.⁷² He simultaneously decreed the restitution of Celidonius and Projectus to their respective

---

65 Council of Orange (a. 441), c. 28 (29).
66 Council of Vaison (a. 442), *Subscr.* On Uzès' ties to Arles, Loseby 1992, 147–148.
67 On the accusations and the process against Celidonius, Leo M. epist. 10, 3; Honoratus of Marseille, Vita Hil. Arel. 21. De Leo 1983, 25–27.
68 Loftus 2011, 425. 430.
69 Leo M. epist. 10, 4. Heinzelmann 1992, 240–241.
70 Mathisen 1989, 113.
71 Leo M. epist. 10, 2. Heinzelmann 1992.
72 Leo M. epist. 10, 7. Heinzelmann 1992, 241.

sees.⁷³ These resolutions would also be sanctioned by a civil decree made by Valentinian III.⁷⁴

This is how the threatening bishop began to occupy a threatened position. But to what extent? Nothing indicates that the papal resolutions had taken effect. It is true that there are no other overreaches by Hilary in the time that was left to him. A different case is that of his successor Ravenius, who claimed a supra-provincial jurisdiction from quite early on, as we will see later.⁷⁵ The security shown by Ravenius only makes sense if it had followed a previous trend. On the other hand, Pope Leo's own actions in dealing with this cause reflects a certain degree of impotence when it comes to asserting his orders and authority over the Gallic episcopate. For example, instead of issuing a resolution on his own authority, he first summoned a council in Rome to judge the cause and then appealed to the imperial authority, which issued a parallel sentence.⁷⁶

Leo's behaviour reflects the enormous internal power that Hilary enjoyed in Gaul. But what was the basis of his power? The answer lies in the dense networks of influence that he wove from a large part of the Gallic episcopate, especially among those from the monastery of Lérins;⁷⁷ with that network, he was able to form a powerful faction around him, against which no other metropolitan bishop could compete. Hilary's networks extended in the secular sphere; as an example they included those who promoted him to the chair of Arles, such as the *magister militum*.⁷⁸ Because of them, Hilary had enormous capacity for manoeuvring on a supra-provincial scale that allowed him to relieve and appoint bishops at will without the need for a legal basis.⁷⁹ A particularly important factor in the construction of these networks was his intervention in the episcopal appointments of all possi-

---

73 Leo M. epist. 10, 3–4.
74 *Constitutio Valentiniani III Augusti*, in Leo M. epist. 11. As Mathisen 1989, 164–165, states: "it merely acted as an enforcement arm for the church in Rome".
75 Mathisen 1989, 170.
76 Hilary himself would have gone to Rome, but left as soon as he saw that he had no way to assert his position. Honoratus of Marseille, Vita Hil. Arel. 22. Heinzelmann 1976, 79–80; Mathisen 1989, 158–159.
77 See Mathisen 1989.
78 Heinzelmann 1976, 78–82; Heinzelmann 1992, 246. On Hilary's secular supports, see also Mathisen 1989, 155–156.
79 Leo himself acknowledged the importance of these personal networks when he alludes to the fact that it is personal affinity that determined the exercise of a supra-metropolitan jurisdiction to Hilary. Leo M. epist. 10, 6.

ble dioceses, regardless of their territory and entity.[80] In order to secure the support of the greatest possible number of bishops he would go as far as to found new dioceses, some of them short-lived, as is the case of Castellane and Thorame. The creation of such networks was a slow process, which is why we do not have evidence of Hilary's first transgressions until well into his episcopate. This is also why it took years to gather the necessary support to convene the first supra-provincial councils, specifically one decade after his ascent to the episcopate. He would then hold three councils in a very short space of time: one in Riez (439), another in Orange (441) and another in Vaison (442). By then he had already consolidated ties with bishops of all ranks and from different territories, thanks to which he obtained a majority in the councils in his favour. Being aware of his control over the conciliar debates, means that his interest in raising all episcopal disputes to council is comprehensible.[81] As David Natal stated for a somewhat earlier context, "the objectives of councils were not to facilitate debate, but to legitimise the opinion of the most powerful episcopal group."[82] By extension, councils would only have been encouraged when their promoter was sure that the result would be resolved in a manner favourable to their interests. Furthermore, in a clear display of force, but also in a provocation to his opponents, Hilary summoned these councils in territories over which Arles had long claimed jurisdiction.

For Hilary, the councils were merely instrumental – used for ecclesiastical primacy in Gaul. Consequently, canonical regulations would have been of a similar nature. Within this system, Hilary would have resorted to the canonical argument when it benefited him, but, without fear of consequences, he would have transgressed when it did not suit him, knowing that all internal complaints were destined to fail. In the end, regulations were pushed into the background when there was majority support. The first assumption was applied at the time of deposing Armentarius of Embrun, while the second is evident in the case of Besançon. This is how, according to Peter van Nuffelen, the canonical regulation functioned, and although different to the rules of the game, it was still part of the game itself.[83]

---

80 Honoratus of Marseille, Vita Hil. Arel. 30. As such, we find him appointing bishops in minor nuclei such as Toulon or Carpentras. About this activity, Loseby 1992, 147–148. Many of the ordained bishops had trained directly with Hilary. Honoratus of Marseille, Vita Hil. Arel. 11.
81 Council of Vaison (a. 442), cc. 7–8. However, such a majority was not synonymous with consensus, so the councils laid the groundwork for the aggrieved parties to appeal to the pope. The success of the Council of Turin was due to it being a council that had the intervention of Italian agents, presumably impartial, whose decision, due to its arbitrary nature, had a greater chance of being accepted by the parties. Only an impartial council could achieve a mutually acceptable solution. On the subsequent acceptance of the Council of Turin, Mathisen 2013, 304–307.
82 Natal 2015b, 41.
83 Van Nuffelen 2011, 245.

Hilary's networks would have spread over numerous dioceses, which, regardless of their original affiliation, were suffragans of Arles. Some metropolitan bishops would not have had the power to contradict the authority of Hilary, and had no choice but to allow his interference within their provinces.[84] It is thus striking that the aforementioned Projectus, a suffragan bishop, addressed his complaint directly to the pope and not to the aggrieved metropolitan, possibly Claudius of Vienne.[85] In fact, Claudius of Vienne and the metropolitan of Lyon attended some of the councils chaired by Hilary,[86] a sign that they had become part of his powerful networks of influence, or that, at least, they attributed a higher moral authority to him.[87] We can thus deduce how some metropolitans, even seeing their jurisdiction diminished, were impassive and even docile in the face of the continuous violations against their authority.[88] Perhaps Claudius kept his rank by accepting the new situation, a rank with which he signed conciliar proceedings. This was not the case of Ingenuus of Embrun, who in exchange for his episcopal promotion freely ceded all his metropolitan rights to Hilary,[89] to the point of signing the proceedings as a suffragan.[90] Pope Leo himself would reproach the attitude of these metropolitans who renounced their rights and describe them as deserters of their rank, precisely for allowing Hilary to ordain bishops in their provinces.[91] Ingenuus' approval of the Council of Orange in 441 contrasts with that of the other two metropolitans present, Claudius of Vienne and Eucherius of Lyon, who sign after Hilary.[92] We can deduce two different metropolitan bishop profiles based on the different ways they approve the councils: the first are those metropolitans, such as the holder of Vienne, who would maintain their rights but afford Hilary a higher authority and allow him to interfere in their provinces and, on the second, those who re-

---

84 As proposed by Mathisen 1989, 157, for the second profile, "Hilary's extended metropolitan rights, therefore, even according to Leo, had not been seized from unwilling metropolitans, but had been ceded willingly to him by the metropolitans concerned".
85 Perhaps now we can understand the papal accusation that he usurped metropolitan rights in the Vienne province. Leo M. epist. 10, 7. We rule out that the aforementioned Projectus had been a metropolitan bishop, as defended by Mathisen 1989, 151–152.
86 Regarding his relationship with the bishop of Lyon, we know that he had corresponded with him and that literary compositions were exchanged. *PCBE* 4, 1000.
87 Griffe 1966, 140.
88 Highlighting episcopal support for Hilary, Heinzelmann 1976, 81.
89 Mathisen 1989, 106–107. 220. It is not surprising that some have attributed Ingenuus with a certain attitude of indifference: Griffe 1966, 166. Cf. Mathisen 1989, 223.
90 *PCBE* 4, 1039.
91 Leo M. epist. 10, 6.
92 Council of Orange (a. 441), *Subscr.*

nounced all their privileges and became mere suffragans, as happened with Ingenuus of Embrun.

Of course, not all metropolitans would have willingly accepted this order of things, but they would have been a minority and with little authority. Faced with this situation, some of them would have simply resigned themselves to it, and included themselves in Hilary's networks. Others, particularly those who were able to escape Hilary's authority, would have been indifferent. Then there would be those who, even under the authority of the bishop of Arles, tried to resist, albeit passively, for example, by not attending his councils.[93] Lastly, there would be the most affected, such as Celidonius, who opted to oppose Hilary's autarkic policies. They only had one option: to appeal to Rome. The fact that they ended up resorting to external interference by the pope is an indication of Celidonius' failure to build dense personal networks not only among his own suffragan episcopate, but among the local population itself.[94] If this were true, perhaps Hilary's threat would not have had such weight or, at least, Celidonius could have addressed the issue in better conditions.[95] We could say that his precarious situation was a consequence of his lack of proactivity.[96] The deposed bishop of Besançon only reacted when it was too late, leaving him one last and the least effective resort: an appeal to Rome.[97]

In contrast, Rusticus of Narbonne was able to retain his position and jurisdiction, while freeing himself from any of Hilary's influence. This is evidenced by his absence, and the absence of his suffragans – with the exception of Constantius of Uzès – in the councils presided over by Hilary,[98] a symptom of the strong control that Rusticus exercised over his bishops.[99] Perhaps as a response to Hilary's aspirations, in Rusticus there are unprecedented claims of his authority and independ-

---

[93] This could have been the case with Aix, who never attended Hilary's councils, although some of his theoretically suffragan bishops did. Mathisen 1989, 118. 220. See *infra*.

[94] This situation is especially evident in the case of Besançon.

[95] As stated by Wood 2019, 239, even though he was referring to the Hispanic case, "cultivating connection to local populations was vital if the bishop was to establish his power in the first place and later to resist outside interference or challenges from within the bishopric".

[96] Wood 2019, 234: "Those who sought to resolve disputes were clearly reactive rather than proactive".

[97] Metropolitans themselves may not have looked favourably on papal meddling in their affairs, but their powerlessness in dealing with the dense personal networks of their adversaries left them no choice.

[98] Heinzelmann 1992, 250; *PCBE* 4, 1658.

[99] Rusticus' networks would have spread outside his province, for example, to the diocese of Marseille, with whose bishop Venerio he had close contacts. *PCBE* 4, 1924.

ence from the bishop of Arles himself,[100] being the first prelate to date the religious buildings promoted by him, such as the Basilica of Saint-Félix of Narbonne and the altar of Minerva, from his years as episcopate.[101]

Aware of his strengths, Hilary mobilised his networks to challenge Pope Leo's attempts to undermine his authority. For example, he ordered that the response to Leo be led by an entourage made up of bishops from outside the Viennensis, such as Constantius de Uzès, in a clear provocation to the pope, aimed at making his internal forces visible.[102] For this he also turned to the secular powers that supported him.[103] What is striking is that the entourage did not address the pope, but the imperial powers. Hilary's concern was not so much the papal resolution, but the decree of Valentinian III, which reaffirmed the bishop of Rome's limited powers when it came to enforcing his orders in Gaul.

The personal networks of different agents of power thus became the determining factor in better coping with the threats to metropolitan authority and, in particular, those that came from Rome. This same situation occurred during the time of Hilary's successor at the Arles see, Ravenius. The new bishop inherited the episcopal networks of his powerful predecessor, which gave him a greater capacity for influence than the rest of his Gallic counterparts, although it is true that the change of head in the Arles see caused Ravenius to lose control of other sees. However, Ravenius was able to ordain a bishop at Vaison, which was theoretically under the jurisdiction of Nicetas of Vienne. The latter would be much less complacent than his predecessor Claudius, but, knowing the strength of Ravenius, he had no choice but to turn to Pope Leo to resolve this interference in his jurisdiction.[104] In a new display of strength, and showing that his power was similar to that of his predecessor, Ravenius mobilised his episcopal networks, ensuring that 19 bishops from the southern Gaul, and from different provinces, demanded metropolitan rights from the pope for the Arlesian see over the Vienne provinces, the two Narbonensis provinces and Alpes Maritimae.[105] The request was still a formality in a *de facto* situation, despite previous papal resolutions. In fact, it is possible that Rav-

---

100 Riess 2013, 83.
101 Marrou 1970; Riess 2013, 80–92.
102 Honoratus of Marseille, Vita Hil. Arel. 22.
103 The Romanus' of Condat *vita*, from the beginning of the sixth century, confirms the support that the most powerful secular agents gave him. Heinzelmann 1992, 242.
104 It is interesting to note that it was the bishops Nicetas of Vienne and Narbonne who anointed Ravenius, perhaps with the hope that he would not show the same aspirations as his predecessor. Leo, *Ep. Coll. Arelat.* 9. Mathisen 1989, 173.
105 Zosimus, *Epistolae Arelatenses genuinae* 12.

enius' intention was to show the pope his willingness to continue exercising supraprovincial jurisdiction, whether he had approval from Rome or not.

On this occasion, instead of betting again on a lost cause, Pope Leo would end up recognising the factual power of Ravenius and the see of Arles. Thus, in a new decree dating from 450, he attributed the dioceses of Tarentaise, Valence, Geneva and Grenoble to Vienne, while the rest of the Viennensis sees, including Die and Viviers, were handed over to Arles.[106] In an indirect acknowledgement of his helplessness, Leo accepts the current state of affairs, including Ravenius' authority over Vaison's see.[107] Despite being the appellant, Nicetas of Vienne would end up humiliated. Beyond the fact that Leo tried to make his decree serve as a compromise between both parties, he was aware that his orders would only be followed if his resolution pleased Ravenius. Otherwise, he risked them falling on deaf ears.

5 The Chronic Precariousness of Certain Metropolitan Sees

Despite his primacy, Ravenius would have had some difficulty maintaining Hilary's networks. The bishop of Vienne was not alone in claiming metropolitan rights for Embrun, the bishops of the Alpes Maritimae, led by Veranus of Vence, also defended them.[108] It is not unreasonable to suggest that behind this claim was Ingenuus of Embrun, who had no other option but to act behind the scenes due to his inability to directly confront his main supporter. Unlike the sees of Vienne and Narbonne, the bishops of Embrun were unable to easily impose themselves on their counterparts in Arles.

Embrun would thus enter the group of metropolitan sees that, despite attempts, showed a chronic inability to establish a real jurisdiction over neighbouring dioceses. The Aix see would also fall into this category. Both metropolitan sees were able to intermittently influence their theoretical suffragan bishoprics throughout the fifth century, and often treated the bishop of Arles as their metropolitan.[109] Ravenius of Arles, for example, presided over a council addressing a dispute between the abbot Faustus of Lerins and the bishop Theodore of Fréjus, who

---

106 Leo M. epist. 66.
107 It has been said that Ravenius had the pope's support. Griffe 1966, 160–161. However, if that were the case, the bishops' actions would not have been necessary.
108 Hil. Arel. epist. 12, 1.
109 Griffe 1966, 154–155. Aix would end up losing its metropolitan rank in the sixth century. Duval, Fevrier, and Guyon 1986, 67–68.

was within the jurisdiction of Aix.¹¹⁰ As far as Embrun is concerned, we have already mentioned the voluntary subordination of its bishop Ingenuus to Hilary. Before the power of Arles, they could only show a passive or veiled resistance when circumstances allowed it, as occurred in the case of Ingenuus during the time of Ravenius of Arles. This is how we also understand the absence of Aix at the council proceedings chaired by Hilary or Ravenius.¹¹¹ To face their precariousness, and given the impossibility of competing with powerful metropolitan sees, both Aix and Embrun opted to compete between themselves.¹¹² We know, for example, that Auxanius of Aix acted against Ingenuus of Embrun, invading his jurisdiction over the diocese of Cimiez by promoting a bishop in the enclave of Nice.¹¹³ His intervention in other dioceses is not ruled out either.¹¹⁴ Here we can see how, for a time, there were two bishops in the same territory, each dependent on a different metropolitan. Faced with such an invasion, Ingenuus appealed to the bishop of Rome, who dealt with the matter in a council and would conclude by ordering Auxanius to desist in his aspirations on Nice.¹¹⁵

Later, there would be those other metropolitan sees whose bishops showed, not so much incapacity, but a certain disinterest, in exercising their theoretical prerogatives. This is the attitude that we perceive in the case of Bourges, the see that we find under the orbit of Tours during the time of Bishop Leo.¹¹⁶ Faced with Bourges' apathy, it is possible that Clermont had adopted a *de facto* metropolitan role from the episcopate of Sidonius Apollinaris that was never answered by Bourges, or at least has not transpired, which is a symptom of his weakness. Perhaps also out of disinterest, Tours found it difficult to assert his metropolitan rights under Bishop Brice. It would not be until the episcopates of his successors, Eusto-

---

110 *Exemplar epistulae generalis quae ad episcopos inuitandos in causa insulae Lerinensis missa est*; *Institutio sanctorum episcoporum Ravennii, Rustici, Nectari, Flori, Constanti(i), Ascelpi(i), Maximi, iusti, Saloni(i), Ingenui, Enanti(i), Zotici, Chrysantii, in causa insula Lerinensis*.
111 On absence, Griffe 1966, 164–165.
112 On this competition, Griffe 1950, 71–74; Griffe 1966, 164–166. We do not rule out that this competition had also occurred with Marseille after Proculus. Mathisen 1989, 219–220. Others, however, rule out that Proculus' successors had tried to reproduce a metropolitan jurisdiction for their sees. Griffe 1950, 67.
113 Hil. Arel. epist. 12, 1.
114 Griffe 1966, 166.
115 Hil. Arel. epist. 12, 1. Griffe 1950, 73–74; Duval, Fevrier, and Guyon 1986, 68.
116 We find him attending the Council of Angers in 453, presided over by Eustochius of Tours, a council which, apart from the aforementioned Leo, was only attended by suffragan bishops of Tours. He also attended the Council of Tours in 461, but this was attended by more bishops from other provinces, possibly because of the celebration of the *receptio Martini* in this city. Pietri 1983, 145.

chius and Perpetuus, that Tours would begin to claim and exercise a real metropolitan authority.[117] Just as in Belgica Secunda, we did not observe a clear metropolitan activity until the time of Remigius of Reims, that is, from the second half of the fifth century, when we observed the first appointments of suffragan bishops.[118] A similar case is that of Trier, whose metropolitan role was diluted throughout the fifth century, with no signs of reactivation until the Merovingian period.[119] One factor that might have influenced the dissolution of the metropolitan role of both sees could have been the little Christianisation of these areas, and also their greater exposure to barbarian incursions. However, this had a lower incidence compared to the first, since in the case of Trier, for example, there continued to be a regular succession of bishops throughout the century.[120] Germania had less luck, where we have no record of the presence of any bishop, not even in its metropolitan see, Mayence, as did Strasbourg, Spire and Worms.[121]

6 The Instrumentalisation of the Pope by the New Secular Power

It was not only episcopal agents who would appeal to Rome. Certain secular powers also saw a possible way to preserve their interests in the papacy. This happened in 463 as a result of the consecration of Marcellus as the new bishop of Die by Mamertus of Vienne.[122] This appointment was a violation of the previous resolutions of Pope Leo, but also of the will of the Die people, whose opinion would not have been taken into account.[123] This interference led to intervention by Gondioc, king of the Burgundians and ultimately *magister militum* of the Empire in Gaul, who appealed to Pope Hilary (461–468) to denounce Mamertus' behaviour.[124] The bishop

---

117 Pietri 1983, 143–152. In a similar vein, *PCBE* 4, 713: "il [Eustochius] est le premier évêque de Tours à revendiquer, sans employer encore le terme, l'autorité d'un métropolitain". On the metropolitan activity of Perpetuus, Bourges 2012.
118 Until then, we only know of the Châlons-sur-Marne and Senlis sees in operation. This map will be multiplied, in time with the evangelisation of the region, at the end of the episcopate of Remigius with the addition of Amiens, Beauvais, Soissons, Arras, Laon, Senlis, Tournai and Saint-Quentin. Isaïa 2011, 140–161.
119 On such reactivation, Poveda Arias 2021.
120 Griffe 1966, 135. Cf. Anton 1989, 61.
121 Gauthier 1980, 129. As this author shows, at that time it would have been the bishops of Belgica Prima who were in charge of the pastoral care and evangelisation of the region.
122 On the identification of this Marcellus with the bishop of Die, Stüber 2020, 78–88.
123 Leo M. epist. 66; Ven. Fort. Vita Marcell. 3.
124 Hil. Arel. *Epistolae Arelatenses genuinae* 19–21.

of Rome responded by addressing the alleged main aggrieved party, Leontius of Arles, whose jurisdiction was ultimately being violated. Leontius was also given a warning for not having made him aware of the bishop of Vienne's movements. He was also required to address the problem in a council chaired by himself.[125] Thus, we see a resignation on the part of Rome to take justice into their own hands in matters of Gaul, limiting itself to only ordering the Gallic episcopate to resolve their affairs. The final resolution of the conflict confirms this. The Gallic bishops met and settled this episode in council. However, far from denouncing Mamertus' behaviour, they accepted Marcellus' appointment and, therefore, the interference of the bishop of Vienne in Die. Faced with this episcopal resolution, Hilary was forced to accept the *status quo*, requesting only that the ordination of Mamertus be confirmed by Leontius.[126]

In line with this event, Leontius of Arles' attitude is striking: he was completely impassive in the face of Mamertus' interference in his supposed area of influence. We thus get the impression that Leontius was much less ambitious than his famous predecessors, and that not only did he not aspire to exercise supra-provincial rights,[127] but he may have even neglected the exercise of his metropolitan functions within its own province.[128] The fact that both Leontius and the bishops gathered in the aforementioned council accepted the current reality is an indication that it had been normalised. The legal arguments were thus swept under the carpet when the different parties accepted a *status quo* supported solely by social practice,[129] in this case in the *de facto* exercise of a metropolitan jurisdiction over Die by a strong and ambitious personality such as Mamertus. In the end, the only one interested in appealing to Rome was Gondioc. It has been argued that the king acted solely to fulfil his functions as *magister militum*,[130] but this contrasts with the general attitude of his predecessors in office, who showed a total indifference towards ecclesiastical affairs. For this reason, we understand that Gondioc's behaviour was a strategy aimed at extending Burgundian influence over this region. His interest in Die would have been to promote a candidate related to him,[131] but also in attracting the population of this city who were dissatisfied with the nomination

---

125 Hil. Arel. *Epistolae Arelatenses genuinae* 19.
126 Hil. Arel. *Epistolae Arelatenses genuinae* 21. Stüber 2020, 82–83. See also Griffe 1966, 163.
127 In fact, the Embrun and Aix sees seem to have enjoyed a few years of stability and independence from Arles, and not because of their greater strength, but because Pope Hilary acknowledged their rank. Hil. Arel. epist. 8; 11. Mathisen 1989, 220.
128 Cf. Mathisen 1989, 205.
129 In a similar vein, Van Nuffelen 2011, 245.
130 Stüber 2020, 82.
131 Nimmegeers 2014, 47; Stüber 2020, 82.

of Marcellus as the new bishop of Die. Thus, Gondioc, through his appeal to Rome, would have become the champion of the popular will in a movement aimed at achieving the support of the city at a nascent moment of his power. Additionally, the episode would have served him to confront Mamertus of Die, with whom we believe he had a tense relationship.

Visigothic prince Frederic would have been pursuing the same intentions when he also appealed to the same pope because of the appointment of Hermes as the new bishop of Narbonne,[132] a city that had just been taken over by the Visigoths.[133] Frederic took advantage of the irregular nature of the appointment of Hermes, who, contrary to canonical norms, had left the episcopal chair of Béziers to become metropolitan of Narbonne, to champion the cause and bring it to Rome. Again, it is striking that it was a secular agent who appealed to the pope and that – as in the previous case – the other bishops did not voice their opposition to the promotion of Hermes, despite the fact that it violated canonical regulations.[134] What is more, certain bishops, such as Faustus of Riez and Auxanius of Aix, would travel to Rome to defend him.[135] It is possible that the controversy generated around the election of Hermes had been exploited by the new Visigothic power as a way to legitimise and vindicate itself in front of the Narbonne community, in this case through assuming a role of arbitration,[136] while gaining the sympathies of groups opposed to Hermes. At the same time, if successful, Frederic would manage to rid himself of someone who opposed Visigothic rule.

Hilary would respond to this new violation of the rules. In a first letter, he would again reproach Leontius of Arles for his passivity in the face of a new violation of the *status quo*, to then issue a resolution unfavourable to the interests of Hermes. In it, Hermes was allowed to keep the Narbonnean chair, but he was deprived of his metropolitan rank, which was granted temporarily, until the death of Hermes himself, to the most veteran bishop of the province, in this case the prelate of Uzès. Hilary could not risk being humiliated before a harsher resolution that deposed Hermes that he could not comply with, so he chose an in between. Knowing whether the papal resolution had any effect is more difficult, but without a doubt

---

[132] Hil. Arel. epist. 7. See Langgärtner 1964, 93–94. 98–90, who denies that he was actually Theodoric's brother. Among those who advocate the contrary option, Mathisen 1989, 207. About Frederic, Serrano Madroñal, 2020.
[133] Hyd. chron. 212 [217]; Isid. hist. 33.
[134] This factor shows how social reality used to prevail over what was prescribed in canonical norms. See Van Nuffelen 2011.
[135] Griffe 1966, 184.
[136] Cf. Mathisen and Sivan 1999, 42.

the Visigothic power would have struggled to enforce it and prevent Hermes from exercising a metropolitan position.[137]

7 The Rising of the New *Regna* and the Fragmentation of the Ecclesiastical Provinces

The cases of Gondioc and Frederic reveal the growing weight that the new barbarian powers began to have from the second half of the fifth century as potential threats to the metropolitan bishops. However, some prelates saw in the incursion of these new actors as an opportunity rather than a potential danger.[138] Remigius of Reims, for example, would approach the Frankish king Clovis, the temporal coincidence of the extension of his metropolitan authority with his approach to the Merovingian was not accidental.[139] Less promising was the outlook for the metropolitans with the Visigothic occupation in the southern half of Gaul, which led to the decomposition of the current ecclesiastical and administrative order. The ecclesiastical provinces were thus exposed to a fragmentation of their territory.[140]

The see of Narbonne was especially damaged, until it was finally conquered by the Visigoths. Its metropolitan maintained the ascendancy over the sees which, like her, were still under the control of the Empire, as is the case of Béziers, Lodève, Nîmes and, theoretically, Uzès as well, but the western part of her province, which included Toulouse, was under the control of the Visigoths, which in practice meant the loss of all influence over them.[141] Already integrated into the Visigothic kingdom, Narbonne would on this occasion lose control over those dioceses that were under Burgundian control. Arles also saw its province fragmented, as we will see below. For its part, Aix – also integrated into the Visigothic kingdom – ended up losing control over Gap, Sistero and Apt, which remained under Burgundian rule. Embrun, annexed to the Burgundian kingdom, also suffered the consequences of the expansionism of both kingdoms, losing its control over its entire province, particularly over Digne and Senez, which fell under Visigothic domination. Lacking strength, it is understood that for a time it depended directly on Vienne.[142]

---

137 Hil. Arel. epist. 7–8. Langgärtner 1964, 95; Griffe 1966, 185; Mathisen 1989, 208–210.
138 Mathisen 1993, 153–158; Díaz 2016.
139 See Poveda Arias, 2019.
140 Schäferdiek 1967, 38–41; Nimmegeers 2014, 50.
141 Mathisen 1989, 120; Riess 2013, 83.
142 Duval, Fevrier, and Guyon 1986, 67–68; Nimmegeers, 2014: 57.

A priori, political boundaries should not influence the internal functioning of the Church but, in reality, they resulted in an isolation of churches according to their political affiliation. In particular, the bishoprics integrated into the Visigothic kingdom did not participate in the Gallic councils that were held outside the areas controlled by the Visigoths, perhaps in a conscious attempt by the the latter to isolate their bishops.[143] Faced with such a threat, the metropolitans had little room for manoeuvre, but they would not resign themselves to accepting the new situation. Basilius of Aix and Leontius of Arles, for example, together with the bishops Graecus of Marseille and Faustus of Riez, would be personally involved in the negotiations that the Visigoth king Euric had with the Empire between the years 474 and 475 to agree on the annexation of new territories.[144] In principle, these bishops attended the negotiations on behalf of the Gallic Church that had not yet fallen under Visigothic domination. However, it is to be expected that they ended up prioritising their personal interests, particularly in regard to maintaining the territorial integrity of their provinces, and put collective interests in the background. Sidonius Apollinaris himself – who in the course of these negotiations attended the Visigothic annexation of his see, Clermont – reproached these bishops for their selfishness.[145] However, the order defined in such negotiations would be destined to be quite ephemeral, since the fall of the Empire in the West left the way clear for the Visigoths to take Arles, Aix and part of their respective territories.

It was especially difficult for Eonius of Arles to accept the fragmentation of his ecclesiastical province. The dioceses north of Durance (St. Paul-Trois-Châteaux, Vaison, Orange, Carpentras, Avignon, Cavaillon) were integrated into the Burgundian kingdom, which allowed the metropolitan of Vienne to take control of them.[146] The bishop of Rome, in this case Anastasius (496–498), would end up recognising the new political order, confirming to Avitus of Vienne his jurisdiction over such dioceses. Eonius of Arles would appeal the papal resolution to Anastasius' successor in the Petrine chair: Symmachus (498–514). To settle the dispute, the bishop of Rome summoned the parties, but apparently neither of them appeared. Consequently, Symmachus did not dare issue a final judgement.[147] We are surprised to see Eonius' claim to his jurisdiction over dioceses that, because of political borders, he

---

[143] Mathisen and Sivan 1999, 41. The isolation of the churches in the Visigothic kingdom contrasts with the active participation in the Gallic councils of those ones integrated into the Burgundian kingdom.
[144] Sidon. epist. VII, 6, 10.
[145] Sidon. epist. VII, 7, 4.
[146] Nimmegeers 2014, 50.
[147] Symmachus, *Epistolae Arelatenses genuinae* 23–24. Mathisen 1997, 546–547; *PCBE* 4, 56; Nimmegeers 2014, 50.

could not control, in what we understand as a denial of the new order. In fact, Avitus expressed a desire to resolve the dispute through the conciliar way, but he knew holding a council with the different parties was impossible because of these same political borders.[148]

8 Conclusions

The metropolitan bishops had to face the same dangers as their suffragans: barbaric invasions, natural catastrophes, internal factionalism and exiles, among others. However, because of the idiosyncrasies of their position, they were also exposed to dangers that were particular to their rank, specifically to questions and violations of their metropolitan jurisdiction. In such situations, we have seen that the social factor – specifically the creation of a complex network of personal ties with the surrounding episcopate, as well as with the local population – were decisive when it came to being able to face such threats, but also to prevent them from arising. Regardless of the institutional order in force, the only thing that guaranteed the metropolitans real exercise of their authority was internal support. Not even intervention from the pope, despite his authority, could reverse this reality. In fact, the bishops of Rome were consistently unable to enforce their orders,[149] except when they folded and accepted the *status quo*. Appeals to Rome always comprised a certain helplessness on the part of certain metropolitans who were incapable of asserting their rights and aspirations through internal channels. Only political vicissitudes could render social factors irrelevant. In particular, the formation of the new *regna* in Gaul brought with it a fragmentation of the ecclesiastical provinces that prevented the metropolitans from exercising a real authority over the territories located in a different political reality; dynamics that, far from abating, will intensify during the Merovingian dynasty immediately afterwards.[150]

---

[148] Alc. Avit. epist. 34.
[149] In a way, the words of B. Neil (2018, 97) become true when he stated the following: "The church of Gaul had sufficient wealth and power of its own to be able to ignore papal bluster". In a line similar to that defended here, Marcos 2013, 160.
[150] Some of these problems are treated in: Poveda Arias 2021.

Bibliography

Primary Sources

Avitus of Vienne, *Epistulae:* Rudolf Peiper, ed. 1883. *Alcimi Ecdicii Aviti Viennensis episcopi. Opera quae supersunt. Monumenta Germaniae Histórica, Auctores antiquissimi (MGH AA).* VI, 2. Berlin: Weidmann.

Boniface I, *Epistulae:* Jacques-Paul Migne, ed. 1967. *Quinti saeculi scriptorum ecclesiasticorum qui ad S. Hieronymum usque floruerunt, opera omnia: nunc primum in unum corpus et ordine chronologico digesta. Patrologia Latina (PL)* 20. Turnhout: Brepols.

Celestine I, *Epistulae:* Jacques-Paul Migne, ed. 1865. *Joannis Cassiani opera omnia: cum amplissimis commentariis Alardi Gazaei; accedunt S. Coelestini I, S. Xysti III, Romanorum pontificum, S. Vincentii Lirinensis, S. Eucherii Lugdunensis, S. Hilarii Arelatensis, Antonini Honorati, Vigilii Diaconi, Fastidii, etc. scripta quae exstant universa; Cassiani tomus posterior, caeterorum tomus unicus. Patrologia Latina (PL)* 50. Paris : Migne.

Concilia Galliae a. 511 – a. 695: Charles De Clercq, ed. 1963. *Corpus Christianorum Series Latina (CCSL)*, 148 A. Turnhout: Brepols.

Epistolae Arelatenses genuinae: Wilhelm Gundlach, ed. 1892. *Epistolae Merowingici et Karolini Aevi Tomus I. Monumenta Germaniae Histórica, Epistolae (MGH Epp.).* III, 1–83. Berlin: Weidmann.

Gregory of Tours, *Decem libri historiae (DLH)*: Bruno Krusch and Wilhelm Levison. eds. 1951. *Monumenta Germaniae Histórica, Scriptores rerum Merovingicarum (MGH SS rer. Merov.).* I, 1, *Gregorii episcopi Turonensis libri historiarum X.* Hannover: Impensis Bibliopolii Hahniani.

Hydatius, *Chronicon:* R. W. Burgess, ed. 1993. *The 'Chronicle' of Hydatius and the 'Consularia Constantinopolitana': Two Contemporary Accounts of the Final Years of the Roman Empire.* Oxford: Clarendon Press.

Hilary, *Epistulae:* Andreas Thiel, ed. 1868. *Epistolae Romanorum Pontificum genuinae et quae ad eos scriptae sunt a S. Hilaro usque ad Pelagium II. T. 1: A S. Hilaro usque ad S. Hormisdam, ann. 461–523.* Brunsbergae: Peter.

Hilary of Arles, *Sermo de uita s. Honorati Arelatensis ep.:* Marie-Denise Valentin, ed. 1977. *Vie de Saint Honorat. Introduction, texte critique, traduction et notes.* Paris : Éditions du Cerf.

Honoratus of Marseille, *Vita s. Hilarii Arelatensis:* Samuel Cavallin and Paul-André Jacob, eds. 1995. *La vie d'Hilaire d'Arles. Introduction, texte latin, traduction et notes.* Paris : Éditions du Cerf.

Innocent I, *Epistulae:* Jacques-Paul Migne, ed. 1967. *Quinti saeculi scriptorum ecclesiasticorum qui ad S. Hieronymum usque floruerunt, opera omnia: nunc primum in unum corpus et ordine chronologico digesta. Patrologia Latina (PL)*, 20. Turnhout: Brepols.

Isidore of Seville, *Historiae:* Cristóbal Rodríguez Alonso, ed. 1975. *Las historias de los godos, vándalos y suevos de Isidoro de Sevilla.* León: Centro de Estudio e Investigación "San Isidoro".

Leo the Great, *Epistulae:* Jacques-Paul Migne, ed. 1966. *Sancti Leonis Magni Romani pontifices opera omnia post Pascharii Quesnelli recensionem in accurante et denuo*, Vol. 1. *Patrologia Latina (PL)*, 54. Turnhout: Brepols.

Paulinus of Nola, *Epistulae:* Wilhelm von Hartel and Margit Kampter, eds. 1999. *Sancti Pontii Meropii Paulini Nolani Epistulae. Corpus Scriptorum Ecclesiasticorum Latinorum (CSEL)* 29. Vindobonae: Verlag der Österreichischen Akademie der Wissenschaften.

Sidonius Apollinaris, *Epistulae:* André Loyen, ed. 1970. *Sidoine Apollinaire, T. 3: Lettres (livres VI–IX).* Paris : Les Belles Lettres.

Victricius of Rouen, *De laude sanctorum:* Roland Demeulenaere, ed. 1985. *Corpus Christianorum Series Latina (CCSL)* 64. Turnhout: Brepols.

Vita Marcelli: François Dolbeau, ed. 1983. "La vie en prose de sain Marcel évêque de Die. Histoire du texte et édition critique." *Francia* 11:97–130.

Secondary Sources

Andrieu-Guitrancourt, Pierre. 1970. "Essai sur saint Victrice, l'église et la province ecclésiastique de Rouen aux derniers temps gallo-romains." *L'année canonique* 14:1–23.

Anton, Hans-Hubert. 1989. "Die Trierer Kirche und das nördliche Gallien in spatrömischer und fränkischer Zeit." In *La Neustrie: les pays au nord de la Loire de 650 à 850*, Vol. 2, edited by Harmut Atsma, 53–73. Sigmaringen: J. Thorbecke.

Bourges, André-Yves. 2012. "Conseul, Carhais et l'activité métropolitaine de Perpetuus de Tours: archéologie, liturgie et canons conciliaires (Ve siècle)." *Britannia monastica* 16:11–39.

De Leo, Pietro. 1983. "Deposizioni vescovili ed ecclesiologia nei sinodi della Gallia premerovingia." *Annuarium Historiae Conciliorum* 15:15–29.

Delaplace, Christine. 2012. "Pour une relecture de la *Vita Caesarii* : le role politique de l'évêque d'Arles face aux représentants des royaumes burgonde, wisigothique et ostrogothique." *Annales du Midi* 124–279:309–324.

Díaz, Pablo C. 2016. "El obispo y las invasiones de los pueblos bárbaros." In *El obispo en la Antigüedad Tardía. Homenaje a Ramón Teja*, edited by Silvia Acerbi, Mar Marcos, and Juana Torres, 146–149. Madrid: Trotta.

Dunn, Geoffrey D. 2011. "Canonical Legislation on the Ordination of Bishops: Innocent I's Letter to Victricius". In *Episcopal Elections in Late Antiquity*, edited by Johan Leemans, 145–166. Berlin: De Gruyter.

Dunn, Geoffrey D. 2013. "Zosimus and the Gallic Churches." In *Religious Conflict from Early Christianity to the Rise of Islam*, edited by Wendy Mayer and Bronwen Neil, 169–186. Berlin: De Gruyter.

Dunn, Geoffrey D. 2014. "Flavius Constantius and Affairs in Gaul between 411 and 417." *Journal of the Australian Early Medieval Association* 10:1–22.

Dunn, Geoffrey D. 2015a. "*Quid habuerit antique consuetudo:* Zosimus of Rome and Hilary of Narbonne." *Revue d'histoire ecclésiastique* 110:31–55.

Dunn, Geoffrey D. 2015b. "*Placuit apostolicae* (*Ep.* 1) of Zosimus of Rome and the Ecclesiastical Reorganization of Gaul". *Journal of Early Christian Studies* 23.4:559–582.

Dunn, Geoffrey D. 2015c. "Zosimus' Synod of Rome in September 417 and his Letter to Western Bishops (*Cum aduersus*)." *Antiquité Tardive* 23:395–406.

Dunn, Geoffrey D. 2016. "The Ecclesiastical Reorganisation of Space and Authority in Late Antique Gaul: Zosimus Letter *Multa contra* (JK 334)." *Journal of the Australian Early Medieval Association* 12:1–34.

Duval, Yvette, Paul-Albert Février, and Jean Guyon. 1986. *Topographie chrétienne des cités de la Gaule des origines au milieu du VIIIe, 2. Provinces ecclésiastiques d'Aix et d'Embrun Narbonensis Secunda et Alpes Maritimae.* Paris: De Boccard.

Frye, David. 1991. "Bishops as Pawns in Early Fifth-Century Gaul." *The Journal of Ecclesiastical History* 42:349–361.

Gauthier, Nancy. 1980. *L'évangélisation des pays de la Moselle : la province romaine de Première Belgique entre Antiquité et Moyen Âge: IIIe–VIIIe siècles.* Paris : De Boccard.

Griffe, Élie. 1950. "La primatie d'Arles et les métropoles d'Aix et d'Embrun au Vème siècle." *Bulletin de littérature ecclésiastique* 51:65–74.
Griffe, Élie. 1964. *La Gaule chrétienne à l'époque romaine 1: Des origines à la fin du IVe siècle*. Paris : Letouzey et Ané.
Griffe, Élie. 1966. *La Gaule chrétienne à l'époque romaine 2: L'Église des Gaules au Ve siècle; l'Église et les barbares; la hiérarchie ecclésiastique*. Paris : Letouzey et Ané.
Heinzelmann, Martin. 1976. *Bischofsherrschaft in Gallien. Zur Kontinuität römischer Führungsschichten vom 4. bis zum 7. Jahrhundert: soziale, prosopographische und bildungsgeschichtliche Aspekte*. Zürich: Artemis Verlag.
Heinzelmann, Martin. 1992. "The 'Affair' of Hilary of Arles (445) and Gallo-Roman Identity in the Fifth Century." In *Fifth-Century Gaul: A Crisis of Identity?*, edited by John F. Drinkwater, 239–251. Cambridge: Cambridge University Press.
Hunter, David G. 1999. "Vigilantius of Calagurris and Victricius of Rouen: Ascetics, Relics, and Clerics in Late Roman Gaul." *Journal of Early Christian Studies* 7:401–430.
Isaïa, Marie-Céline. 2010. *Remi de Reims: une mémoire d'un saint, histoire d'une Église*. Paris: Éditions du Cerf.
Langgärtner, Georg. *Die Gallienpolitik der Päpste im 5. und 6. Jahrhundert. Eine Studie über dem apostolischen Vikariat von Arles*. Bonn: Peter Hanstein Verlag.
Loftus, Susan. "Episcopal Elections in Gaul: The Normative View of the *Concilia Galliae* versus the Narrative Accounts." In *Episcopal Elections in Late Antiquity*, edited by Johan Leemans, 423–436. Berlin: De Gruyter.
Loseby, Simon T. 1992. "Bishops and Cathedrals: Order and Diversity in the Fifth-Century Urban Landscape of Souther Gaul". In *Fifth-Century Gaul: A Crisis of Identity?*, edited by John F. Drinkwater, 144–155. Cambridge: Cambridge University Press.
Marcos, Mar. 2013. "Papal Authority, Local Autonomy and Imperial Control: Pope Zosimus and the Western Churches (a. 417–18)." In *The Role of the Bishop in Late Antiquity: Conflict and Compromise*, edited by Andrew Fear, José Fernández Ubiña, and Mar Marcos, 145–166. London: Bloomsbury.
Marrou, Henri-Irénée. 1970. "Le dossier épigraphique de l'évêque Rusticus de Narbonne." *Rivista di archeologia cristiana* 46:331–349.
Mathisen, Ralph W. 1989. *Ecclesiastical Factionalism and Religious Controversy in Fifth-Century Gaul*. Washington, D.C.: Catholic University of America Press.
Mathisen, Ralph W. 1997. "The 'Second Council of Arles' and the Spirit of Compilation and Codification in Late Roman Gaul." *Journal of Early Christian Studies* 5.4:511–554.
Mathisen, Ralph W. 2013. "The Council of Turin (398–399) and the Reorganization of Gaul ca. 395/406." *Journal of Early Christian Studies* 6:264–307.
Mathisen, Ralph W. and Hagith S. Sivan. 1999. "Forging a New Identity: The Kingdom of Toulouse ad the Frontiers of Visigothic Aquitania (418–507)." In *The Visigoths. Studies in Culture and Society*, edited by Alberto Ferreiro, 1–62. Leiden: Brill.
Müller, Christoph. 2003. *Kurialen und Bischof, Bürger und Gemeinde: Untersuchungen zur Kontinuität von Ämtern, Funktionen und Formen der "Kommunikation" in der gallischen Stadt des 4.- 6. Jahrhunderts*. Freiburg: Albert-Ludwigs-Universität [unpublished PhD].
Natal, David. 2012. "De *Proculi damnatione:* Próculo de Marsella y la construcción de la Iglesia gala a principios del siglo V." *Ilu. Revista de ciencias de las religiones* 17:101–117.
Natal, David. 2015a. "'A Suitable Successor': Building Legitimacy in Hilary's Sermon on the *Life of Honoratus*." *Reti Medievali* 16.1:147–168.

Natal, David. 2015b. "Curando las heridas: redes episcopales y herejía priscilianista." In *Mare Nostrum. Studia Iberia, Italica, Graeca*, edited by Ánges Ludmann, 43–58. Budapest: ELTE Eötvös József Collegium.

Natal, David. 2018. "Putting the Roman Periphery on the Map: the Geography of Romanness, Orthodoxy, and Legitimacy in Victricius of Rouen's *De Laude sanctorum*." *Early Medieval Europe* 26.3:304–326.

Natal, David and Jamie Wood. 2016. "Platying with Fire: Conflicting Bishops in Late Roman Spain and Gaul." In *Making Early Medieval Socities: Conflict and Belonging in the Latin West, 300–1200*, edited by Kate Cooper and Conrad Leyser, 33–57. Cambridge: Cambridge University Press.

Neil, Bronwen. 2018. "Addressing Conflict in the Fifth Century: Rome and the Wider Church." *Scrinium. Revue de patrologie* 14:92–114.

Nimmegeers, Nathanaël. 2014. *Évêques entre Bourgogne et Provence: la province ecclésiastique de Vienne au haut Moyen Âge, V^e–XIe siècle*. Rennes: Presses Universitaires de Rennes.

Pietri, Luce. 1983. *La ville de Tours du IVe au VIe siècle : naissance d'une cité chrétienne*. Rome : École française de Rome.

Poveda Arias, Pablo. 2019. "Clovis and Remigius of Reims in the Making of the Merovingian Kingdoms." *European Review of History* 26.2:197–218.

Poveda Arias, Pablo. 2021. "Patrones de relación entre los reyes merovingios y el episcopado galo (511–561)." *Antiquité Tardive* 29: 211–224.

Riess, Frank. 2013. *Narbonne and Ist Territory in Late Antiquity*. Farnham: Ashgate.

Schäferdiek, Knut. 1967. *Die Kirche in den Reichen der Westgoten und Suewen bis zur Errichtung der westgotischen katholischen Staatskirche*. Berlin: De Gruyter.

Schulz, Fabian. 2019. "Westkirche und Okzident im frühen 5. Jahrhundert." In *Das Christentum im frühen Europa: Diskurse-Tendenzen-Entscheidungen*, edited by Uta Heil, 51–66. Berlin: De Gruyter.

Serrano Madroñal, Raúl. 2020. "Frederico, un miembro de la familia visigoda de los baltingos." *Habis* 51:245–263.

Stüber, Till. 2020. *Der inkriminierte Bischof: Könige im Konflikt mit Kirchenleitern im westgotischen und fränkischen Gallien (466–614)*. Berlin: De Gruyter.

Ubric Rabaneda, Purificación. 2013. "Bishops, Heresy, and Power: Conflict and Compromise in *Epistula* 11* of Consentius to Augustine." In *The Role of the Bishop in Late Antiquity: Conflict and Compromise*, edited by Andrew Fear, José Fernández Ubiña, and Mar Marcos, 127–144. London: Bloomsbury.

Van Dam, Raymond. 1985. *Leadership and Community in Late Antique Gaul*. Berkeley: University of California Press.

Van Nuffelen, Peter. 2011. "The Rhetoric of Rules and the Rule of Consensus." In *Episcopal Elections in Late Antiquity*, edited by Johan Leemans, 243–258. Berlin: De Gruyter.

Villegas, Raúl. 2017. "La primacía de Arlés en las Iglesias galas durante el episcopado de Patroclo (411/413–426)." In *Costellazioni geo-ecclesiali da Costantino a Giustiniano: Dalle chiese 'principali' alle chiese patriarcali*, 307–317. Roma: Institutum Patristicum Augustinianum.

Wood, Jamie. 2019. "Building and Breaking Episcopal Networks in Late Antique *Hispania*." In *Episcopal Networks in late Antiquity: Connection and Communication across Boundaries*, edited by Carmen A. Cvetković and Peter Gemeinhardt, 227–247. Berlin: De Gruyter.

Kevin Grotherr
Between Royal Power and Legitimacy – The Bishops of Mérida (6th–7th c.)

Abstract: The development of the episcopate into the highest ecclesiastical office of leadership lead to an increased confrontation of bishops by diverse and often significant threats, both from outside and from within their own Christian communities. During the *regnum gothorum*, this phenomenon can be observed also in the Iberian Peninsula. An anonymous author reports on the lives of several bishops (6th and early 7th c.) of Augusta Emerita (Mérida) in the so-called *Vitas Sanctorum Patrum Emeritensium*. The bishop Masona and his confessional counterpart Sunna came into conflict with the Visigothic kings Leovigild and Raccared and as a result had to go into exile. But not only royal power becomes a threat to the bishops, also other high secular dignitaries try to overcome the episcopal authority, and even murder seems to be a suitable mean. In addition to external threats even the bishop's own parish can become a peril. As can be seen in the example of bishops Fidelis and Nepopis. In both cases their episcopate is endangered by a damaged basis of legitimacy and, in the case of the latter, leads to an expulsion by the faithful and especially his own clergy.

1 Introduction

By the 3rd century, the episcopate had developed into the highest ecclesiastical directorial office, making it the decisive entity for nearly all conflicts of the Christian cosmos.[1] It is in this context that bishops fought with their peers at councils and their like about principles of teaching, guarded the peace of their congregations and represented them in altercations with the realities of Roman life. Yet such ac-

---

[1] In the *Traditio Apostolica* (3rd c. AD), the bishop is provided with the other offices simply as lower-ranking advisors and personal helpers. Moreover, the bishop was now the decisive officiant, concentrating the highest core competencies of teaching, baptism, the Eucharist and *caritas* in his hands. It is thus little wonder that the projected 'monarchic bishop' of this ecclesiastical order is understood as the dominant office holder for worship and teaching, whose "Machtfülle" resembled that of "alttestamentlichen Hohepriester", as Wilhelm Geerlings 2000, 207, claims; on the 'monepiscopate's' development, see particularly: Dassmann 1994, 47–73; see also: Saxer 2010, 309–336. – This contribution evolved in the framework of the Center for Advanced Study "RomanIslam – Center for Comparative Empire and Transcultural Studies", funded by the German Research Foundation (Deutsche Forschungsgemeinschaft, DFG), at Universität Hamburg.

tivities frequently brought significant dangers to the congregation leaders': a bishop's understanding of the correct teaching could lead him into exile, failure in his congregation could strip him of authority, and an altercation with the representatives of his pagan surroundings could even cost him his life.

Even significantly later, in the 6th and 7th centuries when Christianity was more deeply rooted in society, the episcopal office remained connected with a "gefährlichen Glanz" – as Hartmut Leppin has characterised it.[2] The post-Roman Visigothic kingdom on the Iberian Peninsula is a case in point, when an anonymous author reported in detail the lives of several bishops who operated within the former provincial capital of Hispania, Augusta Emerita (Mérida). The author's reports have been preserved in a collection of Latin saints' lives, the *Vitas Sanctorum Patrum Emeretensium* (*VSPE*), its narratives covering the period from c. 530 to 632.[3] Most scholars date its creation to the tenure of the Emeritensian bishop Stephanus (633–638), although the exact date of its composition cannot be determined with certainty.[4] The work's author also remains shrouded in anonymity, although it seems plausible to identify him as a local deacon, as his detailed knowledge of Augusta Emerita's ecclesiastical structures and self-description as a *levita* suggests.[5] The work comprises five opuscula in total, which the *praefationes* divide into

---

2 Leppin 2018, 196–205 (trans. dangerous lustre).
3 The '*Vitas Sanctorum Patrum Emeretensium*' is subsequently abbreviated to *VSPE*. All quotes from the *VSPE* in this work refer to Maya Sánchez's edition 1992. As the source's section units, however, are quite large, the exact page numbers are given in brackets after each quote. Demarcation of the period in question varies slightly: Panzram 2007, 179, gives a time span of 530–630, while Wood 1999, 193, sets it as 530–605 and Van Nuffelen and Van Hoof 2020, 687, as 550–632 AD. The detailed study of all manuscripts' transmission, preservation state and location is provided by: Maya Sánchez 1992, X–LVIII; on this, see also: Van Nuffelen & Van Hoof 2020, 687. On the author's style and use of language, see e.g.: Garvin 1946, 36; Martyn 2008, 121. A very helpful overview of the referenced sections as well as the significance of the author's word choice is given by: Martínez Pastor et al. 2001.
4 E.g. Koch 2012, 274; Velázquez 2008a, 12–13; Arce 1999, 3; Garvin 1946, 2; on the composition period: Since it has been persuasively proven that the *VSPE* was inter alia designed to bridge a gap in the Emeritensian episcopal list, it seems plausible to date its composition to the tenure of Stephanus, as he was the successor of Renovatus, whom the *VSPE* names as the last bishop of Augusta Emerita. Koch 2012, 275; Stephanus's tenure is presumed to have stretched from 633 to 637(8) AD. Panzram 2007, 209; Kampers 1979, 142; García Moreno 1974, 171.
5 *VSPE* 1. (12): *Quam ob rem ego indignus et omnium peccatorum primus, leuita Xpi, quemammodum narrabit scribere malui, uerbis licet aliis, sensibus tamen ipsis.* The word "*levita*" is a term for a deacon. Martínez Pastor et al. 2001, 229. The authorship is sometimes also ascribed to a deacon named Paulus, although he is primarily accounted as a compiler (Maya Sánchez 1992, LV; Arce 1999, 3) who linguistically reworked the *VSPE* between 670 and 680 AD. Although Panzram 2007, 208, considers it at least possible that Paulus was the anonymous deacon, Koch 2012, 274, states that he cannot be identified as the author.

two elements, with the vitae of a boy and two monks succeeding the first *praefatio*. The following second *praefatio* bridges the way to the significantly more comprehensive episcopal vitae, which share a similar structure but clearly differ from each other in scope.[6] The anonymous author begins by describing the two 'Greek' bishops.[7] He tells of Paulus, the Greek doctor, who arrives in Augusta Emerita as a *peregrinus* and there scales the heights of the episcopal office.[8] When the bishop subsequently succeeds in rescuing the wife of the richest senator in all of Lusitania, the couple declare him their heir out of gratitude and ultimately bestow their entire fortune on him.[9] After several years, a group of Greek merchants arrive in the city accompanied by a young assistant whom Paulus, through pure chance, identifies as his nephew Fidelis, subsequently keeps by his side, places into the service of the Church and ultimately singlehandedly declares him as his episcopal successor.[10] The author follows these vitae directly with the *VSPE*'s main section – that is, the vita of the bishop Masona, a *nobilis gotus* – which is marked inter alia by confessional quarrels and the related conflict between the bishop and the Visigothic king Liuvigild.[11]

The *VSPE* is extraordinary amongst the literary sources of the 7th century: As Javier Arce has noted, despite its hagiographic character it resists a general categorisation. "It is hagiography; but not exclusively. It is also biography […], an unusual piece, because it is neither ecclesiastical history, nor is it a chronicle, nor an account of the lives of distinguished men and women."[12] Through all this, the *VSPE* offers a deep insight into the daily realities of a Late Antique city and, in relation to the episcopal office, clarifies diverse conflicts with high-ranking secular and ecclesiastical authorities, manifold financial sources, confessional quarrels, a comprehensive episcopal *caritas* (a credit system for the needy, the distribution of oil,

---

6 On the same structure, see Panzram 2007, 199; on the opuscula's text proportion of the *VSPE* as a whole: Masona's vita, c. 54 %; Paulus and Fidelis's vita, c. 24 %; narratives on Innocentius and Renovatus, c. 2.5 %; remaining vitae, c. 17.5 %.

7 No clear references to the bishops Paulus and Fidelis can be found outside the *VSPE*. Panzram 2007, 199–200. 220. 223; 2010, 126–127, therefore assumes, among other things, that these bishops were the author's own invention.

8 *VSPE* 4, 1. (25–26).

9 *VSPE* 4, 2. (26–30).

10 *VSPE* 4, 3. (31–33).

11 Council acts (*Concilium Toletanum III* [Vives 1963, 136]) attest to the bishop Masona's (c. 573–606) existence: The bishop signed the Third Council of Toledo's resolutions before all other Hispanic metropolitans, as well as right after King Reccared. Eight years later (597) at a synod (*Concilium Toletanum* [Vives 1963, 157]), Masona was once again the first bishop to sign. He is also mentioned in John of Biclaro's chronicle (chron. 30).

12 Arce 1999, 5; see also Koch 2012, 276.

honey and wine, and the manumission of slaves) and construction work (Xenodochium, Church endowments).[13] These detailed and manifold depictions can be used to crystallise what threats confronted an Hispanic bishop during the "late Long Antiquity".

2 Pressure from Outside – Bishops under Threat of Other Authorities

When it comes to exposing themselves to danger, those Emeritensian bishops who clashed with high-ranking secular authorities ran the most obvious risks. Yet the *VSPE* offers no clear insight into such altercations, though concretely naming the relevant actors, until the episode about the metropolitan Masona. Here, the topic of the altercation between episcopal and other secular authority forms a central element of the vita, primarily reflected in the bishop's struggle with the Arian king Liuvigild (568/9–586).[14]

Although the anonymous author primarily relates this conflict from a religious-confessional perspective, he also reveals the king's strategy of consolidating his kingdom, weakened in an approximately 60-year crisis period through fights over succession, rebellions and clashes with Franks and East Romans.[15] Liuvigild was the first to succeed in re-establishing the territorial unity of the *regnum gothorum*, earning military victories against local and Gothic nobles, Suebi, Basques, Cantabrians, as well as partial success against the East Roman *Spaniae*'s occupations.[16] Moreover, he strengthened his kingship with reforms and elevated his two sons to co-regents in order to establish his own dynasty.[17] Yet this did not pre-

---

[13] *VSPE* 5, 1–3. 13. (47–54. 94–98).
[14] The strongly negative depiction of Arian representatives draws the eye, which is why the *VSPE* has been perceived as an "anti-Arian pamphlet" (Arce 1999, 7), although it can by no means be reduced to such.
[15] Wolfram 2010, 101–104, dates the crisis period between 507 and 568 AD, also detailing the term *morbus Gothicus*, a "gotische Krankheit [, die] grassierte, wonach sich das Gotenvolk wie im Wahnsinn der Könige durch Absetzung oder Mord entledigte [...]. Angefangen bei Alarich I. gab es knapp vierzig Könige und Gegenkönige der Westgoten; kaum die Hälfte ist eines natürlichen Todes gestorben oder unabgesetzt gestorben." On this crisis, see also Kampers 2008, 164–168.
[16] Panzram 2014, 473–474; Ioh. Bicl. chron. 10. 20; According to Isidore (hist. 51), Liuvigild trumped over the Gothic nobility partially by either beheading or exiling those he deemed powerful, and confiscating their fortune. John of Biclaro (chron. 51) claims that the king defeated all his opponents and Spain's external foes, as well as brought great peace to himself and his people.
[17] Arce 2011, 49; Ioh. Bicl. chron. 27; Liuvigild's consolidation measures can be partially understood as *imitatio imperii* (compare Collins 2004, 53). Isidore (hist. 51) accordingly claims that Liuvi-

vent the royal family from falling into a feud that in 579 escalated into the open, though unsuccessful, rebellion of the king's eldest son, Hermenegild.[18] Although dynastic interests may have fuelled this uprising, this did not prevent the conflict from taking on a religious tint as it ran its course. Among other aspects, Hermenegild emphasised his conversion to the Nicene Creed to gain followers among the Catholic Hispano-Romans.[19] This situation already reveals a potential for conflict between Visigothic Arianism and the Hispano-Roman population, influenced by Nicaea and in the majority, whom Liuvigild too sought to approach.[20] To do so, he made use of a policy of integration aimed, inter alia, at establishing a religious unity across his kingdom under the banner of Arian Christianity.[21] On the one hand, the king strove to modify the Arian theology to allow Catholic Christians an easier transition; on the other, he set to work on Catholic bishops, some of whom he successfully encouraged to convert.[22] It is in this context, for example, that Isidore of Seville criticised Vincentius, the bishop of Caesaraugusta (Zaragoza), for his re-baptism under Liuvigild and subsequent apostate status.[23] Even here, one can already hazard that the king viewed the episcopal office as a fitting key to move as many Catholics as possible to convert. For this alone could create a suitable pedestal for building something approaching religious unity.

---

gild was the first Gothic king to introduce kingly insignia like a throne or royal regalia. Liuvigild also founded a city – Reccopolis – which he named after his second son and revised the laws through the *Codex Euricianus*. On this, see e.g.: Kampers 2008, 174–175; an overview of the term's reception is found in Eger 2009, 152.

18 Collins 2004, 56–59; on this, see also Isid. hist. 49.

19 Kampers 2008, 175–177; 13. However, important Catholics also judge the rebellion negatively. John of Biclaro (chron. 55), for example, speaks of an illicit power grab that brought Romans and Goths more destruction than any attack by external foes. Even Gregory of Tours (hist. 6, 43), who wasn't exactly favourably inclined towards Liuvigild and praised Hermenegild's conversion, criticised the king's son: he had exposed himself to God's judgement by plotting such things against his father, even if that father was a heretic.

20 Panzram 2014, 464, thus names the numbers estimated by Ripoll López, according to which approximately 130,000 Visigoths faced seven to twelve million Romans by the late 5th and 6th centuries.

21 Koch, 2012, 202; Kampers 2008, 177–179; see also: Wolfram 2010, 105–106.

22 Faber 2014, 226–229. 15. Faber thus clarifies that Liuvigild's policies of 'Arianisation' were not a violently implemented persecution, which may be generally correct. After all, the king was more inclined to pursuing policies through gold and gifts, as Isidore writes (hist. 50). Yet Gregory of Tours (Franc. 5, 38) reveals that violence was certainly used: many were exiled, robbed of their fortunes, tortured through hunger, imprisoned, suffered blows and executed in manifold ways. However, Gregory places the blame for this not on Liuvigild, but on his wife Goswintha. On the contemporary historians Isidore's and John of Biclaro's judgement of Liuvigild's religious policies, see: Mülke 2016, 99–128.

23 Isid. hist. 50.

The equivalent can also be observed in Augusta Emerita. It was the far-reaching renown of Masona's deeds that drew Liuvigild's attention. In response, he sent the bishop several messengers, who urged him to turn towards Arianism. Yet he is to do so not alone, but *cum universitate plebes* [...] *commissae* – a demand he decisively rejects.²⁴ This involves the assumption of an authoritative relationship between the bishop and the Emeritensian Catholics in which a congregation leader's conversion triggers his followers to switch their confession.²⁵ Liuvigild does not seek to destroy this authoritative relationship, but rather put it use for his plans. The king therefore undertakes another attempt to win the bishop by sending him various gifts and flatteries.²⁶ This, too, aligns with the picture Isidore paints of Liuvigild's religious ambitions, of a man who reached more success through policies of gold and gifts than through persecution.²⁷ In Augusta Emerita, however, such success remains out of the king's reach, as the *episcopus* categorically rejects anything he receives. He also does not stop speaking out against Arianism in order to avoid giving the impression of agreeing with the king through silence. When Liuvigild subsequently realises that his efforts will bear no fruit, he flies into a rage and begins to threaten the bishop, although no details are given about the exact nature of these threats.²⁸ Yet this situation already reveals the potential danger to which the bishop exposes himself by refusing to be integrated into the Visigothic king's policies. The intensity and quality of this potential remain in question, although Masona clearly has no serious cause to worry about being removed from his position through external force.

This, at least, is suggested by the next steps adopted by the king, who makes use of a more subtle strategy. For when he accepts that neither temptation nor threats will convince Masona to convert, he resolves to establish his own Arian bishop in Augusta Emerita. He accordingly brings the Goth Sunna into office to stir up unrest and drag Masona *vel totius populi* into difficulties.²⁹ The king thus

---

24 VSPE 5, 4. (55): *Cuius et poculi letalis austu protinus consilio diabolico armatus, stimulante inuidia, supradicto sanctissimo uiro, legatos intercurrentibus, iterum iterumque mandauit ut, relicta fide catholica, ad Arrianam heresem cum uniuersitate plebis sibi conmisse diuerteret.*
25 A thoroughly justified assumption that those under protection generally followed their ruling authority's conversion. King Reccared thus did not switch confessions by himself, but was joined by the remaining *gens gothorum*. On this, see e.g.: Collins 2004, 64–67; Ioh. Bicl. chron. 85.
26 VSPE 5, 4. (54).
27 Isid. hist. 50.
28 VSPE 5, 4. (55).
29 VSPE 5, 4. (56–57): *Quendam scilicet uirum pestiferum Arriane hereseos prauitatem per omnia uindicantem, cui nomen erat Sunna, pro seditiosis simultatibus excitandis et pro conturbationem sanctissimi uiri uel totius populi in eadem ciuitatem episcopum Arriane partis instituit [...];* The Arian bishop Sunna's existence is attested by John of Biclaro's chronicle (chron. 92).

creates a counter-authority in the city, one that royal power certainly gave the chance of weakening the authority relationship between Masona and his congregation, or even of supplanting it should Sunna succeed in replacing the Catholic bishop as the authoritative entity long term. This state of affairs can clearly be categorised as a danger to the influence and position of the Catholic episcopal office in Augusta Emerita.

Sunna's orchestration as a counter-authority is then tightly interwoven within the city's ecclesiastical buildings. This is not surprising in view of Claudia Rapp's assertion that "the structures associated with the old, pagan way of life – the theatre, hippodrome, forum, public bath – were replaced in their function as social centres by the churches."[30] It therefore also seems plausible that Liuvigild and Sunna view taking possession of urban cult buildings – and thus important centres – as an effective means of sapping Masona's authority and strengthening their own. Right at the start of his tenure, Sunna accordingly lays claim to several basilicas for his confessions, which he could indeed have acquired along with all their respective privileges from the *potestate proprii pontificis*.[31] Unfortunately, no more exact description of the concrete process of this take-over can be formulated, leaving unsolved whether it was enacted with threats of violence or whether the king's authority in the form of a decree proved sufficient.

Yet matters play out differently when Sunna attempts to take over the prestigious basilica of Saint Eulalia, which holds special significance for the Emeritensians.[32] This site comprises the graves not only of Masona's episcopal predecessors, but also of Saint Eulalia, and as the vitae's author explains, miracles can be expected at all of them – miracles even mentioned in Late Antique historiography.[33] For Isidore reports that when Theoderic II strove to sack Augusta Emerita, Saint Eulalia gave a sign that frightened him so much that he and his entire army rapidly retreated to Gaul.[34] Whoever wields control over the grave of the powerful city patron and thus over an important source of spiritual *beneficia* can be certain of possessing a good foundation for strengthening their authority, which is presumably

---

30 Rapp 2005, 10; Monfrin 2010, 1012, also writes that ecclesiastical buildings replaced functions previously filled by the forum; Augusta Emerita gave up its theatres and fora by the second half of the 5th century at the latest. Compare Panzram 2002, 311. The surrounding ecclesiastical structures outside of the city also formed such centres, with which the rural sphere could open and control "en términos socio-políticos, sino también ideológicos o económicos". Poveda Arias 2019, 12–14.
31 *VSPE* 5, 5. (57); Teja 2019, 202–214, here 212, describes this state as a "guerra ente nicenos y arrianos por el control de los espacios públicos y religiosos".
32 On the excavations in the basilica of Saint Eulalia, see e.g. Caballero Zoreda and Mateos Cruz 1995, 297–307.
33 *VSPE* 5, 15. (101).
34 Isid. hist. 32.

why Sunna claims the basilica for himself. Yet this seems to equally provide sufficient reason to oppose the take-over, which Masona does. The Catholic bishop and his *universum populum*, offering heavy resistance, foil the attempt.³⁵ It is only with this attempted takeover of the special basilica that the Catholics and their bishop seem to consider a line to have been crossed that legitimates heavy resistance even against a royal favourite, and eventually against the authority of the king himself. For when Sunna sees himself confronted with resistance he immediately involves the king and asks him to directly place the basilica under his authority through a decree, which Liuvigild however does not do. Instead, he decides that both bishops are to hold a *disputatio* in the Emeritensian episcopal residence, with the basilica as the winner's prize.³⁶ If one is to assume that the king is striving to weaken Masona's authority, why should he pass up this opportune moment for bringing the city's most important basilica directly under his own bishop's control? Yet a glance at his choice of judges, tasked with declaring the debate's winner, suffices to make clear that Liuvigild has little interest in a fair confrontation: they are mostly *fautores Arrianae partis et impiissimi regis*.³⁷ Presumably, the king sees a need to conquer this specific basilica not through violence but through trickery that bestows the appearance of legitimacy. For while the use of force could produce martyrs and resistance and strengthen the authority relationship between Masona and his congregation, a victory by Sunna could form a foundation for legitimacy on which a far-reaching authority could be built.³⁸

Yet the plan fails: miraculously, Masona succeeds in winning the disputation, bringing Liuvigild to a point where he is certainly ready to use violence against the bishop – but only after Masona's episcopal opponent accuses him of many crimes. The king decides to have the unruly bishop brought to him and sends *ministri* to

---

35 *VSPE* 5, 5. (58): *Cui quum sanctus Masona episcopus uel uniuersus cum eo populus resisteret ac uehementer obpugnaret,* [...] *Sunna antefato principi multa in accusationem sancti uiri scripsit* [...]; If the Hispanic Christians thus believed that the sainted martyr had saved the city from being sacked, the threat that the source of her benevolences would dry up would equal a catastrophe to be decisively prevented – and in the author's way of thinking, they would certainly dry up if the basilica were desanctified by a 'heretical' Christian community. After all, the author himself clarifies in the *VSPE* that heavenly *beneficia* are to be expected at martyrs' graves, and that the saints can refuse to bestow them if they consider themselves inadequately worshipped in the basilicas consecrated in their names. Compare *VSPE* 4, 10. (44–46).
36 *VSPE* 5, 5. (58–59); on Augusta Emerita's episcopal residence, see e.g., Mateos Cruz 2000, 504. 507; Godoy Fernández and Tuset Bertrán 1994, 221.
37 *VSPE* 5, 5. (60): *Tum deinde, residentibus episcopis, residerunt et iudices, illi quam maxime qui erant fauctores Arriane partis et impiissimi regis*; on the distribution of the Arian clergy in the *regnum gothorum:* Mathisen 2014, 163.
38 *VSPE* 5, 5. (61–62).

Augusta Emerita to fetch Masona to Toletum (Toledo) by force.[39] Upon his arrival, Liuvigild once again attempts – this time in person – to urge him to convert, wielding both insults and threats, but is again rebuffed. The Visigothic regent also demands that Masona hand over an important Emeritensian relic, the *tunicam sanctissimae virginis Eulaliae*, which the bishop also decisively refuses.[40] After the king sends his men to Augusta Emerita on a futile search for the relic, he begins to threaten the bishop once more; for the first time, the exact nature of these threats is detailed. Masona is informed that he will be severely tortured and banished into exile, where he will suffer many pains and endure an unnecessary and gruesome death. Yet the *episcopus* informs the king that he is not afraid, driving the monarch into another rage and provoking even more drastic threats: he will quarter the bishop if he refuses to provide the demanded relic.[41] But the "soldier of Christ" remains unimpressed and counters: *Iam dixi tibi semel et iterum quia minas tuas non formidabo.*[42] He also claims to have burned the tunic to ash, mixed the ash with water and drank it down, although he carried the relic unhurt and hidden on his body. When the king finally accepts that he will get nowhere with the unrelenting bishop, he has his men remove him and sends him into exile as an enemy of the faith.[43] Ultimately, the king thus succeeds in forcibly removing the bishop from his positions as metropolitan of Lusitania and bishop of Augusta Emerita. Masona is completely at the mercy of Liuvigild's power and has nothing comparable to counter it.[44] The bishop therefore has no choice but to respond to the royal threats by emphasising his own piety and fearlessness as well as his readiness for martyrdom, and to accept his exile.[45]

Yet the anonymous author adds a sequel to this confrontation. For the king considers the exile he himself had ordered too mild a punishment and attempts to kill the bishop by orchestrating an accident. He has Masona put on a very wild horse, hoping that the bishop will fall and break his neck. Yet this plan, too, is foiled by heavenly forces, for the horse suddenly turns as meek as a

---

[39] *VSPE* 5, 6. (63–64).
[40] *VSPE* 5, 6. (65–66).
[41] *VSPE* 5, 6, (66): *Aut dic ubi est quod requiro aut, si non dixeris, cognosce te grauibus afficiendum esse iniuriis et post in regionem longinquam in exilium proficisci, ubi multis erumnis affectus omnibusque necessitatibus intolerabiliter cruciatus crudeli morte deficies.*
[42] *VSPE* 5, 6 (68.) "I have already told you once and again that I shall not fear your threats." (trans. Garvin 1946, 215).
[43] *VSPE* 5, 6. (68–69).
[44] 'Power' is here to be understood in Weber's sense. According to Weber 1980, 124, "Macht" is the chance "innerhalb einer sozialen Beziehung den eigenen Willen auch gegen Widerstreben durchsetzen [zu können], gleichwohl worauf diese Chance beruht."
[45] On Masona's exile, see also: Arce 2011, 160–164.

lamb and carries the bishop safely into exile.⁴⁶ This only leaves the question of why Liuvigild, if he seemingly desired the bishop's death, does not decide in favour of the death penalty, despite ultimately threatening it.⁴⁷ After all, the king could show mercilessness in other matters concerning his policy of consolidation, including beheading those of his people he considered powerful, as Isidore reveals.⁴⁸ Yet Isidore simultaneously stresses that Liuvigild's measures against the Catholic Christians punished several bishops with nothing worse than exile.⁴⁹ If the king thus used the death penalty against Gothic rebels from the high-ranking aristocracy as well as against Catholic Christians but not against their bishops, one can conclude that the episcopal office served as a kind of protection against the death penalty.⁵⁰ This may be explained with the already delineated religious context and political situation on the Iberian Peninsula, which did not simply permit Liuvigild to officially execute a Catholic bishop while consolidating his realm. It would have promoted neither relations with the Franks and East Romans nor the aim of religious unity to help one or even more congregation leaders to achieve martyrdom and thus sharpen the general potential for rebellions and conflicts.⁵¹ Instead, Liuvigild favours policies of balancing and gifting to reach his domestic policy goals.⁵² He obviously fears that measures taken against a renowned bishop that exceed exile could spell consequences for the stability of his own rule.⁵³ If one can now assume that the anonymous author was also aware of the king's restricted possi-

---

46 *VSPE* 5, 6. (70–71).
47 *VSPE* 5, 6. (67): *Aut presenta mici ipsam tunicam quam fraudulenter surripuisti aut, si non presentaueris, diuersis suppliciis faciam diuaricari membra tua.*
48 Isid. hist. 51.
49 Isid. hist. 50. If the brief paragraph further stresses only that Caesaraugusta's bishop's re-baptism made him an apostate, it seems unlikely that Liuvigild ordered the execution of Catholic bishops. Contemporaries like Gregory of Tours would hardly have judged the king comparatively mildly had he been reputed a butcher of bishops.
50 One can infer that Nicene Christians faced the death penalty from Gregory of Tours's (Franc. 5, 38) statement: *diversis suppliciis trucidati sunt*.
51 On the religious tendencies of Hermenegild's rebellion: "Obschon der konfessionelle Gegensatz also weder Ursache noch Auslöser des Konfliktes war, so erhielt [...] [dieser] in seinem Verlauf doch eine dezidiert religiöse Komponente, indem Hermenegild sich als Anhänger des katholischen Glaubens gerierte, der aus diesem Grund der Verfolgung durch seinen arianischen Vater ausgesetzt gewesen sei. Wenn der Bekenntnisgegensatz also nicht am Anfang der Auseinandersetzung stand, so wurde er von Hermenegild doch bald zur ideologischen Rechtfertigung seines Aufstandes politisch instrumentalisiert." Koch 2012, 196–200, here 199.
52 On the Visigothic policy of religious balancing, see Faber 2014, 225–229.
53 It thus seems possible that such a case could have further heightened the religious conflict and would, at a minimum, have been connected with the Catholic Christian's lacking enthusiasm towards Arian conversion attempts, or even with active resistance against the king.

bilities of action, this could explain why in his vita description he limits himself to opening up a path for Liuvigild to remove Masona with the help of an orchestrated accident. The bishop and the *rex* then have one last encounter as part of Masona's return from exile. Saint Eulalia herself calls the bishop back from exile, appearing to the king at night and moving him to let Masona return, who concretely orders *ut uir Dei, qui frustra fuerat a civitate sua remotus, rursus ad suam accederet regendam ecclesiam.*[54] In the *VSPE*, the bishop thus does not return from exile through his own efforts, but is freed through the power of a higher entity that even the Visigothic king is unable to counter.

Yet Masona's return from exile marks no end to all threats the bishop faces, even though Liuvigild has died in the meantime. His son Reccared (586–601) succeeded him to the Visigothic throne and he, too, presumed that religious unity would be a blessing to his *regnum*.[55] The new king thus pursued a similar policy of integration as had his father, though he was more adept at taking into consideration the Iberian Peninsula's religious circumstances. For Liuvigild's religious policies had been deemed a failure, shattering the decisive resistance of the Hispanic episcopate as well as the dominating numbers and cultures of the provincial-Roman portion of the population.[56] This may have induced Reccared to now achieve such unity through Catholic Christianity rather than the Arian creed.[57] The young king himself accordingly converts in 587 and in 589 brings the remaining Gothic *gens* to conversion as well at the Third Council of Toledo, at which several Arian bishops and Gothic persons pledge themselves to Catholic Christianity.[58] Reccared's actions suit the elite of the Hispanic cities, as they can once again imagine they have a *"christianissimus"* on the throne.[59] Yet it must be mentioned that the local ruling elite from this time are no longer composed of traditional Hispano-Roman *gentes* with magistratures and provincial offices, as can be see for example in epigraphic findings. Rather, they seem to be increasingly drawn from clerics and specifically the Hispanic episcopate, which underlines the king's accommodating attitude.[60] For while Liuvigild – to use Weber's terminology – had used his

---

54 *VSPE* 5, 8. (75): "[Leovigild] [...] ordered that the man of God who had in vain been removed from his city come back again to rule his church" (trans. Garvin 1946, 225).
55 Cf. Faber 2014, 229–235.
56 Cf. Kampers 2008, 177–179. 182; Faber 2014, 229; Cf. also Koch 2012, 203–204.
57 Kampers 2008, 182–183.
58 Collins 2004, 64–67; Ioh. Bicl. chron. 85; Isid. hist. 52; on the Third Council of Toledo, see: Orlandis and Ramos-Lissón 1981, 95–116; *Concilium Toletanum III* [Vives 1963, 107–145].
59 John of Biclaro designates both Reccared and the East Roman emperor Mauricius (582–602 AD) as *christianissimus*. Ioh. Bicl. chron. 92; on this, see also: Steinacher 2019, 213–214.
60 For example, an inscription (Ramírez Sádaba and Mateos Cruz, 2000, no. 10 = ICERV 363) from Augusta Emerita (5th c.), which mentions the reconstruction of the city walls and of the bridge over

power to conquer cities, sometimes repeatedly, and rule them, Reccared offered the primarily Catholic urban elites a future and used his conversion to signal that he wanted to be a king willing to integrate them into an institutionalised form of his rule.[61]

But like the Catholics before them, the Arian Christians too offered resistance, as in 588/589 in Septimania, where the king successfully destroyed the resulting rebellion.[62] The Arian faction of August Emerita rebelled as well, with Bishop Sunna playing a central role. John of Biclaro, who also mentioned the rebellion, additionally names an Arian named Segga, who however does not appear in the *VSPE*.[63] This work relates the rebellion mainly as a conspiracy between Gothic nobles working for Sunna who aimed to kill Masona.[64] This proves that the Catholic bishop could be threatened not just by the king, but also by other secular authorities; one such threat was the Goth Witteric, who would later rise to become the Visigothic king himself (603–610).[65] Official office holders, too, were counted amongst the conspirators. The work then mentions several nameless *comites* from various cities, revealing few other details about them. Yet the text does not explicitly report one, much less 'the', Emeritensian *comes*.[66] The threat thus stems at least partially from secular authorities unlikely to reside in Augusta Emerita themselves. The conspirators' concrete plan seems very simple: Masona is to be invited to Sunna's house under some pretext and killed there. But the Catholic bishop, suspecting evil intentions, refuses the invitation. He instead orders the group to come to his own episcopal residence for the conversation. Masona thus seems to have been well aware of the looming danger, willing to entertain his rivals only in a secure location. He also invites Claudius, Lusitania's dux, to the episcopal residence, and the dux arrives shortly after with his men.[67] The *episcopus* thus counters the potential danger by inviting to his home a high-ranking representative of the king's sovereignty, one who can exercise power in the form of military aid. Masona thus

---

the Ana, names only the Visigothic *dux* Salla and the municipal bishop Zenon (483) as the responsible parties. On this: Arce 2011, 301–306; Arce 2008, 121–126; Velázquez 2008b, 127–135; on the *dux* Salla: Zerjadtke 2019, 105–106.

61 Cf. Panzram 2014, 483–485.
62 Isid. hist. 54; Ioh. Bicl. chron. 88–91; on this, see also *VSPE* 5, 12; Kampers 2008, 183.
63 Ioh. Bicl. chron. 88.
64 *VSPE* 5, 10. (81): *Sunna [...] quosdam Gotorum nobiles genere opibusque perquam ditissimos, e quibus etiam nonnulli in quibusdam ciuitatibus comites a rege fuerant constituti, consilio diabolico persuasit [...]*.
65 García Moreno 1974, 86–87.
66 *VSPE* 5, 10. (81): *[...] in quibusdam ciuitatibus comites a rege fuerant constituti [...]*; on 'comes' in the Visigothic kingdom, see: Zerjadtke 2019, 110–111.
67 *VSPE* 5, 10. (82–83); on the *dux* Claudius, see García Monero 1974, 41.

seems to now hope for protection from the same royal power that had harmed him during Liuvigild's rule.

During the ensueing debate, Witteric attempts to turn the plans into reality, intending to kill both Masona and Claudius.[68] Given the chance, the conspirators thus want to rid themselves not only of the bishop but also of the *dux*.[69] This would suggest that the plans surrounding Sunna are more an attempted rebellion than a simple murder plot, though one hindered both by the bishop's authority and the *dux*'s military possibilities. Since Claudius, as a strict Catholic, could hardly be persuaded to support the murder of a Catholic bishop or an Arian rebellion against his lord, Reccared, the conspirators think it wise to remove the representative of 'royal power' in Augusta Emerita.[70] But the assassination fails, since Witteric is miraculously prevented from drawing his sword.[71] He is subsequently flooded with remorse, throws himself on Masona's mercy and confesses the planned murder. In doing so, he also reports that a second assassination was to follow the first, failed plot, in which the conspirators planned to murder the *episcopus* during an Easter feast procession. After confirming these reports, Masona seeks council with the *dux* and both decide to set a trap for the conspirators. Here, Claudius and his men succeed in either killing or capturing the Gothic nobles, thereby also bringing to an end the threat to the Catholic bishop.[72]

Yet the Arian Sunna, who is after all also an Emeritensian bishop. now finds himself facing a great danger that threatens not just his office but his life. The *dux* and his followers fetch Sunna from his house and bring him to Masona, who takes his opponent and the other conspirators into custody.[73] The positions of the two bishops Masona and Sunna now reverse. Most obviously, Masona and Reccared now nurture a mutual relationship very similar to that previously observable between Sunna and Liuvigild. For it is now the Catholic bishop who has the king's favour and, through the *dux*, can seek his protection. Sunna meanwhile falls into disgrace, which brings with it all the unpleasant things that Masona, too, suffered under Liuvigild. For it is now Reccared who ousts the Arian *episcopus* from office, exiles him and places his basilicas and fortune under the control of his con-

---

68 *VSPE* 5, 10. (84).
69 On this episode, see also Zerjadkte 2019, 114; Castillo Lozano 2020, 113–116.
70 *VSPE* 5, 10. (83): *existebat* [sc. Claudius] *prossus fide catholicus et religionis uinculis fortiter adstrictus.*
71 *VSPE* 5, 10. (82–85): *Wittericus [...] gladium [...] e uagina sua educere maluit, ut sanctum Masonam simulque et Claudium secundum quod definitum fuerat trucidaret.*
72 *VSPE* 5, 11. (85–87).
73 *VSPE* 5, 11. (87).

fessional opponent.[74] Even the king's precise methods call to mind his father's religious policies, with the confessional perspective alone having altered. Reccared thus also seems first interested in balancing the unruly Sunna, who similar to Masona is granted special treatment by virtue of his office. For while the king sends all other agents of the rebellion into exile, he presents Sunna with an alternative – a remarkable fact, considering that the *VSPE* at least describes him as the conspiracy's head, and explicable only through the special significance of the episcopal office.[75] The king accordingly suggests that Sunna convert, do penance and, after a fresh evaluation of the fervour of his faith, may be consecrated as bishop in another city.[76] Sunna is thus presented with the chance of continuing to exercise his office in another city, as a Catholic. Like his father, Reccared is thus attempting to integrate the bishop of another confession into his domestic policies by dangling freedom in front of him, instead of simply stripping him of his official status. Once more, one can see the king's hope of utilising the episcopal authority Sunna may wield in the Arian congregation to further his goal of unity across his kingdom. Yet like Masona, Sunna, too, rejects the king's offer of conversion and simultaneously stresses his readiness for martyrdom: he will never become a Catholic, instead either living in the rite he always held or dying.[77] And here again Liuvigild's and Reccared's methods are the same, for Reccared also creates no martyrs but rather sends Sunna into an African exile.[78] This shows that the potential dangers for bishops that arose from conflict with high-ranking authorities could take on supra-confessional significance.

---

[74] *VSPE* 5, 11. (90): *Baselicas quas sanctus Masona dudum iniuste caruerat, iuste cum omuibus priuilegiis recipere meruit et omne patrimonium supradicti heretici, concedente clementissimo principe Recaredo, adeptus est.*

[75] *VSPE* 5, 10. (81).

[76] *VSPE* 5, 11. (88): *Sunnanem uero pseudoepiscopum exortarentur conuerti ad fidem catholicam et, si conuerteretur, tunc demum ei preciperent ut penitentiam agere deberet et satisfactione lacrimarum sua delicta defleret, ut acta penitudine, quum eum iam cognoscerent perfectum esse catholicum, eum postmodum in quaquumque alia ciuitate ordinarent episcopum.*

[77] *VSPE* 5, 11. (88–89): *Ego quid sit penitentiam ignoro. Ob hoc conpertum uobis sit quia penitentiam quid sit nescio et catholicus numquam ero, sed aut ritu quo uixi uiuebo aut pro religione in qua nunc usque ab ineunte etate mea permansi libentissime moriar.*

[78] *VSPE* 5, 11. (90).

3 Pressure from Within – Bishops Threatened by Lack of Legitimacy and Authority

Further confrontations between Emeritensian bishops and concretely named authority figures cannot be traced. Yet this does not mean that influential persons in Augusta Emerita did not yet exist during the tenures of Paulus and Fidelis. The anonymous author, for example, does not write that Paulus's inheritance made him the only power holder, just more powerful than all the others (*cuntis potentibus patentor*).[79] Moreover, the inheritance itself – stemming from the private fortune of the richest senator of Lusitania, a *nobilissimus vir* – can serve as proof of a well-off local elite, one with at least the financial potential to challenge episcopal authority.[80] So although the vitae of Paulus and Fidelis contain no concrete descriptions of other authority figures, they do throw up significant conflict potentials that could prove dangerous for an *episcopus*.

A case in point is Fidelis taking over the episcopal office, a process in which his inherited fortune from Paulus plays a key role. These riches are not subsumed into the Church's holdings, but rather remain part of the bishops's private fortune, as evident in his testamentary instructions, which he wields as a source of pressure against the municipal clergy.[81] For Paulus wants to name his office's successor himself, designating his own nephew Fidelis as such and consecrating him personally during his lifetime.[82] He additionally secures his choice by instructing that the Emeritensian Church is to inherit his entire fortune if the clergy proves willing to accept the new bishop. If not, Fidelis may do as he sees fit with the entire inheritance.[83] After Paulus's death, that which he had feared comes to pass: several

---

[79] VSPE 4, 2. (30): *Et qui peregrinus nicilque habens aduenerat factus est cunctis potentibus potentior in tantum ut omnis facultas eclesie ad conparationem bonorum illius pro nicilum putarentur.*
[80] VSPE 4, 2. (26): *contigit cuiusdam primarii ciuitatis ex genere senatorum nobilissimi uiri egrotasse matrona*; (30) *Tanta namque illis inerat copia rerum, ut nullus senatorum in prouincia Lusitanie illis repperirietur locupletior*; Evidence for a well-off local elite can also be found in Augusta Emerita's 'epigraphic habit', as the grave inscription (CICMe 37 = AE 2001, 1169) of a *vir illustri* from 492 AD illustrates. On this, see: Vegh 2017, 93.
[81] On this case, see also: Roca 2015, 10–11.
[82] VSPE 4, 4. (34–35): *Interim dum auspice Deo constituisset eum antestitem, ita ei adstare et deseruire cupiebat sicut diaconatus tempore ministrare consueuerat, ita ut exuens sibi casullam more ministri coram eo adsistens seruitium omne persolberet*; The term '*antistes*' is here translated with the bishop. Martínez Pastor et al. 2001, 32–33.
[83] VSPE 4, 4. (34): *hunc sibi successorem elegit (sc. Paulus) moxque etiam in loco suo, se uiuente, ordinauit*; on the episcopal testament: It was not unusual for bishop to bestow his property via a testament. Canon 12 of the Council of Tarragona (516 AD), for example, prescribes that if a bishop

Emeritensians speak out against Fidelis and try to force him out of office. Yet when the new bishop responds by planning to leave the city for good, taking Paulus's entire fortune with him, his critics ultimately give way. Fearing that they would be left with nothing, they supposedly threw themselves at his feet, more unwilling than willing, and pleaded with him to stay.[84] Fidelis agrees to continue to exercise his office and to bestow his uncle's entire wealth on the Church.[85] This clearly shows, first that both Paulus and Fidelis could wield financial power in the form of a private fortune, utilising it to effectively pursue policymaking. But it also clearly reveals the threats the bishops faced, as expressed through discontent in their own congregation, especially amongst the clergy.

The *VSPE* traces the resistance to the new bishop back to only a few odious men (*quidam invidiae homines*), whose treachery Paulus had already predicted through a prophetic grace.[86] Yet it seems more likely that the dissatisfaction with Fidelis can be explained not through a general enmity on the part of the clergy, but stems from the manner in which Paulus determined his succession, which deviated significantly from both Christian tradition and the canons of several councils.[87] The records of the Second Council of Braga prove that this also applies to the Iberian Peninsula, as they declare such action impermissible.[88] Several pow-

---

leaves no testament behind, presbyters and deacons are to inventory his entire fortune after his death. The possibility of a bishop making testamentary bequests is thus established. Orlandis and Ramos-Lissón 1981, 56; Council of Tarragona 11 (Vives 1963, 37–38).

84 *VSPE* 4, 5. (35–36); The Council of Braga II, canon 11 (Vives 1963, 89), technically forbade a bishop from abandoning his parish, under the threat of excommunication.

85 *VSPE* 4, 5. (36): *Quibus ille non usquequaque repugnans prebuit adsensum, ut et curam regiminis gereret et in postmodum omne patrimonium suum eclesie derelinqueret*; Marcelo Martínez Pastor et al.'s comprehensive philosophical study of the *VSPE* demonstrates that the bishop does not give the properties to the Church directly, but rather bequeaths them to it at a later point (*in postmodum*). Martínez Pastor et. al 2001, 96–97. 192.

86 *VSPE* 4, 5. (34–35): *Post cuius discessum quidam pestiferi homines iuxta id quod uir Dei predixerat uerbis malignis contra beatissimum Fidelem episcopum musitare ceperunt, ut eum de loco quo constitutus fuerat per quaquumque occasione pellerent.*

87 Yet the practice of a bishop designating a relative does not seem to have been a rarity in Hispania, on this see Castillo Maldonado 2012, 25: "En fin, tras la existencia de auténticas dinastías episcopales, monopolizando una silla catedralicia catedralicia o copando los obispado se una determinada provincia eclesiástica, cabe sospechar no pocos casos de lo que pudiéramos llamar el episcopus designatus."

88 *Concilium Bracarense* II (c. 8): "No le está permitido al obispo designar sucesor a otro en su lugar antes del fin de la vida, y si alguno intentare hacerlo, tal determinación sea inválida. [...]" (trans. Vives 1963, 84); on the Council of Braga II, see also Orlandis and Ramos-Lissón 1981, 86–94. Fuentes Hinojo (2012, 28–30) has a created a more exact list of Late Antique voices who condemned this practice, particularly naming the Roman popes, who warn the Spanish bishops to adhere the Canons' norms in decisions of succession.

erful entities could thus see Fidelis's pontificate as illegitimate, weakening his claim to legitimacy and accordingly the scope of his authority. Moreover, the anonymous author also seems to be downplaying the resistance in Augusta Emerita when he writes that only a few individuals turned against the new *episcopus*.[89] Yet if Fidelis is clearly forced to consider abdicating the highest ecclesiastical office in the city and even to threaten to take his uncle's fortune with him, one must assume he faces a suitably high pressure. Paulus's decision to name a family member as his episcopal successor is therefore connected to a certain potential for conflict that almost costs Fidelis his office and also illuminates a limit to episcopal authority. For the bishop does not seem to have the right to settle a question as vital as the episcopal succession in a manner too distant from canonised Christian practice without expecting complications. Accordingly, Paulus secures his selection with a financial incentive.

Of particular interest in this episode is now the timing when the unrest breaks out. For it does not begin until after Paulus's death, although Fidelis is already presented as his successor during his tenure. If the bishop's approach was perceived as illegitimate nepotism, why did the members of the Emeritensian clergy not express their dissatisfaction earlier? The testamentary instructions concerning the bestowal of the bishop's fortune can hardly serve as sufficient explanation, for these continue to be valid under Fidelis's tenure but do not prevent the clergy from opposing the bishop. This leaves the assumption that the two Greeks' episcopal authority do not meet with the same acceptance in the congregation, though both are consecrated office holders.[90] For the congregation appears to submit to the authority of Paulus, and that of his decisions, until his death extinguishes it; despite his consecration, Fidelis does not succeed in seamlessly building on this authority, as the unorthodox manner of his designation has weakened his legitimacy. In addition, Fidelis is only at the start of his pontificate and thus will hardly have had a chance to prove himself worthy of his office or to shore up his authority.

Yet the bishop may have done precisely this later, for there is not the smallest indication that any form of resistance flared up again. This is particularly interesting as the text makes clear that the clergy submitted to the bishop with gritted teeth and only under the threat of force in the form of financial pressure. But the further descriptions of the bishop's life relate only the exact opposite of general discontent, as expressed in an almost exaggerated claim of harmony between

---

[89] Fuentes Hinojo 2012, 30, also estimates that the number of unsatisfied residents was higher: "Es posible que también se produjesen algaradas populares, como era habitual en estos casos."
[90] Fideles's authority does not seem to have stemmed from his Greek heritage, as Paulus, who had also come to Augusta Emerita as a Greek *peregrinus*, had the same claim.

the bishop and his congregation. The text claims that everyone held such pure and honest love for Fidelis that all burned for him with an unmeasurable brotherly love and with him formed *unum cor et labium*; nor could they permit the development of division or the slightest deviation from this mutual love.[91] Fidelis, who had once come to the city as a stranger, thus succeeds in building a strong and lasting connection (*fides*) to the Emeritensian congregation that even stretches beyond his death. For when Fidelis dies, the Emeritensians supposedly mourned his death but also rejoiced that he had been sent to heaven ahead of them, able to act for their salvation.[92] This statement contains a common conception of a bishop as a heavenly *patronus* that had gained increasing currency in the Christian West from the 4th century onwards.[93] According to this view, Fidelis had now passed through his earthly existence to advocate for his congregation's salvation in the heavenly realm.[94] Despite the questionable circumstances of his ordination, Fidelis thus succeeds in creating a strong *fides* between himself and his congregation. This may have been partially the result of numerous secular *beneficia* Fidelis bestows as episcopal patron, through which he not only proves his legitimacy but also wins the Emeritensians' loyalty in the sense of antique reciprocity.[95] Fidelis enriches his Church, securing his congregation's financial wellbeing by giving alms, forgiving debts and taking care of the prestigious basilica of Saint Eulalia, restoring and expanding it.[96] Nor does the bishop seem to lack heavenly legitimation, since God's grace allows him to fend off demons and miraculously save many lives when a building collapses.[97]

Indeed, the Emeritensian bishops' ability to provide their congregations with secular and heavenly *beneficia* forms a decisive basis for their legitimacy and au-

---

[91] *VSPE* 4, 5. (36).
[92] *VSPE* 5, 1. (47–48): [...] *sed gemminato gaudio congauderet, diuina tribuente miseratione, dum et illum sui pro salutem premisit ad celos et istum eximie uirtutis uirum suscepit gratulanter in terries*; on 'fides', see: RAC 26 (2014), 1112 "Patronage" (Busch, Nicols, and Zanella); see also Ganter 2015, 21.
[93] Rebenich 2001, 35. This conception was supposedly first limited to the apostles and martyrs, which quickly no longer sufficed and thus expanded to include saints and ultimately bishops; on the significance of the heavenly patron, see e.g. the example of Ambrosius of Milan: Martin 1990, 448–450.
[94] The conception of this heavenly patronage elevated secular patronage structures to a supernal level, as Stefan Rebenich 2008, 164, notes: "War im Diesseits der Kaiser der höchste und mächtigste *patronus*, so war es im Jenseits Jesus Christus. Wie unterhalb des Kaisers zahlreiche mächtige Aristokraten als Fürsprecher auftraten, so war es in der spiritualisierten Patronage-Beziehung der Heilige respektive der Märtyrer."
[95] On the antique system of patronage, see: Saller 1982; Krause 1987; Ganter 2015. On the bishop's role as patron, see: RAC 26 (2014), 1110 "Patronage" (Busch, Nicols, and Zanella).
[96] *VSPE* 4, 6. (38–39); 4, 10. (44–45).
[97] *VSPE* 4, 6. (38); 4, 9. (43).

thority. This is particularly demonstrable in the case of the bishop Nepopis, who faced a similar legitimacy problem to Fidelis. For Nepopis, too, receives his episcopal position in Augusta Emerita not through a regular process, but is established as the city's bishop through external authority while Masona resides in exile. Although Nepopis is described as a *pseudosacerdos* and *profanus*, he is doubtlessly a regular Catholic bishop who had previously received and executed his office in another city.[98] When Nepopis takes over episcopal duties in Augusta Emerita, the Emeritensians at first seem to accept their congregation's new leader, for there is nothing to the contrary to suggest resistance. If one further assumes that the city's Christian day-to-day life continues during Masona's exile, there is nothing to suggest that the Emeritensian Church did not also accept Nepopis's episcopal authority for a period of almost three years.

Not until Masona's return is announced does this change. For Nepopis, who had already prepared to leave the city himself, was chased from the city through *omni clero vel populo*.[99] One may now speculate why Nepopis was chased away only shortly before his predecessor's arrival: it seems plausible that the Emeritensians may have expected Liuvigild to enact consequences had they attempted anything similar before. After all – as previously described – Saint Eulalia herself must secure her servant's return by forcing Liuvigild through heavenly power to allow Masona to return to his church. The king sanctioning Masona's return would thus also be the Emeritensians' signal that the time had come to rid themselves of the replacement they had been forced to accept. Leaving speculation aside, however, Masona's return reveals a strong loyalty between him and his Church, one that had remained intact despite the years, and distance, of separation. This is especially clear in the first encounter between the returning bishop and several Emeritensian Catholics, forced to transport out of the city treasures that Nepopis had removed from the city's ecclesiastical buildings.[100] When these Emeritensians crossed paths with Masona and recognised their returning lord in him, they

---

98 VSPE 6, 6. (70–71): *Post hec subrogatur ei pseudosacerdos Nepopis quidam nomine atque in locum uiri Dei in Emeretensem urbem substituitur, homo namque profanus, seruus sane diaboli, angelus Satane, prenuntius Antixpi et hic erat aliene ciuitatis episcopus*; That the deputation between Masona and Sunna also solved the question of the city's religious primacy can been seen in the fact that Liuvigild did not make Sunna the city's sole bishop when Masona was in exile, but rather appointed a Catholic bishop, Nepopis, as Masona's replacement. On this: Bueno Rocha 1972, 1–14. On Nepopis: García Moreno 1974, 170.
99 VSPE 5, 8. (76): *Ipse uidelicet Nepopis infeliciter ab omni clero uel populo pulsus ab Emerita ad suam ciuitatem festinus perrexit ac, ne eum uir Dei Masona in sua eclesia inuenisset et cum omni ignominia pelleret, quantocius egredi festinabit.*
100 VSPE 5, 8. (75–76).

were supposedly filled with great joy and told him *Servi tui sumus, domine.*[101] The bishop then himself travels on to Augusta Emerita, where his church, having regained their *gubernator*, received him with great joy. The last section of this chapter particularly indicates the source of Masona's authority, as well as the possible cause of Nepopis's expulsion: The Church rejoiced at the old bishop's return because the sick had found succour, the suppressed had received help and the needy had received nourishment.[102] This certainly supports the assumption that Nepopis apparently neglected to fulfil his duties as episcopal patron and guarantee the general wellbeing through *beneficiis*.

Judging from Fidelis's case, one could now assume that despite the circumstances of his assuming office, Nepopis's three-year pontificate should theoretically have provided him with sufficient possibilities for significantly strengthening his authority in Augusta Emerita. After all, the Greek bishop managed to overcome the initial doubts of his person to lastingly consolidate his authority. But Fidelis was something that remains out of Nepopis's reach: a good episcopal patron. Nepopis, meanwhile, is presented as a kind of 'anti-patron', as eager to pursue bad deeds as Masona was to pursue good ones.[103] It thus seems plausible that Masona can immediately take up his role of patron again upon meeting the first Emeritensians, and that they do not hesitate to offer him *obsiquium*.[104] It is thus no longer curious that the bishop's mere return to Augusta Emerita unleashes great joy and the expectation of new secular *beneficia* that had been lacking during Nepopis's tenure.

But the foundations of the *fides* between Masona and the Emeritensians were formed not just by the secular *beneficia* a congregation could receive, but also of the spiritual ones, as the bishop's return also reveals. For his renewed presence suffices to reactivate a heavenly grace for the entire city, which had been missing under Nepopis. One should first note what is granted at the very beginning of Masona's pontificate: thanks to the new bishop's prayers, God supposedly kept sickness and hunger at bay not just from Augusta Emerita, but from *omni Lusitania*.[105]

---

101 *VSPE* 5, 8. (77).
102 *VSPE* 5, 8. (78): *Ita nimirum eclesia Emeretensis exultans summa cum iucunditate suum gubernatorem recepit. Gaudebant enim quod repperisset egrotus medellam, solacium quod inuenisset oppressus, alimentum quod non deesset egeno.*
103 *VSPE* 5, 6. (71): *Sed quantum uir Dei crescebat uirtutibus copiosis, e contra ille fedabatur actibus nefandis.*
104 On the '*obsequium*' in the patronage relationship, see Krause 1987, 21.
105 *VSPE* 5, 2. (48–49): *Huius itaque temporibus morbum pestem inedieque inopiam ab urbe Emeretensi uel omnem Lusitaniam eius precibus Dominus procul abegit* [...].

Of particular interest here is the last sentence on Masona's return, when he retakes his place as Augusta Emerita's bishop. The renewed presence of the holy man supposedly put an end to the ominous adversity, the frequently devastating plagues as well as the unusual storms that raged over the entire city, which had doubtlessly been caused by his absence.[106] Through his mere presence, Masona thus grants the Emeritensians access to spiritual *beneficia* in the form of heavily protection that seems to extinguish only when the wrong person sits on the city's Cathedra. The *VSPE* thus legitimates the justified nature of Masona's episcopal tenure directly through higher spiritual entity – one denied to Nepopis, who, after all, at no point is the recipient of any kind of grace. If the Christians of the time believed that heavenly *beneficia* require a legitimate bishop, one can understand why both Nepopis's and Fidelis's episcopal authorities are so vulnerable to attack, and why the congregation and clergy speak out against these bishops and, in Nepopis's case, even resort to banishment.

Overall, a picture now forms of a congregation that accepts a bishop's authority as higher and decisive if it entails, for them, a greater benefit. Moreover, one can argue that although the episcopal office was per se furnished with defined competencies and a fundamental authority, these could easily wobble in times of conflict if not strengthened by charismatic deeds performed by their carrier that reveal his utility for the congregation. Thus, Fidelis at the start of his tenure could only escape the looming loss of his office by using power in the form of financial pressure to force his critics to give way. Nepopis even loses the episcopal office of Augusta Emerita after three years because he fails to make good the legitimacy deficit his appointment had created as well as neglects the duties expected of him as bishop, and thus inter alia has nothing to counter the authority of Masona, which rests partially on heavenly legitimation. It thus becomes clear that a lack of authority caused by deficient legitimacy represents a threat that must be taken seriously, yet spells danger not for the Catholic episcopal office of Augusta Emerita per se, but specifically for its incumbent.

4 Conclusion

The *Vitas Sanctorum Patrum Emeritensium* contains numerous descriptions of threats facing bishops that are concrete and partially independent of their confes-

---

[106] *VSPE* 5, 9. (78): *Reddita sunt a Domino Emeretensi eclesie copiosa suffragia, nam calamitatum penurias et crebras pestilentie clades insolentesque totius urbis procellas sancti uiri presentia Domino miserante suspendit, quas indubie remoto pastore causa eius absentie pressit.*

sion. First are the bishops' conflicts with other authority figures. In these, the bishop's authority in his congregation forms the starting point for a possible threat, yet one that becomes concrete only if the bishop refuses to integrate that authority into the policies of another authority figure, such as the king. This does not, however, lead to the bishop's immediate violent removal, but rather to the opposition attempting to weaken the episcopal authority. Only when the bishop has proven himself a vehement hindrance to such policies does he run the danger of being removed by force from his position and sent into exile. Mindful of his own domestic policy goals, the king, at least, seems to refuse to subject a bishop to measures any more severe than exile. Yet the remaining authority figures – like the Gothic aristocrats around Sunna – think differently. They too attempt to overcome the bishop's authority for their own political goals, but do not shrink back even from episcopal murder.

Another strong threat manifests in the loss of episcopal authority in one's own congregation, triggered by a lack of legitimacy. This can root either in an unorthodox assumption of office or the bishop's neglect of his expected duties (patronage duties, the absence of divine support, etc.). Although the office per se furnishes the bishop with certain competencies and a fundamental authority, these can be easily attacked both externally and internally if legitimacy is lacking, which among other things can lead to the bishop's expulsion by his own congregation.

One may therefore conclude the existence of two types of episcopal threat, though both are aimed at the authority of the episcopal office. First, there is the 'external threat': actors from outside the congregation either attempting to extinguish the bishop's authority or subsume it for themselves. This is juxtaposed by an 'internal threat': actors from inside the congregation attacking the bishop's authority if he has misbehaved or lacks legitimacy. Both types are interconnected and can condition the other. For example, a bishop submitting to an 'external threat' can trigger an 'internal threat'. A bishop fleeing from a physical confrontation with royalty could be judged a dereliction of his patronal duty of protection, negatively impacting the bishop's authority. A visible 'internal threat', meanwhile, could motivate external powers to attack the bishop. This connection can force the bishop to engage in a balancing act of not giving way too strongly to either threat. Otherwise, he must fear the respective extreme of both types and be forced to decide between the loss of his office or even his life and the complete loss of his authority in his congregation.

Bibliography

Primary Sources

Gregory of Tours, *Decem Libri Historiarum:* Bruno Krusch and Wilhelm Levison. ed. 1951. *Monumenta Germaniae Historica, Scriptores rerum Merovingicarum (MGH SS rer. Merov.).* I, 1, *Gregorii Episcopi Turonensis Libri Historiarum X.* Hannover: Hahnsche Buchhandlung.

Isidore of Seville, *Historia Gothorum Wandalorum Suebum:* Theodor Mommsen. ed. 1894. *Monumenta Germaniae Historica, Augtores antiquissimi (MGH Auct. ant.).* XI, *Chronica minora saec. IV. V. VI. VII. (II).* Berlin: Weidmann.

John of Biclaro, Chronicle: Kenneth Baxter Wolf. trans. 1990. *Conquerors and chroniclers of early medieval Spain. Translated with notes and introduction by Kenneth Baxter Wolf.* Translated Texts for Historians 9. Liverpool: Liverpool University Press.

Traditio Apostolica (Geerlings 2000): Georg Schöllgen and Wilhelm Geerlings. eds. ³2000. *Zwölf-Apostel-Lehre; Apostolische Überlieferung; Didache; Traditio Apostolica.* Fontes Christiani 1. Freiburg im Breisgau: Herder.

Vitas Sanctorum Patrum Emeretensium: Antonio Maya Sánchez. ed. 1992. *Corpus Christianorum, Series Latina (CCSL).* 116. Turnhout: Brepols; Joseph N. Garvin. ed. trans. 1946. *The Vitas Sanctorum patrum Emeretensium: text and translation, with an introduction and commentary.* Studies in Medieval and Renaissance Latin Language and Literature 19. Washington: Catholic University of America Press.

Vives, Jose. ed. 1963. *Concilios visigóticos e hispano-romanos.* España cristiana 1. Barcelona/Madrid: Consejo Superior de Investigaciones Científicas.

Secondary Sources

Arce, Javier. 1999. "The City of Mérida (Emerita) in the Vitas Patrum Emeritensium (VIth Century A.D.)" In *East and West: Modes of Communication. Proceedings of the First Plenary Conference at Merida.* The Transformation of the Roman World 5, edited by Evangelos K. Chrysos and Ian Wood, 1–14. Leiden: Brill.

Arce, Javier. 2008 "La inscripción del puente de Mérida de época del rey Eurico (483 d.C.)" *Pyrenae* 39, 2:121–126.

Arce, Javier. 2011. *Esperando a los árabes. Los visigodos en Hispania (507–711).* Madrid: Marcial Pons Historia.

Bueno Rocha, José. 1972. "La cuestión del obispo Nepopis de Mérida." *Asociación Cultural Coloquios Históricos de Extremadura, Trujillo,* 1–14.

Caballero Zoreda, Luis, and Pedro Mateos Cruz. 1995. "Excavaciones arqueológicas en la basílica de Sta. Eulalia de Mérida." In *IV Reunió d'Arqueologia Cristiana Hispànica.* Monografies de la Secció Històrico-Arqueológica 4, edited by Josep M. Gurt, 297–307. Barcelona: Institut d'Estudis Catalans.

Castillo Lozano, José Ángel. 2020. "Luchas de poder en la Mérida visigoda." *Intus-Legere Historia* 14, 2:104–123.

Castillo Maldonado, Pedro. 2012. "'In hora mortis' deceso, duelo, rapiña y legado en la muerte del obispo visigótico." *Hispania Sacra* 64:7–28.

Collins, Roger. 2004. *Visigothic Spain 409–711*. Malden: Blackwell.
Dassmann, Ernst. 1994. Ämter und Dienste in den frühchristlichen Gemeinden. Hereditas 8. Bonn: Borengässer.
Eger, Christoph. 2009. "Zur Imperialisierung des westgotischen Königtums aus archäologischer Sicht." In *Spolien im Umkreis der Macht: Akten der Tagung in Toledo vom 21.–22.9.2006*, edited by Thomas Gregor Schattner and Fernando Valdés Fernández, 151–169. Mainz: Philipp von Zabern.
Faber, Eike. 2014. *Von Ulfila bis Rekkared. Die Goten und ihr Christentum*. Potsdamer altertumswissenschaftliche Beiträge 51. Stuttgart: Steiner.
Fuentes Hinojo, Pablo. 2012. "Sucesión dinástica y legitimidad episcopal en la Mérida visigoda. Dynastic succession and Episcopal Legitimacy in Visigoth Mérida." *En la España Medieval* 35:11–33.
Ganter, Angela. 2015. *Was die römische Welt zusammenhält. Parton-Klient-Verhältnisse zwischen Cicero und Cyprian*. KLIO 26. Berlin/Boston: De Gruyter.
García Moreno, Luis A. 1974. *Prosopografía del reino visigodo de Toledo*. Acta Salmanticensia. Filosofía y Lettras 77. Salamanca: Universidad de Salamanca.
Godoy Fernández, Cristina, and Francesc Tuset Bertrán. 1994. "El Atrium en las Vitas Sanctorum Patrum Emeretensium. ¿Una fórmula de la llamada arquitectura del poder?" *Archivo Español de Arqueología* 67:209–222.
Kampers, Gerd. 2008. *Geschichte der Westgoten*. Paderborn/München/Wien/Zürich: Schöningh.
Koch, Manuel. 2012. *Ethnische Identität im Entstehungsprozess des spanischen Westgotenreiches*. Ergänzungsbände zum Reallexikon der Germanischen Altertumskunde 75. Berlin/Boston: De Gruyter.
Krause, Jens-Uwe. 1987. *Spätantike Patronatsformen im Westen des Römischen Reiches*. München: Beck.
Leppin, Hartmut. 2018. *Die frühen Christen. Von den Anfängen bis Konstantin*. München: Beck.
Martin, Jochen. 1990. "Die Macht der Heiligen." In *Christentum und antike Gesellschaft*. Wege der Forschung 649, edited by Jochen Martin and Barbara Quint, 440–475. Darmstadt: Wissenschaftliche Buchgesellschaft.
Martínez Pastor, Marcelo, Anna Maria Aldama Roy, Maria Dolores Castro Jiménez, Manuel Martínez Quintana, and José Muñoz Jiménez. eds. 2001. *Vitas Sanctorum Patrum Emeretensium. Léxico latino-español*. Alpha – Omega, Reihe B 19. Hildesheim: Olms-Weidmann.
Martyn, John R. C. 2018. *King Sisebut and the Culture of Visigothic Spain, with Translations of the Lives of Saint Desiderius of Vienne and Saint Masona of Merida. Vita vel Passio Sancti Desiderii a Sisebuto Rege composita and Vita Sancti Masonae Emeretensis*, Lewiston: Mellen.
Mateos Cruz, Pedro. 2000. "Augusta Emerita, de capital de la diocesis Hispaniarum a sede temporal visigoda." *Memorias de la Real Academia de Buenas Letras de Barcelona* 25:491–520.
Mathisen, Ralph W. 2014. "'Arian' Clergy, Church Organization, and Church Practices." In *Arianism: Roman Heresy and Barbarian Creed*, edited by Guido M. Berndt and Roland Steinacher, 145–191. Farnham: Ashgate.
Monfrin, Françoise. "Die räumliche Ausbreitung des Christentums in Stadt und Land." In *Die Geschichte des Christentums. Religion, Politik, Kultur.* 3, Der Lateinische Westen und der byzantinische Osten (431–642), edited by Luce Pietri, Norbert Brox and Jean-Marie Mayeur, 1011–1074. Freiburg im Breisgau: Herder.
Mülke, Markus. 2016. "Guter König und doch Verfolger? Die Religionspolitik des Westgotenkönigs Leovigild im Urteil der zeitgenössischen Historiker (Johannes Biclarensis und Isidor von Sevilla)." *Frühmittelalterliche Studien* 50:99–128.

Orlandis, Jose, and Domingo Ramos-Lissón. *Die Synoden auf der Iberischen Halbinsel bis zum Einbruch des Islam (711)*. Konzilgeschichte, Reihe A: Darstellungen. Paderborn: Schöningh.

Panzram, Sabine. 2002. *Stadtbild und Elite: Tarraco, Corduba und Augusta Emerita zwischen Republik und Spätantike.* Historia, Einzelschriften 161. Stuttgart: Steiner.

Panzram, Sabine. 2007. "Eulalia und die Bischöfe von Merida. Von der 'Handlungsmacht' einer Heiligen zur Zeit der Westgoten." In *Formen und Funktionen von Leitbildern*. Altertumswissenschaftliches Kolloquium 17, edited by Johannes Hahn and Meinolf Vielberg, 177–225. Stuttgart: Steiner.

Panzram, Sabine. 2010. "Mérida contra Toledo, Eulalia contra Leocadia: listados 'falsificados' de Obispos como medio de autorepresentación municipal." In *Espacios Urbanos en el Occidente Mediterráneo (S. VI–VIII)*, edited by Alfonso García, Ricardo Izquierdo, Lauro Olmo, and Diego Peris, 123–130. Toledo: Toletum Visigodo.

Panzram, Sabine. 2014. "Die Iberische Halbinsel um 500 – Herrschaft 'am Ende der Welt'. Eine Geschichte in neun Städten." In *Chlodwigs Welt. Organisation von Herrschaft um 500.* Roma Aeterna 3, edited by Mischa Meier and Steffen Patzold, 449–486. Stuttgart: Steiner.

Poveda Arias, Pablo. 2019. "La diócesis episcopal en la Hispania visigoda: concepción, construcción y disputas por su territorio." *Hispania Sacra* 71:9–24.

Ramírez Sádaba, José Luis, and Pedro Mateos Cruz. 2000. *Catálogo de las inscripciones cristianas de Mérida*. Cuadernos Emeritenses 16. Mérida: Museo Nacional de Arte Romano.

Rapp, Claudia. 2005. *Holy Bishops in Late Antiquity. The Nature of Christian Leadership in an Age of Transition.* The Transformation of the Classical Heritage 37. Berkeley/Calif: University of California Press.

Rebenich, Stefan. 2001. "Wohltäter und Heilige. Von der heidnischen zur christlichen Patronage." In *Epochenwandel? Kunst und Kultur zwischen Antike und Epochenwandel*, edited by Franz Alto Bauer and Norbert Zimmermann, 27–35. Mainz: Philipp von Zabern.

Rebenich, Stefan. 2008. "Pars melior humani generis – Aristokratie(n) in der Spätantike." In *Die Macht der Wenigen, Aristokratische Herrschaftspraxis, Kommunikation und 'edler' Lebensstil in Antike und Früher Neuzeit*. Historische Zeitschrift, Beihefte 47, edited by Hans Beck, Peter Scholz and Uwe Walter, 153–175. München: Oldenbourg.

Roca, María J. 2015. "La distinción entre patrimonio eclesiástico y privado de obispos y clérigos en la España visigoda" *e-Legal History Review* 20:1–16.

Saller, Richard P. 1982. *Personal Patronage under the Early Empire*. Cambridge: Cambridge University Press.

Saxer, Victor. 2010. "Die Organisation der nachapostolischen Gemeinden (70–180)." In *Die Geschichte des Christentums. Religion, Politik, Kultur.* 1, Die Zeit des Anfangs (bis 250), edited by Luce Pietri, Thomas Böhm, Norbert Brox and Jean-Marie Mayeur, 269–339. Freiburg im Breisgau: Herder.

Steinacher, Roland. 2019. "Vom Ketzerkönig zum *christianissimus rex*. Politische Dimensionen der homöischen Christologie: Afrika im 5. und 6. Jahrhundert mit einem Ausblick nach Spanien." In *Das Christentum im frühen Europa. Diskurse – Tendenzen – Entscheidungen*. Millennium-Studien 75, edited by Uta Heil, 195–218. Berlin/Boston: De Gruyter.

Teja, Ramón. 2019 "Intra muros y extra muros, La 'guerra' entre nicenos y arrianos por el control de los espacios públicos y religiosos en la Mérida de Leovigildo y Masona." *Studi e materiali di storia delle religioni* 85:202–214.

Van Nuffelen, Peter and Lieve Van Hoof. eds. 2020. *Clavis Historicorum Antiquitatis Posterioris. An Inventory of Late Antique Historiography (A.D. 300–800)*. Corpus Christianorum, Claves-Subsidia (CCCS) 5. Turnhout: Brepols.

Végh, Judit. 2017. "Inschriftenkultur und Christianisierung im Spätantiken Hispanien. Ein Überblick." In *The Epigraphic Cultures of Late Antiquity*. HABES 60, edited by Katharina Bolle, Carlos Machado, and Christian Witschel, 55–110. Stuttgart: Steiner.

Velázquez Soriano, Isabel. 2008a. *Vidas de los Padres de Mérida. Introducción, traducción y notas de Isabel Velázquez*. Colección Estructuras y Procesos, Serie Religion. Madrid: Editorial Trotta.

Velázquez Soriano, Isabel. 2008b. "El puente de Mérida: algo más que un problema de traducción." Pyrenae 39,2:127–135.

Weber, Max. ^{5}1980. *Wirtschaft und Gesellschaft. Grundriss der verstehenden Soziologie*. Tübingen: Mohr Siebeck.

Wolfram, Herwig. ^{3}2010. *Die Goten und ihre Geschichte*. München: Beck.

Wood, Ian. 1999. "Social Relations in the Visigothic Kingdom from the Fifth to the Seventh Century: The Example of Mérida." In *The Visigoths from the Migration Period to the Seventh Century. An Ethnographic Perspective*. Studies in Historical Archaeoethnology 4, edited by Peter J. Heather, 191–206. Woodbridge/Suffolk: Boydell Press.

Zerjadtke, Michael. 2019. *Das Amt des 'Dux' in Spätantike und frühem Mittelalter. Der 'ducatus' im Spannungsfeld zwischen römischem Einfluss und eigener Entwicklung*. Ergänzungsbände zum Reallexikon der germanischen Altertumskunde 110. Berlin: De Gruyter.

Charles Mériaux
Bishops under Pressure: Priests and Episcopal Authority in Carolingian Francia

Abstract: In the eyes of historians, the threat to the bishops during the Early Middle Ages is generally embodied by the higher authorities, civil or ecclesiastical: king, pope and archbishop, as shown by the presentations of the great crises that led, for example, to the deposition of Hincmar of Laon or Rothade of Soissons under the aegis of archbishop Hincmar and King Charles the Bald. However, the ninth century also saw the intervention of an increasingly autonomous actor who claimed a participation in diocesan affairs which could even cause difficulties for the bishop: this was the local clergy and more precisely the clergy installed in the countryside, whose means of action are becoming better known thanks to the work of Steffen Patzold and Carin Van Rhijn. This paper will therefore focus on cases in the province of Reims which show how clerics were able to put pressure on their bishop, whether it be the priests of Soissons who were invited in 861 to testify in favour of one of their number against their bishop Rothade at the provincial synod; The clerics of Laon compiling a singular canonical collection against their bishop in the spring of 869; or the priest Trisingus who forced Hincmar of Reims to justify himself rather piteously to Pope Hadrian II in the autumn of 871.

The threats faced by bishops in the Early Middle Ages stemmed mainly from the civil or ecclesiastic authorities above them, or so is the view of historians who have studied the issue. Kings, popes, and archbishops (as of the Carolingian period) are depicted as the lead protagonists in the serious crises affecting certain dioceses, on occasions culminating in the officeholder being deposed.[1] The most famous such affair was no doubt the lengthy conflict starting in 868 in which Bishop Hincmar of Laon clashed with Charles the Bald and especially with his uncle Archbishop Hincmar of Reims. Despite the papacy acting as moderator and arbiter, the feud became embittered, resulting in the bishop of Laon being deposed in 871 and blinded in 875.[2] But another increasingly autonomous set of agents played a part in this quarrel, who were demanding greater involvement in diocesan affairs more generally, namely the local clergy, and more precisely the clergy based in the country-

---

[1] Kaiser 1993; Fouracre 2003. See also Soria 2005.
[2] Devisse 1976, 726–785; McKeon 1978.

side, about whose means of action we now know far more thanks to the work of Steffen Patzold and Carine Van Rhijn.[3]

In the Early Middle Ages, the number of clerics in the West increased considerably after local churches, already called parishes, became the place for the routine practice and management of the faithful. This change is generally traced back to the Council of Vaison in 529, when Metropolitan Caesurius of Arles authorised the priests of his province to preach.[4] The only source giving an idea of the number of rural clergy in the Early Middle Ages are the acts of the diocesan synod of Auxerre called shortly after 585 by Archbishop Aunarius and undersigned by 34 priests, 7 abbots, and 3 deacons.[5] But there is little doubt that Carolingian reforms over the course of the ninth century caused this number to increase significantly in all dioceses across the Empire.

The purpose of this paper is to show that while there clearly were threats hanging over bishops in the Merovingian period, these acquired a new form over the course of the ninth century, issuing at times from the more numerous diocesan clergy who, though admittedly subject to closer oversight, were also more conscious of their scope for autonomous action.

1 The Threats Hanging over Bishops in Merovingian Gaul

Merovingian documentation clearly records certain places of tension – and conflict even – between a bishop and clerics, mainly priests.[6] There could be many causes for this: cohabitation with a woman and the non-respect of continence, misuse of ecclesiastical assets, or the infringement of certain liturgical prescriptions. These situations mostly resulted in disciplinary sanctions reasserting the bishop's authority, even though we may at times doubt how effective these were. When such situations arose, they seem to have stemmed mostly from individual opposition to the bishop's authority. In Clermont, priest Evodius clashed violently with Bishop Gallus of Clermont during a meal; a similar case arose between priest Cato and Bishop Cautinus, whose office he hankered after.[7] Threats could nevertheless ac-

---

3 Van Rhijn 2007; Mériaux 2014; Patzold and Van Rhijn 2016; Patzold 2020.
4 Gaudemet and Basdevant 1989, 1:192.
5 Gaudemet and Basdevant 1989, 2:488–504.
6 Godding 2001, 284–293.
7 Greg. Tur. vit. patr. VI, 4 for Evodius and *Decem Libri Historiarum* (Franc.), IV, 6–7 for Cato. See Godding 2001, 287–288 and Goetz 2018, 53.

quire scale when opposition was conducted by an influential member of the clergy, particularly the archdeacon, such as the one who planned to murder Bishop Aetherius of Lisieux,[8] or a certain Frontonius who was involved in the assassination of Maracharius of Angoulême.[9] Gregory of Tours personally experienced such opposition from his archdeacon, Riculfus.[10] This was likewise the case in the seventh century for Bishop Leodegarius of Autun whose main opponent was Abbott Hermenarius of Saint-Symphorien, who endeavoured and finally managed to succeed him, and in this role wrote the first Passio of his unfortunate predecessor.[11]

For these threats to be put into action, they generally needed to build on other oppositions, resonating at court for instance, in what Paul Fouracre calls "a conjunction of high politics and local initiative".[12] Bishop Praetextatus of Rouen fell victim to opposition from the court of Chilpéric I, relayed in his city by his own archdeacon.[13] If Riculfus caused difficulties for Gregory in Tours, it is because the latter's Austrasian sympathies were not commonly shared in 579–580. Just as in the case of opposition to Hermenarius, it was rivalry between Leodegarius and Ebroin, mayor of the palace of Neustria, which caused the situation to take a dramatic turn for the worse, leading to the fall then death of the bishop of Autun. This was not an isolated fate: Reinhold Kaiser and Paul Fouracre estimate about twenty bishops were killed during the Merovingian period. Bearing in mind that over the course of the sixth and seventh centuries there were in all a thousand or so bishops in the Frankish kingdom, this figure indicates the very real nature of the threats hanging over bishops.[14]

While the sources insist on the individual and non-systematic character of the opposition encountered by certain bishops, as of the Merovingian period one may also observe forms of solidarity operating relatively independently of episcopal authority. Otto Gerhard Oexle has pointed out that the documentation of Merovingian councils attests to a large number of orders banning clerics' "conjurations".[15] These prohibitions were not specific to the Frankish kingdom, for they invoked and added substance to an interdict issued in 451 in canon 18 of the Council of Chalcedon. One may of course think that such conjurations amounted to "veritable

---

8 Greg. Tur. Franc. VI, 36. See Goetz 2018, 54.
9 Greg. Tur. Franc. V, 36.
10 Greg. Tur. Franc. V, 49. See Godding 2001, 288–289.
11 Mériaux 2018, 75.
12 Fouracre 2003, 23. See Rosenwein 2021.
13 Greg. Tur. Franc. VIII, 31; 41. See Mériaux 2018, 64.
14 Kaiser 1993; Fouracre 2003. Positing an average episcopacy of twenty years for the hundred or so Gallic dioceses over a period of two centuries, one obtains a minimum of one thousand bishops.
15 Oexle 1985, 169–184.

conspiracies by priests against their bishop", and such situations may very well have existed.[16] But one may also envisage that these groups of clergy bound by oaths were not driven so much by hostility towards episcopal authority as by rural clerics' wish to establish close ties of mutual support, as suggested by canon 24 of the Council of Orleans (538). This suggests that the purpose of these conjurations – which gave rise to a charter (*cartula*) – was to practice *caritas* between group members.[17] Criticism of bishops related precisely to the fact that clerics needed to display charity universally, not within the restricted setting of a sworn brotherhood. As Otto Gerhard Oexle suggests, the increasing number of such interdicts over the sixth and seventh centuries may be related to the new situation of the rural clergy, scattered around the countryside of their diocese, and who thereby had weaker ties to the town-based bishop and clerics, and who while not necessarily seeking to express a degree of, or, outright opposition, were nevertheless seeking to partake autonomously in the management of the diocese.[18]

2 Clerical Hierarchy and Control in the Ninth Century

The acts of Frankish councils of the sixth and seventh centuries reveal a still fairly loose hierarchy with a clergy placed under the sole oversight of the archdeacon, as indicated in the late eighth century by a formula concerning him remaining in charge of investigations about rural priests.[19]

However, the introduction of deans (*decani*) in Carolingian dioceses in the following century shows that the episcopacy wished to have intermediaries capable of better controlling the local clergy. This initiative is particularly documented by the episcopal legislation of Hincmar of Reims, and especially the second "capitu-

---

16 Godding 2001, 284–293.
17 Gaudemet and Basdevant 1989, 1:250–251: *Si qui clericorum, ut nuper multis locis diabolo instigante actum fuisse perpatuit, rebelli auctoritate se in unum coniuratione intercedente collegerint et aut sacramenta inter se data aut chartulam conscriptam fuisse patuerit, nullis excusationibus haec praesumtio praeueletur, sed res detecta, cum in sinodo uentum fuerit, in praesumtoribus iuxta personarum et ordinum qualitatem a pontificibus, qui tunc in unum collecti fuerint, uindicetur; quia, sicut caritas ex praeceptis dominicis corde, non cartulae conscriptione est uel coniurationibus exhibenda, ita, quod supra sacras admittitur scripturas, auctoritate et districtione pontificali est reprimendum.*
18 Oexle 1985, 177–180.
19 Zeumer 1886, 263.

lary" of 852 which lists twenty-six points that the *magistri et decani presbiteri* are requested to carefully examine in "mother-churches" and "chapels" in the diocese, reporting back to the archbishop in early July each year.[20] The importance Hincmar attached to the mission of these deans is also emphasized in the capitulary of 874 enjoining archdeacons not to hesitate in removing any "negligent", "useless", or "incorrigible" deans.[21] Elsewhere there were an increasing number of statements about deans over the second half of the ninth century. Additionally, according to the capitulary of Toulouse in 844, Aquitaine already had "archpriests" in charge of "deaneries".[22]

In places without deans, a more informal hierarchy nevertheless existed, as suggested by a chapter in the capitulary of Ver issued in 884 by Carloman, king of West Francia, which mentions the need for each bishop to send priests who were *reverendi et cauti atque prudentia morum temperati* to villages furthest from the episcopal city, to whom younger and less experienced clerics in the vicinity could turn for assistance.[23]

Furthermore, Carolingian bishops could also draw on the regular gathering of the diocesan synod. According to Theodulf of Orleans (797–817), a meeting with the bishop or his representative made it possible to check whether the priest fulfilled his ministry correctly. The priest was even requested to bring liturgical vases, books, and ornaments, and be accompanied by two or three people (either clerics or laymen) who could testify to how he performed his ministry.[24] Furthermore, certain bishops also got into the habit of gathering a small assembly during their diocesan visits, which could function as a sort of itinerant tribunal, referred to in German scholarship as *Sendgericht*.[25] The earliest *ordo* relating to this practice dates from the last quarter of the ninth century. It provided for questioning seven *veriores et prudentiores* witnesses about the church, its endowment, its tithes, and the priest's behaviour. Three *idonei et veridici* priests were then to explain how their peer conducted his ministry. The investigation terminated with a public meeting during which all – clerics and laypeople alike – were reminded of their obligations.[26] A formula in the collection of Solomon III of Constance of the same period also attests to the holding of this sort of episcopal investigation.[27]

---

20 Pokorny and Stratmann 1995, 45–70. See Stratmann 1991; Van Rhijn 2007.
21 Pokorny and Stratmann 1995, 89.
22 Hartmann (1984, 20) concerning the place where fees were to be paid, *statuant episcopi loca convenientia par decanias, sicut constituti sunt archipresbyteri*.
23 Boretius and Krause 1890, 374.
24 Brommer 1984, 106.
25 Hartmann 2008, 245–260.
26 Krause 1894, 118–121. See Hartmann 2008, 253–254.

This enterprise to impose order on the rural clergy was accompanied by an attempt to define the duties of priests ever more precisely, as indicated as of the late 820s by a very detailed investigation formula for candidates to the priesthood: *Institutio ecclesiaticae auctoritatis, quam hi, qui provehendi sunt ad sacerdotium, profiteri debent se observaturos, et, ab his postea deviaverint, canonica auctoritate plectentur*, attributed to Bishop Halitgar of Cambrai.[28] There are also a large number of other, often more concise formulae about clerics' obligations.[29] In the early years of the tenth century, all these documents were gathered in the liminary synodal questionnaire *Libri duo de synodalibus causis et disciplinis ecclesiasticis* compiled between 906 and 913 by Abbot Regino of Prüm at the request of Archbishop Ratbod of Trier,[30] then summarised in the famous *Admonitio synodalis* inserted in the mid-tenth century into the Roman-Germanic Pontifical, compiled by the entourage of Archbishop William of Mainz (954–968).[31]

3 The Diocesan Clergy's Autonomy and Agenda

The instruments and practices put in place to ensure ever closer control over the diocesan clergy attest to the autonomy to which the latter laid claim, though without necessarily acquiring it. Bishops were well aware of this, and sought to involve the priests ever more closely in the running of the diocese.[32] Shortly after 878, in a letter to Bishop Hedenulf of Laon, who had been administrating the diocese of Cambrai since the death of Bishop Jean, Hincmar of Reims reminds his correspondent that when elections were to be held for the new bishop, it would be necessary to include the *vota* brought by the representatives (*vicarii*) of rural priests unable to travel in person to the episcopal city.[33] Furthermore, many of the episcopal capitularies formally promulgated by bishops were issued during meetings of the diocesan synod, suggesting that the chapters were discussed beforehand.[34] The same is true of other decisions taken by the synod, such as the building of new churches, like the church of Favars in the diocese of Limoges in 897, for in-

---

27 Zeumer 1886, 415–416. See Hartmann 2008, 254–255.
28 Hartmann 1979, 392–394. See Van Rhijn 2007, 84–86 and Mériaux 2014, 486–488.
29 Vykoukal 1913, 81–96 and Van Rhijn 2012.
30 Hartmann 2004. See Hartmann 2008, 149–160.
31 Vogel and Elze 1963–1972, 286–289; Amiet 1964; Pokorny 1985.
32 Mériaux 2014
33 Mériaux 2014, 880.
34 Avril 2003; Avril 1991.

stance,[35] or that of Saint Hunegund in the diocese of Laon in the tenth century,[36] as indicated by the charters and narrative sources.

The above-mentioned works by Otto Gerhard Oexle have long drawn attention to the fact that the forms of local organisation of the clergy dating from the "conjurations" of clerics – as attested in sixth- and seventh-century legislation – continued to exist over the following centuries. In the ninth century, meetings between priests and their dean – known as calends (*calendae*) – were additionally a time of conviviality for establishing ties of solidarity, which could at times escape episcopal control.[37] In a letter Hincmar sent to his suffragan John of Cambrai in 874, he expressed concern at the possibility that certain priests might collude to bear false witness to exculpate one of their fellows, and issued orders for an episcopal *missus* "in whom we trust" (*missus nobis credibilis*) to be present.[38] In the Carolingian period, the process of imposing order and hierarchising the local clergy had not extinguished the independence to which the clerics laid claim.

One additional element to take into account is the position of authority that priests acquired within local society, initially gauged in terms of learning and culture as indicated in the existent manuals for priests about which Carine Van Rhijn and Steffen Patzold have produced many works over recent years.[39] This position of authority was also due to a good number of priests being wealthy, thanks to substantial family assets, as well as to their controlling local church resources and tithes. In the mid-ninth century, priest Norbert in Ville-en-Selves in the diocese of Reims was head of an estate including a manse and four slaves, as well as receiving other revenue belonging to his church, particularly the revenue generated by a small landholding assigned to him for his lifetime, and a vineyard given *pro loco sepulturae*. He had also received two manses and a field in benefice from the monastery of Saint-Remi (a church property). We only know about part of this priest's assets, and it is quite possible that he also had family property. As noted by Jean-Pierre Devroey, this depicts "a little *dominus* who was part of the social elite of the village".[40] Additionally, investigations conducted by Susan Wood about the West from the ninth to the eleventh centuries has revealed a fairly sizeable category of priests who owned or co-owned their own churches.[41]

---

35 Aubrun 1981, 350–353.
36 Mériaux 2017, 52.
37 Oexle 1981, 341–348; Avril 2007.
38 Mériaux 2014, 888–889; Mériaux 2015, 170–171.
39 Van Rhijn 2014; Van Rhijn 2016; Patzold 2020, 305–388.
40 Devroey 2003, 201.
41 Wood 2006, 659–680.

In short, we should not generalize the very pejorative terms in which Agobard of Lyon (816–840) portrayed the situation of rural priests exploited by their lords. A fair share of the parish clergy came from families belonging to the local elite, and could thus draw on the support of a family network.[42] Few priests owed their position solely to the bishop, which meant they could be designated to convey broader protests issuing from local society.

4 The Local Clergy: A New Threat?

Hence the rural clergy in Carolingian dioceses could have looked like a new threat. A first illustration of this is the conflict between Archbishop Hincmar of Reims and his suffragan Rothad of Soissons. Rothad had deposed a priest in his diocese, whose defence Hincmar took in summoning a provincial synod in 861 to which priests from the diocese of Soissons were invited to take part. Flodard, in his *Historia Remensis Ecclesiae*, analyses the letter the archbishop sent to the deans of Soissons telling them to summon the priests.[43] The clergy of Soissons were just as great a threat as the archbishop, and they finally obtained Rothad's deposal the following year. According once again to Hincmar's correspondence analysed by Flodoard, ten years previously, in 853/856, priests in the diocese of Soissons had already appealed to the provincial synod, deeming that Rothad had unjustly deprived them of their assets.[44] Hincmar had clearly managed to exploit a long-standing misunderstanding between the bishop of Soissons and his clergy to get the former deposed, even though this was contested before Pope Nicholas I. It is significant that Rothad felt it worthwhile winning over his cathedral chapter by requesting its members be added *en bloc* to the confraternity book of the San-Salvatori-Santa-Giulia monastery in Brescia, in all probability during a voyage to Rome in 865.[45]

The lengthy conflict between Hincmar of Reims and his nephew Hincmar of Laon, which ran from 858 to 871, may be read in a similar light. The main protagonists were initially the two bishops, King Charles the Bald, and Pope Hadrian II. The archbishop gave his full backing to the king who was accusing the bishop of Laon of having withdrawn benefices from royal vassals. The situation took a turn for the worse. In 869, the bishop of Laon placed his own diocese under interdict, a seemingly clumsy move for he was taking the clergy and faithful hostage in a conflict that far exceeded them. He also appealed to Rome, which did not prevent

---

42 Bougard, Bührer-Thierry and Le Jan 2013, 1094–1095; Tinti and Van Rhijn 2020.
43 Stratmann 1998, 329–330. See Devisse 1975–1976.
44 Stratmann 1998, 280.
45 Becher 1983, 384–385.

his being found guilty by the Council of Douzy in 871.[46] Letters exchanged by the two Hincmars seem to accord a minimal role to the local clergy, instead insisting on the four protagonists. But Klaus Zechiel-Eckes's discovery and publication of a small anonymous canonical collection copied in the Paris BNF NAL 1746 manuscript sheds new light on this affair.[47] It is composed of 61 canons taken from pseudo-Isidore's decretals, from the *Herovalliana* collection, from pseudo-Cyprian's *De duodecim abusivis saeculi*, and a passage from the acts of the Council of Tusey in 860. This work extensively reworks its sources, for in addition to defending the rights of a bishop contested by a higher authority, it also defends those of clerics "mistreated" by the bishop: indeed, the title given to canon 6 of the collection – which Klaus Zechiel-Eckes suggests attributing to the work as a whole – is *De male tractatis clericis*. This canon significantly reworks the false decretal attributed to Pope Clement I, which banned stripping a bishop of his function and assets prior to judgement by an "honest council" (*honorabile concilium*), for, under the quill of the authors of this collection, the provision henceforth sets out to defend a cleric deprived of his church by his "brothers" and whose cause was pending examination by a legitimate synod (*legitima synodus*).[48] Canons 58 and 60 point out that a cleric accused unjustly by his bishop may appeal to the synod and neighbouring bishops (*finitimi episcopi*).[49]

Although the collection does not explicitly refer to its authors or whom it was intended for, internal and external criticism suggest it was composed in spring 869, and that it was a response by the clerics of Laon to the interdict placed on the diocese by the bishop which deprived them of their churches.[50] More generally, the authors explicitly refer to the conditions for appointing a bishop – an election *cum consensu cleri vel civium* and ordination by the metropolitan and his suffragans[51] – no doubt in anticipation of the forthcoming deposal of the bishop of Laon, while simultaneously placing themselves from the outset in the Archbishop of Reims' good books. As noted by Cédric Giraud, "the clergy of Laon, placed under a sentence of exclusion, turned the legal arm back against its bearer to exclude him in turn".[52] This internal threat voiced by the clergy of Laon no doubt did just as much as the external threat from the archbishop and king in undermining the bishop's position and hastening the outcome of the affair at the Council of

---

46 Devisse 1976, 726–785; McKeon 1978; Keygnaert 2015.
47 Zechiel-Eckes 2009.
48 Zechiel-Eckes 2009, 59.
49 Zechiel-Eckes 2009, 83–84.
50 Zechiel-Eckes 2009, 44–52.
51 Zechiel-Eckes 2009, 62–63.
52 Giraud 2015, 162.

Douzy two years later. Nevertheless, the collection would appear not to have made any immediate impression on Hincmar of Laon, who once again, in spring 870, placed an interdict on the parish of Folembray to which the neighbouring priest of Coucy laid claim,[53] and unceremoniously excommunicated priest Hadulfus and closed his church on the grounds that he had refused a mission to Augsburg.[54]

In the case concerning us here, it would nevertheless be rash to imagine a threat from the diocesan clergy as a whole. Excellent knowledge of the law was no doubt required to repurpose canons in this way, and it seems likely that this initiative emerged from within the cathedral chapter, with which the bishop had strained relations according to other sources.[55] But once rural priests (and their faithful) became the main victims of the interdict, it seems very likely that they were involved in this initiative, especially as some of them displayed very good knowledge of the law. Still, Frederik Keygnaert is no doubt right in asserting that not all the clergy were opposed to the bishop, given the difficulty the archbishop had in raising the interdict his nephew had placed on the diocese of Laon.[56]

While the two affairs just presented show the Archbishop of Reims exploiting his suffragans' internal difficulties with the clergy, the third and final case shows Hincmar placed in difficulty by his own diocese. The end of a long letter to Pope Hadrian II, dated late September 871, sets out the situation of priest Trisingus who had gone to Rome to complain about how Hincmar had treated him. The letter betrays a certain embarrassment on Hincmar's part.[57] This priest had been denounced for having slept with his brother's wife's daughter from a first marriage. As Trisingus had denied the facts in front of a first synod, Hincmar had refrained from condemning him on so slender a rumour, instead basing his decision on the attempted homicide of which Trisingus was guilty during a fight after a drinking spree in a tavern in Mouzon. As the priest had not presented himself before the provincial synod that was to decide his fate, Hincmar had waited one year before deposing and excommunicating him. Trisingus had then left for Rome and had brought back a letter from the pope – the reason for this long and reasoned justification Hincmar was giving to Hadrian II. Mayke De Jong has recently suggested that Trisingus might have been aware of the flurry of canons spawned over the preceding months by the conflict between Hincmar of Reims and his suffragans, which he was now turning to his advantage to threaten the archbishop. Trisingus was clearly not an isolated case, for a few years later Hincmar felt compelled to

---

53 Schieffer 2018, 332–366. See West 2015.
54 Devisse 1976, 749; McKeon 1978, 77–78.
55 Keygnaert 2015, 71–73.
56 Keygnaert 2015, 76.
57 Schieffer 2018, 434–436. See De Jong (2015, 281–283) for an English translation of the letter.

compile a small collection of canons specifically against *presbiteri criminosi*;[58] then another treatise, *De iudiciis et appellationibus*, denouncing the many priests who sought to get Rome overturn a condemnation by their ordinary bishop.[59] While one cannot admire such a man as Trisingus, the fact that he pleaded his cause in Rome and obliged Hincmar to laboriously justify himself to the pope leads paradoxically to a positive reappraisal not only of the training he had acquired in the field of canon law, but also of the curiosity he must have displayed for the new legal texts which circulated abundantly as of the 850s, especially the vast corpus of False-Isidorians perhaps forged in Corbie in the 830s. When the Trinsigus case arose, Hincmar had been running his diocese for nearly 25 years: in all probability it was he who was responsible for this priest's good knowledge of the law.

5 Conclusion

And so we must conclude that the Carolingian reform conducted by bishops in their dioceses, seeking to better train, oversee, and discipline the rural clergy, also fed a new threat that could turn back against these same bishops. On its own, this threat rarely gave rise to severe crises culminating in the deposal of a bishop, but when aligned with other difficulties affecting certain priests it could produce consequences, as shown by the outcome of the conflict between the two Hincmars. As noted by Frederik Keygnaert, the appearance of this local threat was the consequence of deeper structural changes affecting the Carolingian Church in the second half of the ninth century, for "on the one hand, the bishops aspired to strict control over the local clergy, and on the other, clerics were increasingly confidence due to their swelling number and the creation of new clerical offices".[60] These changes progressively established a new equilibrium in relations between bishops and the clerics, and it is local conditions which explain the very different ways in which these were negotiated.

---

[58] Schmitz 2004.
[59] De Jong 2015, 276–277.
[60] Keygnaert 2015, 76.

Bibliography

Primary Sources

Boretius, Alfred, and Victor Krause, eds. 1890. *Monumenta Germaniae Histórica, Capitularia regum Francorum (MGH Capit.)*. II. Hannover: Hahn.

Brommer, Peter. ed. 1984. *Monumenta Germaniae Historica, Capitula Episcoporum, (MGH Capit. episc.)*. I. Hannover: Hahn.

Gaudemet, Jean, and Brigitte Basdevant. eds. 1989. *Les canons des conciles mérovingiens (VIe –VIIe siècles)*. Vol. 1. Paris: Éditions du Cerf.

Gaudemet, Jean, and Brigitte Basdevant. eds. 1989. *Les canons des conciles mérovingiens (VIe –VIIe siècles)*. Vol. 2. Paris: Éditions du Cerf.

Hartmann, Wilfried, ed. 1984. *Monumenta Germaniae Historica, Concilia (MGH Conc.)*. III. Hannover: Hahn.

Pokorny, Rudolf, and Martina Stratmann, eds. 1995. *Monumenta Germaniae Historica, Capitula Episcoporum (MGH Capit. episc.)*. II. Hannover: Hahn.

Schieffer, Rudolf, ed. 2018. *Monumenta Germania Historica, Epistolae (MGH Epp.)*. VIII, 2, *Die Briefe des Erzbischofs Hinkmar von Reims*. Wiesbaden: Harrassowitz.

Stratmann, Martina, ed. 1998. *Monumenta Germaniae Historica, Scriptores (MGH SS)*. XXXVI, *Flodoardi Historia Remensis Ecclesiae*. Hannover: Hahn.

Zeumer, Karl, ed. 1886. *Monumenta Germaniae Historica, Formulae Merowingici et Karolini aevi (MGH Formulae)*. Hannover: Hahn.

Secondary Sources

Amiet, Robert. 1964. "Une *Admonitio synodalis* de l'époque carolingienne. Étude critique et édition." *Medieval Studies* 26:12–82.

Aubrun, Michel. 1981. *L'ancien diocèse de Limoges des origines au XIVe siècle*. Clermont-Ferrand: Publication de l'Institut d'études du Massif central.

Avril, Joseph. 1991. "La participation du clergé diocésain aux décisions épiscopales." In *À propos des actes d'évêques. Hommage à Lucie Fossier*, edited by Michel Parisse, 251–263. Nancy : Presses universitaires de Nancy.

Avril, Joseph. 2003. "L'institution synodale et la législation épiscopale des temps carolingiens au IVe concile du Latran." *Revue d'histoire de l'Église de France* 89:273–307.

Avril, Joseph. 2007. "Une association obligée: l'archiprêtré ou doyenne." *Revue d'histoire de l'Église de France* 93:25–40.

Becher, Hartmut. 1983. "Das königliche Frauenkloster San Salvatore/Santa Giulia in Brescia im Spiegel seiner Memorialüberlieferung." *Frühmittelalterliche Studien* 17:299–392.

Bougard, François, Bührer-Thierry, Geneviève, and Régine Le Jan. 2013. "Les élites du haut Moyen Âge. Identités, strategies, mobilité." *Annales. Histoire, sciences sociales* 68:1079–1112.

De Jong, Mayke. 2015. "Hincmar, priests and Pseudo-Isidore. The case of Trising in context." In. *Hincmar of Rheims. Life and Work*, edited by Rachel Stone and Charles West, 268–288. Manchester: Manchester University Press.

Devisse, Jean. 1975. *Hincmar, archevêque de Reims (845–882)*. Vol. 1. Genève : Droz.

Devisse, Jean. 1976. *Hincmar, archevêque de Reims (845–882)*. Vol. 2. Genève : Droz.
Devroey, Jean-Pierre. 2003. *Économie rurale et société dans l'Europe franque (VIe–IXe siècles)*. Paris : Belin.
Fouracre, Paul. 2003. "Why were so many bishops killed in Merovingian Francia?" In *Bischofsmord im Mittelalter*, edited by Natalie Fryde et Dirk Reitz, 13–35. Göttingen: Vandenhoeck & Ruprecht.
Giraud, Cédric. 2015. "*Criminosus, falsus testis et sacrilegus*. L'affaire Hincmar de Laon (858–871)." In *La pathologie du pouvoir: vices, crimes et délits des gouvernants*, edited by Patrick Gilli, 146–163. Leiden: Brill.
Godding, Robert. 2001. *Prêtres en Gaule mérovingienne*. Bruxelles: Société des Bollandistes.
Goetz, Hans-Werner. 2018. "Grégoire de Tours: (comment) a-t-il perçu une 'coopétition'?" In *Coopétition. Rivaliser, coopérer dans le sociétés du haut Moyen Âge (500–1100)*, edited by Régine Le Jan, Geneviève Bührer-Thierry and Stefano Gasparri, 49–60. Turnhout: Brepols.
Hartmann, Wilfried. 1979. "Neue Texte zur bischöflichen Reformgesetzgebung aus den Jahren 829/31. Vier Diözesansynoden Halitgars von Cambrai." *Deutsches Archiv* 35:368–394.
Hartmann, Wilfried, ed. 2004. *Das Sendhandbuch des Regino von Prüm*. Darmstadt, Wissenschaftliche Buchgesellschaft.
Hartmann, Wildried. 2008. *Kirche und Kirchenrecht um 900. Die Bedeutung der spätkarolingischen Zeit für Tradition und Innovation im kirchlichen Recht*. Hannover: Hahn.
Kaiser, Reinhold. 1993. "Mord im Dom. Von der Vertreibung zur Ermordung des Bischofs im frühen und hohen Mittelalter." *Zeitschrift der Savigny-Stiftung für Rechtsgeschichte. Kanonistische Abteilung* 79:95–134.
Keygnaert, Frederik. 2015. "L'excommunication collective du diocèse de Laon par l'évêque Hincmar (869): une 'nouvelle' sanction en vue de la défense de l'autorité épiscopale aux temps carolingiens." In *Exclure de la communauté chrétienne. Sens et pratiques sociales de l'anathème et de l'excommuication (IVe–XIIe siècle)*, edited by Geneviève Bührer-Thierry and Stéphane Gioanni, 59–86. Turnhout: Brepols.
Krause, Victor. 1894. "Die Münchener Handschriften 3851. 3853 mit einer Compilation von 181 Wormser Schlüssen." *Neues Archiv* 19:87–139.
McKeon, Peter. 1978. *Hincmar of Laon and Carolingian Politics*. Chicago: University of Illinois Press.
Mériaux, Charles. 2014. "*Consacerdotes et cooperatores*. L'évêque et ses prêtres dans le monde franc (VIe–Xe siècles)." In *Chiese locali e Chiese regionali nell'alto Medioevo*. Vol. 2, 865–894. Spoleto: Centro italiano di studi sull'alto Medioevo.
Mériaux, Charles. 2015. "L'exclusion des prêtres locaux à l'époque carolingienne." In *Exclure de la communauté chrétienne. Sens et pratiques sociales de l'anathème et de l'excommunication (IVe–XIIe siècle)*, edited by Geneviève Bührer-Thierry and Stéphane Gioanni, 157–174. Turnhout: Brepols.
Mériaux, Charles. 2017. "Fêtes et jours chômés dans le monde carolingien (VIIIe–Xe siècles)." In *'Orare aut laborare ?' Fêtes de précepte et jours chômés du Moyen Âge au XIXe siècle*, edited by Philippe Desmette and Philippe Martin, 45–57. Villeneuve d'Ascq: Presses universitaires du Septentrion.
Mériaux, Charles. 2018. "La competition pour l'épiscopat en Gaule mérovingienne." In *Coopétition. Rivaliser, coopérer dans le sociétés du haut Moyen Âge (500–1100)*, edited by Régine Le Jan, Geneviève Bührer-Thierry and Stefano Gasparri, 61–76. Turnhout: Brepols.
Oexle, Otto Gerhard. 1981. "Gilden als soziale Gruppen in der Karolingerzeit." In *Das Handwerk in vor- und frühgeschichtlicher Zeit*, edited by Herbert Jankuhn. Vol. 1, 284–354. Göttingen: Vandenhoeck & Ruprecht.

Oexle, Otto Gerhard. 1985. "Conjuratio et Gilde im frühen Mittelalter. Ein Beitrag zum Problem der sozialgeschichtlichen Kontinuität zwischen Antike und Mittelalter." In *Gilden und Zünfte. Kaufmännische und Gewerbliche Genossenschaften im frühen und hohen Mittelalter*, edited by Berent Schwineköper, 151–214. Sigmaringen: Thorbecke.

Patzold, Steffen. 2020. *Presbyter. Moral, Mobilität und die Kirchenorganisation im Karolingerreich*. Stuttgart: Anton Hiersemann.

Patzold, Steffen, and Carine van Rhijn. eds. 2016. *Men in the Middle. Local priests in Early Medieval Europe*. Berlin: Walter de Gruyter.

Pokorny. Rudolf. 1985. "Nochmals zur Admonitio synodalis." *Zeitschrift der Savigny-Stiftung für Rechtsgeschichte. Kanonistische Abteilung* 71:20–51.

Rosenwein, Barbara H. 2021. "*Condolens doloribus meis*. Threats to bishops in the age of Gregory of Tours". In *Les communautés menacées au haut Moyen Âge (VIe-XIe siècles)*, edited by Geneviève Bührer-Thierry, Annette Grabowsky and Steffen Patzold, 99–109. Turnhout: Brepols.

Schmitz, Gerhard. 2004. *De presbiteris criminosis. Ein Memorandum Erzbischof Hinkmars von Reims über straffälliger Kleriker*. Hannover: Hahn.

Soria Audebert, Myriam. 2005. *La crosse brisée. Des évêques agressés dans une Église en conflits (royaume de France, fin X^e – début XIIIe siècle)*. Turnhout: Brepols.

Stratmann, Martina. 1991. *Hinkmar von Reims als Verwalter von Bistum und Kirchenprovinz*. Sigmaringen: Thorbecke.

Tinti, Francesca, and Carine van Rhijn eds. 2020. "Shepherds, uncles, owners, scribes: priests as neighbours in early medieval local societies.", In *Neighbours and strangers. Local societies in early medieval Europe*, Bernhard Zeller, Charles West, Francesca Tinti, Marco Stoffella, Nicolas Schroeder, Carine van Rhijn, Steffen Patzold, Thomas Kohl, Wendy Davies, and Miriam Czock, 120–149. Manchester: Manchester University Press.

Van Rhijn, Carine. 2007. *Shepherds of the Lord. Priests and Episcopal Statutes in the Carolingian Period*. Turnhout: Brepols.

Van Rhijn, Carine. 2012. "Karolingische priesterexamens en het probleem van correctio op het platteland" *Tijdschrift voor Geschiedenis* 125:158–171.

Van Rhijn, Carine. 2014. "The local church, priests' handbooks and pastoral care in the carolingian period." In *Chiese locali e chiese regionali nell'alto Medioevo*. Vol. 2, 689–706. Spoleto: Centro italiano di studi sull'alto Medioevo.

Van Rhijn Carine. 2016. "Carolingian rural priests as local (religious) experts." In *Gott handhaben. Religiöses Wissen im Konflikt um Mythisierung und Rationalisierung*, edited by Steffen Patzold and Florian Bock, 131–146. Berlin: De Gruyter.

Vogel, Cyrille, and Reinhard Elze. eds. 1963–1972. *Le pontifical romano-germanique du dixième siècle*. Vol. 1. City of Vatican: Biblioteca apostolica Vaticana.

Vykoukal, Ernest. 1913. "Les examens du clergé paroissial à l'époque carolingienne." *Revue d'histoire ecclésiastique* 14:81–96.

West, Charles. 2015. "Hincmar's parish priests." In *Hincmar of Rheims. Life and Work*, edited by Rachel Stone and Charles West, 228–246. Manchester: Manchester University Press.

Wood, Susan. 2006. *The proprietary church in the medieval West*. Oxford: Oxford University Press.

Zechiel-Eckes, Klaus. 2009. *Rebellische Kleriker? Eine unbekannte kanonistisch-patristische Polemik gegen Bischof Hinkmar von Laon in Cod. Paris, BNF, nouv. acq. lat. 1746*. Hannover: Hahn.

Katy Cubitt
Episcopal Authority and Diocesan Structure in England (c. 650–1050)

Abstract: Perhaps the most distinctive feature of the early English church was the enormous size of many of its dioceses. This posed a pastoral problem for bishops in their sacred ministry and their responsibility for clerical correction and spiritual correction in their sees. Early medieval texts are eloquent concerning the threat which pastoral failures posed to the eternal salvation of a bishop. This paper explores the reasons for the creation of these great sees and for their endurance and looks at the religious, political, and economic threats posed when efforts were made for their diminution and the creation of new sees. The paper will range across the Anglo-Saxon period, but primarily focus on the seventh to ninth centuries, examining calls for the creation of new sees such as Bede's Letter to Bishop Ecgbert of York (734 CE) and the letter of Pope Formosus to the English bishops (891–96), tensions over the creation of new metropolitan provinces and the impact of the Viking invasions and settlement.

A distinctive characteristic of the Church in the Anglo-Saxon kingdoms from the seventh to the eleventh centuries was the great size of its dioceses, although it has occasioned little comment or analysis. This paper will begin to fill this gap and explore why these large sees came into existence and why they were so enduring. It examines the early history of the English Church, the seventh and eighth centuries where the diocesan structure of the Church was effectively established and explores the challenges involved in the creation of new sees and the difficulties they posed for the authority and prestige of bishops.

Historical sources for tracing the development of English dioceses before the Norman Conquest are not plentiful nor always very informative. For the early history of English Christianity, Bede's *Ecclesiastical History of the English People* is exceptionally valuable and interesting. Bede does chart the growth of the diocesan Church in each kingdom, naming bishops and bishoprics and sometimes providing dates or datable evidence. His account is shaped by his desire to show the growth of a unified Church, divided amongst the different kingdoms, but united in obedience to the Archbishop of Canterbury and to the universal Church under the authority of the papacy.[1] Bede completed his *Ecclesiastical History* in 735, shortly

---
1 Thacker 2010.

after he had written a lengthy letter of admonition to the bishop of York, Ecgbert, which includes criticism of the lifestyle of bishops and of the excessive size of their dioceses, a text that is therefore also of great value for an examination of Anglo-Saxon ecclesiastical structures.

Bede's *Ecclesiastical History* enables us to reconstruct episcopal succession and follow the creation and mixed fortunes of dioceses up to 735. Thereafter these tasks become more difficult, as the sources are sporadic and not always informative. A number of Anglo-Saxon episcopal lists survive and these, supplemented by the secular and ecclesiastical charters, provide some picture of the sequence of bishops at individual dioceses.[2] These sources are patchy. For example, the reconstruction of episcopal succession is very often dependent on the subscriptions of bishops to royal diplomas so that sees the bishops of which less regularly attended royal councils are poorly recorded.[3] The proceedings of English Church councils are an important source but are again sporadic even before they lapse completely in the later ninth century.[4] There is an occasional flurry of documentation, for example, concerning the shortlived elevation of the see of Lichfield to an archbishopric in the late eighth and early ninth century, or the creation of three new West Saxon sees in the early tenth century, but these caches of documents are an exception.

The territorial limits of early English sees were not recorded by contemporary writers and therefore cannot be traced with certainty. Records of the geographical boundaries of sees do not appear until the eleventh century and the best information available is the thirteenth-century papal taxation record of Pope Nicholas.[5] Florian Mazel has powerfully argued that an interest in the geographical definition of dioceses did not develop until the Gregorian reforms, a thesis that it is hard to test for England in the Early Middle Ages because of the paucity of evidence.[6] It is certainly true that, for example, the canons of the important Southumbrian reforming Council of *Clofesho* in 747 lay down many recommendations for the performance of pastoral care but conceive of this according to the office of the minister rather than in territorial terms.[7] Bede does mention the territorial boundaries in relation to dioceses but only when these are major physical features, such as the River Thames which separated the province of the East Saxons to which

---

2 Keynes 1999.
3 See Keynes, http://dk.robinson.cam.ac.uk/node/115 (accessed 30.10.2022).
4 Cubitt 1995.
5 Brooks 2008, 31–33. For the *Taxatio*, see https://www.dhi.ac.uk/taxatio/ (accessed 30.10.2022). For useful maps of dioceses, see Hill 1981, 147–164.
6 Mazel 2008 and 2016, and see the review by Barrow 2012.
7 Cubitt 1992, 204–205.

Bishop Mellitus had been appointed from that of Kent.⁸ He rarely uses the words 'diocesis' and 'parruchia', preferring to speak of 'episcopatus', the office of a bishop.⁹ As I will argue below, Bede tends to think of bishops as appointed for a people, a 'gens' ruled by a king and granted a see in a specific location. On the other hand, as Julia Barrow, has pointed out when three new sees were set up in West Saxon around 909, their diocesan boundaries were fixed by those of the secular division of the shire. A bishop's spiritual jurisdiction was mapped onto to secular administrative boundaries. Questions of territoriality were definitely of concern in the eleventh century when records survive of parts of the boundaries of the dioceses of Hereford and Worcester, and Canterbury and Rochester, possibly documented because of disputes.¹⁰

Bede's Letter to Bishop Ecgbert of York was written in November 734, not long before the monk's own death. It encapsulates Bede's fears concerning the state of the contemporary Northumbrian Church and sets out measures for how it can be reformed. Bede's reforming agenda, expressed here with such urgency and concision, had developed over a longer period of time and been articulated not only through his *Historia Ecclesiastica* but also in earlier biblical commentaries.¹¹ His letter was prompted by the appointment to the see of York of Ecgberht, a powerful figure whose brother was Eadbert, the king of Northumbria. Ecgberht, who was learned in canon law and had travelled to Rome, was thus well positioned to heed Bede's admonitions.¹² Among the many failings of the Church and episcopate, Bede warned the bishop concerning the spiritual perils resulting from the huge size of his see, and advocated that he collaborates with the king to create new sees with adequate endowments. He urged him to ordain more priests and teachers to provide ministry to the villages and hamlets of his see:

> the distances between the places belonging under the rule of your diocese are too great for you alone to be able to traverse them all and preach the word of God in the several hamlets

---

8 Bede, *Historia ecclesiastica gentis Anglorum* II, (ed. Colgrave and Mynors 1969, subsequently abbreviated to HE).
9 Jones 1929, 145 *'diocesis'*. 375 *'parruchia'*. 375 *'episcopatus'*; see Padel 2011, 66–69; Blair 2005, 427–433 on *'parruchia'* and terminology generally.
10 Barrow 2011, 148; for Hereford-Worcester, see 'The Electronic Sawyer Online Catalogue of Anglo-Saxon Charters' (subsequently abbreviated to S), 1564; Keynes 2000, 18; for Canterbury-Rochester, Brooks 2008, 28–43.
11 DeGregorio 2004.
12 Mayr-Harting 2004.

and homesteads even in the full course of the whole year, it is very necessary that you appoint several assistants for yourself in the sacred work, by ordaining priests [...].[13]

With greater asperity, Bede complained that many remote areas received no ministry but still paid their ecclesiastical dues to the bishop:

> For we have heard, and it is rumoured, that many villages and hamlets of our people are situated in inaccessible mountains and dense woodlands, where there is never seen for many years at a time a bishop to exhibit any ministry or celestial grace; not one man of which, however, is immune from rendering dues to the bishop.[14]

Bede suggests that Egbert and the Northumbrian king petition the pope to be allowed to create more sees and situate them in suitable monasteries, endowing them with properties to be confiscated from the so-called pseudo-monasteries which Bede roundly condemned as purely lay establishments without any spiritual merit. Ecgbert's see of York was indeed vast as were also the other two Northumbrian dioceses of Hexham and Lindisfarne. Bede had suggested to Egbert that if the Northumbrian sees were increased, the bishop could successfully apply to the pope to be elevated to an archbishop of a metropolitan see. Despite Egbert's failure to create more bishoprics, he was successful in gaining papal permission for the creation of a new English province, so that in 735 he became Archbishop of York and leader of the Northumbrian province.[15]

Bede had reminded Egbert of the Church plan of Pope Gregory the Great in which Gregory instructed Augustine to create two metropolitans, one at London and one at York, with two ecclesiastical provinces of 12 sees.[16] It is highly questionable how much the pope knew of English topography and geography and his scheme probably reflected his experience of small, city-based sees in Italy, a far

---

13 Translation from Whitelock 1979, 801; Bede, *Epistola* 131: *Et quia latiora sunt spatia locorum quae ad gubernacula tuae diocesis pertinent, quam ut solus per omnia discurrere, et in singulis uiculis atque agellis uerbum Dei praedicare, etiam anni totius emenso curriculo, sufficias, necessarium satis est, ut plures tibi sacri operis adiutores asciscas presbyteros unidelicet ordinando* [...].
14 Translation from Whitelock 1979, 802; Bede, *Epistola* 134: *Audiuimus enim – et fama est – quia multae uillae et uiculi nostrae gentis in montibus sint inaccessis ac saltibus dumosis positi, ubi numquam multis transeuntibus annis sit uisus antistes, qui ibidem aliquid ministerii aut gratiae caelestis exhibuerit; quorum tamen ne unus quidem a tributis antistiti reddendis esse possit immunis* [...].
15 *Continuatio Baedae* 735 (ed. Colgrave and Mynors 1972). 573 records that Ecgbert received the pallium. On the creation of the northern archdiocese, see the important article Story 2012.
16 HE I, 29. (104–107).

cry from the vast rural dioceses that caused Bede so much anxiety.[17] Indeed, the papal instruction and the rulings of canon law that bishoprics must be situated in cities probably perplexed the architects of English diocesan structure faced with an absence of urbanism and competing political demands. The English missionary to the continent, Boniface, experienced resistance from Pope Zachary over his creation of sees in rural Bavaria, fixing new bishoprics in 'oppida', 'castella' and an 'urbs'. Zachary reminded Boniface that sees should not be situated 'in uillulas vel in modicas civitates' lest the dignity of the status of the bishop be damaged.[18] The number of English sees never reached the giddy heights of Gregory's league of 24. In Egbert's day there were five or possibly six bishoprics in his province: York, Lindisfarne, Hexham, Whithorn and perhaps Mayo in Ireland, a refugee outpost of the Northumbrian Church.[19] The Southumbrian province appears by comparison with Northumbria to boast a plethora of sees, 13 in total, including Canterbury, but this is scarcely an abundance and the sees were still extensive.[20]

Why did the English Church favour such large ecclesiastical territories? The essentially non-urban topography of Anglo-Saxon England did not fit the Mediterranean model of city-based diocesan territories, rather sees were shaped by the English political landscape and particularly by the emergence of major kingdoms in the seventh century which subsumed a patchwork of lesser polities.[21] The new kingdoms of Northumbrian and Mercia, for example, united the lesser territories of Bernicia and Deira, and of the Mercians and Middle Angles. And beneath these provinces lay a multiplicity of small, regional polities.[22]

Bede's account of the formation of the early English dioceses unfolds in a number of phases, as the conversion of the English surged and stalled in different kingdoms.[23] The Gregorian mission initiated the process, with the establishment of sees at Canterbury, Rochester, London and slightly later York. These bishoprics were all located in *civitates* – Bede's vocabulary is precise here – and founded through collaboration between the Roman missionaries, Augustine and Paulinus, and kings Æthelberht and Edwin.[24] London and York lapsed temporarily as a result of the

---

17 Stancliffe 1999, 114–115. 138; Wallace-Hadrill 1988, 44; and see Flechner 2015; Brooks 1984, 10; see Gregory as better informed about English political realities.
18 See the letter exchange between Boniface and Pope Zachary over the creation of three new sees in Bavaria, Boniface, *Epistolae*, no. 50–51.
19 On Mayo, see Charles-Edwards 2000, 320.
20 Cubitt 1989 and 2000.
21 See above, 97–98.
22 Bassett 1989; Campbell 1979; Yorke 1999; Scull 1999. 2001.
23 Mayr-Harting 1991; Yorke 2006, esp. 149–156.
24 Yorke 2006; Canterbury, Rochester and London: HE I, 26–27. 29. 33; II, 3. 5; York and Lindisfarne: HE I, 29; II, 18; III, 3. 28.

accession of pagan rulers. The next phase was one of more piecemeal growth as individual kings sponsored mission in their kingdoms. Bishoprics were created in East Anglia, Northumbria, Wessex, Middle Anglia and Mercia through the sponsorship of an individual bishop by a king. To give just two examples, Bede relates how the convert kings Sigeberht of East Anglia and Oswald of Northumbria having learnt their Christian faith in exile, appointed bishops and set them up with sees, so that in Northumbria Aidan became bishop with his see at Lindisfarne, and for East Anglia Felix was consecrated with his see at *Dommuc*.[25] Further, the territorial extent of a see was defined by the king's personal dominion. The vast sees of Northumbria and the Midlands were, for example, the product of this development. Just as the royal authority of King Wulfhere of Mercia extended over Mercia, Lindsey and the Middle Angles so too did that of his bishops, first Diuma and then his successors Ceollach, Trumhere, and Jaruman.[26] On Jaruman's death (?667), Wulfhere sought a new bishop, in Bede's phrase, 'for himself and his people' – *sibi quoque suisque* – from Archbishop Theodore.[27] Wilfrid's expansive diocese mirrored the dominion of King Oswiu, extending over the whole of Northumbria and part of the Pictish kingdom, 'as far', in the words of Bede, 'as Oswiu's power extended'.[28] Wilfrid's actual appointment as bishop was made earlier, in the reign of King Alhfrith, when in the phrasing of Bede, he was established for the king and his people, *sibi suisque*. This phrase neatly encapsulates the alignment of the bishop's authority with a king's – bishops were appointed as the spiritual adjuncts to a king's political authority. The institution of a bishop for a kingdom was apparently seen as a mark of independence, as the sad story of the South Saxon see of Selsey illustrates. This was set up for Wilfrid by the South Saxon king, Æthelwealh, in 680/1 but did not survive the invasions of King Caedwalla of Wessex who subjected the kingdom to servitude, as did his successor King Ine. Bede comments 'So it came about that during all this time it could have no bishop of its own' and was subject to the West Saxon see of Winchester.[29] Despite efforts for its re-establishment in the early eighth century, the bishopric of Selsey lapsed again for many years, probably from c. 716 to 733.[30]

The political monopolization of episcopal authority diverged from the model of ecclesiastical structure favoured by the Gregorian missionaries and the Church of Canterbury. In the early days of the conversion, when Augustine's mission was un-

---

25 HE II, 15; III, 3.
26 HE III, 7. 21, 24; HE III, 24.
27 HE III, 24; IV, 2.
28 HE IV, 2–3. (336–337): *quousque rex Osuiu imperium protendere poterat*.
29 HE IV, 15. (380–381): *Quare factum est, ut toto illo tempore episcopum proprium habere nequiret*.
30 HE IV, 13; V, 18.

derpinned by the political control of Æthelberht of Kent whose overlordship extended to the Humber, sees were created at London for the East Saxons and at Rochester, subdividing the kingdom of Kent in accordance with its tradition of joint kingship based in western and eastern Kent.[31] This is a telling contrast to the policies of Oswiu and Wulfhere and this pattern of smaller sees, salami-slicing Æthelberht's hegemony, was clearly not attractive to them. Indeed, when Theodore of Tarsus arrived to lead the English Church in 668 and attempted to increase the number of dioceses, he met with some resistance both from kings and prelates. Theodore's first move was to create a second see for East Anglia at Elmham, pushed through with the retirement for health reasons of the current bishop of *Dommuc*. Theodore's major project, the subdivision of the great Northumbrian diocese, necessitated the cooperation of King Ecgfrith and was achieved by what looks like a pact with the king in which Bishop Wilfrid, who had fallen out of favour with Ecgfrith, was expelled. Collaboration with the archbishop presumably facilitated his departure. In 678, new sees were carved out of Wilfrid's diocese so that the provinces of Bernicia and Deira were each provided with their bishop. Lindsey, which had been subject to the Bishops of Mercia, was provided with its own bishop, and in 681 a bishop appointed to Whithorn in Pictish territory.

The Church struggled to implement diocesan reform: Theodore was appointed to Canterbury by the pope himself and was not indebted to any king for his elevation. His papal appointment seems to have buttressed his authority with kings. Kings were reluctant to accept sees in subjugated territories: the new bishopric of Lindsey survived only for the duration of Northumbria's control of the region and was again subsumed by Mercia when its king regained the region.[32] An attempt to resurrect the bishopric of Selsey was made in the early eighth century 'by a decree of a synod', but its independence only lasted for the pontificates of two bishops and then lapsed again. Bede's allusion to the synodal decree perhaps hints that the revival of Selsey was pushed through by the combined authority of some or all of the English episcopate manifested at a synod.[33] Reforming archbishops had to seize their moment. The creation of new sees out of existing dioceses not only affected royal authority but was also a diminution in the revenues and dignity of the bishop whose see was reduced and required his permission. The most opportune moment was upon the death of a bishop when it might be possible to gain the agreement of his successor.[34] Bede's letter to Ecgberht advocating the

---

31 HE II, 3; and see Yorke 1990, 32–34.
32 HE IV, 12.
33 HE V, 18. (514–515): *statutum est synodali decreto.*
34 Patzold 2008.

elevation of York to archiepiscopal status was deliberately timed: Archbishop Tatwine of Canterbury had died on 30 July 734, a few months before Bede's letter was penned in November and Tatwine's successor, Nothelm, was not consecrated until 735, presumably after Ecgbert's promotion.[35] As we have seen, the creation of the second East Anglian see was done on the retirement of the bishop of *Dommuc*; the see of Sherborne was carved out of that of Winchester on the death of Bishop Haedde (c. 705). The lapsed see of Leicester was revived and removed from the control of the bishop of Lichfield in 737, following the death of Aldwine (Uor).[36]

The coincidence between powerful superkingdoms and dioceses forged in the mid-seventh century posed a number of significant and enduring threats to the development of the Church. One of these was the tensions caused by the fossilisation – when the topography of political power no longer fitted that of religious authority. The most conspicuous example of this is the conflict between the Mercian king, Offa, and the archbishopric of Canterbury in the late eighth century. The Mercians had extended their power across the kingdoms of Southumbria, taking over London and reaching down into Kent which attempted to resist, defeating Offa in 776 and restoring their king to independence for a few years. Archbishop Jaenberht of Canterbury, an associate of the Kentish king, was opposed to Mercian overlordship. A non-compliant archbishop could seriously challenge and undermine royal power – the Archbishop of Canterbury commanded the obedience of his suffragans, each drawn from different kingdoms, some subject to Mercian authority and some not. He held the power not only of the consecration of bishops but also of kings. Offa was not tolerant of the challenge contained in Canterbury's metropolitan authority and successfully lobbied the pope for the creation of his own archbishopric at Lichfield which was granted in 789. The establishment of the new metropolitan in the lifetime of the current Archbishop of Canterbury, Jaenberht, who was in opposition to Offa, was an act of humiliation. It is a remarkable indication of the power of ecclesiastical tradition in eighth-century England that Lichfield's elevation could not be sustained and was abolished by a synodal decree in 803, after the retirement of Archbishop Hygeberht of Lichfield, probably in 801.[37] There are indications that the tensions rumbled on for at least another decade with schemes to implement Gregory's plan for a metropolitan at London.[38]

The huge importance for Anglo-Saxon kings of control of bishops and dioceses can be seen in the fate of sees in the aftermath of the Viking invasions and con-

---

35 *Continuatio Baedae* (ed. Colgrave and Mynors 1972) 572–573, and see Mayr-Harting 2004.
36 HE IV, 5; V, 18; Simeon of Durham, *Historia regum* (Whitelock 1979, 264).
37 Brooks 1984; Cubitt 1995; Noble 2014.
38 Cubitt 1999.

quests of the 890s. The Viking takeover of the Midlands and North of England exacerbated the already meagre provision with the disappearance of the sees of Hexham in the North, the midland see of Leicester and the East Anglian see of *Dommuc*, and the lengthy lapse in bishops in the sees of Elmham and Lindsey. The monster see of Dorchester was created replacing Leicester and Lindsey; it reached across the Midlands and into Lincolnshire.[39] The longterm absence of bishops for these places cannot be blamed on the Viking settlers – the West Saxon kings exerted their control over much of the Midlands and East Anglia in the first decades of the tenth century and the former kingdom of Northumbria was annexed to West Saxon power in the mid tenth century. West Saxon control did not result in ecclesiastical revival or in the revitalization of sees, as Julia Barrow has argued.[40] In the middle of the tenth century, there was one attempt to revive the lapsed sees of Lindsey and Elmham which both received bishops in the 950s.[41] This was perhaps an initiative on the part of the reforming Archbishop Oda of Canterbury (941–958). However, in the later tenth century the episcopal lists for both sees show gaps and Lindsey was ultimately reabsorbed by Dorchester which came to govern most of the Midlands.[42] The preference of the West Saxon kings was for the religious governance of sees to be carried out from bases nearer to their heartlands: the see of Leicester was transferred to Dorchester, Oxfordshire, and East Anglia seems to have been administered from London for a time in the tenth century.

Rather than follow older historiography in blaming the Vikings for the disruption of English sees, one can argue that the Viking conquests ultimately provided an opportunity for the West Saxon kings to diminish the number of bishops and bring the control of dioceses firmly into their homelands, presumably gaining economic benefits as a result and avoiding the risk of rogue bishops in newly conquered regions supporting revolts against them. The West Saxons would have certainly learnt this lesson as a result of the conduct of Archbishop Wulfstan I of York who, with the Northumbrian council, made peace in 947 with King Eadred following the king's successful campaigns in Northumbria. However, according to the 'D' version of the Anglo-Saxon Chronicle, the Northumbrians repudiated this compact and accepted the Norwegian Eric Blood-Axe as king. In 952, Archbishop Wulfstan was imprisoned for disloyalty and subsequently seems to have been moved to the see of Dorchester, closer to the centre of West Saxon power. The archbishop's position of authority and influence, and his ability to consecrate a king, made

---

[39] Barrow 2000, 155–179; Hadley 2006, 207–208.
[40] Barrow 2000, 155–179.
[41] For Lindsey, see Sawyer 1998, 149–154.
[42] Keynes 1986, 216–217, 219.

him a particularly dangerous figure. Whitelock suggests that Wulfstan I's behaviour may have prompted later English kings to ensure the archbishop's fidelity by combining the archbishopric of York with the see of Worcester so that the archbishops had firm roots within the south.[43]

Such steely control of dioceses may have eliminated threats to the West Saxon dynasty and their power beyond the Thames but it opened the English Church to papal censure and the threat of an anathema. In the 890s, Pope Formosus wrote to the English bishops castigating them for the growth of pagan practices and for long vacancies in Anglo-Saxon sees.[44] Was Formosus prompted to write because of the lapsed succession in sees such as *Dommoc* and Elmham? Later English tradition – recorded in the late tenth century – remembered Formosus as demanding the creation of new sees although this is not mentioned in his letter. Although there are problems with this late tradition, Formosus's intervention may very well have included a demand for more sees or have resulted in their creation. Two documents from the later tenth century, one of unknown origin and the other a letter to King Æthelred penned by Archbishop Dunstan in the 980s, claimed that Formosus had written to King Edward the Elder threatening excommunication unless he instituted bishops in destitute sees and that Edward and Plegmund had responded by the consecration of seven bishops in one day. Elements of this story are manifestly wrong – Formosus died before Edward acceded to the throne. The consecration of the bishops in question did in fact take place, probably in 909 (but not necessarily on one and the same day) when the sees of Crediton, Ramsbury and Wells were created out of the dioceses of Winchester and Sherborne.[45] The latter had expanded greatly from the early ninth century when the West Saxon kings brought Cornwall under their rule.[46] It is possible that the impetus for the subdivision of Winchester and Sherborne did indeed come from Pope Formosus. As noted earlier, it was not customary to carve out new sees from existing dioceses while a bishop was alive. The bishoprics of Sherborne and Winchester were occupied respectively by Asser from sometime in the 890s to 909 and Denewulf from c. 878 to 908.[47] Thus if Formosus's mandate in the 890s included the creation of new sees, it would have been controversial to carry it out before 909, during the reign of Edward the Elder.

The two later tenth-century documents were drafted because of an enduring dispute over the possession of three estates awarded to the new see of Crediton, later claimed by the diocese of Cornwall. They nicely illustrate the difficulties in

---

43 Whitelock 1981, 71–74.
44 Whitelock, Brett, and Brooke 1981, I.8:35–38.
45 Whitelock, Brett, and Brooke 1981, I.35:165–171, with helpful commentary; Robinson 1918.
46 Padel 2010, 121.
47 Keynes 1986, 222–223.

the creation of new sees. Cornwall was placed firmly under West Saxon control in 838 when the West Saxon king, Ecgberht, suppressed a revolt against his authority there. He asserted his royal right to grant land there, assigning three estates to the bishop of Sherborne which then bore pastoral responsibility for the area, a grant which massively increased Sherborne's pastoral territory. Then in 909, the see of Crediton was created out of that of Sherborne with responsibility for the ministry to Cornwall. These three estates at Lawhitton, Pawton and *Cœllincg* (unidentified) were granted, according to later tenth-century documents, to 'the authority of Devon [i.e. Crediton] because [the Cornish people] had previously been disobedient, without fear of the West Saxons'.[48] They were given to facilitate the annual visitation of the Cornish regions by the bishop of Crediton. However, a decade or so later the Cornish were provided with their own bishop and see at St Germains by King Æthelstan, removing Cornwall from Sherborne's jurisdiction. These three estates were therefore claimed by successive bishops of Cornwall.[49] Dunstan's letter to King Æthelred was probably prompted by his consecration of a new bishop of Cornwall, Ealdred, sometime between in the 980s. Dunstan petitioned the king to confirm the new bishop's right to the estates but it is not known whether Æthelred did so. Half a decade or so later in 994, King Æthelred did issue a diploma, confirming Ealdred of Cornwall's full episcopal rights in his see but does not mention the see's endowment.[50] Both Dunstan's letter of the 980s and Æthelred's charter of 994 indicate that the bishops of Cornwall struggled to assert their rights and status. The two estates that can be identified – Lawhitton and Pawton – were held by Exeter in the Domesday Book but since the see of Cornwall had been amalgamated with that of Crediton in 1027 it is unclear which sees these estates had belonged to.[51] The status of the Cornish see based at St Germains seems to have remained problematic, as in 994 King Æthelred issued a charter to its bishop, Ealdred, granting him full episcopal authority over his see.[52] Neither the see of Cornwall nor that of Crediton were wealthy: neither could probably afford to lose the income from these estates.

It was more common in the tenth and eleventh centuries for sees to be amalgamated or held in plurality than for sees to be divided, despite their great size. Even the advent from the later tenth century of reforming bishops who not only advocated for Benedictine monasticism but also promoted pastoral renewal did

---

48 Whitelock, Brett, and Brooke 1981, I.35:165–171, at 171: *to innstinge inn to Defenun, forþam þe hi ær þam unhyrsume wæron buton Westseaxna ege.*
49 Padel 2010, 121–123.
50 S 880.
51 Orme 2010, 11.
52 S 880; Padel 2010, 122.

not result in smaller sees, rather the opposite.[53] St Dunstan, the future archbishop of Canterbury, seems to have retained the see of Worcester when promoted to London. St Oswald held both Worcester and York, establishing a practice that endured for nearly a hundred years.[54] The last bishop to hold both sees was Ealdred, who was also bishop of Hereford (1056–1060). He only relinquished Worcester and York apparently under pressure from the pope when he arrived in Rome to seek his pallium in 1061.[55] In 1027, Lyfing amalgamated the sees of Crediton and Cornwall, and, for a couple of years, also held the see of Worcester.[56] Archbishop Ælfric of Canterbury retained the see of Ramsbury from which he was promoted.[57] Among the various wrongs and canonical failings of Stigand (d. 1072), the notorious archbishop of Canterbury is the fact that he retained his previous see of Winchester after his elevation to the archbishopric. Here, however, the fault is only one of degree since the two sees in England he held were the wealthiest in the country.[58]

Territorially extensive dioceses became an embedded characteristic of the English Church before the Norman Conquest. The reasons for this characteristic are complex and obscure. There was a preference for extensive sees in the Danelaw, in the Midlands and Yorkshire, with a particular desire to keep the archbishopric of York closely linked to West Saxon authority through its tie to Worcester. The reasons here may have been both political and economic as the combined sees almost doubled the bishop's resources.[59] The landed endowment of English dioceses apart from the two richest sees of Canterbury and Winchester were relatively small compared to those of the great monastic houses.[60] The cost of endowing new sees must also have been a considerable issue; bishoprics gained most of their landed property before the early tenth century and had to fight to preserve it from losses in the tenth and eleventh centuries. Further, providing a suitable landed endowment for a new or restored see was not a simple task as bishops needed estates as bases for the itineration of their dioceses and for travel to assemblies and on other business outside their sees.[61] The creation of the three new West Saxon sees illustrates these issues, recording how estates were allocated to Crediton for pastoral work in Corn-

---

53 Barlow 2004.
54 Barlow 1979, 215–216. 226–229.
55 Tinti 2019
56 Barlow 1979, 212–215.
57 Brooks 1984, 279. 383.
58 Cowdrey 2004; Giandrea 2007, 126.
59 Giandrea 2007, 126.
60 Giandrea 2007, 126 and Knowles 1950, 702.
61 Barrow, 2012; for an example of bishops using estates as the basis for travel within their sees, see Dyer 2005.

wall. Moreover, the new sees do not seem to have well endowed. When the Lotharingian royal priest, Hermann, was appointed to Ramsbury, he regarded it as impoverished and eventually combined it with Sherborne. Crediton, under Lyfing, was amalgamated with Cornwall.[62] At Wells and Ramsbury, for some of their occupants, this disadvantage may have been compensated for by their function as stepping-stones on the path to Canterbury. They furnished seven archbishops up to the Norman Conquest.[63] The struggles of these sees in the late tenth and eleventh century is a contrast with the success of the great monastic foundations, such as Ely, which gained their endowment in this period.[64] Kings seem to have preferred to allow bishops to hold sees in plurality and to combine them rather than equip them with more estates.

How did the large Anglo-Saxon dioceses affect episcopal authority and how did they threaten episcopal status and legitimacy? The issue of diocesan structure lies at the fulcrum of the intersection of pastoral and political geography with the conflicts and tensions arising from the bishop's need to work with kings and the *Realpolitik* of secular power. Bede's letter to Ecgbert highlights the pastoral challenges of geographically extensive diocese. He chastised the bishop concerning the fact that his see was so vast that it was impossible for the bishop to travel round it to carry out his ministry of teaching and preaching. He urged Ecgbert to consecrate more priests and institute teachers to baptize and teach the faithful of his dioceses.[65] However, not all aspects of the cure of souls could be performed by lesser clergy, ordinations of clergy, confirmations and the dedication of churches were solely episcopal responsibilities. Bede was particularly anxious that bishops profited from church taxes on the laity while failing to carry out their ministry, singling out confirmation.[66] Episcopal oversight was a pressing question – the Southumbrian reforming council at *Clofesho* in 747, followed by the papal legatine synod in Northumbria in 786 repeated the canonical regulation that bishops should circumambulate their dioceses every year not only to teach and preach but also to supervise, examine and correct the diocesan clergy. According to the 747 Council, bishops were to keep watch over the people, summoning them to assemble to receive episcopal teaching. The papal legates in 786 (in a text partially drafted by Alcuin) elaborated upon this command, specifying that bishops should preach, confirm and condemn pagan practices and separate those in incestuous relation-

---

62 Barlow 1979, 212–215. 220–221.
63 Cubitt 2011, 121–126.
64 Giandrea 2007, 131; Knowles 1950, 702, see for example, Ely and Bury.
65 See the passages quoted above, 97–98.
66 Bede, *Epistola* 134–135.

ships.⁶⁷ In 747 and in 786 the bishops were therefore reminded of the centrality of diocesan visitation to their responsibility for their flocks. By the later tenth century, diocesan synods had become the main mechanism for the bishop's responsibility for clerical discipline, the scrutiny of pastoral care and the exercise of episcopal judicial authority.⁶⁸ Nevertheless, this did not necessarily ameliorate the difficulties of distant travel – even in the relatively small see of Canterbury, there is evidence that the obligation on the part of local priests to collect the Chrism on Maundy Thursday – a popular time for the diocesan synod – was shared out and carried out only by major churches.⁶⁹

It is possible that in some sees, the bishop was assisted by chorepiscopi or by rural bishops. A charter of 930 in which King Athelstan grants land in Lancashire to the cathedral church of York is attested by three otherwise unknown bishops in addition to the roster of 14 bishops whose sees are known. These bishops – Alfred, Cynsi and Wulfhelm – may have been bishops without sees, working to support the ministry of an established bishop.⁷⁰ The incomplete nature of our knowledge of bishops, particularly in areas remote from the West Saxon heartlands, has recently been underlined by the discovery of the Galloway Hoard in Scotland. This included a rock crystal jar embellished with gold bearing an inscription (probably from the ninth century) with the name of a bishop Hyguald who cannot be identified.⁷¹ It seems probable that there were bishops without sees providing ministry in Northumbria and perhaps elsewhere in England who have not been recorded.

A bishop's failure to carry out his pastoral oversight and ministry within his diocese fundamentally undermined his fitness for office, damaging his reputation, and endangered the salvation of the laity and religious within the see, putting also his own salvation in peril. Bishops were warned of the consequences of the failure to exercise the episcopal duty of correction and discipline for their own salvation. Their failure to rebuke and discipline the sins of others could result in their own damnation for those sins. This was a constant theme of episcopal polemic, manifest for example in the eighth-century letters of the English missionary, Boniface, and in the eleventh-century preaching Archbishop Wulfstan of York.⁷² Pastoral failure

---

67 Haddan and Stubbs 1868–1878, 3:360–361; Dümmler 1895, *Epistolae carolini*, 3:21; Cubitt 1995, 152–190; Carella 2012.
68 Cubitt 2023 (forthcoming).
69 Brooks 1984, 203–204.
70 S 407; Woodman 2012, 86–97.
71 https://www.nms.ac.uk/explore-our-collections/stories/scottish-history-and-archaeology/galloway-hoard/sections/the-galloway-hoard-rock-crystal-jar/ (accessed 30.10.2022).
72 Bethurum, no. 16a. 16b. 17. (239–245); Wilcox 2000; Boniface, *Epistolae* no. 78, 161–171. This motif is derived from Ezechiel 3: 18–19, and see, for example, Greg. M. epist. I, 33.

reflected negatively upon a bishop and could linger in the collective memory: a mid-eighth-century vision of hell transmitted with Boniface's correspondence describes the presence there of 'a great multitude of sad and grieving children who had died without baptism' under Bishop Daniel of Winchester (704–755), whose diocese not only covered most of Wessex but also incorporated the lapsed see of Selsey.[73] Although Daniel was a bishop of some note, described by Bede as 'fully instructed in ecclesiastical matters', and consulted by Boniface with great respect on missionary strategy, in some circles at least he was remembered with less respect.[74]

To what extent does the predominance of large dioceses in the pre-Conquest English Church reflect the importance of monasteries in pastoral work? The pattern of extensive dioceses was established in the seventh to eighth centuries when, according to the minster model, monastic communities were responsible for pastoral care. These communities, now called minsters, possessed great landed estates which can be considered proto-parishes for which the religious community provided pastoral ministry.[75] These were founded both by kings and lay aristocrats and by bishops. Many minsters came into episcopal ownership in the eighth and ninth centuries.[76] At a local level, minster churches were a more significant part of the Church's ministry than bishops. In his paper on Castile, Julio Escalona raises the issue of how episcopal power and importance were affected by the presence and power of monasteries. It may be the prevalence of minster-parishes that relieved the challenges of such great dioceses. By the later tenth centuries, when English diocesan structures had become relatively fixed, bishop and cathedral communities were less attractive as recipients of grants than the new Benedictine houses such as Ely.[77] While, in this respect, these may have undercut the ability of bishoprics to win grants, this development was hardly resisted by the bishops, many of whom in the later tenth century were monks. The leading tenth-century bishops, Æthelwold of Winchester and Oswald of Worcester and York, were prime movers in the foundation of monasteries.

---

73 Boniface, Ep. 115 (249): *infantium numerosam multitudinem sub Danielo episcopo maxime sine baptismo morientium tristem et merentem*; and see above 100–101 for the size of Daniel's diocese.
74 HE V, 18.
75 Blair 2006; for caution see Cubitt 1995; Rollason and Cambridge 1995.
76 Cubitt 1995, 223–234; Sims-Williams 1990, 135–145. 155–168.
77 See above 107.

Conclusion

The pattern of extensive dioceses that characterized the early English Church was established in the seventh century when kings whose political and military control extended over many provinces and had absorbed once-independent polities appointed bishops to provide spiritual rule for their dominion. In the seventh and eighth centuries, the possession of a bishop with his see was a defining feature of a kingdom. This territorial pattern of one bishop per kingdom was the result of dioceses mirroring political structures. The Church, however, played a much more dynamic role – the creation of dioceses gave religious legitimacy to the territorial expansion of ambitious kingdoms, strengthening their boundaries, endowing them with spiritual prestige and suppressing the status of smaller polities. Rather than kingdoms creating dioceses, dioceses played a role in creating kingdoms. Without this policy, one might imagine the development of the political and religious territorial structures of early England as looking like those of early medieval Ireland with its small kingdoms with monastic bishops, and looser overlordships by greater kingdoms.

Although there were changes to diocesan structure in later churches, the existence of geographically expansive dioceses was established. There was a North-South divide in this picture as the sees in the south, especially in the West Saxon heartlands, were far smaller. It is notable that the West Saxons failed to revive lapsed sees in the Danelaw, in Northumbria and East Anglia, they did in 909 subdivide their core sees of Sherborne and Winchester. The reasons behind the enduring existence of such great sees are complex and a combination of political and economic factors. In the tenth century, similarly to the seventh, kings were reluctant to appoint bishops to the archbishopric of York who might become agents of resistance to their authority. It may also have been difficult for them to endow new or revived sees with sufficient estates to ensure that they would prosper. There were many challenges to the creation of new sees. Bede's Letter to Bishop Egbert is extremely revealing in this respect. It reads like sweet reason but lurking underneath, like magma beneath a volcano, were simmering issues of status and prestige and wealth. Bede knew this: the volcano had erupted before in the events of the 680s when Archbishop Theodore divided the great Northumbrian diocese governed by St Wilfrid. The profound disruption caused by the diminution of one diocese to create others lay behind the turbulence and tumult of his career.

The letter of Pope Formosus and the forged documents created in the later tenth century are revealing of tensions underlying the new sees of Crediton, Ramsbury and Wells. The pope had rebuked the Archbishop of Canterbury for his pastoral failures. The new sees do not seem to have been lavishly endowed and at least one dispute over the estates assigned continued for decades. The relative impoverishment of English sees continued to be troublesome in the eleventh century when a number of sees were held in plurality, a practice which once again brought papal censure on the English Church. Archbishop Ealdred also received a papal censure in the eleventh century when he travelled to Rome to receive the pallium and was refused unless he gave up the sees of Hereford and Worcester.

Bibliography

Primary Sources

Bede, *Historia ecclesiastica gentis Anglorum* (HE): Bertram Colgrave and Roger A. B. Mynors. eds. 1969. *Bede's Ecclesiastical History of the English People*. Oxford: Clarendon Press.
Bede, *Epistola ad Ecgbertum episcopum:* Christopher Grocock and Ian N. Wood. eds. 2013. *Abbots of Wearmouth and Jarrow*, 124–126. Oxford: Clarendon Press.
Boniface, *Epistolae:* Michael Tangl. ed. 1916. *Sancti Bonifatii et Lulli Epistolae, Monumenta Germaniae Historica, Epistolae selectae (MGH EE sel.).* I. Berlin: Weidmann.
Continuatio Bedae: Bertram Colgrave and Roger A. B. Mynors. eds. 1969. *Bede's Ecclesiastical History of the English People*, 572–577. Oxford: Clarendon Press.
Charters of Christ Church, Canterbury, 2 Vols.: Nicholas P. Brooks and Susan E. Kelly. eds. 2013. London: British Academy and Oxford University Press.
Charters of Northern Houses: David A. Woodman. ed. 2012. London: British Academy and Oxford University Press.
Councils and Ecclesiastical Documents relating to Great Britain and Ireland, 3 Vols: Arthur W. Haddan and William Stubbs. eds. 1868–1878. Oxford: Clarendon Press.
Dümmler, Ernst. ed. 1895. *Monumenta Germaniae Historica, Epistolae (MGH Epp.).* IV. 2, *Epistolae Karolini Aevi.* Berlin: Weidmann.
Gregory the Great, *Registrum epistularum libri XIV:* Dag Norberg. ed. 1982. *Corpus Christianorum Series Latina (CCSL).* 140 (1–7) et 140 A (7–14). Turnhout: Brepols.
Homilies of Wulfstan: D. Bethurum. ed. 1957. Oxford: Clarendon Press.
Simeon of Durham, *Historia Regum:* Thomas Arnold. ed. 1882–1885. *Symeonis monachi opera omnia.* 2. Rolls Series 75, 3–283.
The Electronic Sawyer Online Catalogue of Anglo-Saxon Charters (S). https://esawyer.lib.cam.ac.uk/about/index.html (charters cited by number) (accessed 30.10.2022).
Whitelock, Dorothy. 1979. ed. *English Historical Documents c. 500–1042*. London: Eyre Methuen.
Whitelock, Dorothy, Martin Brett, and Christopher N. L. Brooke. eds. 1981, *Councils and Synods with Other Documents relating to the English Church*. 2 Vols. Oxford: Clarendon Press.

Secondary Sources

Armitage Robinson, Joseph. 1918. "The Plegmund Narrative." In *The Saxon Bishops of Wells A Historical Study in the Tenth Century*. British Academy Supplemental Papers IV, 18–28. London: Oxford University Press.

Barlow, Frank. ²1979. *The English Church 1000–1066*. London: Longman.

Barlow, Frank. 2004. "Lyfing [Living] (d. 1046)." In *Oxford Dictionary of National Biography*. Oxford: Oxford University Press. (online) https://www.oxforddnb.com/page/1413 (accessed 30.10.2022).

Barrow, Julia S. 1994. "English cathedral communities and reform in the late tenth and eleventh centuries" In *Anglo-Norman Durham 1093–1193*, edited by David W. Rollason, Margaret Harvey, and Michael Prestwich, 25–39. Woodbridge: Boydell.

Barrow, Julia S. 2000. "Survival and mutation: ecclesiastical institutions in the Danelaw in the ninth and tenth centuries" In *Cultures in Contact Scandinavian Settlement in England in the Ninth and Tenth Centuries*, edited by Dawn M. Hadley and Julian D. Richards, 155–176. Turnhout: Brepols.

Barrow, Julia S. 2011. "Review of Mazel, Florian. 2008. 'L'Espace du diocèse Genèse d'un territoire dans l'Occident médiéval (V^e–XIIIe siècle)'" *Journal of Ecclesiastical History* 62.1:147–148.

Barrow, Julia S. 2012. "Way-stations on English episcopal itineraries, 700–1300." *English Historical Review* 127:549–165.

Bassett, Steven. ed. 1989. *The Origin of Anglo-Saxon Kingdoms*. Leicester: Leicester University Press.

Blair, John. 2005. *The Church in Anglo-Saxon Society*. Oxford: Oxford University Press.

Brooks, Nicholas. 1984. *The Early History of the Church of Canterbury: Christ Church from 597 to 1066*. Leicester: Leicester University Press.

Brooks, Nicholas. 2008. "An early boundary of the diocese of Canterbury and Rochester." In *A Commodity of Good Names Essays in Honour of Margaret Gelling*, edited by Oliver James Padel and David N. Parsons, 28–43. Donington/Lincolnshire: Shaun Tyas.

Cambridge, Eric and David W. Rollason. 1995, "Debate: the pastoral organization of the Anglo-Saxon Church: a review of the 'minster hypothesis'." *Early Medieval Europe* 87:87–104.

Campbell, James. 1986a. *Essays in Anglo-Saxon History*. London: Hambledon Press.

Campbell, James. 1986b. "Bede's Reges and Principes." In *Essays in Anglo-Saxon History*, James Campbell, 85–98. London: Hambledon Press.

Campbell, James. 1986c. "Bede's words for places." In *Essays in Anglo-Saxon History*, James Campbell, 99–119. London: Hambledon Press.

Charles-Edwards, Thomas M. 2000. *Early Christian Ireland*. Cambridge: Cambridge University Press.

Carella, Bryan. 2012. "Alcuin and the legatine capitulary of 786: the evidence of scriptural citations." *Journal of Medieval Latin* 22:221–256.

Cowdrey, Herbert E. J. 2004. "Stigand (d. 1072)." In *Oxford Dictionary of National Biography*. Oxford: Oxford University Press. (online) https://www.oxforddnb.com/page/1413 (accessed 30.10.2022).

Cubitt, Catherine. 1989. "Wilfrid's 'usurping bishops': episcopal elections in Anglo-Saxon England, c. 600–c. 800." *Northern History* 25:18–38

Cubitt, Catherine. 1992. "Pastoral Care and Conciliar Canons: the provisions of the 747 Council of Clofesho." In *Pastoral Care before the Parish*, edited by John Blair and Richard Sharpe, 193–121. Leicester: Leicester University Press.

Cubitt, Catherine. 1995. *Anglo-Saxon Church Councils c. 650–c. 850*. London: Leicester University Press.

Cubitt, Catherine. 1999. "Finding the Forger: an alleged decree of the 679 Council of Hatfield." *English Historical Review* 114:1217–1248.

Cubitt, Catherine. 2011. "Bishops and succession crises in tenth- and eleventh-century England." In *Patterns of Episcopal Power Bishops in Tenth- and Eleventh-Century Western Europe, Strukturen bischöflicher Herrschaftgewalt im westlichen Europa des 10. und 11. Jahrhunderts*, edited by Ludger Körntgen and Dominik Waßenhoven, 111–126. Berlin: De Gruyter.

Cubitt, Catherine. 2023 (forthcoming). *Sin and Society in Tenth- and Eleventh- Century England*. Cambridge: Cambridge University Press.

De Gregorio, Scott. 2004. "Bede's In Ezram et Neemiam and the reform of the Northumbrian church." *Speculum* 79:1–25.

Dyer, Christopher. 2005. "Bishop Wulfstan and his estates." In *St. Wulfstan and his World*, edited by Julia S. Barrow and Nicholas P. Brooks, 137–149. Aldershot: Ashgate.

Flechner, Roy. 2015. "Pope Gregory and the British: mission as a canonical problem." In *En Marge*, edited by Hélène Bouget and Magali Coumert, 47–65. Brest: Centre de Recherche Bretonne et Celtique.

Hadley, Dawn M. 2006. *The Vikings in England Settlement, Society, and Culture*. Manchester: Manchester University Press.

Hill, David. 1981. *An Atlas of Anglo-Saxon England*. Oxford: Basil Blackwell.

Jones, Putnam Fennel. 1929. *A Concordance to the Historia ecclesiastica of Bede*. Cambridge/Massachusetts: Medieval Academy of America.

Keynes, Simon. [3]1986. "Episcopal succession in Anglo-Saxon England." In Handbook of British Chronology, edited by Edmund B. Fryde, Diana Eleanor Greenway, Stephen Porter and Ian Roy, 209–224. London: Royal Historical Society.

Keynes, Simon. 1999. "Episcopal lists." In *The Blackwell Encyclopedia of Anglo-Saxon England*, edited by Michael Lapidge, John Blair, Simon Keynes and Donald Scragg, 172–174. Oxford: Blackwell Publishers.

Keynes, Simon. 2000. "Diocese and cathedral before 1056." In *Hereford Cathedral: a History*, edited by Gerald Aylmer and John Tiller, 3–20. London: Hambledon Press.

Keynes, Simon. "An Atlas of Attestations in Anglo-Saxon Charters." (online) http://dk.robinson.cam.ac.uk/node/115 (accessed 30.10.2022).

Loyn, Henry Royston. 2000. *The English Church 940–1154*. Harlow: Longman.

Mayr-Harting, Henry. [3]1991. *The Coming of Christianity to Anglo-Saxon England*. University Park/Pa: Pennsylvania State University Press.

Mayr-Harting, Henry. 2004. "Ecgberht [Egbert] (d. 766)." In *Oxford Dictionary of National Biography*. Oxford: Oxford University Press. (online) https://www.oxforddnb.com/page/1413 (accessed 30.10.2022).

Mazel, Florian. 2008. *L'Espace du diocèse Genèse d'un territoire dans l'Occident médiéval (Ve-XIIIE siècle)*. Rennes : PU Rennes.

Mazel, Florian. 2016. *L'Eveque et le Territoire*. Paris : Editions du Seuil.

Noble, Thomas F. X. 2014. "The rise and fall of the archbishopric of Lichfield in English, papal and European perspective." In *England and Rome in the Early Middle Ages*, edited by Francesca Tinti, 291–305. Turnhout: Brepols.

Orme, Nicholas. 2010. "From the Romans to the Norman Conquest." In *A History of the County of Cornwall II Religious History to 1560*, edited by Nicholas Orme, 1–20. London/Woodbridge: University of London and Boydell Brewer.

Padel, Oliver J. 2010. "Christianity in medieval Cornwall: Celtic aspects." In *A History of the County of Cornwall II Religious History to 1560*, edited by Nicholas Orme, 110–125. London/Woodbridge: University of London and Boydell Brewer.

Padel, Oliver J. 2011. "Asser's *parochia* of Exeter." In *Tome Studies in Medieval Celtic History and Law in Honour of Thomas Charles-Edwards*, edited by Fiona Edmonds and Paul Russell, 65–72. Woodbridge: Boydell.

Patzold, Steffen. 2008. "L'archdiocèse de Magdebourg. Perception de l'espace et identité (X^e–XIe siècle)." In *L'Espace du diocèse Genèse d'un territoire dans l'Occident médiéval (V^e–XIIIe siècle)*, edited by Florian Mazel, 167–193. Rennes: PU Rennes.

Sawyer, Peter. 1998. *Anglo-Saxon Lincolnshire*. Lincoln: Society for Lincolnshire History and Archaeology.

Scull, Christopher. 1993. "Archaeology, early Anglo-Saxon society and the origins of the Anglo-Saxon kingdoms." *Anglo-Saxon Studies in Archaeology and History* 6:65–82.

Scull, Christopher. 1999. "Social archaeology and Anglo-Saxon kingdom origins." *Anglo-Saxon Studies in Archaeology and History* 10:17–24.

Scull, Christopher. 2001. "Local and regional identities and processes of state formation in fifth- to seventh-century England: some archaeological problems." In *Kingdoms and Regionality: Transactions from the 49 Sachsensymposium 1998 in Uppsala*, edited by Birgit Arrhenius, 121–125. Stockholm: Stockholm University Archaeological Research Laboratory.

Sims-Williams, Patrick. 1990. *Religion and Literature in Western England 600–800*. Cambridge: Cambridge University Press.

Stancliffe, Clare. 1999. "The British Church and the mission of St Augustine." In *St Augustine and the conversion of England*, edited by Richard Gameson, 106–151. Stroud/Gloucestershire: Sutton Publishing Stroud.

Story, Joanna. 2012. "Bede, Willibrord and the letters of Pope Honorius I on the genesis of the archbishopric of York." *English Historical Review* 127:783–813.

Thacker, Alan. 2010. "Bede and history." In *The Cambridge Companion to Bede*, edited by Scott De Gregorio, 170–190. Cambridge: Cambridge University Press.

Tinti, Francesca. 2019. "The pallium privilege of Pope Nicholas II for Archbishop Ealdred." *Journal of Ecclesiastical History* 70.4:708–730.

Wallace-Hadrill, John Michael. 1988. *Bede's Ecclesiastical History of the English People: A Historical Commentary*. Oxford: Oxford University Press.

Whitelock, Dorothy. 1981. "The Dealings of the Kings of England with the Northumbria in the Tenth and Eleventh Centuries." In *History, Law and Literature in 10th–11th Century England*, edited by Dorothy Whitelock, 70–88. London: Variorium Reprints.

Wilcox, Jonathan. 2000. "The wolf on shepherds: Wulfstan, bishops and the context of the *Sermo Lupi ad Anglos*." In *Old English Prose: Basic Readings*, edited by Paul E. Szarmach, 395–418. New York: Garland.

Yorke, Barbara. 1990. *Kings and Kingdoms of early Anglo-Saxon England*. London: Seaby.

Yorke, Barbara. 2006. *The conversion of Britain: religion, politics and society in Britain, c.600–800*. Harlow: Pearson Longman.

Katharina Winckler
Suspicious Minds: Bishops without Seat and Canonical Bishops in Eighth-Century Bavaria

Abstract: The sources of eighth-century Bavaria mention bishops who cannot be linked to a bishop's seat, as required by the church. In some sources they are addressed as if being a normal part of the Bavarian church. However, in other sources such as in the letters of Boniface and the Breves Notitiae of Salzburg they met fierce opposition. But at least until the end of the 8th century they still played an important part in the Bavarian church. The paper investigates those bishops and the conflicts they had with the newly established bishoprics of Bavaria.

In most areas of the Late Antique Roman Empire a proper Church structure existed: archbishoprics, bishoprics, and their dioceses. Yet for some areas we only have limited information about the organisation of the Church. One such region are the provinces of Raetia secunda and Noricum ripense. These areas along the upper Danube had been under Roman rule for centuries, but in the case of Raetia, curiously, there seems only limited Roman organisational structures.[1] Although they were near the Roman heartland or surrounded by deeply Christianised areas such as Pannonia and valleys of the eastern Alps such as Churraetia, the Etschvalley and Noricum mediterraneum almost no information exists about the Christian organisation. The only contemporary source about Christianity in Raetia secunda and Noricum ripense is the Vita Severini, a text dating from the beginning of the 6th century. However, this text largely fails to elucidate the Christian organisation: the only bishopric that is mentioned north of the Alps is Lauriacum. Although it implies that it had vanished by the end of the 5th century.[2]

Only from the early 8th century sources flow more abundantly for this area, now the early medieval dukedom of Bavaria. They refer to a newly founded Christian organisation and the foundation of the canonical bishoprics of Bavaria: Regensburg, Freising, Salzburg, Passau and, from 772 on, Säben. In addition to the bishops of these dioceses, more bishops appear in the sources until the beginning of the 9th century. They cannot be linked to a fixed bishop's seat as connected to

---
1 Gottlieb 1989, 79–80. 86.
2 Eugipp. Sev. 31, 6 (ed. Régerat 1991, 262).

several places at once. It is not clear the canonical or organisational background those clerics had: were they bishops tied to an influential, even ducal, family, some sort of courtly bishops? Were they itinerant bishops, such as the founding bishops of the future sees in Regensburg, Freising and Salzburg? Or chorbishops – special bishops that were sent from a bishop's seat to remote areas of the diocese?[3] Sometimes they appear in more than one place and sometimes seem to be monastic bishops, located in a monastery as abbot.

All of these bishops were not acting according to Church rules, as defined by the Council of Nicea. This council set the duties of a bishop and determined what a bishop's seat should be like.[4] But even though those canons were quite clear, the situation in many areas of the former Roman Empire had required new and flexible forms of the ecclesiastical organisation, especially when the Roman *civitas* structure, upon which the dioceses were based, had ceased to exist – and with it the specific territorial structure of a Diocese.[5] In areas, such as the Raetia secunda, there remain doubts if they existed at all. As there was a Christian population the Church had to be organised somehow. In other areas, the inflow of heathen people and/or the distance to Rome and its canonical orders had allowed heretical practices to be accepted by local priests. Disputes such as that of the Three Chapters (see below) further deepened the distance between local Church structures. We know that the bishoprics and monasteries in Merovingian Gaul enjoyed much autonomy, and uncanonical behaviour became quite common.[6] Some bishops became close to the kings and dukes and apparently did not need a fixed seat any longer: they were attached to people and not to territory.[7]

For most Church reformers from the late 7th century, the existence of such bishops meant those areas were not canonical anymore. As a consequence, these reformers worked to eliminate such bishops. From the 8th century, starting in the Carolingian court, we find many synods and letters that try to define the responsibilities of a bishop and his obligations in his diocese. The functions of a bishop were clearly expressed and lists of their duties were sent to every corner of the Empire. Bishops who were not acting according to those rules met strong opposition: foremost by canonical bishops of the regions, who were direct competitors

---

3 German "Wanderbischof", Koller 1991, 63. 67.
4 The council of Nicaea of 325 defines that a bishopric had to be located in a worthy place, that is in Roman times only a *civitas*, and had to have an adjacent territory. Also, bishops and priests were not allowed to move. They should stay at the place where they were ordinated. Mazel 2016, 33. 42–44.
5 Wood 1994, 71.
6 Wood 1994, 75–79.
7 Streich 1984, 19; Corbinian as a "Hofbischof": Vogel 2000, 123–124.

over power and territory, but also by Church reformers, missionaries and occasionally even the pope. However, uncertainties remained, especially when assessing the worldly powers of a bishop.[8] It was not always easy to eliminate a bishop who did not act in accordance with Church laws, since those bishops often acted with the consent of local elites, dukes and kings. In 8th-century Bavaria, we find several such bishops and sources reveal the competition and disputes with canonical bishops. Ultimately, the bishopric in the Nicaean, canonical sense was successful, but it took more than a hundred years to accomplish this.

1 No Bishops? Christian Roots of 8th-Century Bavaria

The lack of Late Antique bishoprics in the territory of the *ducatus Baiuvariorum*, at least in its core area, is peculiar. Neither known Late Antique bishoprics of Lauriacum/Lorch nor Sabiona/Säben are located within the territory of 6th- and 7th-century Bavaria. The area was Christianised, however, as not only the Vita Severini tells us. Some local traditions hint toward the survival of cults of Late Antique saints: St. Afra of Augsburg, St. Florian of Lorch and St. Maximilian of Bischofshofen.[9] From the 6th century we have archaeological finds in graves that can be interpreted as signs of Christianity, the so-called Goldblattkreuze, small crosses in gold.[10] Late Antique archaeological findings of churches are conspicuously rare and often are questionable, but remains of churches can be dated from the 7th century.[11]

Finally, we do have some rare written accounts of Christianity in Bavaria. Most prominent is the story of Theudelinda, daughter of the duke of Bavaria. She married the Lombard king Authari and, after his death, King Agilulf. We have contemporary sources for her life and deeds, stating that Theudelinda was Christian and Catholic. As there is no evidence of a conversion as an adult, we can assume that she was baptized and raised as a Christian in Bavaria.[12] It is a wonder who was responsible for her baptism – if it was not the bishop, as would have been appro-

---

8 Patzold 2009, 263; Angenendt 2009, 128–130.
9 Wolfram 1995, 111–114; Jahn 1991, 552.
10 Oderweller 2019, 137–139.
11 Later 2018, 825–837.
12 Greg. M. epist. no. IV, 4; no. IX, 67; no. XIV, 12; Pohl 2005, 412–413; Jahn 1991, 14–17.

priate for a duke's daughter[13] – who would have ordained a priest for the baptism? Unfortunately, the sources remain silent.

At approximately the same time the Irish saint Columbanus travelled from Francia to Rome. He took a route over the Eastern parts of the Alps and chose to rest for a while in Brigantium (Bregenz). According to his biographer, Jonas, he found churches there alongside heathen practises. After Columbanus, more Frankish monks and missionaries visited Bavaria. In the second book of the Vita Columbani the travels, before his death in 629, of the missionary Eustasius to the Bavarians are narrated. Later his pupil, the monk Agrestius, also went to Bavaria. He chose to adhere to the heretical side of the Three Chapter schism and subsequently moved to Aquileia.[14] And finally, during the reign of King Dagobert (623–639), Saint Amandus (d. 675) from Aquitaine, later bishop of Maastricht, travelled through Bavaria. His vita, written at the end of the 7th century, does not refer to a mission there. He founded a Christian region, yet no bishops or monasteries are mentioned.[15] After Amandus, the sources remain silent for the rest of the 7th century. The legacy of the Luxeuil monks was not explicitly fostered in later centuries, but their memory was not forgotten. In the 8th century Arbeo of Freising wrote that Saint Emmeram chose not to go to the pagan Slavs and Avars east of Bavaria. This was surely written with the vitae of Columbanus and Amandus in mind, who made similar decisions, although the author did not mention those missionaries.[16] Thus we cannot talk of a mission in Bavaria in the 8th century.[17]

Although we have enough evidence that Bavaria was at least partially Christianised, we do not know who consecrated the churches and monasteries and who ordained and organised the priests in their wooden churches.

2 The Beginning of the 8th Century: Theodo's and Boniface's Plans

Only in the beginning of the 8th century, in 716, do we finally hear from the first Bavarian bishops – although hypothetically: Duke Theodo went to Rome "as the first of his people" to organise the Bavarian Church in a canonical diocesan struc-

---

13 For baptism as sacral foundation of worldly power see Jahn 1991, 52–53 and footnote 110.
14 Wood 2001, 35–37; Wood 1994, 196–197; Vogel 2000, 117–122.
15 Wood 2001, 39–42; Wolfram 1995, 43; *Vita Amandi episcopi* I c. 16 (*MGH* 1910, 39–40).
16 *Vita Haimhrammi* (1953, 12); Wood 2001, 151.
17 Wood 2011, 11.

ture.[18] In accordance with the pope "three or four" bishops should be installed.[19] Duke Theodo had divided his duchy between his three sons, it is therefore assumed that the early ecclesiastical division corresponds to the worldly division. In turn, this relates to the later known canonical bishop's seats and their ecclesiastical territory: Regensburg, Freising, Salzburg and Passau.[20] But when in 732 and 739 the Anglo-Saxon missionary Boniface came to Bavaria, he claimed to have found only one real bishop in Bavaria, Vivilo of Passau, who had been consecrated by the pope himself. According to Willibbord's Vita Bonifatii, written in the year 765, how he organised the Bavarian Church in the year 739 is described: he divided it – again – into four dioceses.[21] This reminds us of the description in the *Liber pontificalis*. Therefore, Boniface had only re-established or reinforced an already existing structure that either had fallen apart – or was ignored by him.[22]

For Salzburg we have a list of bishops in the *liber confraternitatum*, where we find two bishops of Salzburg after Saint Rupert (see below) and before Bishop Johannes, who was ordained in 739 by Boniface[23]: Vitalis and Flobargisus/Flobrigis.[24] In another papal letter written in 738 by Gregory III, further bishops of Alemannia and Bavaria are named, but unfortunately not with their seat,[25] and local traditions speak of at least three bishops under Duke Theodo (more in the section "Wandering/Itinerate Bishops").

So, why did Boniface choose to ignore those bishops? In 739, Pope Gregory III wrote to Boniface, recalling that Boniface went to the Bavarians whom he found "extra ordinem ecclesiasticum viventes, dum episcopos non habebant in provincia" – "living outside of the church order and having no bishop in the province". So, it seems that the operating words in this letter are not "episcopos non habebant" but "extra ordinem ecclesiasticum viventes" – that is, for Boniface, and after his interventions to the pope, existing Bavarian bishops were entirely uncanonical and thus non-existent. We have further indications of this opinion when looking at the quarrels of Boniface with Bishop Virgil (749–784, see below).[26] In 748 even the pope mentions false bishops, although not in any specific area.[27]

---

18 Lib. pontif. (1886, 1:398); Paulus Diaconus, *Historia Langobardorum* VI, 44; Jahn 1991, 74–75; Freund 2004, 24–34.
19 Gregory II, Papal decree for Bavaria, 452 (*MGH* 1863).
20 Jahn 1991, 73–75; Freund 2004, 31–44.
21 *Vita Bonifatii* (2011, 502).
22 Freund 2004, 50–55. On p. 67 he argues that the plans of 716 were still known and even discussed with Boniface in Rome.
23 *Vita Bonifatii* 2012, 502; Freund 2004, 54.
24 *Liber Confraternitatum* 41, 1; Wolfram 1995, 252–253; Koller 1991; 60–61.
25 Letters of Boniface 2011, 127; Freund 2004, 56.
26 Wolfram 1995, 253–257.

This opinion did not meet the approval of the Bavarian ecclesiastical and worldly elite. That might be the reason why, in 743, Odilo asked the pope for a new emissary: Sergius, perhaps thought of as a replacement for Boniface by the duke.[28] Willibord took these accusations even further in the Vita Bonifati. There a scismatic is mentioned – Eremvulf. When narrating the creation of the Bavarian Church province by Boniface, he writes how the missionary had removed those who had wrongly taken the dignity of a bishop "falso se episcopatus gradu praetulerunt".[29] There remains the question whether these bishops were real schismatics or heretics, or if this was just an exaggeration by Boniface and his biographer to highlight the saint's achievements. We could speculate at this point if this might have been a reference to the Three Chapter schism, the fall out between the bishops under the lead of the patriarchate of Aquileia and the pope that had started in 553 and, at least in Langobardia, had ended in 698. Already Theudelinda had sympathised with the Three Chapter side.[30] The abovementioned Luxeuil monk Agrestius – and apparently even Columbanus – were also siding with Aquileia.[31] That Theodo, as the first of the Bavarians, travelled to Rome roughly two decades after the end of this schism could be linked with this end. That around a decade later the Bavarian bishops were still schismatic (or seen as schismatic) is a possibility and might even be the reason why the memories of those (hypothetical) 7th-century bishops were erased.[32]

In Boniface's time, the main reason for his and the pope's concerns were not only heretics and possible schismatics, but also Irish monks, who were called *scotti*, and who were probably also meant by the term *brittoni*, in contrast to Anglosaxon missionaries. Boniface and his companions were explicitly and positively addressed by Pope Zachary as coming from the "gens Anglorum et Saxonum in Brittania insula".[33] Of significance is the conflict Boniface had with Bishop Virgil

---

27 Pope Zachary writes to Boniface in 748: *erroneos simulatores sub nomine episcoporum vel presbiterorum, qui numquam ab episcopis catholicis fuerunt ordinati*, Letters of Boniface 2011, 260–262; Jahn 1991, 139.
28 Jahn 1991, 168–170 and 188–191. The episode is narrated, with a strong Carolingian bias, in the Annales Mettenses (*MGH* 1905, 327–328).
29 *Vita Bonifatii* c. 6., 2011, 500–502.
30 As visible in her letters to Pope Gregory the Great. Pohl 2005, 412.
31 Wood 1994, 196–197; Wolfram 1995, 43.
32 Gleirscher 2000 speculates that the impact in Bavaria and Carantania might have been profound.
33 Letters of Boniface 2011, 128; see also below, chapter "Monastic bishops". The origin of Boniface as Anglosaxon in letter Nr. 80 of pope Zachary to Boniface in 748, Letters of Boniface 2011, 258. See also the heretical *scotti* Samson in the Letters of Boniface 2011, 264, and the exepiscopus Clemens in the Roman Synod of 745, letters of Boniface 2011, 398.

of Salzburg: in his eyes, this Irish cleric was a dangerous heretic who tolerated wrong baptism in his diocese, and even had strange theories on the shape of the world.[34]

3 Wandering/Itinerant Bishops

After Boniface's death, and probably connected with the composition of his *vita* by Willibald in the second third of the 8th century, the Bavarian bishops Arbeo and Virgil started their own narrative of the origin of the ecclesiastical organisation in Bavaria.[35] We have three texts stemming from the late 8th-century telling of saints who were active in Bavaria around the year 700: the Vita Corbiniani and Passio Haimhrammi, written in the second third of the 8th century by Arbeo, bishop of Freising (764–784), and the Vita Ruperti, which was possibly created by Virgil himself as early as the second half of the 8th century. This text surely originated from the second half of the 8th century.[36] These texts chose to ignore Boniface completely.[37] The *damnatio memoriae* could stem from this disregard of bishops and episcopal traditions in Bavaria before 739. But the narratives also chose to ignore 7th-century Christianity in Bavaria, leaving out Theudelinda and not mentioning the Luxeuil traditions of Amandus, Agrestius and others – although it is very likely that the narrators knew about them.[38]

In the narratives Duke Theodo was largely responsible for the implementation of a proper Christian organisation in Bavaria. But in their version, this ruler did not personally initiate the foundation of bishoprics. In his narrative it was wandering/missionary bishops from Francia who established the episcopates of Bavaria. Three saints, Corbinian of Freising, Rupert of Salzburg and Emmeram of Regensburg, and a fourth with a lost tradition, Erhardt,[39] are all from Francia but are only known in Bavaria. All three texts have a strong territorial aspect and stand in close relationship with the need to create a proper, that is territorial, diocese.[40]

---

34 Wood 2001, 146; Wolfram 1995, 255–257; Also, in Letter Nr. 80/748, Letters of Boniface 2011, 266–268.
35 Wood 2001, 53; Wood 1994, 74. for the method of establishing a cult to legitimize the power of the bishopric in general.
36 Wood 2001, 146–148.
37 Only TF 234ab mentions Boniface, Kohl 2010, 207. For the disregard of Boniface in Bavarian historiography see Freund 2004, 72–76. esp. footnote 232 on page 75.
38 For example, Arn was abbot in St. Amand, Wolfram 1995, 43.
39 Freund 2004, 13–14.
40 See Winckler 2019.

Additionally, they share similar narrative specifics: they tell a story of a holy man who had already been ordained as a bishop for a Frankish place and only afterwards decided to bring true Christianity to the Bavarian people. But those saints have a broken, not necessarily Carolingian/ Merovingian, frankishness: Rupert leaves his proper seat, Worms, without consent of the king[41]; Emmeram, according to Arbeo, originated in Poitiers of Aquitania;[42] and even Corbinian is, in one variant of the text, denounced as "Brittanorum origine ortum".[43]

In only one version of one text, do we hear about the conversion of the Bavarians from paganism. The saint Rupert also baptises Duke Theodo, a story modelled after such illustrious stories as Bishop Silvester and the baptism of Emperor Constanine and Bishop Remigius, who baptised the Merovingian king Chlodvig.[44] In all other texts and variants we hear only of the affirmation of an already existing, but crude and superficial, Christianity.[45] This is corresponding to the laments of Boniface in the 730s about the state of Christianity in Bavaria and the activities of "British" missionaries. But the texts locate the events about a generation earlier than Boniface, around the year 700. By this dating, the Bavarian bishops of the second half of the 8th century belittle the acts of Boniface by attributing his accomplishments to otherwise unknown bishops. The authors aimed at giving the seats proper traditions, independent of this missionary.[46]

At the same time, they also ignored the already existing Christianity at the time of those "founding fathers". They did not mention Theudelinda, the legacies of the Luxeuil monks, Theodo's travel to Rome – and each other.[47] So, these narratives served further purposes. One is to position themselves as bishoprics with their own prestigious traditions. It is no coincidence that the two other bishoprics of Bavaria did not have such saints: Säben was known to have roots dating back to the 5th/6th century,[48] Vivilo of Passau had been ordained by the pope before Boni-

---

41 Wolfram 2012, 93–97.
42 *Vita et passio Sancti Haimhrammi Martyris*, c. 1.3 (Bischoff 1953, 6–10). For the *topos* of saints coming from Aquitania as misisonaries, see Helvétius 2010, 50–54.
43 *Vita Corbiniani* c. 26 (*MGH* 1920, 218).
44 Breves Notitiae c. 1 (ed. Lošek 2006, 88); Angenendt 1984, 165–170. The version where Rupert converts the Bavarians from paganism seems to be driven by the urge of the bishopric of Salzburg to establish its superiority over the other Bavarian bishoprics in 798. Wolfram 1995, 234.
45 Rupert: *Gesta Hrodberti* c. 4 (*MGH* 1913, 159), Conversio, c. 1 (Wolfram 2012, 58); *Vita et passio Sancti Haimhrammi Martyris* c. 7 (Bischoff 1953, 14–16); Vita Corbiniani c. 15 (*MGH* 1920, 203).
46 Wood 2011, 148–150. for Rupert and Virgil.
47 Jahn 1991, 35–36; Wood 2001, 148.
48 Albertoni 2003, 58–60.

face. In Passau there might have been even older traditions still alive in the 8th century.[49]

Another purpose might be the need to distance themselves from an uncanonical and possibly heretical past. Interestingly, as consciously shaped as those texts are they still carry on uncanonical ideas about a bishop and his seat. One is the abovementioned uncanonical movement of the bishops to a foreign place in another ecclesiastical territory,[50] where they acted as bishops –seeming like itinerant bishops[51] or, in the case of Emmeram, even courtly bishops.[52] Furthermore, Corbinian and Rupert were involved in founding important monasteries and even led monastic lives, which put them dangerously close to the contested Irish traditions of monastic abbot bishop (see the chapter about monastic bishop). The texts focus on other aspects that made them apt as saints[53], but it makes us wonder why the authors did not leave out those uncanonical aspects – even though they left out so much else.

The answer probably lies in the fact that, even at the time of the composition of these texts, such bishops still roamed around in Bavaria – with the still strong backing by elite families and even the duke. They were not perceived as uncanonical in this time.

4 A Bishop without a Seat: Salzburg, Bischofshofen and Liuti

The Breves Notitiae and Notitia Arnonis were both written around the year 800 in the aftermath of Duke Tassilo's fall and the takeover by Charlemagne. The deeds were used as a summary of Salzburgian property – but disputed property was also listed in the hope to gain favour from the new rulers.[54] One conflict dealt with the monastery of Bischofshofen, founded, built and consecrated in or near the year 711 with the support of Bishop Rupert of Salzburg. Property for the endowment of the monastery was donated to both the monastery and Salzburg by mem-

---

[49] As proven by the so-called Rottachgau-fragment, Erkens 2008, 497–498. This idea was revisited by Passau in the 9th century, when Bishop Pilgrim did huge forgeries to claim that his bishopric the successor of the Late Antique of Lauriacum. Roach, 2021, 72–78.
[50] For the discussion canonical/uncanonical acting of Rupert, see Wolfram, 1995, 236–237.
[51] Koller 1991, 63–64.
[52] This position even led to the martyrdom of the saint: *Vita Haimhrammmi* (ed. Bischoff 1953, 16 and 24–26).
[53] Wood 2001, 154.
[54] Kohl 2010, 98; Brown 2001, 83–84.

bers of the Albina family. But (according to the bishop) the property was alienated soon afterwards and came back into the hands of the family. When the texts were written, the property was still disputed and claimed by the archbishop Arn of Salzburg.[55]

Under Duke Odilo, the dispute escalated between his chaplain Ursus, also a member of the Albina, and Bishop Virgil of Salzburg.[56] Here, the narration of the Notitia Arnonis stops, but the Breves Notitiae projects the tale further and in more detail:[57] when Virgil managed to receive back at least half of the property, Ursus built, with the help of Duke Odilo, another church. To consecrate the church, they sent for "unum vacantem episcopum nomine Liuti" – a bishop without a seat called Liuti.[58] The name Liuti/Liudi appears also in other sources of the time: as "Liudinus" in the *liber confraternitatum* of Salzburg[59] and as "Liudo" in the letter of Pope Gregory III to the bishops of Bavaria and Alemannia. Neither source mentions a seat.[60] If these references refer to the same person, Liuti was recognised by the other bishops and even the pope.

Nevertheless, his actions against the bishopric of Salzburg was uncanonical, as he was consecrating a church in a different diocese. Or was he? We have no sources that explicitly dictate the borders of the Bavarian dioceses of the 8th century. For two dioceses – Freising and Salzburg – we have excellent sources listing the 8th-century property and churches of those sees. Their property lies within a certain radius around the bishops seat, the supposed centre of the diocese, and thus seem to follow a certain territorial outline. But there is still enough space between the so-defined core areas of the dioceses to suggest that the borders were neither obvious nor clearly defined.[61] Often we find a monastery in those distended spaces, such as Staffelsee or Chiemsee. And it is exactly in those monasteries where we find bishops of unclear affiliation (see Abbot Bishop below).

---

55 Wolfram 1995, 201–204.
56 *Notitia Arnonis* c. 8 (Lošek 2006, 82–85).
57 *Breves Notitiae* c. 3 (Lošek 2006, 90–92 and c. 8. 96–100).
58 Brown 2001, 46–50; *Breves Notitiae* c. 3, 90–93 and c. 8. 96–101. esp. c. 8, 10., 98–99. It is not entirely clear, where this church was located: either directly at Bischofshofen – which would make more sense in regard of the story, or, according to H. Wolfram, in today Oberalm, where the noble family Albina resided. Jahn 1991, 407.
59 *Liber confraternitatum* (*MGH* 1904, 26. 63. "Liudinus ep.").
60 Letters of Boniface 2011, 126; Freund 2004; Jahn 1991, 136–139.
61 If we just count the churches who were explicitly consecrated in the charters (Traditions of Freising) or called "ecclesia parrochiale", that means less a parochia in modern sense but more "church of a certain bishopric" in the *Breves Notitiae* and *Notitia Arnonis*, we get an even clearer picture of the diocese's borders. Winckler 2019, 36–40.

That suggests that in 8th-century Bavaria there were enough 'free' spaces where a bishop without a seat could consecrate and act without violating canon law. For Liuti this implies that he was neither a chorbishop nor from another known diocese of Bavaria. He could have been an abbot-bishop. When looking at the geographical closeness to Salzburg and Bischofshofen, Chiemsee would be an option.[62] But his closeness to the family of the Albina and also to Duke Odilo poses another possibility: that he was a court bishop, a bishop without a see and tied to a family and their main residence(s) or even to the duke himself.[63]

5 Dobdagrecus, a Monastic Bishop

Bishops who were abbots of a monastery at the same time came from two traditions: one is the institution of a monastic cathedral chapter, that is a monastery that was adjacent to a bishop's seat. This is a canonical institution of the Catholic Church and already mentioned in Late Antiquity. The second tradition might be linked to this but got a life on its own in early medieval Ireland where abbot-bishops emerged. Those bishops were the abbots of a monastery that had no diocese attached, at least not in a traditional, territorial sense, and were positioned often far from settlements. Such bishops originated in Irish Christianity and were not common in early and Roman-Catholic Christendom, thus leading to rifts. It spread also to the Frankish empire, where it was especially common at the margins of the realms and their missionary areas. This institution was never seen as canonical (though seemingly tolerated by the pope) and would be contested at the moment when a proper bishop's see had been established.[64] In Bavaria we find such bishops at first in the narratives of the legendary founders, especially

---

[62] Wolfram interprets Liuti as chorbishop because of his mention in the liber confraternitatum of Salzburg (see footnote 57). Letter of Gregory III to the bishops of Alemannia and Bavaria addresses a "Liudo", Letters of Boniface 2011, 126, in the Footnote in footnote 44 he is taken as bishop of Chiemsee.

[63] This is confirmed by another recently formulated theory by Stih 2021. He suggests that the earliest Bavarian mission to Carantania was mainly carried out by the duke and not the bishoprics of Salzburg and Freising – hence the importance of the cell of St. Maximilian as a ducal monastery, that was positioned on the route to this region and, furthermore, the significance of Liuti as the personal bishop of Odilo and the Albina; Winckler 2012, 313–314.

[64] Angenedt 2005, 97–98; Bitel 2020, 301–302; Sharpe, 1984, 231–234; for the territoriality of the Roman bishoprics see Mazel 2016, 97–105. Frankish monasteries founded in the tradition of Columban did not have abbot bishops. Diem 2020, 181–184.

Corbinian.[65] However, the monasteries they established became the basis of the monastic cathedral chapters of the bishopric, so when the narratives were written down this no longer appeared uncanonical.

A generation later, at the latest in 745, Virgil and his companions came from Ireland by the route over Francia and the court of Pippin III to Bavaria and settled in Salzburg.[66] They are the first Irish missionaries we know of for sure, although there might have been predecessors: when Gregory III wrote in 738 a letter to Alemannic and Bavarian bishops, he reminds them to ignore "gentilitatis ritum et doctrinam vel venientium Brittonum vel falsorum sacerdotum hereticorum" – the rites of the pagans, the incoming Britons, and false and heretic priests,[67] with "Brittonum" apparently meaning the Irish.

Virgil came to Salzburg as abbot, and took a bishop with him, Dobdagrecus (died before 788), who was probably consecrated already in Ireland and who acted as bishop in Salzburg. In 746 or 747, Virgil became a bishop himself, and from then on was more bishop of Salzburg than abbot.[68] Dobdagrecus became abbot of Chiemsee. There he acted also as a bishop. We meet him again in a charter of Freising, where his uncanonical actions had caused conflict. In 804 at the southeastern corner of the diocese, the bishop of Freising clashed with the monastery of Chiemsee over several parochial churches. The abbot of Chiemsee stated that a certain Tuti Grecus, a bishop from Ireland ("Tuti Grecus advena episcopus scottus"), had built and probably consecrated those churches – against canonical laws, as Freising explicitly stated.[69] There exists also a royal charter that calls Dobdagrecus abbot of Chiemsee, so this "Tuti Grecus" is the same person, maybe with a pun intended. In Chiemsee he acted as abbot-bishop in Irish tradition, leading the monastery independent of surrounding bishoprics.[70] Although the diocese of Freising complained over the uncanonical behaviour of this bishop, it could settle its con-

---

65 This monastic episcopate let older research conclude, starting with Krusch, that Corbinian was from Ireland, see Vogel, 2000, 80–120 and the many arguments against it.
66 Wolfram 1995, 253.
67 Letters of Boniface 2011, 128; Freund 2004, 56, see also above, chapter "The beginning of the 8th century".
68 Wolfram 1991, 253–255, 258 and esp. 263 for the strong tie between the bishop and monastery of Salzburg, according to Wolfram due to the Irish heritage of Virgil. Also, another of this company became bishop, Sidonius who was bishop in Passau from ca. 754–763/4, Jahn 1991, 86.
69 Traditionen Freisings Nr. 193 (Bitterauf 1905, 182–184, esp. 183): *Tuti Grecus advena episcopus Scottus ipsa parrochia et ecclesias iniuste et contra canonica institutione proprisisset*.
70 Jahn 1991,146–147. In Agilolfingian times, Chiemsee was never subordinated under Salzburg or Freising; Wolfram 1995, 252–254. See also *DD Karol* I, Nr. 162, 219: Charlemagne gives the monastery of Chiemsee to the church of Metz. The charter defines Chiemsee as *monasterium virorum nomine Kieminsea, quod Doddogrecus peregrinus habuit.*

flict with Chiemsee only over half a century, after Charlemagne had taken over Bavaria and backed the canonical dioceses when reclaiming property. Some monasteries, however, remained strong opponents against the bishops and their dioceses, with the abbots being influential figures fighting for autonomous rights and territory. Nevertheless, abbots were usually not also bishops.

6 Bishop of Two Places: Langres-Passau and Neuburg/Staffelsee

There are yet other surplus bishops and ecclesiastical networks that were parallel to the canonical dioceses and bishop's seats in Bavaria. One seems to stem from older links between the Bavarian nobility and the wider Frankish area. Already mentioned were the ecclesiastical links to Aquitania.[71] But the other, more concrete link of the 8th century is to Burgundy, to be more precise to the bishopric of Langres. This see traditionally was also occupied by someone who was abbot of the monastery of Saint Bénigne in Dijon at the same time and, for a while, also Moutier Saint Jean.[72] After Charles Martell received Burgundy, he transferred the administration of the bishopric of Auxerre, according to an 9th-century source, to six Bavarian nobles.[73] This connection gains salience in the second half of the 8th century: from 769 to 838 the bishops of Langres were indeed from Alemannia and Bavaria.[74] One family, known as the "Waltrichs", seems even to have acquired positions as abbots and bishops in Burgundy and Bavaria at the same time. Why the Carolingian kings took men from Bavaria, a region that at this time had strong autonomous ideas, is best explained by the complicated relationship between Carolingian kings and the Agilolfingian from Alemannia and Bavaria.[75]

The first Waltrich is known from a deed of 772, where the monastery of Schäftlarn was 'officially' founded, although it had existed at least for a decade.[76] The monastery was consecrated in the name of Saint Denis, the patron saint of the Frankish realm, but it celebrated on the 9th of October – the day of the saint Benigne of Dijon. And it is at that place where we find Waltrich again. In 774 he acted as bishop of Langres and abbot of St. Benigne in Dijon. His successor, Petto, also

---

71 Most notably Amandus (see above, footnote 40), but also, and maybe in his tradition, the saints Emmeram and maybe even Ehrhart of Regensburg, see Gaillard 2010, 159–161.
72 Semmler 1986, 31 and footnote 84.
73 *Gesta episcoporum Autissiodorensium* (MGH 1881, 395–398); Semmler 1986, 33.
74 Störmer 1986, 45–46.
75 For a short summary in relation to Langres see Störmer 1986, 48–51.
76 Jahn 1991, 358–365; Traditionen Schäftlarn Nr. 1 (Weissthanner 1953, 1–6).

held both positions.[77] Furthermore, this Waltrich also had possibly been bishop of Passau at the same time (774–791 in Langres, 777–804 Passau).[78] Waltrich in the final years of Tassilos's reign additionally would act as bishop and abbot of the monastery Schäftlarn, a position that put him at odds with the surrounding diocese of Freising. Nevertheless, we have no evidence of a conflict there. One possibility might be that this family was related to the Carolingians.[79] J. Jahn states that Schäftlarn remained a monastery free of Freising's influence until the beginning of the 9th century.[80]

Finally, we have three bishops who are located in the West of the Bavarian duchy, in the overlapping spheres of the bishopric of Augsburg (which was not part of the Bavarian Church province of this time) and Freising: Manno, Odalbert and Sintpert. Manno is the first to appear in the sources: we find him as "episcopus" in a charter of 759/760 in the traditions of Freising.[81] When in 770 a *pactum fraternitatis* between Bavarian bishoprics and monasteries is established, he signs along with other Bavarian bishops and abbots. We can assign to each of the names one of the episcopal sees of Bavaria – except Manno.[82] Though a later list of Augsburg bishops mentions a Bishop Manno.[83] In the area between Augsburg and Freising we find in 784 a bishop called Odalhart, who signs another charter in the traditions of Freising.[84] A later addition in the Vita Bonifatii sees Oadalhart as the successor of Manno as bishop of Nova Civitate/Neuburg.[85] And, to make matters even more complicated, in 804 Odalhart signs together with Hiltiger, an *episcopus vocatus*.[86] This term usually designates someone who is not yet ordained as bishop. However, the 8th century's use of this term is quite vague.[87]

---

77 Traditionen Freisings Nr. 88 (Bitterauf 1905, 108); Traditionen Schäftlarn Nr. 2–6, 7–11 (Jahn 1991, 361–362).
78 Jahn 1991, 154, 364. Maybe this connection came from the marriage in 741 of Duke Odilo with Charlesmartell's sister Swanahilt. Störmer 1986, 47, 58–60; Semmler 1986, 38–39. At the foundation of Kremsmünster in 777 we find Waltrich as bishop, presumably of Passau. Wolfram 1995, 377.
79 Störmer 1986, 72.
80 Jahn 1991, 366.
81 Traditionen Freisings Nr. 15 (Bitterauf 1905, 43): *Signunm Mannoni episcopi*, along Bishop Joseph of Freising.
82 *Concilia aevi Karolini* 2. 1 (*MGH* 1906, 96–97) added after a summary of the Synod of Dingolfing in 770.
83 *Series episcoporum Augustensium* (*MGH* 1881, 333).
84 Traditionen Freisings Nr. 86, AD 777 (Bitterauf 1905, 107): Bishop Virgil with the bishops Arbeo and Odalhart as witnesses; Traditionen Freisings Nr. 118 (Bitterauf 1905, 131): *Signum Oadalharti episcopi* directly after duke Tassilo and without any other bishop.
85 Jahn 1991, 405 and 513.
86 Traditionen Freisings Nr. 197, 16 June 804 (Bitterauf 1905, 189).
87 Halfond 2010, 206–208; Koller 1991, 62 and 70.

And finally, Sintpert: when Arn of Salzburg was appointed archbishop in 798, the other bishops of Bavaria protested against this order. In a letter Pope Leo III reminds the Bavarian bishops to subordinate themselves under the new archbishop. In this letter, curiously, he addresses not only the usual suspects, that is the bishops of Freising, Regensburg, Passau and Säben but also a Bishop Sindpert of Neuburg on the Danube – "Sintperto ecclesiae Niwinburcgensis", one of the "provinciae Baiowariorum Epsicopis".[88] Only two years later the pope had to again remind the same bishops to subordinate themselves to Archbishop Arn – yet this time, Sintpert is adressed as "Sintpertus staffnensis ecclesie".[89] We know, that Staffelsee was an Augsburg monastery, so this led to the common conclusion that this person is the same as Sintpert, bishop of Augsburg (ca. 778 to 807).[90] As we have seen, in 8th-century Bavaria bishops habitually resided in a monastery, so it is no surprise that we find one actually being called bishop *of* the monastery. Those "surplus" bishops seem to combine all the abovementioned types: courtly bishops, abbot bishops and wandering bishops, with several seats.

All the abovementioned bishops demonstrate that the canonical order in 8th-century Bavaria was far from being consolidated.[91] The mention of Sintpert's name in a papal letter documents that the position of these bishops was not contested at this time. But it is also the papal letter of 800 that ultimately indicates the end of uncanonical and anarchistic episcopal organisations: the letter reminds the bishops of Bavaria that they finally had to subordinate themselves under a superior archbishop.

7 Episcopus Missus: Salzburg and the Chorbishops

Although (or maybe because) the position of Salzburg as the first among the Bavarian bishoprics was contested, the bishopric made use of yet another form of

---

88 *Epistolae Karolini aevi* III, Nr. 3, dates April 20 798 (*MGH* 1899, 58).
89 *Epistolae Karolini aevi* III, Nr. 5 (*MGH* 1899, 60).
90 Freund 2004, 85–86; Freund 2010, 472–473; Elmshäuser 1989, 344–348. However, Jahn 1991, 405 and 449, seems to see Sintpert of Staffelsee/Neuburg as a different person than Sintpert of Augsburg. Also, a bishop of Regensburg is called Sintpert (after 756/768–791), probably the Sintpert in the foundation act of Kremsmünster in 777, Wolfram 1995, 361 and 377. As the name seems to have been quite common at that time there is always the possibility, that all these Sintperts were – like Waltrich – different persons.
91 Jahn 1991, 407.

bishops without a seat: the chorbishops. This institution was canonical[92] and came more into use in the 8th century and in the early Carolingian empire.[93] The *Codex Carolinus* contains a letter of Pope Zachary to Pippin and the Frankish bishops, written in 747, in which the pope clearly defined the duties of a bishop. The pope emphasised the territoriality of a diocese. He added instructions regarding the duties of chorbishops. They were consecrated bishops, but they did not have the right to ordain priests, should only administer churches that were assigned to them and they were subordinate to the *episcopus civitatis*.[94] At a later point, the chorepiscopate met fierce opposition, most notably from Hincmar of Reims.[95]

In Bavaria, the first chorbishops appear from the middle of the 8th century. Their most important area of operation were the eastern regions of the Bavarian duchy, that is from ca. 740 on the mostly pagan region of Carantania, and, from 796 on, the former Avarian realm east of the river Enns and the former Roman province of Pannonia.[96] These regions were far away from the long established Christian organisational structures of Bavaria, Italia and Francia. Even from the outpost of the monastery of St. Maximilian in Bischofshofen, far within the Alps, two high passes had to be crossed in order to reach Carantania. Nevertheless, Salzburg was very ambitious to extend its power to this area and even beyond, in constant competition with the bishoprics of Freising (Innichen) and the patriarchate of Aquileia. Later it tried to extend its influence also along the Danube, where it clashed with the bishopric of Passau, and in the former Pannonia, where Salzburg met the Byzantine missionaries Constantin and Method.

We learn about the chorbishops of Salzburg mainly in the so-called *Conversio*, written in ca. 870. This text that was created decades later than the narrated events and after the chorbishops were already no longer in use. The text pursued a political aim: it should establish the right of the archbishopric of Salzburg over Pannonia. So, the account should be read with a grain of salt.[97] According to that narrative, Bishop Virgil sent in the 740s a bishop called Modestus to Carantania. This bishop is called *episcopus missus* and his duties were explained in the conversio: "[...]dans ei licentiam ecclesias consecrare, clericos ordinare iuxta canonum diffinitionem nihilque sibi ursupare, quod decretis sanctorum partum contrairet [...]",

---

92 Although the specific rights and powers remained a matter of dispute. See Percival [1899] 1995, 21–23.
93 The Synod of Paris also dealt with the chorbishops by acting against them, *MHG Conc* 2/2, 1906, 629–630.
94 Letter of pope Zachary, in: Letters of Boniface 2011, 420–422.
95 Hinkmar of Reims (*MGH* 2003, 198).
96 Pohl 2018, 387–389.
97 Wolfram 2012, 27–33.

that is, consecrate churches and clerics according to the canons and they should not claim what is not allowed by the decrees of the holy fathers.[98] This description reads more as a justification than a list of duties. When we compare the conversio to the letter of Zachary, it seems that even at the time of Virgil the duties of Modestus did not comply with church law.[99]

The next bishop for the eastern areas, who is mentioned in the conversio, is Deodricus/Theoderic. He was called *episcopus* and explicitly ordained upon request of Charlemagne by Archepiscope Arn for missionary work in Avaria and, according to the conversio, Carantania. In 833 Luois "the German" grants property in the "provintia Auarorum" to the bishopric of Passau which had formerly belonged to a Theodoric. If this is the same Theodoric of the conversio, it would possibly subordinate him not to Arn as bishop of Salzburg but to Arn as archbishop of the ecclesiastical province of Bavaria.[100] This subordination is also underlined by the fact that this area was never an uncontested part of Salzburg: Passau also claimed it.[101] Arn also addressed choreptiscopi in general, without specifically naming anyone, in the synod of Reisbach in 800.[102]

After an otherwise unknown Otto the conversio mentions Oswald, the last of the Carantanian chorbishops. He disappeared after 863 and was probably at least in part responsible for the abolishment of chorbishops.[103] From the papal archives we know that Bishop Oswald wrote to the pope in person – and thereby ignored his superior, Archbishop Adalwin of Salzburg – to ask for advice in rather mundane matters about the lives of missionaries in remote areas. He asked what to do with a priest who had hit a deacon and how to respond to another cleric who had killed a pagan. The answer of the pope was very mild, highlighting the difficult conditions in a still very pagan environment.[104] Later Salzburgian traditions talk about further, grave conflicts between Oswald and the archbishop.[105] Chorbishops threatened the authority of the diocese over this area and the pros-

---

98 Wolfram 2012, 64–66; Wolfram, 1995, 264–265.
99 Wolfram 2012, 127 and Koller 1991, 67.
100 Charter of Louis the German Nr. 9 (*MGH* 1934, 11); Conversio c. 8 (ed. Wolfram 2012, 71/ ed. Lošek 1997, 114–117. esp. footnote 90).
101 Wolfram 2012, 32 and 160–162. for Theoderic (similar Wolfram, 1995 291–295).
102 *MGH* 2, 1: *Concilia aevi Karolini* (742–842), part 1 (742–817), Nr. 22, 196.
103 *Conversio* c. 9 (Wolfram 2012, 70–72. 164).
104 Letter of Nicolaus I. Nr. 142 (*MGH* 1925, 660–661).
105 Wolfram 2012, 215–216, Wolfram 1995, 297–299.

pect for a new, independent bishopric loomed. Therefore, Salzburg chose to abolish the chorbishops after Oswald, at least for the moment.[106]

8 Resumé

In early medieval Bavaria we find several sources talking about bishops without a fixed seat, with uncanonical seats in monasteries or in the vicinity of noble families. Those bishops still existed at a time when the canonical episcopal order was established in Bavaria, at the latest in 739. Often, they were involved in disputes with the canonical seats of Bavaria. But especially at the end of the 8th century, after the Carolingian takeover, they were seen as equals, for example by the pope. For the canonical bishops, these "alternative structures" were not only contradicting ecclesiastical rule, they were threatening their power and diminishing their territory. They ignored the work of Boniface in their writings but ultimately used Boniface's devotion to the Church rules for their own benefit. But despite their conflicts with itinerant or abbot-bishops, they venerated itinerant bishops as saints and founding fathers of their diocese, strengthening Christianity in Bavaria.

Ultimately, such a chaotic structure with no clear organisation and dubious practices was no longer up to date in the early 9th-century Carolingian Church.[107] Carolingian clerics worked on the uniformisation of the Church rules and by doing so changed the position and duties of the bishop – not at least because of their importance in ruling the empire.[108] Also in Bavaria those new rules were soon put into practice, starting with the appointment of Arn as Archbishop of Bavaria. A late relict of 8th- and maybe 7th-century practises seem to be the chorbishops. Although they were subjugated under the archbishop/bishops of Salzburg, they seem to have enjoyed a great idea of autonomy. As this led to conflicts, this institution was, at least for a while, stopped. In the beginning of the 9th century, the itinerant bishops, court bishops and abbot-bishops, vanished and their memory was either canonized in tales about the Bavarian saints Rupert, Corbinian and Emmeram – or forgotten.

---

106 They were reinstated in the beginning of the 10th century. In 1072 the bishopric of Gurk was founded as an "Eigenbistum", that is a bishopric under the sole subjection of Salzburg and without a proper diocese, as it was located within the diocese of Salzburg. Angenendt 1984, 236.
107 See also the laws that explicitly forbid to consecrate churches in a 'foreign' diocese.
108 Patzold 2006, 140–146.

There remains the question, where did those bishops come from? Were they a result of the chaotic conditions of a newly founded Church province or a remainder of habits from older times?

When looking at the evidence, I believe that we can pinpoint the emergence of those autonomous itinerant and court bishops in the 7th, perhaps even the 6th century.[109] The territorial diocesan structure of the late Roman Empire was destroyed, if it had ever existed in this region. But there was an organisational need for structures, as parts of the population were still Christian, at least in some rudimentary way. Also, connections with Christian regions that always had a diocesan organisation and bishops, for example the Frankish realms or Langobardia, were strong. So, also the 7th-century dukes and powerful families of Bavaria wanted a bishop to consecrate their churches and monasteries, ordain priests or abbots and to baptize their children. Those bishops might have resided in monasteries or at the courts of nobles, or were wandering around turning to places where their service was needed. For a proper diocese and bishop's seat in the Roman-Catholic sense and with a territorial aspect there was neither a need nor did the Bavarian nobles seem to have wanted it. Only starting with Theodo and his successors was the Bavarian Church integrated into the larger Church structures. The strong position of the uncanonical bishops throughout the whole 8th and early 9th centuries show that this was a longstanding process with many disputes and conflicts on the way.

Bibliography

Primary Sources

Annales Mettenses: Bernhard von Simson, ed. 1905. *Monumenta Germaniae Historica, Scriptores rerum Germanicarum in usum scholarum (MGH SS rer. Germ.).* X. Hannover/Leipzig: Hahn.

Arbeo of Freising: *Vita Corbiniani:* Bruno Krusch, ed. 1920. *Monumenta Germaniae Historica, Scriptores rerum Germanicarum in usum scholarum (MGH SS rer. Germ.).* XIII. Hannover: Hahn.

Arbeo of Freising, *Vita Corbiniani:* Franz Brunhölzl, ed/trans. 1983. Vita Corbiniani, Bischof Arbeo von Freising und die Lebensgeschichte des hl. Korbinian, 84–154. München: Schnell &Steiner.

Arbeo of Freising: *Vita Haimhrammi:* Bruno Krusch, ed. 1920. *Monumenta Germaniae Historica, Scriptores rerum Germanicarum in usum scholarum (MGH SS rer. Germ.).* XIII. Hannover: Hahn.

Arbeo of Freising, *Vita Haimhrammi:* Bernhard Bischoff, ed/trans. 1953. *Vita et passio sancti Haimhrammi martyris, Leben und Leiden des heiligen Emmeram.* München: Ernst Hermann Verlag.

Boniface, Life and Letters: Michael Tangl, ed. 1916. *Bonifatii et Lulli Epistolae, Monumenta Germaniae Historica,* Epistolae *selectae (MGH EE sel.).* I. Berlin: Weidmann.

---

[109] See also the idea of Micro-Christendoms in Brown, 2003/2013, 378–379; Angenendt 2009, 130.

Boniface, Life and Letters: Wilhelm Levison. ed. 1905. *Vita Sancti Bonifatii, Monumenta Germaniae Historica, Scriptores rerum Germanicarum in usum scholarum (MGH SS rer. Germ.).* LVII. Hannover/Leipzig: Hahn.

Boniface, Life and Letters: Reinhold Rau, ed/trans. 2011. *Briefe des Bonifatius, Willibalds Leben des Bonifatius. Nebst einigen zeitgenössischen Dokumenten. Ausgewählte Quellen zur deutschen Geschichte des Mittelalters.* Freiherr-vom-Stein-Gedächtnisausgabe IVb. Darmstadt: Wissenschaftliche Buchgesellschaft.

Breves Notitia and *Notitia Arnonis:* Fritz Lošek, ed/trans. 2006. *Quellen zur Salzburger Frühgeschichte. Veröffentlichungen des Instituts für österreichische Geschichtsforschung 22. Ergänzungsband*, edited by Herwig Wolfram. Wien: R. Oldenbourg Verlag.

Concilia aevi Karolini I (742–817): Albert Werminghoff, ed. 1906. *Monumenta Germaniae Historica, Concilia (MGH Conc.)* 2, 1. Hannover/Leipzig: Hahn.

Concilia aevi Karolini II (819–842): Albert Werminghoff, ed. 1906. *Monumenta Germaniae Historica, Concilia (MGH Conc.).* II, 2. Hannover/Leipzig: Hahn.

Conversio Bagoariorum et Carantanorum: Herwig Wolfram, ed/trans. 2012. *Conversio Bagoariorum et Carantanorum: das Weißbuch der Salzburger Kirche über die erfolgreiche Mission in Karantanien und Pannonien.* Ljubljana: Slovenska akdemija znanosti in umetnosti Zveza zgodovinskih društrev Slovenije.

Conversio Bagoariorum et Carantanorum: Fritz Lošek, ed/trans. 1997. *Die Conversio Bagoariorum et Carantanorum und der Brief des Erzbischof Theotmar von Salzburg. Monumenta Germaniae Historica*, Studien und Texte. XV. Hannover: Hahn.

Royal Charters, Nr. 162: Engelbert Mühlbacher, ed. 1906. *Monumenta Germaniae Historica,* Die Urkunden der Karolinger 1 *(MGH DD Karol)* I, 219. Hannover: Hahn.

Royal Charters, Nr. 9: Paul Kehr, ed. 1934. *Monumenta Germaniae Historica,* Die Urkunden der Deutschen Karolinger *(MGH DD LdD).* Berlin: Weidmann.

Paulus Diaconus, *Historia Langobardorum:* Georg Waitz, ed. 1878. *Monumenta Germaniae Historica, Scriptores rerum Germanicarum in usum scholarum (MGH SS rer. Germ.).* XLVIII. Hannover: Hahn.

Epistolae selectae Pontificum Romanorum Carolo Magno et Ludowico Pio regnantibus scripta: Karl Hampe, ed. 1899. *Monumenta Germaniae Historica, Epistolae* **(MGH Epp.).** V, *Karolini aevi* III. Berlin: Weidmann.

Formulae Alsaticae: Karl Zeumer, ed. 1886. *Monumenta Germaniae Historica, Formulae Merowingici et Karolini aevi (MGH Formulae).* Hannover: Hahn.

Gesta episcoporum Autisiodorensium: Georg Waitz, ed. 1881. *Monumenta Germaniae Historica, Scriptores (MGH SS).* XIII. Hannover: Hahn

Gesta s. Hrodberti confessoris: Wilhelm Levison, ed. 1913. *Monumenta Germaniae Historica,* criptores rerum Merovingicarum *(MGH SS rer. Merov.).* VI. Hannover/Leipzig: Hahn.

Gregorius I, *Registrum epistularum:* Paul Ewald and Ludwig Hartmann. eds. 1891. *Monumenta Germaniae Historica, Epistolae (MGH Epp.).* I. Berlin: Weidmann.

Gregory II, *Papal decree of for Bavaria:* Georg Pertz, ed. 1863. *Monumenta Germaniae Historica, Leges in folio (MGH LL).* III. Hannover: Hahn.

Hinkmar von Reims, *Opusculum LV capitulorum:* Rudolf Schieffer, ed. 2003. *Monumenta Germaniae Historica, Concilia (MGH Conc.).* IV, Suppl. 2, Die Streitschriften Hinkmars von Reims und Hinkmars von Laon 869–871. Hannover: Hahn.

Liber Confraternitatum s. Petri Salisburgensis vetustior: Siegmund Herzberg-Fränkel, ed. 1904. *Monumenta Germaniae Historica, Necrologia (MGH Necr.).* II. Berlin: Weidmann.

Nicolai I., *Papae Epistolae:* Ernst Perels, ed. 1925. *Monumenta Germaniae Historica, Epistolae (MGH Epp.). Epistolae Karolini Aevi* IV. Berlin: Weidmann.

Series episcoporum Augustensium: Georg Wait, ed. 1881. *Monumenta Germaniae Historica, Scriptores (MGH SS).* XIII. Hannover: Hahn.

Traditionen des Hochstiftes Freising 1: Theodor Bitterauf. ed. 1905. *Die Traditionen des Hochstiftes Freising (Vol. 1–2).* Quellen und Erörterungen zur bayerischen Geschichte NF 4. München: Rieger'sche Universitätsbuchhandlung

Traditionen des Klosters Schäftlarn: Alois Weissthanner, ed. 1953. *Die Traditionen des Kloster Schäftlarns 1: 760–1305.* Quellen und Erörterungen zur bayerische Geschichte NF 8. München: Beck

Vita Amandi episcopi: Bruno Krusch, ed. 1910. *Monumenta Germaniae Historica, Scriptores rerum Merovingicarum (MGH SS rer. Merov.).* V. Hannover/Leipzig: Hahn.

Vita Severini, Eugippius: Philippe Régerat. ed/trans. 1991. *Vie de Saint Séverin/Eugippe.* Sources Chrétiennes No 374. Paris : Éditions du Cerf.

Secondary Sources

Albertoni, Giuseppe. 2003. *Die Herrschaft des Bischofs. Macht und Gesellschaft zwischen Etsch und Inn im Mittelalter.* Bozen: Verlagsanstalt Athesia.

Angenendt, Arnold. 1984. *Kaiserherrschaft und Königstaufe. Kaiser, Könige und Päpste als geistliche Patrone in der abendländischen Missionsgeschichte.* Berlin: Walter de Gruyter.

Angenendt, Arnold. 2005. "Liudger. Lehrer – Missionar – Klostergründer – Bisschof – Heiliger." In *805: Liudger wird Bischof. Spuren eines Heiligen zwischen York, Rom und Münster,* edited by Gabriele Isenberg and Barbara Rommé, 91–104. Mainz: Verlag Phillipp von Zabern.

Angenendt, Arnold. 2009. "Kirche als Träger der Kontinuität." In *Von der Spätantike zum frühen Mittelalter. Kontinuitäten und Brüche, Konzeptionen und Befunde*, Vorträge und Forschungen, Band 70, edited by Theo Kölzer and Rudolf Schieffer, 101–142. Ostfildern: Jan Thorbecke.

Bischoff, Bernhard. 1959. "Dub-dá-chrich." *Neue Deutsche Biographie 4*, 145. URL: https://www.deutsche-biographie.de/pnd135718457.html#ndbcontent (accessed 30.10.2022)

Bitel, Lisa. 2020. "Monastic Identity in Early Medieval Ireland." In *The Cambridge History of medieval monasticism in the Latin West, Volume I: Origins to the Eleventh Century*, edited by Alison I. Beach and Isabelle Cochelin, 297–316. Cambridge: Cambridge University Press.

Brown, Peter. 2013. *The rise of western Christendom: triumph and diversity, A.D. 200–1000.* Tenth anniversary revised edition. Chichester: Wiley-Blackwell.

Brown, Warren. 2001. *Unjust seizure: conflict, interest, and authority in an early medieval society.* Ithaca, NY: Cornell University Press.

Diem, Albrecht and Rousseau, Philip. 2020. "Monastic Rules (Fourth to Ninth Century)." In *The Cambridge History of medieval monasticism in the Latin West, Volume I: Origins to the Eleventh Century*, edited by Alison I. Beach and Isabelle Cochelin, 162–194. Cambridge: Cambridge University Press.

Elmshäuser, Konrad. 1989. "Untersuchungen zum Staffelseer Urbar." In *Strukturen der Grundherrschaft im frühen Mittelalter,* edited by Werner Rösener, 335–369. Göttingen: Vandenhoek & Ruprecht.

Erkens, Franz-Reiner. 2008. "Actum in vico fonaluae die consule: Das Rottachgau-Fragment und die romanische Kontinuität am Unterlauf des Inns." In *Nomen et fraternitas: Festschrift für Dieter*

Geuenich zum 65. Geburtstag edited by Uwe Ludwig and Thomas Schilp, 491–510 Berlin: De Gruyter.

Freund, Stephan. 2004. *Von den Agilolfingern zu den Karolingern. Bayerns Bischöfe zwischen Kirchenorganisation, Reichsintegration und karolingischer Reform (700–847)*. München: C.H. Beck.

Freund, Stephan. 2010. "Sintpert(us)." *Neue Deutsche Biographie* 24, 472–473. URL: https://www.deutsche-biographie.de/pnd118797352.html#ndbcontent (accessed 30.10.2022).

Gaillard, Michèle. 2010. "Erhard, évêque de Ratisbonne, un saint aquitain en Bavière ?" In *Saints d'Aquitaine. Missionnaires et pèlerins du haut Moyen Âge*, edited by Edina Bozoky, 159–172. Rennes: Presses Universitaires de Rennes.

Gleirscher, Paul. 2000. "Der Drei-Kapitel-Streit und seine baulichen Auswirkungen auf die Bischofskirchen im Patriarchat von Aquileia." *Der Schlern* 74:9–18.

Gottlieb, Gunther. 1989. "Die regionale Gliederung in der Provinz Rätien." In *Raumordnung im Römischen Reich. Zur regionalen Gliederung in den galllischen Provinzen in Rätien, Noricum und Pannonien*, edited by Gunther Gottlieb, 75–88. München: Verlag Ernst Vögel.

Halfond, Gregory I. 2010. *Archaeology of Frankish Church Councils, ad 511–768*. Leiden: Brill.

Helvétius, Anne-Marie. 2010. "L'origine aquitaine des saints dans l'hagiographie franque des VIIIe – IXe siècles : réalité ou allégation ?" In *Saints d'Aquitaine. Missionnaires et pèlerins du haut Moyen Âge*, edited by Edina Bozoky, 45–62. Rennes: Presses Universitaires de Rennes.

Jahn, Joachim. 1991. *Ducatus Baiuvariorum. Das bairische Herzogtum der Agilolfiger*. Monographien zur Geschichte des Mittelalters 35. Stuttgart: Hiersemann.

Kohl, Thomas. 2010. *Lokale Gesellschaften: Formen der Gemeinschaft in Bayern vom 8. Bis zum 10. Jahrhundert*. Ostfildern: Jan Thorbecke.

Koller, Heinrich. 1991. "Bischof, Wanderbischof, Chorbischof im frühmittelalterlichen Baiern." *Jahrbuch des Oberösterreichischen Musealvereins* 136:59–71.

Later, Christian. 2019. "Kirche und Siedlung im archäologischen Befund – Anmerkungen zur Situation in der Baiovaria zwischen Spätantike und Karolingerzeit." In *Gründerzeit. Siedlung in Bayern zwischen Spätantike und Frühmittelalter*, edited by Jochen Haberstroh and Irmtraut Heitmeier, 823–864. St. Ottilien: Eos-Verlag.

Lauwers, Michel. 2008. "Territorium non facere diocesim. Conflits, limites et représentation territoriale du diocèse (V^e–Xe siècle)." In *L'espace du diocese. Genèse d'un territoire dans l'Occident medieval (V^e–XIIIe siècle)*, edited by Florian Mazel, 23–68. Rennes : Presses Universitaires de Rennes.

Mazel, Florian. 2016. *L'évêque et le territoire. L'invention médiévale de l'espace (V^e–XIIIe siècle)*. Paris : Éditions du Seuil.

Odenweller, Michael. 2014. "Goldmünze und Goldblattkreuz. Die Obolus-Beigabe in frühmittelalterlichen Bestattungen als Zeugnis der Christianisierung." *Frühmittelalterliche Studien* 48:121–154.

Patzold, Steffen. 2006. "Die Bischöfe im karolingischen Staat. Praktisches Wissen über die politische Ordnung im Frankenreich des 9. Jh." In *Staat im frühen Mittelalter. Forschungen zur Geschichte des Mittelalters* 16, edited by Stuart Airlie, Walter Pohl and Helmut Reimitz, 133–162. Wien: Verlag der österreichischen Akademie der Wissenschaften.

Patzold, Steffen. 2009. "Bischöfe als Träger der politischen Ordnung des Frankenreichs im 8./9. Jahrhundert." In *Der frühmittelalterliche Staat – europäische Perspektiven. Forschungen zur Geschichte des Mittelalters* 16, edited by Walter Pohl and Veronika Wieser, 255–270. Wien: Verlag der österreichischen Akademie der Wissenschaften.

Percival, Henry. 1899/1995². *The seven Ecumenical Councils of the undivided church: their canons and dogmatic decrees, together with the canons of all the local synods which have received ecumenical acceptance*. Seven Ecumenical Councils, Second Series, Nicene and Post-nicene Fathers 14, New York 1900/ Peabody Mass. 1995², https://www.ccel.org/ccel/schaff/npnf214.vii.vi.xiii.html (accessed 30.10.2022).

Pohl, Walter. 2005/2010. "Theodelinde." Germanische Altertumskunde Online: Kulturgeschichte bis ins Frühmittelalter – Archäologie, Geschichte, Philologie, edited by Sebastian Brather, Wilhelm Heizmann and Steffen Patzold, 412–413. Berlin: De Gruyter. https://www.degruyter.com/data base/GAO/entry/RGA_5702/html (accessed 30.10.2022).

Pohl, Walter. 2018. *The Avars. A Steppe Empire in Central Europe, 567–822*. Ithaca/London: Cornell University Press.

Roach, Levi. 2021. *Forgery and Memory at the End of the First Millennium*. Princeton: Princeton University Press.

Semmler, Josef. 1986. "Die Aufrichtung der karolingischen Herrschaft im nördlichen Burgund im VIIIe Jahrhundert." In *Aux origines d'une seigneurie ecclésiastique. Langres et ses évêques VIIIe–XIe siècles. Actes des Colloques Langres-Ellwangen, Langres, 28 juin 1985*, 19–40. Langres : Société historique et archéologique de Langres.

Sharpe, Richard. 1984. "Some problems concerning the organization of the church in early medieval Ireland." *Peritia* 3:230–270.

Štih, Peter. 2021. "Der heilige Maximilian von Celeia, die Maximilianszelle und die Anfänge der Karantanenmission." *Mitteilungen der Gesellschaft für Salzburger Landeskunde* 160/161:38–58.

Störmer, Wilhelm. 1986. "Bischöfe von Langres aus Alemannien und Bayern. Beobachtungen zur monastischen und politischen Geschichte im ostrheinischen Raum des 8. Und frühen 9. Jahrhunderts." In *Aux origines d'une seigneurie ecclésiastique. Langres et ses évêques VIIIe–XIe siècles. Actes des Colloques Langres-Ellwangen, Langres, 28 juin 1985*, 45–74. Langres : Société historique et archéologique de Langres.

Streich, Gerhard. 1984. *Burg und Kirche während des deutschen Mittelalters. Untersuchungen zur Sakraltopographie von Pfalzen, Burgen und Herrensitzen Teil I: Pfalz- und Burgkapellen bis zur staufischen Zeit*. Vorträge und Forschungen, Sonderband 29,1. Ostfildern: Jan Thorbecke.

Vogel, Lothar. 2000. *Vom Werden eines Heiligen. Eine Untersuchung der Vita Corbiniani des Bischofs Arbeo von Freising*. Arbeiten zur Kirchengeschichte 77. Berlin: Walter de Gruyter.

Winckler, Katharina. 2012. *Die Alpen im Frühmittelalter: Die Geschichte eines Raumes in den Jahren 500 bis 800*. Wien: Böhlau.

Winckler, Katharina. 2019. "The Territory of the Bishop: Ritual and Diocesan Boundaries in Early Medieval Bavaria." In *Power in landscape. Geographic and digital approaches on historical research*, edited by Mihailo Popović, Veronika Polloczek, Bernhard Koschicek, Stefan Eichert, 33–44. Leipzig: Eudora.

Wolfram, Herwig. 1995. *Salzburg, Bayern, Österreich. Die Conversio Bagoariorum et Carantanorum und die Quellen ihrer Zeit*. Wien: Oldenbourg Verlag.

Wolfram, Herwig. 2012. *Conversio Bagoariorum et Carantanorum: Das Weißbuch der Salzburger Kirche über die erfolgreiche Mission in Karantanien und Pannonien*. Ljubljana: Slovenska akdemija znanosti in umetnosti Zveza zgodovinskih društrev Slovenije.

Wood, Ian. 1994. *The Merovingian Kingdoms 450–751*. London: Longman.

Wood, Ian. 2001. *The missionary life: saints and the evangelisation of Europe, 400–1050*. Harlow: Pearson.

Julio Escalona
The Tenth-Century Castilian Church in the Wider Iberian Context: The Large Gap between Ideal and Reality

Abstract: The ecclesiastical organisation of the County of Castile shows an acute contrast with the patterns inherited from the Visigothic period. The Visigothic Church was a large-scale, complex organisation, founded upon a strong episcopate. There were a large number of monasteries, some of them great houses with strong connections to the ecclesiastical hierarchies, but also many small, ill-known foundations, whose subordination to their bishops was not an easy task. The Visigothic period produced a complex body of legislation, as well as liturgical and disciplinary texts, that were copied and circulated in the kingdom of León in the tenth century. However, despite the emphasis made by Spanish and foreign traditional historians to unveil the tenth-century process of restoration of the ideal Visigothic past, the reality seems to point in quite another direction. The County of Castile is an extreme example of how the Church of the Kingdom of León developed its own organisational structure, and one that was far removed from its Visigothic predecessor. Bishops and monasteries operated in a remarkably different way, and they produced a territorial pattern that was hard to adapt to the ideal fostered by the Gregorian reform, by the late eleventh century.

Bishops are a familiar feature of the social landscape of Late Antiquity and the Early Middle Ages. Our sources present them carrying out a leading role in a variety of aspects of the high ecclesiastical and secular politics as well as in the daily life of their communities. Yet, no single pattern will fit each and every bishop. Their significance and influence varies dramatically from one region and one moment to another. In this article, I aim to briefly examine the ninth- to tenth-century Castilian Church, a case that not only reveals the extent to which the roles of bishops were determined by their socio-political context, but also presents an acute contrast between past traditions and present realities.

1 Echoes from the Past

1.1 The Inheritance from Late Antiquity

In its heyday, around the mid-seventh century, the Hispanic Church was a major component of the ecclesiastical map of the post-Roman West, along with the Churches of North Africa, Gaul and Italy, and developed a strongly idiosyncratic doctrinal, liturgical, and intellectual tradition. As in other regions of the West, the organisation of the Visigothic Church mirrored that of the Late Roman state. The episcopate was structured on two levels: the province, governed by a metropolitan, and the dioceses, by a bishop. This scheme remained operational despite the fact that the extent of the provinces – along with their number – evolved at a pace marked by political events such as the creation of the Suevic kingdom in Galicia, or the Byzantine take-over of the Southeast, both of which severed significant blocks of the territory of *Hispania*.[1] At the second level, the theoretical equation between bishopric and city, with its dependent territory, only worked in those regions of *Hispania* where city-to-countryside links remained operative, and much less so in those regions, particularly the Iberian northwestern quadrant, where the urban network had ceased being the basic matrix for territorial control.[2] Nevertheless, the episcopate (the role of the abbots of major monasteries is comparatively little known), formed a tightly knit power elite that governed Church and kingdom and often provided the latter with the minimum institutional framework necessary to keep feuding and rivalries among the secular aristocracy at bay.[3] Law making, whether ecclesiastical or secular, was largely a task for the clerics, as was the legitimation of royal power. The council canons describe a strongly centralised Church, firmly submitted to the episcopate.[4] However, the generally idealistic character of Visigothic legislation (whether secular or ecclesiastical) calls for sound scepticism regarding practice.[5] In less urbanised regions, the local presence of the bishops may have been much less capillary, and monasteries – especially those of middle and small rank – may have been more autonomous than the canons would suggest.

---

1 Barbero 1992.
2 Díaz 2000.
3 See Arce 2011, 261–281.
4 Díaz 2014.
5 Díaz and Valverde 2000.

1.2 A Northwestern Periphery

Regional variation is a crucial factor in understanding not only the Church, but also the whole structuration of the Visigothic kingdom.[6] The Toledan kings' realm was an amalgamation of territories with very different geographical, economic and social conditions. The actual drivers of the political system – and home to the kingdom's strongest aristocracies – were *Baetica* and *Septimania*, and to a lesser extent the middle and lower Ebro valley and the rest of the Mediterranean coastal strip. By contrast, the economies of the inlands were much less dynamic, and the urban decline was much more intense. The opposite end of this scale was the northwest, that is, the Late Roman province *Gallaecia*, which comprised all the lands from Iberia's central mountain range to the shore (roughly modern Galicia, Castilla y León, Asturias, Cantabria and the north of Portugal).[7] This region was significantly less developed, even in pre-Roman times, and the urbanization promoted by Rome produced a network of oversized municipal territories that articulated a mass of local economies that were strongly dependent on the workings of the state. In turn, the demise of Roman rule in the early fifth century meant a blow that the region would never recover from.[8] After the Suevi cut off the extreme northwest, the plateau suffered a profound crisis. The largest and most lavish Roman *villae* were abruptly and definitively abandoned.[9] The cities suffered a sharp decline and fortified settlements (*castra*) proliferated in the surrounding rural areas.[10] The trade circuit that operated in the so-called Atlantic Arc until the sixth century prolonged a certain economic pulse in the coastal ports from Portugal to the Gulf of Biscay, but with little capillary penetration in the interior.[11]

This territorial fragmentation had an ecclesiastical dimension too. In the small, highly fragmented Suevic kingdom, an episcopate independent from the rest of *Hispania* allowed a relatively large number of bishoprics to emerge in the course of the sixth century, some of them in secondary locations.[12] By contrast, in the eastern half of *Gallaecia* (roughly from the modern province of Palencia to the east), the Hispanic episcopate did not bow to the sweeping fragmentation process, and kept a firm grip on the creation of new bishoprics, even dismantling those

---

6 Wickham 2005, 37–41; Koon and Wood 2009.
7 Díaz 2006.
8 Escalona 2006.
9 Chavarría Arnau 2007.
10 Castellanos García and Martín Viso 2005; Escalona 2006.
11 Fernández Fernández 2014; Quirós Castillo et al. 2009; Sánchez-Pardo 2020.
12 Díaz 2011, 230–244; Sánchez-Pardo 2014.

that emerged more or less spontaneously.[13] This was a general trend in the post-Roman West that the Iberian bishops had long tried to block, as the well-known fifth-century episodes of the letter from the towns of the Upper Ebro valley to Pope Hilarius, and Silvanus of Calahorra's episcopal ordinations, revealed.[14] Consequently, for most of the sixth century, Palencia was the single bishopric east of Astorga, and only at the end of the century, and after the conversion of Reccared in the III Council of Toledo (589), a crown of new sees appeared around it: Ávila, Segovia, Osma and Oca.[15] This pattern reflects profound territorial changes. The regional capital, Clunia, vanished almost completely,[16] and the sees of Osma and Oca were both born on second-order settlements.[17] The case of *Auca* (Oca) is especially striking. Why *Auca*, of all places, when there were other more suitable settlements nearby, some of which – such as *Virovesca* (modern Briviesca) – had already cherished aspirations to the episcopal rank in the fifth century?[18]

2 A New Landscape

The Arab conquest of 711 destroyed the Visigothic state and replaced it with another where the Christian Church played the diminished political role of channelling relations between the rulers and the conquered population. This demise, preceded by that of the North African Church, drastically modified the map of Latin Christendom, leaving Francia and Rome as the only major players (albeit with a growing presence of the insular Churches).[19] The leverage of the Hispanic Church dropped accordingly, as evidenced from the 780s by the political implications of the Adoptionist controversy.[20] However, between the eighth and tenth centuries, in the regions of Iberia under Muslim rule, the episcopate remained active. The Toledan metropolitan and primate continued to be the head of the Iberian Church, although, over the ninth century, Toledo gradually became increasingly peripheral and the ecclesiastical centrality moved to the old *Baetica*, where the Ummayad

---

13 Martin 1998.
14 Vilella Massana 1994; Castellanos García 1997.
15 Díaz 2008.
16 Cepas Palanca 2006.
17 Martín Viso 1999. On the archaeological context of Osma, see Dohijo 2010, 224–226.
18 Escalona 2006, 191–192.
19 Moorhead 2015, 260–261.
20 D'Abadal i de Vinyals 1949; Barbero 1984; Isla Frez 1998; Isla Frez 2004; Chandler 2002; Deswarte 2010.

state power resided.[21] The bishops interacted with their Muslim rulers, controlled their communities, held councils, and often kept in contact with their continental counterparts. These religious leaders seem to have cherished the notion of a unitary *Hispania* that in the discourse of the clerical sources became identified more with the "Church of *Hispania*", and less with a "Kingdom of the Goths" that had gradually turned into a feature of the past. Ideal and reality, though, were not quite in accordance. Whatever authority the episcopate could claim over all of *Hispania*, during the eighth century their grip on the regions beyond the frontiers of Al-Andalus clearly faded out.[22]

In parallel, northwest Iberia became even more peripheral. After the Arab take-over and the failure of the conquerors to control the northwest, state power disappeared altogether to be replaced by an amalgam of micro-territorial identities, based either on what remained of the cities and their hinterlands, or on rural districts.[23] Across this vast and internally diverse region, the situation of the Church is known only in a very fragmentary way. Historians more or less agree that within the territory of modern Galicia some sort of ecclesiastical network, even if highly fragmented, lived on; some bishoprics persisted, although the fate of the urban sites in this period remains largely in obscurity, and a conservative ecclesiastical culture survived, as evidenced in the survival of ancient book production and charter writing traditions, for example.[24] Some consensus exists too on the fact that in the core of the Asturian kingdom (modern Asturias and western Cantabria) a new ecclesiastical organisation emerged, closely linked to the monarchy. Although naturally moulded on the Hispanic tradition, this branch was more open to Frankish influence, especially between the 780s and the 840s.[25] Conversely, on the situation of the plateau there is hardly a consensus. The once popular notion of a wholesale depopulation is now entirely discredited, but any overall image of plateau settlement in this period is largely hypothetical.[26] Some Late An-

---

21 Aillet 2010, 45–48. 69–80.
22 Escalona 2004; Isla Frez 2004.
23 Martín Viso 2021. With this general panorama, it may seem ironic that the bulk of the surviving textual and monumental evidence of the Iberian Church prior to AD 1000 comes precisely from the region least connected to the rest of the former Visigothic territory. This must be attributed to the almost total loss of the Latin manuscript production from the rest of Iberia (except the Pyrenean foothills and the Frankish-dominated Catalan counties), as well as to the destruction of most of the Christian buildings that took place from the eleventh century onwards, a time by which the Christian population of Al-Andalus had dwindled to a minimum.
24 On charters, see Davies 2019; on books, Rodríguez Díaz 2011.
25 Isla Frez 1998; Bronisch 1999.
26 Escalona and Martín Viso 2020.

tique urban centres, such as Astorga or León, might have continued in operation,²⁷ but the archaeological evidence is still too thin to allow for nuance, and there is precious little evidence about episcopal structures.²⁸

A combination of factors forced a drastic turn in the second half of the ninth century. On the one hand, after a phase of internal reinforcement during Alfonso II's reign (791–842), the Asturian monarchy began to incorporate the lands south of the Cantabrian mountains under Ordoño I (850–866), a process during which the kingdom transformed itself into a more complex political aggregate. On the other hand, in Al-Andalus Emir 'Abd-al-Rahmān II (822–852) carried out a policy of centralisation based on taxation.²⁹ While this strengthened the tightly knit Cordoban power circles, it generated much contestation too. In parallel, the fiscal pressure upon the Christian population also accelerated the ongoing process of conversion to Islam. At some point in the ninth century, the Christians gradually turned from being the vast majority of the population of Al-Andalus into a diminishing minority by the mid-tenth century.³⁰ This threatened the position of the remaining Christians, at about the same time that the Carolingian monarchs ceased to be a significant reference for those who hoped to eventually rid themselves of their Muslim rulers.³¹ While this sentiment was probably shared for a long time by most Andalusi Christians, a small fraction of them turned to more exalted positions in the 850s, giving rise to the so-called movement of the voluntary martyrs.³² The representativeness of those radical militants was probably very uneven. In Córdoba, where they seem to have been relatively numerous and the Church played a delicate game of balance vis-a-vis central power, the radicals could be perceived by most of the hierarchy as a nuisance, if not a liability. By contrast, in Toledo, with a long-running history of rebelliousness against Córdoba, they found much more support, hence the strong political gesture of choosing as metropolitan none other than Eulogio of Córdoba, the key leader of the martyrs movement (although he was executed before he could take office).

---

27 González González 2017.
28 Gutiérrez González 2006.
29 Acién and Manzano 2009; Manzano 2015.
30 The classical reference on conversion – though much contested – is Bulliet 1979; see also Manzano 2006, 287–292. On the legal dimensions of conversion see Fernández Félix and Fierro 2001.
31 Since the late eighth century, Charlemagne and Louis the Pious had promoted a discourse according to which the Visigothic kingship had ended at the hands of the unfaithful due to their own sins, and the only hope of recovery for the Iberian Christians was the king of the Franks, as champion of Christianity. See Barbero and Vigil 1978, 240–242; Escalona 2004, 229–232; Conant 2014.
32 The bibliography is abundant. See Wolf 1988; Coope 1995; Christys 2002; See also Isla Frez (2015) for a particularly sharp analysis.

In the following decades, a completely new situation unfolded. The Andalusi emirs' position deteriorated in an unprecedented way and a wave of rebellions followed one after the other, until in the 920s 'Abd-al-Rahmān III brought the situation under control again. In parallel, and probably drawing on a previous relationship between the Asturian kings and the people of Toledo (recalcitrant rebels against Córdoba), groups of Andalusi radical clerics migrated northwards, where they became the designers of a complete ideological renovation of the Asturian monarchy. By transplanting to Asturias the expectations cherished by many southern Christians of a "Visigothic revival" that would do away with Muslim rule,[33] they developed the backbone of the Neo-Gothic identity that would become the signature of the Kingdom of León for centuries. The finest product of this "new deal" were the so-called Chronicles of Alfonso III,[34] a wholesale update of the Asturian history carefully tailored to serve the purposes of a monarchy that, by claiming to be destined to expel the Muslims from Iberia, actually called for a unanimous acceptance of their rule by the northern Christians, within their realm and beyond.

Just as the Asturian monarchs took the Visigothic kings as their model, their Church looked up to their ancient predecessors too. Manuscripts circulating across the northwest from the early tenth century reveal that the fundaments of the Toledan ecclesiastical regime – councils, liturgical material, monastic rules, hagiographical works – were known and studied in at least some of the northern ecclesiastical centres.[35] The ideal of restoring the secular and ecclesiastical order of the Kingdom of Toledo is pervasive in the Asturian chronicles, but the kind of Church that actually developed there was not really an Isidoran one. Firstly, there were no metropolitans (as was to be expected, given that the metropolitan sees that had held authority over parts of the region in the past – Braga, Mérida, Tarragona and Toledo – all remained under Muslim rule and beyond the reach of the Asturian king). Secondly, any attempt to restore the ancient bishoprics had to face the fact that new centres like Oviedo, Santiago or León had emerged and were now key components of the ecclesiastical map, which rendered the task pointless.[36] With all this in mind, shortly after 880, one anonymous author composed a poem in praise of King Alfonso III that eventually closed the so-called Crónica Albeldense,[37] and which presented the monarch surrounded by a circle of bishops in

---

33 García Moreno 1999; Deswarte 2001.
34 Bonch Reeves 2016; Isla Frez 2019; Cf. Deswarte 2003.
35 Díaz y Díaz 1969.
36 Fernández Conde 2008, 349–356; De Ayala Martínez 2008, 150–172.
37 On the poem's original position in the chronicle see Gil, Moralejo and Ruiz de la Peña 1985, 93.

the apostolic number of twelve.[38] With a minimum of words, the poem deploys the fundamentals: the transfer of sees from Muslim-controlled regions explains the demise of Braga in favour of Lugo and of Dumio in favour of Mondoñedo. Santiago is explained as a transfer from Iria, while other novelties, like Oviedo or León, just go unaccounted for. Finally, but not less interestingly, the depiction of the eastern side of the kingdom suggests that the poet tiptoed in haste around the issue: east of León only two sees are recorded: Osma and Veleia. I have suggested elsewhere that this duet does not reflect necessarily the existence of two bishoprics, but rather the fact that at this time two distinct political units existed on the eastern fringes of the kingdom: Castile and Álava.[39] To this must be added the fact that other sees, like Palencia, Salamanca or Simancas, were assigned bishops, sometimes ephemerally, in the following decades. No neo-Gothic ideal would fully represent the landscapes of *Realpolitik* in the late ninth-century Iberian northwest.

Nevertheless, at least from the time of Alfonso III (866–910), the Asturian kings and their ecclesiastical aides initiated a political programme aimed at strengthening the organisation of the Church, even if they necessarily had to build upon the actual framework of an extremely undeveloped episcopal network, and a cloud of monasteries (mostly in the hands of various secular powers) that rarely worked at more than a micro-regional scale, but had great capacity to reach into the localities. This situation must have conditioned the earliest developments, which seem to have been aimed not so much at reinforcing the direct agency of bishops themselves as at ensuring the creation of a high sphere of very powerful monasteries – such as Sahagún, Celanova or Escalada – which were strongly connected to the king and his bishops, even if the main aristocratic families never ceased to interfere. In terms of material culture, the spread of lavish religious buildings in the so-called Mozarabic style, directly or indirectly promoted by the monarchy in the central decades of the tenth century, may well be marking the elevation of this upper

---

38 *ITEM NOTITIA EPISCOPORUM CUM SEDIBUS SUIS: Regiamque sedem Ermenegildus tenet / Flaianus Bracare Luco episcopus arce / Rudesindus Dumio Mendunieto degens / Sisnandus Hyrie sancto Iacobo polens / Naustique tenens Conimbrie sedem / Brandericus quoque locum Lamecense / Sabastianus quidem sedis Auriense / Iustusque similiter in Portucalense / Albarus Uelegie Felemirus Uxome / Maurus Legione necnon Ranulfus Astorice / Prefatique presules in eclesie pleue / Ex regis prudentia emicant clare / Rex quoque clarus omni mundo factus / Iam supra fatus Adefonsus uocatus / Regni culmine datus, belli titulo abtus, / Clarus in Astures, fortis in Uascones, / Ulciscens Arabes et protegens ciues, / Cui principi sacra sit uictoria data, / Christo duce iubatus semper clarificatus / Polleat uictor seculo, fulgeat ipse celo, / Deditus hic triumpho, preditus ibi regno. Amen. Chronicon Albeldensis*, XII (ed. Gil, Moralejo and Ruiz de la Peña 1985, 158).
39 Escalona 2020, 172–174.

layer of major monastic houses that were the true backbone of the Leonese Church before the Gregorian reformation.[40]

3 Castile: A Periphery within a Periphery

When considered in this multi-scalar context, the Church within the county of Castile represents an extreme version of the same contradiction between the Visigothic ideal and a much more unarticulated reality that has been described above for the Asturian-Leonese Church more generally. The widespread vision of Castile as a mere administrative district of the Asturian kingdom is not, to my mind, a very useful point of departure.[41] Castile is better understood as a frontier satellite principality. Its rulers only very rarely claimed formal autonomy from their kings (for example, they never assumed a royal title until the takeover by the Pamplonese dynasty in 1038),[42] but the landed resources that the Leonese monarchs employed elsewhere in the kingdom to secure the allegiance of the different regional elites[43] were entirely lacking in Castile, where there simply was no royal property to redistribute, and what little revenues could be collected in the king's name – such as judicial fees – never actually reached his hands. The acceptance of royal superiority in Castile was not a matter of top-down imposition, but rather the result of a political consensus to create a stable scenario for the regional aristocrats.[44]

A passage of the Chronicle of Alfonso III that describes the extension that the kingdom had in the time of Alfonso I (739–757) mentions Castile among other territorial units, such as Asturias [de Santillana], Trasmiera, Sopuerta or Carranza, that seem to have constituted the micro-regional breakdown of the realm.[45] Castile however, was not exactly like the others. Firstly, it was a recently coined spatial notion: "*Bardulies qui nunc appellatur Castella*". Since there is no clear evidence of a territory called Bardulias before the eighth century, this appears to be an attempt to account for the rise of a new unit, through an antiquarian reference to the pre-Roman tribe of the Varduli. Rather than as a specific territory, Castile should be understood as the shifting space occupied by a network of poorly understood, small-scale aristocracies that emerged throughout the ninth century at the inter-

---

40 Rielo Rincón 2017. On the term, see the critical reassessment by Caballero Zoreda and Moreno Martín 2016.
41 See a paramount example in Martínez Díez 2004.
42 Estepa Diez 2007.
43 On this issue see especially Carvajal Castro 2017; Martín Viso and Carvajal Castro 2013.
44 Escalona 2016.
45 *Chronica Adefonsi tertii regis* 14 (ed. Gil, Moralejo and Ruiz de la Peña 1985, 132–133).

face between a series of regional powers: the Asturian kingdom, the kingdom of Pamplona, the Muslim powers of the Middle Ebro valley (either the Emirate and their delegates or the rebels who opposed them), and other networks of related warlords, such as Álava.[46] Secondly, while the other territories mentioned in the chronicle remained basically unchanged, Castile expanded enormously within two generations. Roundabout the 860s it must have been little more than a handful of valleys in the north of the modern province of Burgos; by the 880s it had expanded southwards as far as Burgos and Castrojeriz, while probably also incorporating an undetermined amount of territory towards the Cantabrian see; in the early tenth century it had reached the main strongholds on the Duero river, by which time the reaction of the Caliphate led to the creation of a stable frontier on the upper Duero valley. Such an expansion clearly indicates that Castile was not just another administrative district and that whatever political identity was associated to the name Castile, it did not refer to a defined territory, but to the space eventually controlled by the aristocratic compound ruled by the counts of Castile.[47]

The political development of Castile can be broken down in three phases. From the mid-ninth century to the 880s, it was a small territory – or rather a small network of warrior elites – under a ruler who held a theoretically unmediated relationship of subordination to the Asturian kings (hence the title "count"). In the 880s, a period of instability (often called "the first fitna") started in Al-Andalus. With rebellions sprouting everywhere, the emirs lost control of the Ebro valley, which fell in the hands of warlord networks. This seems to have given the warrior elites of Castile and Álava the opportunity to expand. Expansion began under Count Diego Rodríguez, but, tellingly, after his death in 885 a new phase opened when a number of individuals claimed the title of count and apparently competed for supremacy among themselves.[48] This phase lasted until the 920s and by the end of it Castile had roughly achieved the territorial extension that it would maintain for the rest of the comital period, until 1038. Around 930, when the most significant protagonists of that generation of competition and territorial growth were already dead, the territory so abruptly acquired could just as well have exploded into multiple small principalities of a size similar to the northern territories mentioned above. It did not, though. By 932 a single leadership had been restored under Count Fernán González (932–970). I have suggested elsewhere that traditional explanations for this outcome, such as an imposition by King Ramiro II, and/or

---

[46] On this view of the ninth-century frontier dynamics, see Larrea Conde and Pastor Díaz de Garayo 2012; Lorenzo Jiménez 2007, and Escalona (2023).
[47] Escalona (2023).
[48] Martín Viso 2002; Estepa Díez 2009; Santos Salazar 2018; Quirós Castillo 2021.

the emergence of a particularly able and charismatic leader, have no documentary support and are even at odds with the rationale of Leonese royal authority at the time.[49] The move to establish and maintain a single rule over such a huge territory should be seen as a push for unity by the regional aristocracies that had thitherto been competing. There is no space here to address the socio-political rationale underlying this decision. Suffice it to say that it opened a period of strong centralisation, focused on the comital seat of Burgos, where the main secular and ecclesiastical elites formed a rather stable halo around the count, giving way to a comital dynasty that lasted four generations, until 1029.

One could legitimately question the extent to which there was a Castilian Church before 932 or rather a series of unconnected religious institutions. The only episcopal see clearly evidenced is Valpuesta, but the extent of episcopal authority beyond the domains of their monastic headquarters is unclear (see below). The most visible elements in the documentary record are a large number of small monasteries, whose interests ranged from the strictly local to the micro-regional. Apparently, they were connected to secular elites of varying relevance, and their subjection to any higher authority probably was little more than formal, if at all. However, already in the late ninth century there are traces of monastic hierarchisation processes, with some houses gaining control of smaller ones.[50] Unlike the mid-Ebro valley, where some monastic houses are known to have had libraries and active *scriptoria*, in Castile charter making was probably widespread, but there are hardly any traces of codex production before the tenth century.[51] However, there are documentary hints such as the charter of 867 in which Abbot Guisando bequeathed to his monastery of Orbañanos "…libros […] id est: antiphonario, missale, comnico, ordinum, orationum, ymnorum, psalterium, canticorum, precum, passionum".[52] Do we need to assume that all books in circulation in ninth-century Castile had to be of foreign provenance?

---

49 Escalona 2016; Escalona (2023).
50 On the complex relationship between monasteries, local communities and elites in early Castile, see, among many others, Peña Bocos 1993; Díez Herrera 1994; Martín Viso 2000; Larrea Conde 2007a; Díez Herrera 2007; Larrea Conde 2008; Escalona 2020.
51 Scraps of a ninth-century treatise on medicine/divination are preserved among the leaves of the *Cartulario Gótico de Valpuesta*, a facticious codex that also contains tenth-century material. This of course, does not imply that it was written there, nor that the book circulated in northern Castile in the ninth century. See Ruiz Asencio, Ruiz Albi, and Herrero Jiménez 2010, 1:153–156; For a possible remainder of a codex that could have belonged to the monastery of Orbañanos, see Fernández Flórez and Serna 2017, 1:47–48.
52 *BGal* 424 (www.ehu.eus/galicano/id424 [accessed 30.10.2022]). See Fernández Flórez and Serna 2017, 1:44–45.

3.1 Where Are the Castilian Bishops?

The most obvious constraint in investigating the early Castilian bishops is that virtually all extant charters are of monastic provenance.[53] There are no traces of episcopal archives before the foundation of Burgos Cathedral in 1075. Historians have gone to great extents in order to identify the Castilian sees and their bishops in the extant monastic charters, and they have had to face the fact that the individuals that bear the title *episcopus* most frequently do not express their see, unlike their Leonese counterparts.[54] The aforementioned widespread assumption that the kings of León and their officers, the counts of Castile, sought to restore the episcopal pattern of the Visigothic period, led to an intricate jigsaw puzzle, because each bishop recorded in the sources had to be assigned to one of three sees: Oca, Valpuesta (allegedly successor to the ancient see of Osma), or Muñó (an innovation from the Visigothic tradition). Episcopal lists were thus composed for all three sees.[55]

In a recent publication, I have argued that a critical re-assessment of the sources leads to different conclusions.[56] Of the aforesaid episcopal sees, only Valpuesta presents long-term connections to bishops, although the evidence is clearer for the late ninth to mid-tenth centuries than later, and there is little to say about their territorial outreach. There are no reliable mentions of bishops of Oca throughout the comital period, except for a few documents from San Millán de la Cogolla that seem to have been doctored in the eleventh century or later. The case of Muñó (modern Villavieja de Muñó, Burgos) is particularly striking. The best known Muñó bishop is Basilio, in the mid-tenth century. However, no extant charter de-

---

53 Only a series of ninth- to tenth-century charters issued by or for the bishops of Valpuesta are preserved in the cartulary of their monastery of Santa María de Valpuesta. Likewise, a set of eleventh-century charters linked to the bishops of Burgos seem to have remained at the archive of San Pedro de Cardeña, and ultimately found their way into its cartulary too. For Valpuesta, see Ruiz Asencio, Ruiz Albi, and Herrero Jiménez 2010, docs. 6. 8. 10–12. 14–15. 16. 18–19. 32–35; for Cardeña, see Fernández Flórez and Serna 2017, 1:195–196.
54 The bishops are not alone in this. Abbots only rarely mention their monastery, and aristocrats do not express any territorial reference. Likewise, synchronisms in dating clauses only mention the king (of León or Oviedo) and the count of Castile. There are very rare exceptions, like a San Millán charter of 952 that mentions the king, the count, and the bishop of Valpuesta in the synchronisms: *Regnante rex Ordonio in Legione, et comite Fredinando Gundessalvez in Castella; Didaco episcopus, in Valle Posita*. BGal 423 (www.ehu.eus/galicano/id423 [accessed 30.10.2022]). On the problems of the Castilian charter corpus, see Escalona 2012; Escalona 2016.
55 See, in general, Serrano 1935; and more specifically, Martínez Díez 1984; Carriedo Tejedo 2002; Dorronzoro 2013.
56 Escalona 2020.

clares a connection of Basilio to Muñó, nor the mere existence of a bishopric there. The whole idea derives from an *explicit* in a codex of 949 from Cardeña, that has Basilio holding the episcopate in the see of the castle of Muñó.[57] The fact that at that time Basilio was using the castle of Muñó as his see obviously does not imply that there was a stable bishopric there. Muñó is no more a stable bishopric than the see of Sasamón, cited ephemerally in the eleventh century, and never to reappear. Yet, much has been made of this mention, by painstakingly seeking Basilio's possible predecessors and successors, thus creating a long-running episcopal series out of thin air.

In short, there is not enough evidence to support the idea that the Church in the county of Castile was at any time organised in three bishoprics. Instead, it seems that a number of individuals carried the episcopal title, but we cannot be certain of how many of them existed at any given moment, nor about the territorial dimensions of their authority, although it seems a fair assumption to see them as members of the high political entourage of the counts.[58] They conceivably followed the counts when they itinerated across the territory. If they had separate territorial jurisdictions, this has left no traces.

3.2 What Did the Castilian Bishops Do?

So, there were multiple bishops in the county of Castile, but what exactly did they do? It is really difficult to see them in action in the roles one would expect from an early medieval prelate. To start with, how they were appointed to office is totally unknown, other than one case of succession from uncle to nephew in Valpuesta in the early tenth century.[59] It makes sense to think of them as members of the Castilian aristocracy, especially from the times of Count Fernán González (932–970) onwards, but this is completely conjectural. As for their actions, in theory one would expect to see bishops ordaining priests and abbots, but again there is no documentary trace of such ceremonies. Consecrating churches is maybe the clearest event when we may expect seeing a bishop in action. However, by contrast to Catalonia,[60] where numerous acts of consecration of churches survive, Castile is again a total

---

[57] *Explicitus est liber iste a notario Sebastiano diacono notum praefixionis diem, quatordecimo kalendas februarii, era DCCCCLXXXVII regnante serenissimo Ramiro in Legione et egregio comite Fredinando Gundisalui in Castella atque pontificatum gerente Basilio episcopo sedis Munnioni Castelli.* (Manchester, John Rylands Library, ms. lat. 89). See Díaz y Díaz 1983, 39.
[58] On this kind of bishops, see Larrea Conde 2007b.
[59] Escalona 2020, 184–185.
[60] Ordeig i Mata 1993–1994.

void. A few charters, though, contain passing mentions of bishops involved in the creation of new churches. For example, in 867, Abbot Guisando recalled that he and his followers had the church of San Juan de Orbañanos built with the blessing of Bishop Felmiro of Valpuesta.[61] This probably implies an episcopal consecration. In contrast, a charter of 937 seems to declare that Abbot Salitus had founded and consecrated the church of San Juan de Boneli in an unspecified time in the past, and then had his actions confirmed by Count Fernán González and Bishop Vincencius.[62]

The Castilian bishops are much more conspicuous instead in what could be called their *political roles*, as figures of authority. For instance, they are seen presiding over courts of justice, and not only in disputes over ecclesiastical matters, but also in secular ones. They take part too in high-level political assemblies, like the one held in 931 when King Alfonso IV – whose power was much contested at the time – made one of a very few royal appearances in Castille and, as a political gesture, confirmed the boundaries of a property to Cardeña, the top Castilian monastery: "*In quo loco plurimis aepiscopis, abbatibus et comitibus fuerunt coniuncti...*".[63] Political assemblies of the comital entourage in which, besides discussing the issues in order, pious gifts were made to the Church, may well be the background of some high-status donations to monasteries involving not only the counts and their noblemen, but also bishops and abbots, even if the charters of donation are all that survives from such gatherings.[64] In fact, in high-status deeds, the witness lists often include one or more bishops accompanied by a narrow circle of abbots – never abbesses – representing the main monasteries, like Cardeña, Arlanza or Valeránica. It seems that aristocrats, abbots, and bishops actually formed the ruling elite of the county.

If the canonical functions of the Castilian bishops are elusive, the diocesan structures are quite invisible. On the one hand, a complete obscurity surrounds the issue of episcopal revenues.[65] To judge by the context, the very few mentions

---

[61] *Ego igitur Guisandus abba simul cum sociis meis aliis fratribus, sub benedictione domno Elmiro episcopo, nunper fabricavimus ecclesia* [...]. BGal 424 (www.ehu.eus/galicano/id424 [accessed 30.10. 2022]).
[62] *Ego, igitur, Salitus abbate* [...] *hedificavi monasterio ad vocatione Sancti Iohanne Baptiste* [...] *hec que condidi et sacravi* [...] *Vincencius episcopus confirman* [...]. BGal 377 (www.ehu.eus/galicano/id377 [accessed 30.10.2022]). See further Escalona 2020, 186.
[63] On the political significance of Leonese royal confirmations, see Carvajal Castro 2017, 75. On the lack of royal property in Castile, see Escalona 2016, 100–101.
[64] On one such possible assembly linked to two donations to monasteries, see Escalona, Velázquez and Juárez 2012, 265.
[65] The only mention of episcopal *tertiae* before the eleventh century refers to the neighbouring territory of Álava, and is dated to as early as 871, but could be a later interpolation. BGal 220

of *decimae* or *primiciae* in charters cannot be interpreted as ecclesiastical, but rather as royal or comital revenues, which were eventually transferred to churches.[66] Moreover, there is hardly any trace of an episcopal clergy.[67] Maybe the most eloquent example is that of Jimeno, who bore the title *archipresbyter*, and worked as a scribe in the first half of the tenth century. He seems to have copied codices at both the *scriptoria* of Valeránica and San Millán de la Cogolla. In 946 he titles himself "archpriest" twice in a San Millán codex (Madrid, RAH, Emil. 25, fol. 160v and 295r). However, there is no trace of Jimeno's activity as a diocesan cleric.[68] All we know about him points instead to monastic contexts. His case seems to indicate that titles such as "archpriest" or "dean" could express the rank or prestige of individual clerics, more than a proper diocesan structure.[69]

3.3 Bishops and Monasteries, a Zero-Sum Relationship?

At this point, it is interesting to establish a contrast with the information from the surviving tenth-century codices. In the first half of this century, at least two of the main monasteries in the county, Cardeña and Valeránica, had *scriptoria* that produced top-quality codices, and were in close communication with other codex-producing centres in the neighbouring Rioja region, such as Albelda or San Millán.[70] More hypothetically, Valpuesta may well have had a *scriptorium* capable of producing codices, and other middle-ranking houses, such as Pedroso, might have too. Contrary to what is usually assumed, I see no firm evidence to support the widespread idea that Silos had an active *scriptorium* in the tenth century, and the evidence for Arlanza is also very thin.[71] While there is nearly no trace of the original Cardeña building, entirely obliterated by its enormous Romanesque and Gothic

---

and 221 (www.ehu.eus/galicano/id220 [accessed 30.10.2022]). Pastor Díaz de Garayo and Larrea Conde 2015, 273–275.

66 See, for example, Condes 71 (1011), a charter only preserved fragmentarily, by which Count Sancho García donated to San Salvador de Oña the village of Solas *cum calumpniis, homicidiis, decimis, primiciis et cum omnibus directuris ad dominium meum pertinentibus*. On this issue see also Gómez Gómez and Martín Viso 2021.

67 Exceptionally, a text from 984 mentions a priest acting as dean of Bishop Munio [...] *decano de episcopo, Oveco, presbiter de Bergale* [...]: *BGal* 221 (www.ehu.eus/galicano/id221 [accessed 30.10. 2022]).

68 Pérez de Úrbel 1977 offers an exceedingly fictionalised reconstruction of Jimeno's biography. An entirely different view in Díaz y Díaz 1979, 115–121.

69 Contrast with the much more organized diocesan clergy of León: Del Ser Quijano 1986.

70 For Cardeña, see Shailor 1978–1979; Martínez Díez 1999; For Valeránica, García Molinos 2004.

71 Escalona 2002, 125–126. For Arlanza, see Díaz y Díaz 1983, 348–349. 415–419.

successors,[72] the extant remains of the long disappeared Valeránica point to the so-called "Mozarabic" style promoted by the monarchy, maybe indicating that this was not only one of the top monasteries in the county, but also well in tune with the general trends of the Leonese Church.[73] Valeránica is exceptional in this respect, but the not so distant Santa María de Retortillo, built in a neat Mozarabic style, of which there is hardly any documentary trace, is a fine reminder that much of our information is lost, and it is advisable not to draw sharp conclusions from the absence of evidence.

The books copied in those centres reveal that there was an intense circulation of exemplars, and that in these regions codices originated in Al-Andalus crossed paths with others of Frankish provenance.[74] Although no antiphonary copied in Castile has survived in its entirety, there are charter mentions to prove they did circulate, as we have seen. If the parallel with the famous León Antiphonary is correct, then the Castilian clerics must have been familiar with rituals such as the *Officium in ordinatione episcopi*,[75] or the *Officium de sacratione baselicae* it contains.[76] In other words, whether they were actually practised in Castile or not, the proper procedures for canonical ordinations and consecrations were known in the region. The same is true of ecclesiastical revenues, such as the first-fruits offerings, for which there is a specific service in the León Antiphonary (*Officium de primitiis*),[77] but also in the Castilian copies of the *Liber Commicus*.[78] The services for tithes and first fruits, therefore, were known in Castile, and surely their underlying legal notions were too.

Since these liturgical texts derive from the Visigothic tradition, as do the collections of council canons and the secular *Liber Iudicum*, one could be easily tempted to put the stress on the neo-Gothic ideal as the main driver of the higher ecclesiastical spheres. However, this should be tested against the evidence of the monastic rules.[79] We simply do not know the normative framework that applied in most of the Castilian monasteries, but it is clear that some *codices regularum* did circulate, especially from the second half of the century, and, for all the weight of the Hispanic tradition, the absolute favourite was none other than the Benedic-

---

72 Menéndez Pidal 1908.
73 Moreno Martín 2015.
74 See an overview in Díaz y Díaz 1969. For a discussion of libraries in the kingdom of León, Díaz y Díaz 1983, 151–246. A quantification by type of book in Díaz y Díaz 1983, 179.
75 Brou and Vives 1959, 448.
76 Brou and Vives 1959, 431–444.
77 Brou and Vives 1959, 370.
78 Pérez de Úrbel and González Ruiz-Zorrilla 1955, LXXXII.
79 Díaz y Díaz 1983, 193–194.

tine rule, particularly through the works of Smaragdus of Saint Mihiel.[80] Historians have long debated to what extent the popularity of Smaragdus reveals an early diffusion of Benedictine observance that predated the stronger wave of Cluniac influence and the Gregorian reform in the eleventh century, or whether it was a mere scholarly component in an ecclesiastical culture otherwise firmly attached to its Visigothic ideal. This line of argument based on contrasting Visigothic vs. Carolingian/Roman influence seems to me to entirely miss the point. The Smaragdus manuscripts and the sporadic mentions of the Benedictine rule in charters should be seen in the light of canon 2 of the Council of Coyanza (1055).[81] Coyanza is often interpreted alternatively as an attempt to restore entirely the ecclesiastical order that was in force in the Visigothic period, or as the end of an era, a sort of forerunner to the Leonese kingdom's joining the Roman rite and the Continental usages to the detriment of the Visigothic tradition under Alfonso VI.[82] However, much of its contents rather suggest the culmination of the tenth-century ecclesiastical organisation, which was not Roman or Carolingian, but neither purely Visigothic. Coyanza 2 established that whenever possible, the kingdom's monasteries should keep to either the Isidoran or the Benedictine rule. If Benedict's rule is only rarely mentioned in tenth-century León, Isidore's is virtually unheard of, but the striking balance that the canon makes between both rules is not the most important aspect of this canon anyway. What is really crucial is that, either rule – each in its own way – emphasizes a model of monasticism that was highly structured: well organised communities, governed by abbots appointed through neatly formal procedures, and firmly subjected to episcopal authority. Coyanza's support of the Benedictine rule needs to be understood in the context of the northwestern Iberian Church, where the bishops did not have the resources to implement a purely diocesan network that reached into the local.[83] In many areas they could not even maintain a clear territorial definition for their bishoprics. The only institutions that penetrated deep into the localities were the monasteries, and it was through them that the bishops exercised control. Castile is an extreme case, with a large number of monasteries of different rank (some hugely powerful), but a very ill-defined episcopacy. In this context, the bishops needed to control the major monas-

---

80 One of the earliest examples is Silos, ms. 1, was copied from a model in caroline script, according to Díaz y Díaz 1983, 468.
81 Coyanza, 2 (Martínez Díez 1992, 117–188): *Deinde statuimus ut omnia monasteria nostra secundum possibilitates suas adimpleant ordinem Sancti Isidori uel Sancti Benedicti et nichil habeant proprium nisi per licentiam sui episcopi aut sui abbatis. Et ipsi abbates suis episcopis sint obedientes* [...].
82 García y García 1988, 386–387; Ayala 2008, 270–283.
83 See also the nuances to this ideal model posed by Mazel 2016.

teries, and the frequency with which their abbots accompany their prelates in charter witness lists suggests that they did constitute a tightly knit clerical ruling elite (though not without tensions, for sure). The only way of strengthening this network was by having the middle- and low-rank monasteries subjected to major ones by means of aggregations. And precisely this process is one of the most visible in the extant charters. All throughout the tenth century, kings, counts and aristocrats favoured the subjection of small monasteries to bigger ones in a continuous movement that was notably accelerated by Fernando I, both before and after the Council of Coyanza.[84] Just as Richard Sharpe dismissed long ago the idea of a purely monastic Irish church, and emphasised the bishops' often overlooked importance,[85] the tenth-century Castilian Church cannot be defined simply by siding along with either bishops or monks. They both operated together and they did so over an almost exclusively rural landscape (only Burgos stands as a noticeable town) with very lax territorial structures.[86] The clerical elites strove to make this system work by reinforcing the monastic networks as well as the links between bishops and abbots. In this kind of system, more powerful monasteries did not necessarily mean weaker bishops as it did in a Carolingian context (and certainly in the Visigothic church too).[87]

4 Conclusion

The tenth-century Castilian Church (as did the Church of the Leonese kingdom, more generally) lived in a permanent contrast between ideal and reality. The ideal was not so much – to my mind – a nostalgic gaze towards the Visigothic past as it was the expectation of a more structured and powerful Church, more strongly connected to royal power, and freer from the ties of the secular aristocracies. Visigothic, Carolingian, or something in between was secondary. In its turn, the reality was the lack of a proper urban-based episcopal network, and the extreme porosity between secular and monastic interests at the local scale. Ultimately, the Gregorian reform would provide the essential drive towards a stronger, more formalised, and more independent Church, but in the tenth century the northwestern Iberian clerics were already pursuing that in their own, alternative ways.

---

[84] Díez Herrera 2007; García de Cortázar 2006; García de Cortázar 2007.
[85] Sharpe 1984.
[86] Escalona 2020, 197–199.
[87] Wood 2006, 198: "Wherever monasteries owned numerous lesser churches, as in Bavaria, or provided most of the pastoral care, as in England, the bishop's authority in his diocese would be much reduced by monastic independence".

Bibliography

Primary Sources

Chronicon Albeldensis: Gil Fernández, Juan, José Luis Moralejo and José Ignacio Ruiz de la Peña, eds. 1985. *Crónicas Asturianas: Crónica de Alfonso III (Rotense y "A Sebastián"), Crónica albeldense (y "profética")*. Oviedo: Universidad de Oviedo.

Chronica Adefonsi tertii regis: Gil Fernández, Juan, José Luis Moralejo and José Ignacio Ruiz de la Peña, eds. 1985. *Crónicas Asturianas: Crónica de Alfonso III (Rotense y "A Sebastián"), Crónica albeldense (y "profética")*. Oviedo: Universidad de Oviedo.

Becerro Galicano: Becerro Galicano Digital – www.ehu.eus/galicano (accessed 30.10.2022).

Ruiz Asencio, José María, Irene Ruiz Albi, and Mauricio Herrero Jiménez. 2010. *Los Becerros Gótico y Galicano de Valpuesta*. 2 Vols. Madrid: Real Academia Española – Instituto Castellano y Leonés de la Lengua.

Secondary Sources

Acién Almansa, Manuel and Manzano Moreno, Eduardo. 2009. "Organización social y administración política en al-Ándalus bajo el emirato." *Territorio, Sociedad, y Poder Anejo* 2:331–348.

Aillet, Cyrille. 2010. *Les mozarabes: christianisme, islamisation et arabisation en Péninsule Ibérique (IXe-XIIe siècle)*. Madrid: Casa de Velázquez.

Arce, Javier. 2011. *Esperando a los árabes. Los visigodos en Hispania (507–711)*. Madrid: Marcial Pons Historia.

Barbero de Aguilera, Abilio. 1984. "Los 'síntomas españoles' y la política religiosa de Carlomagno." *En la España Medieval, 4. Estudios dedicados al profesor d. Angel Ferrari Núñez* 1:87–138.

Barbero de Aguilera, Abilio. 1992. "Las divisiones eclesiásticas y las relaciones entre la Iglesia y el Estado en la España de los siglos VI y VII." In *La sociedad visigoda y su entorno histórico*, edited by Abilio Barbero de Aguilera, 168–197. Madrid: Siglo XXI. Original edition, 1989.

Barbero de Aguilera, Abilio and Marcelo Vigil Pascual. 1978. *La formación del feudalismo en la Península Ibérica*. Barcelona: Crítica.

Bonch Reeves, Ksenia. 2016. *Visions of Unity after the Visigoths. Early Iberian Latin Chronicles and the Mediterranean World*. Turnhout: Brepols.

Bronisch, Alexander Pierre. 1999. "Asturien und das Frankreich zur Zeit Karls des Grossen." *Historisches Jahrbuch* 119:1–40.

Bulliet, Richard W. 1979. *Conversion to Islam in the Medieval Period. An Essay in Quantitative History*. Cambridge, Massachusetts/London: Harvard University Press.

Caballero Zoreda, Luis and Francisco José Moreno Martín. 2016. "Sobre la dimensión epistemológica e histórica de una propuesta historiográfica. El modelo explicativo mozarabista." In *Im Schnittpunkt der Kulturen. Architektur und ihre Austattung auf der Iberischen Halbinsel im 6.-10./11. Jahrhundert (Cruce de culturas. Arquitectura y su decoración en la Península Ibérica del siglo VI al X/XI)*, edited by Ines Käflein, Jochen Staebel and Matthias Untermann, 299–330. Frankfurt/Madrid: Vervuert/ Iberoamericana.

Carriedo Tejedo, Manuel. 2002. "Cronología de los obispos de Castilla en los siglos VIII–X (Osma-Muñó, Veleya-Valpuesta y Oca-Burgos)." *Edad Media. Revista de Historia* 5:69–116.

Carvajal Castro, Álvaro. 2017. *Bajo la máscara del Regnum: la monarquía asturleonesa en León (854–1037)*. Madrid: Consejo Superior de Investigaciones Científicas.

Castellanos García, Santiago. 1997. "Calagurris cristiana. Sobre el concepto ideológico de civitas en la Antigüedad Tardía." *Kalakorikos* 2:55–68.

Castellanos García, Santiago and Iñaki Martín Viso. 2005. "The local articulation of central power in the north of the Iberian Peninsula (500–1000)." *Early Medieval Europe* 13, 1:1–42.

Cepas Palanca, Adela. 2006. "The ending of the Roman City: the case of Clunia in the Northern Plateau." In *People and Space in the Middle Ages, 300–1300*, edited by Wendy Davies, Guy Halsall and Andrew Reynolds, 187–207. Turnhout: Brepols.

Chandler, Cullen J. 2002. "Heresy and Empire: The Role of the Adoptionist Controversy in Charlemagne's Conquest of the Spanish March." *The International History Review* 24, 3:505–527.

Chavarría Arnau, Alexandra. 2007. *El final de las villae en Hispania (siglos IV–VII d. C.)*. Bibliotèque de l'Antiquité Tardive 7. Turnhout: Brepols.

Christys, Anne. 2002. *Christians in al-Andalus, 711–1000*. Richmond (Surrey): Curzon Press.

Conant, Jonathan P. 2014. "Louis the Pious and the contours of empire." *Early Medieval Europe* 22, 3:336–360.

Coope, Jessica. 1995. *The Martyrs of Córboba: Community and Family Conflict in an Age of Mass Conversion*. Omaha, NE: University of Nebraska Press.

D'Abadal i de Vinyals, Ramón. 1949. *La batalla del adopcionismo y la desintegración de la Iglesia Visigoda*. Barcelona. Real Academia de Buenas Letras de Barcelona.

Davies, Wendy. 2019. "Regions and micro-regions of scribal practice." In *Polity and Neighbourhood in Early Medieval Europe*, edited by Julio Escalona, Orri Vésteinsson, and Stuart Brookes, 305–323. Turnhout: Brepols.

De Ayala Martínez, Carlos. 2008. *Sacerdocio y reino en la España altomedieval. Iglesia y poder en el Occidente peninsular, siglos VII–XII*. Madrid: Silex.

Del Ser Quijano, Gregorio. 1986. "La renta feudal en la Alta Edad Media: el ejemplo del cabildo catedralicio de León en el período asturleonés." *Studia Historica. Historia Medieval* 4:59–75.

Deswarte, Thomas. 2001. "La prophétie de 883 dans le royaume d'Oviedo: Attente adventiste ou espoir d'une liberation politique." *Mélange de Science Religieuse* 58:39–56.

Deswarte, Thomas. 2003. *De la destruction à la restauration: l'idéologie du royaume d'Oviedo-León (VIIIe–XIe siècles)*. Cultural Encounters in late Antiquity and the Middle Ages 3. Turnhout: Brepols.

Deswarte, Thomas. 2010. "Une minorité chrétienne en occident: la Chrétienté hispanique et l'adoptianisme." In *Minorités et régulations sociales en Méditerranée médiévale*, edited by Stéphane Boissellier, François Clément and John Victor Tolan, 251–268. Rennes: Presses Universitaires de Rennes.

Díaz, Pablo C. 2000. "City and Territory in Hispania in Late Antiquity." In *Towns and Their Territories between Late Antiquity and the Early Middle Ages*, edited by Gian Pietro Brogiolo, Nancy Gauthier and Neil Christie, 3–35. Leiden/Boston/Köln: Brill.

Díaz, Pablo C. 2006. "*Extremis mundi partibus. Gallaecia* tardoantigua: Periferia geográfica e integración política." In *Comunidades locales y dinámicas de poder en el norte de la Península Ibérica durante la Antigüedad Tardía*, edited by Urbano Espinosa Ruiz and Santiago Castellanos García, 201–216. Logroño: Univ. de La Rioja, Servicio de Publicaciones.

Díaz, Pablo C. 2008. "Sedes episcopales y organización administrativa en la cuenca del Duero (siglos IV–VII)." In *De Roma a los bárbaros: poder central y horizontes locales en la cuenca del Duero*,

edited by Santiago Castellanos García and Iñaki Martín Viso, 123–143. León: Universidad de León.
Díaz, Pablo C. 2011. *El reino suevo (411–585)*. Madrid: Akal.
Díaz, Pablo C. 2014. "Concilios y obispos en la Península Ibérica (siglos VI–VIII)." In *Chiese Locali e Chiese Regionali nell'Alto Medioevo*. Settimane di Studio della fondazione Centro Italiano di Studi sull'Alto Medioevo 61, 1095–1158. Spoleto: Centro Italiano di Studi sull'Alto Medioevo.
Díaz, Pablo C. and María Rosario Valverde. 2000. "The theoretical strength and practical weakness of the Visigothic Monarchy of Toledo." In *Rituals of Power. From Late Antiquity to the Early Middle Ages*, edited by Frans Theuws and Janet Nelson, 59–93. Leiden/Boston: Brill.
Díaz y Díaz, Manuel Cecilio. 1969. "La circulation des manuscrits dans la Péninsule Ibérique du VIIIe au XIe siècle." *Cahiers de civilisation médiévale* 4:219–241/383–392.
Díaz y Díaz, Manuel Cecilio. 1979. *Libros y librerías en la Rioja altomedieval*. Biblioteca de Temas Riojanos. Logroño: Instituto de Estudios Riojanos.
Díaz y Díaz, Manuel Cecilio. 1983. *Códices Visigóticos en la Monarquía Leonesa*. Fuentes y Estudios de Historia Leonesa 31. León: Centro de Estudios e Investigación "San Isidoro".
Díez Herrera, Carmen. 1994. "Las actividades del abad Guisando: Un modelo de organización del espacio en la Castila de Alfonso III." In *La época de Alfonso III y San Salvador de Valdediós*, edited by Francisco Javier Fernández Conde, 165–186. Oviedo: Universidad de Oviedo.
Díez Herrera, Carmen. 2007. "La agregación de monasterios: una forma de organización social del espacio en la Alta Edad Media." In *El monacato en los reinos de León y Castilla (siglos VII–XIII)*, X Congreso de Estudios Medievales, 389–402. León: Fundación Sánchez-Albornoz.
Dohijo, Eusebio. 2010. "Evolución y transformación urbana de las ciudades del alto valle del Duero durante la Antigüedad Tardía." In *Espacios urbanos en el occidente mediterráneo (s. VI–VIII)*, edited by Alfonso García, Ricardo Izquierdo, Lauro Olmo and Diego Peris, 219–228. Toledo: Toletvm Visigodo.
Dorronzoro Ramírez, Pablo. 2013. "La creación de la sede de Burgos en el siglo XI. Una nueva perspectiva " *Estudios Medievales Hispánicos* 2, 2:47–87.
Escalona, Julio. 2002. *Sociedad y territorio en la Alta Edad Media castellana: la formación del alfoz de Lara*. 1079 Vols. Oxford: J&E Hedges.
Escalona, Julio. 2004. "Family Memories. Inventing Alfonso I of Asturias." In *Building legitimacy. Political discourses and forms of legitimation in medieval societies*, edited by Isabel Alfonso, Hugh Kennedy and Julio Escalona, 223–262. Leiden/Boston: Brill.
Escalona, Julio. 2006. "Patrones de fragmentación territorial: el fin del mundo romano en la Meseta del Duero." In *Comunidades locales y dinámicas de poder en el norte de la Península Ibérica durante la Antigüedad Tardía*, edited by Urbano Espinosa and Santiago Castellanos García, 165–200. Logroño: Instituto de Estudios Riojanos.
Escalona, Julio. 2012. "La documentación de la Castilla condal: viejos problemas y nuevas perspectivas." In *Mundos medievales. Espacios, sociedades y poder. Homenaje al Profesor José Ángel García de Cortázar y Ruiz de Aguirre*, edited by Beatriz Arízaga Bolumburu and Jesús Ángel Solórzano, 473–488. Santander: Universidad de Cantabria.
Escalona, Julio. 2016. "In the name of a distant king: representing royal authority in the county of Castile, c.900–1038." *Early Medieval Europe* 24, 1:74–102.
Escalona, Julio. 2020. "Organización eclesiástica y territorialidad en Castilla antes de la reforma gregoriana." In *La construcción de la territorialidad en la Alta Edad Media*, edited by Iñaki Martín Viso, 167–201. Salamanca: Ediciones Universidad de Salamanca.

Escalona, Julio. (2023). "*Estados y señores de la guerra en la Península Ibérica altomedieval: una exploración.*" In *El Estado en la Alta Edad Media. Nuevas perspectivas*, edited by Álvaro Carvajal Castro and Carlos Tejerizo-García, 43–65. Bilbao: Universidad del País Vasco.

Escalona, Julio, Isabel Velázquez Soriano and Paloma Juárez. 2012. "Identification of the sole extant charter issued by Fernán González, Count of Castile (932–970)." *Journal of Medieval Iberian Studies* 4, 1:259–288.

Escalona, Julio and Iñaki Martín Viso. 2020. "The Life and Death of an Historiographical Folly: The Early Medieval Depopulation and Repopulation of the Duero Basin." In *Beyond the Reconquista: New Directions in the History of Medieval Iberia (711–1085)*, edited by Simon Barton and Robert Portass, 21–51. Leiden: Brill.

Estepa Diez, Carlos. 2007. "Castilla de condado a reino." In *Alfonso VI y su época. I. Antecedentes del reinado (966–1065)*, edited by E. Fernández González and J. Pérez Gil, 37–67. Léon: Universidad de Léon, Secr. de Publ.

Estepa Díez, Carlos. 2009. "La Castilla primitiva (750–931): condes, territorios y villas." In *Poder y Simbología en Europa, siglos VIII-X (Actas del Symposium Internacional, Oviedo, 22–27 de septiembre del 2008)*, edited by Francisco Javier Fernández Conde and César García de Castro Valdés, 261–278. Oviedo: Trea.

Fernández Conde, Francisco Javier. 2008. *La Religiosidad Medieval en España. Alta Edad Media (siglos VII–X)*. 2 ed. Oviedo: Trea.

Fernández Félix, Ana and Maribel Fierro. 2001. "Cristianos y conversos al Islam en al-Andalus bajo los Omeyas: Una aproximación al proceso de islamización a través de una fuente legal andalusí del s. III/IX." In *Visigodos y Omeyas: Un debate entre la Antigüedad tardía y la Alta Edad Media*, Anejos de Archivo Español de Arqueología 23, edited by Luis Caballero Zoreda and Pedro Mateos Cruz, 415–428. Madrid: Consejo Superior de Investigaciones Científicas.

Fernández Fernández, Adolfo. 2014. *El comercio tardoantiguo (ss. IV-VII) en el Noroeste peninsular a través del registro cerámico de la ría de Vigo*. Roman and Late Antique Mediterranean Pottery 5. Oxford: Archaeopress.

Fernández Flórez, José Antonio and Sonia Serna Serna, eds. 2017. *El Becerro Gótico de Cardeña: el primer gran cartulario hispánico (1086)*. 2 Vols, 32–33. Burgos: Real Academia Española – Instituto Castellano Leonés de la Lengua.

García de Cortázar y Ruiz de Aguirre, José Ángel. 2006. "Los monasterios del reino de León y Castilla a mediados del siglo XI: un ejemplo de selección de las especies." In *Monjes y Monasterios Hispanos en la Alta Edad Media*, edited by José Ángel García de Cortázar and Ramón Teja, 255–288. Aguilar de Campoo: Fundación Santa María La Real. Centro de Estudios del Románico.

García de Cortázar y Ruiz de Aguirre, José Angel. 2007. "Reyes y abades en el Reino de León (años 910 a 1157)." In *Monarquía y sociedad en el Reino de León. De Alfonso III a Alfonso VII*, Fuentes y estudios de historia leonesa 117–118, edited by José María Fernández Catón, 201–264. León: Centro de Estudios e Investigación "San Isidoro".

García Molinos, Elena. 2004. "Florencio de Valeránica, calígrafo y notario del siglo X." In *El Reino de León en la Edad Media, XL*, Fuentes y Estudios de Historia Leonesa 105, edited by José María Fernández Catón, 241–429. León Centro de Estudios e Investigación "San Isidoro".

García Moreno, Luis Agustín. 1999. "Spanish Gothic consciousness among the Mozarabs in al-Andalus (VIII–Xth centuries)." In *The Visigoths: Studies in Culture and Society*, The medieval Mediterranean 20, edited by Alberto Ferreiro, 303–323. Leiden/Boston/Köln: Brill.

Garcia y García, Antonio. 1988. "Concilios y sínodos en el ordenamiento jurídico del reino de León." In *El reino de León en la Alta Edad Media, I. Cortes, Concilios y Fueros*, Fuentes y Estudios de Historia Leonesa 48, edited by José María Fernández Caton, 360–384. León: Centro de Estudios e Investigación "San Isidoro".

Gómez Gómez, Javier and Iñaki Martín Viso. 2021. "Rationes y Décimas: Evidencias sobre la gestión de las sernas en el siglo XI en el noroeste de la Península Ibérica." *Espacio, Tiempo y Forma. Serie III. Historia Medieval* 34:359–382.

González González, Raúl. 2017. *Élites urbanas y relaciones de poder en Oviedo, León y Astorga durante la Edad Media (siglos IX–XIII)*. Oviedo: Universidad de Oviedo, Departamento de Historia.

Gutiérrez González, J. Avelino. 2006. "Las fuentes arqueológicas informadoras del espacio urbano medieval: la ciudad de León como ejemplo." In *El espacio urbano en la Europa medieval*, edited by José Ángel Solorzano Telechea and Beatriz Arízaga Bolumburu, 77–145. Nájera: Instituto de Estudios Riojanos.

Isla Frez, Amancio. 1998. "El adopcionismo y las evoluciones religiosas y políticas en el Reino Astur." *Hispania* 200:971–993.

Isla Frez, Amancio. 2004. "El adopcionismo. Disidencia religiosa en la Península Ibérica (fines del siglo VIII-principios del siglo IX)." *Clio & Crimen* 1:115–134.

Isla Frez, Amancio. 2015. "Los cristianos exaltados en el siglo IX: sociabilidad y memoria." In *Sociabilidades en la Historia*, edited by Santiago Castillo Alonso and Montserrat Duch Plana, 91–114. Madrid: Catarata.

Isla Frez, Amancio. 2019. *La crónica de Alfonso III y el reino astur*. Oviedo: Trea.

Koon, Sam, and Jamie Wood. 2009. "Unity from disunity: law, rhetoric and power in the Visigothic kingdom." *European Review of History: Revue européenne d'histoire* 16,6:793–808.

Larrea Conde, Juan José. 2007a. "Construir iglesias, construir territorio: las dos fases altomedievales de San Román de Tobillas (Álava)." In *Monasteria et Territoria. Élites, edilicia y territorio en el Mediterráneo medieval (siglos V–XI)*, edited by Jorge López Quiroga, A. M. Martínez Tejera and Jorge Morín de Pablos, BAR International Series, 321–336. Oxford: Archaeopress.

Larrea Conde, Juan José. 2007b. "Obispos efímeros, comunidades y homicidio en La Rioja Alta en los siglos X y XI." *Brocar* 31:177–200.

Larrea Conde, Juan José. 2008. "De la invisibilidad historiográfica a la apropiación del territorio: aldeas y comunidades en la España cristiana (siglos X y XI)." In *Cristiandad e Islam en la Edad Media hispana*, Semana de Estudios Medievales de Nájera 18, edited by José Ignacio De la Iglesia Duarte, 169–207. Logroño: Instituto de Estudios Riojanos.

Larrea Conde, Juan José and Ernesto Pastor Díaz de Garayo. 2012. "*Alaba wa-l Qilāʿ*: la frontera oriental en las fuentes escritas de los siglos VIII y IX." In *Asturias entre visigodos y mozárabes (Visigodos y Omeyas, VI)*, Anejos de Archivo Español de Arqueología 63, edited by Luis Caballero Zoreda, Pedro Mateos Cruz and César García de Castro Valdés, 307–329. Madrid: Consejo Superior de Investigaciones Científicas.

Lorenzo Jiménez, Jesús. 2007. "Los ḥuṣūn de los Banu Qasi: Algunas consideraciones desde el registro escrito." *Brocar* 31:79–105.

Manzano Moreno, Eduardo. 2006. *Conquistadores, Emires y Califas: Los Omeyas y la formación de Al-Andalus*. Barcelona: Crítica.

Manzano Moreno, Eduardo. 2015. "Moneda y articulación social en al-Andalus en época omeya." In *Monnaies du Haut Moyen Âge. Histoire et archéologie (Péninsule Ibérique – Maghreb, VIIe–XIe siècle)*, edited by Philippe Sénac and Sébastien Gasc, 133–155. Toulouse: Méridiennes.

Martin, Céline. 1998. "Las cartas de Montano y la autonomía episcopal de la Hispania septentrional en el siglo VI." *Hispania Antiqua* 22:403–426.

Martín Viso, Iñaki. 1999. "Organización episcopal y poder entre la Antigüedad Tardía y el Medioevo (siglos V–XI): las diócesis de Calahorra, Oca y Osma." *Iberia. Revista de la Antigüedad* 2:151–190.

Martín Viso, Iñaki. 2000. *Poblamiento y estructuras sociales en el norte de la Península Ibérica, siglos VI–XIII*. Salamanca: Universidad de Salamanca.

Martín Viso, Iñaki. 2002. "Poder político y estructura social en la Castilla altomedieval: el condado de Lantarón (siglos VIII–XI)." In *Los espacios de poder en la España medieval*, edited by José Ignacio De la Iglesia Duarte. Semanas de Estudios Medievales de Nájera 12, 533–552. Logroño: Instituto de Estudios Riojanos.

Martín Viso, Iñaki. 2021. "Tiempos de colapso y resiliencia: Espacios sin estado en la Península Ibérica (siglos VIII–X)." *Intus-Legere Historia* 15:78–105.

Martín Viso, Iñaki and Álvaro Carvajal Castro. 2013. "Historias regionales de la repoblación: Los reyes asturleoneses y las 'políticas de la tierra' en el oeste de la meseta del Duero." In *El Historiador y la Sociedad. Homenaje al Profesor José María Mínguez*, edited by Pablo C. Díaz, Fernando Luis Corral and Iñaki Martín Viso, 39–52. Salamanca: Universidad de Salamanca.

Martínez Díez, Gonzalo. 1984. "Los obispados de la Castilla Condal hasta la consolidación del obispado de Oca en Burgos en el Concilio de Husillos (1088)." In *El factor religioso en la formación de Castilla. Simposio organizado por el Excmo. Ayuntamiento de Burgos y la Facultad de Teología en el MC aniversario de la Ciudad (884–1984)*, edited by Saturnino López Santidrián, Publicaciones de la Facultad de Teología del Norte de España Sede de Burgos 50, 87–164. Burgos. Aldecoa.

Martínez Díez, Gonzalo. 1992. "La tradición manuscrita del fuero de León y del concilio de Coyanza." *El Reino de León en la alta Edad Media* 2:117–188.

Martínez Díez, Gonzalo. 1999. "Códices visigóticos del monasterio de Cardeña." *Boletín de la Institución Fernán González* 218, 1:33–48.

Martínez Díez, Gonzalo. 2004. *El Condado de Castilla (711–1038). La Historia frente a la leyenda*. 2 Vols. Valladolid: Junta de Castilla y León.

Mazel, Florian. 2016. *L'Évêque et le territoire: L'invention médiévale de l'espace*. Paris : Éditions du Seuil.

Menéndez Pidal, Juan. 1908. *San Pedro de Cardeña: (restos y memorias del antiguo monasterio)*. New York: The Hispanic Society of America.

Moorhead, John. 2015. *The Popes and the Church of Rome in Late Antiquity*. Routledge Studies in Ancient History 8. New York: Routledge.

Moreno Martín, Francisco José. 2015. "Reflexiones en torno al "scriptorium" de Valeránica y a los fundamentos de la edilicia monástica de la Castilla condal." In *El mundo de los conquistadores. La península Ibérica en la Edad Media y su proyección en la conquista de América*, edited by Martín Federico Ríos Saloma, 803–838. México: UNAM – Ediciones Sílex.

Ordeig i Mata, Ramon. 1993–1994. *Les dotalies de les esglesies de Catalunya (s. IX–XII)*. Vic: Estudis Históricos.

Pastor Díaz de Garayo, Ernesto and Juan José Larrea Conde. 2015. "La "Reja de San Millán": transmisión textual y estructura interna." In *Estudios en homenaje al profesor César González Mínguez*, edited by Iñaki Bazán Díaz, José Antonio Munita Loinaz, Ernesto García Fernández and Ernesto Pastor Díaz de Garayo, 257–297. Bilbao: Universidad del País Vasco

Peña Bocos, Esther. 1993. "Las presuras y la repoblación del valle del Duero: algunas cuestiones en torno a la atribución y organización social del espacio castellano en el siglo IX." In *Repoblación* y reconquista: Actas del III Curso de Cultura Medieval, edited by José Luis Hernando Garrido and Miguel Angel García Guinea, 249–259. Aguilar de Campóo: Fundación Santa María La Real, Centro de Estudios del Románico.

Pérez de Úrbel, Fray Justo. 1977. "El escriba Eximeno y los comienzos del escritorio de San Millán de la Cogolla." *Boletín de la Institución Fernán González* 188:75–95.

Pérez de Úrbel, Fray Justo and Atilano González Ruiz-Zorrilla, eds. 1955. *Liber Commicus*. 2 Vols. Madrid: Consejo Superior de Investigaciones Científicas.

Quirós Castillo, Juan Antonio. 2021. "Arqueología de los condados castellanos. Sociedades locales y prácticas políticas en Lantarón (siglos IX–X)." *Spal* 30, 2:308–339

Quirós Castillo, Juan Antonio, Agustín Azkarate Garai-Olaun, Ramón Bohigas Roldán, Iñaki García Camino, Ángel Luis Palomino Lázaro and José María Tejado Sebastián. 2009. "Arqueología de la Alta Edad Media en el Cantábrico Oriental." In *Medio siglo de arqueología en el Cantábrico Oriental y su entorno*, edited by Armando Llanos, 449–500. Vitoria-Gasteiz: Instituto Alavés de Arqueología.

Rielo Rincón, Marta. 2017. "Arquitectura eclesiástica en León en el Altomedievo. Una lectura a través de los materiales y los documentos." *Arqueología y Territorio Medieval* 23:89–114.

Rodríguez Díaz, Elena E. 2011. "Los manuscritos mozárabes: Una encrucijada de culturas." In *Die Mozaraber. Perspektiven und Definitionen der Forschung*, Geschichte und Kultur der Iberischen Welt 7, edited by Matthias Maser and Klaus Herbers, 75–103. Berlin/Münster/Wien/Zürich/London: LIT Verlag.

Sánchez-Pardo, José Carlos. 2014. "Organización eclesiástica y social en la Galicia Tardoantigua. Una perspectiva geográfico-arqueológica del Parroquial Suevo." *Hispania Sacra* 66, 134:439–480.

Sánchez-Pardo, José Carlos. 2020. "Late Antique Atlantic contacts through the case of Galicia." In *Ceramics and Atlantic Connections: Late Roman and Early Medieval imported pottery on the Atlantic Seaboard*, edited by Maria Duggan, Sam Turner and Mark Jackson, 94–107. Oxford: Archaeopress.

Santos Salazar, Igor. 2018. "Competition in the frontiers of the Asturian kingdom: the *comites* of Castile, Lantarón and Álava (860–940)." In *Coopétition. Rivaliser, coopérer dans les sociétés du Haut Moyen Âge (500–1100)*, Haut Moyen Âge 31, edited by Régine Le Jan, Geneviève Bührer-Thierry and Stefano Gasparri, 231–251. Turnhout: Brepols.

Serrano, Luciano. 1935. *El Obispado de Burgos y la Castilla primitiva desde el siglo V al XIII*. Madrid: Instituto Valencia de Don Juan.

Shailor, Barbara Ann. 1978–1979. "The Scriptorium of San Pedro de Cardeña." *Bulletin of the John Rylands Library* 61:444–473.

Sharpe, Richard. 1984. "Some problems concerning the organization of the Church in Early Medieval Ireland." *Peritia* 3:230–270.

Vilella Massana, Josep. 1994. "La correspondencia entre los obispos hispanos y el papado durante el siglo V." *Studia Ephemeridis Augustinianum* 46:457–480.

Wickham, Chris. 2005. *Framing the early middle ages. Europe and the Mediterranean 400–800*. Oxford: Oxford University Press.

Wolf, Kenneth Baxter. 1988. *Christian martyrs in muslim Spain*. Cambridge: Cambridge University Press.

Wood, Susan. 2006. *The Proprietary Church in the Medieval West*. Oxford: Oxford University Press.

Part Two: **Bishops and Politics**

Ian Wood
Burgundians and Bishops

Abstract: Despite contrary claims in the *Histories* of Gregory of Tours and in the letters of Avitus of Vienne, any persecution of Catholic bishops by those 5th–6th century Burgundian rulers of Arian faith seems to have rarely been driven by differences in their beliefs. Those instances of conflict between the Gibichung rulers and bishops in their territories – mostly known thanks to descriptions of them having to flee their sees – may primarily be seen in the context of the struggle over territorial control with the neighboring kingdoms of the Franks and Visigoths. Further sources of conflicts are found within the internal matters of the bishoprics and in different rulings as to the legality of marriages to widowed spouses of close relatives. The transfer of churches and liturgical vessels between Catholic and Arian endowments is a rare case where the difference in faith appears to have triggered a conflict. Otherwise, the relations seem to have been cordial and conflicts based mostly on suspicions due to the maintenance of episcopal contacts across the newly established – and still contested – borders. This did, however, only result in threats to individual bishops and not the episcopate as a whole.

Our main narrative source for the history of Gaul in the late fifth and sixth centuries, the *Histories* of Gregory of Tours, implies that this was a period in which the Catholic episcopate was under threat from Arian rulers, with the exception of territories controlled by the Franks. Euric persecuted the Catholics.[1] During the reign of his son, Alaric II, Volusianus was removed from the diocese of Tours,[2] as was his successor Verus,[3] both dying in exile. Quintianus of Rodez was thought to have favoured Frankish intervention and abandoned his diocese.[4] Aprunculus of Langres was regarded as suspect by the Burgundians, who Gregory presents as Arian,[5] and fled to Clermont where he took over the bishopric following the death of Sidonius.[6] Two other bishops, Theodore and Proculus, were supposedly exiled from *Burgundia*, and were subsequently appointed jointly to the

---

1 Greg. Tur. Franc. II, 25 (ed. Krusch and Levison 1951, 70–71).
2 Greg. Tur. Franc. II, 26; X, 31 (ed. Krusch and Levison 1951, 71; 531).
3 Greg. Tur. Franc. X, 31 (ed. Krusch and Levison 1951, 531).
4 Greg. Tur. Franc. II, 36 (ed. Krusch and Levison 1951, 84–85).
5 Greg. Tur. Franc. II, 28 (ed. Krusch and Levison 1951, 73–74).
6 Greg. Tur. Franc. II, 23 (ed. Krusch and Levison 1951, 68–69).

bishopric of Tours by Chrotechildis.⁷ It has long been recognised, however, that Euric's persecution was shortlived and was essentially political, consistent with his take-over of large parts of Provence.⁸ His predecessors and successors emerge relatively unscathed in hagiographical sources, other than those written by Gregory.⁹ Evidence for the territory under Burgundian control also presents us with a very different image from that implied by the bishop of Tours.

Relations between the Gibichung leaders of the Burgundians and the Catholic episcopate are reasonably well evidenced, even though there is not a great deal of relevant hagiography. The number of episcopal *vitae* that provide us with significant evidence relating to the politico-religious history of the Rhône and Saône valleys in the late fifth and early sixth centuries is relatively low: essentially the *Life of Apollinaris of Valence*¹⁰ and the Carolingian réécriture of the *Life of Marcellus of Die*.¹¹ The *Vita Marcelli* includes information relating to the bishop's exile at the hands of Euric,¹² as well as an anecdote about his relations with the Gibichung court. We are told that when he attended the dedication of a church in Lyon built by Gundobad's wife Caretena, who was a great admirer of the bishop of Die, Marcellus pressed the king for some concession to his city, which he secured only after curing one of the queen's ladies-in-waiting.¹³ The *Life of Avitus of Vienne* is a late text, dependent on that of his brother Apollinaris.¹⁴ Unfortunately, although Eutropius of Orange was alive during the period of Gibichung rule, his fascinating *vita*, from the beginning of the sixth century, has nothing to say about his relations with secular powers.¹⁵ Ennodius' *Vita Epiphanii* does have valuable information on the dealings of the bishop of Ostrogothic Pavia with Gundobad, and provides us with a detailed account of the role of a bishop as diplomat. However, it has little to say about the bishops of the Rhône valley, other than to praise Avitus.¹⁶ Nor

---

7 Greg. Tur. Franc. X, 31 (ed. Krusch and Levison 1951, 531).
8 Stroheker 1937, 40. The most recent discussion is Stuber 2019, esp. 41–88.
9 See Wood, "Arianism and identity among the early medieval gentes: variations in time and space" (forthcoming); Wood, "The development of the Visigothic court in the hagiography of the fifth and sixth centuries" (forthcoming); Wood, "The lives of episcopal saints in Gaul: models for a time of crisis, c.470–550" (forthcoming).
10 *Vita Apollinaris episcopi Valentinensis* (ed. Krusch 1896, 194–203); Kinney 2014, 157–177.
11 Dolbeau 1983, 97–130.
12 *Vita Marcelli Diensis*, 4–5 (ed. Dolbeau 1983, 117–121).
13 *Vita Marcelli Diensis*, 9 (ed. Dolbeau 1983, 124–126); Kampers 2000, 1–32; see also Vulfinus, *Carmen de Marcello episcopo Diensi*, ll. 214–228 (ed. Strecker 1923, 963–976, at 971–972).
14 *Vita Aviti* (ed. Peipe 1883b, 177–181).
15 Verus, *Vita Eutropii* (ed. Varin 1849, 53–64). A new edition by Barrett is forthcoming in the *Journal of Medieval Latin*.
16 Ennodius, *Vita Epiphanii*, 173 (ed. Vogel 1885, 84–109, at 106).

does Gregory of Tours tell us anything about contacts between his great-grandfather, Gregory of Langres, and the Gibichungs in the section dedicated to his saintly ancestor in the *Liber Vitae Patrum*.[17] Bishops do appear interacting with kings in a number of non-episcopal *lives*, in particular the *Vita Abbatum Acaunensium* and the *Life of Eptadius of Cervon*. In the *Life of the Abbots of Agaune* Bishop Maximus plays a key role in encouraging Sigismund to found the monastery of St Maurice,[18] and in the *Vita Eptadii* Clovis is said to have asked Gundobad, unsuccessfully, that Eptadius be consecrated bishop of Auxerre.[19] Unfortunately, however, the *Vita Eptadii* is an extremely problematic work. It may date from the end of the sixth or the beginning of the seventh century, but the text is unquestionably corrupt and its narrative is not easily squared with what else is known of the period; its information has, therefore, to be regarded as suspect.[20]

The non-hagiographical material, however, makes up for the relative absence of episcopal *vitae*. The evidence of letter-collections is extremely rich, beginning with Sidonius' comments on the dealings of Patiens of Lyon with Chilperic,[21] as well as his own contacts with the Gibichung court after his election as bishop of Clermont.[22] Richer still is the correspondence of Avitus of Vienne,[23] to which one can add information provided by Gregory of Tours from letters of Avitus that no longer survive.[24] In addition, there are various tantalising references to both Gundobad and to Sigismund in the dedication homilies of Avitus, most of which are, sadly, fragmentary.[25] And there are a few nuggets to be found in the *Epistolae Arelatenses genuinae*.[26] Further, there are the canons of two Church councils, that of Epaon held in 517 and, more siginificantly, that of the Council of Lyon in the period 518/23,[27] as well as the *Liber Constitutionum*, the collection of Gibichung

---

17 Greg. Tur. vit. patr. VII (ed. Krusch 1885, 236–240).
18 *Vita Abbatum Acaunensium absque epitaphiis*, 3 (ed. Krusch 1920, 322–336, at 331).
19 *Vita Eptadii presbyteri Cervidunensis*, 8 (ed. Krusch 1896, 184–194, at 189).
20 Favrod (1997, 16–18) asserted the authenticity of the *Vita Eptadii*. There are, however, considerable problems with the narrative, as noted by Wilkinson 2020, 18–20, whose notes 13 and 15 draw attention to the extraordinary nature of Krusch's emendations to the text.
21 Sidon. epist. VI, 12, 3 (ed. Loyen 1960–1970, 3:26–27).
22 Sidon. epist. V, 6 and 7 (ed. Loyen 1960–1970, 2:182–185).
23 *Alcimi Ecdicii Aviti Opera quae supersunt* (ed. Peiper 1883a; ed. Malaspina and Reydellet 2016: trans. Shanzer and Wood 2002).
24 Greg. Tur. Franc. II, 34 (ed. Krusch and Levison 1951, 81–84).
25 Alc. Avit. hom. 17–33 (ed. Peiper 1883a, 125–153); Perrat and Audin 1956–1957, 2:433–451; Wood 2014, 81–97.
26 *Epistolae Merowingici et Karolini Aevi* (ed. Gundlach 1892, 1–83). On the collection see Wood 2018, 45–61, at 54–55.
27 Council of Epaon (ed. Gaudemet and Basdevant 1989, 93–125); Council of Lyon I (ed. Gaudemet and Basdevant 1989, 127–135).

law that includes one edict issued in 517 at the request of a bishop.[28] The episcopal epitaphs, which are relatively numerous for the bishops of Lyon, and which provide a particular statement of the image of the ideal bishop, have nothing to say, however, about relations with kings.[29]

For the most part relations between the Gibichungs and their bishops were cordial, even though Gundobad and Godegisel were Arians (or more correctly Homoean), as initially was Gundobad's son Sigismund, although he converted to orthodoxy early in his political career.[30] Gundobad's second son, Godomar, was most probably a Homoean and may have remained so – Avitus certainly feared that the successor of the Catholic Sigismund might be an Arian.[31] Despite the impression given by Gregory of Tours,[32] Gundobad's father, Gundioc, and uncle, Chilperic, were probably both Catholic – Gundobad's adherence to Arianism is likely to have been inspired by his uncle and mentor Ricimer.[33]

The first dealings of the Gibichungs with the Catholic hierarchy were positive. In 463 Gundioc, as *magister militum per Gallias*, wrote to the pope to inform him about the problematic election and consecration of Marcellus of Die.[34] The ceremony had been performed by the metropolitan bishop of Vienne, Mamertus, although the diocese of Die was within the jurisdiction of Arles. In later years, when Arles was under the control of the Visigoths, the Gibichungs may, however, have supported the bishop of Vienne in any conflict with his southern neighbour – in a judgement of 513 dealing with the claims of the two metropolitans the pope refers to *saecularia patrocinia*.[35] It is highly likely that the Gibichungs backed the claims of the metropolitan of Vienne, a city under their control, once Arles was in the hands of the rival Visigothic regime. Gundioc's brother, and successor as *magister militum*, Chilperic, was on good terms with Patiens of Lyon,[36] and with Sidonius Apollinaris, both before and after his election as bishop of Clermont, until the transfer of Clermont to the Visigoths by Julius Nepos in 474.[37]

At least one bishop, however, fell out of favour with a Gibichung ruler in the late 470s. When Sidonius died in 479[38] he was succeeded as bishop of what was by

---

28 Burg. lib. const., extr. 20 (ed. Von Salis 1892, 119).
29 Heinzelmann 1976.
30 Alc. Avit. epist. 8 (ed. Peiper 1883a, 40–43: Shanzer and Wood 2002, 220–224).
31 Alc. Avit. epist. 7, (ed. Peiper 1883a, 35–39: Shanzer and Wood 2002, 295–302).
32 Greg. Tur. Franc. II, 28 (ed. Krusch and Levison 1951, 73–74).
33 Wood 2019, 301–315, at 306–311.
34 *Epistolae Arelatenses genuinae*, 19 (ed. Gundlach 1892, 28–29).
35 *Epistolae Arelatenses genuinae*, 25 (ed. Gundlach 1892, 35–36).
36 Sidon. epist. VI, 12, 3 (ed. Loyen 1960–1970, 3:26–27).
37 Sidon. epist. V, 6 and 7 (ed. Loyen 1960–1970, 2:182–185).
38 Furbetta 2015, 243–254.

that time Visigothic Clermont by Aprunculus, who had previously been bishop of Langres, and had just fled to the Auvergne from the Burgundian city. Gregory of Tours claims that Aprunculus was regarded with suspicion at a time when the people of north Burgundy were hoping that the Franks would take over the region.[39] This is clearly fantasy on Gregory's part, and it is part of his promotion of the Franks as a "Chosen People".[40] In 479 Childeric (who was pagan, in any case) posed no threat to the Gibichungs. The flight of Aprunculus, therefore, does not bear comparison with the removal of Volusianus and Verus from the diocese of Tours by Alaric II.[41] Moreover, had Aprunculus been in collusion with the Merovingians, he would surely have fled to Frankish territory (which is a good deal closer to Langres than is the Auvergne). Interestingly, however, Sidonius and Aprunculus were correspondents. In a letter to Aprunculus that Sidonius seems to have written either during his exile at Liviana, or, more probably, after his return to Clermont in the last year of his life, he talks of mutual friends including Caelestius, who had been in Béziers.[42] Moreover the letter of Sidonius implies some arrangement over a minor cleric who was to join Aprunculus in Langres – although its meaning is unclear. It may well be that it was Aprunculus' contacts in the heart of Visigothic territory that made him suspect in the eyes of the Gibichungs.

Another bishop who probably fell foul of the Gibichungs is Faustus of Riez. He was forced into exile in Aquitaine, where he stayed with various acquaintances, including Ruricius of Limoges.[43] It is usually asserted that he was driven out of his see by Euric.[44] However, there is nothing in the sources to identify the ruler responsible for the persecution of the bishop of Riez. Moreover, there is no evidence that Riez was in Visigothic rather than Burgundian hands. Unfortunately no bishop of Riez signed the canons of the Visigothic Council of Agde or the Burgundian Council of Epaon, but bishops from the adjacent sees of Apt and Sisteron were present at the latter gathering.[45] Also Gundobad was involved in the appointment of the abbot of the monastery of Bevons in the diocese of Sisteron.[46] Further,

---

39 Greg. Tur. Franc. II, 23 (ed. Krusch and Levison 1951, 68–69).
40 Wilkinson 2020, 22, was unfortunately not aware of Sidonius' epitaph, and thus accepts an incorrect chronology. As a result his reconstruction of events cannot stand.
41 Greg. Tur. Franc. X, 31 (ed. Krusch and Levison 1951, 531). On Volusianus and Verus, Stüber 2019, 89–100.
42 Sidon. epist. IX, 10, (ed. Loyen 1960–1970, 3:154).
43 Faust. Rei. epist. 2–5 (ed. Luetjohann 1887, 265–297, at 266–271).
44 See Stroheker 1937, 34. A Visigothic take-over is assumed by Stüber 2019, 68–77.
45 Council of Epaon (ed. Gaudemet and Basdevant 1989, 120–125).
46 Dynam. *Vita Marii*, 2 (Patrologia Latina 80, cols. 25–32, at col. 27).

Sidonius, speaks of the problems of communication, implying that he and Faustus were in different kingdoms after the Visigothic take-over of Clermont in 474.[47]

It might be argued that the exile of Marcellus of Die provides a parallel to that of Faustus:[48] the prose *Vita Marcelli*, as it survives in a réécriture of an earlier text, states that Euric drove the saint and the whole population from the city, and that Marcellus himself was held in exile, first in Arles, then at Couserans, and finally at Toulouse.[49] The Carolingian verse *life* confirms the bishop's exile in Aquitaine, but does not identify his persecutor.[50] The whole episode, however, is problematic. Historians have struggled to find a context for the exile, given that Die was in Gibichung hands, and have had to hypothesise a brief Visigothic take-over,[51] which is difficult to envisage given the geographical position of the city. François Dolbeau described Euric's conquest as an "épisode peut-être calqué sur la Vita Bibiani, ... car il n'existe aucun autre témoignage sur l'occupation de Die par les Wisigoths".[52] That Marcellus did spend some time in exile seems likely, as it is mentioned in a number of sources, although none of them early. But the detail supplied in his prose *life* is highly questionable, and it is impossible to reconstruct what actually happened.

It is perfectly possible, however, that Faustus was driven into exile by the Burgundian Gibichungs because of his role in the transfer of various Provençal cities, along with Clermont, to Euric, at the behest of the emperor Julius Nepos. Bishops were often used as envoys in the fifth and sixth centuries,[53] but that could leave them in awkward political positions. Faustus was the one bishop from Gibichung-controlled territory involved in negotiations between the Empire and Euric[54] – after the cession of territory by Nepos the bishops of Aix, Arles and Marseille would have become subject to the new Visigothic rulers of Provence. It may also be that the close association of Faustus with Ruricius, and perhaps also with the Cahors region,[55] made the bishop of Riez look like a potential fifth-columnist, likely to betray Gibichung territory to Euric. During times of tension having connections in neighbouring kingdoms was dangerous. We see this in the correspond-

---

47 Sidon. epist. IX, 3, 2 (ed. Loyen 1960–1970, 3:134–135).
48 The case of Marcellus is analysed by Stüber 2019, 78–88.
49 *Vita Marcelli Diensis*, 4–5 (ed. Dolbeau 1983, 117–121).
50 Vulfinus, *Carmen de Marcello episcopo Diensi*, ll. 314–30, 347–50 (ed. Strecker 1923, 974–975).
51 The various interpretations are considered by Stüber 2019, 78–88.
52 Dolbeau 1983, 118, n. 22: on other possible borrowing from the *Vita Bibiani*, see 119, n. 30.
53 Gillett 2003, 113–171.
54 Sidon. epist. VII, 6, 10 (ed. Loyen 1960–1970, 3:46).
55 Mathisen 1998, 163–94.

ence of Sidonius,[56] as well as that of Avitus.[57] Inevitably members of the Gallo-Roman upper classes had contacts that stretched across new political frontiers, contacts that rendered them open to suspicion. The point is most clearly illustrated in the *Life of Caesarius of Arles*, who came from Chalon-sur-Saône, and was thus thought likely to collude with the Burgundians. He was accused by the notary Licininius of wanting to turn his city over to the Gibichungs.[58] In moments of crisis it was prudent to avoid contact across borders. Aprunculus clearly did not. Even worse, Faustus had negotiated with an alien regime, and had done so on behalf of an emperor who was not recognised by the Gibichungs. Neither of these bishops suffered for theological reasons: indeed, it is possible that the Gibichung in control when they left Burgundian territory was Chilperic, a Catholic, while the territory in which they spent their exiles was under the rule of an Arian monarch.

Our sources are silent on Gundobad's establishment in what had been Chilperic's post – even the date is unclear – although there may have been a power struggle. The new ruler's Arianism does not seem to have caused much difficulty, despite a reference to persecution in two letters of Avitus.[59] Exactly what this persecution was in unclear. We may, however, get some indication of the cause of the problem from a letter in which Avitus insisted that the Catholics should not take over Arian basilicas in 516 when Gundobad died and his Catholic son succeeded him, in case a subsequent Arian ruler might take retaliatory action.[60] Avitus indeed states explicitly that if the Catholics took over Arian basilicas the Arians could reasonably claim to have been persecuted: this may suggest that the establishment of an Arian (or rather Homoean)[61] Church had caused problems. If, as seems likely, Gundobad's Arianism derived from his maternal uncle Ricimer and not from his (probably Catholic) father, it would have been after his return from Italy in c. 474[62] that provision was made for Arian worship. It may be that Gundobad requisitioned church buildings and liturgical vessels in the period between his return and the end of the century, and that this was regarded as persecution by the Catholics. Certainly there is some evidence that Gundobad alienated sections of the

---

56 Sidon. epist. IX, 3, 2 (ed. Loyen 1960–1970, 3:134–135).
57 Alc. Avit. epist. 24; 36; 51; 52 (ed. Peiper 1883a, 56. 66. 79–82).
58 Cyprian of Toulon, Firminus, Viventius, Messianus and Stephen, *Vita Caesarii episcopi Arelatensis* I, 21 (ed. Krusch 1896, 434–501, at 465). On Caesarius, see Stüber 2019, 100–129.
59 Alc. Avit. epist. 7; 8 (ed. Peiper 1883a, 35–43).
60 Alc. Avit. epist. 7 (ed. Peiper 1883a, 35–39: Shanzer and Wood 2002, 295–302).
61 Heil 2011.
62 Escher 2005, 2:733: provides a succinct statement of the evidence: "Les sources n'indiquent pas la date de la retour de Gondebaud dans le royaume, mais il est généralement admis que c'était à l'époque de l'arrivée de Nepos, en 474".

Catholic aristocracy, since some members of the Roman nobility joined a rebellion against him in 500.[63]

It may be that we should associate the exile of bishops Theodore and Proculus with this same persecution. Gregory of Tours relates that the two of them had been expelled from their cities in Burgundia because they were faced with hostility (*ab hostilitate de urbibus suis expulsi fuerant*), and that they followed Chrotechildis to Francia when she married Clovis.[64] Subsequently, she arranged for their joint appointment to the diocese of Tours after the death of Licinius, probably in 520, or perhaps after that of Leo in c. 526.[65] The only chronological indicator we have for the exile of the two bishops is the marriage of Chrotechildis to Clovis, which should probably be dated to 501.[66] Unfortunately, Gregory does not tell us which were the original sees of the two exiles. Moreover, the account he gives of their appointment in the closing chapter of the *Histories* is at odds with the statement in Book III, where no reference is made to their earlier troubles or even to their previous episcopal appointments. Since the bishop of Tours makes no attempt to use their story to blacken Gundobad, we might hypothesise that rather than falling foul of the Gibichungs, Theodore and Proculus may have antagonised their own congregations: this would fit with Gregory's words, *ab hostilitate*. That bishops did fall out with their congregations is clear from the history of Quintianus, who, like Aprunculus, fled from his first episcopal see of Rodez to Clermont, where he became bishop. In the *Decem Libri Historiarum* Gregory claims that he was accused of plotting to hand over his city to the Franks.[67] In the *Liber Vitae Patrum*, however, the bishop of Tours adds the information that Quintianus, an African, angered his dead predecessor, Amantius, by moving his bones.[68] The *life* of the earlier bishop of Rodez, seems to confirm that the translation was not popular.[69] We should remember, therefore, that local tensions, rather than any conflict with a ruler, could lead to the removal of bishops. On the other hand, it is possible that Theodore and Proculus were simply clergy who accompanied Chrotechildis, and that

---

63 Greg. Tur. Franc. II, 33 (ed. Krusch and Levison 1951, 80–81); Mar. Avent. chron. s.a. 500 (ed. Favrod 1991, 68–69).
64 Greg. Tur. Franc. X, 31 (ed. Krusch and Levison 1951, 532).
65 Greg. Tur. Franc. III, 17 (ed. Krusch and Levison 1951, 117).
66 Weiß 1971, 44. 53.
67 Greg. Tur. Franc. II, 36; III, 2 (ed. Krusch and Levison 1951, 84–85. 98–99). Edward James (1985, 139, at n. 2) offers a plausible reconstruction of the context in which Quintianus might have been suspected of collusion with the Franks.
68 Greg. Tur. vit. patr. IV, 1 (ed. Krusch 1885, 224–225).
69 *Vita Amantii*, XI, 76–83 (ed. Krusch 1885, 55–64, at 62).

Gregory incorrectly fitted their move to the Frankish kingdom into his model of Arian persecution.

Whatever the cause of the persecution mentioned by Avitus, according to the bishop in a letter addressed to the pope the problem ended with Sigismund's conversion to Catholicism, probably in 501/2.[70] Thereafter, Gundobad was on good terms with his bishops, although Avitus was wary when dealing with him over the issues of a runaway slave and of a man who refused to return a deposit:[71] his care to exculpate himself suggests that he was determined to avoid getting on the wrong side of the ruler. Strikingly he acknowledged that the Church was dependent on Gundobad for its endowment and the safeguarding of its property. The *Vita Marcelli* does recount a minor conflict between the bishop and Gundobad, but this seems to have been no more than an initial refusal by the ruler to remit some burdens oppressing the citizens of Die.[72]

The exile of Faustus and the flight of Aprunculus belong to the period in which Gaul was being divided following the implosion of imperial authority. Whatever persecution of Catholics in the early part of Gundobad's rule may have been related to the endowment of the Homoean Church for the new ruler and his Arian followers. After 501/2 relations between the Gibichungs and the episcopate of the Rhône-Saône basin were cordial, as even Gregory of Tours admitted.[73] Despite his wariness in dealing with the Arian Gundobad, Avitus appears to have been close terms with the king.[74] The good relations of his son Sigismund with the Catholic hierarchy during Gundobad's lifetime are apparent not just in the letters of Avitus, but also in the foundation of the monastery of Agaune in 515, where the prince was influenced primarily by Bishop Maximus of Geneva,[75] although there is some evidence that Victorius of Grenoble was unhappy with the arrangements – the transfer of leading ascetics from different parts of the Gibichung province to the new foundation caused resentment.[76] When Gundobad died the year after the foundation of Agaune, it must have seemed as if the territory under Burgundian rule was about to enter a Golden Age of Catholicism, although Avitus, in his *de basilicis haereticis non recipiendis*, counselled against triumphalism.[77] Initially Sigis-

---

70 Alc. Avit. epist. 8 (ed. Peiper 1883a, 40–43: Shanzer and Wood 2002, 220–224).
71 Alc. Avit. epist. 44 (ed. Peiper 1883a, 73–74: Shanzer and Wood 2002, 216–219).
72 *Vita Marcelli Diensis*, 9 (ed. Dolbeau 1983, 124–126); Vulfinus, *Carmen de Marcello episcopo Diensi*, ll. 214–228 (ed. Strecker 1923, 971–972).
73 Greg. Tur. Franc. II, 34 (ed. Krusch and Levison 1951, 81–84).
74 Alc. Avit. epist. 2–6; 21–22; 30; 44 (ed. Peiper 1883a, 15–35. 54–55. 60–62. 73–74).
75 *Vita Abbatum Acaunensium absque epitaphiis*, 3 (ed. Krusch 1920, 331–332).
76 *Vita Abbatum Acaunensium absque epitaphiis*, 5 (ed. Krusch 1920, 332–333).
77 Alc. Avit. epist. 16–18 (ed. Peiper 1883a, 48–50).

mund seems to have lived up to expectations: in response to a plea of Bishop Gimellus of Vaison he issued an edict protecting foundlings.[78] Not long after, however, his actions led to an astonishing confrontation with his bishops.

The issue at the heart of the confrontation was a legal one: how to deal with marriages that were defined in certain rulings as incestuous. The question had arisen shortly before 517 when Avitus and Victorius of Grenoble discussed the case of a man marrying the sister of his dead wife, and whether it constituted incest.[79] This was followed by a piece of secular legislation issued by Sigismund in 517, condemning marriage to a dead wife's sister as incestuous.[80] The Council of Epaon in 517 also condemned marriage to the sister of one's dead wife, as well as to the widow of one's brother, to one's step-mother, cousin, cousin's offspring, to the widow of one's uncle, and to one's step-daughter.[81] The secular legislation and the canon, however, were breached a year or so later (at some point around the time of, or just after, the death of Avitus in February 518, but before 523) by Sigismund's treasurer, Stephanus, who married Palladia, the sister of his dead wife. Eleven bishops, under the leadership of Viventiolus of Lyon, responded by gathering in Lyon to condemn Stephanus and his wife. And they went further, announcing that the bishops would unite to support each other if any of them was subject to any harassment (*tribulationem quamcumque vel amaritudinem aut commotionem*) as a result of the decision, and that each bishop would withdraw to a monastery of his choice if the king continued in breach of communion.[82] There is a postscript to the canons to say that following the intervention of the king, Stephanus and Palladia were to be allowed to continue to pray *in locis sanctis* until the prayer that followed the reading of the Gospel. This is signed by nine bishops: among the absent names is that of Viventiolus. Whether he and Florentius (of Orange?), the other non-signatory to the addendum, withheld their names, or whether they were unable to sign, is unclear.

The canons of the Council of Lyon provide us with the official ecclesiastical account of the stand-off between the king and his bishops. There is, in addition, a narrative account contained in the *Vita Apollinaris* that presents a much more severe picture of the break-down of relations. Here, following the incestuous marriage, Avitus and Apollinaris summoned a council that excommunicated Stephanus. This enfuriated the king, who had the bishops imprisoned in the Lyonnais *oppidum* of Sardinia. But on seeing their obduracy he allowed them to return to their

---

78 Burg. lib. const., extr. 20 (ed. Von Salis 1892, 119).
79 Alc. Avit. epist. 16–18 (ed. Peiper 1883a, 48–50); Mikat 1994; Wood 1998, 291–303.
80 Burg. lib. const. 36 (ed. Von Salis 1892, 69).
81 Council of Epaon, can. 30 (ed. Gaudemet and Basdevant 1989, 114–117).
82 Council of Lyon I (518–523), can. 1 (ed. Gaudemet and Basdevant 1989, 128–129).

dioceses. Apollinaris, however, remained in Lyon, where he performed a miracle. Meanwhile, the king was seized with a fever: the queen begged Apollinaris to cure him, which he did. The king realised his error and begged forgiveness.[83]

There are numerous problems with the narrative of the *Vita Apollinaris*. Avitus was unquestionably dead by the time that the bishops met in Lyon: the bishop of Vienne who signed the canons of the Council of Lyon was his successor, Julian. But Avitus may have been living when the marriage of Stephanus and Palladia took place. The conciliar records suggest a rather different pattern of events from that provided by the hagiographical narrative, with Viventiolus of Lyon as the prime mover. The place where Sigismund supposedly had the bishops imprisoned has not been identified: the name Sardinia looks as if it has been borrowed from an account of the Vandal persecutions (exile from Africa to Sardinia is well attested)[84] – but attempts at identification have been made, including the suggestion that Sardinia is a spelling mistake for the site of the later monastery of Savigny-les-Lyonais. Moreover, the history of Stephanus and Palladia is followed in the *Vita Apollinaris* by a completely separate account of a tour of cities of Provence completed by the bishop before his death. If, as is possible, given that we have no death date for Apollinaris, the second section of the *Vita* relates to the period after the Gibichung loss of control over Valence, perhaps in c. 523, it illustrates the reestablishment of contacts by a bishop from the highest level of the old aristrocracy, following the redrawing of the political boundary. It looks as if two free-standing narratives relating to the saint have been stitched together. Not surprisingly, Bruno Krusch, in his edition of the *Vita*, condemned it as a later fabrication.[85] Angela Kinney, however, has provided a detailed analysis of the language of the text, which suggests that it was written in the sixth, or perhaps seventh, century.[86]

The *Vita Apollinaris* certainly presents an image of Sigismund that is not to be found in the canons, but the king may well have reacted furiously. The addendum to the Lyon canons does, however, suggest that agreement was reached – the word used is *temperamentum*.[87] Stephanus and Palladia must have separated, in order to be allowed to remain in church until after the reading of the Gospels. And this was an arrangement that was agreed in response to the *sententia* of the king (*domni quoque gloriosissimi regis sententia*). We can, therefore, be sure that the episcopal threat of excommunication and of monastic withdrawal had the required effect. It is possible that Viventiolus and Florentius had held out for a more severe punish-

---

83 *Vita Apollinaris episcopi Valentinensis*, 2–6 (ed. Krusch 1896, 198–199).
84 Conant 2012, 161–166; Whelan 2018, 16. 147.
85 Krusch 1896, 194–197.
86 Kinney 2014.
87 Council of Lyon I (518–523) (ed. Gaudemet and Basdevant 1989, 134–135).

ment than was inflicted on Stephanus. Despite the claims of the *Vita Apollinaris* that the bishop of Valence was a prime-mover in the affair, he signed the addendum to the canons, which may imply that he took a less hard line than Viventiolus and Florentius. But there had been enough of a united front among the bishops to secure considerable concessions on the part of the king. When they acted in unison, the bishops of a region could force concessions from a ruler.

Yet greater disaster was to strike Sigismund almost immediately after the affair of Stephanus and Palladia. The king murdered his own son, and then, full of remorse, retired to the monastery of Agaune.[88] The Franks and the Ostrogoths took advantage of the situation and invaded Burgundian territory. Sigismund himself was dragged off and murdered. His brother, Godomar, however, did manage to defeat the Franks, and the Burgundian state survived for another decade, before falling to the Merovingians.

The history of Gibichung relations with the episcopate of the Rhône and Saône valleys is remarkable for its variety. For the most part rulers and bishops were on good terms, but there were instances of conflict. There is some slight evidence for the persecution of Catholics by an Arian ruler, but that seems to have been relatively insignificant and confined to a short period of time. There is no evidence that Catholic clergy suffered for doctrinal reasons, although questions of the endowment of a rival Church with buildings and liturgical vessels would seem to have caused problems. In fact, the letters of Avitus of Vienne suggest that there was civilised and amicable debate between the bishop and Gundobad.[89] A more significant cause of conflict between the episcopate and the Gibichung rulers was political. As frontiers became drawn between the new Successor States there was always a danger that someone with a wide network of contacts might be thought to be colluding with a neighbouring power. But in the Burgundian case, the most dramatic conflict between a king and his bishops arose over a moral issue, which was a matter of both secular and ecclesiastical law. Sigismund's decision to support his incestuous treasurer was the trigger for what was effectively a strike by the ecclesiastical hierarchy. Acting in unison the episcopate could force a royal climb-down. As in the Visigothic kingdom of Toulouse, although there were moments during the period of Gibichung rule when individual bishops were under threat, the episcopate as a whole was not in danger.

---

[88] Greg. Tur. Franc. III, 5–6 (ed. Krusch and Levison 1951, 100–103); *Passio Sigismundi regis*, 8–9 (ed. Krusch 1888, 329–340, at 337–338).
[89] Heil 2011; Wood 2019.

Bibliography

Primary Sources

Avitus of Vienne: Rudolf Peiper ed. 1883a. *Alcimi Ecdicii Aviti Opera quae supersunt*, Monumenta Germaniae Historica, Auctores Antiquissimi *(MGH AA)*. VI, 2. Berlin: Weidmann; Elena Malaspina and Marc Reydellet ed. 2016. *Avit de Vienne, Lettres*. Paris : Belles Lettres; Danuta Shanzer and Ian Wood. trans. 2002. *Avitus of Vienne, Letters and Selected Prose*. Liverpool: Liverpool University Press.

Council of Epaon: Jean Gaudemet and Brigitte Basdevant. eds. 1989. *Les canons de conciles mérovingiens (VI-VIIe siècles)*. Vol. 1. Sources Chrétiennes 353, 93–125. Paris : Éditions du Cerf.

Council of Lyon I : Jean Gaudemet and Brigitte Basdevant. eds. 1989. *Les canons de conciles mérovingiens (VI-VIIe siècles)*. Vol. 1. Sources Chrétiennes 353, 127–135. Paris : Éditions du Cerf.

Cyprian of Toulon, Firminus, Viventius, Messianus and Stephen, *Vita Caesarii:* Bruno Krusch. ed. 1896. *Monumenta Germaniae Historica, Scriptores Rerum Merowingicarum (MGH SS rer. Merow.)*. III, 434–501. Hannover: Hahn.

Dynamius Patricius, *Vita Marii:* Jacques-Paul Migne ed. 1863. *Patrologia Latina (PL)*. 80, cols. 25–32. Paris : Migne.

Ennodius, *Vita Epiphanii:* Friechrich Vogel ed. 1885. *Monumenta Germaniae Historica, Auctores Antiquissimi (MGH AA)*. VII, 84–109. Berlin: Weidmann.

Epistolae Arelatenses Genuinae, Epistolae Merowingici et Karolini Aevi: Wilhelm Gundlach. ed. 1892. *Monumenta Germaniae Historica, Epistolae (MGH EE)*. III, 1–83. Berlin: Weidemann.

Faustus of Riez: Christian Luetjohann. ed. 1887. *Fausti alliorumque epistulae ad Ruricium aliosque*, Monumenta Germaniae Historica, Auctores Antiquissimi *(MGH AA)*. VIII. Berlin: Weidmannm.

Gregory of Tours, *Decem Libri Historiarum:* Bruno Krusch and Wilhelm Levison. eds. 1951. *Monumenta Germaniae Historica, Scriptores Rerum Merovingicarum (MGH SS rer. Merov.)*. I. Hannover: Hahn.

Gregory of Tours, *Liber Vitae Patrum:* Bruno Krusch. ed. 1885. *Monumenta Germaniae Historica, Scriptores Rerum Merovingicarum (MGH SS rer. Merov.)*. I, 1, 211–294. Hannover: Hahn.

Liber Constitutionum: Ludwig Rudolf von Salis ed. 1892. *Leges Burgundionum*, Monumenta Germaniae Historica, Leges Nationum Germanicarum *(MGH LL nat. Germ.)*. II, 1. Hannover: Hahn.

Marius of Avenches, Chronicle: Justin Favrod. ed. 1991. *La Chronique de Marius d'Avenches (455–581)*. Cahiers Lausannois d'histoire médiévale 4. Lausanne : Université de Lausanne.

Passio Sigismundi: Bruno Krusch. ed. 1888. *Monumenta Germaniae Historica, Scriptores Rerum Merovingicarum (MGH SS rer. Merov.)*. II. Hannover: Hahn.

Sidonius Apollinaris: André Loyen. ed. 1960–1970. *Sidoine Apollinaire*. 3 Vols. Paris, Belles Lettres.

Verus, *Vita Eutropii:* Pierre Varin ed. 1849. "Vie de Saint Eutrope, évêque d'Orange, par Verus, son successeur." *Bulletin du Comité Historique des monuments écrits de l'histoire de France. Histoire-Sciences-Lettres.* I, 53–64. Paris : Comité.

Vita Abbatum Acaunensium absque epitaphiis: Bruno Krusch. ed. 1920. *Monumenta Germaniae Historica, Scriptores Rerum Merovingicarum (MGH SS rer. Merov.)*. VII, 322–336. Hannover: Hahn.

Vita Amantii: Bruno Krusch. ed. 1885. *Venanti Honori Clementiai Fortunati, Opera Pedestria*, Monumenta Germaniae Historica, Auctores antiquissimi *(MGH AA)*. IV, 2, 55–64. Berlin: Weidmann.

Vita Apollinaris: Bruno Krusch. ed. 1896. *Monumenta Germaniae Historica, Scriptores Rerum Merovingicarum (MGH SS rer. Merov.)*. III, 194–203. Hannover: Hahn.

Vita Aviti: Rudolf Peiper ed. 1883b. *Alcimi Ecdicii Aviti Opera quae supersunt, Monumenta Germaniae Historica, Auctores antiquissimi (MGH AA).* VI, 2, 177–181. Berlin: Weidmann.

Vita Eptadii presbyteri Cervidunensis: Bruno Krusch. ed. 1896. *Monumenta Germaniae Historica, Scriptores Rerum Merovingicarum (MGH SS rer. Merov.).* III, 184–194. Hannover, Hahn.

Vita Marcelli Deiensis: François Dolbeau. ed. 1983. "La vie en prose de saint Marcel, évêque de Die: Histoire du texte et édition critique." *Francia* 11:97–130.

Vulfinus, *Carmen de Marcello episcopo Diensi:* Karl Strecker. ed. 1923. *Monumenta Germaniae Historica, Poetae Latini medii aevi (MGH Poetae), Poetae Latini aevi Carolini.* IV, 963–976. Berlin: Weidmann.

Secondary Sources

Conant, Jonathan. 2012. *Staying Roman: conquest and identity in Africa and the Mediterranean, 439–700.* Cambridge: Cambridge University Press.

Dolbeau, François. 1983. "La vie en prose de saint Marcel, évêque de Die: Histoire du texte et édition critique." *Francia* 11:97–130.

Escher, Katalin. 2005. *Genèse et évolution du deuxième royaume burgonde (443–534). Les témoins archéologiques.* Vol. 2, British Archaeological Reports, International Series 1402, 2 Vols. Oxford: Archaeopress.

Favrod, Justin. 1997. *Histoire politique du royaume burgonde (443–534).* Lausanne : Bibliothèque historique vaudoise.

Furbetta, Luciana. 2015. "L'epitaffio di Sidonio Apollinare in uno nuovo testimone manoscritto." *Euphrosyne* 43:243–54.

Gillett, Andrew. 2003. *Envoys and Political Communication in the Late Antique West, 411–533.* Cambridge: Cambridge University Press.

Heil, Uta. 2011. *Avitus von Vienne und die homöische Kirche der Burgunder.* Patristische Texte und Studien 66. Berlin: Walter de Gruyter.

Heinzelmann, Martin. 1976. *Bischofsherrschaft in Gallien: Zur Kontinuität römischer Führungsschichten vom 4. bis zum 7. Jahrhundert. Soziale, prosopographische und bildungsgeschichtliche Aspekte.* Beihefte der Francia 5. München: Artemis.

Kampers, Gerd. 2000. "Caretena – Königin und Asketin." *Francia* 27:1–32.

Kinney, Angela. 2014. "An appeal against editorial condemnation: a reevaluation of the *Vita Apollinaris Valentinensis.*" In *Edition und Erforschung lateinischer patristischer Texte,* edited by Victoria Zimmerl-Panagl, Lukas J. Dorfbauer, and Clemens Weidmann, 157–177. Berlin: Walter de Gruyter

Mathisen, Ralph. 1998. "The Codex Sangallensis 190 and the transmission of the classical tradition during Late Antiquity and the early Middle Ages." *International Journal of the Classical Tradition* 5:163–94.

Mikat, Paul. 1994. *Der Inzestgesetzgebung der merowingisch-fränkischen Konzilien (511–626/27).* Paderborn: Schöningh.

Perrat, Charles and Amable Audin. 1957. "Alcimi Ecdicii Aviti viennensis episcopi homilia dicta in dedicatione superioris basilicae." In *Studi in onore di Aristide Calderini e Roberto Paribeni.* Vol 2, 433–451. Milano: Casa ed. Ceschina.

Stroheker, Karl Friedrich. 1937. *Eurich, König der Westgoten.* Stuttgart: Kohlhammer.

Stuber, Till. 2019. *Der inkriminierte Bischof. Könige im Konflikt mit Kirchenleitern im westgotischen und fränkischen Gallien (466–614).* Berlin: Walter de Gruyter.

Weiss, Rolf. 1971. *Chlodwigs Taufe: Reims 508. Versuch einer neuen Chronologie für die Regierungszeit des ersten christlichen Frankenkönigs unter Berücksichtigung der politischen und kirchlich-dogmatischen Probleme seiner Zeit.* Frankfurt: Lang.

Whelan, Robin. 2018. *Being Christian in Vandal Africa: the politics of orthodoxy in the post-Roman West.* Oakland: University of California Press.

Wilkinson, Ryan H. 2020. *The last horizons of Roman Gaul: communication, coin circulation, and the limits of the second Burgundian kingdom.* British Archaeological Reports, International Series 3006. Oxford: BAR Publishing

Wood, Ian. 1998. "Incest, law and the Bible in sixth-century Gaul." *Early Medieval Europe* 7:291–303.

Wood, Ian. 2014. "The homilies of Avitus." In *Sermo doctorum: compilers, preachers and their audiences in the early medieval West*, edited by Maximilian Diesenberger, Yitzhak Hen, and Marianne Pollheimer, 81–97. Turnhout: Brepols.

Wood, Ian. 2018. "Why collect letters?" In *Zwischen Alltagskommunikation und literarischer Identitätsbildung: Studien zur lateinischen Epistolographie in Spätantike und Frühmittelalter*, edited by Gernot M. Müller, 46–61. Göttingen: Franz Steiner.

Wood, Ian. 2019. "Discussions with kings: the Dialogues of Avitus of Vienne", In *Das Christentum im frühen Europa. Diskurse – Tendenzen – Entscheidungen*, edited by Uta Heil, 301–315. Berlin: Walter de Gruyter.

Wood, Ian. (forthcoming). "Arianism and identity among the early medieval gentes: variations in time and space."

Wood, Ian. (forthcoming). "The development of the Visigothic court in the hagiography of the fifth and sixth centuries."

Wood, Ian. (forthcoming). "The lives of episcopal saints in Gaul: models for a time of crisis, c. 470–550."

Marco Cristini
Sailing to Byzantium: Sixth-Century Popes under Threat in Constantinople

Abstract: Sailing to Byzantium was a hazardous but not unusual task for sixth-century bishops of Rome. Three popes traveled to Constantinople in the space of twenty years: John I and Agapitus on behalf of the Ostrogothic kings, Vigilius of emperor Justinian. John I was sent to the East in order to convince Justin to end the persecution of the Arians, Agapitus had to discuss both the ongoing Gothic War and the accession to the Constantinople see of Anthimus, whereas Vigilius was summoned in order to deal with the Three-Chapter Controversy, not to mention Silverius, who was exiled by the emperor in Lycia ostensibly because of his anti-monophysite attitude. Papal travels to the East between 525 and 545 indicate that political issues were at least as important as theological ones. They also show that the symbolic relevance of the popes depended upon the balance of power between Ravenna and Constantinople, since both the Gothic sovereigns and the emperor needed the support of papal authority in order to substantiate their claims over Italy. Justinian's conquest of Rome was a setback for the pontiffs: previously persuasion and religious concessions were as important as threats to secure their cooperation, thereafter sheer coercion sufficed.

1 Introduction

The second half of the fifth century witnessed a remarkable increase in the pope's authority and prestige, which went hand in hand with the decreasing power of the Western Roman emperors.[1] When the Huns threatened Italy in 452, it was Pope Leo I who led the embassy that convinced Attila to turn back.[2] Three years later, the pontiff again left Rome to negotiate with an invading army, namely Geiseric's Vandals, who agreed to spare the inhabitants of the city in exchange for the permission

---

[1] On fifth-century popes, see Sessa 2012, and Moorhead 2015. – I am grateful to the conference participants and Kristina Sessa, in particular, for their comments on and feedback to my paper. This article was written during my tenure as a Fellow at the Center for Advanced Studies. "Migration and Mobility in Late Antiquity and the Early Middle Ages" (Eberhard Karls Universität Tübingen). I am grateful to all colleagues and staff there.
[2] Wessel 2008, 45–47.

to plunder it at will.³ In both cases, the pope acted as an envoy and took part in the resolution of a hazardous situation which Italian secular authorities were unable (or unwilling) to face by themselves. A couple of decades later, the authority of the pope was further strengthened by the deposition of the last Western emperor Romulus, which enabled the bishop of Rome to gain a fair degree of independence from the religious and secular policies of the (Eastern) emperor. For instance, Felix III refused to endorse the Henotikon and thereby triggered the first schism between the Churches of Old and New Rome.⁴ His successor Gelasius went so far as to write to Emperor Anastasius that the world was governed by the authority of the pontiffs and the power of the emperor, yet of these the former was the more important.⁵

Of course, popes had to deal with the rulers of Italy after 476, but both Odoacer and Theoderic, although Arian, showed no desire to imitate the Vandalic kings and their harsh persecutions of their Catholic subjects.⁶ They needed the support of the Catholic Church to rule over Italy and obtained it by pursuing a policy of tolerance, which was reciprocated by the pontiffs, who abstained from taking a stand against the heterodoxy of Odoacer's followers or the Goths.⁷ For most of his reign, Theoderic intervened in religious disputes only when it was absolutely necessary, as for instance in 501 when the controversy concerning the election of Symmachus to the position of bishop of Rome threatened to escalate into a full-scale civil war between his supporters and those of the 'anti-pope' Laurentius.⁸ Theoderic summoned Symmachus to Ravenna to prove that he was not guilty of the charges brought against him. The pope went as far as Rimini, before suddenly turning back because he feared (in all likelihood correctly) that his enemies had laid a plot against him. Once again in Rome, he was able to emerge from the trial against him unscathed and have a synod accept the principle that the pope cannot be judged by anyone. It is far from certain that the verdict would have been the

---

3 Steinacher 2016, 196–205; Roberto 2020, 111–116.
4 The reference work on the Acacian Schism is Kötter 2013, but see also Deliyannis 2014.
5 Gelasius papa Epist. 12 (Thiel 1868, 350–351): *Duo quippe sunt, imperator auguste, quibus principaliter mundus hic regitur: auctoritas sacrata pontificum, et regalis potestas. In quibus tanto gravius est pondus sacerdotum, quanto etiam pro ipsis regibus hominum in divino reddituri sunt esamine ratione.*
6 On Odoacer, see Caliri 2017, 126–130. The religious tolerance of Theoderic has been studied extensively during the last few decades. See most recently Ożóg 2016; Canella 2017, 229–283; Kötter 2020. On the Vandalic persecutions against the Catholics, see Whelan 2018; Fournier 2019.
7 The ethnonym 'Goths' is adopted here to designate the Ostrogoths, who in the sixth century were distinguished from the Visigoths by using two different terms only in Jordanes' *Getica* and in the *Vita Caesarii episcopi Arelatensis*, see Gillett 2000, 495–500.
8 Sardella 1996, 26–36.

same had the trial taken place in Ravenna. Even in such difficult circumstances, Theoderic did not arrest or depose the pope when he refused to come to him, since such a move would have jeopardized the support of part of the senate and the Roman people.[9]

The delicate power-balance between the Gothic king and the pope was suddenly tilted after the execution of Boethius and Symmachus, which was in all likelihood caused by the untimely death of the heir to the Gothic throne, Eutharic, and the ensuing struggle for his succession, which involved both the neighbouring kingdoms and the Empire. The instability caused by this crisis had fateful consequences and placed the bishop of Rome at the centre of a complex net of embassies, secular ambitions and ecclesiastical disputes, forcing both him and his successors to play a prominent role in sixth-century politics. In the space of twenty years, three popes reached Constantinople and none of them saw Rome again. John I was sent to the East by Theoderic and died in Ravenna after his return to Italy; Agapetus travelled to Constantinople on behalf of King Theodahad and died there; Vigilius was summoned by Justinian to Byzantium, where he remained for nine years, dying in Syracuse on the return journey. In the meantime, a fourth pope, Silverius, was exiled by Justinian.

These papal travels to the East are noteworthy for at least two reasons. First, no bishop of Rome had ever arrived in Constantinople before John I, yet three popes reached the Bosphorus and another was exiled to Lycia within two decades. Secondly, all these popes were compelled to travel to Constantinople either by the Gothic kings or by the emperor, and were often threatened by both. Contemporary sources such as the *Liber pontificalis* or Liberatus' *Breviarium* focus mainly on religious controversies, which is understandable considering that they were written for a clerical audience. However, modern scholarship has also given attention to ecclesiastical and theological disputes over diplomatic and military issues.[10] The chief purpose of this paper is to offer a reappraisal of sixth-century papal travels, arguing that they should be studied in the context of the relations between the Empire and the Goths, thereby integrating the traditional reconstruction of these embassies with a more precise analysis of their political and military background.

---

9 See Lizzi Testa 2013.
10 See for instance Moorhead 2015, 66–69 (John I). 74–76 (Agapetus). 87–89 (Vigilius); Wiemer 2018, 551–559.

2 John I: The First Papal Visit to Constantinople

John I was elected pope in 523, a year of high importance for Ostrogothic Italy. Eutharic, Theoderic's son-in-law and appointed heir, may have died in 522/523; then, a few months later, Boethius was accused of treason and executed, together with his father-in-law Symmachus, one of the most influential Roman aristocrats. The reasons behind this unprecedented attack against the senatorial aristocracy have long been discussed. What we know for certain is that a senator, Albinus, wrote a compromising letter to Constantinople and that Boethius tried to defend him. The most convincing explanation is that offered by Barnish, who states that a few senators wrote to the emperor about the possible regency or succession of Theodahad, Theoderic's nephew, whereas the king had already designated his grandson Athalaric as his heir.[11] Some scholars have also argued that Albinus dealt with controversial religious issues,[12] but this reconstruction is unconvincing since a former consul would hardly have encouraged Justinian to persecute his Arian subjects. Moreover, Pope Hormisdas died on August 6th 523, and a week later John I became the next bishop of Rome, so there was no time to discuss the papal election with Constantinople.[13] In all likelihood, the succession to Hormisdas had already been decided beforehand, with the approval of the king.

It is impossible to establish whether the election of the pope took place before or after the arrest of Boethius, but the former is more likely, since John seems to have been a friend of the philosopher.[14] The relationship between the king and pope is shrouded in obscurity until late 525/early 526, when Theoderic suddenly summoned John to Ravenna and asked him to go to Constantinople together with a few senators as his envoy.[15] According to the *Liber pontificalis*, the king said that he would put the whole of Italy to the sword if the pope refused,[16] a gross-

---

[11] On Boethius' death, see Robinson 2004. On the reasons for his arrest and execution, see Barnish 1990, 30: "the letter of Albinus to the east concerned the possible regency or succession of Theodahad". This reconstruction has been accepted by among others Heather 1996, 250–254, and Vitiello 2014, 55–56.
[12] See e.g. Bertolini 1941, 88–89; Amory 1997, 216–218; Saitta 1999, 208.
[13] Lib. pontif. 54, 12 and 55, 1 and 6. Stein 1949, 255–256, unconvincingly argues that the letters dealt with the papal election of John I, a candidate whom Theoderic did not support. However, the rapidity of the choice of Hormisdas' successor indicates that it had been agreed upon in advance, and it is unlikely that either the senate or the Roman clergy dared to openly contradict Theoderic in an issue of such importance.
[14] Sardella 2000; Moorhead 2015, 65. Boethius dedicated three of his theological works to a deacon named John, who may be identical with the would-be pope John I.
[15] See Ensslin 1951.
[16] Lib. pontif. 55, 2: *omnem Italiam ad gladio perderet*.

ly exaggerated threat that echoes Theodahad's alleged plan to murder the senators and their families if Pope Agapetus did not convince Justinian to recall his army from Italy in 535–536.[17] It is beyond doubt that Theoderic never uttered such words, but he did possibly threaten the pope and the senators with the same fate as Boethius, since it cannot be ruled out that they were involved in Albinus' treacherous negotiations with Constantinople.

The sources do not agree on the instructions given to the pope. According to the *Liber pontificalis*, he should have convinced the emperor to give their churches back to the Arians,[18] whereas Marcellinus Comes and the *Excerpta Valesiana* mention only the Arians living within the Empire, who should have been allowed to continue practising their faith.[19] Interestingly, all sixth-century Eastern authors except Marcellinus are silent about an imperial persecution of the Arians and John Malalas writes that in 528 (three years later) the emperor seized all Arian churches except those of the Exakionites, a term used to refer to the Arianism of the Gothic sovereigns.[20] On this basis, one may conjecture that the pope's mission was successful and that for this reason Justinian did not seize the churches of the Exakionites. However, the *Liber pontificalis* relates the following information:

> The venerable pope John and the senators came home in glory after obtaining everything from the emperor Justin; King Theoderic the heretic received them with great treachery and hatred and he wanted to put them too to the sword, but in fear of the emperor Justin's

---

17 Liberat. 21 (*ACO* 2.5, 135), see below.
18 Lib. pontif. 55, 2: *ut redderentur ecclesias hereticis in partes Orientis*.
19 Marcell. chron. a. 525: *pro Arrianis suae caeremoniae reparandis*; Anon. Vales. 88–91. The interpretation of the latter passage is not straightforward due to different readings. Mommsen (*MGH, AA* 9, 328) reconstructs the text as follows: *Ambula Constantinopolim ad Iustinum imperatorem, et dic ei inter alia, ut reconciliatos in Catholica restituat religione* (Anon. Vales. 88; see also Festy 2020, 18), whereas Moureau and Velkov (1968, 25) prefer to include a controversial reading which is present in a few manuscripts (although enclosing it in square brackets): *Ambula Constantinopolim ad Iustinum imperatorem, et dic ei inter alia, ut reconciliatos [hereticos nequaquam] in Catholica restituat religione*. The meaning of this passage is clarified by Anon. Vales. 91: Justin *omnia repromisit facturum praeter reconciliatos, qui se fidei Catholicae dederunt, Arrianis restitui nullatenus posse*. See the commentary by König 1997, 201–202. Almost three centuries later, Theophanes the Confessor, chron. AM 6016, offers an account which is similar to that of the *Excerpta Valesiana*, since he reports that John should have ensured that the Arian subjects of the emperor were not forced to abandon their faith, yet he writes that Justinian did not confiscate the churches of the Exakionites shortly afterwards (chron. AM 6020), probably following Malalas' narrative.
20 John Malalas 18, 7. Cf. John Malalas. 15, 10, who calls Athalaric (or perhaps Theoderic) Ἀρειανὸς τῷ δόγματι, ὁ ἐστιν Ἐξακίονιτης. See Goltz 2008, 202.

wrath he destroyed them all by maltreatment in prison, so that blessed Pope John [...] grew weak and died.[21]

John had allegedly obtained everything from the emperor, but nevertheless the king put him in prison. This striking contradiction can be explained by comparing the embassy of Pope John with the embassies that went to Constantinople in 518–519. After his accession to the throne, Justin immediately tried to heal the Acacian Schism, which had divided the Church of Rome and Constantinople for three decades. Justin was a former soldier of humble origins and had no ties with the aristocracy of Constantinople.[22] He was therefore in dire need of a legitimization in a way that could strengthen his authority, and so he decided to come to terms with the Church of Rome. He granted the pope's requests and convinced the Patriarch of Constantinople to sign a document recognizing that "nobody can overlook the words of our Lord Jesus Christ, who said: 'You are Peter, and upon this rock I will build my church' (*Mt* 16:18)".[23] However, the pope was able to conclude the negotiations with Constantinople only after Theoderic had obtained the imperial recognition for his would-be heir, Eutharic, who was created consul together with the emperor himself, one of the greatest honours for a man of Late Antiquity.[24]

Religious and political aims coexisted during the negotiations of 518–519, but the latter were more important than the former, at least for Theoderic. It is likely that the same was the case again seven years later. In 525, succession was the most pressing problem for both Theoderic and Justin, who intended to leave the throne to his nephew Justinian. The Gothic king was aware of this situation and took advantage of it. He forced the pope to travel to Constantinople where, in the words of the *Liber pontificalis*, "Justin was filled with joy because he had deserved as emperor to see the vicar of St Peter the apostle in his own realm; and at his hands the

---

21 Lib. pontif. 55, 6: *Revertentes Iohannes venerabilis papa et senatores cum gloria, dum omnia obtinuissent a Iustino Augusto, rex Theodoricus hereticus cum grande dolo et odio suscepit eos, id est papam Iohannem et senatores, quos etiam gladio voluit interficere; sed metuens indignationem Iustini Augusti, quos tamen in custodia omnes adflictos cremavit, ita ut beatissimus Iohannes [...] deficiens moreretur.* The English translation is taken from Davis 2000, 50.
22 The reference work on Emperor Justin is still Vasiliev 1950, but see also Greatrex 2007, and Szidat 2019.
23 Avell. 159, 3. The same quotation occurs also in Avell. 116b, 1, app. 4, 1 (the *libellus fidei* which the Oriental bishops had to subscribe) and in Avell. 230, 1, written by the African bishop Possessor.
24 See Cristini 2019a.

emperor Justin was gloriously crowned".²⁵ The legitimization obtained through this coronation undoubtedly increased the prestige of the emperor and made Justinian's accession to the throne easier.

It is reasonable to conjecture that Theoderic, by allowing the pope to go to Constantinople and crown Justin, expected the end of the persecution against the Arians in exchange and, most importantly, imperial recognition of his heir, the young Athalaric.²⁶ According to two older versions of the *Liber pontificalis*, the so-called *Epitome Feliciana* and *Epitome Cononiana*, Justin did give back the churches to the Arians,²⁷ a success that is summarized in the last version of the *Book of the Pontiffs* by the statement that he obtained everything from the emperor. Yet, Theoderic imprisoned the pope as soon as he set foot in Italy. If John had had only one task, this behaviour would be hardly understandable.²⁸ But if we conjecture that the king mainly wanted to obtain Justin's recognition for his heir, John's failure to achieve it can explain his arrest.

Cassiodorus' *Variae* reports that Athalaric wrote to the emperor as soon as he came to the throne, a year after the pope's embassy, in order to ask for imperial recognition. For Theoderic, succession was much more pressing than a few vague laws against the Arians, so it is likely that he took advantage of Justin's need to strengthen his authority in order to achieve his goals, which were both political and religious. Furthermore, he chose as his envoys not only the pope, who may have been a close friend of Boethius, but also Inportunus and Theodorus,

---

25 Lib. pontif. 55, 4: *Iustinus imperator tamen gaudio repletus est quia meruit temporibus suis vicarium beati Petri apostoli videre in regno suo: de cuius manibus cum gloria coronatus est Iustinus Augustus.* See also Vitiello 2005.
26 See Moorhead 1992, 238, who suggests "the possibility that there was a hidden political agenda involved in the mission as to which our sources are silent". More explicit Heather 1996, 257: "the pope's embassy [...] may have been designed to win Justin's recognition for Athalaric", and Wiemer 2018, 554: "Denkbar wäre, dass Theoderich versuchte, die Zustimmung des Kaisers für eine Regelung der Nachfolge zu gewinnen".
27 Duchesne 1886, 104: *Epitome Feliciana* 55: *propter sanguinem Romanorum reddidit hereticis ecclesias*; *Epitome Cononiana* 55: *propter sanguinem Romanorum reddidit hereticis ecclesias suas*. The date of composition of these epitomes is still under discussion. The most convincing reconstruction has been offered by Verardi 2016, 31–76, who argues that both the Felician and the Cononian abbreviations were composed in the early sixth century before the full *Liber pontificalis*. For other hypotheses, see McKitterick 2020, 195–201.
28 Wiemer 2018, 555–558, suggests another explanation, namely that Theoderic resented Justin's coronation by the hand of the pope, considering it as an act of treason. However, it is unlikely that such an important ceremony had not been planned well in advance and, moreover, Theoderic was undoubtedly aware that the emperor would try to take advantage of the pope's visit, therefore his reaction would have been by far too harsh if John had fully achieved the main goal of the embassy.

who were brothers of Albinus, the senator who had first been accused of treason,[29] as if Theoderic intended to show to the emperor that those who had supported Theodahad a few years earlier were now willing to take part in an embassy aimed at securing Justin's recognition for the choice of Athalaric as the next king of the Goths.

Theoderic's plan proved unsuccessful, since he only managed to secure religious concessions for the Arians living within the Empire, and had an unexpected result, of significantly increasing the pope's prestige. Although first threatened and later arrested by the Ostrogothic king, John I managed to present himself as the head of the whole Catholic Church to the bishop of Constantinople a few years after the latter had been forced to acknowledge the pope's primacy. On the other hand, Justin was undoubtedly pleased with the outcome of the embassy, since he had strengthened his legitimacy and at the same time further alienated the Church and senate of Rome from Theoderic. John I and Justinian emerged as the winners from the embassy, whereas the Gothic king was unable to repeat the success of 519, namely winning the imperial recognition of his successor in exchange for the pope's support for Justin.

3 Agapetus: An Embassy for Christ and Theodahad

Theoderic's failure did not discourage Theodahad from pursuing a similar strategy a few years later. However, the relationship between the Goths and the Empire had changed dramatically in the meantime. In 526, Theoderic's grandson Athalaric came to the throne, but he was still a child and therefore his mother Amalasuintha became the *de facto* ruler of Italy.[30] Her regency lasted until 534, when her son died. Italy could not be ruled by a woman, therefore Amalasuintha appointed her cousin Theodahad as *consors regni*, that is "colleague of the realm", after he had sworn that "while the name of the office was to be bestowed upon him, she herself would in fact hold power no less than before".[31] Unsurprisingly, this joint-rule was short-lived. After just seven months or so, Amalasuintha was mur-

---

29 *PLRE* II, 592, Inportunus and 1097–1098, Theodorus 62. See also Wiemer 2018, 554.
30 See the seminal monograph by Vitiello 2017. The difficult legitimization of Athalaric has been examined by two recent papers: Wiemer 2020 and Bonamente 2020.
31 Procopius, *bellum Gothicum* 1, 4, 8 (the translation is taken from Dewing and Kaldellis 2014, 260, slightly modified): ἐς Θευδάτον μὲν τὸ τῆς ἀρχῆς ὄνομα ἄγοιτο, αὐτὴ δὲ τῷ ἔργῳ τὸ κράτος οὐκ ἔλασσον ἢ πρότερον ἔχοι. On the title of *consors regni*, see La Rocca 2012.

dered by Theodahad.³² Justinian took advantage of this *coup d'état* and declared war upon the Goths.³³ His troops took Sicily and Salona (in Dalmatia) within a few months, after which Theodahad tried to reach a deal with the emperor.³⁴ There is no space here for a full discussion of the ensuing negotiations, but suffice it to say that Pope Agapetus was in all likelihood sent to the East by the king to persuade the emperor to accept the deal.³⁵ He also had another purpose there, namely to force the Patriarch Anthimus to resign, since he was considered close to the Monophysites.³⁶

Liberatus of Carthage in his *Breviarium* states quite explicitly that the pope led two embassies: one for the king (*causa legationis susceptae*) and another for Christ (*Christi legatio*).³⁷ Liberatus is more interested in the dispute concerning the bishop of Constantinople than he is in Agapetus' role during the negotiations with the emperor about the ongoing war, yet he first relates (in a few words) the latter and only then considers the deposition of Anthimus and the appointment of a new patriarch, Menas.

According to his report, Agapetus was forced to leave Rome for Constantinople by the king, who threatened to put the whole of Italy to the sword if the pope did not undertake the embassy.³⁸ Again, his threat is undoubtedly exaggerated, but it is likely that Theodahad compelled the pope to travel to Constantinople against his will. Cassiodorus' *Variae* reports that Agapetus had to pawn several Church vessels to the royal treasury in order to obtain the money that was necessary to carry out the embassy.³⁹ This practice is quite unusual, especially since it was Theodahad who had ordered the pope to go to Constantinople without notice and therefore one could expect that the king would provide financial support for the embassy.

---

32 Vitiello 2014, 94–111.
33 This was the beginning of the so-called Gothic War, a conflict that lasted for two decades and laid waste to most of Italy. The most detailed overview of the war is still that of Rubin 1995, 59–200, but see also Heather 2018, 147–179 and 251–268, as well as Whitby 2021, 205–254.
34 Procopius, *bellum Gothicum* 1, 6.
35 Vitiello 2014, 128–132.
36 See Ensslin 1958, who focuses almost entirely on religious issues. The same is true for Powell 2020, 139–146.
37 Liberat. Brev. 21 (*ACO* 2.5, 135). The account of Lib. pontif. 59, 2 is more focused on the political aims of the embassy: *Hic missus est a Theodato rege Gothorum ad domnum Iustinianum Augustum in legationem, quia eodem tempore imperator domnus Iustinianus Augustus indignatus est Theodato regi, eo quod occidisset reginam Amalasuenta, filiam Theodorici regis, commendatam sibi, qui eum regem fecerat.*
38 Liberat. 21 (*ACO* 2.5, 135): *Theodatus rex Gothorum scribens ipsi papae et senatui Romano interminatur non solum senatores, sed et uxores et filios filiasque eorum gladio se interempturum, nisi egisserit apud imperatorem ut destinatum exercitum suum de Italia summoveret.*
39 Cassiod. Var. 12, 20.

In all likelihood, he appropriated the Church vessels with the aim of forcing the pope to act as his envoy. Interestingly, Cassiodorus also notes that he ordered them to be given back to papal officials once the embassy had achieved (some of) its goals.⁴⁰

Upon his arrival in Constantinople, Agapetus was greeted with the utmost respect, but his dealings with the emperor did not go as smoothly as those of John I ten years earlier. At first Justinian refused to depose Patriarch Anthimus and went so far as to threaten the pope with exile if he did not bend to his will, at least according to the *Liber pontificalis*. But the emperor accepted to do as Agapetus suggested after an apparently animated exchange.⁴¹

It is not completely clear whether the pope was successful or not, since the *Liber pontificalis* reports that he achieved all his goals, whereas Liberatus states that Justinian refused to recall his troops from Italy.⁴² The debate on the second (and main) aim of the embassy is further complicated by the uncertainty that surrounds the negotiations between Theodahad and Justinian, since Procopius reports that two different deals were discussed at the same time and that the king changed his mind more than once.⁴³ Moorhead remarks that the abovementioned passage of the *Liber pontificalis* "recalls the assertion in the same text that John I and his senatorial colleagues had returned from Constantinople having obtained everything. Perhaps the text attempted to make Agapetus's doings in the East conform to a model of how things should have been".⁴⁴ On the other hand, it is possible that the pope did convince Justinian to accept one of the agreements proposed by Theodahad, but then the king went back on his word.⁴⁵

However, for the sake of this paper the embassy itself is relevant rather than its outcome. The bishop of Rome went to Constantinople on behalf of the Goths for the second time in the space of less than ten years and both Theodahad and Justinian tried to take advantage of this visit. The Gothic king intended to put an end to the war by seeking the direct intercession of the pope, whereas the emperor

---

40 See also the detailed commentary by Lizzi Testa in Giardina 2015, 278–284. However, it is not certain that the embassies were commonly funded by the envoys themselves, see Gillett 2003, 188: this letter "can be generalised only tentatively for regular practice in the Ostrogothic kingdom, or other areas or times [...] There is no indication what arrangements for *tuitio* and financing of missions were made for embassies undertaken by non-senatorial court functionaries".
41 Lib. pontif. 59, 3–5.
42 Lib. pontif. 59, 6: *Agapitus papa omnia optenuit ex qua causa directus fuerat*; Liberat. 21 (*ACO* 2.5, 136): *imperator autem pro multis fisci expensis ab Italia destinatum exercitum avertere nolens supplicationem papae noluit audire*.
43 Procopius, *bellum Gothicum* 1, 6. See also Vitiello 2014, 119–128.
44 Moorhead 2015, 76.
45 Procopius, *bellum Gothicum* 1, 7, 11–12.

had to accept albeit unwillingly the pope's intervention in the affairs of the Church of Constantinople. His very submission to the authority of the bishop of Rome had great political significance,[46] as Justinian was eager to stress the difference between him, a pious Catholic sovereign who obeyed the pope, and Theodahad, an Arian king who had threatened to slaughter the Roman senators and their families. The pope was again able to take advantage of a quite difficult situation and re-assert his superiority over the bishop of Constantinople, whom he forced to leave his see. Theodahad's threats and the fact that Agapetus had been compelled to sail to Constantinople against his will did not affect his authority, which was rather strengthened by the emperor's deference to him.

4 Silverius: A Pope in Exile

Justinian's decision to grant the pope's requests soon bore fruit. Agapetus died in Constantinople shortly after the end of the negotiations, in April 536, and at the end of the same year the inhabitants of Rome opened the gates to the East Roman troops led by Belisarius. According to Procopius, the new pope Silverius "more than anyone else urged them to do this".[47] Silverius was the son of Pope Hormidas, who had enjoyed an excellent relationship with Theoderic, and had undoubtedly been elected with Theodahad's consent. After the latter's murder by Witigis, he possibly feared that the new king would take some action against him, so his decision to welcome Belisarius' troops into Rome is partly ascribable to the consequences of the fratricidal infighting between the Goths, yet the favourable outcome of Agapetus' embassy also played an important role.

Once the emperor had achieved his goal, namely the surrender of the ancient capital of the Roman Empire, he could afford to be less deferential towards the pope, who in the meantime found himself in the front-line of the conflict. In fact, both Silverius and the Romans expected that Belisarius would soon leave their city and bring the war to Ravenna, as had happened during the conflict between Odoacer and Theoderic, but they were mistaken.[48] The general decided to

---

[46] See Capizzi 1994, 65–66, who points out "la necessità di Giustiniano di non figurare come persecutore dei calcedoniani proprio all'inizio della guerra in Italia". See also Demacopoulos 2013, 119: in 535–536, "Justinian was deliberately promoting Roman ecclesiastical claims as a *quid pro quo* to lobby for Agapetus' support".

[47] Procopius, *bellum Gothicum* 1, 14, 4: μάλιστα δὲ αὐτοὺς Σιλβέριος ἐς τοῦτο ἐνῆγεν, ὁ τῆς πόλεως ἀρχιερεύς. See also Sotinel 2000a "Silverio".

[48] Procopius, *bellum Gothicum* 1, 14, 16–17.

entrench himself in Rome, which was shortly after besieged by Witigis.[49] A few months later, Silverius was suddenly accused of treason, deposed and exiled. Sixth-century sources offer two different explanations: the pope was either plotting with the Ostrogoths against the general or he was in disagreement with Empress Theodora on ecclesiastical matters.[50]

From the account of the *Liber pontificalis*, Silverius' deposition looks like an abduction, since it was carried out in the utmost secrecy for fear of causing an uprising. According to this report, the main reason behind the pope's dramatic removal from office was his refusal to re-accept Anthimus as Patriarch of Constantinople. Interestingly, it seems that Justinian first asked Silverius to come to Constantinople, and that he ordered to depose him only after the pope declined the invitation. This move caused a heated controversy in the Roman Church, as the new pope, Vigilius, was (in all likelihood correctly) suspected to have favoured Silverius' deposition in order to be appointed as his successor, and the controversial beginning of his pontificate evidently exerted a strong influence on sixth-century sources.[51]

Both ancient authors and modern scholarship tend to dismiss the charge of treason and focus on the dispute over the Patriarch of Constantinople, but the hagiographical account of Silverius' exile should not be followed blindly[52]. Procopius, who was an eye-witness of the first Gothic siege of Rome, reports that after a few months the population became unhappy with Belisarius, who had turned the city into a fortress and was exposing the Romans to the dangers of war.[53] An emotional testimony to their feelings during this period has also been preserved by Arator, who began a prefatory letter to his *Historia Apostolica* by writing that "When I watched the blazing battles from the resounding walls, I was one of those people who lived in fear of war".[54]

---

[49] On the siege of 537–538, see Breccia 2020.
[50] See Procopius, *bellum Gothicum* 1, 25, 13 (treason), Lib. pontif. 60, 6–9 (reinstatement of Anthimus as Patriarch of Constantinople), and Liberat. 22 (*ACO* 2.5, 136–137), who offers the most detailed account.
[51] See Hildebrand 1922 and Moorhead 2015, 79–80.
[52] Grazianskij 2021, 206–210, rightly doubts the traditional reconstruction, which is based on Procopius and Liberatus' accounts, but he argues that the pope was deposed by order of Justinian since the emperor hoped that Vigilius would prove more amenable to his wishes and aid his attempts of coming to a reconciliation with the monophysites. Salzman 2021, 261, rightly conjectures that "Silverius may have been trying to mediate some sort of truce, as Leo had done in 455".
[53] Procopius, *bellum Gothicum* 1, 20, 5–7.
[54] Arator, *ad Vigil.* 1–2: *Moenibus undosis bellorum incendia cernens, / pars ego tunc populi tela paventis eram.* The English translation is taken from Hillier 2020, 119 (slightly modified).

During the siege, Witigis tried more than once to win over the Romans; Procopius reports that, immediately after Silverius' deposition, Belisarius "banished some of the senators from Rome on the same charge", that is on the charge of treason.[55] It is likely that the dispute over Anthimus was little more than a pretext and that the real reason for Silverius' deportation was the fear that he could again open the gates of the city, this time to the Goths. The *Liber pontificalis* mentions a compromising letter of the pope, who was said to have promised to open the *Porta Asinaria* to the Ostrogoths.[56] As Moorhead remarks, "its location, just to the east of the Lateran, would have made it an ideal place for the city's bishop to admit enemies"[57] and nine years later the king Totila would enter Rome through this very gate.[58] Of course, this does not mean that the letter mentioned by the sources really existed, but only that an understanding between the pope and the senate, on the one hand, and the Goths on the other, should not be ruled out. The inhabitants of Rome were well aware of what happened to the Neapolitans after the storming of their city in 536[59] and were understandably eager to avoid incurring a similar fate, so it is possible that they contacted the Goths to discuss the terms of surrender.

Justinian could not afford to lose Rome and the support of its bishop at the same time, so he asked him to come to Constantinople as proof of his loyalty. A similar situation had occurred two years earlier. On this occasion, King Theodahad asked the senators to come to Ravenna since he was unsure about their attitude towards him, especially after the murder of Amalasuintha. The senators refused and the king did not force them to leave the city, instead seeking a compromise.[60] However, Justinian did not hesitate to assert his authority over Rome by deposing and exiling the pope, a step which the Gothic sovereigns had never taken. It was a

---

55 Procopius, *bellum Gothicum* 1, 25, 14: τινὰς δὲ καὶ τῶν ἐκ βουλῆς ἐπ᾽ αἰτίᾳ τῇ αὐτῇ ἐνθένδε ἐξελάσας. The English translation is taken from Dewing and Kaldellis 2014, 309. On Vitiges and his propaganda aimed at the Romans, see e.g. Procopius, *bellum Gothicum* 1, 20, 7–14; 2, 6.
56 Lib. pontif. 60, 7: *Et urguente iussione exierunt quidam falsi testes qui et dixerunt quia nos vicibus invenimus Silverium papam scripta mittentem ad regem Gothorum: 'Veni ad portam qui appellatur Asinariam, iuxta Lateranis, et civitatem tibi trado et Vilisarium patricium'*. See also Liberat. 22 (*ACO* 2.5, 136): *fertur autem Marcum quendam scholasticum et Iulianum quendam praetorianum fictas de nomine Silverii composuisse litteras regi Gothorum scriptas, ex quibus convinceretur Silverius Romanam velle prodere civitatem*.
57 Moorhead 2015, 80.
58 Procopius, *bellum Gothicum* 3, 20, 15. See Cristini 2022, 73–74.
59 Procopius, *bellum Gothicum* 1, 10, 29. On Neaples during the first phase of the Gothic War, see Tabata 2009, 225–231; Lillington-Martin and Stewart 2021, 290–295.
60 See Cassiod. *Var.* 10, 13–14. 16–18. And Vitiello 2014, 111–119.

move with few precedents,[61] which was in all likelihood not foreseen by the pope when he agreed to open the gates of Rome to Belisarius. Silverius' deportation thereby set a dangerous precedent and cast a disturbing shadow on the relationship between the Roman bishop and the emperor.

5 Vigilius: A Pope under Siege

The election of Silverius' successor, Vigilius, was determined by Belisarius, who was likely carrying out an order of Justinian. The Roman clergy had no choice but to obey, although quite a few priests and deacons voiced their disagreement.[62] Vigilius was a member of one of the most important Italian senatorial families.[63] His father had been praetorian prefect, his mother was a daughter of Olybrius, a leading member of the senate and praetorian prefect in 503, and his brother Reparatus had a distinguished career under both the Gothic sovereigns (Athalaric appointed him as *praefectus urbis Romae* in 527) and Justinian (becoming praetorian prefect in 538/539), until he was brutally murdered by the Goths after the fall of Milan in 539.[64] Vigilius was hence the perfect candidate to replace Silverius, since he could strengthen the ties between Justinian and the senatorial aristocracy, whose support was of paramount importance to rule Italy. Yet, the new pope did not follow Justinian's theological positions without a thought. As usual, contemporary sources dwell upon the religious controversies between pope and emperor and pay little attention to the political rivalry between them, which was an unforeseen consequence of having allowed a leading exponent of the senatorial aristocracy to become pontiff.

Pope Vigilius soon claimed not only a spiritual authority over Rome, but also a secular one, as is shown by Arator's *Historia Apostolica*.[65] According to a prefatory letter which was addressed to Vigilius, Rome was saved from the Goths by the pope, and not by Belisarius.[66] Here, Arator depicts the pope as a new Roman em-

---

61 Emperor Constantius II exiled Pope Liberius around 355. The most famous deportation of a pope during Late Antiquity occurred in 653, when Pope Martin I was exiled first to Constantinople and then to Cherson, in Crimea.
62 Liberat. 22 (*ACO* 2.5, 137): *quibus dubitantibus et nonnullis resistentibus favore Bilisarii ordinatus est Vigilius.*
63 Sotinel, 2000b "Vigilio"; Moorhead 2015, 84–94.
64 See *PLRE* II, 609–610, Ioannes 67; 795–796, Olybrius 5; 939–940, Reparatus 1.
65 Sotinel 1992.
66 Arator, *ad Vigil.* 3–6: *Publica libertas, sanctissime papa Vigili, / advenis incluso solvere vincla gregi. / De gladiis rapiuntur oves pastore ministro, / inque humeris ferimur te revocante piis.*

peror, using words which are reminiscent of Ovid's portrait of Augustus in his *Tristia*, as it has long been noticed.[67] Arator and his public were undoubtedly able to appreciate such learned quotations. The intertextual shift between an epic poem on the *Acts of the Apostles*, written in the mid-sixth century and a work written during the Age of Augustus contributed to portray Peter (as well as his successors) with imperial overtones.[68]

The purpose of this literary play is quite explicit, yet it can be further clarified with another example of papal *imitatio Imperii*. Arator presents Vigilius as *publica libertas* ("common freedom") in what is manifestly an allusion to the imperial past of Rome, since these words appear on coins minted under Galba, Vespasian, Nerva and Constantine.[69] Interestingly, the defence of Roman freedom was one of the most important ideological themes during the Gothic War: both Theoderic's successors and Justinian proclaimed that they were fighting to protect the freedom of Rome.[70] It is therefore likely that Arator imitated here a common motif of sixth-century propaganda, but he did so by using a clause that can be traced back to the times of the earlier Empire.

However, Vigilius was walking on thin ice, since he had been elected thanks to his ties with the imperial court, but had refused to accept Justinian's theological positions and acknowledge his control over the Church and the city of Rome. His situation became increasingly awkward when the emperor condemned the so-called Three Chapters, the works of three theologians who were said to be inclined towards Nestorianism.[71] This is not the place to dwell upon this controversy, suffice it to say that the Latin bishops and the pope strongly opposed this decision. The date of Justinian's edict is uncertain, but there are good reasons to believe that it was issued in 544.[72] A year later, Vigilius was arrested and brought first to Sicily and then to Constantinople, where he remained until the end of the Gothic War. According to the *Liber pontificalis*, Vigilius' exile was decided by Empress Theodora because the pope had refused to restore Anthimus to his office,[73] yet the pope re-

---

67 Deproost 1990, 60–63 (with bibliography).
68 See Deproost (1990, 217), who writes about "une *translatio imperii* qui confère au pontife romain l'ancien ascendant attaché à la souveraineté de l'empereur". On imperial echoes in Arator, see also McKitterick (2020), 63–65.
69 See e.g. Sutherland 1984, 233. 235–236. 239 (Galba); Mattingly and Sydenham 1926, 46. 65. 68 (Vespasian). 223–225. 227–229 (Nerva); Bruun 1966, 572–573. See also Angelucci 1990, 79–87.
70 See Moorhead 1987 and Cristini 2019b.
71 For an introduction to the Three Chapter Controversy, see Capizzi 1994, 97–149. More detailed Chazelle and Cubitt 2007.
72 Capizzi 1994, 99–100; Chazelle and Cubitt 2007, 3.
73 Lib. pontif. 61, 4.

mained in Sicily for many months in spite of Justinian's alleged urgency to settle these religious disputes.

Again, the political and military background of Vigilius' exile should be taken into consideration in order to understand its causes. In 545, the Goths led by King Totila had subjugated most of Italy and were threatening Rome.[74] Interestingly, Procopius reports that around the same time of Vigilius' deportation (in late 545), a suspicion of treason arose against Cethegus. The patrician, who was *caput senatus* at that time, had to move to Civitavecchia and then Constantinople.[75] There is not enough evidence to conclude that his exile and that of Vigilius were somehow connected, but one could entertain the possibility that the leaders of both the Church and the senate had fallen into disgrace after attempting to open negotiations with Totila. An agreement between Vigilius and the Gothic king was unlikely, but cannot be entirely ruled out. When the war came close to Rome again, its bishop had to reckon with the possibility that the Goths might take it and possibly tried to avoid a violent sack, following a practice that was quite normal in Late Antiquity.[76] Of course, Justinian could (and did) interpret this as an act of treason, but it would be misleading to think that the bishop of Rome hoped for a victory of Theoderic's people, since Silverius had acted in the same way when Belisarius had approached Rome. The choice of opening the gates was mostly dictated not by personal preferences, but by the desire to avoid a bloodbath.

Moreover, it did not escape Justinian that Totila could have used the pope to undermine Constantinople's authority over Italy if the Gothic king had conquered Rome, as is indicated by what happened in 546. After taking the city, Totila immediately dispatched the would-be pope Pelagius, the highest-ranking priest he found in Rome, to Constantinople with the aim of convincing the emperor to reach a deal.[77] Obviously, this embassy, not unlike those which preceded it, had political aims, but its symbolic dimension was equally important. By acting as envoys, Roman bishops and priests implicitly (and often unwillingly) acknowledged the Gothic rule over Italy and showed that the Church of Rome supported Theoderic's successors.

---

74 Rubin 1995, 165–170; Cristini 2022, 66–71.
75 Procopius, *bellum Gothicum* 3.13.12.
76 Caesarius of Arles was accused of treacherous dealings with the Burgundians during the War of Provence, see Klingshirn 1994, 106–110. Delaplace 2012 believes that the charges against Caesarius were groundless, yet it was a common practice for a bishop to look after the safety of his people if the secular autority was unable to do so, see e.g. Procopius, *bellum Persicum* 2, 5, 13; 2, 6, 17; 2, 11, 21–24.
77 Procopius, *bellum Gothicum* 3, 21, 18–25. See Cristini 2022, 112–115.

Justinian could not afford to lose the support of the bishop of Rome at a time when Totila had reconquered most of the Italian peninsula, so he decided to deport the pope for the second time in less than a decade. At the same time, he neutralized a possible rival for the symbolic inheritance of Rome and obtained a precious hostage who could guarantee the loyalty of the Roman Church in the coming years, since imperial threats might have been less effective in a city besieged (or controlled) by the Goths[78].

6 Conclusion

Sixth-century popes travelled unwillingly. They usually left their see only after being threatened or forced by a secular authority, and they were hardly to blame for their reluctance to venture beyond the Aurelian walls. As long as they were in Rome, they could count upon the support of (at least part of) the Roman clergy and senators, whereas outside the city they were more vulnerable. Furthermore, popes played an increasingly important role in ensuring the safety of the inhabitants of Rome from the fifth century onwards, so leaving the city often put their flock and the Church properties at risk. Age represented a further disincentive: long voyages were endurable for young clerics, but could (and did) prove fatal for bishops who were past their prime. In the sixth century, Constantinople proved to be "no country for old men", to quote the opening line of Yeats' famous poem *Sailing to Byzantium*, which provides a good – although entirely accidental – summary of early medieval papal travels to Constantinople.[79]

At the same time, the above-examined embassies show the increasing importance of the bishops of Rome, whose connections with the senatorial aristocracy became more evident between 525 and 545. John I was a personal friend of Boethius; Agapetus belonged to a distinguished Roman family; and Vigilius counted three praetorian prefects among his close relatives. Theoderic and his successors were able to take advantage of the charismatic authority of the pope to pursue their own goals, while at the same time preserving the appearance of a close cooperation between them and the senate, whose members were not entirely reliable after the execution of Symmachus and Boethius. Gothic sovereigns were ready to force the popes to act as their envoys by resorting to threats, yet they never de-

---

[78] For a more detailed analysis of the relationship between Vigilius, Justinian, and Baduila, see Cristini 2022, 139–142.
[79] Finneran 1989, 193.

posed or exiled them, since they needed their support in order to be able to rule over the Catholic population of Italy.

On the other hand, Justin and Justinian were glad to take advantage of papal visits to Constantinople to strengthen their power, complied with the wishes of the popes and made considerable concessions to them, often to the detriment of the Patriarch of Constantinople, but only as long as it suited their goals. Once Rome was in the hands of Belisarius, the emperor could afford to depose one pope and exile another. Justinian's conquest of Italy was a setback for the pontiffs: previously persuasion and religious concessions were as important as threats to secure their cooperation, but thereafter sheer coercion sufficed.

The embassies led by Pope John I and Agapetus, as well as the deportation of Silverius and Vigilius, clearly indicate that political issues were at least as important as theological ones, if not more so, and that the latter were often used to hide the main purpose of the pope's travel. The bishops of Rome took advantage of their role as envoys to increase their prestige, but at the same time they fell victim to their own fame, since the propagandistic value of their support became so great that both the Gothic sovereigns and the emperor were prepared to break with centuries-old traditions in order to achieve (or not to lose) it.

When Justinian forced the bishop of Rome to come to the East for the second time in less than a decade, he won a remarkable victory and at the same time conceded defeat. Unlike Theoderic and his successors, he had been able to exile (one might say to abduct) two popes without losing either the city of Rome or the support of its inhabitants. Yet he also proved himself unable to turn them into docile instruments of his foreign or ecclesiastical policy. Thus, two Arian rulers managed to convince the Roman pontiffs to act as their envoys, whereas Justinian gained only two illustrious (and troublesome) prisoners when he tried to bend them to his will, in spite of his threats and unrelenting pressure.

Bibliography

Primary Sources

Arator, *Ad Vigilium:* Richard Hillier. trans. 2020. Arator, *Historia Apostolica.* Liverpool: Liverpool University Press.
Collectio Avellana: Otto Günther. ed. 1895–1898. *Epistulae imperatorum pontificum aliorum inde ab a. CCCLXVII usque ad a. DLIII datae. Avellana quae dicitur collectio.* 2 Vols. Prague/Vienna/Lepizig: F. Tempsky.
Cassiodorus, *Variae:* Andrea Giardina. ed. 2015. Flavio Magno Aurelio Cassiodoro Senatore, *Varie.* Vol. 5. Roma: L'Erma di Bretschneider.

Epitome Cononiana and *Epitome Feliciana:* Louis Duchesne. ed. 1886. *Le Liber pontificalis.* Vol. 1. Paris : Thorin.
Excerpta Valesiana: Theodor Mommsen. ed. 1892. *Monumenta Germaniae Historica, Auctores antiquissimi (MGH AA).* IX, *Chronica minora saec. IV. V. VI. VII. (I).* Berlin: Weidmann; Moreau, Jacques, and Velizar Velkov. eds. 1968. *Excerpta Valesiana.* Leipzig: Teubner; Festy, Michel, ed. 2020. *Anonyme de Valois II. L'Italie sous Odoacre et Théodoric.* Paris : Les Belles Lettres.
Gelasius, *Epistolae:* Andreas Thiel. ed. 1868. *Epistolae Romanorum pontificum genuinae.* Vol. 1. Brunsbergae: in aedibus Eduardi Peter.
John Malalas: Johann Thurn. ed. 2000. Ioannis Malalae *Chronographia.* Berlin/New York: De Gruyter.
Liberatus, *Breviarium:* Eduard Schwartz. ed. 1936. *Acta Conciliorum Oecumenicorum. Concilium universale Chalcedonense, Collectio Sangermanensis (ACO).* 2, 5. Berlin/Leipzig: De Gruyter.
Marcellinus Comes: Theodor Mommsen. ed. 1894. *Monumenta Germaniae Historica, Auctores antiquissimi (MGH AA).* XI, *Chronica minora saec. IV. V. VI. VII. (I).* Berlin: Weidmann.
Procopius, *Bellum Gothicum:* Jakob Haury, and Gerhard Wirth. eds. 1963. *Procopii Caesariensis Opera omnia.* Vol. 2. Leipzig: Teubner; Dewing, Henry B., and Anthony Kaldellis. trans. 2014. Prokopios, *The Wars of Justinian.* Indianapolis/Cambridge: Hackett.
Procopius, *Bellum Persicum:* Jakob Haury, and Gerhard Wirth. eds. 1962. *Procopii Caesariensis Opera omnia.* Vol. 1. Leipzig: Teubner.
Theophanes, *Chronographia:* Carl de Boor. ed. 1883. Theophanis *Chronographia.* Vol. 1. Leipzig: Teubner.

Secondary Sources

Amory, Patrick. 1997. *People and Identity in Ostrogothic Italy, 489–554.* Cambridge: Cambridge University Press.
Angelucci, Paolo. 1990. *Centralità della Chiesa e primato romano in Aratore.* Roma: Herder.
Barnish, Samuel J.B. 1990. "Maximian, Cassiodorus, Boethius, Theodahad: Literature, Philosophy and Politics in Ostrogothic Italy." *Nottingham Medieval Studies* 34:16–32.
Bertolini, Ottorino. 1941. *Roma di fronte a Bisanzio e ai Longobardi.* Bologna: Licinio Cappelli Editore.
Bonamente, Giorgio. 2020. "*Puer in regia civitate:* Atalarico e la difficile legittimazione del regno (Cassiod. *Variae* VIII 1–8)." *Occidente/Oriente* 1:83–105.
Breccia, Gastone. 2020. "La difesa di Roma. Il capolavoro di Belisario, 536–538 AD." *Nuova Antologia Militare* 1:211–242.
Bruun, Patrick M. 1966. *The Roman Imperial Coinage.* Vol. 7: *Constantine and Licinius, A.D. 313–337.* London: Spink and Son.
Capizzi, Carmelo. 1994. *Giustiniano I tra politica e religione.* Soveria Mannelli: Rubettino.
Caliri, Elena. 2017. *Praecellentissimus rex. Odoacre tra storia e storiografia.* Roma: DICAM.
Canella, Tessa. 2017. *Il peso della tolleranza. Cristianesimo antico e alterità.* Brescia: Morcelliana.
Chazelle, Celia, and Catherine Cubitt, eds. 2007. *The Crisis of the Oikoumene. The Three Chapters and the Failed Quest for Unity in the Sixth-Century Mediterranean.* Turnhout: Brepols.
Cristini, Marco. 2019a. "*In ecclesiae redintegranda unitate:* re Teoderico e la fine dello Scisma Acaciano." *Rivista di Storia della Chiesa in Italia* 73:367–386.
Cristini, Marco. 2019b. "La *libertas* nell'Italia del VI secolo." In *Libertas. Secoli X–XIII. Atti del Convegno Internazionale, Brescia, 14–16 settembre 2017*, edited by Nicolangelo D'Acunto and Elisabetta Filippini, 215–229. Milano: Vita e Pensiero.

Cristini, Marco. 2022. *Baduila: Politics and Warfare at the End of Ostrogothic Italy*. Spoleto: Centro italiano di Studi sull'alto medioevo.

Delaplace, Christine. 2012. "Pour une relecture de la *Vita Caesarii* : le rôle politique de l'évêque d'Arles face aux représentants des royaumes burgonde, wisigothique et ostrogothique." *Annales du Midi* 124:309–324.

Deliyannis, Deborah. 2014. "The Roman *Liber Pontificalis*, Papal Primacy, and the Acacian Schism." *Viator* 45:1–16.

Demacopoulos, George E. 2013. *The Invention of Peter: Apostolic Discourse and Papal Authority in Late Antiquity*. Philadelphia: University of Pennsylvania Press.

Deproost, Paul-Augustin. 1990. *L'apôtre Pierre dans une épopée du VIe siècle : l'Historia apostolica d'Arator*. Paris : Institut d'Études Augustiniennes.

Ensslin, Wilhelm. 1951. "Papst Johannes I. als Gesandter Theoderichs des Grossen bei Kaiser Justinos I." *Byzantinische Zeitschrift* 44:127–134.

Ensslin, Wilhelm. 1958. "Papst Agapet I. und Kaiser Justinian I." *Historisches Jahrbuch* 77:459–466.

Finneran, Richard J. ed. 1989. *The Collected Poems of W.B. Yeats*. New York: Palgrave Macmillan.

Fournier, Éric. 2019. "Persecuting Heretics in Late Antique North Africa: Tolerant Vandals and Intolerant Bishops?" In *Inclusion and Exclusion in Mediterranean Christianities, 400–800*, edited by Yaniv Fox and Erica Buchberger, 147–166. Turnhout: Brepols.

Gillett, Andrew. 2000. "Jordanes and Ablabius." In *Studies in Latin Literature and Roman History X*, edited by Carl Deroux, 479–500. Bruxelles: Latomus.

Gillett, Andrew. 2003. *Envoys and Political Communication in the Late Antique West, 411–533*. Cambridge: Cambridge University Press.

Goltz, Andreas. 2008. *Barbar – König – Tyrann: Das Bild Theoderichs des Großen in der Überlieferung des 5. bis 9. Jahrhunderts*. Berlin/New York: De Gruyter.

Grazianskij, Michail. 2021. *Kaiser Justinian und das Erbe des Konzils von Chalkedon*. Stuttgart: Steiner.

Greatrex, Geoffrey. 2007. "The Early Years of Justin I's Reign in the Sources." *Electrum* 12:99–113.

Heather, Peter. 1996. *The Goths*. Oxford/Cambridge [Mass.]: Blackwell.

Heather, Peter. 2018. *Rome Resurgent. War and Empire in the Age of Justinian*. Oxford: Oxford University Press.

Hildebrand, Paul. 1922. "Die Absetzung des Papstes Silverius – 537 – Eine quellenkritische Untersuchung." *Historisches Jahrbuch* 42:1–37.

Klingshirn, William E. 1994. *Caesarius of Arles: the Making of a Christian Community in Late Antique Gaul*. Cambridge: Cambridge University Press.

König, Ingemar. 1997. *Aus der Zeit Theoderichs des Großen. Einleitung, Text, Übersetzung und Kommentar einer anonymen Quelle*. Darmstadt: Wissenschaftliche Buchgesellschaft.

Kötter, Jan-Markus. 2013. *Zwischen Kaisern und Aposteln: Das akakianische Schisma (484-519) als kirchlicher Ordnungskonflikt der Spätantike*. Stuttgart: F. Steiner

Kötter, Jan-Markus. 2020. "Katholische Geistliche, homöischer König. Gedanken zu konfessioneller Differenz und politischer Kooperation." In *Theoderich der Große und das gotische Königreich in Italien*, edited by Hans-Ulrich Wiemer, 175–191. Berlin/Boston: De Gruyter.

La Rocca, Cristina. 2012. "*Consors regni:* a Problem of Gender? The *consortium* between Amalasuntha and Theodahad in 534." In *Gender and Historiography: Studies in the earlier middle ages in honour of Pauline Stafford*, edited by Janet L. Nelson, Susan Reynolds and Susan M. Johns, 127–143. London: Institute of Historical Research.

Lillington-Martin, Christopher, and Michael Stewart. 2021. "Turning Traitor: Shifting Loyalties in Procopius' Gothic Wars." *Byzantina Symmeikta* 31:281–305.

Lizzi Testa, Rita. 2013. "Rome during the Ostrogoth Kingdom: Its Political Meaning as Apostolic See." In *Der Fall Roms und seine Wiederauferstehungen in Antike und Mittelalter*, edited by Henriette Harich-Schwarzbauer and Karla Pollman, 131–149. Berlin: De Gruyter.
Mattingly, Harold, and Edward A. Sydenham. 1926. *The Roman Imperial Coinage*, Vol. 2, *Vespasian to Hadrian*. London: Spink and Son.
McKitterick, Rosamond. 2020. *Rome and the Invention of the Papacy: The Liber pontificalis*. Cambridge: Cambridge University Press.
Moorhead, John. 1987. "*Libertas* and *nomen Romanum* in Ostrogothic Italy." *Latomus* 46:161–168.
Moorhead, John. 1992. *Theoderic in Italy*. Oxford: Clarendon Press.
Moorhead, John. 2015. *The Popes and the Church of Rome in Late Antiquity*. London/New York: Routledge.
Ożóg, Monika. 2016. *Inter duas potestates: The Religious Policy of Theoderic the Great*, trans. Marcin Fijak. Frankfurt am Main: Peter Lang.
Powell, Joshua. 2020. *Justinian's Indecision. How Social Networks Shaped Imperial Policy*. Piscataway (NJ): Gorgias Press.
Roberto, Umberto. 2020. *Il secolo dei Vandali: storia di un'integrazione fallita*. Palermo: 21 Editore.
Robinson, Phoebe. 2004. "Dead Boethius: Sixth-Century Accounts of a Future Martyr." *Viator* 35:1–19.
Rubin, Berthold. 1995. *Das Zeitalter Iustinians*, Vol. 2, Aus dem Nachlass herausgegeben von Carmelo Capizzi. Berlin/New York: De Gruyter.
Saitta, Biagio. 1999. "The Ostrogoths in Italy." *Polis. Revista de ideas y formas políticas de la Antigüedad Clásica* 11:197–216.
Salzman, Michele Renee. 2021. *The Falls of Rome: Crises, Resilience, and Resurgence in Late Antiquity*. Cambridge: Cambridge University Press.
Sardella, Teresa. 1996. *Società Chiesa e Stato nell'età di Teoderico. Papa Simmaco e lo scisma laurenziano*. Soveria Mannelli: Rubettino.
Sardella, Teresa. 2000. "Giovanni I, santo." *Enciclopedia dei papi* 1:483–487.
Sessa, Kristina. 2012. *The Formation of Papal Authority in Late Antique Italy. Roman Bishops and the Domestic Sphere*. Cambridge: Cambridge University Press.
Sotinel, Claire. 1992. "Autorité pontificale et pouvoir impérial sous le règne de Justinien : le pape Vigile." *Mélanges de l'Ecole française de Rome. Antiquité* 104:439–463.
Sotinel, Claire. 2000a "Silverio." *Enciclopedia dei papi* 1:508–512.
Sotinel, Claire. 2000b "Vigilio." *Enciclopedia dei papi* 1:512–529.
Stein, Ernest. 1949. *Historie du bas-Empire*, trans. Jean-Remy Palanque, Vol. 2. Paris/Bruges: Desclée de Brouwer.
Steinacher, Roland. 2016. *Die Vandalen. Aufstieg und Fall eines Barbarenreichs*, Stuttgart: Klett-Cotta.
Sutherland, Carol H.V. 1984^2. *The Roman Imperial Coinage*, Vol. 1, *From 31 BC to AD 69*. London: Spink and Son.
Szidat, Joachim. 2019. "Gewohnheiten der Diplomatie und die Wiederaufnahme des theologischen Dialogs durch Iustinus 518 n. Chr. (*Coll. Avell., Ep.* 141–148)." In *The Collectio Avellana and Its Revivals*, edited by Rita Lizzi Testa and Giulia Marconi, 190–209. Newcastle upon Tyne: Cambridge Scholars Publishing.
Tabata, Kayoko. 2009. *Città dell'Italia nel VI secolo d.C.* Roma: Bardi Editore.
Vasiliev, Alexander A. 1950. *Justin the First. An Introduction to the Epoch of Justinian the Great*. Cambridge [Mass.]: Harvard University Press.
Verardi, Andrea A. 2016. *La memoria legittimante. Il Liber pontificalis e la Chiesa di Roma del secolo VI*. Roma: Istituto Storico Italiano per il Medio Evo.

Vitiello, Massimiliano. 2005. "*Cui Iustinus imperator venienti ita occurrit ac si beato Petro.* Das Ritual beim ersten Papst-Kaiser-Treffen in Konstantinopel: eine römische Auslegung." *Byzantinische Zeitschrift* 98:81–96.

Vitiello, Massimiliano. 2014. *Theodahad. A Platonic King at the Collapse of Ostrogothic Italy.* Toronto/Buffalo/London: University of Toronto Press.

Vitiello, Massimiliano. 2017. *Amalasuintha. The Transformation of Queenship in the Post-Roman World.* Philadelphia: University of Pennsylvania Press.

Wessel, Susan. 2008. *Leo the Great and the Spiritual Rebuilding of a Universal Rome.* Leiden/Boston: Brill.

Whelan, Robin. 2018. *Being Christian in Vandal Africa. The Politics of Orthodoxy in the Post-Imperial West.* Oakland: University of California Press.

Whitby, Michael. 2021. *The Wars of Justinian.* Yorkshire – Philadelphia: Pen & Sword.

Wiemer, Hans-Ulrich. 2018. *Theoderich der Grosse König der Goten – Herrscher der Römer. Eine Biographie.* München: Beck.

Wiemer, Hans-Ulrich. 2020. "Von Theoderich zu Athalarich: das gotische Königtum in Italien." In *Theoderich der Große und das gotische Königreich in Italien,* edited by Hans-Ulrich Wiemer, 239–294. Berlin/Boston: De Gruyter.

Bruno Dumézil
Victims, Actors or Spectators? The Bishops of the Merovingian Kingdom during the Civil War of 575–613

Abstract: The so-called "royal bloodfeud" is often described as the most violent period in Merovingian history. But threats to bishops do not differ appreciably from the usual ones if we consider the cases of several individuals such as Aetherius of Lisieux, Egidius of Reims or Desiderius of Vienne. The real dangers are the result of a sum of matching factors. First, different actors must work against the bishop, both at the local level, among the Frankish episcopate and within the Palace. The king or queen never seems to act alone. Secondly, to be truly threatened, the bishop must himself constitute a threat to a leading player in the Civil War. Therefore, the bishops of the periphery have little to fear: they are mostly unconcerned spectators or actors of their own local game. Very few are victims. Finally, until the beginning of the 7th century, a strong argument is always needed to obtain the deposition of a bishop in a council and death never seems to be the goal. Unlike the murder of a king or a magnate, the assassination of a bishop is very bad publicity, which civil war actors are unwilling to see used against them.

The period between the death of Sigebert I in 575 and the execution of Brunhild in 613 is often seen as one of the most turbulent times in Merovingian history. Perhaps this judgment is a bit too harsh: the so-called royal bloodfeud was not a continuous process and it was not even the most violent period in the history of the dynasty, especially compared to the troubles of the 670s and 680s.[1] However, it does constitute a particularly well documented moment. The main witness is, of course, Gregory of Tours, who was both an observer and a protagonist of political affairs until the early 590s.[2] But we also have several series of contemporary epistolary documents, notably the *Austrasian letters* and the correspondence of Gregory the Great. A retrospective account of the events is provided by late Merovingian hagiography, by the extraordinary testament of Bertrand of Le Mans and, finally, by Fredegar.

---

1 Wood 1994, 88–101; Wood 2006.
2 Murray 2015, 61–101.

Admittedly, all these testimonies do not have the same value; none is neutral. But they offer an exceptional window over four decades, when the bishops of the Frankish world had to contend with a harsh political context. There are several ways to encompass the situation, but game theory can provide an interesting point of view.[3] Frankish bishops, like other actors in society, can be seen as players who have specific goals and who interact with other players who have their agendas as well. This interrelation can lead to conflicts, alliances or temporary collaborations, allowing each to move forward towards their own goals.[4] In this context, bishops can be seen as threatened pieces in the game, but also threatening pieces, alongside kings and lay aristocrats. In addition, all players do not have the same goals. Some bishops seem to occupy an essential place in the heart of the kingdom, while others had purely local ambitions; the link between the two levels, however, may prove essential to all policies.[5]

Let's start at the end, meaning the game's outcome in 613. Were the bishops among the major casualties of the civil war? From the point of view of observers, the first victims were the royals. We know the famous quotation of Fredegar in which King Clotar II accuses Brunhild of having caused the death of ten kings.[6] Even if the old queen is probably not the only culprit, the record is not entirely false. Significantly reduced, the Merovingian dynasty was the main victim of the Merovingian civil war: several kings were put to death, including Sigebert I, Chilperic, Theodebert II and Sigebert II. During the same period, more than a dozen princes also died violent or suspicious deaths. To a lesser extent, the secular aristocracy seems to have lost many members. Prominent personalities such as Guntram Boso or Rauching did not survive the troubles of the 580s; their family groups even seem to have been eliminated or so greatly reduced that they are no longer noticeable.[7]

Now let's consider the bishops. With almost one hundred cities in Merovingian Gaul, they were numerous. Using the method of Martin Heinzelman and Charles Mériaux, one can estimate that about two hundred and fifty were in office between 575 and 613.[8] The nature of our sources makes them well known, better than several kings and better than most secular aristocrats. However, even considering broadly the meaning of "threats", the toll in the sources remains remarkably small. Between 575 and 613, only three bishops are known to have been murdered:

---

3 Myerson 1997; Dagnino and Rocco 2009.
4 Le Jan, Bührer-Thierry, and Gasparri 2018.
5 Revel 1996.
6 Chronicle of Fredegar IV, 42.
7 Wood 1994, 99–100.
8 Heinzelmann 1993, 76; Mériaux 2018, 65–66.

Praetextatus of Rouen, Desiderius of Vienne and Sagittarius of Gap. The number is even lower considering that Desiderius and Sagittarius weren't bishops anymore when they were put to death. This number is also low if we consider the eighteen cases of bishops killed during Merovingian times, studied by Paul Fouracre: the era of the Neustrian dynasty killed more than during the moment of rivalry between the two branches of the Merovingian family.[9] Of course, between 575 and 613 around a dozen bishops suffered deposition, some of them provisionally as they later returned to their posts. But in quantitative perspective, the dangers that could strike down a bishop were relatively few compared to those incurred by the laity. So, we should not be trapped in the discourse of victimization that we find in our texts. In terms of survival, the bishops were certainly favoured players.

Beyond this general assessment, the place the actors occupy determines the risks they run. If we consider for example the case of the kingdom of Austrasia, the violent death of Sigebert I in 575 constitutes a crisis, which breaks the territory into two zones. First, there is the capital region, between Trier and Reims, which remains under the direct control of the Palace, that is, young king Childebert II and several courtiers. Then, there are the southern and western cities, over which the Palace exerts only a weak control, and which sometimes even escape it.[10] In the centre, we see the assertion of the power of three bishops: old Agericus of Verdun, the ambitious Egidius of Reims and, a little later, Magnericus of Trier. These three men have in turn the opportunity to participate in the regency organized around little Childebert. And it is in this capacity that they gain advantages, but also suffer major threats.

Magnericus is the least well known, although he is the successor and spiritual heir of the great Nicetius of Trier.[11] With the death of Count Gogo, his political faction suffers between 581 and 583; at times, he is perhaps led to take risks. If he is to be identified as the author of the *Austrasian Letters*, this collection shows that he had little significant activity during this period.[12] From 584, his group returned to power with Magnericus becoming a leading figure. In 586, he became the godfather of Theodebert II, son of Childebert II, and in 587 he participated in the negotiation of Andelot on behalf of Austrasia. This is when he came close to dying as Guntram Boso tried to use him to save his life.[13] But the threat he suffers is therefore a sign of triumph, not of downfall.

---

9 Fouracre 2003, 13–37.
10 Cardot 1987.
11 *PCBE* 4, 1223–1224, Magnericus.
12 Dumézil, 2019.
13 Greg. Tur. Franc. X, 10.

Let's consider Egidius of Reims, who became bishop before 566.[14] Trusted man of the late Sigebert I[15] and ruling a city located in the central region of Austrasia, he manages to take control of the Palace between 581 and 583, against the faction of Duke Lupus of Champagne and, probably, of the bishop of Trier.[16] But in 583, Egidius loses power; at a meeting of the Austrasian army, he is accused of conspiring against the king's interests and must flee in haste. Gregory of Tours tells us that the bishop of Reims loses a shoe and doesn't concern himself in hopes of reaching the safety of his city walls.[17] Egidius later became a secondary player, but that did not mean he was eliminated. The king still uses him in 584 as an ambassador.[18] In 587, he is suspected of having joined the plot of Rauchingus, without conclusive proof; he is forsaken by the king and makes his peace with Duke Lupus.[19] It was long after the victory of the faction of Magnericus that a council was organized in November 590 to condemn Egidius. This deposition undoubtedly owes a lot to a local group, that of the family of Lupus of Champagne, which seizes the occasion to obtain the see of Reims.[20]

For his part, the old Agericus of Verdun was the godfather of young king Childebert II.[21] No doubt of real importance during the reign of Sigebert I and at the start of the reign of his godson, but it gradually disintegrated, first against the faction of Egidius and then against that of Queen Brunhild. In 587, Agericus grants his protection to Guntram Boso, then to the children of Guntram Boso, but without results.[22] He also tries to protect Berthefredus, another enemy character of Brunhild, but to no avail. Gregory often describes Agericus as having been bitter at the time of his death in 588.[23] Despite all that, it is not his person that was threatened, but his succession: the palace imposes the *referandarius* Charimer as bishop, against the local candidate, Bucciovaldus, who was Agericus' abbot.

The situation is almost the same in Neustria. For example, Praetextatus of Rouen appears as an important bishop, who became godfather of prince Merovech.[24] In 576, he supported Merovech against his father Chilperic, but paid dearly by the downfall of his godson: in 577, Childeric convened a council of 45 bishops

---

14 *PCBE* 4, 615–618, Egidius 4.
15 Halfond 2014.
16 Isaïa 2009, 89–101; Dumézil, 2008, 249–252.
17 Greg. Tur. Franc. VI, 31.
18 Greg. Tur. Franc. VII, 14.
19 Greg. Tur. Franc. IX, 14.
20 Greg. Tur. Franc. X, 19.
21 *PCBE* 4, 71–72, Agericus 1.
22 Greg. Tur. Franc. IX, 8 and IX,10.
23 Greg. Tur. Franc. IX, 12.
24 *PCBE* 4, 1515–1519, Praetextatus 5.

against him. Praetextatus is accused of high treason, of uniting by marriage Merovech to his aunt Brunhild, and of stealing valuables. Probably led by Bertrand of Bordeaux, the council pronounces destitution, excommunication and exile.[25] His see goes to one Melantius.[26] But in 584, Praetextatus takes advantage of Chilperic's death to return from exile. King Guntram allows him to regain his see and it is Melantius who is exiled and goes into retirement to join Queen Fredegund, also in a difficult situation, at the *villa* of Vaudreuil.[27] In the spring of 586, Praetextatus is assassinated in his own cathedral by an unknown murderer, perhaps in the service of Fredegund, Melantius, or both.[28] In any case, it was Melantius who regained the post, with the support of part of the episcopate. It is seen once again that the fall of the bishop is not only connected with the civil war: internal and external factors unite.

We have to notice that the centre of the game isn't always dangerous. An example is Ragnemodus of Paris.[29] Godfather in 583 to one of Chilpéric's sons, Theodoricus, one might have expected he would be the victim of the twists and turns of the civil war. But Ragnemodus seems to follow the mainstream: he condemns and then absolves Praetextatus of Rouen, he threatens then supports Gregory of Tours, helps Queen Fredegund and then King Guntram. But he does not seem to have any major ambition, except to stabilize himself in Paris as the true heir of the great Germanus of Paris, which he easily survives.

Usually, of course, the fate of the main players follows that of the factions to which they belong. However, these bishops always fare better than kings or lay aristocrats. The cases of Egidius of Reims and Praetextatus remain exceptions. Their deposition is the result of an accumulation of threats: at the level of the realm, their faction has been defeated; at the city level, they fall victims to a rival group. And finally, they do not enjoy a consensus within the episcopate.

Now let's look at the edges of the game board to consider first Bishop Aetherius, who occupies the city of Lisieux, a city of no strategic or political importance.[30] In 584, Aetherius is the victim of a plot by his archdeacon and his schoolmaster. He flees to the kingdom of Guntram but remains accused in front of King Childeric, on whom the city depends. But there is no local consensus against him. So Childeric refuses to take part in the plot to appoint the schoolmaster as the new bishop. It seems that Aetherius is also supported by most of the Frankish episcopate. So Chil-

---

25 Greg. Tur. Franc. VII, 18. See Pontal 1989, 175.
26 Greg. Tur. Franc. VIII, 31.
27 Greg. Tur. Franc. VII, 19.
28 Greg. Tur. Franc. VIII, 31.
29 *PCBE* 4, 1585–1587, Ragnemodus.
30 *PCBE* 4, 65–66, Aetherius 6.

peric warns Guntram that there are no charges against Aetherius, who can return to Lisieux. Therefore, Aetherius regains his city.[31] Another case is that of Avitus from Clermont.[32] He had been elected in 571 with great difficulty, at the will of Sigebert I and against canon law. Facing him stood a local faction led by the priest Eufrasius.[33] One would have thought that the death of Sigebert I would weaken Avitus. It's quite the opposite. Isolated by the civil war, the bishop of Clermont can carry out completely autonomous operations and in particular expels Jews from his city.[34] These probably supported his local enemies.[35] In short, the civil war gives him a free hand to threaten whomever he wishes.

Of course, the problem is greater when bishops from the periphery endeavour to take a central position, or even try to create a new game of which they are masters. This is the case with some bishops who supported the usurper Gundovald.[36] In October 585, Guntram had five of his supporters sentenced. Faustinus of Dax is deposed; Bertrand of Bordeaux, Orestes of Bazas and Palladius of Saintes are condemned to pay 100 *solidi* of gold per year (ironically, to serve as a pension for Faustinus!). As for Ursinus of Cahors, he is excommunicated for three years.[37] These condemnations undoubtedly result from the will of King Guntram. But not only. Bishop Palladius was the victim of opposition from part of his clergy.[38] During their trial, he and Bertrand of Bordeaux insult each other copiously.[39] Obviously, the condemnation results from a lack of consensus around their person, which weakens them in the face of the anger of the Merovingian king. In 585, the only bishop who dies because of his adherence to the usurpation of Gundovald is Sagittarius of Gap, sentenced to death by Guntram.[40] However, one can wonder if his contemporaries still saw him as a bishop. He had been deposed six years before for adultery, homicide, lese majesty and high treason. And he had publicly wielded arms. His behavior disqualified him in the eyes of many. No one counted him as a martyr, even in the Church of Lyons where he had been the disciple of the great Nicetius around 560.[41]

---

31 Greg. Tur. Franc. VI, 36.
32 *PCBE* 4, 266–268, Avitus 5.
33 Wood 1983.
34 Greg. Tur. Franc. V, 11; Ven. Fort. Carmen V, 5; Goffart 1989.
35 Wood 1983, 44–48.
36 The Gundovald affair has been the subject of multiple interpretations, see: Goffart 2012. Bishops implicated in the affair are studied by Halfond 2000, 284–293.
37 Greg. Tur. Franc. V, 20.
38 Greg. Tur. Franc. VIII, 22.
39 Greg. Tur. Franc. VII, 39.
40 Greg. Tur. Franc. VIII, 7.
41 *PCBE* 4, 1680–1683, Sagittarius 2.

In the aftermath of the Gundovald affair, King Guntram's main target remains Bishop Theodorus of Marseille, not perhaps because he was the most involved, but because he is the subject of accusations that come from everywhere: from the Marseilles clergy, from the faction of rector Dynamius, from part of the Provençal episcopate, from the king of Burgundy who suspects him of treason and, finally, from Pope Gregory the Great who reproaches his forced conversion.[42] Let us add that Theodorus' situation is extremely complex since his city belongs partly to Austrasia, and partly to Burgundia. Despite all of this, Theodorus retains his post until his death. As he plays on two sets, there is no consensus to replace him, perhaps because there are too many candidates. And we know that Gregory of Tours sympathizes with him, because both are in the same geopolitical situation.[43]

From the point of view of Gregory of Tours, the bishop most threatened by the clashes of civil war is of course himself.[44] No doubt he dreamed of becoming a top player by giving his support to prince Merovech in 576 and by continuing to maintain friendship with Austrasia. He played and lost. The most important threat he suffers takes place in 580 when Childeric calls the Council of Berny against him where he is accused of having spread rumors against Fredegund.[45] No doubt Gregory of Tours pays for the support he gave to Childeric's enemies, but above all he has to endure the rivalry of several bishops, the hatred of part of his clergy and the personal rivalry of a count.[46] But the opposition is divided and King Childeric prefers to negotiate the rallying of Gregory, who ultimately emerges absolved. Then, he returns to what he always was: a second-tier player.

This far, in this best-known phase of the civil war, the opposition between kings and bishops seems less strong than the competition between local clerics and bishops, or even between bishops among themselves.[47] Keeping this in mind, one can envision the following decades, which are less documented. I will limit myself to the most famous cases.

The misfortunes suffered by Bertchram of Le Mans are mainly known from his will.[48] In 586 he becomes bishop. Le Mans falls under the kingship of Clotar II, but he does not seem to have any difficulty with King Guntram, whom he serves on several occasions. On the other hand, he must face the family of his predecessor

---

[42] *PCBE* 4, 1876–1679, Theodorus 7; Wood 1994, 84–86. On the local antagonism with Dynamius: Dumézil 2009.
[43] Greg. Tur. Franc. VIII, 12.
[44] See Goffart 1988; Wood 1993.
[45] Greg. Tur. Franc. V, 49.
[46] Heinzelmann 2015, 7–34.
[47] Mériaux 2018.
[48] Weidemann, 1986; *PCBE* 4, 345–351, Berthechramnus 2.

Baudigiselus for questions of heritage. In March 592, when Le Mans comes under the control of Childebert II, Bertchram is forced into exile and is replaced by one Berthigiselus, probably a relative of Baudigiselus.[49] Around 595, Clotar II takes over the city and Bertchram regains his see. He loses it in 600, when Clotar II is defeated by Theodoric II and Theodebert II. However, he eventually returns from exile in 604, thanks to an agreement between Clotaire II and Theodebert II. This time, Bertchram takes the opportunity to ruin his opponent Berthigiselus. It is difficult to know to what extent Bertchram of Le Mans' difficulties result from his involvement in Clotar II's party and to what extent they are the product of local rivalries. It should be noted that Bertchram is not at all threatened during the political crisis of 612, obviously because he no longer has a local opponent likely to ask Theodoric II for his deposition. Le Mans is by no means a central city, even on the scale of the petty Neustria of Clotar II. Bertchram, even though he is allied with the royal family, does not seem to have had such an important political role that would justify his woes. Civil war is simply the background of a clash between two local players.

The case of Desiderius of Vienne is more complex.[50] If we follow the account of the two *Passiones* composed on this character as well as the testimony of Fredegar, Desiderius is a victim of Queen Brunhild. But if other sources are used, his misadventures can be interpreted somewhat differently. Desiderius received the see of Vienne before 596. It is not impossible that he owed his post to Theodoric II and Brunhild, which would explain why the *Passiones* remain unclear about the time of his consecration. Soon, Desiderius comes into conflict with one of his deacons, Pancratius, who wants to retire to a monastery. Pancratius brings the matter to the attention of the pope, who decides in his favor.[51] This suggests that Desiderius is at least in conflict with some of his clergy. Desiderius also resumes an old struggle of the Church of Vienne by claiming the *pallium* in 599.[52] At that time, this petition went against the ancient rights of the bishop of Arles, but also against the claims of Syagrius of Autun; the latter is supported by Queen Brunhild.[53] Gregory the Great ends up denying the pallium to Desiderius.[54] At the same time, the pope signals to Desiderius that a great Gallic council will be convened under the leadership of Syagrius of Autun and Aregius of Gap.[55] We can see tensions in

---

49 *PCBE* 4, 352, Berthegisilus.
50 *PCBE* 4, 566–569, Desiderius 13; Nimmegeers 2014, 184–186.
51 Greg. M. epist. IX, 157.
52 Greg. M. epist. IX, 220.
53 Dumezil 2009, 338–340.
54 Greg. M. epist. IX, 220.
55 Greg. M. epist. IX, 218.

the episcopate, and the bishop of Vienne probably plays the troublemaker. At his own risk. In 601, rumors begin to reach Gregory the Great about the behavior of Desiderius.[56] In 602–603, Desiderius is accused of rape and is deposed by a council meeting in Chalon. Who is in charge? The sources mention several actors: Queen Brunhild, the mayor of the palace, Protagius, the bishop of Lyons Aridius, one Domnolus who recovers the see of Vienne.[57] A consensus seems to have been found to cause his downfall, but no direct connection between Desiderius and Clotar II can be identified; he is not a victim of the civil war between Brunhild and the Neustrian king. In 606 or 607, the queen meets a council that rehabilitates Desiderius.[58] But he is again accused by Bishop Aridius of Lyons. Desiderius is arrested by three counts and killed.[59] It remains unclear whether it was an accident or a disguised execution. The proclamation of his holiness is the result of a collective will: that of the clergy of Vienne, which intends to demonstrate his piety; that of the Wisigoth Sisebut, who wrote one of the *Passiones*, and wants to show Brunhild's death as that of a persecutor; that of Burgundian authors of the "Columbanian movement", who highlight the martyrdom of Desiderius to justify their rallying to Clotar II.[60]

Finally, we have to point out that none of the bishops who were supporters of Brunhild suffers from the downfall of the queen, even if they were main players in it. Aridius of Lyons and Desiderius of Auxerre keep their sees and even benefit from the benevolence of Clotar II[61]. Even Domnolus keeps Vienne.

In short, the threats to bishops during the royal bloodfeud do not differ appreciably from the usual ones. Even in the most restless decades, the danger does not seem particularly great. The real threats are the result of a sum of matching factors. First, several different actors must work against the bishop, both at the local level, at the level of the Frankish episcopate and within the palace. The king or queen never seems to act alone. In the 670s, the well-known case of Leudegarius of Autun confirms this impression.[62] Secondly, to be truly threatened the bishop must himself constitute a threat to a leading player in the civil war. Therefore, the periphery has little to fear: there, most bishops are unconcerned spectators, not actors. Very few are victims. Finally, until the beginning of the seventh century, a strong argument was needed to obtain the deposition of a bishop in

---

56 Greg. M. epist. XI, 34.
57 Sisebut. *Vita uel Passio Desiderii*, 4; Anonymous, *Vita II Desideri*, 2; Chronicle of Fredegar IV, 24. Martín 1995.
58 Sisebut. *Vita uel Passio Desiderii*, 10; Anonymous, *Vita II Desideri*, 8.
59 Anonymous, *Vita II Desideri*, 8.
60 Fouracre and Gerberding 1996, 22–24; Dumezil 2009, XIV–XVII; Fox 2010.
61 *PCBE* 4, 196–198, Aridius; 570–571, Desiderius 15.
62 Fouracre and Gerberding 1996; Dumézil 2017; Mériaux 2018.

a council.[63] And even a strong conviction is not necessarily an exit from the game. Mobilizing Roman law and synodal canons, the bishops sought to declare themselves sacrosanct, especially during the late sixth century.[64]

Deposition, exile or excommunication are often temporary situations: for the players, there are more losses than eliminations. A bishop's death never seems to be the goal. Unlike the murder of a king or a magnate, the assassination of a bishop is bad publicity, which civil war actors are unwilling to see used against them. So, in the political game of the Merovingians, it is not the king who constitutes an impossible piece to take, it's the bishop.

Bibliography

Primary Sources

Berthramn of Le Mans, *Testament:* Weidemann ed. 1986. Margarete *Das Testament des Bischofs Berthramn von Le Mans vom 27. März 616*. Main, Verl. der Römisch-germanischen Zentralmuseums.

Epistolae Austrasicae: Malaspina, Elena. ed. 2001. *Il Liber epistolarum della cancelleria austrasica*, Rome: Herder.

Fredegar, *Chronicarum libri IV cum continuationibus:* Bruno Krusch. ed. 1888. *Monumenta Germaniae Historica (MGH SS rer. Merov.)*. II. Hannover: Hahn.

Gregory of Tours, *Decem libri historiarum:* Bruno Krusch. ed. 1965. *Monumenta Germaniae Historica (MGH SS rer. Merov.)*. I. Hannover: Hahn.

Gregory the Great, *Registrum epistularum libri XIV:* Dag Norberg. ed. 1982. *Corpus Christianorum Series Latina (CCSL)*. 140 (1–7) et 140 A (7–14). Turnhout: Brepols.

Sisebut, *Vita uel Passio Desiderii ep. Viennensis:* Bruno Krusch. ed. 1896. *Monumenta Germaniae Historica (MGH SS rer. Merov.)*. III. Hannover: Hahn.

Venantius Fortunatus, *Carmina:* Marc Reydellet. ed. 1994–1998. 3 Vols. Paris : Les Belles Lettres.

Vita II Desiderii Cadurcae urbis episcopi: Bruno Krusch. ed. 1902. *Monumenta Germaniae Historica (MGH SS rer. Merov.)*. IV. Hannover/Leipzig: Hahn.

Secondary Sources

Cardot, Fabienne. 1987. *L'espace et le pouvoir. Études sur l'Austrasie mérovingienne*, Paris : Publications de la Sorbonne.

Dagnino, Giovanni Battista and Elena Rocco. eds. 2009. *Coopetition strategy: Theory, Experiments and Cases*, London–New York: Routlegde.

---

63 See the well documented case of Nicetius of Trier: Uhalde 1999.
64 Esders and Reimitz 2019, 85–111.

Dumézil, Bruno. 2008. *La reine Brunehaut*, Paris : Fayard.
Dumézil, Bruno. 2009. "Le patrice Dynamius et son réseau : culture aristocratique et transformation des pouvoirs autour de Lérins dans la seconde moitié du VIe siècle." In *Lérins, une île sainte de l'Antiquité au Moyen Âge*, edited by Yann Codou et Michel Lauwers. Turnhout: Brepols.
Dumézil, Bruno. 2019. "Private Records of Official Diplomacy: The Franco-Byzantine Letters in the Austrasian Epistolar Collection." In *The Merovingian Kingdoms and the Mediterranean World: Revisiting the Sources*, edited by Stefen Esders, Yitshak Hen, Pia Lucas and Tamar Rotman, 55-62. London: Bloomsbury.
Dumézil, Bruno. ed. 2017. *Le dossier saint Léger*, Paris : Les Belles Lettres, La roue à livres.
Esders, Stefan, and Helmut Reimitz. 2019. "After Gundovald, before Pseudo-Isidore. Episcopal jurisdiction, clerical privilege and the uses of Roman law in the Frankish kingdoms." *Early medieval Europe* 27:85-111.
Fouracre, Paul. 2013. "Why were so many bishops killed in Merovingian Francia?" In *Bischofsmord im Mittelalter. Murder of Bishops*, edited by Nathalie Fryde and Dirk Reitz, 13-37. Göttingen: Vandenhoeck & Ruprecht.
Fouracre, Paul, and Richard A. Gerberding. 1996. *Late Merovingian France. History and Hagiography 640-720*, Manchester-New York: Manchester University Press.
Fox, Yaniv. 2010. "The bishop and the monk: Desiderius of Vienne and the Columbanian movement." *Early Medieval Europe* 20:176-194.
Goffart, Walter. 1988. *The Narrators of Barbarian History (AD 550-800): Jordanes, Gregory of Tours, Beda and Paul the Diacon*, Princeton: Princeton University press.
Goffart, Walter. 1989. "The Conversion of Avitus of Clermont and Similar Passages in Gregory of Tours." In *Rome's Fall and After*, edited by Walter Goffart, 293-317. London: Hambledon Continuum.
Goffart, Walter. 2012, "The Frankish Pretender *Gundovald*, 582-585. A Crisis of Merovingian Blood." *Francia* 39:1-27.
Halfond, Gregory. 2014. "Negotiating episcopal Support in the Merovingian Kingdom of Reims (AD 561-575)." *Early Medieval Europe* 22:1-25.
Halfond, Gregory. 2000. "Corporate solidarity and its limits within the Gallo-Frankish episcopate." In *The Oxford Handbook of the Merovingian World*, edited by Bonnie Effros and Isabel Moreira, 278-298. Oxford: Oxford University Press.
Heinzelmann, Martin. 1976. *Bischofsherrschaft in Gallien. Zur Kontinuität römischer Führungsschichten von 4. bis 7. Jahrhundert*, München: Artemis Verlag.
Heinzelmann, Martin. 1993. "Les évêchés entre Loire et Rhin jusqu'à la fin du VIIe siècle." In *La christianisation des pays entre Loire et Rhin (IVe-VIIe siècle)*, edited by Pierre Riché, 75-90. Paris : Éditions du Cerf.
Heinzelmann, Martin. 2015. "Gregory of Tours: The Elements of a Biography." In *A Companion to Gregory of Tours*, edited by Alexander C. Murray, 7-34. Leiden-Boston, Brill.
Isaïa, Marie. 2009. "Egidius de Reims, le traître trahi ? En relisant Grégoire de Tours." In *La trahison au Moyen Age*, edited by Maïté Billoré et Myriam Soria, 89-101. Rennes : Presses Universitaires de Rennes.
Le Jan, Régine, Geneviève Bührer-Thierry and Stefano Gasparri. eds. 2018. *Coopétition. Rivaliser, coopérer dans les sociétés du haut Moyen Âge (500-1000)*. Turnhout: Brepols.
Martín, José Carlos. 1995. "*Quendam pestiferae mentis hominem*, un personaje sin nombre de la *Vita Desiderii*." In *Actas del I Congreso Nacional de Latín Medieval (León, 1-4 Diciembre de 1993)*, edited by Maurilio Pérez González, 307-313. León: Universidad de León.

Mériaux, Charles. 2018. "La compétition pour l'épiscopat en Gaule mérovingienne." In *Coopétition. Rivaliser, coopérer dans les sociétés du haut Moyen Âge (500-1000)*, edited by Régine Le Jan, Geneviève Bührer-Thierry and Stefano Gasparri, 61-76. Turnhout: Brepols.

Murray, Alexander Callander. 2015. "The Composition of the *Histories* of Gregory of Tours and Its Bearing on the Political Narrative." In *A Companion to Gregory of Tours*, edited by Murray, Alexander Callander, 61-101. Leiden-Boston: Brill.

Myerson, Roger. 1997. *Game Theory. Analysis of Conflict*. Harvard: Harvard University Press.

Nimmegeers, Nathanaël. 2014. *Évêques entre Bourgogne et Provence. La province ecclésiastique de Vienne au haut Moyen Âge (V^e-XIe siècle)*, Rennes : Presses Universitaire de Rennes.

Pontal, Odette. 1989. *Histoire des conciles mérovingiens*, Paris : Éditions du Cerf-IRHT.

Revel, Jacques, ed. 1996. *Jeux d'échelles. La micro-analyse à l'expérience*. Paris : Seuil.

Uhalde, Kevin. 1999. "Proof and Reproof: The Judicial Component of Episcopal Confrontation." *Early Medieval Europe* 8:1-11.

Wood, Ian. 1983. "The Ecclesiastical Politics of Merovingian Clermont." In *Ideal and Reality in Frankish and Anglo-Saxon Society, Studies presented to J. M. Wallace-Hadrill*, edited by Patrick Wormald, 34-57. Oxford: Blackwell.

Wood, Ian. 1993. *"The secret histories of Gregory of Tours." Revue belge de philologie et d'histoire, 71:* 253-270.

Wood, Ian. 1994. *The Merovingian Kingdoms 459-751*. London: Longman.

Wood, Ian. 2006. "The *Bloodfeud* of the Franks: a historiographical legend?" *Early Medieval Europe* 14:489-503.

Francesco Veronese
Bishops, Relics and Multi-Directional Pressures in Carolingian Northern Italy: The Cases of Verona and Milan

Abstract: In the aftermath of the conquest of the Lombard kingdom by Charlemagne (774), a number of figures coming from different regions of the Carolingian world were appointed as counts and bishops in Italy. They were called to act as intermediaries between local contexts and the new royal power, and to foster the integration of the kingdom's élites in the broader horizon of the Carolingian polity. In order to achieve that, they had first to negotiate their own integration within their new contexts of political, social, and cultural action. The cult of local saints and relics was one of the key issues they addressed to boost their own self-inclusion. A renewed care for the memory, celebration, and monumental settings of the special dead and their remains was one of the key elements in their struggle to establish channels of communication and cooperation with local élites and societies. Saints and relics were also the object of disputes and sometimes conflicts, and were used to support competing claims for ecclesiastical primacy. My paper will focus on two case-studies, the Carolingian bishops of Verona and Milan, highlighting their uses of saints, relics, and hagiography as tools to cope with the pressures, demands, and disputes resulting from their unsteady position as non-local figures holding authority over contexts they were initially unfamiliar with.

1 Stranger Things (and Bishops) in Carolingian Italy

The manuscript Saint Gall, Stiftsbibliothek, 733, most probably produced in Alamannia (Saint Gall itself?) in the first quarter of the 9th century, contains a collection of capitularies issued by Charlemagne and his son Pippin of Italy.[1] The collection opens with the capitulary of Herstal of 779 followed by the *Capitulare cum*

---

[1] The manuscript is available for online consultation at https://www.e-codices.unifr.ch/it/searchresult/list/one/csg/0733 (accessed 30.10.2022). – Research for this paper has been undertaken in the context of the PRIN 2017 project *Ruling in hard times. Patterns of power and practices of government in the making of Carolingian Italy*, P.I. Giuseppe Albertoni (University of Trento), research unit of Padova.

episcopis Langobardicis deliberatum (780–790), the *Admonitio generalis* of 789, a double capitulary *missorum* also issued around 789, Charlemagne's letter *in Italiam emissa* (779–781), and excerpts from Pippin's capitulary of Pavia (787).[2] This collection includes texts specifically concerning Italy, associated with some of the most important legislative issues of Charlemagne's reign such as the capitulary of Herstal and the *Admonitio generalis*, where the path and the general guidelines for Carolingian *correctio* found expression.[3] The small book, quite short (81 pages), is portable and clearly written by a single hand who took special care to highlight the beginnings of the capitularies and single chapters.[4] In his transcription of the *Admonitio generalis* the copyist carefully distinguished the addressees of each chapter (bishops, counts, the clergy, the people as a whole) with a peculiar graphic mark.[5] The mark recurs in following sections of the book, but not in those preeceeding the *Admonitio*. The final section of the book recorded under the title of *Collectio de decimis dandum* [sic] gathers passages from the *Liber scintillarum* by Defensor of Ligugé and decrees from Merovingian and Carolingian councils dealing with the duty to pay tithes, the most important source of income for bishops. The initial purpose of this collection is not entirely clear. Philippe Depreux, who recently provided an edition of this final section of Saint Gall 733, suggested it was composed for a royal *missus* on his way to Italy, where he was to transmit it to bishops.[6] If so, the manuscript now in Saint Gall must have either been a preparatory copy or in any case found its way back to Alamannia at some time. One should consider that from the *Divisio regnorum* of 806 to 829, Saint Gall and Alamannia were effectively part of the kingdom of Italy. Alamannian monks thus had good reasons to be interested in Italian capitularies. Hubert Mordek, though locating its production in "Südwestdeutschland", accorded equal plausibility to an Italian origin, as well as to a composition at Charlemagne's court for an Italian audience.[7] As underlined by Depreux, what seems to be common to all the texts of the collection, and quite probably determined the compiler's choices, is the general concern for bishops – and for Italian bishops specifically.[8] The Italian capitularies included in the collection mostly focus on bishops' public functions and duties. The capitulary of Herstal and the *Admonitio generalis* were likely included in order to provide the ideal

---

2 A full description of the codex and its contents is provided by Mordek 1995, 676–680.
3 On the circulation of Carolingian capitularies in Italy, Bougard 1995, 30–52; Davis 2015, 279–281.
4 Mostert 2016, 112–127, esp. 124.
5 On the position of the codex in the transmission of the *Admonitio generalis*, Mordek, Zechiel-Eckes, and Glatthaar 2012, 97.
6 Depreux 2018, 19–41, esp. 28–30 and 39–41. Also McKitterick 2009, 253–268, esp. 263.
7 Mordek 1995, 678.
8 Depreux 2018, 28–30.

framework in which bishops' public activities found their grounding and legitimacy from a Carolingian perspective. What clearly emerges from the choice of its contents is that somewhere – be it Alamannia, Aachen, or Italy – someone felt the need to provide bishops working in Carolingian Italy with a collection mostly legal but also with doctrinal sanctions of the roles and responsibilities connected with their charge and position, *ici compris* the payment of tithes, their key means of economic sustenance.

In the first decades of Carolingian power over Italy, bishops could be perceived as in need of such a collection. The Carolingian conquest of 774 deeply affected episcopal authority, responsibilities and roles in what had been the Lombard kingdom of Italy.[9] Both individual bishop's careers and their identity as belonging to a social group experienced deep changes, affecting the ways in which some were recruited. The new rulers established a number of trusted and culturally prominent men coming from beyond the Alps as bishops in Italy – mostly from Francia, Bavaria, Alamannia, and Burgundy – often trained in monastic milieus.[10] This establishment did not take place simultaneously in all episcopal seats of the kingdom. Appointments mostly involved Northern Italy and, somewhat later, Tuscany.[11] The bishoprics most concerned by the rulers were those seen as prestigious or ones that needed to be cast under direct and close control because of their strategic position or previous connections to the memory of the (Lombard) royal authority. The sources are almost totally silent about the procedures for appointments, although it seems that previous bishops were not removed by force. Rather, once they died candidates were chosen and supported as successors, probably imposed, by the Carolingian rulers. Destitutions only occurred in cases of open uprisings against Carolingian power. After the defeat of Bernard of Italy's rebellion of 817–818 some of the bishops who had supported Pippin's son, such as Anselm of Milan, were actually deposed, but that had more to do with their political leanings than with their episcopal responsibilities and activities.[12] The installation of non-local bishops frequently went hand in hand with that of other public officers, in the first place counts coming from beyond the Alps and taking the place of previous Lombard dukes or *gastaldi*.[13] In their cases, forced removal is more frequently attested, especially after the anti-Carolingian uprising lead by Hrotgaud, duke of Friuli, in 776.[14]

---

9 On bishops in Lombard times, Gasparri 2008, 137–159.
10 Hlawitschka 1960; Castagnetti 1995.
11 Bougard 2021, 54–81, esp. 60–61; on Tuscany (especially Lucca): Tomei 2019, 359–362.
12 De Jong 2009, 28–29; Santos Salazar 2021, 84–89.
13 Pohl 2008, 67–78; Bougard 2021, 59–60.
14 Davis 2015, 136–139; Gasparri 2021, 85–93, esp. 85–87.

Those installed by rulers as bishops and counts in the political and social landscape of the kingdom in Italy found themselves in ambivalent positions. Men of power, featuring highly advanced religious and juridical abilities, were called upon to cooperate in the integration of the kingdom within the Carolingian world and in the inclusion of Italian élites in its social networks and communications with the rulers. The capitularies issued for the kingdom echoed this urgency, expressing more generally Carolingian legislative actions, that counts and bishops work together in order to secure justice for local populations, maintain public buildings and support social peace and concord.[15] In other words, they were called upon to share responsibilities and tasks of government, and to support the rulers in the fulfillment of their ambitious *ministerium* of leading the Christian people to eternal salvation.[16] These public charges and the support granted by rulers set them in a condition of preeminence in their local activities. Yet their non-local provenance could undermine such a condition. At least initially these bishops were probably unknown to local society, and were urged to establish a dialogue in order to establish themselves as effective channels of communication between the localities and Carolingian power. They were required to build new connections, develop social networks and negotiate inclusion among the people they were meant to govern. These 'men in the middle' were exposed to pressures and expectations coming from both rulers and local societies.[17] In other words, they appeared both strong and weak at the same time. That is why a book such as the collection of legal and doctrinal texts of the manuscript Saint Gall 733, stating the bishops' public roles and the collective duty to pay tithes for their upkeep, would have been extremely precious in their eyes.

Another means by which many, but not only foreign, bishops of early Carolingian Italy used to respond to these needs was the cult of local saints and relics.[18] The memory of saintly figures belonging to the distant past and the glorious traditions of their sees was recovered and reasserted – and often reshaped. New ecclesiastical buildings were erected, or ancient ones restored using new architectural solutions and embellished with precious materials. These operations were frequently enhanced by the translation or relocation of saints' remains. New hagiographical texts dedicated to saints' holy lives and relics were composed. Their protagonists were thus provided with one of the mandatory conditions set by Car-

---

15 For instance Pippin's *Capitulare italicum* of 801–810: *MGH Capitularia regum Francorum*, I, ed. Boretius 1883, 209–211, n. 102.
16 On Carolingian royal *ministerium*, De Jong 2019.
17 I use here an effective definition developed for Carolingian local clergy (below the level of bishops) in Patzold and van Rhijn 2016.
18 An overview in Vocino 2014, 26–52.

olingian councils and capitularies for the cult of saints, that is, the existence (preferably written) of documentation attesting the long-lasting tradition of their veneration.[19] Carolingian Italy experienced a season of intense hagiographical production.[20] The care for local saints, their resting places, and their written memories became for non-local bishops a key to prove and celebrate the continuity between the past, in which those saints had lived and died, and the Carolingian present. The figures whose cults they venerated were usually martyrs and/or bishops from Late Antiquity, and thus effective for present-day bishops to present themselves as ideal successors. The dialogue with local societies for self-inclusion developed the formulation of new identities mixing both old and new. A sense of shared belonging to a common historical and spiritual tradition, usually and purposefully traced to the first centuries of the dissemination of the Christian religion, was meant to connect the new bishops and their flocks. In this perspective, the Carolingian present was to be seen as a natural continuation, and even fulfilment, of this long Christian history. In so doing these bishops embraced, and reworked according to their personal needs, those approaches to the Frankish past in Christian terms that played a key role in the political rhetorics and legitimacy of power in Carolingian times.[21]

In what follows I will focus my attention on two specific case-studies in which the activity of non-local bishops working in Carolingian Italy between the late 8th and the first half of the 9th century involved the use of saints, their relics, their resting places, and their written memories to negotiate their self-inclusion in local societies. I will attempt to illustrate different functions attributed to expressions of the cult of saints in contexts of unsteady balances of power, in which bishops were exposed to pressure and, sometimes, open threat.

2 Saint Bishops and Martyrs in Carolingian Verona

Between the 780s and 840s, the episcopal seat of Verona was consistently held by bishops having come from beyond the Alps, especially Francia and even more Alamannia.[22] Verona was thus one of the first places to experience the introduction of non-local royal officers following the Carolingian conquest.[23] This is hardly sur-

---

19 Veronese 2020a, 327–338.
20 Vocino 2014; with special concern for central Italy, Vocino 2017, 95–268.
21 McKitterick 2004; Reimitz 2015; Kramer, Reimitz, and Ward 2021.
22 Castagnetti 1990; La Rocca 1995.
23 Zettler 2009b, 89–114; Stoffella 2020a, 175–184.

prising. Even though officially it was never a capital, Verona had hosted rulers and their representatives since the time of the Ostrogothic king Theoderic in the 6th century, continuing through Lombard and Carolingian times.[24] Its position as a crossroads of communication routes linking the two sides of the Alps, as well as the extent of the Po valley both by land and water, made it strategically important from Carolingian rulers' perspective. The local Church featured a long and prestigious history, starring prominent figures such as the bishop (and saint) Zeno, a contemporary and correspondent of Ambrose of Milan.[25] The activity of a cathedral *scriptorium* and library, equally attested since the 6th century, as well as a school for the formation of the local clergy, guaranteed that the history, traditions and liturgical needs of the Church of Verona could be celebrated by the means of written texts.[26]

At least two of the earliest Carolingian bishops, Egino (ca 780–ca 802) and Ratold (ca 802–ca 840), were suitable choices to appreciate and make use of the culture available in Verona.[27] They were also connected with another context of significant cultural activity in Carolingian times, the powerful monasteries around the *Bodensee*, especially Reichenau.[28] It was here that Egino and Ratold most probably received their formation and, according to later hagiographical texts, had decided to spend their final years after retiring from episcopal duties.[29] Networks were established between Verona and Alamannia, allowing the exchange of books, texts, ideas, items (*ici compris*, as we will see, relics) and people. Reichenau and nearby Saint Gall, hubs for the production, preservation and dissemination of texts corresponding to the guidelines of Carolingian *correctio*, provided these bishops with the useful means in their struggle for inclusion. Verona thus became a vanguard position in the introduction of *correctio* and its textual production in Italy. An analysis of the liturgical books produced and/or in use in Verona in the late 8th to early 9th century demonstrates that.[30] The codex XCII of the Cathedral library, copied in the early 9th century, contains a collection of Roman *ordines*, liturgical formularies for rituals specifically pertaining to bishops.[31] *Ordines* experi-

---

24 Brogiolo 2005, 233–250.
25 Anti 2009; Piepenbrink 2015, 565–584.
26 Bassetti 2018; Bassetti 2018, 7–23, esp. 22–23.
27 Biographical data on Egino and Ratold resp. in Zettler 2009a, 363–385; and Hlawitschka 1997/1998, 5–32.
28 One of the most recent overviews on Carolingian Alamannia and its monastic communities is Weber and Zotz 2020.
29 Especially the 10th-century *De miraculis et virtutibus sancti Marci evangelistae* (ed. Klüppel 1980, 143–151).
30 Polloni 2007, 151–228.
31 Santoni 2009, 173–211, esp. 194–198; Polloni 2012, 349–350.

enced a large diffusion – and strong adaptations – in the Carolingian world precisely because of the allure of Roman authority attached to them, though their origin was not always Roman.[32] The codex XCII is a witness of the collection, labelled by Michel Andrieu as "Collection B", probably composed in the Rhineland.[33] Reichenau and the Alamannian bishops of Verona were the likely mediators for the transmission of these liturgical materials to Northern Italy. A contemporary local hand amended and commented on the texts of the *ordines*, especially highlighting deacons' liturgical roles, thus the interventions have been tentatively attributed to the archdeacon Pacificus, once credited as the scribe of the entire book.[34] Whatever their attribution, these corrections are interesting as they show that Verona's local clergy was actively involved in the negotiation, scrutiny and adaptation of liturgical materials brought by the early Carolingian bishops from their places of origin. Corrections were made on the grounds of another manuscript of the collection, probably the one now preserved in Cologne, ms 138 of the Erzbischöfliche Diözesan- und Dombibliothek.[35] In early 9th-century Verona no less than two copies of this collection were available and were consulted in order to adapt the Roman *ordines* to local liturgical customs and needs. Precisely because of its Roman origin – more constructed than actual – and identity of its liturgical formularies, Collection B was a book charged with the meanings that the Carolingians attributed to Romanness as a key element in their legitimacy.[36] Rome was presented as a repository of ancient, prestigious and authentic traditions, and Carolingian calls for *correctio* were nourished with references to Rome and what was believed to be Roman texts,[37] such as Collection B of Roman *ordines*. It functioned as one of the tools that early Carolingian foreign bishops deployed in Verona in order to establish a dialogue with the local clergy.

Egino and Ratold were also responsible for the production of sacramentaries in the *Gregorianum-Hadrianum* form, so called because a copy had been sent by Pope Hadrian to Charlemagne. This sacramentary was later reworked by Benedict of Aniane or, according to a recent attribution proposed by Franck Ruffiot, by Theodulf of Orléans, and was enriched with a number of formularies for specific votive masses.[38] Two exemplars are now preserved in the cathedral library, manu-

---

32 Andrieu 1931–1961.
33 Westwell 2018, 60–63.
34 Meersseman, Adda, and Deshusses 1974, 5. 62–65.
35 The manuscript is available for online consultation at http://www.ceec.uni-koeln.de/ceec-cgi/kleioc (accessed 30.10.2022).
36 Westwell 2019, 63–79. Also Sarti 2016, 1040–1058; Maskarinec 2018, 138–153.
37 Hen 2011, 111–124.
38 Ruffiot 2021.

scripts XCI and LXXXVI, dating respectively to the early and mid-9th century.[39] In these sacramentaries the supplement by Benedict of Aniane or by Theodulf of Orléans is missing. Their votive masses were taken instead from a so-called 8th-century Gelasian sacramentary, another book produced in the mode of Carolingian *correctio*, but from a different tradition and environment than the *Gregorianum-Hadrianum*.[40] Once again, the introduction of this sort of mixed sacramentary in Verona is usually explained by links connecting it to Alamannia. The archetype of ms XCI was most probably produced in Reichenau before the composition of the supplement by Benedict or Theodulf, and was then taken to Verona.[41] As Yitzhak Hen has repeatedly underlined, despite its Roman provenance the *Gregorianum-Hadrianum* was never formally imposed as an official product of Carolingian liturgical reforms.[42] Other textual shapes of sacramentaries, such as the forementioned 8th-century Gelasian, were developed and widely circulated at least until the mid-9th century. Carolingian rulers did nothing to prevent its transmission nor to patronize the circulation of the *Hadrianum*. In other words, the late 8th and early 9th-century bishops of Verona strongly supported the local implementation of Carolingian religious reforms in many different textual variations. Their choice of textual products was strictly connected to, perhaps limited by, books available in Reichenau. Yet the Roman identity of the *Hadrianum* sacramentary, declared on its title page as *a sancto Gregorio papa Romano editum*, was heavily emphasized, as can be seen in what remains of f. 2r of ms LXXXVI. Roman *ordines* and a sacramentary explicitly described as Roman were at the core of Egino and Ratold's efforts to introduce Carolingian reforms in Verona. As a result Verona was especially precocious in receiving and using these books in the territory of early Carolingian Northern Italy.[43] Verona became a hub for the Italian dissemination of liturgical books imbued with the Carolingian ideas of *correctio* and Romanness. Liturgy was thus key to these bishops' interventions tailored around the ideals of Carolingian *correctio*. The introduction of new liturgical practices was the ground upon which the Alamannian bishops established relations with the local clergy, thereby negotiating their integration in order to overcome their ambiguous condition. Liturgy was of common interest and shared responsibilities between bishops and their clergy. The texts they took to Verona were used, commented upon, and reproduced throughout the whole 9th century and beyond.

---

39 Polloni 2012, resp. 269–285. 337–341.
40 Moreton 1976.
41 Meersseman, Adda, and Deshusses 1974, 29–31; Polloni 2007, 169.
42 Hen 2001, 74–95; Hen 2018, 203–212.
43 Ferrari 1979, 265–279, esp. 269–272; Bougard 2021, 72.

In late 8th- to early 9th-century Verona, hagiography was equally affected by innovations. The manuscript XCV is a collection of hagiographical texts stitched together between the late 9th and early 10th century.[44] Its current structure is the result of an assemblage of 9th-century hagiographical booklets (*libelli*), previously circulating independently, and the final part of an early 9th-century passionary covering the whole liturgical year.[45] On the grounds of palaeographical considerations, the compilation can be located in Verona. What remains of this passionary is the earliest Italian example of this sort of hagiographical compilations.[46] Conspicuous collections of hagiographical texts are initially attested as originally conceived in the Frankish world towards the mid-8th century,[47] from where they rapidly spread to Bavaria and Alamannia. Once again this new means of transmitting hagiographical texts was presumably taken to Verona by its early Carolingian bishops and made Verona a pioneer in the diffusion of this new pattern of hagiographical books. The book witnesses that in Carolingian Verona, at least until the 1st half of the 9th century, both the traditional diffusion of hagiographical texts as *libelli* and as parts of larger collections coexisted. This is another expression of the negotiations between local and newly introduced customs that took place in Verona as a result of the activities of its early Carolingian bishops. Their investment in hagiography embraced a more general celebration of Verona's Christian past and its Carolingian present. The wealth of saintly memories and relics preserved in the city was exploited according to new needs. In the late 8th or early 9th century a *Life* of Saint Zeno, bishop of Verona in the 4th century, was written in the cathedral's cultural milieu by an author introducing himself as *Coronatus notarius*.[48] Later traditions point to a cooperative involvement of Bishop Ratold and Pippin, king of Italy, in the foundation of a monastery close to the basilica where Zeno's body was buried.[49] The monastery was richly endowed, ecclesiastical buildings were reconstructed, and Zeno's relics were translated following a fire.[50] Though the monastery's first appearance in documentary sources dates to 841, and evidence for the fire is later, the establishment of a monastic life in St Zeno can be attributed to Egino and Ratold – with or without King Pippin's involvement. This operation presents similarities with other cases of monastic foundations in Caro-

---

44 Polloni 2007, 178–181; 2012, 362–379.
45 Chiesa 1987, 123–153.
46 Bougard 2021, 68.
47 Dolbeau 2008, 13–35. On booklets as a material way of transmitting hagiographical texts, Poulin 2006, 15–193; Pilsworth 2010, 175–195.
48 *Sermo de vita sancti Zenonis* (ed. Marchi 1972, 18–23). Also Vocino 2014, 46–47.
49 Zettler (forthcoming).
50 On the whole issue now Stoffella 2020b, 543–596.

lingian Northern Italy, as we will see with Milan and St. Ambrose. Zeno's memory was promoted outside Verona as well. His cult probably diffused beyond the Alps already in the 8th century, due to political relationships between the Lombard kingdom and Bavaria.[51] Still the Alamannian bishops supported its further dissemination to areas with which they were tied, Alamannia and the Rhineland. The oldest surviving witness of Coronatus's *Life* is contained in a passionary produced at Reichenau in the 1st half of the 9th century.[52] Relics of Zeno were placed in the new basilica of the monastic compound of Fulda, as recorded by the *Tituli Fuldenses*, once attributed to Rabanus Maurus.[53] In the 850s Rabanus himself included the feastday of Saint Zeno in his martyrology.[54] Egino and Ratold used their saintly predecessor, his relics, and his written memories as if their own business cards. In this way they presented themselves in their new identity as bishops of Verona to the places and communities with which they were in touch.

In his martyrology, Rabanus recalled the death of the martyrs Firmus and Rusticus on the 9th of August, killed in Verona during the persecution of Maximianus – or Maximinus, according to other textual traditions.[55] For the composition of his entry Rabanus clearly relied on the *Passio et translatio Firmi et Rustici*, written in Verona.[56] The events described in this text, the trial and passion of the two martyrs and the long journey of their bodies back to Verona, took place between Late Antiquity and the late Lombard times.[57] The final translation of the relics to Verona is located during the joint kingdom of the two last Lombard rulers, Desiderius and Adelchis (759–774), thus dating the text to the third quarter of the 8th century[58]. Recently a thorough reassessment of the cultural and textual production of Carolingian Verona highlighted strong commonalities between this text and other products of that time, so that a composition of the *Passio et translatio* between the late 8th and the early 9th century seems equally plausible.[59] Whatever the case, the Carolingian bishops of Verona used these two martyrs' textual and material memories in a way similar to their treatment of Zeno. The earliest witness

---

51 Stoffella 2008, 73–85.
52 The manuscript is available for online consultation (accessed 30.10.2022) at https://digital.blb-karlsruhe.de/blbhs/content/titleinfo/3413876. Also Holder 1970, 119–131; Chiesa 2008, 105–125, esp. 109–110.
53 Kloft 2010, 367–387.
54 Rabanus Maurus, *Martyrologium* (ed. McCulloh 1979, 1–161, esp. 35 [12 April], 127 [8 December] and possibly 60 [20 June]).
55 Rabanus Maurus, *Martyrologium* (ed. McCulloh 1979, 78).
56 *Passio et Translatio sanctorum Firmi et Rustici* (ed. Golinelli 2004, 13–23: 13–19).
57 On this text, Veronese 2015, 85–114.
58 Golinelli 2004.
59 Veronese 2021, 219–249, esp. 222–230.

of their *Passio* (even though deprived of the *Translatio*) can be found in a manuscript from Saint Gall dating to the second half of the 9th century, now St Gall, Stiftsbibliothek, 566.[60] As we have seen, Rabanus Maurus most probably had a copy of this text. It probably reached Fulda together with the relics of the two martyrs that were installed in one of the altars of the new basilica – the same one containing Zeno's remains – in 818.[61] Local sanctity in all its shapes was at the core of Egino and Ratold's efforts to celebrate themselves as bishops of an ancient and prestigious seat in the eyes of their correspondents from the other side of the Alps.

The Carolingian bishops of Verona celebrated the memory of local saints through the means of hagiography. In so doing they also provided written documentation attesting their cult, as requested by Carolingian conciliar decrees and capitularies on saints' veneration. Two categories of audience were thus addressed. On the one hand these bishops were showing to Carolingian rulers their acceptance and respect of the new rules on saints and their cults, and their adherence to the principles of *correctio*. On the other hand they intended to prove to the local society of Verona that they were effectively willing to care for local memories and glories of their seat, to exploit its cultural resources, and to elevate local cults to standards imposed by the Carolingian legislation. New texts and religious experiences – such as the monastic community of St. Zeno – were tools they used to claim and appropriate the care for Verona's saints in their efforts for integration and their self-integration. In other words, saints and their celebration (both liturgical and textual) were the means of intervention the Alamannian bishops chose to face the pressures coming from both Carolingian kings and from the local society, efforts that appear at least partially successful. The cult and fame of the saints they celebrated reached beyond the Alps. From several points of view, the Alamannian bishops' self-integration seems effective during both Egino's episcopacy and the first period of Ratold's. The gradual dissemination of minuscule scripts with clear Raetian features among subscribers of Verona's charters points in that direction.[62] It was only later that pressures erupted, together with tensions within the Carolingian family. During the revolts against Louis the Pious by Bernard of Italy (817–818) and the emperor's sons (830–834), Ratold firmly took the position of Louis's side, thus losing the support of the Carolingian ruler of Italy, Lothar, who most probably forced him out of the kingdom.[63] His presence in Verona is no lon-

---

[60] The manuscript is available for online consultation (accessed 30.10.2022) at https://www.e-codices.unifr.ch/it/searchresult/list/one/csg/0566.
[61] Rabanus Maurus, *Carmina* (ed. Dümmler 1884, 154–258, esp. 208).
[62] Santoni 2009.
[63] Hammer 2007, 328–334.

ger attested after 834 – and very scantily already in the 820s.[64] Political outbursts of the Carolingian world produced pressures quite different from those that Ratold had managed in previous years. New priorities overcame his efforts at integration – and at self-integration.

3 Reshaping Ambrose in Carolingian Milan

Another place that precociously experienced Carolingian interventions in the appointment of ecclesiastical authorities was Milan – less surprising than in the case of Verona.[65] Milan, an imperial capital in Late Antiquity, was the metropolitan seat of North-Western Italy. Its long Christian tradition was strongly tied to the figure of Saint Ambrose, a Church Father, but also an active worshipper and purveyor of relics. In the Lombard era, Milan struggled in competition with Pavia, a suffragant seat according to ecclesiastical hierarchies but also capital of the kingdom. With the support of the Lombard kings, in the 7th and 8th century Pavia managed to rise to conspicuous autonomy from Milan.[66] The hagiographical celebration of local saints, firstly the bishop Syrus, played a crucial role in this competition, both in the Lombard and Carolingian periods.[67] Under the Carolingians' rule, the balances of power changed dramatically. Some scholars argue that Pavia paid for its former role as the Lombard capital, and more for the resistance it opposed to Charlemagne and his armies in 773–774.[68] On the contrary, relationships between Milan and the Carolingian rulers were close since Charlemagne's times, when Archbishop Thomas baptized the king's daughter Gisla (781).[69] A spiritual kinship was thus established between Charlemagne and Thomas. In the same year, a few months earlier, another spiritual tie linked the ruler to Pope Hadrian, who baptized Charlemagne's sons Carloman (renamed Pippin) and Louis (the Pious) in Rome, also elevating them to sub-kings of respectively Italy and Aquitaine.[70] Milan and Rome, in the range of months, were thus established as two key ecclesiastical partners of the Carolingian power in Italy. In the 780s, Thomas's successor Peter, for whom Frankish origins have been argued, founded in Milan a monastic community serving the basilica that preserved the body of Saint Am-

---

64 Depreux 1997, 358–360.
65 On Carolingian Milan, Castagnetti 2017.
66 Majocchi 2008, 17–37.
67 Everett 2002, 857–957; Vocino 2011, 169–186.
68 Settia 1987, 69–158, esp. 74–75; Vocino 2011, 171.
69 On this episode, Balzaretti 2019, 177–180.
70 Nelson 2019, 181–186.

brose.[71] Some years later (790) Peter had his foundation and land endowment to the monastery confirmed and enriched by Charlemagne.[72]

Milan soon became one of the key sites of Carolingian power and of its memory in Italy. According to a later and questionable tradition, both King Pippin and his son Bernard were buried in the basilica of St. Ambrose.[73] Yet – and this is clearly different from Verona – the appointment of non-local archbishops ceased with Peter and was reassessed only some decades later, for contingent reasons. Odelpertus, Peter's successor, spent his whole ecclesiastical career, from subdeacon to archbishop, in Milan.[74] The same events that increasingly precluded Ratold's presence and activity in Verona equally and deeply affected Milan. In 818, Archbishop Anselm was accused of supporting Bernard's uprising and paid for his affiliation with the loss of his charge.[75] The process of integration of Milan and its élites within Carolingian balances of power possibly experienced a backlash in the immediate aftermath of the rebellion. Yet Anselm's choice seems to suggest that he was integrated enough to take a conscious decision concerning his relations with the Carolingian rulers. His successor Bonus, in any case, was chosen from among the local clergy.[76] In other words, the need for the rulers' direct intervention in the imposition of an external candidate was not perceived as a direct consequence of Anselm's participation to the rebellion. Things changed, however, once Lothar came to Italy as its king in 822.[77] The archepiscopal seat was selected as a pivotal place in the establishment of his own agents and network of power as king.[78] Two homonymous figures of Frankish origins, Angilbert I (822–823) and II (823–859), perhaps relatives, were appointed as archbishops, most probably through Lothar's intervention. Especially the second Angilbert, during his long episcopacy, rose to a leading role in the political life of the kingdom both with Lothar and his son and successor Louis II.[79] In his late 9th-century chronicle, Andreas of Bergamo described Angilbert II as a consistent supporter of Lothar during his revolts against Louis the Pious, and chosen as Lothar's representative in negotiating the peace with his father. In a flattering episode, Andreas casts credit for Louis's forgiveness

---

71 Balzaretti 2019, 177–191.
72 *MGH Diplomata Karolinorum*, 1: *Pippini, Carlomanni, Caroli Magni Diplomata* (ed. Dopsch et al. 1906, 221–222, n. 164).
73 Balzaretti 2019, 81; and Nelson 2000, 131–184, esp. 160–161.
74 Ambrosioni 1986, 85–118, esp. 98.
75 Balzaretti 2019, 188–189.
76 Ambrosioni 1986, 98–99.
77 De Jong 2009, 32–33; Sernagiotto 2017, 215–246.
78 Vocino 2015, 135–154, esp. 137.
79 Bertolini 1961, 260–263; Tessera 2019a, 7–29.

of Lothar to Angilbert's demonstration of rhetorical skills and theological knowledge.[80]

Andreas' portrait of Angilbert is especially interesting – and well known. The chronicler described the first meeting between Angilbert and Lothar, when the king decided to ask the archbishop to be his intercessor at his father's court, as less than sympathetic. When he came to the ruler's presence, Angilbert bowed his head and respectfully greeted him, but didn't kneel as a form of reverence for his own ecclesiastical dignity as archbishop. A disappointed Lothar rebuked him, intimating that Angilbert believed to be Ambrose in person. Angilbert replied that he was no Ambrose, and that Lothar was not God the Lord.[81] The connection established by Andreas between Angilbert and his renowned predecessor Ambrose clearly reflects on the identity that Angilbert developed for himself as an archbishop and in order to consolidate the position of his Church in the ecclesiastical hierarchies of the Carolingian kingdom of Italy. The memory and cult of Ambrose, but also of other, not necessarily Milanese, saints were core to his endeavours, which took different shapes.

Angilbert's involvement in sanctity and Ambrose was not immediate. His first – actually his only – gift to the monastery of St. Ambrose is dated to 835, according to a *praeceptum* surviving in later interpolated copies.[82] The general validity of its contents can be proven by the confirmation of Angilbert's donations, enhanced by further donations of land, issued in that same year by Lothar in an original diploma[83] a few months before Lothar endowed the monastery with the estate of Limonta.[84] The gift was mediated and requested by the queen Ermengard on behalf of the soul of her little brother Hugh, who died at a young age and was buried in St. Ambrose. Angilbert and the royal couple's joint interventions were another step in the establishment of Ambrose's shrine as a place of memory for the Italian branch of the Carolingian family, including relatives from Ermengard's side.

Lands were not the only gift of the archbishop to the monastic community of St. Ambrose. Angilbert's charter most probably was consistent with the manufacturing of the famous altar in gold, silver and precious stones, signed by master

---

[80] Andreas of Bergamo, *Historia* (ed. Waitz 1878, 220–230, esp. 225–226, ch. 7); transl. in Berto 2021, 60–61. For a reading of this episode in its context, Noble 2021, 19–35, esp. 24–25.

[81] Andreas of Bergamo, *Historia* (ed. Waitz 1878, 225, ch. 7): *Tunc imperator dixit: "Sic contenis te, quasi sanctus Ambrosius sis!" Archiepiscopus respondit: "Nec ego sanctus Ambrosius, nec tu dominus Deus"*.

[82] Edited in *Codex Diplomaticus Langobardiae* (ed. Lambertenghi 1873, 218–219, n. 122).

[83] *MGH Diplomata Karolinorum, 3: Lotharii I et Lotharii II Diplomata* (DD LoI) (ed. Schieffer 1966, 99–101, n. 26).

[84] DD LoI, 93–95, n. 23. On these episcopal and royal gifts, Balzaretti 2019, 196–202.

Wolvinus, that still stands as the main altar of the basilica of St. Ambrose.[85] Recent studies by Miriam Tessera and Ivan Foletti have focused on this extremely precious and complex work of art, recasting it within its cultural and political context and suggesting new interpretative readings.[86] The golden altar was imbued with a range of meanings.[87] Its very existence and the formidable amount of resources spent for its production were a demonstration of Angilbert's generosity, but also of his will to commemorate the one who appeared to him as his most important predecessor. A line of continuity between the Late Roman, imperial past and the Carolingian, and once again imperial, presen times of his Church was thus established. The altar was also conceived as a reliquary for containing and preserving the bodies of Ambrose and two of the martyrs whose relics he had discovered, Gervasius and Protasius. The three saints' remains were placed together into the altar in a re-used Late Antique porphyry sarcophagus, another reference to the imperial past of Milan.[88] The deposition of the relics in the altar, most probably presided over by Angilbert himself, gave them centrality in the monastic basilica's space and reconfigured the ways in which pilgrims and the faithful had access to them. The decoration of the altar was programmed accordingly[89]: its front, facing the nave, records episodes from the Gospel. The faithful were thus addressed with the idea that the basilica, the saints buried inside it, and those who governed it – the archbishop, his clergy, and the monks – were part of the same stream of continuity, a parallel and even longer one than the link between different imperial moments. This was a history of salvation, connecting the Biblical and early Christian past and the Carolingian present.[90] This image of continuity, also embracing the Old Testament, was at the core of the rulers' strategies of self-legitimation, and was widely expressed and diffused in both Carolingian historiography and legislation.[91] On the back of the altar, episodes from Ambrose's life were carved and endowed with explanatory inscriptions. Interestingly, despite the presence of Gervasius and Protasius' bodies in the altar, their discovery by Ambrose does not appear among these episodes, even though it was described by Paulinus in his *Life of Ambrose*, one of the main sources for the saint's celebration on the altar's icono-

---

85 Among the rich bibliography on the golden altar, Hahn 1999, 167–187; Thunø 2006, 63–78; and the bibliography quoted in the next two footnotes.
86 Tessera 2019b, 216–225; Foletti 2020, 107–160.
87 Also Boucheron 2019, 103–126.
88 Cupperi 2004, 141–175.
89 For what follows, Foletti 2020, 138–146.
90 Tessera 2019a, 17–18.
91 Garrison 2000, 114–161; Reimitz 2015, 320–326; Heydemann 2020, 89–131.

graphic programme.⁹² Attention was to be dedicated to Ambrose. But whose attention? The altar's back could be seen almost exclusively by the monks, the clergy performing the liturgy and, less frequently, by high-ranking guests, such as kings, emperors, lay and ecclesiastical magnates. The basilica was visited by Carolingian kings since 781, when Charlemagne's daughter Gisla was baptized by the archbishop Thomas. Probably in preparation of that visit Ambrose's resting place was included in a list of places of interest for pilgrims to Italy, the *Itinerarium Salisburgense*, now preserved in Vienna.⁹³ These were among the categories of audience who could be physically in the position to appreciate the celebration of Ambrose orchestrated by Angilbert.⁹⁴ The personal relationship he established with his predecessor was equally highlighted.⁹⁵ One of the images on the *fenestella confessionis*, on the center back, shows Angilbert offering the altar to and being crowned by Ambrose.

The altar also offered the artistic opportunity and space for a celebration of the entire Christian history of Milan, what its sides clearly show. *Clipei* with the portraits of Milanese saints were arranged around central crosses and surrounded by angels. Ambrose, his successor Simplicianus, Gervasius and Protasius appear on the south side. One more bishop – Maternus or Mansuetus – and two more martyrs – Nabor and Nazarius – were carved on the opposite side, together with Saint Martin of Tours.⁹⁶ Angilbert thus produced his own interpretation of the glorious past (and present) of the Church of Milan, recalling its glories and protectors in a sort of metalwork *laus civitatis*, on the model of the 8th-century *Versum de Mediolano* or the early Carolingian *Versus de Verona*.⁹⁷ The archbishop crafted his celebration by both inclusion and exclusion. In his choice of the episodes concerning Ambrose, Angilbert decided to include the archbishop's oniric presence at the funeral of Saint Martin. This episode was not reported by Ambrose's traditional hagiography, the one composed by Paulinus of Milan, the source for other scenes and inscriptions surrounding them. Only Gregory of Tours, in his *Miracles of Saint Martin*, mentions the appearance of Ambrose at the burial.⁹⁸ This is the only episode that Angilbert took not from Paulinus, but from Gregory. Somehow he provided a

---

92 Paul. Med. vita Ambr. (ed. Bastiaensen 1975, 51–125, esp. 70–72, ch. 14). Also Petoletti 2019, 202–215.
93 Balzaretti 2019, 178–179.
94 Foletti 2020, 148–150.
95 Foletti 2020, 145–146.
96 The identification of the bishop as Mansuetus was suggested in Ferrari 2008, 281–291.
97 Both texts are edited in *Versus de Verona. Versum de Mediolano civitate* (ed. Battista 1960). Also Granier 2004, 131–154; 2009, 35–56.
98 Greg. Tur. *Miracula sancti Martini* (ed. Krusch 1885, 134–211, esp. 141, ch. 1.5).

sort of counterbalance to Gregory of Tours' account: while the *Miracles of Saint Martin* describes Ambrose spiritually present at Martin's grave, Angilbert made Martin's image physically present and (more or less) visible on the altar containing Ambrose's body. What is more, by choosing this scene the archbishop consciously established a connection between the saint he meant to celebrate and one of the key figures of Frankish sainthood in both Merovingian and Carolingian (as well as later) times, Martin of Tours.[99] The special relationship between the two saints is highlighted on the altar's sides, where their images are placed in the same positions within the crosses decorating them. Angilbert's inclusive efforts had not only artistic and literary but also (and most of all) social and political purposes. The representation of the Frankish Martin at Ambrose's shrine aimed to underline the integration of Milan in the Carolingian world.

Exclusion concerned the choice of the events of the life of Ambrose (whatever the source), featuring disputes and conflicts with the imperial power. The most famous of these episodes was the public penance imposed on Theodosius (390) by the saint after the slaughter of the citizens of Thessalonica.[100] The memory of this clash between episcopal and imperial authority, especially in the version offered by Cassiodorus in his *Historia tripartita*, was widely known in Carolingian times, when it was quoted to offer political advice to rulers.[101] Yet in Angilbert's programme celebrating Milan in Carolingian terms there was no place for memories of archbishops opposing, or humiliating, emperors. That was even more the case in 835, when the revolts against Louis the Pious came to an end and Lothar, together with a notable part of his key supporters, were sent (confined, according to the *Gesta Hludowici* by Thegan) to Italy by his father.[102] One of these *fideles* of Lothar was Hugh, former count of Tours, father of Queen Ermengard and thus Lothar's father-in-law[103]. His setting in Brianza together with his wife Ava strengthened the presence of Ermengard's family in the area around Milan, but could also offer the suggestion and chance to emphasize links between Milan and Tours.[104] For Angilbert and his struggle for (self-)integration those were years of extreme political tensions, and the new, full-time presence of Lothar and his followers could only increase them. The archbishop's gift to the monastery was conceived as a way to establish a dialogue between the glorious past of his seat and its Carolingian, even Lotharian, present. The golden altar was the place and object where

---

99 Farmer 1991; Van Dam 1993, 13–28; McKinley 2006, 173–200.
100 Meens 2014, 21–23; Van Renswoude 2019, 87–108.
101 Ward 2015, 68–83.
102 Thegan, *Gesta Hludowici* (ed. Tremp 1995, 167–277: 250, ch. 55).
103 Depreux 1997, 262–264.
104 Hlawitschka 1960, 221–226; Balzaretti 2019, 199; Veronese 2020b, 155–163.

the identity of his Church was re-designed in order to adapt it to these new conditions and dilute, even take advantage, of the pressures they created.

Angilbert's role in this new season of the cult of Ambrose in Milan has lead medieval authors, as well as later scholars, to note his involvement in other endeavours concerning Milanese saints and their relics. Precisely because of his multi-faceted interest, Angilbert is one of the candidates, together with his successors Tado (860–868) and Anspertus (868–881), as the addressee of the new and Carolingian version of the *Life of Ambrose*, only witnessed in the ms Saint Gall, Stiftsbibliothek, 569 and thoroughly analyzed by Giorgia Vocino.[105] Miriam Tessera recently provided a list of episodes of relics' displacements that, according to different sources, involved Angilbert II.[106] Relics of Quirinus and Nicomedis were given by Angilbert to the monastery of San Vincenzo in Prato. In 836, the archbishop presided over the transfer of Saint Calogerus' body from Albenga to Civate as a way to safeguard it from the Saracene raids on the coasts of Liguria. An inscription still preserved in Leggiuno on Lake Maggiore, some 60 kms North-West of Milan, attests that the royal *vassus* Erembertus, *ordinante domino Angilberto archiepiscopo*, placed relics of the martyrs Primus and Felicianus in the local church of St Syrus, on that occasion re-consecrated to the two saints.[107] Finally the 12th-century *Historia Hirsaugiensis Monasterii* reports that the relics of Aurelius, that Bishop Notingus took to his foundation of Hirsau, had been given to him by Angilbert. Some of these translations are witnessed only by later sources, so there is the possibility that in this list episodes actually involving Angilbert merged with later narrative constructions. Yet this very process of accumulation reflects the key role played by the cult and the mobilization of relics in Angilbert's activities as an archbishop, as well as long lasting success in the eyes of later authors and audiences.

Angilbert's efforts were apparently addressed to reassess and reinforce his Church's control over the territories and institutions of Milan's ecclesiastical province. Monastic reform as prompted by Carolingian *correctio* was one of the principles driving his interventions.[108] He exploited his personal network of relationships from the other side of the Alps, for highly trained reinforcements. When Bishop Rampertus of Brescia addressed him requesting help to establish a regular life at the basilica of the Sts. Faustinus and Giovita, Angilbert sent him the Frankish monks Hildemar and Leodegar, both imbued with the spirit of Carolingian monastic reforms.[109] Later Hildemar was also the author of a commentary on the Rule

---

[105] Vocino 2015. Also Vocino 2016, 331–349, esp. 343–345.
[106] For what follows, Tessera 2019a, 8–10. For an overview also Tomea 2006, 159–189.
[107] Edited in Petoletti 2001, 1–45, esp. 5. Also Castagnetti 2004; Castagnetti 2005, 139–153.
[108] On Carolingian monastic reforms, Kramer 2020, 432–449.
[109] Gavinelli 2005, 1–27; Archetti 2006, 113–124; Archetti 2018, 310–319.

of Benedict.[110] Once they accomplished their task in Brescia, they were asked to take reform to the community of Civate.[111] Angilbert thus set himself as a reference point for the institution or redefinition of religious experiences in the ecclesiastical province of Milan on the grounds of Carolingian principles. He was active in both the projection of Milan on the imperial stage and the injection of imperial discourses and practices in Milan.

4 Conclusions

In August 875 the emperor Louis II died near Brescia, one of Milan's suffragan seats. According to (once again) Andreas of Bergamo, the bishop Anthony of Brescia buried Louis's body in the local church of St. Mary.[112] This church also hosted the relics of one of Anthony's predecessors, Philastrius, bishop and saint in the late 4th century, a contemporary of Ambrose of Milan.[113] His relics had been relocated, and his cult reassessed, in 838 by Bishop Rampertus, who also took care to celebrate the event by writing a *Historia de Translatione beati Philastrii*.[114] Anspertus, archbishop of Milan, immediatley sent his archdeacon to claim the emperor's body, but Anthony refused to give it up. So Anspertus took the lead in an expedition gathering two more suffragan bishops of Milan, Garibaldus of Bergamo and Benedict of Cremona, and went to Brescia. Louis's body was lifted from its initial resting place and taken to the basilica of St. Ambrose in Milan. Andreas, whose text is our only source of this episode, was eager to underline his own role, not only as an eye-witness but also as one of those who materially carried the coffin over their shoulders. His text gives no other details about himself and his involvement in the events he relates. Andreas was a priest at the service of one of the bishops who escorted the emperor's body to Milan, Garibaldus, so was probably celebrating the loyalty of his Church and its head to its metropolitan seat.[115] In any case, this passage is especially interesting for my purposes. In Andreas' *Historia* the competition between Brescia and Milan for the possession of Louis's body becomes an episode in the definition of the relationships and balances of power between ecclesiastical authorities in late 9th-century Lombardy. This is highly indicative of the role assigned

---

110 Diem 2016, 243–261. Also Valtorta 2020, 229–259.
111 Piva 2002, 125–136.
112 Andreas of Bergamo, *Historia* (ed. Waitz 1878, 18. 229).
113 Spinelli 2004, 7–19.
114 Bettelli Bergamaschi 1975, 18–140, providing an edition of the text at 125–137. Also Vocino 2011, 174–175.
115 On Bergamo in Garibaldus's times, De Angelis 2009, 56–69.

by the Carolingian bishops of Northern Italy – both local and foreign – to the resources of the dead. Claims over their control could produce competitions, oppositions, conflicts, even between an archbishop and his suffragans. In a case such as this, in which the possession of a body was at stake, Anthony of Brescia could have perceived himself to be under open threat. To be sure, Louis II was not a saint, but he was an emperor, so he was in any case special, especially in the eyes of the archbishops of Milan, who since the late 8th century worked to establish a close relationship between their Church and Carolingian rulers. In Paolo Delogu's words, "Anspert seems to have aimed at creating a centre of royal devotion in Milan, whose guardian he planned to become".[116]

Royal devotion was flanked by saints' devotion. The Carolingian archbishops of Milan, especially those of non-local origins, invested considerable economic and cultural resources in their sponsoring of local saints. They identified themselves with the history of their Church, or with a version of it that could respond to their needs. The Alamannian bishops of Verona acted in similar ways. They exploited the ideal and material resources provided by local saints in order to build their identity as bishops. They then spread it via the network linking them to the other side of the Alps. Of course the two cases I focused on are not the only Italian contexts where such efforts for inclusion/integration (and self-integration) through the care for saints are evident. Yet the activities of the Alamannian bishops of Verona and the Frankish archbishops of Milan are especially well-documented by a range of sources, both written and material, and reflect a variety in the expression of this care. The non-local bishops (and archbishops) of Carolingian Italy were not necessarily, or not always, bishops under threat, even though their political choices could, and sometimes did, expose them to actual threats or, in any case, negative consequences. They were, however, bishops consistently under strong pressures, coming from both the royal power and local societies. Taking care of the saints and relics connected to places where they were active was perceived as a potentially effective way to prove to their local interlocutors that inclusion in the Carolingian politics could advantage all those who were involved. The special dead, their remains, their memories and their spaces provided these bishops with tools to overcome the pressures hanging over them.

---

[116] Delogu 2021, 36–55, at 49.

Bibliography

Primary Sources

Andreas of Bergamo, *Historia:* Georg Waitz. ed. 1878. *Monumenta Germaniae Historica, Scriptores rerum Langobardicarum (MGH SS rer. Lang.).* I. Hannover: Hahnsche Buchhandlung.

Andreas of Bergamo, *Historia:* transl by Luigi Andrea Berto. ed. 2021. *Franks and Lombards in Italian Carolingian Texts. Memories of the Vanquished.* London/New York: Routledge.

Capitulare italicum: Alfred Boretius. ed. 1883. *Monumenta Germaniae Historica, Capitularia regum Francorum (MGH Capit.).* I. Hannover: Hahn.

Codex Diplomaticus Langobardiae: Giulio Porro Lambertenghi. ed. 1873. Turin: E Regio Typographeo.

De miraculis et virtutibus sancti Marci evangelistae: Theodor Klüppel. ed. 1980. *Reichenauer Hagiographie zwischen Walahfrid und Berno.* Sigmaringen: Thorbecke.

Die Admonitio *generalis* Karls des Grossen: Hubert Mordek, Klaus Zechiel-Eckes and Michael Glatthaar. eds. 2012. *Monumenta Germaniae Historica, Fontes iuris Germanici antiqui in usum scholarum separatim editi (MGH Font. iur. Germ.).* XVI. Hannover: Harrassowitz.

Gregory of Tours, *Miracula sancti Martini:* Bruno Krusch. ed. 1885. *Monumenta Germaniae Historica, Scriptores rerum Merovingicarum (MGH SS rer. Merov.).* I, 2. Hannover: Hahnsche Buchhandlung.

Monumenta Germaniae Historica, Diplomata Karolinorum (MGH DD). I, *Pippini, Carlomanni, Caroli Magni Diplomata.* Engelbert Mühlbacher ed. 1906. Hannover: Hahnsche Buchhandlung.

Monumenta Germaniae Historica, Diplomata Karolinorum (MGH DD). III, *Lotharii I et Lotharii II Diplomata (Lo I).* Theodor Schieffer. ed. 1966. Berlin-Zürich: Weidmann.

Nell'anno del Signore 517. Verona al tempo di Ursicino: crocevia di uomini, culture, scritture: Massimiliano Bassetti. ed. 2018. Spoleto: Centro Italiano di Studi sull'Alto Medioevo.

Passio et Translatio sanctorum Firmi et Rustici: Paolo Golinelli. ed. 2004. "Passione e Traslazione dei santi Fermo e Rustico." In *I Santi Fermo e Rustico: un culto e una chiesa in Verona. Per il 17° centenario del loro martirio,* edited by Caterina Gemma Brenzoni and Paolo Golinelli. Verona: Parrocchia di San Fermo Maggiore.

Paulinus, *Vita Ambrosii:* Antonius Adrianus Bastiaensen. ed. 1975. *Vite dei santi.* 3, edited by Christine Mohrmann. Milano: Fondazione Lorenzo Valla.

Rabanus Maurus, *Carmina:* Ernst Dümmler. ed. 1884. *Monumenta Germaniae Historica, Poetae latini medii aevi (MGH Poetae).* 2. Berlin: Weidmann.

Rabanus Maurus, *Martyrologium:* John McCulloh. Ed. 1979. Rabani Mauri *Martyrologium – De Computo,* Corpus Christianorum, Continuatio mediaevalis (CCCM). 44. Turnhout: Brepols.

Sermo de vita sancti Zenonis: Gian Paolo Marchi. Ed. 1972. In *Il culto di San Zeno nel veronese,* edited by Gian Paolo Marchi, Angelo Orlandi and Maurizio Brenzoni. Verona: Banca Mutua Popolare di Verona.

Thegan, *Gesta Hludowici:* Ernst Tremp. Ed. 1995. *Thegani Gesta Hludowici imperatoris – Astronomi Vita Hludowici imperatoris,* edited by Ernst Tremp. *Monumenta Germaniae Historica, Scriptores rerum Germanicarum (MGH SS rer. Germ.).* LIV. Hannover: Hahnsche Buchhandlung.

Versus de Verona. *Versum de Mediolano civitate:* Giovanni Battista Pighi. ed. 1960. Studi pubblicati dall'Istituto di Filologia Classica 7. Bologna: Zanichelli.

Secondary Sources

Ambrosioni, Annamaria. 1986. "Gli arcivescovi nella vita di Milano." In *Atti del 10° congresso internazionale di studi sull'alto medioevo*, 85–118. Spoleto: Centro Italiano di Studi sull'Alto Medioevo.

Andrieu, Michel. 1931–1961. *Les Ordines romani du Haut Moyen Âge*, 5 vols. Louvain : Spicilegium sacrum Lovaniense.

Anti, Eduard. 2009. *Verona e il culto di san Zeno tra il IV e il XII secolo*. Verona: Edizioni dell'Abazia di San Zeno.

Archetti, Gabriele. 2006. "Ildemaro a Brescia e la pedagogia monastica nel commento alla Regola." In *San Faustino Maggiore di Brescia: il monastero della città*. Brixia Sacra 11/1, edited by Gabriele Archetti and Angelo Baronio, 113–124. Brescia: Associazione per la storia della Chiea bresciana.

Archetti, Gabriele. 2018. "Monasteri episcopali e cura delle anime: tre casi a confronto (secoli IX–XI)." *Hortus artium medievalium* 24:310–319.

Balzaretti, Ross. 2019. *The lands of Saint Ambrose: monks and society in early medieval Milan*. Turnhout: Brepols.

Bassetti, Massimiliano. 2018. "Cultura e scuola nella società dell'alto Medioevo: per una critica dei luoghi comuni." *Reti Medievali Rivista* 19/2:7–23.

Bertolini, Margherita Giuliana. 1961. "Angilberto." In *Dizionario Biografico degli Italiani*, 3, 260–263. Roma: Treccani.

Bettelli Bergamaschi, Maria. 1975. "Ramperto, vescovo di Brescia, e la *Historia de translatione beati Philastrii*." *Archivio Ambrosiano* 28:18–140.

Boucheron, Patrick. 2019. *La trace et l'aura. Vies posthumes d'Ambroise de Milan (IVe–XVIe siècle)*. Paris : Seuil.

Bougard, François. 1995. *La justice dans le royaume d'Italie. De la fine du VIIIe au début du XIe siècle*. Bibliothèque des Écoles Françaises d'Athènes et de Rome 291. Rome : École Française de Rome.

Bougard, François. 2021. "Was There a Carolingian Italy? Politics, Institutions and Book Culture." In *After Charlemagne: Carolingian Italy and its rulers*, edited by Clemens Gantner and Austrian Pohl, 54–81. Cambridge/New York: Cambridge University Press.

Brogiolo, Gian Pietro. 2005. "Capitali e residenze regie nell'Italia longobarda." In *Alto medioevo mediterraneo*, edited by Stefano Gasparri, 233–250. Firenze: Firenze University Press.

Castagnetti, Andrea. 1990. *Minoranze etniche dominanti e rapporti vassallatico-beneficiari, Alamanni e Franchi a Verona e nel Veneto in età carolingia e postcarolingia*. Verona: Libreria Universitaria Editrice.

Castagnetti, Andrea. 1995. *Teutisci nella Langobardia carolingia*. Verona: Libreria Universitaria Editrice.

Castagnetti, Andrea. 2004. *Una famiglia di immigrati nell'alta Lombardia al servizio del regno (846–898)*. Verona: Libreria Universitaria Editrice.

Castagnetti, Andrea. 2005. "Il vassallo regio Eremberto e la traslazione di reliquie nella chiesa privata di San Siro di Leggiuno (846)." In *Chiesa, vita religiosa, società nel medioevo italiano. Studi offerti a Giuseppina De Sandre Gasparini*. Italia Sacra 80, edited by Maria Clara Rossi and Gian Maria Varanini, 139–153. Roma: Herder.

Castagnetti, Andrea. 2017. *La società milanese in età carolingia*. Verona: Libreria Universitaria Editrice.

Chiesa, Paolo. 1987. "Note su un'antica raccolta agiografica veronese (Verona, Bibl. Capitolare, ms. XCV)" *Studi medievali*, 3. s. 28:123–153.

Chiesa, Paolo. 2008. "I manoscritti delle *passiones* aquileiesi e istriane." In *Le passioni dei martiri aquileiesi e istriani*, 1. Fonti per la Storia della Chiesa in Friuli dell'Istituto Pio Paschini – Udine,

Serie medievale 7, edited by Emanuela Colombi, 105–125. Rome: Istituto Storico Italiano per il Medioevo.

Cupperi, Walter. 2004. "Regia purpureo marmore crusta tegit: il sarcofago reimpiegato per la sepoltura di sant'Ambrogio e la tradizione dell'antico nella Basilica Ambrosiana di Milano." In *Senso delle rovine e riuso dell'antico*. Classe di Lettere e Filosofia, Quaderni 14, edited by Walter Cupperi, Annali della Scuola Normale Superiore di Pisa, 141–175. Pisa: Scuola Normale Superiore.

Davis, Jennifer. 2015. *Charlemagne's Practice of Empire*. Cambridge: Cambridge University Press.

De Angelis, Gianmarco. 2009. *Poteri cittadini e intellettuali di potere. Scrittura, documentazione, politica a Bergamo nei secoli IX–XII*. Studi di storia 5. Milano: Unicopli.

De Jong, Mayke. 2009. *The Penitential State. Authority and Atonement in the Age of Louis the Pious, 814-840*. Cambridge: Cambridge University Press.

Delogu, Paolo. 2021. "The Name of the Kingdom." In *After Charlemagne: Carolingian Italy and its rulers*, edited by Clemens Gantner and Austrian Pohl, 36–55. Cambridge/New York: Cambridge University Press.

Depreux, Philippe. 1997. *Prosopographie de l'entourage de Louis le Pieux (781-840)*. Instrumenta 1. Sigmaringen: Thorbecke.

Depreux, Philippe. 2018. "Charlemagne et les capitulaires : formation et réception d'un corpus normatif." In *Charlemagne : les temps, les espaces, les hommes*. Haut Moyen Âge 34, edited by Rolf Grosse and Michel Sot, 19–41. Turnhout: Brepols.

Diem, Albrecht. 2016. "The Carolingians and the *Regula Benedicti*." In *Religious Franks: religion and power in the Frankish kingdoms: studies in honour of Mayke de Jong*, edited by Rob Meens, Dorine van Espelo, Bram van den Hoven van Genderen, Janneke Raaijmakers, Irene van Renswoude and Carine van Rhijn, 243–261. Manchester: Manchester University Press.

Dolbeau, François. 2008. "Naissance des homéliaires et des passionnaires. Une tentative d'étude comparative." In *L'antiquité tardive dans les collections médiévales. Textes et représentations, VIe-XIVe siècle*. Collection de l'École Française de Rome 40, edited by Stéphane Gioanni and Benoît Grévin, 13–35. Rome: École Française de Rome.

Everett, Nicholas. 2002. "The Earliest Recension of the Life of S. Sirus of Pavia (Vat. lat. 5771)." *Studi Medievali*. 3. s. 43/2:857–957.

Farmer, Sharon. 1991. *Communities of Saint Martin. Legend and Ritual in Medieval Tours*. Ithaca: Cornell University Press.

Ferrari, Mirella. 1979. "Libri liturgici e diffusione della scrittura carolina nell'Italia settentrionale." In *Culto cristiano, politica imperiale carolingia*. Convegni del centro di studi sulla spiritualità medievale, Università degli Studi di Perugia 18, 265–279. Todi: Accademia Tudertina.

Ferrari, Mirella. 2008. "Il nome di Mansueto arcivescovo di Milano (672–681)." *Aevum* 82:281–291.

Foletti, Ivan. 2020. *Objects, relics, and migrants. The Basilica of Sant'Ambrogio in Milan and the cult of its saints (386–972)*. In between 2. Rome: Viella.

Garrison, Mary. 2000. "The Franks as New Israel? Education for an Identity from Pippin to Charlemagne." In *The Uses of the Past in the Early Middle Ages*, edited by Yitzhak Hen and Matthew Innes, 114–161. Cambridge: Cambridge University Press.

Gasparri, Stefano. 2008. "Recrutement social et rôle des évêques en Italie du VIe au VIIIe siècle." In *Hierarchie et stratification sociale dans l'Occident médiéval (400-1100)*. Haut Moyen Âge 6, edited by François Bougard, Dominique Iogna-Prat and Régine Le Jan, 137–159. Turnhout: Brepols.

Gasparri, Stefano. 2021. "The Government of a Peripheral Area. The Carolingians and North-Eastern Italy." In *After Charlemagne: Carolingian Italy and its rulers*, edited by Clemens Gantner and Austrian Pohl, 85–93. Cambridge/New York: Cambridge University Press.

Gavinelli, Simona. 2005. "Il gallo di Ramperto: potere, simboli e scrittura a Brescia nel secolo IX." In *Margarita amicorum. Studi di cultura europea per Agostino Sottili*, 1. Bibliotheca erudita 26, edited by Fabio Forner, Carla Maria Monti and Paul Gerhard Schmidt, 1–27. Milano: Vita e pensiero.

Granier, Thomas. 2004. "Á rebours des *laudes civitatum* : les *Versus Romae* et le discours sur la ville dans l'Italie du Haut Moyen Âge." In *Le médiéviste devant ses sources. Questions et méthodes*, edited by Claude Carozzi and Huguette Taviani-Carozzi, 131–154. Aix-en-Provence : Presses Universitaires de Provence.

Granier, Thomas. 2009. "La *renovatio* du modèle rhétorique antique dans les éloges urbains de l'Italie du haut Moyen Âge." In *Au Moyen Âge, entre tradition antique et innovation*. CTHS Histoire 36, edited by Michel Balard and Michel Sot, 35–56. Grénoble : Éditions du Comité des travaux historiques et scientifiques.

Hahn, Cynthia. 1999. "Narrative on the Golden Altar of Sant'Ambrogio in Milan: Presentation and Reception." *Dumbarton Oaks Paper* 53:167–187.

Hammer, Carl I. 2007. *From ducatus to regnum: Ruling Bavaria under the Merovingians and early Carolingians, Haut Moyen Âge 2*. Turnhout: Brepols.

Hen, Yitzhak. 2001. *The Royal Patronage of Liturgy in Frankish Gaul. To the Death of Charles the Bald*. London: Boydell and Brewer.

Hen, Yitzhak. 2011. "The Romanization of the Frankish Liturgy: Ideal, Reality and the Rhetoric of Reform." In *Rome Across Time and Space. Cultural Transmission and the Exchange of Ideas, c. 500–1400*, edited by Claudia Bolgia, Rosamond McKitterick and John Osborrne, 111–124. Cambridge: Cambridge University Press.

Hen, Yitzhak. 2018. "When Liturgy Gets Out of Hand." In *Writing the Early Medieval West. Studies in Honour of Rosamond McKitterick*, edited by Elina Screen and Charles West, 203–212. Cambridge: Cambridge University Press.

Heydemann, Gerda. 2020. "The People of God and the Law: Biblical Models in Carolingian Legislation." *Speculum* 95/1:89–131.

Hlawitschka, Eduard. 1960. *Franken, Alemannen, Bayern und Burgunder in Oberitalien (774–962): Zum Verständnis der fränkischen Königsherrschaft in Italien*. Freiburg im Breisgau: Albert.

Hlawitschka, Eduard. 1997/1998. "Ratold, Bischof von Verona und Begründer von Radolfzell." *Hegau* 54/55:5–32.

Holder, Alfred 1970. *Die Handschriften der Badischen Landesbibliothek in Karlsruhe. Neudruck mit bibliographischen Nachträgen*, 5/1: *Die Reichenauer Handschriften, Die Pergamenthandschriften*. Wiesbaden: Harrassowitz.

Kloft, Matthias Th. 2010. "Hrabanus Maurus, die 'tituli' und die Altarweihen." In *Raban Maur et son temps*. Haut Moyen Âge 9, edited by Philippe Depreux, 367–387. Turnhout: Brepols.

Kramer, Rutger. 2019. *Rethinking Authority in the Carolingian Empire. Ideals and Expectations during the Reign of Louis the Pious (813–828)*. Amsterdam: Amsterdam University Press.

Kramer, Rutger. 2020. "Monasticism, Reform, and Authority in the Carolingian Era." In *The Cambridge History of Medieval Monasticism in the Latin West*, edited by Alison I. Beach and Isabelle Cochelin 432–449. Cambridge: Cambridge University Press.

Kramer, Rutger, Helmut Reimitz, and Graeme Ward, eds. 2021. *Historiography and Identity III. Carolingian Approaches*. Cultural Encounters in Late Antiquity and the Middle Ages 29. Turnhout: Brepols.

La Rocca, Cristina. 1995. *Pacifico di Verona. Il passato carolinglo nella costruzione della memoria urbana*. Nuovi studi storici 31. Rome: Istituto Storico Italiano per il Medioevo.

Laury, Sarti. 2016. "Frankish Romanness and Charlemagne's Empire." *Speculum* 91/4:1040–1058.

Majocchi, Piero. 2008. *Pavia città regia. Storia e memoria di una capitale altomedievale*. Altomedioevo 6. Roma: Viella.

Maskarinec, Maya. 2018. *City of Saints. Rebuilding Rome in the Early Middle Ages*. Philadelphia: University of Pennsylvania Press.

McKinley, Allan S. 2006. "The First Two Centuries of Saint Martin of Tours." *Early Medieval Europe* 14:173–200.

McKitterick, Rosamond. 2004. *History and Memory in the Carolingian World*. Cambridge: Cambridge University Press.

McKitterick, Rosamond. 2009. "Charlemagne's *missi* and their books." In *Early Medieval Studies in Memory of Patrick Wormald*, edited by Stephen David Baxter, Patrick Wormald and Stephen Baxter, 253–268. Farnham: Ashgate.

Meens, Rob. 2014. *Penance in Medieval Europe, 600–1200*. Cambridge: Cambridge University Press.

Meersseman, Gilles Gerard, Edvige Adda, and Jean Deshusses. 1974. *L'orazionale dell'arcidiacono Pacifico e il* carpsum *del cantore Stefano*. Spicilegium Friburgense 21. Friburgo: Edizioni Universitarie.

Mordek, Hubert. 1995. *Bibliotheca capitularium regum Francorum manuscripta. Überlieferung und Traditionszusammenhang der fränkischen Herrschererlasse*. Hilfsmittel 15. München: Monumenta Germaniae Historica.

Moreton, Bernard. 1976. *The Eighth-Century Gelasian Sacramentary: A Study in Tradition*. Oxford: Oxford University Press.

Mostert, Marco. 2016. "'… but they pray badly using corrected books': errors in early Carolingian copies of the *Admonitio generalis*." In *Religious Franks: religion and power in the Frankish kingdoms: studies in honour of Mayke de Jong*, edited by Rob Meens, Dorine van Espelo, Bram van den Hoven van Genderen, Janneke Raaijmakers, Irene van Renswoude and Carine van Rhijn, 112–127. Manchester: Manchester University Press.

Nelson, Janet L. 2000. "Carolingian Royal Funerals." In *Rituals of Power. From Late Antiquity to the Early Middle Ages*. The Transformation of the Roman World 8, edited by Frans Theuws and Janet L. Nelson, 131–184. Leiden/Boston/Köln: Brill.

Nelson, Janet L. 2019. *King and Emperor. A New Life of Charlemagne*. Oakland: University of California Press.

Noble, Thomas F.X. 2021. "Talking about the Carolingians in Eighth- and Ninth-Century Italy." In *After Charlemagne: Carolingian Italy and its rulers*, edited by Clemens Gantner and Austrian Pohl, 19–35. Cambridge/New York: Cambridge University Press.

Patzold, Steffen, and Carine van Rhijn, eds. 2016. *Men in the Middle. Local Priests in Early Medieval Europe*. Berlin/Boston: De Gruyter.

Petoletti, Marco. 2001. "Contributo all'epigrafia lombarda del IX secolo: le iscrizioni altomedievali dei ss. Primo e Feliciano a Leggiuno." *Italia medioevale e umanistica* 42:1–45.

Petoletti, Marco. 2019. "Nequimus esse martyres, sed repperimus martyres. Le reliquie di Ambrogio, Protaso e Gervaso nelle fonti antiche e medievali." In *Apparuit Thesaurus Ambrosius. Le reliquie di Sant'Ambrogio e dei martiri Gervaso e Protaso tra storia, scienza e fede*, edited by Carlo Faccendini and *Carlo* Capponi, 202–215. Milano: Silvana editoriale.

Piepenbrink, Karen. 2015. "Christliche Gemeinden in *Venetia et Histria.* Verona und Aquileia in der Perzeption der Bischöfe Zeno und Chromatius." *Athenaeum. Studi periodici di letteratura e storia dell'antichità* 103:565–584.

Pilsworth, Claire. 2010. "Vile Scraps: 'Booklet' style manuscripts and the transmission and use of the Italian martyr narratives in early Medieval Europe." In *Zwischen Niederschrift und Wiederschrift: Frühmittelalterliche Hagiographie und Historiographie im Spannungsfeld von Kompendienüberlieferung und Editionstechnik*, Forschungen zur Geschichte des Mittelalters 18, edited by Richard Corradini, Maximilian Diesenberger and Meta Niederkorn-Bruck, 175–195. Wien: Österreichische Akademie der Wissenschaften.

Piva, Paolo. 2002. "Sulle tracce di un'abbazia carolingia: Civate" *Hortus artium medievalium* 8:125–136.

Pohl, Walter. 2008. "'Gens ipsa peribit'. Kingdom and identity after the end of Lombard rule." In *774. Ipotesi su una transizione.* Seminari internazionali del Centro interuniversitario per la storia e l'archeologia dell'alto medioevo 1, edited by Stefano Gasparri, 67–78. Turnhout: Brepols.

Polloni, Susanna. 2007. "Manoscritti liturgici della Biblioteca Capitolare di Verona (secolo IX)." In *Medioevo. Studi e documenti*, 2, edited by Andrea Castagnetti, 151–228. Verona: Libreria Universitaria Editrice.

Polloni, Susanna. 2012. *I più antichi codici liturgici della Biblioteca Capitolare di Verona (secc. V–XI), Catalogo descrittivo.* Studi e documenti di storia e liturgia 45. Verona: Archivio Storico Curia Diocesana.

Poulin, Jean-Claude. "Les *libelli* dans l'édition hagiographique avant le XIIᵉ siècle." In *Livrets, collections et textes. Études sur la tradition hagiographique latine.* Beihefte der Francia 6, edited by Martin Heinzelmann, 15–193. Ostfildern: Thorbecke.

Reimitz, Helmut. 2015. *History, Frankish Identity and the Framing of Western Ethnicity, 550–850.* Cambridge: Cambridge University Press.

Ruffiot, Franck. 2021. *Théodulf d'Orléans, compilateur du Supplementum au Sacramentarium Gregorianum Hadrianum. Le témoignage du corpus des préfaces eucharistiques.* Liturgiewissenschaftliche Quellen und Forschungen 111. Münster: Aschendorff.

Santoni, Francesca. 2009. "Scrivere documenti e scrivere libri a Verona." In *Le Alpi porta d'Europa. Scritture, uomini, idee da Giustiniano al Barbarossa. Atti del convegno internazionale di studio dell'Associazione italiana dei paleografi e diplomatisti, Cividale del Friuli (5-7 ottobre 2006).* Studi e ricerche 4, edited by Laura Pani and Cesare Scalon, 173–211. Spoleto: Centro Italiano di Studi sull'Alto Medioevo.

Santos Salazar, Igor. 2021. *Governare la Lombardia carolingia (774–924).* Altomedioevo 9. Roma: Viella.

Sernagiotto, Leonardo. 2017. *Spes optima regni. L'azione politica di Lotario I (795–855) alla luce delle fonti storico-narrative del secolo IX*, unpublished PhD thesis. Trento: University of Trento.

Settia, Aldo A. 1987. "Pavia carolingia e post-carolingia." In *Storia di Pavia, 2: L'alto medioevo*, 69–158. Pavia: Banca del Monte di Lombardia.

Spinelli, Giovanni. 2004. "Intorno alla cronologia dei vescovi Filastrio e Gaudenzio." *Brixia Sacra* 9:7–19.

Stoffella, Marco. 2008. "Le relazioni tra Baviera e Toscana tra VIII e IX secolo: appunti e considerazioni preliminari." *Mélange de l'Ecole Française de Rome. Moyen Âge* 120/1:73–85

Stoffella, Marco. 2020a. "In vico Gussilingus. Comunità locali, ufficiali pubblici minori e amministrazione della giustizia nella Verona carolingia." In *I Longobardi a Venezia. Scritti per Stefano Gasparri.* Haut Moyen Âge 40, edited by Irene Barbiera, Francesco Borri and Annamaria Pazienza, 175–184. Turnhout: Brepols.

Stoffella, Marco. 2020b. "La basilica e il monastero di S. Zeno nel contesto veronese di fine VIII e inizio IX secolo." *Studi Medievali*, 3. s. 61/2:543–596.

Tessera, Miriam Rita. 2019a. "Ambroise et Martin. L'autel d'or de la basilique Saint-Ambroise et le programme épiscopale d'Angilbert II de Milan." *Annales de Bretagne et des Pays de l'Ouest* 126/1:7–29.

Tessera, Miriam Rita. 2019b. "Angilbertus ovans. L'altare d'oro e la memoria di Ambrogio in età carolingia." In *Apparuit Thesaurus Ambrosius. Le reliquie di Sant'Ambrogio e dei martiri Gervaso e Protaso tra storia, scienza e fede*, edited by Carlo Faccendini and *Carlo* Capponi, 216–225. Milano: Silvana.

Thunø, Erik. 2006. "The Golden Altar of Sant'Ambrogio in Milan. Image and Materiality." In *Decorating the Lord's Table. On the dinamic between Image and Altar in the Middle Ages*, edited by Søren Kaspersen and Erik Thunø, 63–78. Copenhagen: Museum Tusculanum Press.

Tomea, Paolo. 2006. "Nunc in monasterio prefato Clavadis nostro tempore conditus requiescit. Il trasferimento di Calocero a Civate e altre traslazioni di santi nella provincia ecclesiastica di Milano e nei suoi dintorni tra VIII e X secolo." In *Età romanica. Metropoli, contado, ordini monastici nell'attuale provincia di Lecco (XI–XII secolo). Atti del convegno*, edited by 159–189. Milano: Skira.

Tomei, Paolo. 2019. *Milites elegantes. Le strutture aristocratiche nel territorio lucchese (800–1100 c.)*. Reti Medievali E-Book 34. Firenze: *Firenze* University Press.

Valtorta, Benedetta. 2020. "Anecdota Veronensia. Un dossier ildemariano alla Biblioteca Capitolare." *Revue Bénédictine* 130/2:229–259.

Van Dam, Raymond. 1993. *Saints and Their Cults in Late Antique Gaul*. Princeton: Princeton University Press.

Van Renswoude, Irene. 2019. *The Rhetoric of Free Speech in Late Antiquity and the Early Middle Ages*. Cambriddge: Cambridge University Press.

Veronese, Francesco. 2015. "Foreign Bishops Using Local Saints. The Passio et translatio sanctorum Firmi et Rustici (BHL 3020–3021) and Carolingian Verona." In *Saints and the City. Beiträge zum Verständnis urbaner Sakralität in christlichen Gemeinschaften (5.–17. Jh.)*. FAU Studien aus der Philosophischen Fakultät 3, edited by Michele C. Ferrari, 85–114. Erlangen: FAU University Press.

Veronese, Francesco. 2020a. "Tra rispetto delle leggi e furti notturni. Narrazioni di mobilità di reliquie nelle *translationes* carolinge." *Mélanges de l'École Française de Rome. Moyen Âge* 132/2:327–338.

Veronese, Francesco. 2020b. "Un franco (anzi, due) in Brianza. Gli ultimi anni di Ugo di Tours e sua moglie Ava (834–39)." In *I Longobardi a Venezia. Scritti per Stefano Gasparri*. Haut Moyen Âge 40, edited by Irene Barbiera, Francesco Borri and Annamaria Pazienza, 155–163. Turnhout: Brepols.

Veronese, Francesco. 2021. "Rome and the others. Saints, relics and hagiography in Carolingian North-Eastern Italy." In *After Charlemagne: Carolingian Italy and its rulers*, edited by Clemens Gantner and Austrian Pohl, 219–249. Cambridge/New York: Cambridge University Press.

Vocino, Giorgia. 2011. "Hagiography as an Instrument for Political Claims in Carolingian Northern Italy: The Saint Syrus Dossier (*BHL* 7976 and 7978)." In *An Age of Saints? Power, Conflict and Dissent in Early Medieval Christianity*. Brill's Series on the Early Middle Ages 20, edited by Peter Sarris, Matthew Dal Santo and Phil Booth, 169–186. Leiden/Boston: Brill.

Vocino, Giorgia. 2014. "Under the aegis of the saints. Hagiography and power in early Carolingian northern Italy." *Early Medieval Europe* 22/1:26–52.

Vocino, Giorgia. 2015. "Framing Ambrose in the resources of the past. The late antique and early medieval sources for a Carolingian portrait of Ambrose." In *The Resources of the Past in Early Medieval Europe*, edited by Clemens Gantner, Rosamond McKitterick and Sven Meeder, 135–154. Cambridge: Cambridge University Press.

Vocino, Giorgia. 2016. "Bishops in the mirror: from self-representation to episcopal model. The case of the eloquent bishops Ambrose of Milan and Gregory the Great." In *Religious Franks: religion and power in the Frankish kingdoms: studies in honour of Mayke de Jong*, edited by Rob Meens, Dorine van Espelo, Bram van den Hoven van Genderen, Janneke Raaijmakers, Irene van Renswoude and Carine van Rhijn, 331–349. Manchester: Manchester University Press.

Vocino, Giorgia. 2017. "L'agiografia dell'Italia centrale (750–950)." In *Hagiographies. Histoire internationale de la littérature hagiographique latine et vernaculaire en Occident des origines à 1550*, 7, edited by Monique Goullet, 95–268. Turnhout: Brepols.

Ward, Graeme. 2015 "Lessons in leadership: Constantine and Theodosius in Frechulf of Lisieux's Histories." In *The Resources of the Past in Early Medieval Europe*, edited by Clemens Gantner, Rosamond McKitterick and Sven Meeder, 68–83. Cambridge: Cambridge University Press.

Weber, Edwin Ernst, and Thomas Zotz, eds. 2020. *Herrschaft, Kirche und Bauern im nördlichen Bodenseeraum in karolingischer Zeit*. Stuttgart: Kohlhammer.

Westwell, Arthur. 2018. *The dissemination and reception of the Ordines Romani in the Carolingian Church, c. 750–900.* unpublished PhD thesis. Cambridge: University of Cambridge.

Westwell, Arthur. 2019. "The *Ordines Romani* and the Carolingian Choreography of a Liturgical Route to Rome." *Acta ad archaeologiam et artium historiam pertinentia* 31:63–79.

Zettler, Alfons. 2009a. "Die karolingischen Bischöfe von Verona I. Studien zu Bischof Eghio († 802)." In *Historia archaeologica. Festschrift für Heiko Steuer zum 70. Geburtstag*. Ergänzungsbände zum Reallexikon der Germanischen Altertumskunde 70, edited by Sebastian Brather, Dieter Geuenich and Christoph Huth, 363–385. Berlin/New York: De Gruyter.

Zettler, Alfons. 2009b. "Die karolingischen Grafen von Verona. Überlegungen und Annäherungsversuche." In *Adel und Königtum im mittelalterlichen Schwaben. Festschrift für Thomas Zotz zum 65. Geburtstag*. Veröffentlichungen der Kommission für geschichtliche Landeskunde in Baden-Württemberg 175 (Reihe B), edited by Andreas Bihrer, Mathias Kälble and Heinz Krieg, 89–114. Stuttgart: Kohlhammer.

Zettler, Alfons. (forthcoming). "Über die Verbindungen König Pippins von Italien mit Verona." In *Spes Italiae. Il regno di Pipino, i Franchi e l'Italia (781–810)*, edited by Francesco Borri and Giuseppe Albertoni.

Part Three: **Individualising Threats and Strategies**

Isabelle Mossong
Italy's Late Antique Bishops in Exile (3rd–Beginning of 7th c.): The Epigraphic Point of View

Abstract: Generally speaking, the phenomenon of Late Antique bishops in exile is mainly known from literary sources. Usually, the reader does not only learn something about the circumstances that led to an expulsion, but he can also occasionally be informed on the duration, possible travel companions or the living conditions in the new environment. However, not only literary sources contribute to this topic, epigraphical testimonies also preserve the memory of these clerical exiles (at least in Italy), even if they are much scarcer in this regard: hardly more is volunteered than the fact that the bishop has eventually been in exile. If we are not informed by other sources on the exile, it is very difficult to extract historical valuable facts from these epigraphical texts. But as shall be demonstrated, it is not impossible. Several inscriptions of different genres will be presented, mainly from Rome, but not exclusively, and belonging to a time span extending from the 4th to the 6th century. Some of these texts remind of exiles that have taken place long before the confection of the inscription, but that were still alive in the collective memory, others refer to exiles that are more or less contemporary to the epigraphical texts.

In Late Antiquity, some of the most famous and often controversial bishops are known to have spent time in exile at least once during their episcopal office. This group includes renowned personalities, among which can be found: Athanasius, bishop of Alexandria (328–373), who was in exile in Trier, Rome and Egypt;[1] John Chrysostomus, patriarch of Constantinople (398–407), exiled respectively to Kukusus, Arabissus (both in *Armenia Secunda*) and Pityus on the eastern shore of the Black Sea;[2] and Hilary, bishop of Poitiers from 350–367, who was exiled to Phrygia.[3] These displaced clerics certainly had to deal with the insecurities of modified living circumstances, but the threat – the central attention of this volume

---

[1] Gentz 1950; Anatolios 2018. – I want to warmly thank the organizers of the conference "Bishops under Threat. Contexts and Episcopal Strategies between Late Antiquity and the Early Middle Ages in the West", Prof. Dr. Sabine Panzram and Dr. Pablo Poveda Arias, for the kind invitation and the possibility to publish my contribution in this volume, as well as their patience.
[2] Brändle 1998, on his exile specifically, see col. 438; Mayer 2018.
[3] Doignon 1991; Hunter 2018; Melo 2021.

– does not necessarily arise from the exile as such, which was merely a destabilizing consequence. The threat emanated more concretely from the powerful people who initiated, or at least suggested, the exile and may have determined the conditions during banishment.

Since Republican times, exile was a conventional method to remove a *persona non grata* from his familiar environment.[4] The reasons behind such decisions may have differed depending on time and circumstances: treason, controversy, competition, and misconduct are some elements that may have lead to exile. Exile might embrace various forms: it could be forced or deliberately chosen (though in that circumstance it should rather be considered as a flight), it could be permanent or temporary and could take place in the vicinity or in territories far away. Often the destination could not be chosen freely, but was determined by the exiling authority. The exiled person could be under a more or less extensive control or might be allowed to live a more unmolested life. These circumstances varied from one specific case of exile to another and constituted the framework for the exile. A simple eviction from a city was, however, not enough to classify the displacement as an exile, since control by a third party might affect the timing, the conditions of the journey or its destination. In Late Antiquity, the act of exiling was a secular punishment as the order generally came from a high authority with a non-ecclesiastic background in deciding on the fate of a clergyman. This meant that the spheres of secular administration and the church were closely entangled over the centuries. Within the Christian community excommunication was a more common punishment. This was not necessarily a displacement, but was rather the exclusion of a community member, who generally remained on site. However, as one ascended higher within the Christian society and more specifically within the Christian clergy, exile became the stronger weapon to exclude someone from the local community.

Episcopal exile is well documented throughout Late Antiquity and is set geographically throughout the Roman Empire. In this instance, however, a specific region is the focus of our attention: the Italian peninsula. It is particularly suitable for a closer analysis, since its episcopal sees are outstanding, both in respect of their numbers as well as their chronological distribution. The Roman see, in particular, occupies an exceptional position among the Christian Church: over time, its primacy became increasingly evident and was more or less accepted overall within Christianity. A certain number of questions can be addressed to the Italian mate-

---

4 The exile as a political instrument is a well investigated topic: for the Republican times, see Kelly 2006; for the imperial period, see Stini 2011; for Late Antiquity particularly, see the monograph by Washburn 2013 and the two edited volumes by Vallejo Girvés, Bueno Delgado and Sánchez-Moreno Ellart 2015 and by Rohmann, Ulrich and Vallejo Girvés 2018.

rial: who exactly were the banished Italian bishops? Why did they go into exile? What authority decided on the exile? Was there possibly a rival bishop vying for the episcopal see? Where have they been exiled to? Did they return or die in exile? All these inquiries will become relevant at some point in this paper as ties to the epigraphical material will be established. On a chronological level, the time span from the 3rd to the beginning of the 7th century is taken into account, in order to consider in equal measure the pre- and post-Constantinian situation, when fundamental changes affected political and social realities, as also the Christian Church.[5]

Generally speaking, aspects of exile in Late Antiquity as an item of investigation is not a new research domain. Several publications from the last fifteen years show an increasing scientific interest in the topic.[6] Among these important contributions is especially an article by Margarita Vallejo, which is a useful starting point for what is to follow as it concentrates explicitly on inscriptions.[7] Several scholars have treated the topic of episcopal exile from one aspect or another but there has been no comprehensive study that exclusively concentrates on Italian bishops.

1 Italian Bishops in Exile (235–555)

Firstly, a hopefully exhaustive list of Italian bishops known to have spent time in exile will be useful. Beginning with the city of Rome, nine bishops are shown by historical sources to have been exiled at some point during their tenure of office.[8]

---
[5] These are also the chronological borders of my thesis, see now Mossong 2022.
[6] See especially the conference proceedings edited by Blaudeau 2008 and Hillner, Ulrich and Engberg 2016; furthermore, the monographs by Handley 2011, Washburn 2013 and Barry 2019. To this must be added the very useful database of the project "Migration of faith. Clerical exile in Late Antiquity" by Julia Hillner (University of Sheffield), Jörg Ulrich (Universität Halle-Wittenberg) and Jakob Engberg (Aarhus University): https://www.clericalexile.org/ (last consulted on 30.10.2022).
[7] Vallejo Girvés 2007.
[8] Literary sources only are mentioned in the footnotes corresponding to Table 1 and 2, as the epigraphic testimonies will be presented separately at a later stage in this contribution; bishops with a relevant inscription are highlighted by spaced letters. Another remark must be made with respect to the list in Table 1: it does not consider "antipopes" such as Ursinus, the opponent of Damasus (*PCBE* 2, 2356–2358 [Vrsinus 1]; for a chronology of the events leading to his exile, see Ménard 2008, 245–246; 251–252, Wirbelauer 2008a, 42–43 and Wirbelauer 2008b, 264–265), Eulalius, the opponent of Bonifatius (*PCBE* 2, 680–682 [Eulalius 2]), or the Donatist Bishop Claudianus (*PCBE* 2, 446–447 [Claudianus 2]). For Silvester (314–355; *PCBE* 2, 2071 [Silvester 1], Kreilos 2002; Rüpke 2005, n. 3099 [Silvester]), the Lib. pontif. informs us about a stay at the Mount Soracte, qualified as exile and preceding Constantine's baptism (Lib. pontif. I, 170 states: *Hic exilio fuit in monte Seracten et postmodum rediens cum gloria baptizavit Constantinum Augustum, quem curavit Dominus*

Table 1: Exiled Bishops of Rome[9]

Name	bishop of	from/to	exiled to	exiled by	reason	duration	exile ended by
Pontian[10]	Rome	230–235	Sardinia	Maximinus Thrax (?)	persecution	235 (exact duration unknown)	resigns first, then dies in exile

---

a lepra, cuius persecutionem primo fugiens exilio fuisse cognoscitur), from which the bishop returns to Rome. However, this seems to be a conjecture from the *Vita S. Silvestri* (thus Duchesne in Lib. pontif. I, CXI–CXII). Silvester's (though not direct) successor, Iulius (337–352; *PCBE* 2, 1201 [Iulius 1]; Rüpke 2005, n. 1981 [Iulius (3)]), has also been excluded from the table, since the only hint about a possible exile is Lib. pontif. I, 205 (*Hic multas tribulationes et exilio fuit mensibus X; et post huius Constantini mortem cum gloria reversus ad sedem beati Petri apostoli*). It seems that this text passage is corrupted though, referring rather to his direct successor Liberius (see Lib. pontif. I, CXXIII), because there is no other historical evidence for an exile by Iulius. What is more, the indicated duration (*mensibus X*) is purely factitious, since most likely Iulius was not banned at all and Liberius' exile lasted at least two years. What is more, the Cat. Lib. 89–94 (ed. Divjak/Wischmeyer 2014, 328) does not contain any relevant information to this regard. Another bishop who has been excluded from this table is John I (523–526; *PCBE* 2, 1080 [Iohannes 28]), since his imprisonment (*custodia*) by Theoderic in Ravenna in 526 can not be qualified as a proper exile (Lib. pontif. I, 276: *sed metuens indignationem Iustini Augusti, quos tamen in custodia omnes adflictos cremavit, ita ut beatissimus Iohannes, episcopus primae sedis, papa, in custodia adflictus deficiens moreretur. Qui tamen defunctus est Ravennae in custodia, XV kal. iunias, martyr*).

9 A similar table can be found in Wirbelauer 2008b, 270–272, although with the following divergencies: Cornelius, Marcellus, Eusebius and Bonifatius are not mentioned; instead John III (561–574; *PCBE* 2, 1098 [Iohannes 53]; in my opinion, the passage in Lib. pontif. I, 305–306 does not refer to a proper exile: the formulation *Tunc sanctissimus papa retenuit se in cymeterio sanctorum Tiburtii et Valeriani* seems to suggest an active part of John himself, rather than undergoing a punishment by somebody else; similarly Wirbelauer 2008a, 44 n. 37) and Martinus (649–653; outside my chronological frame) are recorded.

10 For the biographical data, see Hamm 2002 and Rüpke 2005, n. 2791 (Pontianus). The events can be found in Cat. Lib. 40–42 (ed. Divjak/Wischmeyer 2014, 527): *eo tempore Pontianus episcopus et Yppolitus presbyter exoles sunt deportati in Sardinia in insula nociva Severo et Quintiano con(sulibus). in eadem insula discinctus est iiii kal(endas) octobr(es)* [...] and Lib. pontif. I, 145: *Eodem tempore Pontianus episcopus et Yppolitus presbyter exilio sunt deportati ab Alexandro (!) in Sardinia insula Bucina, Severo et Quintiano consulibus. In eadem insula adflictus, maceratus fustibus, defunctus est III kal. novemb.* [...]. The emperor (Severus) Alexander, who dies in March 235, is mentioned erroneously in this last text, as it was probably Maximinus Thrax who sent Pontian into exile, as can be deduced by the consular date: Cn. Claudius Severus and L. Ti. Claudius Aurelius Quintianus were the consuls of the year 235. From the Cat. Lib. it is known that Pontianus resigned first (*discinctus est*), before dying in exile at an unknown date (the chronological indications in the Lib. pontif. are not reliable, see Lib. pontif. I, p. XCIV). Later on, his body is brought to Rome by Bishop Fabianus and laid to rest in the *coemeterium Calixti* (Lib. pontif. I, 145).

Table 1: Exiled Bishops of Rome *(Continued)*

Name	bishop of	from/to	exiled to	exiled by	reason	duration	exile ended by
Cornelius[11]	Rome	251–253	Centumcellae (mod. Civitavecchia)	Trebonianus Gallus	persecution	252–253 (exact duration unknown)	dies in exile
Lucius[12]	Rome	253–254	unknown	Unknown	unknown	253 (exact duration unknown)	returns to Rome
Marcellus[13]	Rome	308–309	unknown	Maxentius	unknown	unknown	Unknown
Eusebius[14]	Rome	309 or 310	Sicily	Maxentius	unknown	unknown	dies in exile

---

11 Short biographies can be found in Hammerich 2002 and Rüpke 2005, n. 1304 (Cornelius [2]). The Cat. Lib. 54–55 (ed. Divjak/Wischmeyer 2014, 528) relates the following events: *post hoc Centumcellis expulsi ibi cum gloria dormitionem accepit*. The events related by Lib. pontif. I, 150 (*Post hoc Cornelius episcopus Centumcellis pulsus est* [...]. *Post hoc ambulavit noctu Centumcellis. Eodem tempore audivit Decius eo quod epistulam accepisset a beato Cypriano, Cartaginensi episcopo. Misit Centumcellis et exhibuit beatum Cornelium episcopum* [...]) are fictional and do not depict the real events, since Decius has already died in June 251. But at least the episode set in Centumcellae seems to bear some credibility.

12 On his life, see Windau 2002a and Rüpke 2005, n. 2296 (Lucius [1]). The historical data on his exile is rather scarce, the Cat. Lib. 57–58 (ed. Divjak/Wischmeyer 2014, 528) relates: *hic exul fuit et postea nutu dei incolumis ad ecclesiam reversus est* [...] and the Lib. pontif. I, 153 only states the following: *Hic exilio fuit*. A letter by Cyprian, contemporary to the events, seems to attest his return to Rome from an unknown exile place: [...] *ut pascendo gregi pastor et gubernandae navi gubernator et plebi regendae rector redderetur et appareret relegationem vestram sic divinitus esse dispositam, non ut episcopus relegatus et pulsus ecclesiae deesset, sed ut ad ecclesiam maior rediret* (epist. 61, I, 2; ed. Bayard 1961–1962). Thus, the first Roman bishop to go into exile and return to Rome is Lucius (and not Liberius, as stated by Wirbelauer 2008b, 261).

13 For a short biography, see Rüpke 2005, n. 2359 (Marcellus [1]). The Cat. Lib. 77–78 (ed. Divjak/Wischmeyer 2014, 528) does not contain any relevant information. According to Lib. pontif. I, 164, Maxentius' punishment takes place in a stable in Rome, whereto Marcellus is condemned twice. This course of events is however not confirmed by other sources. Furthermore, it must be stressed that the only source mentioning Marcellus' exile is the Damasian epigram ED 40 (see below p. 256–257).

14 For a short biography, see Rüpke 2005, n. 1558 (Eusebius [2]). The Cat. Lib. 79 (ed. Divjak/Wischmeyer 2014, 528) and the *vita Eusebii* in Lib. pontif. I, 167 do not contain any relevant information. The only source mentioning an exile is the Damasian epigram ED 18 (see below p. 257). The exact dates of his episcopate as well as of his death are unknown.

Table 1: Exiled Bishops of Rome *(Continued)*

Name	bishop of	from/to	exiled to	exiled by	reason	duration	exile ended by
Liberius[15]	Rome	352–366	Milan, then Beroia (Thracia)	Constantius II	Condemnation of Athanasius	355/56–358	returns to Rome
Bonifatius[16]	Rome	418–422	Coem. Maximi (Rome/ Via Salaria)	Honorius?	Schism for the Roman see	Jan.– Apr. 419	returns to Rome

---

15 On his life before his episcopal election, see *PCBE* 2, 1297–1298 (Liberius 1). Dümler 2002a, Rüpke 2005, n. 2216 (Liberius) and Natal 2018 give the essential biographical data. His exile is to be situated in the context of the condemnation for heresy of the bishop of Alexandria, Athanasius. See Wirbelauer 2008a, 33–34, Wirbelauer 2008b, 258–264, and Ulrich 2018. This episode is reported by Ammianus Marcellinus (Amm. 15, 7, 6–10) and Theodoreth (Theodoret of Cyrus, *historia ecclesiastica* 2, 16–17). And the exile is mentioned in Lib. pontif. I, 207: *Hic exilio deportatur a Constantio eo quod noluisset heresi arrianae consentire, et fecit in exilio annos III.* [...] *Post paucos autem dies zelo ducti Ursacius et Valens rogaverunt Constantium Augustum ut revocaret Liberium de exilium* [...]. *Tunc revocaverunt Liberium de exilio. Rediens autem Liberius de exilio, habitavit in cymeterio sanctae Agnae apud germanam Constanti Augusti* [...]. On this last episode set in the Roman cemetery of S. Agnese and its validity, see Cohen 2018. Furthermore, we are informed by Hier. chron. *ad a.* 356 (ed. Helm 1913, 240: *Liberius episcopus romanus in exilium mittitur.*) about the exile, whereas the Cat. Lib. 95–96 (ed. Divjak/Wischmeyer 2014, 528) does not contain any relevant information. Sulpicius Severus mentions Liberius' return to Rome (chron. II, 39, 8), as does the Collectio Avellana I, 3. During his exile he has written four letters to several bishops, preserved in the works of Hilary of Poitiers, that have been much debated (Liberius, epist. *Studens paci, Pro deifico, Quia scio* and *Non doceo*; CSEL 65: 155–156. 168–173). On the inscription mentioning his exile, see below p. 258.

16 On his life before his episcopal election, see *PCBE* 2, 318–319 (Bonifatius 3); for a short biography, see Kampert 2002 and Rüpke 2005, n. 946 (Bonifatius [1]). Lib. pontif. I, 227 informs us about the events that took place during the conflict confronting Bonifatius and Eulalius: *Eodem tempore ambo Augusti missa auctoritate hoc praeceperunt ut ambo exirent civitate. Qui cum pulsi exissent, habitavit Bonifatius in cymeterio sanctae Felicitatis martyris, via Salaria, Eulalius vero in civitate Antio, ad sanctum Hermen.* [...] *Hoc audientes Augusti utrumque miserunt et erigerunt Eulalium et missa auctoritate revocaverunt Bonifatium in urbem Romam et constituerunt episcopum; Eulalium vero miserunt foris in Campaniam.*

Table 1: Exiled Bishops of Rome *(Continued)*

Name	bishop of	from/to	exiled to	exiled by	reason	duration	exile ended by
Silverius[17]	Rome	536–537	Patara/Lycia	Belisarius/ Justinian	high treason	9 months	dies on his return on the Pontine island of Ponza when returning
Vigilius[18]	Rome	537–555	Sicily, then Constantinople	Justinian	Three-Chapter Controversy	545–7 June 555	dies in Syracusa when returning to Rome

Not surprisingly, more than half of the exiled bishops, namely Pontian, Cornelius, Lucius, Marcellus and Eusebius, belong to the pre-Constantinian era, a time when several imperial persecutions heavily affected the Christian community and constrained some of its bishops to go into exile. It appears that at this point in time the respective bishops were exiled to nearby regions in Italy (Sardinia, Centumcellae, Sicily), a habit that would change in the centuries to come. What is more, the main reason these bishops were exiled was due to persecutions, a factor that would no longer exist after the Edict of Milan in the year 313. The remaining four bishops belong to the 4th, 5th and 6th centuries: they were exiled to farther away territories (Thrace, Lycia, Constantinople; only Bonifatius spent his exile in the nearby *Coemeterium Maximi* on the Via Salaria). What is more, there were a variety of reasons for their exiles: condemnation of Athanasius, schism for the Roman see, high treason or the Three Chapter Controversy. However, what is strik-

---

17 On his life before his episcopal election, see *PCBE* 2, 2069 (Silverius 1). The Lib. pontif. I, 293 states the following: *Quem suscepit Vigilius archidiaconus in sua quasi fide et misit eum in exilio in Pontias et sustentavit eum panem tribulationis et aqua angustiae. Qui deficiens mortuus est et confessor factus est.* Further primary sources are Liberat. brev. 22 (ACO II/5, 138, 21–22. Schwartz); Procopius, *historia arcana* I 14 and 27; Procopius, *bellum Gothicum* I 25.13. See also Wirbelauer 2008a, 44.

18 On his life before his episcopal election, see *PCBE* 2, 2298 (Vigilius 6), on his episcopate Bruns 2002 and Neil 2018. Lib. pontif. I, 297–299: *tentus est et deposuerunt eum ad Tiberim; miserunt eum in navem.* [...] *Qui ingressus Siciliam in civitate Catinense* [...]. *Et valefaciens omnibus ingressus est Constantinopolim vigilias domini nostri Iesu Christi.* [...] *Tunc dimisit omnes cum Vigilio. Venerunt Siciliam in civitate Syracusis. Adflictus, calculi dolorem habens, mortuus est.* On the exile, Wirbelauer 2008a, 44; on the inscription alluding his exile, see below p. 259–260.

ing is, that for almost all of these exiles of Roman bishops, regardless of the point in time they took place, the emperor seems to have played a crucial role.

For the remaining 239 Italian sees that existed at some point in the 4th to the beginning of the 7th century,[19] we know of only 4 (or maybe 5) more bishops that had been exiled.[20]

Table 2: Exiled Bishops from Italy

Name	bishop of	from/to	exiled to	exiled by	reason	duration	exile ended by
Eusebius[21]	Vercelli	before 353–369/70	Scythopolis in Palestine, then in Cappadocia, finally in Egypt	Constantius II	Condemnation of Athanasius	355–361/3	returns to Vercelli
Lucifer[22]	Cagliari	c. 353–370	Germanikeia, Eleutheropolis, then Cappadocia	Constantius II	Condemnation of Athanasius	355–362	returns to Sardinia

---

19 They are listed in the "Fastes épiscopaux de l'Italie" within the Annexes of the *PCBE* 2, 2404–2427.
20 I want to thank Robert Wiśniewski (Warsaw) for drawing my attention to Maximus of Naples and the *Libellum precum*.
21 *PCBE* 2, 692–697 (Eusebius 1); Dümler 2002b, who indicates that Eusebius already became bishop of Vercelli in 345, Rüpke 2005, n. 1559 (Eusebius [4]) and MacEachnie 2018. On Eusebius' exile, see Hier. Chron. ad a. 355 (ed. Helm 1913, 239–240): *Eusebius Vercellensis episcopus et Lucifer ac Dionysius Caralitanae et Mediolanensis ecclesiae episcopi, Pancratius quoque Romanus presbyter et Hilarius diaconus distantibus inter se ab Arrianis et Constantio damnantur exiliis*, and Hier. vir. ill. 96 (ed. Migne 1883, 735): *Eusebius, natione Sardus, et ex lectore urbis Romanae, Vercellensis episcopus, ob confessionem fidei a Constantio principe Scythopolim et inde Cappadociam relegatus, sub Juliano imperatore ad Ecclesiam reversus, edidit in Psalmos Commentarios Eusebii Caesariensis, quos de Graeco in Latinum verterat. Mortuus est Valentiniano et Valente regnantibus*. The exact end of the exile does not seem to be clear: indications vary from 361 (Rüpke, Dümler) to 363 (MacEachnie). On the inscriptions mentioning his exile, see below p. 260–261.
22 *PCBE* 2, 1324–1328 (Lucifer 1) and Windau 2002b.

Table 2: Exiled Bishops from Italy *(Continued)*

Name	bishop of	from/to	exiled to	exiled by	reason	duration	exile ended by
Dionysius[23]	Milan	352–361	Armenia	Constantius II	Condemnation of Athanasius	355–361?	dies in exile
Maximus[24]	Naples	c. 355–before 362	?	Constantius II	Condemnation of Athanasius	355–before Feb. 362	dies in exile
Marcianus?[25]	*?*	*?*	*Grado (?)*	*?*	*pro causa fidei*	*40 years*	*death?*

Four of these exiled bishops (Eusebius, Lucifer and Dionysius, as well as Maximus) belong to the same historical context, whereas the testimony of the remaining one (Marcianus) is extremely uncertain (above in italics). At this stage in our analysis we know of thirteen, maybe fourteen Late Antique bishops from all over the peninsula that were exiled at some point of their episcopate. Five of these bishops were exiled as a result of events that led to the condemnation of Athanasius at the Council of Milan in the year 355: Liberius, Eusebius of Vercelli, Lucifer of Cagliari, Dionysius of Milan and Maximus of Naples.

It is much easier to get relevant information on exiles for the bishops of Rome, since there are useful primary sources, for example, the *Catalogus Liberianus* from the Chronograph of the year 354 and the *Liber pontificalis*. In addition, several ancient authors such as Cyprian of Carthage, Ammianus Marcellinus and Procop provide useful details. Outside of Rome, this task is more difficult, since pertinent information is much more dispersed.[26]

---

23 *PCBE* 2, 563–565 (Dionysius 1).
24 *PCBE* 2, 1466–1467 (Maximus 4). *Libellum precum* 25 (ed. Whiting 2019, 84): *Maximus quoque de Neapoli Campaniae* […]; *deinde, ubi ob constantiam animi fideique virtutem carnis infirmitate non vincitur, ductus est in exilium atque illic martyr in Domini pace requievit*.
25 *PCBE* 2, 1385 (Marcianus 10). On the inscription alluding his exile, see below p. 261.
26 Thus, it is not guaranteed that somebody relevant may have erroneously been left out, especially within the non-Roman sees. Strikingly, the "Migration of Faith"-Database does not provide any further cases.

2 Epigraphically Documented Exiles by Italian Bishops

Since all of these *episcopi* are well documented by literary sources, in order to get the most complete picture, it is advisable to turn to another type of material: epigraphical testimonies. Of these fourteen bishops, ten are recorded in inscriptions in some manner[27] when taking into account all 871 inscriptions of the Late Antique clergy known from Italy for the 3rd until the beginning of the 7th century.[28] It is essential, nevertheless, to reduce these testimonies in order to obtain useful material for the present purpose, i.e. the episcopal exile.

Inscriptions are certainly a less common documentary source and are not the first type of evidence a scholar would consider when doing research on exiled clerics, or, more specifically, bishops. Despite this, a handful contain pertinent information. The exiles of six bishops are attested in inscriptions, four originating from Rome, namely testimonies concerning Marcellus, Eusebius, Liberius and Vigilius, and two belonging to two other Italian cities, Eusebius of Vercelli and a rather mysterious Marcianus attested in Grado.

The two inscriptions mentioning the earliest exiles of Roman *episcopi* belong to the era of Bishop Damasus, on the *cathedra Petri* from 366 until 384, and refer to two of his predecessors from the beginning of the 4th century: Marcellus and Eusebius. The former was bishop of Rome from 308 until 309. He had the difficult task of reorganizing the Christian community after the persecutions of Diocletian. He carried this out with skill and thoroughness, since he insisted on the fact that the *lapsi* should do penance for their guilt. More than half a century later we learn from an epigram by Bishop Damasus what the consequences of this engagement were: *finibus expulsus patriae est feritate tyranni* (v. 6).[29] The tyrant here is obviously the emperor Maxentius (306–312), who expelled Marcellus from Rome to an unknown place. Whether *finibus patriae* is to synonymize with *finibus imperii* is undecided, but rather probable, since Marcellus originated from Rome, as stated

---

[27] Of the listed bishops in Table 1 and 2 only Silvester of Rome, Lucifer of Cagliari, Dionysius of Milan and Maximus of Naples do not have left any epigraphical trace.

[28] See the catalogue in Mossong 2022.

[29] ED 40 = ICUR n.s. IX 24830 (Rome/Coem. Priscillae): *Veridicus rector lapsos quia crimina flere / praedixit miseris fuit omnibus hostis amarus / hinc furor hinc odium sequitur discordia lites / seditio caedes solvuntur foedera pacis /⁵ crimen ob alterius Chr(istu)m qui in pace negavit / finibus expulsus patriae est feritate tyranni / haec breviter Damasus voluit comperta referre / Marcelli ut populus meritum cognoscere possit.* See also now Mossong 2022, n. 608.

by the *Liber pontificalis*.[30] Thus, exiling him to a foreign land would surely have had a larger impact than merely sending him to just outside the *Vrbs*. However, we do not know where he was sent, nor whether Marcellus returned from his exile.[31]

The second Damasian inscription concerns Eusebius, the direct successor of Marcellus, who functioned for only a few months in 310.[32] Eusebius had to deal with an opposing faction within the Christian community, led by a certain, and otherwise unknown, Heraclius, also mentioned in this epigraphical text. This division caused a further intervention by the emperor Maxentius – again qualified as *tyrannus* (v. 5) – who exiled them both. The text is of great value for Eusebius' episcopate and exile, since information from other sources is non-existent. Thus, the reader learns that Marcellus died in exile on the Sicilian shores (*litore Trinacrio*; v. 8–9); the fate of Heraclius is unknown.

This text was not only created by Damasus half a century after the events, but interestingly was carved a second time in the 6th century, probably when the relevant area of the Catacombs of Saint Calixtus were restored.[33] Most probably the Damasian inscription had already suffered at that time, so that the creation of a new slab with the same text was put into practice, with a lack of skill but nevertheless trustworthy. This is important since the fragments preserved from the Damasian original do not include the parts referring to the exile. It is only thanks to the manuscript versions – copied with great probability from the 6th century slab[34] – that the relevant part has been preserved and handed down to us. If

---

30 Lib. pontif. I, 164: *Marcellus, natione Romanus, ex patre Benedicto, de regione Via Lata [...]*.
31 Ménard 2008, 247–248 privileges the idea of a return to Rome, since Marcellus is not qualified as a martyr in his Damasian epigram, contrary to Eusebius (see the following note). But this is highly speculative and we have no evidence neither for a death in exile nor for a return to Rome.
32 ED 18 = ICUR n.s. IV 9515 (Rome/Coem. Calixti): *Da[m]asu[s episcopus fecit] | | Herac[lius] vet[uit labsos peccata dolere] / Euse[bi]us [mis]e[ros docuit sua crimina flere] / [sci]ndit[ur] in p[artes] populus [gliscente furore] / [sedi]t[io caedes] bellum [discordia lites] /* [5] *[exte]mplo [pariter p]ulsi [ferit]a[te tyranni] / [inte]gra c[um rector s]erva[ret f]oed[era pacis] / [pertulit exil]iu[m domino s]ub iudic[e l]ae[tus] / [litore Trinacrio mundum] vitamq(ue) r[el]iqu[it] / [Eusebio episcopo et] ma[rt]yr[i]*. Left to the text, in vertical order: *[Dama]si pa[pae cultor adque amator]*. Right to the text, in vertical order: *[Furius Dionysius Filocalus scripsit]*. See also now Mossong 2022, n. 21.
33 A. Ferrua states in the ICUR edition: "Titulus ipse cum barbarorum incursione, ut videtur, comminutus esset, religiose collectis et compositis in aversa magna tabula cm. 87 x 163 fere [...] rursus incises sed mendose est, saec. fere VI ex. puto." On this later inscription specifically, see ED 18[1]. On the back of this opistographic slab an honorific inscription dating to 214 for the emperor Caracalla can be found (CIL VI 1067).
34 This includes the sylloge Turonensis transmitted by the Göttweihensis 64 and Closterburgensis 723 as well as the sylloge Laureshamensis in cod. Vat. Pal. 833 f. 61' (A. Ferrua in ICUR n.s. IV 9515).

this later copy had not existed, the record of Eusebius' exile in Sicily would have been completely lost.

These two inscriptions show an obvious interest in events that took place several decades before. The Damasian epigrams are a very special group of evidence that constitute an incomparable pool of information for different subjects within the Christian community of the 4th century and earlier. Interestingly, the *Liber pontificalis* does not mention explicitly either of the exiles of these two Roman bishops, in contrast to what it may attest later for Liberius and Silverius.

From several manuscripts of the middle of the 4th century, we know of a metrical epitaph of 54 verses that is supposed to be the funerary inscription of Bishop Liberius.[35] This attribution is not entirely secure, since the name of the departed is not included in the text. However, the attribution to Liberius can be considered as a consensus. The *elogium* mentions several stages of his life before alluding to his exile: his familiar background is referenced, as well as his clerical career as a *lector* and a *presbyter*, before referring to his exile (v. 42). He was expelled from Italy for his stance during the conflict linked to Athanasius of Alexandria. Furthermore, interesting about this exile is that Liberius was replaced on the episcopal see by his archdeacon Felix, with whom he had to deal when returning home from foreign shores, probably in 358. It must be stressed that Liberius is most probably not the author of his own epitaph, since it is written in the second person singular throughout, but rather that the text was written at some point after his death, although it is difficult to say when or by whom. Thus, it is not an autobiographical mention of an exile, in contrast to the four letters Liberius wrote during his exile in Thrace.[36] He is the only Roman bishop for whom we have an epigraphical trace that mentions the exile and at the same time are in possession of his own epistolary production. Furthermore, we are informed about the events from the report of the historian Ammianus Marcellinus[37] and Theodoret of Cyrus,[38] who give detailed information about the circumstances leading to the Liberian exile.

Potentially, although with caution, a second inscription may be linked to the Liberian banishment from Rome. It is a funerary inscription from Spoleto in Umbria, where a neophyte named Picentia Legitima is explicitly said to have

---

35 ICUR n.s. IX 24831 (Rome/Coem. Priscillae). For practical reasons, only the relevant verses of this long metrical text are given here (v. 42–44): *insuper exilio decedis martyr ad astra, / adque inter patriarchas p(rae)sagosq(ue) prophetas, / inter apostolicam turbam martyrumq(ue) potentum*. Vallejo 2007, n. 8 (bears erroneously "n. 7"); Cohen 2018, 157–158 and now Mossong 2022, n. 13.
36 On these letters, see above footnote n. 16.
37 Amm. 15, 7, 6–10.
38 Theodoret of Cyrus, *historia ecclesiastica* 2, 16–17.

been recently *consignata a Liberio papa:* baptized by this bishop.[39] Is there a realistic chance that Liberius conferred this sacrament on his way to the Milanese court, the first stop on his way into exile in the East? In my opinion, it should be taken into consideration, since it is less probable that Picentia made a journey to Rome to get baptized and then return to Spoleto. Unless we consider that at some point there was another undocumented journey by Liberius to Spoleto, other than from the exile context. In any case, Picentia was buried at an unknown age by her husband Flavius Hospitianus, who provided a double sarcophagus with inscription. When considering the remaining epigraphical material on clerics, there is no other neophyte known who was baptized by a Roman bishop, regardless of it being on his way into exile or not.

The next testimony considers Bishop Vigilius, who was bishop of Rome from 537 until 555.[40] Vigilius was expelled by Emperor Justinian because of his positions during the monophysite debate and the following schism of Three Chapters. He was exiled first to Sicily, then to Constantinople, and was allowed to return to Rome only after ten years. From an inscribed marble slab, today preserved at the Roman church of S. Maria in Trastevere but originally probably from a cemetery of the Via Salaria, we know that a presbyter named Mareas represented Bishop Vigilius during his absence.[41] We see that, although the exile was much longer than that of Liberius, Vigilius was not replaced on the episcopal see, but was represented by another member of the clergy: *praesulis in vicibus clausisti pectora saeva* (v. 3). Mareas obviously did an excellent job, as stated on the inscription: *tu fueras meritus pontificale decus* (v. 8). Did the experience two centuries earlier regarding Liberius and Felix influence the decision not to replace a Roman bishop too early? Was this former episode, which led to several problems in the middle of the 4th century, perceived as an *exemplum* that must not be followed? This is difficult to say, but definitely worth consideration. As we learn from the last line of

---

39 ICI VI 63 (Spoleto/church of S. Gregorio): *D(e)p(ositio) | Picentiae | Legitimae | neofytae | die V Kal(endas) Sep(tembres) | consignata | a Liberio papa | Fl(avius) Hospitianus | maritus | uxori | bene merenti | duplicem | sarcofagum | cum titulo | hoc loco [sanct]o e[t s]i[bi] | posuit | [in quo cum] marito | [quiesc]et.* See now Mossong 2022, n. 372.

40 For the details of his exile, see the contribution of Marco Cristini in this volume.

41 ICUR n.s. VIII 23065 (Rome/Via Salaria; now S. Maria in Trastevere): *Digne tenes premium Marea pro nomine Xp(ist)i / vindice quo vivit sedes apostolica / praesulis in vicibus clausisti pectora saeva / ne mandata patrum perderet ulla fides /⁵ tuque sacerdotes docuisti crismate sancto / tan⸢ g⸣ere bis nullum iudice posse deo / te querunt omnes te saecula nostra requirunt / tu fueras meritus pontificale decus / pauperibus largus vixisti nulla reservans /¹⁰ dedisti multis quae modo solus habes / hoc tibi care pater pietate notavi / ut rele⸢ g⸣ant cuncti quam bene clarus eras / [hic] requiescit in pace Mareas pr(esbyter) qui [vixit ann(is) pl(us)] mi[nus – – – XIII post?] cons(ula)t(um) Ba`si⸢ l⸣i ind(i)c(tione) III.* See also now Mossong 2022, n. 95 and for Mareas *PCBE* 2, 1396 (Mareas 2).

the inscription and the respective consular datation, Mareas died in the same year when Vigilius returned from exile – whether this happened shortly before or immediately after, it is impossible to tell – thus, he could not be taken into consideration for the succession on the Roman see when Vigilius died in 555. He would, however, have been a good choice since he had proven himself when the superior authority was far away for a long time.

Now, let us leave Rome and turn to the bishops from other regions of the Italian peninsula. Interestingly, documentation is not very diverse. Two very debatable testimonies come from the northern city of Vercelli. They inform us that a certain Eusebius had spent some time in exile. He is historically known from other sources as bishop of Vercelli from c. 353 until 369/70, with a documented exile in the East from 355–362. It is set in the same context as the exile of Bishop Liberius: Eusebius and several of his disciples refused to condemn Athanasius of Alexandria, a position that led to the intervention of Constantine II and ended in a mandated exile. The first inscription mentioning this banishment is a long metrical text still preserved on stone, although it might be a medieval copy of the Late Antique poem.[42] It bears the interesting, but hidden, hint of an acrostic: *Eusebius episcopus et martur*, which reveals the recipient.[43] In this text, dedicated only to Eusebius, he is *exiliique dolor victi stupuere fidelem* (v. 4). Yet again, we do not learn anything about the exact context of this exile, which fortunately is found in several other sources, among which is a letter Eusebius wrote himself in exile.[44]

The second inscription – now lost and only known by two medieval manuscripts – is an honorific poem that celebrates Bishop Honoratus and his pre-

---

42 See M. Aimone in ICI XVII 68, 149.
43 ICI XVII 68 (Vercelli/Cathedral, where preserved): *Emeritae quantum damnato corpore vitae / vel cunctis exuta malis mens possit inisi / sat dedit agnosci virtus quem mille labores / exiliique dolor victi stupuere fidelem /* [5] *blandus et adfatu facilis sanctusq(ue) sereno / in vultu exponins animum patientior âequo / virtutum specimen dives sub paupere mundo / scribtorum custos rigidus dubiiq(ue) serenus / excusor veri contendens mente beata /* [10] *purgatam in terris animam revocare per âethr[a] / indignum clamans demergi crimine vitas / sulpureasq(ue) undas corrupto corpore adire / candor erat mentis verus semperq(ue) docebat / omnia factorum nostrae rationis habenda /* [15] *participesq(ue) mali facinus qui in fata reclinan[t] / ultor inexpletus fidei bellator in hostes / sincerus cultorq(ue) Dei dominorq(ue) malorûm / errantum lumen qui crimina tolleret ore / talis erat specie quem nec ieiunia longa /* [20] *magnanimum vicere sitim fluvialibus undis / algorem vili solitum depellere veste / robore caelesti mundum calcavit et omnes / terrenas vicit labes purgatior aethra / vitarum maculas puro qui decoquit igni /* [25] *rebus qui docuit populos factisq(ue) vocavit.* See also Vallejo 2007, n. 6 and now Mossong 2022, n. 530.
44 Euseb. Verc. epist. 2 (CCSL 9: 104–109).

decessor Eusebius, who is explicitly mentioned three times.⁴⁵ We learn that *exilii poenas et carceris iste subivit* (v. 13), a banishment that can be set in the context of Eusebius' exile, which took placè when Honoratus was still far from becoming a bishop.⁴⁶ It is not documented by any other source that Honoratus had actually also passed some time in exile but this inscription makes it very plausible.

In order to complete this survey, we should mention a rather insecure testimony belonging to the Adriatic city of Grado: here, in the church of S. Eufemia, an epitaph laid in mosaics states that a certain Bishop Marcianus *peregrinatus est pro causa fidei annos XL*.⁴⁷ Unfortunately, we do not know where Marcianus occupied his episcopal see and if he possibly was exiled in Grado, where he died probably in the year 578 (593 would also be possible according to the indiction). However, he seems to have been buried in the church recently erected by Bishop Helias (571–587). We should handle this inscription with caution, since it is not clear if Marcianus was in peregrination because of his *own* faith (and thus maybe in exile) or if he was on a long-lasting mission in order to propagate Christian faith in general. All in all, we should be very careful with any overinterpretation of this inscription and as a consequence I would not make a case for an identification of Marcianus with the bishop of Augusta Vindelicorum (modern Augsburg), respectively Sabiona (Säben in South Tirol), as did Rudolf Egger a few decades ago or as a partisan of the Three Chapters as presented in the *PCBE* 2, only by referring to the quite nebulous formulation *peregrinatus est pro causa fidei*.⁴⁸ Therefore, this testimony *could* be interpreted as a piece of evidence for an episcopal exile, but this is far from being unquestionable.

---

45 ICI XVII 71 (Vercelli/Cathedral; now lost): *Tercius hanc urbis sedem tenuit Honoratus / antistes, cuius spiritus astra tenet. / Eusebius praesul primus, qui martyr alumpnus / caelorum postquam regna beata petit, /⁵ hic pater ecclesiam docuit hanc dogmate recto, / sermones complens actibus ipse suos. / Terris ac caelo coniunctus ubique magistro / Eusebio consors hic Honoratus adest / Pontificis sancti cineres tenet Honorati /¹⁰ archa hominis vilis quae manet ingenio. / Hunc sanctum docuit, nutrivit pastor alumnus / egregius martyr praesul et Eusebius. / Exilii poenas et carceris iste subivit / Discipulus carus et socius pariter. /¹⁵ Ambo fide digni meritis et nomine patres / Cum Christo iuncti praemia summa tenent*. See Vallejo 2007, n. 7 (bears erroneously "n. 6.") and now Mossong 2022, n. 508.
46 The exact clerical position Honoratus occupied when living in exile is not known; in the poem, he is simply qualified as a *discipulus* (v. 14). Since he is not on the episcopal see yet, he is not included in Table 2 above.
47 AE 1938, 135 (Grado/Cathedral of S. Eufemia, where preserved): *Hic requiescit in pace Christi sanct(a)e me|moriae Marcianus episc(opus), qui vixit in e|piscopato annos XLIIII et peregrinatus | est pro causa fidei annos XL. Deposi|⁵ tus est autem in hoc sepulcro | VIII Kal(endas) Maias, indict(ione) undecima*. See now Mossong 2022, n. 456.
48 Egger 1950; *PCBE* 2, 1385 (Marcianus 10).

3 Conclusion

In conclusion, we can state that, with respect to episcopal exile, Late Antique epigraphical sources are not silent at all, at least within the Italian peninsula. The gathered material can be divided into three categories:
1) Inscriptions that confirm the literary sources
    This category includes the testimonies on Liberius, Vigilius and Eusebius of Vercelli. In these cases, the epigraphical sources are a further (confirming) piece of the puzzle;
2) Inscriptions that are independent from the literary sources
    This category includes the Damasian epigrams on Marcellus and Eusebius of Rome. Since the exiling authority is in both cases the *tyrannus* Maxentius, these texts may be qualified as propaganda against the hated emperor. It is not completely sure if both bishops had eventually been into exile in the stated conditions, since Damasus states more than once in other inscriptions that his level of information is due to *fama*;[49]
3) Inscriptions that attest non-literary persons
    This category includes the epitaph of Marcianus from Grado. Since the decisive and unambiguous information for an exile is lacking, this testimony has to be handled with care.

It must be stressed that none of these texts comes directly from the person that has endured the exile, which is maybe the biggest difference to the letters that bishops may have penned themselves during their banishment. The epigraphical texts seem to have been mostly created after the death of the exiled person and belong predominately to the genre of honorific inscriptions. The three texts that have been transmitted on their original support are funerary inscriptions that in two cases do not consider the exiled person itself (we remember the texts of Picentia Legitima and Mareas) and in the third case constitutes a very insecure testimony.

All of the exiled bishops from the Italian peninsula documented by inscriptions are exiled by a state authority, none has chosen deliberately to dislocate himself, as far as we know. Furthermore, it is important to stress that none of the stated examples can be attributed to a synodal decision, where colleagues of the same rank would have condemned a bishop fallen into disgrace. The proper threat, i.e. the exiling entity, only appears exceptionally within the epigraphic material. The only case is Maxentius, who is alluded to with the very negative expression *tyrannus* in the two Damasian epigrams for Marcellus and Eusebius.

---

49 ED 37 and ED 40: *fama refert.*

Can we deduce from this evidence that Italian bishops had rarely been exiled in comparison to their fellow colleagues from other regions? And what may be the reasons for this? It is difficult to give a final judgement about this but at least it is a remarkable phenomenon.

Finally, a quick look to the situation outside Italy shall be given: here information is even scarcer since there seems to be only one testimony for an exiled bishop. It comes from Algeria and refers to an anonymous bishop who had been in his position for eighteen years during which he had to endure several exiles (*multis exiliis*) for unknown reasons.[50] As can be deduced from the indicated aera, he died in 495. Other testimonies consider two presbyters from the city of Madaura (*Africa proconsularis*), namely Donatianus[51] and Liberatus,[52] but over the entire Western Roman Empire we have no other explicit epigraphical sources attesting an episcopal exile.[53] Thus, Italy provides an exceptional setting for this kind of investigation, which cannot be reproduced in another geographical area. Some further elements come from the archaeological context, but these only concern bishops coming from abroad that are attested in Italy.[54] The opposite – archaeological traces left by Italian bishops during their exile in faraway regions – is not documented. Thus, epigraphy is certainly not the primary source when studying exiled bishops, but if it has more to offer than initially thought the task of this approach is accomplished.

---

50 CIL VIII 9286 (Mouzaia): *[– – – – –] | [– – – mu]ltis exiliis [saepe] | probatus et fidei | catholicae adser|tor dignus inventus | inplevit in episcopatu | an(nos) XVIII m(enses) II d(ies) XII et occi|sus est in bello Mauro|rum et sepultus est die | VI Id(us) Maias p(rovinciae) CCCCLVI*. See Vallejo 2007, n. 1. Because of his anonymity, this bishop is not mentioned in *PCBE* 1. This is a good example why it is not recommendable to completely exclude anonymous people from prosopographical studies: for Italy, I have tried to counterbalance this practice by listing at least the anonymous clergy known by epigraphical testimonies, see Mossong 2022, tab. 2, where 107 anonymous clergymen from all over Italy are recorded.
51 ILCV 1601 A (Madaura): *Donatianus pr(e)sb(yter) | in exilio pro fide ca|t(h)olica hic aput col(oniam) Mad(auros) | relegatus recessit die | nonas Apriles an(no) (ç)I Kartha|g(i)n(is) vixit annis XCVI*. See also Vallejo (2007), n. 3. *PCBE* 1, 283 (Donatianus 1).
52 ILCV 1601B (Madaura): *Presuiter(!) Libe|ratus pro fide | cat(h)olica in exsili|o reces(s)it in pace et v(i)x(it) | annis LXXV | depositus est | die XVII ka(lendas) Iulias*. See also Vallejo 2007, n. 4. *PCBE* 1, 638 (Liberatus 6).
53 This is confirmed by a search of the word "exil" within the *sacerdotes christiani* in the EDCS-database (last consulted on 30.10.2022).
54 See Verstegen 2018.

Bibliography

Primary Sources

Ammianus Marcellinus: John C. Rolfe. ed. 1950–1961. *The Loeb Classical Library. Ammianus Marcellinus*. 3 Vols. London: William Heinemann LTD and Cambridge (MA): Harvard University Press.

Catalogus Liberianus: Johannes Divjak and Wolfgang Wischmeyer. eds. 2014. *Das Kalenderhandbuch von 354. Der Chronograph des Filocalus*. 2 Vols. Wien: Holzhausen.

Collectio Avellana: Otto Guenther. ed. 1895. *Corpus Scriptorum Ecclesiasticorum Latinorum (CSEL)*. 35, *Epistolae Imperatorum Pontificum Aliorum Inde ab a. CCCLXVII usque DLIII datae Avellana Quae Dicitur Collectio*, 2 parts. Prague/Vienna: F. Tempsky and Leipzig: G. Freytag.

Cyprian, *Epistolae:* Le chanoine Bayard. ed. 1961–1962. *Collection des Universités de France (CUF). Saint Cyprien, Correspondance*. 2 vols. 2nd edition. Paris : Les Belles Lettres.

Eusebius, *Epistolae:* Vinzenz Bulhart. ed. 1957. *Corpus Christianorum, Series Latina (CCSL)*. 9, *Eusebii Vercellensis Episcopi quae supersunt*. Turnhout: Brepols.

Faustinus, *Libellum precum:* Colin M. Whiting. ed. 2019. *Documents from the Luciferians: In Defense of the Nicene Creed*. Writings from the Greco-Roman World 43. Atlanta: Society of Biblical Literature.

Liberius, *Epistolae:* Alfred Leinhard Feder. ed. [1916] 1966. *Corpus scriptorum ecclesiasticorum Latinorum (CSEL)*. 65, *Sancti Hilarii Pictaviensis opera*. New York: Johnson.

Jerome, *Chronicum:* Rudolf Helm. ed. 1913. *Die Griechischen Christlichen Schriftsteller der ersten drei Jahrhunderte, Eusebius, Siebenter Band, Erster Teil. Eusebius Werke, Die Chronik des Hieronymus*. Leipzig: J.C. Hinrichs'sche Buchhandlung.

Jerome, *De viris illustribus:* Jean-Jacques Migne. ed. 1883. *Patrologia Latina*. 23, *Sancti Eusebii Hieronymi, Opera Omnia*. Paris : Migne.

Liberatus, *Breviarium:* Eduard Schwartz. ed. 1936. *Acta Conciliorum Oecumenicorum (ACO). Concilium universale Chalcedonense, Collectio Sangermanensis*. 2, 5. Berlin/Leipzig: De Gruyter.

Procopius: Henry B. Dewing. ed. 1914–1940. *The Loeb Classical Library. Procopius*, 7 Vols. London: William Heinemann LTD and Cambridge (MA): Harvard University Press.

Sulpicius Severus, *Chronicorum Libri duo:* Karl Halm. ed. 1866. *Corpus scriptorum ecclesiasticorum Latinorum (CSEL)*. 1, *Sulpicii Severi Libri qui supersunt*. Vienna: Carl Gerold's Sohn.

Theodoret of Cyrus, *Historia ecclesiastica:* Thomas Gaisford. ed. 1854. *Theodoreti Episcopi Cyri Ecclesiasticae Historiae Libri Quinque*. Oxford: E typographeo academico.

Secondary Sources

Anatolios, Khaled. 2018. "Athanasius, Patriarch of Alexandria." In *Oxford Dictionary of Late Antiquity (ODLA)*, 170–172.

Barry, Jennifer. 2019. *Bishops in flight. Exile and Displacement in Late Antiquity*, Oakland: University of California Press.

Blaudeau, Philippe, ed. 2008. *Exil et relégation. Les tribulations du sage et du saint durant l'Antiquité romaine et chrétienne (Ier-VIe s. ap. J.-C.); actes du colloque organisé par le Centre Jean-Charles Picard, Université de Paris XII-Val de Marne (17-18 juin 2005)*. Paris : De Boccard.

Brändle, Rudolf. 1998. "Johannes Chrysostomus I." In *Reallexikon für Antike und Christentum (RAC)* 18, col. 426–503.
Bruns, Peter. 2002. "Vigilius von Rom." In *Lexikon der antiken christlichen Literatur (LACL)*, 3rd edition, 720.
Cohen, Samuel. 2018. "Liberius and the Cemetery as a Space of Exile in Late Antique Rome." In *Mobility and Exile at the End of Antiquity*. Early Christianity in the Context of Antiquity 19, edited by Rohmann, Ulrich and Vallejo Girvés, 141–160. Berlin: Peter Lang.
Doignon, Jean. 1991. "Hilarius von Poitiers." In *Reallexikon für Antike und Christentum (RAC)* 15, col. 139–167.
Dümler, Bärbel. 2002a. "Liberius von Rom." In *Lexikon der antiken christlichen Literatur (LACL)*, 3rd edition, 456–457.
Dümler, Bärbel. 2002b. "Eusebius von Vercelli." In *Lexikon der antiken christlichen Literatur (LACL)*, 3rd edition, 249.
Egger, Rudolf. 1950. "Die ecclesiae Raetiae secundae." In *Reinecke-Festschrift: Zum 75. Geburtstag von Paul Reinecke am 25. September 1947*, edited by Gustav Behrens and Joachim Werner, 51–60. Mainz: Schneider.
Gentz, Günther. 1950. "Athanasius." In *Reallexikon für Antike und Christentum (RAC)* 1, col. 860–866.
Hamm, Ulrich. 2002. "Pontianus von Rom." In *Lexikon der antiken christlichen Literatur (LACL)*, 586.
Hammerich, Holger. 2002. "Cornelius von Rom." In *Lexikon der antiken christlichen Literatur (LACL)*, 165.
Handley, Mark. 2011. *Dying on foreign shores. Travel and Mobility in the Late-Antique West*. JRA Supplementary Series 86. Portsmouth: Journal of Roman Archaeology.
Hillner, Julia, Jörg Ulrich, and Jakob Engberg, eds. 2016. *Clerical exile in Late Antiquity*. Early Christianity in the Context of Antiquity 17. Frankfurt a. M.: Peter Lang.
Hunter, David G. 2018. "Hilary of Poitiers." In *Oxford Dictionary of Late Antiquity (ODLA)*, 721–722.
Kampert, Otmar. 2002. "Bonifatius I. von Rom." In *Lexikon der antiken christlichen Literatur (LACL)*, 3rd edition, 129.
Kelly, Gordon P. 2006. *A history of exile in the Roman Republic*. Cambridge: University Press.
Kreilos, Jutta. 2002. "Silvester I. von Rom." In *Lexikon der antiken christlichen Literatur (LACL)*, 3rd edition, 641.
MacEachnie, Robert. 2018. "Eusebius of Vercelli." In *Oxford Dictionary of Late Antiquity (ODLA)*, 568.
Mayer, Wendy. 2018. "John Chrysostom." In *Oxford Dictionary of Late Antiquity (ODLA)*, 821–823.
Melo, Melissa. 2021. "« Car je ne suis qu'un messager, et non l'auteur » : La communication exilique d'Hilaire de Poitiers." *Ktèma* 46:157–167.
Ménard, Hélène. 2008. "L'exil, enjeu de la sainteté : Réflexions sur la construction de la figure de l'évêque en Italie dans la seconde moitié du IVe s. ap. J.-C." In *Exil et relégation : les tribulations du sage et du saint durant l'Antiquité romaine et chrétienne (Ier-VIe s. ap. J.-C.) ; actes du colloque organisé par le Centre Jean-Charles Picard*, edited by Philippe Blaudeau, 241–253. Paris : De Boccard.
Mossong, Isabelle. 2022. *Der Klerus des spätantiken Italiens im Spiegel epigraphischer Zeugnisse – eine soziohistorische Studie*. Klio Beihefte 36. Berlin: Walter de Gruyter.
Natal, David. 2018. "Liberius." In *Oxford Dictionary of Late Antiquity (ODLA)*, 906.
Neil, Brownen. 2018. "Vigilius." In *Oxford Dictionary of Late Antiquity (ODLA)*, 1563.
Rohmann, Dirk, Jörg Ulrich, and Margarita Vallejo Girvés, eds. 2018. *Mobility and Exile at the End of Antiquity*. Early Christianity in the Context of Antiquity 19. Berlin: Peter Lang.

Rüpke, Jörg. 2005. *Fasti sacerdotum. Die Mitglieder der Priesterschaften und das sakrale Funktionspersonal römischer, griechischer, orientalischer und jüdisch-christlicher Kulte in der Stadt Rom von 300 v. Chr. bis 499 n. Chr.* Potsdamer Altertumswissenschaftliche Beiträge 12, 3 Vols. Stuttgart: Steiner.

Stini, Frank. 2011. *Plenum exiliis mare. Untersuchungen zum Exil in der römischen Kaiserzeit.* Geographica Historica 27. Stuttgart: Steiner.

Ulrich, Jörg. 2018. "How to Gain *indulgentiam*: The Case of Liberius of Rome." In *Mobility and Exile at the End of Antiquity*. Early Christianity in the Context of Antiquity 19, edited by Rohmann, Ulrich and Vallejo Girvés, 199–212. Berlin: Peter Lang.

Vallejo Girvés, Margarita. 2007. "Exilios y exiliados a partir de la epigrafía: un caso peculiar de movilidad geográfica." In *Acta XII Congressus Internationalis Epigraphiae Graecae et Latinae*, edited by Marc Mayer i Olivé, Giulia Baratta, and Alejandra Guzmán Almagro, 1477–1482. Barcelona: Universitat de Barcelona.

Vallejo Girvés, Margarita, Juan Antonio Bueno Delgado, and Carlos Sánchez-Moreno Ellart, eds. 2015. *Movilidad forzada entre la Antigüedad Clásica y Tardía.* Alcalá de Henares: Universidad de Alcalá, Servicio de publicaciones.

Verstegen, Ute. 2018. "Laid to Rest Abroad – Evidence for Forced Movement of Clerics in the Archeological Record." In *Mobility and Exile at the End of Antiquity*. Early Christianity in the Context of Antiquity 19, edited by Rohmann, Ulrich and Vallejo Girvés, 175–196. Berlin: Peter Lang.

Washburn, David. 2013. *Banishment in the Later Roman Empire, 284–476 CE.* Routledge Studies in Ancient History 5. New York/London. Routledge.

Windau, Bettina. 2002a. "Lucius I. von Rom." In *Lexikon der antiken christlichen Literatur (LACL)*, 3rd edition, 465.

Windau, Bettina. 2002b. "Lucifer von Cagliari." In *Lexikon der antiken christlichen Literatur (LACL)*, 3rd edition, 464.

Wirbelauer, Eckhard. 2008a. "Exil für den römischen Bischof." *Saeculum* 59/I:29–46.

Wirbelauer, Eckhard. 2008b. "Comment exiler un pape ?" In *Exil et relégation : les tribulations du sage et du saint durant l'Antiquité romaine et chrétienne (Ier–VIe s. ap. J.-C.); actes du colloque organisé par le Centre Jean-Charles Picard*, edited by Philippe Blaudeau, 255–272. Paris : De Boccard.

Withing, Colin M. 2019. *Documents from the Luciferians. In Defense of the Nicene Creed.* Writings from the Greco-Roman World 43. Atlanta: SBL Press.

Martin Horst
Bishops between Reform and Heresy: Priscillian, Martin of Tours and Magnus Maximus

1 Introduction

Abstract: The teachings of Priscillian of Ávila were a major source of conflict within the church in the late fourth century – at first limited to the Iberian Peninsula, but quickly spreading beyond the Pyrenees and, instigated by a faction of the bishops involved, also beyond the confines of the church. After the denouncement as heresy at the councils of Zaragoza (380) and Bordeaux (384), the episcopal opposition to Priscillianism had its most drastic effect in successfully pushing for the death penalty for Priscillian and some of his followers at Trier in 385 – a judgement for which the secular authority of the Empire was made use of. Far from putting an end to the conflict, this involvement only escalated it and led Martin of Tours and others to condemn the entire process. The councils of Turin (398/399) and Toledo (400) were able to calm it temporarily – but not entirely. To explain the rapid expansion of the conflict and the appeal to the secular authority, tracing the personal contacts of the involved parties can provide valuable insights. They clearly illustrate the dense network spreading across both the Late Antique episcopate and the civil administration.

The large number of bishops involved in clashes over what became known as Priscillianism can only be partly represented by Martin of Tours and Priscillian – already associated with one another by their shared ascetic tendencies. Both came to lead movements offering concepts of religious life, especially clerical life, that drastically differed from what was developing during the late fourth century in their home territories of Hispania and Gaul, respectively. Resistance to their ideas came primarily from the episcopate and resulted in the execution of Priscillian on the orders of Magnus Maximus and serious conflict between the emperor and Martin of Tours. The episcopate of Gaul and Hispania acquired lessons from their actions, having escalated the conflict by their answering each threat with a counterthreat. Martin was not involved[1] until late in the steadily escalating conflict between Priscillianists and their adversaries based on the Iberian Peninsula.

The nature of actions taken in this conflict can be judged through a close look at how they are presented in the available sources. In this regard, much is owed to the fundamental work of Vollmann, who enriched scholarly discussion by revealing the context of the sources, especially in analyzing them with regards to canon law and exploring the authorship of the Würzburg tractates.[2] Equally helpful is the recent article by Girardet in reconstructing events from the council of Saragossa in 380 to the immediate aftermath of Priscillian's execution at Trier around 386.[3] With the publication of the last relevant source in 1889,[4] the likelihood of a chance discovery that would close gaps in the source material seems low. Tantalizing glimpses of lost documents that could fill these gaps in our knowledge of events are seen in some of our sources. Given the later scapegoating of Ithacius of Ossonoba and the resulting bias of the account, his apologetic work mentioned by Isidore of Seville would be of enormous interest.[5] There are three separate sources regarding the events up to and at the Council of Saragossa. Apart from the relevant section of the continuous narrative of Sulpicius Severus' *chronica*, the apologetic *Liber ad Damasum Episcopum*[6] provides an alternative narrative, which differs as to whether Priscillian and his associates were actually condemned by the assembled bishops. While no complete *acta* of the council survives, a list of twelve participants and eight *canones* makes no mention of any particular person being condemned.[7] Developments up to the point when Priscillian, Instantius and Salvianus

---

1 And not as doctrinally close to Priscillianism as the shared catchphrase 'asceticism' might imply, not sharing his preference for apocryphal literature, for example. See Vollmann 1974, 527–531. – This contribution evolved in the framework of the Center for Advanced Study "RomanIslam – Center for Comparative Empire and Transcultural Studies", funded by the German Research Foundation (Deutsche Forschungsgemeinschaft, DFG), at Universität Hamburg.
2 Vollmann 1974.
3 Beginning with Girardet 1974, there are three monographs dealing with the Priscillianist controversy, Chadwick 1976 and Burrus 1995 each providing a comprehensive look at the topic, with Van Dam 1985 offering a more compact English-language overview, as does Jorge 2006. Markauskas 2015 serves to provide a context for episcopal utilization of secular legal resources in Late Antiquity, while numerous articles by Escribano Paño focus on the different aspects of the topic – only some of the more recent ones can be included in the bibliography: 2005, 2019, 2021a, b, c. Girardet 2018/2019, 34–57, summarizes the events.
4 Schepps 1889. Conti 2010 mentions few changes in the text but thankfully provides a complete translation.
5 Isid. vir. ill. 15.
6 Vollmann 1974, 490, ascribes a fair likelihood to Priscillian being the author of the letter.
7 There are two strands of transmission with minor differences: in the *Collectio Hispana* (the 10th-century *Codex Albeldensis seu Vigillianus* [El Escorial D.I.2], which also contains the full *acta* of the

went to Rome to petition Bishop Damasus after unsuccessfully attempting the same with Ambrose in Milan are covered in both the *chronica* and the *Liber ad Damasum*. For the later events, the *chronica* is the only available source for roughly 383 to 385, including the synod at Bordeaux and the trial at Trier.[8] The letter from Magnus Maximus to Bishop Siricius of Rome emphasizing his role in combating "Manicheans"[9] dated to 385 appears to be roughly contemporaneous with the trial. The aftermath, including the synod at Trier in 386 is once again only described by Sulpicius Severus, in his *Dialogi*, where the reaction of Martin of Tours takes center stage.[10] There are inconsistencies with the *chronica* and the *Vita sancti Martini* that can be explained by attempts to paint the subject of his veneration in the most positive light possible. The hagiographical text simply omits numerous aspects of his interactions with fellow bishops and the imperial court in the course of the Priscillianist controversy. As such, it is not very useful for a reconstruction of Martin's strategy in dealing with the threat posed by his doctrinal proximity to the Priscillianists and his actions during and after the trial at Trier. It does, however, serve as a reminder of Sulpicius' bias in reporting on the Priscillianists – attempting to maintain an untarnished image of Martin in the face of widespread condemnation and of similarly inclined ascetics.

2 A Conflict within the Episcopate of the Iberian Peninsula

Concerning the introduction of practices and teachings on the Iberian Peninsula that would come to be described as Priscillianist, the account of Sulpicius Severus is the main source.[11] The social and educational[12] background of Priscillian is de-

---

first *Toletanum*) and in the later *Hispana Gallica Augustodunensis* (depending on a single complete manuscript: Vat. Lat. 1341). See Panzram 2015, 630–632, regarding the general lack of reliability of the latter.
8 Although not a contemporary, Prosper (chron. 1187) places these under the consulate of Arcadius and Bauto – i.e., 385. It is unclear which source he relies on in this case and he doesn't provide any further information beyond that given by Sulpicius Severus.
9 Avell. 40, 4.
10 Sulp. Sev. dial. II (III), 11–13.
11 Isid. vir. ill. 15 shows that both Sulpicius and Isidore seem to depend on an apologetic work of Ithacius, see Chadwick 1976, 21–22; Girardet 2018/2019, 32.
12 Vollmann 1974, 490–494, analyses the Würzburg tractates I–III in order to glean additional insight as to the education of their author – seeing a greater likelihood of them having been produced by Priscillian than for the remaining eight examples. He points out the well-constructed *libellus* accusing Hydatius of Mérida in the second tractate as a sign of considerable knowledge of

scribed as having been one of rich and noble birth, well read and possessing an intellect of great potential, which was corrupted through depraved studies.[13] Rather than having been the origin of his teachings, Priscillian is supposed to have been instructed by a woman named Agape – likewise of noble birth – and a rhetorician by the name of Helpidius,[14] who were in turn instructed by a certain Mark of Memphis, said to have brought the "gnostic heresies" from Egypt to Hispania.[15]

It is not possible to provide a firm timeline for the process by which Priscillian brought his circle of followers together than to place it in the decade leading up to the Council of Saragossa on October 4th 380. By this time, their numbers had grown to such an extent that at least twelve bishops assembled to deal with what had clearly become regarded as a problem –perhaps even beyond the Pyrenees given the attendance of two Aquitanian bishops, Phoebadius of Agen and Delphinus of Bordeaux.[16] Of more worry than the spread among the laity, Priscillian's circle now contained a number of bishops, two of whom – Instantius and Salvianus – are singled out by Sulpicius as particularly close supporters. According to him, Bishop Hyginus of Córdoba brought this state of affairs to the attention of Hydatius of Mérida,[17] whose efforts at containing the movement are summarized as having been wholly unsuccessful, only serving to further spur on its adherents.[18]

Concerning Priscillianist practices, the eight *canones* issued by the majority at Saragossa provide an insight into the practices that were regarded as objectionable. The list of bishops is given in the beginning – instructing one among their number, Lucius, to read out the decisions, each closing with a declaration of uni-

---

canon law. His reading of the author "carefully avoiding" the use of classical allusions would nonetheless imply some familiarity with them.

13 Sulp. Sev. chron. II, 46, 3–5.
14 *PLRE* I, 415, Helpidius 8, who is mentioned again as being condemned with Priscillian at Saragossa (Sulp. Sev. chron. II, 47, 1–3). Despite being of Greek origin, the name is sufficiently common in the Western Empire that a relation with *PLRE* I, Helpidius 9, relation of Theodosius I., or *PLRE* II, Helpidius 1, *proconsul Africae* in 402 and correspondent of Symmachus, cannot necessarily be assumed, see Matthews 1975, 110, n. 2.
15 Sulp. Sev. chron. II, 46, 1–2.
16 *Concilium Caesaraugustanum* I, 16–21. Apart from Hydatius, the personal history of Carterius makes it unlikely that he would support the Priscillianists asceticism, see *PCBE:* Hispania 147–148, Carterivs.
17 Sulp. Sev. chron. II, 46, 7–9.
18 Panzram 2015, 636, argues that the hierarchy of episcopal sees in provincial capitals assuming metropolitan rank was not yet established on the Iberian Peninsula – the appeal from the bishop of one provincial capital to another (*Lusitania* to *Baetica*) may be due to more intangible measures of seniority.

versal assent.[19] The main thrust of the decrees is to prevent religious practices that are independent of the established Church, with a secondary aim to curtail certain ascetic practices associated with the Priscillianists, such as fasting on Sundays, thus receiving the Eucharist but not consuming it as part of the rite.[20] While this would take on importance later in recognizing Priscillianists within congregations, the primary issues appear to have been two tendencies inherent in Priscillianism: to absent oneself from organized prayer and to receive religious instruction through unsanctioned channels.[21] To this end, the *canones* forbid absence from churches during Lent and between December 17th and January 6th, as well as forbidding retreat to cells or the mountains.[22] Clerics were likewise forbidden from abandoning their churches and taking on monastic habits,[23] while women were banned from joining groups of unrelated men to undertake religious instruction.[24] Only women over the age of forty were permitted to take vows of chastity, and only after obtaining permission from a cleric.[25] The prohibition against bearing the title of *doctor* without permission must also be regarded as an attempt at regaining control over the means of religious instruction.[26]

Comparing the sparse report with that of contemporaneous councils, it is impossible to exclude the possibility of Priscillian and his followers Instantius, Salvianus and Helpidius having received individual sentences *"in absentes"*[27], as the *chronica* states, without record of them in later manuscripts. They further are said to have been excluded from communion, with Hyginus additionally being excluded for ignoring this prohibition. Bishop Ithacius of Ossonoba[28] was charged with promulgating the news of the sentence. Given the support provided to the Priscillianist cause by Symposius of Astorga in later years, it seems more likely

---

19 Girardet 2018/2019, 33, points out that little is known about how majority opinions were formed by this point in time. The usual subscription lists disregard any dissenting minority and may thus provide a skewed image of total attendance. Regarding *unanimitas*, see also Weckwerth 2010, 272–283.
20 *Concilium Caesaraugustanum* I, 29–43 (c. II and III), see Chadwick 1976, 14.
21 Vollmann 1974, 498; Girardet 2018/2019, 34–35.
22 *Concilium Caesaraugustanum* I, 29–38 and 44–52 (c. II and IV).
23 *Concilium Caesaraugustanum* I, 59–66 (c. VI).
24 *Concilium Caesaraugustanum* I, 22–28 (c. I).
25 *Concilium Caesaraugustanum* I, 72–76 (c. VIII).
26 *Concilium Caesaraugustanum* I, 67–71 (c. VII). There is no further information on who would have been authorized to award the title – allowing just any single bishop to do so would hardly have been an effective tactic.
27 Sulp. Sev. chron. II, 47, 2.
28 Sulp. Sev. chron. II, 47, 3, *"Ithacio Sossubensi"* changed into *Ossonobensi* in Sigonius' edition of 1581 rather than an alternative reading of *Oxomensi*, see also Escribano Paño 2005, 142, n. 81.

that no such sentence could be agreed upon.[29] The *Liber ad Damasum* at least states clearly that no such sentence had been issued or that any of the Priscillianists were even summoned or accused:

> *Denique in conuentu episcopali qui Caesaraugustae fuit nemo e nostris reus factus tenetur, nemo accusatus, nemo conuictus, nemo damnatus est, nullum nomini nostro uel proposito uel uitae crimen obiectum est, nemo ut euocaretur non dicam necessitatem sed nec sollicitudinem habuit. Datum nescio quod ab Hydatio ibi commonitorium est quod uelut agendae uitae poneret disciplinam: nemo illic nostrum inter illa repraehensus tua potissimum epistula contra inprobos praeualente, in qua iuxta euangelica iussa praeceperas, ne quid in absentes et inauditos decerneretur.*[30]

In a later repetition of the claim, the author explicitly adds that no sentence was passed, even in their absence[31] – something that would have been inadmissible in any case, according to a previous letter sent by Damasus.[32] The quoted section shows two strategies utilized by the Priscillianists to counter efforts of the bishops to deal with a perceived threat to their authority: physically avoiding and otherwise ignoring them. Keeping the *canones* in mind, the claims that they had nothing to do with their way of life seem somewhat disingenuous.[33] If the *canones* had simply proven ineffectual, any further escalation from the bishops assembled at Saragossa can only be speculative – as the Priscillianists also chose a more drastic strategy, such speculation is moot.

Apart from ignoring decisions taken at Saragossa or finding ways around them, as in Instantius and Salvianus raising Priscillian to the episcopal see of Ávila, they set about dealing with a prominent adversary.[34] This may have been in response to Hydatius attempting to punish transgressions against the *canones* of Saragossa with excommunication as threatened at the council.[35] While nonde-

---

29 Unless the *canones* were decided on first, followed by the departure of Symposius (see *Concilium Toletanum* I concerning the events at Saragossa: while Martínez Diez 1984 does not include the *professiones* against the Priscillianists, they are provided in the appendix of Chadwick 1976, 236: "*sola tamen una die praesente Symphosio*", based on his reading of the transcriptions of both de Morales and Bautista Pérez.).
30 Priscill. tract. II, 42–43.
31 Priscill. tract. II, 48.
32 There are no other records of this letter or its contents. It can only be assumed that these are properly represented in this further attempt at communication with Damasus.
33 van Waarden 2014, 137: "Doctrinal ambiguity is simply waved away…".
34 *Concilium Caesaraugustanum* I, 57–60.
35 Girardet 2018/2019, 40–41, holds this to be the most likely explanation for the discrepancy over whether anyone was sentenced at Saragossa – it could truthfully be claimed that this wasn't the case as it only happened later, based on the decisions made there. See also Burrus 1995, 30.

script accusations against Hydatius are claimed to have originated with a presbyter from within his own ranks, the *Liber ad Damasum* describes more serious charges added from within the churches of the Priscillianist bishops. With Hyginus and Symposius now among their supporters, the two were charged with delivering letters to Hydatius and further efforts to arrange a peaceful resolution.[36] Once again, reproduced as part of a supposed reply by Hydatius, the claim that no one was condemned at Saragossa is repeated. Despite all efforts, an inordinate degree of fear of prosecution is said to have led Hydatius to reach out to the imperial court to obtain a decree against the Priscillianists by misrepresenting the nature of their practices.[37] The *chronica* picks up the narrative again, after leaving out the aftermath of the Council of Saragossa except for the appointment of Priscillian as a bishop.[38]

3 Escalation beyond the Diocese and into the Civil Sphere

For once, the two narratives are united in removing the blame from the Priscillianists and placing it squarely on the shoulders of Hydatius, while the *chronica* also holds Ithacius responsible for appealing to secular judges. The claim is that due to Hydatius petitioning Gratian a rescript against *"pseudoepiscopos et Manichaeos"*[39] was issued.[40] Despite their assertions of orthodoxy, defense of congregations choosing their own bishops and attempts at distancing themselves strongly from Manichaeism,[41] this time Priscillian and his episcopal followers appear to have been unable to ignore the charges, forcing them to flee the Iberian Peninsula. The aforementioned success of the movement in Aquitaine may explain their choice of destination– their expulsion from Bordeaux by Bishop Delphinus shows that his stance towards them had not softened since the Council of Saragos-

---

36 Possibly in the form of another council: its decisions would have superseded those from Saragossa, as Vollmann 1974, 499, notes. See also Girardet 2018/2019, 43.
37 Priscill. tract. II, 48–50.
38 Sulp. Sev. chron. II, 47, 4.
39 Priscill. tract. II, 50. Chadwick 1974, 33–34, and Girardet 2018/2019, 41, discuss the validity of Priscillian's consecration as bishop of Ávila, but without knowing the circumstances this cannot be determined. It is unknown whether another bishop apart from Instantius and Salvianus took part in it as required, whether they had been excommunicated at the time and whether a majority of the bishops of the province including the metropolitan agreed with the consecration.
40 Sulp. Sev. chron. II, 47, 7.
41 Priscill. tract. II, 50.

sa.⁴² Elsewhere, the reception was more favorable, as they remained for some time with Euchrotia and Procula, widow and daughter of the rhetorician Delphidius,⁴³ who would accompany them to Trier. Sulpicius reports hearsay that Procula had become pregnant by Priscillian and procured an abortion – something that would have fit suspicions about a group that withdrew from the broader congregations. Priscillian, Instantius and Salvianus went to Rome but could not attain an audience with Damasus, instead preparing the *Liber ad Damasum* to petition the bishop to intervene in their favor.⁴⁴ Having failed in this, they attempted to gain an audience with Ambrose in Milan but were likewise unsuccessful⁴⁵ – assuming that he and Damasus had gained a false impression of their movement through contact with their opponents.⁴⁶

Up to this point, the Priscillianists could claim to have remained wholly within the bounds of the Church, but having failed to appeal to its two most influential leaders, they had a choice of either seeking refuge in exile or support from outside the Church. There is no other source than the *chronica* regarding the means they chose – describing their next action as having been first to bribe the *magister officiorum*, Macedonius⁴⁷ to produce a second rescript countermanding the first and restoring them to their sees, and secondly to have Volventius, proconsul in Hispania deal with Ithacius.⁴⁸ Finding himself accused as a *"perturbator ecclesiarum"*⁴⁹ by the secular authorities, he is said to have taken the same action as his opponents did before and fled to Gaul – finding support from the *praefectus praetorio*

---

42 *PCBE* 4, 552–555, Delphinvs, shows that Delphinus was not generally hostile to asceticism, having baptized and later kept in close contact with Paulinus of Nola who eulogized him as the Aquitanian saint capable of heavenly intercession – alongside Martin of Tours, serving the rest of Gaul, and others (Paul. Nol. carm. 19, 153–154).

43 Auson. prof. 5, 35–38 expresses relief that Delphidius' early death kept him from witnessing the deviance of his daughter and execution of his wife.

44 van Waarden (2014, 141–142) explains it as having failed because Damasus would not have been willing to commit to the unreserved support it argues for. This would have left him no leeway for any diplomatic effort or to extricate himself, should the conflict escalate – as it did.

45 Priscill. tract. 50. As Ambrose maintained friendly contact with Delphinus of Bordeaux and Phoebadius of Agen in later years, treating them like a single person (Ambr. epist. 47), it seems likely that the anti-Priscillianists would have utilized him as a conduct to both Damasus and the imperial court. See also Girardet 2018/2019, 42.

46 Sulp. Sev. chron. II, 48, 1–4.

47 *PLRE* I, 526, Macedonius 3 is recorded as having locked the doors of his office against Ambrose attempting to intercede with him in another matter and in return not finding sanctuary within the church (Paul. Med. vita Ambr. 37) when he was later arrested for misconduct (Symm. rel. 36). See also Matthews 1975, 191.

48 Sulp. Sev. chron. II, 48, 5–49, 1.

49 Sulp. Sev. chron. II, 49, 2.

Gregorius[50] in Trier. The prefect's attempt to imprison those accused of heresy at the urging of Ithacius, placed by Sulpicius in the broader context of combating corruption, was thwarted by another intervention of the *magister officiorum*. Another bribe supposedly motivated him to place the investigation in the hands of the *vicarius Hispaniarum*[51] and to give orders to have Ithacius brought before him. The flight of Ithacius into the protection of the bishop of Trier, Britto,[52] brought the proceedings to a standstill until the usurpation of Magnus Maximus rendered the decisions of the previous court moot. At this juncture, the fact that Ithacius was still in Trier found him well placed to air his grievances against the Priscillianists to the receptive ears of the new emperor, who appears to have jumped at the chance to distinguish himself as a defender of orthodoxy.[53]

He chose to call an imperial council – a means that had been well established since the gathering at Arles in 314 at the urging of Constantine I – at Bordeaux and thus exclude both Prefect Gregorius and the *vicarius Hispaniarum* from the process.[54] Choosing a location outside of the Iberian Peninsula went against precedent,[55] although the prevalence of Priscillianism in Aquitaine was used to argue for its suitability, even though the central parties were all from beyond the Pyrenees. In any case, Bishop Delphinus is most likely to have presided over the council, which did not bode well for the Priscillianists.[56] Except for the uncertain date of 385,[57] all information about the council is contained in just two verses of the *chronica*, providing neither list nor even the number of participants or details of the proceedings.[58] It reports that both Instantius and Priscillian were brought to Bor-

---

50 *PLRE* I, 404, Proculus Gregorius 9, recipient of Symm. epist. III, 17–22 – out of office before the murder of Gratian, August 25th, 383.
51 While he is not named in the *chronica*, it seems reasonable to assume that it was *PLRE* I, 559–560, Marinianvs 2, given that he received Cod. Theod. IX, 1, 14 on May 27th, 383 and the usurpation of Magnus Maximus of August of the same year follows in the narrative. From Symm. epist. III, 23–29, Marinianus appears to have been on friendly terms with Symmachus – (epist. III, 29) *"Stetimus officiis religionis hactenus pares"* suggests that the was also a pagan. Picking an investigator who was not obviously aligned with either side may have been an attempt at de-escalation.
52 *PCBE* 4, 373, Britto, Var. Britannius; Britonnius, the *chronica* uses Britannius.
53 Chadwick 1976, 43; Compare Avell. 39 and 40 – Escribano (2019, 75–76; 2021c, 187–188) give arguments in favor of this having been successful, with him having gained in stature compared to Valentinian II., at least in the eyes of Theodosius I., while Escribano (2021b, 74–75) brings forth less self-serving motivations.
54 Sulp. Sev. chron. II, 49, 3–7.
55 Cod. Thrsod. XVI 2, 23, Gratian had ruled in 376 that such synods were to be held in dioceses concerned.
56 Girardet 2018/2019, 45.
57 Prosp. chron. 1187, not necessarily reliable.
58 For further discussion see Vollmann 1974, 507–512; Chadwick 1976, 42–46; Burrus 1995, 81–84.

deaux, with the former proving unable to defend himself against accusations and defrocked. Rather than giving testimony, Priscillian is reported to have made an appeal to the emperor, with Sulpicius displaying his consternation at this having been allowed. He argues that the accused should either have been judged without his testimony or, if there had been grounds for the assembled bishops to recuse themselves, judgement transferred to another group of bishops – but never to the imperial court.[59] The argument that Priscillian was attempting to have the emperor call another gathering in a more favorable location and with a more favorable composition suffers from the low likelihood that the plea would be granted, given that it had been Maximus who called the council in the first place. Nevertheless, other avenues of appeal open to Priscillian do not readily suggest themselves.[60]

Given that he would certainly have being defrocked like Instantius and probably also exiled, his decision seems unwise in hindsight[61] – however, the possibility of a secular trial with an accusation of *maleficium*,[62] carrying with it the threat of capital punishment, may not have entered his mind. While the leadup to the trial and the timeline[63] are as unclear as they are concerning the events at Bordeaux, the description in the *chronica* is at least somewhat more detailed. It begins with a full assault on Ithacius, who, together with Hydatius, had taken the role of accuser with what Sulpicius characterizes as excessive enthusiasm. Rather than enthusiasm, what prompted this outburst becomes clear in the following section where Ithacius dared to importune Martin of Tours, then residing at the court in Trier, with charges of heresy for attempting to spare the accused the death penalty.

As long as he remained at Trier, the standoff held. Sulpicius reports of a promise made by Maximus to Martin to keep it as such. He was only to break it due to the influence of two bishops by the names of Magnus and Rufus after Martin had departed. The trial was handed over to the new prefect of Maximus, Evodius, who tried and convicted Priscillian after he supposedly admitted to obscene practices.[64] When the sentencing was repeated,[65] Ithacius is said to have stepped aside as an

---

59 Sulp. Sev. chron. II, 49, 8–9.
60 It would have been possible according to precedent, compare Girardet 1974, 435–437; Chadwick 1976, 44; Birley 1983, 33–34; Burrus 1995, 94.
61 Chadwick 1976, 46; Fournier 2006, 159; Girardet 2018/2019, 46–47.
62 Kahlos 2016, 167–168.
63 Beginning in 385 or 386 and stretching into 387 at the outside, see Chadwick 1976, 132–138; Birley 1983, 31–33.
64 Paneg. Lat. XII, 29 suggests that the confession was achieved through torture and strongly criticizes the condemnation of Euchrotia alongside Priscillian. Compare Birley 1983, 34.
65 Reading *iudicium* with this meaning seems more plausible than the entire trial being repeated.

accuser out of fear of the reaction of his fellow bishops and was replaced by a treasury official. Subsequently, the sentences were passed and were carried out – with Priscillian and several of his followers, including Euchrotia, being beheaded. The sentence passed against Instantius at Bordeaux appears to have been upheld, only resulting in banishment. The death of Priscillian is claimed by Sulpicius to have led to him having been worshipped as a martyr in Hispania for the fifteen years that had passed.[66]

4 Dealing with the Effects of the Condemnation at Trier

Not only did the execution fail to put an end to the controversy, but expanded the circle of involved parties beyond the Priscillianists on one side and their opponents on the other – the cases of Hyginus and Symposius have shown that allegiances could shift over time. Beyond retelling the events as a two-sided dispute, a closer look at personal threats that resulted from taking a position during the trial and its aftermath is necessary. The spectrum ranges from Martin of Tours, accused of Priscillianist sympathies by Ambrose of Milan, obliged to position himself against secular interference in what he understood to be ecclesiastical, to Magnus Maximus, being criticized for interference, and to Hydatius and Ithacius having had a part in bringing the trial about. Both suffered the loss of their sees, with Hydatius having felt pressured to give up his bishopric voluntarily, while Ithacius was cast out of the episcopate.[67] Their strategy of answering all attacks with counterattacks had proven only to escalate the conflict,[68] aided by a similar strategy among the Priscillianists after ignoring the opposition was no longer sustainable. While no one openly sided with the Priscillianists, their practices being almost universally condemned, Martin and Ambrose, as well as Maximus, rested their positions on the technicality of whether Priscillian had still been part of the episcopate at the time of the trial. Martin and Ambrose held this to have been the case – thus Ambrose could issue

---

66 Sulp. Sev. chron. II, 50–51; the fifteen years put forward in 51, 8 cannot serve to date the death of Priscillian exactly, as the time of writing is likewise uncertain.
67 Sulp. Sev. chron. II, 51, 5–6. At a later date between 386 and 389 according to Prosp. chron. 1193, see also Chadwick 1976, 148–149; Girardet 2018/2019, 47.
68 Natal and Wood 2016, 40–44.

his critique without direct consequences, seeing more of a general threat to the episcopate, had secular interference been allowed to continue.[69]

The threat to Martin, again residing in Trier, was far more immediate, having already been subject to accusation of heresy, and he further increased it by refusing communion with Ithacius or any of his associates and by arguing against the persecution of heretics in Spain. Justifying his refusal through Ithacius' prosecution of a sitting bishop, his argument against persecution can be explained as his fear that otherwise, orthodox Christians could also be falsely swept up in this endeavor.[70] Associates of Ithacius called upon Maximus' argument to Martin that the sentences had been arrived at lawfully, and that the council concurrently found Ithacius to be without fault.[71] The emperor further threatened executions of heretics to break Martin's resistance, with a compromise in which some aspects of the persecution would be cancelled in return for Martin taking part in communion at the ordination of Felix as successor of Britto at Trier.[72] Rather than being threatened with exclusion from communion, the stature of Martin was such that he was able to pressure opponents by withholding communion, despite his attempts at reforming the clergy along monastic lines making him vulnerable to accusation of doctrinal proximity to the heretics.[73]

Maximus had to defend himself against criticism by Siricius, successor of Damasus on the Petrine chair, for having allowed the trial at Trier to go forward. He was, however, not explicitly criticized for sentencing a sitting bishop, suggesting a level of ambiguity around the question of Maximus choosing to recognize only the first rescript against Priscillian as having taken effect or whether the Council of Bordeaux effectively stripped him of his position before the trial. The emperor furthermore argued that the accused had confessed – sending the corresponding records to the bishop of Rome[74] who had, like his predecessor, wisely chosen to ignore the entire proceedings.

---

69 Ambr. epist. 30; Hier. vir. ill. 121 also supports this interpretation; See also Vollmann 1974, 511; Chadwick 1976, 129; Markauskas 2015, 95–97. 121.
70 Sulp. Sev. dial. II (III), 11.
71 Presumably shortly after the trial, before outrage over the decision had time to build up.
72 Sulp. Sev. dial. II (III), 12–13.
73 Sulpicius Severus (Mart. 10) describes the similar tendency to seek isolation.
74 Avell. 40, 4. See also Girardet 2018/2019, 50–51.

5 From Individual Strategies to a Broader Pacification?

While all sides agreed on episcopal disputes having to be settled internally, an overview of bishops utilizing secular legal means shows that this differed from earlier developments. Unlike Nicene/non-Nicene conflicts, in which imperial patronage tended to sharply favor one party, this clash was characterized by both sides being able to access the highest levels of the administration.[75] The outcry over this escalation enabled Martin and Ambrose to set a trend towards an increase in clerical immunity.[76] A possible motivation for Maximus allowing a civil prosecution was the opportunity to confiscate the fortunes of the condemned,[77] an apparently prudent course of action given his financial situation.

Beyond making the danger of carrying squabbles outside the Church starkly visible, the Priscillianist controversy also resulted in a long-lasting division within the Church. In Gaul this was framed as being between Felician and anti-Felician factions – i.e., those sharing communion with the associates of Felix of Trier, originally of Ithacius, despite his participation in the trial, and those who refused it as Martin of Tours did from the investment of Felix until his death in 397.[78] The division in Hispania remained between anti-Priscillianists and Priscillianist sympathizers. Having been entangled, it then took two separate councils to attempt to settle things in Hispania and Gaul – the latter council being held in Turin in 398 or 399 due to, among other factors,[79] the proximity to the imperial court at Milan and the still pervading influence of the late Ambrose. Earlier attempts at such a gathering had been unsuccessful, as the faction around Martin declined to attend out of fear of being outnumbered.[80] The bishops assembled at Turin issued a *canon* inviting any Felicians willing

---

75 Markauskas 2015, 95–96. Although the lack of integration into inter-provincial episcopal networks limited the access of the Priscillianists to the most prominent bishops, as seen above.
76 Markauskas 2015, 123–124. Natal and Wood 2016, 45, argue for increased differentiation between the episcopal and the imperial sphere that were not easily distinguishable before.
77 Girardet 2018/2019, 49: Cod. Theod. XVI 5, 3; 5, 7; 5, 9.
78 Sulp. Sev. dial. II (III), 13, 5–6. See also Mathisen 1989, 14–15.
79 Mathisen 2013, 291–296, expands on the factors that led to the assembly at Turin and how these support a date of 398/399 for the council rather than alternative propositions. While coming to different conclusions concerning the relocation of the Gallic prefecture from Trier to Arles and resulting ecclesiastical disputes, Bleckmann 2002, 163, also argues for an early date based on the currency of the Felician split.
80 Mathisen 1989, 15–16.

to cut ties with Felix to be received among them,[81] with resignation of Felix around the same time greatly speeding this process.[82]

In Toledo, as a multitude of *canones* aimed at the surviving – if not growing – number of Priscillianists was issued, there was also an attempt at reconciliation. The nineteen bishops assembled there[83] in 400 agreed to receive Symposius and his son Dictinius, in the meantime placed upon a vacant episcopal see, back into their ranks.[84] In return, they condemned their former Priscillianist teachings, as the professions *contra sectam Priscilliani aera ccccxxxviii* show.[85] More bishops with Priscillianists leanings followed them back into the fold.[86] Both efforts may be seen as more than just a healing of longstanding rifts but rather a closing of ranks against what was perceived to be a serious external threat. The dangers of individual bishops stubbornly pursuing their own strategies had been made perfectly clear. In Gaul at least, efforts were made in the fifth century to steer such pursuits along hierarchical channels[87] while in Hispania the process was more protracted.[88] On either side of the Pyrenees, however, calling upon the next authority in line remained a popular tactic when the current one would not fulfil your wishes.[89] As long as nobody strayed from the line, even personal enmities[90] could be dealt with without endangering greater parts of the Church.

Otherwise, bishops aligning themselves with external actors could have done massive damage to the wealth of the Church, with covetous rulers seeking to prosecute its members. The fortunes of those among the episcopate with an aristocratic background would have made tempting targets with the density of their personal networks a constant temptation to gather support against rivals within the Church from outside of it. Without the example of the Priscillianist controversy serving as a deterrent, it might have resulted in far more widespread conflicts.

---

81 *Concilium Turinense* I, 80–86 (c. 6).
82 Mathisen 1989, 18.
83 *Concilium Toletanum* I, 180–198.
84 Natal and Wood 2016, 45–46.
85 Chadwick 1976, 234–239. Hispanic era 438 = 400 AD.
86 Van Dam 1985, 109–110.
87 Natal and Wood 2016, 46.
88 Panzram 2015, 658–661.
89 Natal and Wood 2016, 54.
90 Priscill. tract. I, 40: *"domesticas inimicitias"*.

Bibliography

Primary Sources

Ambrosius, *Epistulae:* Otto Faller and M. Zelzer. eds. 1968–1996. *Corpus Scriptorum Ecclesiasticorum Latinorum (CSEL).* 82/1–4. Vienna: Hölder-Pichler-Tempsky.
Ausonius, *commemoratio professorum Burdigalensium: Ausonii Opera,* Roger P. H. Green. trans. [1991] 2009. Oxford Classical Texts. Oxford: Clarendon Press.
Codex Theodosianus: Paul Krueger and Theodor Mommsen. eds. [1904] 2000. *Codex Theodosianus, Volumen I, Theodosiani libri XVI Cum constitutionibus Sirmondianis.* Hildesheim: Weidman.
Concilia Galliae A. 314–A. 506: Charles Munier. ed. 1963. *Corpus Christianorum Series Latina (CCSL).* 148. Turnhout: Brepols.
Council of Saragossa I: "Concilio I de Zaragoza: Texto critico." In *I Concilio Caesaraugustano, MDC aniversario,* edited by Félix Rodríguez Barbero. 1981. Zaragoza: Institucíon Fernando el Católico.
Epistulae Imperatorum Pontificium Aliorum Datae Avellana quae Dicitur Collectio: Otto Günther. ed. 1895. *Corpus Scriptorum Ecclesiasticorum Latinorum (CSEL).* 35/1. Vienna: F. Tempsky.
Gaudemet, Jean. 2008. *Conciles Gaulois du IVe siècle.* Sources chrétiennes No 241. Paris : Éditions du Cerf.
Isidorus Hispalensis, *De Viris Illustribus: El "De Viris Illustribus" de Isidoro de Sevilla: Estudio y Edición Crítica.* 1964. Salamanca: Consejo Superior de Investigaciones Científicas.
Jerome, *De viris illustribus:* Ernest Cushing Richardson. trans. 1892. Nicene and Post-Nicene Fathers, Second Series, Vol. 3. Buffalo, NY: Christian Literature Publishing Co.
La Colección Canónica Hispana IV: Concilios Galos Concilios Hispanos: Primera Parte, Gonzalo Martínez Diez and Felix Rodríguez. eds. 1984. Monumenta Hispaniae Sacra, Serie Canónica IV. Madrid: Consejo Superior de Investigaciones Científicas.
Latinius Pacatus Drepanius, *Panegyric of Theodosius:* Roger A. B. Mynors ed. [1964] 1990. In *XII Panegyrici Latini.* Oxford Classical Texts. Oxford: Oxford University Press.
Paulinus Mediolanensis, *Vita sancti Ambrosii:* Michele Pellegrino. ed. 1961. *Vita di S. Ambrogio: Introduzione, testo critico e note a cura di Michele Pellegrino.* Verba seniorum N.S. 1. Milan: Editrice Studium.
Paulinus Nolanus, *Carmina:* Wilhelm von Hartel. ed. 1894. *Corpus Scriptorum Ecclesiasticorum Latinorum (CSEL).* 30. Vienna: F. Tempsky.
Priscillian: Georg Schepps. ed. 1889. *Priscilliani quae supersunt. Corpus Scriptorum Ecclesiasticorum Latinorum (CSEL).* 18. Vienna: F. Tempsky; Marco Conti. trans. 2010. *Priscillian of Avila: The Complete Works.* Oxford Early Christian Texts. Oxford: Oxford University Press.
Prosper Tiro, *Epitoma Chronicorum:* Theodor Mommsen. ed. 1892. *Monumenta Germaniae Histórica, Scriptores (MGH SS AA). IX, Chronica minora saec. IV. V. VI. VII.* Berlin: Weidmann.
Q. Aurelius Symmachus: Jean-Pierre Callu. ed. trans. 1982. *Symmaque Correspondance: Tome II: Livres III–IV.* Collection des Universites de France Serie Latine 260. Paris : Les Belles Lettres; Alexandra Forst. trans. 2020. *Q. Aurelius Symmachus. Amtliche Schreiben.* Berlin/Boston: De Gruyter.
Sulpicius Severus, *Dialogi; Chronicorum Libri duo:* Karl Halm. ed. 1866. Sulpicius Severus, *Opera. Corpus Scriptorum Ecclesiasticorum Latinorum (CSEL).* 1. Vienna: Carl Gerold's Sohn.
Sulpicius Severus, *Vita sancti Martini:* Gerlinde Huber-Rebenich. trans. 2010. *Das Leben des heiligen Martin. Lateinisch/Deutsch.* Stuttgart: Philip Reclam jun.

Secondary Sources

Birley, Anthony Richard. 1983. "Magnus Maximus and the Persecution of Heresy." *Bulletin of the John Rylands Library* 66/1:13–43.

Bleckmann, Bruno. 2002. "*Arelate metropolis*: Überlegungen zur Datierung des Konzils von Turin und zur Geschichte Galliens im 5. Jahrhundert" *RQA* 98: 162–173.

Burrus, Virginia. 1995. *The Making of a Heretic: Gender, Authority, and the Priscillianist Controversy*. Berkeley: University of California Press.

Chadwick, Henry. 1976. *Priscillian of Avila: The Occult and the Charismatic in the Early Church*. Oxford: Clarendon Press.

Escribano Paño, María Victoria. 2005. "Heresy and Orthodoxy in fourth-century Hispania." In *Hispania in Late Antiquity: Current Perspectives*. The Medieval and Early Modern Iberian World 24, edited by Kim Bowes and Michael Kulikowski, 121–149. Leiden: Brill.

Escribano Paño, María Victoria. 2019. "Maximus' Letters in the Collectio Avellana: A Comparative Study." In *The Collectio Avellana and Its Revivals*, edited by Rita Lizzi Testa and Giulia Marconi, 50–85. Newcastle upon Tyne: Cambridge Scholars Publishing.

Escribano Paño, María Victoria. 2021a. "El priscillianismo hoy: balance, perspectivas y aportaciones sobre la injerencia imperial en los conflictos eclesiásticos." *Gerión. Revista de Historia Antigua* 39/2:469–484.

Escribano Paño, María Victoria. 2021b. "La intervención de Magnus Maximus (383–388) en el conflicto Priscilianista." *Hispania Sacra* LXXIII:67–76.

Escribano Paño, María Victoria. 2021c. "The Letter from Magnus Maximus to Valentinian II (CA 39): Two Imperial Images in Conflict." In *Emperors and Emperorship in Late Antiquity. Images and Narratives*. Impact of Empire 40, edited by María Pilar García Ruiz and Alberto J. Quiroga Puertas, 177–198. Leiden: Brill.

Fournier, Éric. 2006. "Exiled bishops in the Christian Empire: Victims of Imperial Violence?" In *Violence in Late Antiquity: Perceptions and Practices*, edited by Harold A. Drake, 157–166. Aldershot: Ashgate.

Girardet, Klaus Martin. 2009. "Trier 385. Der Prozeß gegen die Priszillianer." In *Kaisertum, Religionspolitik und das Recht von Staat und Kirche in der Spätantike*. Antiquitas 56, edited by Klaus Martin Girardet, 419–454. Bonn: Habelt.

Girardet, Klaus Martin. 2018/2019. "Das Schicksal Priszillians und seiner Anhänger 380 in Saragossa, 384 in Bordeaux und 385 in Trier." *Annuarium Historiae Conciliorum* 49:30–57.

Jorge, Ana Maria C.M. 2006. "The Lusitanian Episcopate in the 4th Century: Priscilian of Ávila and the Tensions Between Bishops." *e-Journal of Portuguese History* 4/2:1–15.

Kahlos, Maijastina. 2015. *Artis heu Magicis*: "The Label of Magic in fourth-century Conflicts and Disputes." In *Pagans and Christians in Late Antique Rome: Conflict, Competition and Coexistence in the Fourth Century*, edited by Michele Renee Salzman, Marianne Sághy and Rita Lizzi Testa. Cambridge: Cambridge University Press.

Markauskas, Melissa. 2015. *From Privilege to Proscription: The Transformation of Episcopal Conflict across the Long Fourth Century*. PhD Dissertation, University of Manchester.

Mathisen, Ralph Whitney. 1989. *Ecclesiastical Factionalism and Religious Controversy in Fifth-Century Gaul*. Washington, DC: The Catholic University of America Press.

Mathisen, Ralph Whitney. 2013. "The Council of Turin (398/399) and the Reorganization of Gaul ca. 395/406." *Journal of Late Antiquity* 6/2:264–307.

Matthews, John. 1975. *Western Aristocracies and Imperial Court AD 364–425*. Oxford: Oxford University Press.

Natal, David, and Jamie Wood. 2016. "Playing with fire: conflicting bishops in late Roman Spain and Gaul." In *Making Early Medieval Societies: Conflict and Belonging in the Latin West, 300–1200*, edited by Kate Cooper and Conrad Leyser, 33–57. Cambridge: Cambridge University Press.

Panzram, Sabine. 2015. "'Hilferufe' aus Hispaniens Städten – Zur Ausbildung einer Metropolitanordnung auf der Iberischen Halbinsel (4.–6. Jahrhundert)." *Historische Zeitschrift* 301:626–661.

Van Dam, Raymond. 1992. *Leadership & Community in Late Antique Gaul.* Berkeley: University of California Press.

Van Waarden, Joop. *Priscillian of Avila's Liber ad Damasum, and the Inability to Handle a Conflict.* In *Violence in Ancient Christianity: Victims and Perpetrators*, ed. Albert C. Geljon and Rimer Roukema. Vigiliae Christianae Supplements 125. 132–150. Leiden: Brill, 2014.

Vilella, Josep. 1998. "PCBE: Hispania." *Medieval Prosopography 19:*135–176.

Vollmann, Benedikt. 1974. "Priscillianus." RE Suppl. 14: 485–559.

Weckwerth, Andreas. 2004. *Das erste Konzil von Toledo: Ein philologischer und historischer Kommentar zur Constitutio Concilii.* JbAC Ergänzungsband Kleine Reihe 1. Münster: Aschendorff Verlag.

Weckwerth, Andreas. 2010. *Ablauf, Organisation und Selbstverständnis westlicher antiker Synoden im Spiegel ihrer Akten.* JbAC Ergänzungsband Kleine Reihe 5. Münster: Aschendorff Verlag.

Margarita Vallejo Girvés
Bishop Licinianus of Carthago Spartaria, The Monastery of Asán and the Struggle between Visigoths and Byzantines

Abstract: There are few bishops of Byzantine Hispania whose names we know; in addition, there is the curious circumstance that their episcopal governments are concentrated in the last decade of the 6th century, a period in which coincide the Byzantine Emperor Maurice and the Visigoth king Reccared. Due to the time allotted for this intervention, we will focus on the study of one of these bishops, Licinianus of *Carthago Spartaria:* a recently edited document from the monastery of San Victorián (San Martín de Asán) can contribute new lines of study both about the family origin of this bishop as well as about his political position before the conversion of Reccared to Catholicism and the Byzantine commitment to preserve these peninsular territories.

We can confidently say that evidence concerning the bishops of Byzantine Hispania, that part of the Iberian Peninsula dominated by the Empire between 552 and 625,[1] indicates that some were threatened by Byzantine authorities. They suffered physically from these threats, through being overthrown, exiled or, according to some sources, poisoned.[2]

The prosopography of Byzantine Hispania is meager: two are well-known governors, Comenciolus and Caesarius,[3] and five are familiar bishops who occupied ecclesiastical sees dominated by Byzantines in the ancient *Diocesis Hispaniarum*. Severus and Ianuarius were both bishops of *Malaca* (Málaga); Stephanus, of an unknown see, was perhaps from the Baetic city of *Assidona* (Medina Sidonia); Licinianus of *Carthago Spartaria* (Cartagena) and Vincentinus, from the island of *Ebussus* (Ibiza), are well-known. Significantly, all of them occupied their respective bishoprics in the last two decades of the sixth century, a period of interest in the history

---

[1] On Byzantine Hispania, both from historiographical and archaeological point of view, see, among others, Ripoll 1996, 251–267; Díaz 2004, 27–60; Bernal-Casasola 2008, 363–383; Vizcaíno Sánchez 2009; Wood 2010, 292–319; Vallejo Girvés 2012; Fossella 2013, 30–38.
[2] Vilella Masana 1991, 175–176; González Fernández 1997, 287–298; Vallejo Girvés 2012, 297–304 and 311; Salvador Ventura 2013, 245–261; Wood 2020, 353–372; Vallejo Girvés 2020, 451–459; Ferreiro 2020, 173–177.
[3] *PLRE* IIIA, 321–325, Comentiolus 1; 258–259, Caesarius 2, respectively.

of this Mediterranean territory under Byzantine control since 552. This was a period when the reign of Maurice's empire and the administrative reorganisation of the western territories took place. Several significant events occurred in the Visigothic kingdom: Hermenegild's rebellion against Leovigild and his political, military and doctrinal reaction, and Reccared's ascension to the Visigothic throne and the abandonment of the Arian faith to embrace the Nicene-Chalcedonian faith. These were also the years in which the Byzantines pejoratively described the Visigoths as '*hostes* barbari',[4] where Visigoths spoke of the *romana insolentia* to refer to Byzantine troops in peninsular territory,[5] and when King Reccared attempted to acquire a copy of the treaty between Athanagild and Justinian to legally secure his conquests of territories dominated by the Byzantines on the Iberian Peninsula.[6]

As there were approximately 20 to 25 bishops during the existence of Byzantine Hispania we should add several *anonimi* to the list of bishops mentioned. Eclesiastical sees that were undeniably in Byzantine hands, the ancient Roman province of *Carthaginiensis*, the metropolitan area represented by the see of *Carthago Spartaria*, and the bishoprics of *Illici* (known today as Elche), *Dianium* (known today as Denia) and *Urci* (possibly Pechina) are under consideration.[7] Also in the ancient Roman province of *Baetica* were the aforementioned bishoprics of Malaga and *Assidona*, and, in the Balearic Islands, certainly Ibiza and, perhaps, those of Mallorca and Menorca.[8] Considering the seventy-five years of Byzantine

---

[4] CIL II 3420: *Quisquis ardua turrium miraris culmina / vestibulumq(ue) urbis duplici porta firmatum / dextra levaq(ue) binos porticos arcos / quibus superum ponitur camera curia convexaq(ue) / Comenciolus sic haec iussit patricius / missus a Mauricio Aug(usto) contra hostes barbaros / magnus virtute magister mil(itum) Spaniae / sic semper Hispania tali rectore laetetur / dum poli rotantur dumq(ue) sol circuit orbem / ann(o) VIII Aug(usti) ind(ictione) VIII.*

[5] Isid. hist. 54 (long): *Saepe etiam et lacertos contra Romanas insolentias.*

[6] Greg. M. epist. IX, 229, *ad Reccaredum regem Wisigothorum*. Cf. Vallejo Girvés 2020, 431–432; Ferreiro 2020, 170–172.

[7] Between the years 552/555 and 570, the city and territory of *Basti* (Baza), belonging to the *Carthaginiensis*, were under Byzantine control. We know that there was a bishopric in that city in 589, and because its existence can be dated back decades, it seems certain that its bishop or bishops, name also unknown, would for practically two decades have increased the Byzantine *nomina* of Hispania to which we are referring. In 570 that territory was conquered by King Leovigild and became part of the peninsular territories controlled by him (Ioh. Bicl. chron. 12: *Leouigildus rex loca Bastanie et Malacitane urbis repulsis militibus uastat et uictor solio reddit*). See Velázquez 2000, 588–599; Vallejo Girvés 2001, 13–35.

[8] During the period of Vandal domination of the Balearic Islands, the bishoprics of Mallorca, Menorca and Ibiza depended on the Sardinian metropolitan area of *Caralis*. We believe that the bishopric of Ibiza depended on *Carthago Spartaria* at the end of the sixth century, which is why we consider, as we have stated on other occasions, that the Byzantines, when recovering a part of

rule over Hispanic territories and more than two hundred and fifty years of Byzantine rule over the Balearic Islands, it is understandable that the number of Hispano-Byzantine bishops increased exponentially: at least one predecessor of Licinianus of Cartagena and another of Severus of Malaga, two predecessors of Vincentius de Ibiza, and, in addition, several *anonimi* occupying the ecclesiastical sees of *Illici, Dianium* and *Urci.* In addition, there were possibly two *anonimi* ancestors of Stephanus of *Assidona* and his successor and another of Ianuarius of Malaga. At least one successor to Licinianus from Cartagena and several to Vincentius from Ibiza once the Balearic Islands ceased to be Byzantine territory at the end of the eighth or beginning of the ninth century.[9]

Literary or epigraphic sources only transmitted the names of Byzantine bishops who were in charge of the ecclesiastical administration in the last two decades of the sixth century, and not much documentation exists on the ecclesiastical sees of the Iberian Peninsula under Visigothic control prior to the last two decades of the sixth century. This might explain, in part, the concentration of the names of Byzantine prelates during the period, coinciding with more nominal knowledge of Hispanic bishops in general.[10] In the last two decades of the sixth century, Byzantine bishops known by their name and reference to the two main cities of Byzantine Hispania: *Malaca* and *Carthago Spartaria* are evident.[11]

This situation is related to the destabilisation of Visigoths and Byzantines caused by Hermenegild's rebellion.[12] Significantly, two of the aforementioned bishops, Severus of Malaga and Licinianus of Cartagena, have been given their own voice through their writings and from what Isidore of Seville has told us of them.[13] The other three, Vincentius from Ibiza, Ianuarius from Malaga and Stephanus from *Assidona* are known through Licinianus from Cartagena in the case of Vincentius from Ibiza,[14] Gregory the Great in the cases of the Baetic bishops of Ma-

---

the territories of the Roman *Diocese Hispaniarum*, administratively linked the Balearic domains to their Hispanic constituency. See Vallejo Girvés 2005, 15–43; 2012, 302–303.

9 Amengual i Batle 2005, 87–113; Roselló 2006, 307–324; Nadal Cañellas 2006, 325–340; Signes 2005, 45–100; 2007, 597–604.

10 The last council held in Visigothic territory before the III Council of Toledo in 589, was from Valencia, which dates back to c. 549, that is, a few years before the entry of the Byzantine troops into the Iberian Peninsula to "help" Athanagild, claimant to the Visigoth throne. See Vilella Masana 2004, 1–47; Díaz 2014, 1095–1158.

11 Vallejo Girvés 2012, 165–172. 243–249; Vizcaíno Sánchez 2019, 155–164.

12 Castellanos García 2007, 109–140; García Moreno 2008, 95–168.

13 Isid. vir. ill. XXIX (*Licinianus*); Isid. vir. ill. XXX (*Severus*); in relation with Severus, see Zwierlein 1994, and Vallejo Girvés 2012, 246–249.

14 Licinian. *Epistula ad Vincentium* 1.

laga and *Assidona*.¹⁵ Three were under threat: Ianuarius, Stephanus and Licinianus. We will focus on the bishop of *Carthago Spartaria*, since a recently discovered document, originating from the Pyrenean monastery of Asán, has given us a new perspective on complex relationships between this bishop and the Byzantine and Visigothic authorities.

The two phrases *"Si otium nostrum non perturbaret temporis cualitas"* and *"laboro nostro in arcto tempore prouidentes"*[16] belong to an epistle addressed to a deacon named Epiphanius, written jointly between Licinianus and Severus, who would occupy the episcopal see of Cartagena and Malaga, respectively, from the early eighties of the sixth century.[17] Although, thanks to Isidore of Seville, we known that Severus was *"collega et socius Liciniani episcopi"*,[18] we unfortunately do not know whether they were bishops at the time the letter was written. It is clear that they considered it to be a time of difficulties, although they did not specify what kinds of difficulties existed.[19] Such statements may not be merely rhetorically if we look at another epistle written by Licinianus of Cartagena, in which he also mentions that he was living in complicated times.

Licinianus wrote a letter in reply to Bishop Vincentius of Ibiza. Although we cannot specify the time the letter was written, we are certain that Licinianus was already bishop of *Carthago Spartaria* and superior in rank to the Bishop Vincentius.[20] In this letter, regarding the credulity of Vincentius concerning a "letter fallen from heaven" or a "Sunday letter",[21] we find another direct allusion to difficulties not specifically alluded to.

The author indicates that he decided to reply to the letter he received from Vincentius of Ibiza *"inter uarias tribulationum angustias"*.[22] They could relate, of course, to problems related to activities as pastor of his diocese, as contained in the letter he sent to Gregory the Great regarding the prerequisites to be ordained a priest.[23] Considering the period of the bishopric of Licinianus,[24] as well as what

---

15 Greg. M. epist. XIII, 46–47 (*Epistulae II Iohanni defensori*).
16 Licin. Carth. and Sever. Malac., *Epistula ad Epiphanium* 2 and 22, respectively.
17 In relation to these dates cf. *infra*.
18 Isid. vir. ill. XXX.
19 See González Fernández 1995, 279–281.
20 See *supra* n. 8.
21 The two hypotheses emerge when studying the probable content of the epistle that Vincentius of Ibiza sent to Licinianus, which has not been preserved. For the proposals and analysis of the preserved epistle, the lost one and the letter that caused the credulity of the Ebusitan bishop, see Vallejo Girvés 2020, 389–391.
22 Licinian. *Epistula ad Vincentium* 1.
23 Licinian. *Epistula ad Gregorium Papam* 5. Cf. González Fernández 1995, 276–277; Alberto Cánovas 2008, 35–72.

was happening on the Peninsula during the period– the military confrontation between Visigoths and Byzantines –it seems that Licinianus refers to the clear political context of King Reccared's conversion to Catholicism, and his conviction that one of his missions as monarch of the Visigoths was the union of all the Hispanic territories under his rule, implying conquest of the territories dominated by the Byzantines in Hispania, as well as military and political reactions to Visigoth manoeuvres.[25] Reccared could achieve this through war, as Isidore of Seville wrote, through diplomacy, which we read in a letter from Gregory the Great,[26] but also through a desire to convince the Byzantine ecclesiastical authorities to work in favour of Visigoth interests, a possibility from the document we alluded to earlier. We propose that Reccared's intention was to co-opt Licinianus for his cause, in order for the bishop to work in favour of Visigoth unionist interests from within the Byzantine territory of Hispania, from its main city and ecclesiastical see.

A document recently edited by José Carlos Martín-Iglesias and Guillermo Tomás-Faci, although preserved in a medieval copy originally from the Pyrenean monastery of San Victorián (San Martín) in Asán, is a *diploma* from King Reccared ordering the properties that had been donated to the monastery by a bishop named Bagauda and another named Licinianus be returned to the same monastery:

> <D>ominis sanctis ac beatissimis est in Christi honore gloriosis Petro et Paulo apostolis, atque Stephano, Vicentio et Eulalie martyribus, necnon et sancto Martino episcopo et confessori in monasterio Asani constituto Recaredus Rex.
>
> Tunc glorie nostre credimus inuenire apud Deum ueniam peccatorum, dum ecclesiis Dei aliquid de fisco nostro offerimus. Et ideo sanctitati uestre de nostra donamus largitate locella, que condam Bagauda episcopus cellule uestre per suam concessit donacionem et fisco nostro fuerat apllicitum. Similiter et quod Licinianus episcopus in territorio Ylerdensi, Barbutano, Terrantonensi et Boletano tenuisse uisus est, id est, prestante fisco nostro, solidos nouem, cum mancipiis, terris, uineis et stiuola de Bergot <et> Bego cum omni iure suo, sicuti a memoratis episcopis noscitur fuisse possessum, pro luminaribus uel stipendis pauperum uestre beatitudini presente auctoriatis nostre uigore, glorae uestre fusa prece, concedimus atque donamus, quatenus pro hac re in futuro seculo nostre serenitati merces adcrescat copiosa et beatitudo uestra temporum perpetuitate ex nostro munere possidere ualeatis.
>
> Data sub die idus decembris anno primo regni nostri Toleto.[27]

---

24 Isidore of Seville commented that *claruit temporibus Mauricii Augusti* (Isid. vir. ill. XXIX). From this, we understand that his episcopate did not begin before 582, the year Maurice was proclaimed emperor.
25 Navarro Cordero 2000, 97–118; Castellanos García 2007, 295–306; Vallejo Girvés 2012, 264–288.
26 Isid. hist. 54 (long); Greg. M. epist. IX, 229, *ad Reccaredum regem Wisigothorum*.
27 Tomás-Faci and Martín-Iglesias, 2017, 261–286.

In this document, dated in Toledo in the year 586, the king alluded to the fact that the two bishops had given the proprieties to the monastery of Asán at a time not indicated, and that due to unspecified circumstances these proprieties ended up being part of the Visigothic royal treasury. Information provided by John of Biclaro and Isidore of Seville regarding successive decisions of Leovigild and Reccared on ecclesiastical properties, led the editors to conclude that these unspecified circumstances had been associated with Leovigild's policy of confiscation during the period of maximum Arian political propaganda, i.e., during the Hermenegild rebellion.[28] Reccared decided that they would once again be owned and administered by the aforementioned monastery.[29] Likewise, the decision by Reccared to return properties donated by Bagauda and Licinianus to their rightful owner, the monastery of Asán would obey, according to all indications, his approach to the Nicene-Chalcedonian Church, whose faith he would soon embrace. There were only three years left before the celebration of the Third Council of Toledo, where the conversion of the Visigoth people was to be made official, but the king had already taken significant steps to demonstrate that this was his intention and that he did not intend to harm the Catholic hierarchy or alienate its properties.[30]

It is important to identify the donor bishops as part of the analysis of Licinianus of Cartagena. We have no record of the existence of a bishop named Bagauda during the period between the founding of the Asán monastery, which occurred during the reign of King Gesaleic,[31] and the year 586. The only Hispanic bishop of that name that we know is the holder of the see of *Egabrum*, who attended the Eighth Council of Toledo in 653, and who, according to a preserved inscription, consecrated in his diocese a basilica dedicated to Saint Mary in the year 660.[32] This places it outside the chronological range of the donation of property to Asán by the bishop called Bacauda mentioned in the *diploma* by Reccared. Therefore, we cannot rely on the name of this bishop to identify the other donor bishop, Licinianus, and need to look for other indications in the sources.

The medieval copyists believed that the Licinianus appearing in Reccared's *diploma* was a bishop of Ilerda, without specifying the period in which he would ex-

---

28 Isid. hist. 50 (long): [Leovigildus] [...] *ecclesiarum reditus et priuilegia tulit*. See Valverde Castro 124–125; Vallejo Girvés 2003b, 35–48; Castellanos García 2007, 211–212; García Moreno 2008, 125–134; Mülke 2016, 99–128; Barroso Cabrera 2020, 306–308.
29 Ioh. Bicl. chron. 86: *Reccaredus rex aliena a precessoribus direpta et fisco sociata placabiliter restituit*; Isid. hist. 55 (long): [Reccaredus] [...] *adeo liberaris, ut opes priuatorum et ecclesiarum praedia, quae paterna labes fisco adsociauerat, iuri proprio restauraret*; see Díaz 2012, 100.
30 Tomás-Faci and Martín-Iglesias 2017, 267–268.
31 Tomás-Faci and Martín-Iglesias 2017, 262.
32 *ICERV* 308. See García Moreno 1974, 195–106 (nº 209); Salvador Ventura 1998, 45–46 (nº 49).

ercise his episcopate. As the editors of the document state, this stems from the location of the land donated by Licinianus in the Ilerdensis area. This is not a sufficient argument, indicated as such by the editors, who, do not suggest a location or chronology for this Licinianus.[33] However, we know of the existence of a bishop named Licinianus, who was a contemporary of Reccared: the bishop of *Carthago Spartaria*, the main city of the Byzantines in Hispania, to which we have been alluding.

The year 586 coincides with a time in which Licinianus of Cartagena was already bishop of this city: a time when Leander of Seville returned to Hispania from Constantinople, via *Carthago Spartaria*, at which point the two bishops met in the city, albeit briefly.[34] We are tempted to suggest that the Licinianus in Reccared's *diploma* and the Licinianus, bishop of *Carthago Spartaria*, are the same person.

An argument against such a hypothesis could be the great distance between the episcopal see that Licinianus occupied and the location of the properties mentioned in the *diploma* in the areas of Ilerda and Osca. However, the fact that Licinianus of Cartagena or his family owned properties in the Pyrenean area does not necessarily implies they came directly from that area, or even that he had professed in the Asán monastery.

Licinianus of Cartagena has been linked to another peninsular monastery, also located in Visigoth territory: the Servitanus monastery, associated with the diocese of Ercavica, in Visigothic Celtiberia. The hypothesis is based on the existence of an epistolary correspondence between Licinianus and Eutropius, abbot of that monastery.[35] Accordingly, Licinianus and Eutropius would have been monks at that monastery, and later would have been named bishops of Cartagena and Valencia, respectively.[36]

The Servitanus monastery was founded, according to Ildefonsus of Toledo, by the African abbot Donatus, in Ercavica diocese territories, possibly already during the first decade of the reign of Leovigild, therefore approximately in the year 568;[37]

---

33 Tomás-Faci and Martín-Iglesias 2017, 267 and n. 18; also Tomás-Faci 2017, 308 n. 27.
34 This meeting was recorded by Licinianus in the epistle to Gregory the Great (Licinian. Epistula ad Greg. Pap., 6). As we know, Leander of Seville had resided in Constantinople for several years to try to attract the emperor to the cause of Hermenegild, of which that bishop of Seville was a supporter. See Vallejo Girvés 2012, 249–256 and 267; Ubric Rabaneda 2020, 110–111.
35 Isid. vir. ill. XXIX: *Licinianus, Carthaginis Spartariae episcopus, in Scripturis doctus, cuius quidem nonnullas epístolas legimus: de sacramento denique baptismatis unam et ad Eutropium abbatem, qui postea Valentiae episcopus, plurimas*. See García Moreno 1974, 147 (nº 366).
36 Madoz, 1948, 15–16; Barroso Cabrera and Morín de Pablos 1994, 287–306; cf. González Fernández 1995, 275–276.
37 Ildefonsus of Toledo, De Viris illustribus 3. Ioh. Bicl. chron. 18, speaks of Abbot Donatus' fame as a saintly thaumaturge in the context of events dating from approximately 570–571. Regarding the

almost fifteen years after Byzantine troops had taken possession of some areas of the Iberian Peninsula. If Licinianus had been a monk of a Visigothic monastery – the Servitanus monastery – it would seem likely that a monk from Visigothic lands would have been appointed bishop of the main Byzantine ecclesiastical see, *Carthago Spartaria*, a surprising decision at a time when the animosity between Visigoths and Byzantines could not be hidden.[38]

Isidore of Seville affirms, in *De Viris Illustribus*, that, although Licinianus's literary and epistolary work was abundant, he was not able to obtain them.[39] That Licinianus was able to correspond with other Hispanic abbots or bishops, could suggest similar relations with a monastery of which an abbot, who could be the recipient of his correspondence, was the head.

The relations between Visigoths and Byzantines were not cordial at any time between Athanagild's arrival to the throne and 586, the year that serves as our chronological milestone. There were, of course, truces, such as the *statu quo* pact Athanagild and Justinian signed, which must have occurred in the early years of the sixties of the sixth century.[40] Moreover, the Byzantines refrained from helping Hermenegild in the last moments of his rebellion, since Leovigild paid 30,000 *solidi* to Emperor Maurice for his neutrality.[41] There does not appear to have been a time, however, in those decades when relations were cordial enough for the Byzantine authorities to allow a monk from a significant Visigothic monastery to be appointed bishop of their main city in Hispania.[42]

Therefore, one would have to conclude that Licinianus or his family were already based in the area of the *Carthaginiensis* conquered by the Byzantines. This would not have prevented him from having an epistolary relationship with Eutropius when he was abbot of Servitanus, because we know that communications between political areas of the Peninsula were fluid;[43] nor prevented him or his family from owning land in areas of Hispania, such as the Pyrenean area. A close example

---

Servitanus monastery and its location in the diocese of Ercávica, see Barroso Cabrera and Morín de Pablos 2003, 9–25; Barroso Cabrera, Carrobles Santos, Diarte Blasco, Morín de Pablos 2014, 257–294.
38 Vallejo Girvés 2012, 235 *passim*.
39 Isid. vir. ill. XXIX: *Licinianus Carthaginis Spartariae episcopus, in Scripturis doctus, cuius quidem nonnullas epistolas legimus [...] Reliqua vero industriae et laboris eius ad nostrum notitiam minime venerunt.*
40 Vallejo Girvés 1996, 208–218; 2012, 158–163.
41 Greg. Tur. Franc. V, 38; Vallejo Girvés 2012, 252–256.
42 Cf. *supra*.
43 See García Moreno 2008, 163, on the nature of the epistolary relationship between Eutropius and Licinianus; this autor considers that it was in conection with Eutropius' rejection of the pro-Arian politics of Leovigild in 580s.

is that of the family of Bishop Leander of Seville, who, originally from the *Carthaginiensis* province, had properties in this province but also in that of Baetica, where they settled after leaving Byzantine Hispania.[44] Our hypothesis thus is to consider Licinianus to be a member of a Carthaginian aristocratic family, with properties in different parts of the Iberian Peninsula, but who, contrary to the family of Bishop Leander of Seville, did not resist Byzantine control of his lands. For the moment and while the Visigothic Arian government lasted, the family of Licinianus – or he himself – did not consider being under Byzantine rule a disadvantage, especially when the immediate successors of Emperor Justinian, that is Justin II, Tiberius and Maurice, although subjected to heretical Monophysite pressures, were fundamentally Nicene-Calcedonians.[45]

However, something changed after the death of King Leovigild. Reccared's conversion to Catholicism, which, although occurring officially in 589, would have already been planned at his coronation in 586. It was also clear that Reccared wanted to end the Byzantine presence in Hispania. In fact, Isidore of Seville tells us that he acted against the *romana insolentia*, the arrogant Byzantine attitude that still held in Hispania and that, surely, would have taken advantage of Visigoth instability after the fall of Hermenegild and the almost immediate death of Leovigild to further secure their territorial positions.[46]

It is interesting to note the possible impact on Licinianus' loyalty towards the Byzantine authorities since his two main ecclesiastical references in Hispania – Eutropius, bishop of Valencia, and Leander, bishop of Seville – were now the pillars of Reccared in the process of converting his people to Catholicism.[47]

Considering Reccared's relationships with Leander and Eutropius and that of Licinianus with both, but especially with Eutropius, the Visigothic king could have believed having the support of the main bishop of Byzantine Hispania, Licinianus, for the Visigothic unionist cause would be useful. With his decision to return to the Asán monastery the confiscated goods that had initially been the property of bishops Bagauda and Licinianus, Reccared would not only demonstrate to the entire Catholic ecclesiastical hierarchy of his kingdom that his conversion was unques-

---

44 Isid. vir. ill. XXVIII: *Leander, genitus patre Seueriano, Carthaginiensis prouinciae Hispaniae, professione monachus et ex monacho Hispalensis ecclesiae prouinciae Baeticae constitutus episcopus*. Cf. Leander reg. XXXI, 858–884. See Wood 2016, 21–22 and Ubric Rabaneda 2020, 103–104, with reference to all proposals about the geographical origin of Leander's family.
45 Vallejo Girvés 2003a, 775–776.
46 Cf. Isid. hist. 54. See Castellanos García 2007, 301–306; Vallejo Girvés 2012, 269 *passim*.
47 Ioh. Bicl. chron. 91: *Summa tamen sinodalis negocii penes sanctum Leandrum Ispalensis ecclesie episcopum et beatissimum Eutropium monasterii Sirbitani abbatem fuit*. See Castellanos García 2007, 225–233; Ubric Rabaneda 2020, 113–115; cf. Mellado 1995, 329–336; Andrés 2010, 63–68.

tionable and that he wanted to repair the misdeeds of his father, but would also send Licinianus of Cartagena a message that he was a Catholic king, that he was not going to harm the Hispanic Church, and that, consequently, there was no reason to remain loyal to an emperor who resided in distant Constantinople, and who, moreover, was subject to constant pressure from the Monophysite heretics.[48]

We do not know whether such a gesture by Reccared was successful. But we can speak of the concern of the Byzantines with the political manoeuvers being carried out by the Visigoth king that resulted in his conversion, since in 589, Comenciolus, the Byzantine governor of Hispania ordered an inscription in which he stated that he had been sent by the emperor to fight the *hostes barbari*, who were none other than the Visigoths.[49] Although it was a message addressed to the Visigoths, it was also intended for inhabitants of *Carthago Spartaria*, faced with political-ecclesiastical advances from Reccared, who might have begun to show signs of unease with the Byzantine government.[50]

Although our hypothesis is viable, it is true that it did not have the immediate effect sought by Reccared, since Licinianus continued to be bishop of Byzantine Cartagena, and as such he addressed Pope Gregory the Great by letter, possibly in 595 or a little later, to discuss certain doubts he had about the reading of the *Regula Pastoral* written by the pontiff.[51] Surely, the epistolary and literary work of Licinianus had to reflect the feeling of its author as we have seen in passages from two of his three preserved epistles, but, as Isidore of Seville said, his work was barely preserved.[52] Given that *Carthago Spartaria* was destroyed by the Visigoths,[53] we can conclude that most of his work could have been too, depriving us of better understanding the life and government of Bishop Licinianus of Cartagena, as well as the relations he maintained with the Byzantine authorities and, probably, with the Visigoths, whether civil or ecclesiastical.

We do not know in what year Licinianus died. Isidore of Seville affirmed that he died while Maurice was emperor, which leads us to conclude that his death occurred between the years 595 and 602, when the emperor was executed at the hands of the usurper Phocas.[54] Isidore of Seville includes a meaningful commen-

---

48 Cf. Navarro Cordero, 2000, 97–118.
49 CIL II 3420. See Vallejo Girvés 1996–1997, 289–306; Prego de Lis 2000, 97–118; Vallejo Girvés 2012, 294–304.
50 Vallejo Girvés 2012, 270–274.
51 Licinian. *Epistula ad Gregorium Papam*.
52 Isid. vir. ill. XXIX, *supra* n. 39.
53 Isid. ety. XV, 1, 67: *Nunc autem a Gothis subversa atque in desolationem redacta est*. See Vizcaíno Sánchez 2019, 155–164. Cf. Vallejo Girvés 2012, 362–364.
54 Whitby 1988, 24–27 and 165–169.

tary on the short biography that was dedicated to Licinianus, that he *"occubuit Conatantinopoli, ueneno, ut ferunt, extinctus ab aemulis"*.⁵⁵ The expression *"ut ferunt"*, is uncertain whether he died from natural causes or not, although it is clear that Isidore wanted to cast a shadow of suspicion on the behaviour of the Byzantine authorities: from reference to his strange death and to those enemies who are not named, we understand the high opinion he had of Licinianus not only as an intellectual but as a political figure, of which, surely, his brother Leander of Seville was able to speak.⁵⁶

Licinianus' stay in Constantinople had to have been known by the papal apocrisiary, that is, the ambassador of Gregory the Great before the imperial court of that time, which, for chronological reasons, would be either Sabinianus or Anatolius.⁵⁷ A function of the apocrisiaries was to control the flow of clergy from the western patriarchate who arrived in Constantinople, with the intention of exposing their affairs to the imperial authorities.⁵⁸ However, Licinianus was able to reach the city without the need for papal intermediation. Moreover, Gregory the Great was reluctant to help Reccared obtain a copy of the treaty signed between Justinian and Athanagild, which took place close to Licinianus' visit to Constantinople.⁵⁹ Given that we know the high regard that he had for Gregory the Great, it does not seem possible that he would not hasve informed the pope of his intention to travel to Constantinople to present the emperor a matter that concerned him. For this reason, we believe that Licinianus might have been ordered by the Byzantine authorities to move to Constantinople, where he could be heard but warned that his relationship with Visigoth ecclesiastics close to King Reccared was not well regarded, since Emperor Maurice was not willing to have any Hispanic peninsular territory taken away from him. If we focus on Isidore's suspicions, we might conclude that the influence of Byzantine authorities over Licinianus was not powerful enough to change his mind. Thus, eliminating an individual whose attitude was a danger to Byzantine interests in the Iberian Peninsula was essential.⁶⁰ It would not be the first time such a manoeuvre was used in imperial practice: we know that Pope Agapitus – whose pontificate was extended in the 535–536 biennium, and who was opposed to supporting the opinion of Emperor Justinian on the controversial matter that would culminate in the condemnation of the

---

55 Isid. vir. ill. XXIX.
56 Wood, 2016, 35–36; Castellanos García 2020, 21; Ubric Rabaneda 2020, 125–126.
57 *PCBE* 2, 1966–1968, s.v. Sabinianus 3; *PCBE* 2, 1221–1225, s.v. Anatolius 3.
58 See Western 2015, 697–714. Cf. Iustinus. novell. VI, 3.
59 See *supra* n. 6, and Díaz 2008, 59–80.
60 García Moreno 2008, 133–134; Vallejo Girvés 2012, 301–304.

Three Chapters – became mysteriously ill during his stay in Constantinople and passed away several days later.[61]

This would not logically prevent the papal apocrisiary from being aware of the arrival of a Western bishop in Constantinople. Moreover, it is very possible that the work of recovering the body of Licinianus and burying it with dignity fell on the Western clergymen linked to the *officium* of the papal apocrisiary.[62]

Conclusion

In any case, we know for a fact that during the years of Reccared's conversion there was what we could call "the rebellion of the bishops of Byzantine Hispania"; not only because of Licinianus's trip to Constantinople and his suspicious death, but because of the illegal trials, overthrowings, exiles and confiscations to which two other prelates were subjected: Ianuarius, possibly the successor of Severus in the episcopal see of Malaga, and Stephanus, perhaps of the other great Byzantine see of Baetica, *Assidona*. Both bishops suffered at the instigation and personal decision of Comenciolus, a fact that we know from the epistles of Gregory the Great.[63] The same Comenciolus that Maurice had sent to *Carthago Spartaria* to fight the *hostes barbari* during the episcopate of Licinianus. It is clear that leading Hispano-Byzantine bishops showed signs of a desire to have more direct communications with the Visigoths; something that was not seen from Constantinople.

The only points we know for certain is that Licinianus died in Constantinople; that *Carthago Spartaria* continued to be controlled for more than twenty-five years by Byzantine hands; and that Ianuarius of Malaga and Stephanus were removed from their sees for at least eight years (from 595 to 603). The rebellion of the Byzantine bishops did take place, somehow. Contrary to what might be supposed, however, the coercive force of the Byzantine state in peninsular territories was greater than they would have expected.

---

61 Lib. pontif. 59. 6. See Neil 2015, 114.
62 Regarding the specific place, it is difficult to estimate, although it is known that near the seat of the apocrisiary, in the so-called οἶκος τῆς Πλακιδίας, there were two churches in the city associated with the Roman patriarch and the apocrisiary, the churches of Saint Sergius and Bacchus and the adjoining one dedicated to Saint Peter and Paul, which could have reserved areas for the burial of their monks and clergy (Janin 1964, 135–136; ²1969, 451).
63 Cf. *supra* n. 2.

Bibliography

Primary Sources

Gregory of Tours, *Historiae:* Bruno Krusch and Wilhelm Levison, eds. 1951. *Gregorii episcopi Turonensis libri Historiarum X. MGH SRM* I, 1. Hannover: Societas Aperendis Fontibus Rerum Germanicarum Medii Aevi.

Gregory the Great, *Epistulae:* Dag Norberg, ed. 1972. *S. Gregorii Magni Registrum epistularum.* I–II. CC SL 140–140 A. Turnhout: Brepols.

ICERV = José Vives, ed. ²1969. *Inscripciones cristianas de la España romana y visigoda.* Barcelona: Consejo Superior de Investigaciones Científicas.

Ildefonsus of Toledo, *De Viris Illustribus:* Carmen Codoñer Merino, ed. 2007. Valeriano Yarza Urquiola, Carmen Codoñer Merino, *Ildefonsi Toletani episcopi. De uirginitate sanctae Mariae, De cognition baptsimi. De itinere deserti. De uiris illustribus.* Turnhout 2007.

Isidore of Seville, *De Viris Illustribus:* Carmen Codoñer Merino, ed. 1964. *El 'De Viris Illustribus' de Isidoro de Sevilla. Estudio y edición crítica.* Salamanca: Ediciones Universidad de Salamanca.

Isidore of Seville, *Historia Gothorum:* Cristóbal Rodríguez Alonso, ed. 1975. *Las historias de los godos, vándalos y suevos de Isidoro de Sevilla.* León: Centro de Estudios e Investigación "San Isidoro".

Isidore of Seville, *Etymologiae:* Wallace M. Lindsay, ed. 1911. *Isidori Hispalensis episcopi Etymologiarum siue Originum libri XX. I–II.* Oxford: Oxford Clarendon Press.

John of Biclaro, *Chronica:* Carmen Cardelle de Hartmann, ed. 2001. *Victoris Tunnunensis Chronicon cum reliquiis ex Consularia Caesaraugustana et Iohannis Biclarensis Chronicon.* CC SL 173 A. Turnhout: Brepols.

Licinianus of Cartagena, *Epistulae:* José Madoz, ed. 1948. *Liciniano de Cartagena y sus cartas. Edición crítica y estudio histórico.* Madrid: Colegio Máximo de Oña.

Secondary Sources

Alberto Cánovas, José. 2008. "Liciniano y su época." *Scripta Fulgentina* 2:35–72.

Amengual i Batle, Josep. 2005. "Ubi Pars Graecorum: medio milenio de historia relegada de las Baleares y las Pitiusas." *Pyrenae* 36, 2:87–113.

Andrés Sanz, María Adelaida. 2010. "Leandro de Sevilla." In *La Hispania visigótica y mozárabe. Dos épocas en su literatura,* edited by Carmen Codoñer Merino and María Adelaida Andrés Sanz, 63–68. Salamanca: Ediciones Universidad de Salamanca.

Barroso Cabrera, Rafael. 2020. "Between Throne and Altar. Political Power and Episcopal Authority in the Beginning of the Visigothic Kingdom of Toledo." In *The Visigothic Kingdom. The Negotiation of Power in Post-Roman Iberia,* edited by Sabine Panzram and Paulo Pachá, 295–313. Amsterdam: Amsterdam University Press.

Barroso Cabrera, Rafael and Jorge Morín de Pablos. 1994. "La ciudad de Arcávica en época visigoda: fuentes literarias y testimonios arqueológicos." *Actas dos Trabalhos de Antropologia e Etnologia* XXXIV, 3–4:287–306.

Barroso Cabrera, Rafael and Jorge Morín de Pablos. 2003. "El Monasterio Servitano. Auge y caída de un cenobio visigodo." *Codex Aquilarensis* 19:9–25.

Barroso Cabrera, Rafael, Jesús Carrobles Santos, Pilar Diarte Blasco and Jorge Morín de Pablos. 2014. "La evolución del suburbio y territorio ercavicense desde la Tardía Antigüedad a la época visigoda." In *In concavis petrarum habitaverunt. El fenómeno rupestre en el Mediterráneo Medieval. De la investigación a la puesta en valor*, edited by Jorge López Quiroga and Artemio M. Martínez Tejera, 257–294. Oxford: BAR.

Bernal-Casasola, Darío. 2008. "Ciudades del 'Fretum Gaditanum' tardoantiguo: pesquerías y comercio transmediterráneo en época bizantina y visigoda." *Zona Arqueológica* 9:363–383.

Zwierlein, Otto. 1994. *Severi Episcopi (Malacitani [¿]) in Evangelia Libri XII das Trierer Fragmenter der Bücher VII–X*. Munich: Bayerische Akademie der Wissenschaften.

Castellanos García, Santiago. 2007. *Los godos y la cruz. Recaredo y la unidad de Spania*. Madrid: Alianza.

Castellanos García, Santiago. 2020. "Isidore of Seville: Historical Context." In *A Companion to Isidore of Seville*, edited by Andrew Fear and Jamie Wood, 21–41, Leiden/Boston: Brill.

Díaz, Pablo C. 2004. "En tierra de nadie: visigodos frente a bizantinos. Reflexiones sobre la frontera." In *Bizancio y la Península Ibérica. De la Antigüedad Tardía a la Edad Media*, edited by Pedro Bádenas and Inmaculada Pérez Martín, 27–60. Madrid: Consejo Superior de Investigaciones Científicas.

Díaz, Pablo C. 2008. "Gregorio Magno y el reino visigodo: un conflicto de poderes." In *Gregorio Magno, l'impero e i 'regna'*, edited by Claudio Azzara, 59–80. Firenze: SISMEL. Edizioni dell Galluzzo.

Díaz, Pablo C. 2012. "Confiscations in the Visigothic Reign of Toledo: A Political Instrument". In *Expropriations et confiscations dans les royaummes barbares. Une approche regionale*, edited by Pierfrancesco Porena and Yann Riviere, 93–112. Roma: École Française de Rome.

Díaz, Pablo C. 2014. "Concilios y obispos en la Península Ibérica (siglos VI-VIII)." In *Chiese locali chiese regionali nell'alto medioevo. Settimane di Studio* 61, 1095–1158. Spoleto: Centro italiano di studi sull'alto Medioevo.

Ferrerio, Alberto. 2020. *Epistolae Plenae. The Correspondence of the Bishops of Hispania with the Bishops of Rome (Third though Seventh Centuries)*. Leiden/Boston: Brill.

Fossella, Jason. 2013. "Waiting only for a Pretext. A new chronology for the Sixth-Century Byzantine Invasion of Spain." *Estudios Bizantinos* 1:30–38.

García Moreno, Luis A. 1974. *Prosopografía del Reino Visigodo de Toledo*. Salamanca: Ediciones Universidad de Salamanca.

García Moreno, Luis A. 2008. *Leovigildo. Unidad y diversidad de un reinado*. Madrid: Real Academia de la Historia.

González Fernández, Rafael. 1995. "Cultura e ideología del siglo VI en las cartas de Liciniano de Cartagena." In *Lengua e Historia. Homenaje al Profesor Dr. D. Antonio Yelo Templado al cumplir 65 años*. Antigüedad y Cristianismo 12, 269–374. Murcia: Servicio de Publicaciones de la Universidad de Murcia.

González Fernández, Rafael. 1997. "Las cartas de Gregorio Magno al defensor Juan. La aplicación del Derecho de Justiniano." In *La tradición en la Antigüedad Tardía*. Antigüedad y Cristianismo 14, 287–298. Murcia: Servicio de Publicaciones de la Universidad de Murcia.

Janin, Raymond. 1964. *Constantinople Byzantine. Développement urbain et répertoire topographique. Revised and expanded edition*. Paris : Institut Français d'Etudes Byzantines.

Janin, Raymond. ²1969. *La géographie ecclésiastique de l'Empire Byzantin. Première Partie. Le siège de Constantinople et le patriarcat oecuménique. T. III. Les églises et les monastères*. Paris : Institut Français d'Etudes Byzantines.

Nadal Cañellas, Juan. 2006. "Las bulas de plomo bizantinas del Castlllo de Santueri." *Bolletí de la Societat Arqueològica Lul.liana* 62:325–340.

Navarro Cordero, Catherine. 2000. "El Giro Recarediano y sus implicaciones políticas: el catolicismo como signo de identidad del Reino Visigodo de Toledo." *Ilu. Revista de Ciencias de las Religiones* 5:97–118.

Neil, Bronwen. 2015. "Death and the Bishop of Rome: From Hormisdas to Sabinian." *Scrinium. Revue de patrologie, d'hagiographie critique et d'histoire ecclésiastique* 11:109–121.

Mellado, Joaquín. 1995. "Nuevas dudas sobre las relaciones monarquía-episcopado en la época de Recaredo", *Actas I Congreso Nacional de latín medieval*, 329–336. León.

Mülke, Markus. 2016. "Guter König und doch Verfolger? Die Religionspolitik des Wesgotenkönigs Leovigild im Urteil der zeitgenössischen Historiker (Johannes Biclarensis und Isidor von Seville)." *Frühmittelalterliche Studien* 50:99–128.

Prego de Lis, Augusto. 2000. "La inscripción del Comenciolus del Museo Municipal de Arqueología de Cartagena." In *V Reunió d'Arqueologia Cristiana Hispánica* (Cartagena 1998), 97–118. Barcelona: Institut d'Estudis Catalans and Universitat de Barcelona.

Ripoll, Gisela. 1996. "Acerca de la supuesta frontera entre el *Regnum Visigothorum* y la Hispania bizantina." *Pyrenae* 27:251–267.

Rosselló, Guillem. 2006. "Nueva luz sobre los siglos oscuros de Baleares y Pitiusas." *Bolletí de la Societat Arqueològica Lul·liana* 62:307–324.

Salvador Ventura, Francisco. 1998. *Prosopografía de Hispania Meridional. III. Antigüedad Tardía (300–711)*. Granada: Universidad de Granada.

Salvador Ventura, Francisco. 2013. "The Bishops and the Byzantine Intervention in Hispania." In *The Role of the Bishops in Late Antiquity. Conflict and Compromise*, edited by Andrew Fear, José Fernández Ubiña and Mar Marcos, 245–261. Madrid: Bloomsbury.

Signes, Juan. 2005. "Bizancio y las Islas Baleares en los siglos VIII y IX." In *Mallorca y Bizancio*, edited by Rafael Durán Tapia, 45–100. Mallorca: Amigos del Castillo de San Carlos.

Signes, Juan. 2007. "Bis wann waren die Balearen byzantinisch". In *Byzantina Mediterranea. Festschrift für Johannes Koder zum 65. Geburtstag*, edited by Johannes Koder and Klaus Belke, 597–604. Wien: Böhlan.

Tomás-Faci, Guillermo. 2017. "The Transmission of Visigothic documents in the Pyrenean monastery of San Victorián de Asán (6th–12th. Centuries): Monastic Memory and Episcopal Disputes." *Antiquité Tardive* 25:303–314.

Tomás-Faci, Guillermo and José Carlos Martín-Iglesias. 2017. "Cuatro documentos inéditos del monasterio visigodo de San Martín de Asán (522–586)." *Mittellateinisches Jahrbuch* 52,2:261–286.

Ubric Rabaneda, Purificación. 2020. "Leander of Seville and his influence on Isidore of Seville." In *A Companion to Isidore of Seville*, edited by Andrew Fear and Jamie Wood, 101–132, Leiden/Boston: Brill.

Valverde Castro, María Rosario. 1999. "Leovigildo. Persecución religiosa y defensa de la unidad del reino." *Iberia. Revista de la Antigüedad* 2:123–132.

Vallejo Girvés, Margarita. 1996. "The Treaties between Justinian and Athanagild and the Legality of Byzantium's Peninsular Holdings." *Byzantion* 66,1:208–218.

Vallejo Girvés, Margarita. 1996–1997. "*Comenciolus, magister militum Spaniae, missus a Mauricio Augusto contra hostes barbaros*. The Byzantine Perspective of the Visigothic Conversion to Catholicism." *RomanoBarbarica* 14:289–306.

Vallejo Girvés, Margarita. 2001. "Las sedes eclesiásticas hispano-bizantinas en su incorporación al Reino Visigodo de Toledo." *Cassiodorus. Rivista di Studi sulla Tarda Antichità* 6–7:13–35.

Vallejo Girvés, Margarita, 2003a. "El Imperio Romano de Bizancio. Conflictos religiosos." In *Historia del Cristianismo. I. El mundo antiguo*, edited by Manuel Sotomayor and José Fernández Ubiña, 759–814, Madrid/Granada: Editorial Trotta and Universidad de Granada.

Vallejo Girvés, Margarita. 2003b. "Los exilios de católicos y arrianos bajo Leovigildo y Recaredo." *Hispania Sacra* 55:35–48.

Vallejo Girvés, Margarita. 2005. "Inserción de las Baleares en el orbe bizantino." In *Mallorca y Bizancio*, edited by Rafael Durán Tapia, 15–43. Mallorca: Amigos del Castillo de San Carlos.

Vallejo Girvés, Margarita. 2012. *Hispania y Bizancio. Una relación desconocida*. Madrid: Akal.

Vallejo Girvés, Margarita. 2020. "Comentario a las epístolas." In *La Hispania tardoantigua y visigoda en las fuentes epistolares. Antología y comentario*, edited by José Carlos Martín-Iglesias, Pablo C. Díaz and Margarita Vallejo Girvés. Madrid: Consejo Superior de Investigaciones Científicas.

Velázquez, Isabel. 2000. "Zonas y problemas eclesiásticos durante la época de la presencia bizantina en Hispania (una reflexion sobre los textos)." In *V Reunió d'Arqueologia Cristiana Hispánica (Cartagena 1998)*, 588–599. Barcelona: Institut d'Estudis Catalans and Universitat de Barcelona.

Vilella Masana, Josep. 1991. "Gregorio Magno e Hispania." In *Gregorio Magno e il suo tempore. Alle Origini dell'Europa. XIX Incontro di Studiosi dell'antichità cristiana in collaborazione con l'École Française de Rome*, 167–186. Roma: Institutum Patristicum Augustinianum.

Vilella Masana, Josep. 2004. "Los concilios eclesiásticos hispanos del período visigodo-arriano: análisis histórico-prosopográfico." *Medieval Prosopography* 25:1–47.

Vizcaíno Sánchez, Jaime. 2009. *La presencia bizantina en Hispania (siglos VI–VII), La documentación arqueológica*. Murcia. Servicio de Publicaciones de la Universidad de Murcia.

Vizcaíno Sánchez, Jaime. 2019. "Carthago Spartaria, una plaza fuerte bizantina." In *El tiempo de los visigodos en el territorio de Valencia*, edited by Esperança Huguet and Albert Ribera, 155–164. Valencia: Diputación de Valencia.

Western, Joseph. 2015. "The Papal Apocrisiarii in Constantinople during the pontificate of Gregory I. 590–604." *Journal of Ecclesiastical History* 66,4:697–714.

Whitby, Michael. 1988. *The Emperor Maurice and his Historian. Theophylact Simocatta on Persian and Balkan Warfare*. Oxford: Clarendon Press.

Wood, Jamie. 2010. "Defending Byzantine Spain: Frontiers and Diplomacy." *Early Medieval Europe* 18:292–319.

Wood, Jamie. 2016. "A family affair: Leander, Isidore and the legacy of Gregory the Great in Spain." In *Isidore of Seville and his reception in the early Middle Ages. Transmitting and Transforming Knowledge*, edited by Andrew Fear and Jamie Wood, 31–56. Amsterdam: Amsterdam University Press.

Wood, Jamie. 2020. "Conflicts over Episcopal Office in Southern Hispania. Comparative Perspective from Visigothic and Byzantine Territories". In *The Visigothic Kingdom. The Negotiation of Power in Post-Roman Iberia*, edited by Sabine Panzram and Paulo Pachá, 353–373. Amsterdam: Amsterdam University Press.

Pablo C. Díaz
Dumio-Braga. A Functional Duality, a Legal Anomaly

Abstract: The presence of monasteries that were simultaneously episcopal seats is an absolutely exceptional phenomenon in Late Antique Christianity outside the British Isles. In fact, when this reality occurs, it is associated with processes of 'colonisation' of Briton entities, as in the case of early settlements in northern Armorica or the exceptional case of the diocese of Britonia on the Spanish Cantabrian coast. Only one known case, that of the monastery-bishopric of Dumio, near Bracara, seems to escape this model. Founded around 550 by a Pannonian named Martin, the monastery was converted a few years later into an episcopal see. Martin became its titular and in this function exerted an enormous influence on the Suevic conversion to Catholicism. Ten years later, Martin was elected metropolitan bishop of Braga and simultaneously retained the see of Dumio. Both sees, sometimes with independent bishops, sometimes with a shared bishop, survived until the Muslim invasion. An institutionally anomalous history whose durability over time is exceptional and difficult to explain.

Any scholar devoted to the study of Christianity in the Late Antique and medieval periods would find it unnecessary to gloss the essential role that monasteries in marginal areas played as productive centres of cultural preservation and dissemination, instruments for conversion and, very often, essential cogs of political power. It is uncommon to find all these factors linked to a single monastery, and even more difficult to prove it in early stages of monastic development. At this stage monasteries were singular foundations, frequently located in areas of varying political jurisdiction, without the support from powerful orders that coordinated a large number of monasteries and could therefore assimilate the wills of a multitude of individuals. The 'pre-history' of this process encompasses certain monasteries whose relevance in the courtly environments of the first Germanic monarchies is unquestionable, be it in Anglo-Saxon, Italic or Franco-German environments. Iberian examples are less well explored, with emphasis usually placed on the role of the Toledan monastery of Agali and its relationship with the Visigothic Catholic court,[1] but with only occasional attention drawn to the monastery of

---
[1] Cf. Codoñer Merino 1972, 47–49. Díaz 1987, 165–166; Gonzálvez Ruíz 2007, 99–145. – This article was

https://doi.org/10.1515/9783110778649-017

Dumio. A possible explanation is that the province of *Gallaecia* and the Suevic kingdom that had settled there in the early decades of the fifth century have been relegated to oblivion due to their remote location.[2] Nonetheless, the influence of the monastery since the mid-sixth century in the context of the Suevic court, and in the religious history of the later Visigothic province until the early eighth century, is crucial.

The origin of the monastery is associated with the missionary task of Martin, an easterner who arrived in Braga around 550 and would gain essential, although equivocal, prominence in the conversion of the Suevic kingdom to Catholicism.[3] The reasons for his arrival, whether incited from Galia or even by the Byzantine court, or the product of a less probable individual missionary initiative, have been the subject of a variety of considerations.[4] What all sources seem to agree upon is that Martin was a monk and that his activity as a monastic founder is the first that can be attributed to him. Even though Isidore of Seville uses the plural when mentioning his activities,[5] the only monastery that we can directly associate him with is Dumio, whose construction is ascribed to him in the minutes of the Tenth Council of Toledo.[6] The monastery was established in the vicinity of Braga, on the site of a *villa* that dated to the Early Empire and which was probably still in use when the basilica attached to the monastery was built.[7] The elevation of a monastery in the vicinity of the city, royal headquarters of the Arrian kingdom and Catholic metropolis of the province, must have been endorsed by the king and the Catholic hierarchy,[8] relying on whoever provided the property, perhaps the monarch himself. This circumstance suggest that Martin arrived in Braga in the context of a political mission. If not himself part of a delegation, he would have

---

completed under the aegis of the Research Project PID2020–112506GB-C42 (Ministerio de Ciencia e Innovación).

2 Díaz 2011a.

3 Thompson 1980, 77–92; Silva 2008, 50–53.

4 Ferreiro 1980, 243–251; 1988, 226–228; Branco 1999. Considerations that would vary greatly if he had been attributed a Gallic rather than an eastern origin, as is done by López Pereira 2014.

5 Isid. vir. ill. 22: *monasteria condidit*; Isid. hist. 91 (short version): *multa monasteria condita*. Although in the long version he does not refer to monasteries but to the creation of numerous *instituta*.

6 *Concilium Toletanum X, Item aliud decretum: sancti Martini ecclesia Bracarensis episcopi, qui et Dumiense monasterium uisus est construxisse* (Martínez Díez and Rodríguez 1992, 544–545). Although it has also been suggested that the monastery could have existed before the arrival of Martin in Braga; see Díaz y Díaz 1995, 33.

7 Fontes 1991.

8 The founding of a monastery, whoever its promoter, was subject to the diocesan bishop's approval, in compliance with the rules of the *Concilium Calcedonensis* (cc. 4 and 8), also gathered at an earlier date in the Councils of Agde (a. 506) and Orleans (a. 511). See Díaz 2017, 465.

been at least a member of a negotiating group at a time when Byzantium had interests in the southern part of the Peninsula (in 522, troops under the command of Liberius had settled there on request of the pretender Athanagild)[9] and when the Suevi felt threatened by the advance of the Visigoths, who were determined to exert their rule over the entire Peninsula.[10]

The integration of Martin and the monastery into the sphere of the court and their involvement in the kingdom's ecclesiastical matters must have been immediate.[11] Nonetheless, Martin's primary undertaking is likely to have been monastic.

One of his poems, *In refectorio*, is dedicated to the consecration of the monastic building.[12] Among his works is the translation from Greek of a collection of oriental *Apothegmata*, added to which are translations he entrusted to a monk named Pascasio, who apologizes in the prologue for his lack of expertise and that the task was undertaken out of obedience to Martin, whom he addresses as *"Dumio uenerabili Martino presbytero et abbati"*,[13] suggesting that he was not yet a bishop.[14] According to the Breviary of Braga, Martin was consecrated bishop of Dumio on 5 April 556, holding the position for 23 years. The monastery's church acquiring the status of episcopal basilica two years later.[15] The consecration of the monastery as episcopal see and the appointment of its abbot as bishop is an exceptional event in the West. A parallel development in northern *Gallaecia* in those same years was in the see of Britonia, where a Celtic community had a bishopric that was also located in a monastery: *monasterium Maximi*.[16] The possibility that Dumio existed as an episcopal abbey as a result of Irish influence is questionable;[17] however, the co-

---

9 Vallejo Girvés 2012, 140–164.
10 Díaz 2011a, 138–153.
11 Ferreiro 1981; Castillo Maldonado 2017.
12 Hernández Lobato (2012–2013) notes that it is a rewriting of a poem by Sidonius Apollinaris with 'intertextual echoes' of Sedulius.
13 Barlow 1950, 294.
14 Sent. part. (Barlow 1950, 11–51). The codices confer its author the title of *Martinus episcopus Dumiensis*, which could suggest that the work was written after he had become a bishop; however, this could be merely an identifier, since such work would make more sense in the context of an earlier stage of his activity in *Gallaecia*. See Soares 1996, 62–64; Andrés 2010, 71–81.
15 *Actus beati Martini Dumiensis* 9 (Barlow 1950, 304). Gregory of Tours (Franc. V, 37) mentions 30 years of bishopric, although he is probably also counting Martin's stay in *Gallaecia*.
16 Paroch. Suev. XIII, 1: *Ad sedem Britonorum: ecclesias que sunt intro Britones una cum monasterio Maximi et Asturias*. López Alsina 2010, 106, believes that the see would have gone from being a personal diocese over Britton settlers in the area in the sixth century, to becoming a territorial diocese with jurisdiction over the coastal area of Asturias in the seventh century.
17 Livermore 1997 suggests its association with a military settlement. While Alberro 2003 believes that they would have settled there in the fifth century as a group of missionaries who had arrived by sea on a pilgrimage, the last station of an Atlantic Celtic secular flow.

existence of the Church of *Gallaecia* with the Celtic community suggests that the reality of a nonterritorial bishopric, linked to a monastery, would not be novel. It is reasonable to assume that Martin was appointed based on his role as negotiator in the process of converting the Suevic king.[18] According to Isidore, Martin would have already been bishop of the monastery of Dumio when Theudimer's conversion took place.[19] Since there was already a Catholic bishop in Braga, allotting him the see of Dumio could have been a mechanism to integrate Martin into the hierarchical structures of the Church of *Gallaecia*. However, what might have been intended initially as temporary would continue as a vested right.[20] If this followed a model it must have been eastern, as was the floorplan of the temple elevated there.[21] In any case, it is anomalous. In the East it would have been common to choose bishops among renowned hermits, even if they had been abbots at some point, but accepting the position meant giving up monastic life and devoting oneself to the diocesan community, not turning the monastery into a bishopric.[22] The search for ideal candidates to episcopacy among monks had spread early across the West.[23]

Either way, the decision to ordain Martin Catholic bishop should not be interpreted as against the canon, nor against the will of the bishops of *Gallaecia*. An

---

18 The general trend is to consider that, except for the Christian groups in the north of the peninsula of Armorica, bishop-abbots would not have been known outside the British Isles. See Oliger 1958, 20, who is completely unaware of the realities of Britonia and Dumio.

19 Isid. hist. 91 (long version): *Qui confestim Arrianae impietatis errare destructo Suevos catholicae fidei reddidit innitente Martina monasterii Dumiensis episcopo*. At some point he refers to him with the exceptional title of *Dumiensis monasterii sanctissimus pontifex* (vir. ill. 22), where such courtesy is clearly a synonym for *episcopus*, albeit it is usually reserved for metropolitans. See Sánchez Salor 1976, 20.

20 Díaz y Díaz 1995, 34, believes that this could be a continuity of more ancient Hispanic situations, but if such is the case, it is impossible to trace.

21 Cf. Fontes 1992, 234–235; 2006, 21–22, who draws attention to the building's large dimensions, which would be consistent with a royal foundation, while he considers that, although its model is clearly eastern, it was so widespread that it is impossible to accurately define its immediate influence.

22 Sterk 2004, 6. 205.

23 Norton 2007, 50. Such is the case with the aforementioned monastery of Agali, which would supply at least four prominent bishops of the see of Toledo in the seventh century: Eladius, Iustus, Eugenius (I) and Ildefonsus. Ftuctuosus' anonymous hagiographer writes down that, attracted by his holiness, *multas idóneas ac nobiles personas* went to follow his teachings, adding that several such disciples achieved episcopal dignity (*Vita Fructuosi* 8). The evolution of these monks who became bishops was characterized by an unquestionable change in their condition, especially regarding patrimonial capacity, which made it advisable for them to relinquish any right or power they may have previously held in the community, which would extend to the position of abbot. See Oliger 1958, 56–57, on the subject of epist. X, 1 of Gregory the Great.

annex to the minutes of the Council of Braga held in 572, which, as we shall see, would be presided over by Martin himself as metropolitan of Braga, gathers a collection of canons from the eastern churches, adapted by himself to correct errors and obscuring the translators' lack of skill and copyists' negligence. The decrees promulgated at first address matters related to the clergy and subsequently those that affect laypeople. Out of a total of 84 decrees, the first 16 deal specifically with the figure of the bishop and his functions, the first issue raised being concerns of election and ordination. The first canon, taken from the Council of Laodicea,[24] rejects popular tradition in the naming of bishops – in this case, monks would be the Christian *plebs* and such a figure would already be their superior – the decision falling to the rest of the episcopacy.[25] When the ordination took place, the more bishops from the province who could attend, the better, but there were to be at least three present and the signature of the rest was required, although the consecration rested exclusively with the metropolitan.[26] According to the *incipit* that precedes the *capitula*, these would have been selected and arranged by Martin in a previous council held in Lugo whose existence has raised countless questions.[27] Such meeting would have been where the conversion of the Suevi was formally accomplished and where the Church of *Gallaecia* would have been ordered, including the separation of the sees of the kingdom in two provinces with their respective metropolises (Bracara and Lucus),[28] creating new sees and allocating churches and territories to them in the form, at least rudimentary, presented by the *Parrochiale Sueuum*.[29] Without delving into considerations regarding the veracity of this council, it is clear that sometime between 561 and 572 a process of territorial planning took place and the canon law norms that confirmed Dumio as a legitimate see were shaped,[30] in turn corroborating Martin's growing power over the provincial Church.

Nonetheless, it is more difficult to ascertain how Martin's rise from bishop of Dumio to metropolitan of Braga was justified, according to such canons, and, even more so, his simultaneous retention of both sees. The decrees establish that no cleric, including bishops, could change from a minor to a major church: *de inferiore*

---

[24] Martínez Díez 1967, 232.
[25] *Capitula Martini* 1. See Norton 2007, 7–9. 45.
[26] *Capitula Martini* 2–3.
[27] David 1947, 64–68; Mansilla 1968, 38; Fernández Calo 2016, 128–133.
[28] Evidence that the metropolitan geography of Hispania was still adjusting to the political circumstances. See Fernández Calo 2016; Panzram 2018.
[29] Díaz 1998; Sánchez-Pardo 2014.
[30] It would seem less likely to date said Council of Lugo between 576 and 582, a dating that creates more problems than it solves. See Bermúdez Veloso and Ibáñez Beltrán 2020, 182, n. 2.

ciuitate non transeat ad maiorem;[31] apparently, changing diocese was not allowed under any circumstances, and neither was it possible to act outside one's jurisdiction, nor hold a vacant see, not even in the hypothetical case *si populus [...] desiderit illum*.[32] Hence, Martin's promotion must have been the result of an extraordinary legal solution that necessarily resolved must have been by a council procedure; this, in turn, may serve to justify the existence of the abovementioned Council of Lugo.

It is difficult to reconstruct how this monastery/bishopric developed into an essential body in the subsequent Suevic and Visigothic history of *Gallaecia*. The influence of Martin's charisma is unquestionable, but it is also true that royal support, among other factors, would have benefited and increased the monastery's assets. The fact is that, under the Suevi rule and at certain times in the following Visigothic period, the bishopric of Dumio was a gateway to the position of metropolitan of Braga and, when such was the case, both sees were held by the same bishop. We do not know whether this appointment implied the election of a new abbot for the monastery or whether Martin remained in such a position.[33] If we pay attention to the situation in the mid-seventh century, it is possible that Martin's promotion to the office of bishop of Dumio could already have entailed the election of a new abbot to rule over the monks. In the Council of Toledo of 653, the bishop of the see of Dumio, Richimirus, was represented by Abbot Osdulgus,[34] so it is reasonable to assume that he would have been the abbot of the monastery. In any case, placing both sees under the same prelate could solve hypothetical jurisdictional conflicts; we find it difficult to understand how the existence of two bishops in a urban setting could be reconciled, even if the jurisdiction of one of them was exclusively limited to monasterial properties and their dependents.

At any rate, Martin's role in the conversion of the Suevi must have been at the root of this anomaly, although the monastery itself must have become consolidated as an influential entity. Dumio's position as a cultural centre is clear; indeed, it is from where the Egyptian model of monasticism spread across the entire territory of *Gallaecia*, in what would eventually be one of the richest and most original monastic experiences of Late Antiquity. To this we should add Martín's own work. We have mentioned how he collected and adapted the canons that would be included

---

31 *Capitula Martini* 5.
32 *Capitula Martini* 9.
33 The generally accepted view is that the bishop of Dumio was simultaneously (always) the monastery's abbot. As an example Ferreiro 2017.
34 *Concilium Toletanum* VIII: *Item uicarii episcoporum [66] Osdulgus abba Riccimiri episcopi ecclesiae Dumiensis* (Martínez Díez and Rodríguez 1992, 445). Ferreiro 2017 interprets the text in a different way: "Osdulgus Ricimirus, Abbot-Bishop of the Church of Dumium".

in the Hispanic collections as an essential basis for ecclesiastical law; he also published several treatises aimed at providing answers to the queries of certain of his fellow-bishops, which would justify his dedications to some of them,[35] or to the king himself, as is the case with his *Formula Vitae Honestae*, a text that proves extremely valuable to Martin's role as royal advisor.[36] As can be gathered from the preamble, the king himself would have entrusted Martin with assisting him in his task:

> I am not unaware, most merciful king, that the very burning thirst of your spirit insatiably searches in the vessels of knowledge, and that you unflaggingly search in the sources whence the waters of moral science spring; you often stimulate my humbleness with your letters so that I frequently write you some words of solace or appeal.[37]

As it develops, the opuscule includes a series of pieces of advice, warnings and rules of conduct that constitute a treatise of moral instructions that stem from an essential principle: good governance of oneself guarantees a good sovereign. As the text unfolds, the king is described according to terms of the imperial rhetoric of power that were completely foreign to the past of the Suevic monarchy. The text was written in a simple style so that it could be understood by those of good faith and is meant to be recited to the king (we are to assume that the monarch is not qualified to read it himself). Although Martin affirms that, since the king is endowed with natural wisdom, he has not written it for his private cultivation, but that it is intended for those who help him in the task of governing, adding that it is within reach of any of his advisors and ministers, and that it would be fitting for them to read it, understand it and, above all, follow its instructions.[38]

---

35 He sends the collection of eastern canons to his peer Nitigisius of Lugo; the *De Ira* treatise is dedicated to Witimer, bishop of Ourense; *De Correctione Rusticorum* is a letter addressed to Polimius of Astorga; while the opuscule *De trina mersione* was sent to a bishop called Bonifacius, whose bishopric, although unknown, is outside the Suevic kingdom, and who was probably a bishop in Visigothic territory.
36 Silva 2008, 87–135.
37 Mart. Brac. form. vit. 1: *Gloriosissimo ac tranquillissimo et insigni catholicae fidei praedito pietate Mironi regi Martinis humilis episcopus. 1. Non ignoro, clementissime rex, flagrantissimam tui animi sitim sapientiae insatiabiliter poculis inhiare eaque te ardenter, quibus moralis scientiae riuulis manant, fluenta requirere et ob hoc humilitatem meam tuis saepius litteris admoneri ut dignationi tuae crebro aliquid per epistolam scribens aut consultationis aut exhortationis alicuius etsi qualicumque sint offeram dicta.* On Martin's attempt to model the figure of the Suevi monarch according to the moral patterns of the good Christian emperor, see Rodrigues Roedel 1997.
38 Mart. Brac. form. vit. 1: *libellum hunc nulla sophismatum ostentatione politum sed planitie purae simplicitatis exertum capacibus fidenter auribus obtuli recitandum. Quem non uestrae specialiter*

Martin is undoubtedly addressing the king's court, even more obvious if we pay attention to the development of the treatise as a whole, where he reviews the four virtues that he believes should grace good governance: caution, magnanimity, temperance and justice.[39] These are four virtues that make any individual honourable, but in the discursive development of the opuscule it is obvious that he is referring to the virtues of a good ruler.[40] Martin's instructive advice to the king in the *Formula Vitae Honestae* treatise, as well as what he suggests in the *De Ira*, another of his moral treatises, seems taken from the Stoic tradition's description of a good ruler.[41] But Martin also assumes his role as the king's spiritual advisor, which is why the philosophical, ethical perception becomes Christian moral instruction in his treatises *Pro repellenda iactantia, Item de superbia* and, especially, *Exhortatio humilitatis*. There seems to be a consensus as to these being three parts of the same work aimed at teaching those with government duties:[42]

> First and foremost I urge you to profess constant fear of exaggeratedly flattering praise from men [...] It is a king's flaw to be indulgent towards his flatterers, in the same way as it is servile to flatter [...] Hence, I have considered it convenient to provide you with these instruments of humility and add, though you already have it, the replacement of this commanding rudder, because where the height is greater for men, the wind of pride always blows stronger [...] And so this is the true and Christian humility. With it you will excellently rule those under your charge. With it you will merit victory over every vice, ascribing the win to God and not yourself.[43]

---

institutioni, cui naturalis sapientiae sagacitas praesto est, sed generaliter his conscripsi quos ministeriis tuis adstantes haec conuenit legere, intellegere et tenere.

39 "Iustitia" and "Pietas" are, according to Isidore of Seville, the virtues of a good monarch (ety. IX, 3, 5: *Regiae uirtutes praecipuae duae: iustitia et pietas*). The king's piety is included in the dedication of Martin's text, whereas his justice is praised throughout it. The matter is fleetingly approached in another of the author's texts, where he suggests that wrath renders and individual uncapable of considering justice and makes a king a tyrant (Mart. Brac. ira: *1. [Ira] ad considerationem iustitiae inhabilis [...] 3. Ira omnia ex optimo et iustissimo in contrarium mutat [...] Da regi, tyrannus est*).
40 The text was for a long time attributed to Seneca, especially because of its closeness to his Stoic view of political doctrine and natural law. Whether because of its content or because of the philosopher's fame, the fact is that it spread massively throughout the Middle Ages, to the extent of being preserved in more than 600 manuscripts dated between the ninth and the eleventh centuries. By the thirteenth century, it had been translated into all the vernacular languages of western Europe. Cf. Bickel 1905; Barlow 1952, 12–14.
41 Orselli 1999.
42 Fontán 1974.
43 Mart. Brac. humil.: *1. Quisquis nutu Dei cuiuslibet officii dignitate praecelles ac providae gubernationis utilitate ceteris praecedis hominibus, hanc exhortatiunculam meam dignanter [...] 2. Hoc ergo hortor in primis, ut semper delectabilia illa nimis hominum blandimenta permiteas [...] Adulanti siquidem adgaudere regium est; adulari uero seruile est [...] 5. Tibi igitur me oportuit haec humilitatis instrumenta porrigere, tibi gubernaculi, quamuis et ipse habeas, etiam hoc superfluum add-*

While it has been suggested that the text has a generic meaning and is aimed at all rulers[44], any king or political decision-maker, it is necessary to place such moral treatises in their context. Martin practically devoted his entire life to the task of converting and indoctrinating the Suevi of *Gallaecia*, who are, alongside the kingdom's entire Catholic community, the recipients of his work. It is quite clear, however, that the ultimate addressee – much as a generic or indirect rhetoric form was used – was the Suevi king. If the treatise was written after 570, such a recipient would be Miro himself, to whom Martin dedicated his *Formula Vitae Honestae*. This special relationship between Martin and the Suevi king became evident at the time of his death, when he established that his testamentary dispositions be entrusted, to ensure better compliance, to consecutive kings.[45]

Martin's role as the monarch's advisor can be regarded as a personal prerogative, but must be directly associated with the role played by the monastery. In the *Parroquiale Suevum*, the monastery of Dumio is listed as the sixth episcopal see; whereas the others register the churches and *pagi* under their jurisdiction, what now appears is *Ad Dumio familia seruorum*.[46] The bishop of Dumio exercises jurisdiction over its properties and over its dependents, and obviously over its monks. The extension of such properties must have grown throughout the sixth and seventh centuries. An exceptional coincidence has allowed us to learn the hypothetical reach of such an estate. At a council meeting held at the royal headquarters of Toledo on 1 December 656, the bishops had to settle a complaint made by the Church of Dumio on the subject of the liberality shown by Richimirus, late bishop of the see, who in his testamentary dispositions had clearly acted against its interests. The bishops proceed under Recceswinth's instructions who, via the *uir inluster* Wamba, had sent them such testament, but also under Martin's. It can be deduced that the successive kings were entrusted with the task of protecting the monastery of Dumio,[47] probably its very continuance as episcopal see and the integrity of the assets that guaranteed its survival, so that Recceswinth was in charge of such pro-

---

ere moderamen, quia ibi semper elationis fortior uentus est, ubi et honoris fortior altitudo [...] 6. Ecce haec est uera illa et Christiana humilitas. In hac et te et quibus praesides optime gubernabis. In haec uictoriam ex omni uitio poteris promereri, Deo hoc quod uiceris tribuendo, non tibi [...].
44 See Barlow (1950, 52), who draws attention to the repeated use of "quisquis" throughout the entire work. Although, on the other hand, we could mention the use of "tibi" or "te", where he seems to be addressing a specific interlocutor.
45 *Concilium Toletanum* X, *Item aliud decretum* (Martínez Díez and Rodríguez 1992, 544–549). For more on the will and its issues, see Merea 1953; García Gallo 1956.
46 Paroch. Suev. VI, 1. David 1947, 46, notes how some manuscripts include the formula *familia regia*, which means that the bishop of Dumio would be a sort of royal arch-chaplain, probably because the copyists no longer understood what this diocese had originally been.
47 On the *commendatarii* and their role, Pérez de Benavides 1975, 145–146.

tection at the time and transferred the canonical decision to the assembly of bishops.

What had Richimirus done? To begin with, he had established that the church's revenue and the profits from the sale of its products (*illationes tributorum et pretia frugum*) be yearly delivered to the poor. He then established that when he died all the items held inside the church – probably liturgical objects and precious goods of any type (*universae speciei, generis et corporis*) – be likewise given to the poor. It seems that he had previously sold them at such a negligible price that it seemed more of a loss than a deal (*uiliori pretio uendere ordinasse ut negotiatio earum rerum perditio*). He also stipulated that some of the church's servants be declared freedmen, additionally granting them more than 500 slaves,[48] some of them from his private property. The bishops agreed unanimously that Richimirus' decision was unacceptable: his action had been so 'indiscreet' that he had left the church with nothing to honour its dignity,[49] all the more since the poor, as the council saw it, were not in dire need (*qui nullum inminens causa pauperum necessitatis existeret*).[50] Richimirus had breached the canonical norm that forbade bishops from transferring ecclesiastical assets,[51] since he had left the church no compensation for the freed servants and neither had he provided anything as reparation for the slaves and other properties granted to those whom he had given the status of freedmen.[52] By virtue of this, Richimirus' will was declared void;[53] what is more, it seems as though the will drafted by the bishop regarding his private properties was held in abeyance so that his assets could be used to repair the damage suffered by the episcopal *domus*, and that it would only be pos-

---

[48] The information provided in the different manuscripts about this is conflicting. García Gallo 1956, 381, prefers to believe that it was fifty, although the most recent edition by Martínez Díez and Rodríguez 1992, 546, mentions *quingenta* (500).

[49] Cf. Buenacasa 2004.

[50] Undoubtedly, popular expectations regarding the bishop's *caritas* involved hope that this would materialize, but behaviours like Richimirus' are absolutely exceptional. See Kreiner 2011.

[51] *Concilium Toletanum III*, c. 3, after recalling this principle, aids to monks and churches of the diocese were set as exceptions but always in amounts that would not severely damage ecclesiastical property. The role of the bishop as administrator of the diocese can be observed throughout all Hispanic council law, but seldom so clearly as in the minutes of the *Concilium Emeritense* of 666, where a large number of the canons seem designed to specify such task. See Díaz 1995.

[52] The bishop could probably donate goods of the diocesan Church, but provided it was compensated at the expense of his own property. We do not know whether the principle was universally accepted, but such possibility had been stated at the Council of Mérida of 666, provided that there was clear evidence that the bishop had contributed *triplum aut multo plus* to his church of what he had donated (*Concilium Emeritense*, c. 21). See De Juan 1998.

[53] Repeal that was endorsed by civil law, which prohibited fraudulent and secret sales made by bishops or clergymen (LV 5,1, 2–3).

sible to comply with its clauses once the Church had been compensated for its lost property.[54] It was decided that the only concession to be granted to Richimirus would be to entrust the newly appointed bishop of Braga-Dumio, Fructuosus, with the enforcement of the provisions so that he could revoke or confirm the freedom and property gifted to the freed servants according to their merits. It is clearly impossible to estimate what the wealth of the monastery-bishopric could have been: 500 servants are a lot if they were only part of the properties, but, since we have no figures to compare with or diminish its importance, a lot in relation to what?

It is unquestionable that by assigning the task of settling the conflict to the bishops what was being preserved was the property of an episcopal see according to the criteria used by ecclesiastical canons for the protection of diocesan assets,[55] without considering the independent ownership of monasteries – which, on the other hand, had their own mechanisms to safeguard their properties – regarding the diocesan church. In this context, Dumio clearly acted more as an episcopal see than as a monastery and we should imagine that the preservation of such episcopal status, alongside the monastery itself, is what Martin had very probably entrusted to the kings, aware that, for the metropolitan church of Braga, its mere existence was a challenging anomaly. This said, we have seen how Richimirus had been represented in Toledo three years earlier by an abbot, we assume from the monastery, called Osdulgus. The problem is that we do not know whether these two positions were always separate or if they could occasionally be accrued by one individual. It is hard to know the relationship that could exist between bishop and abbot. Apparently, at least while the bishop of Dumio was in such a position for the monastery, he would continue subjected to monastic discipline. Although it seems unlikely that he was ever subjected to the abbot's discipline, as noted by Bede for the community of Iona;[56] in the case of Lindisfarne, however, the offices of bishop and abbot were sometimes held jointly and sometimes separately, but bishops remained faithful to the rule.[57]

What were the implications of a monastery being also an episcopal see? Monasteries had been entitled to *ius possessionis* since the mid-fifth century. At a coun-

---

54 Cf. Castillo Maldonado 2012.
55 Castellanos García 1998; Díaz 2017, 477–480.
56 Beda Venerabilis, *Historia ecclesiastica gentis Anglorum* 3, 4.
57 This would appear so from the different references in his *Historia Eclesiastica. See* Oliger 1958, 66. Even more confusing is the case of Warinbertus, in Gaul in the second half of the 7th century, abbot of the royal monastery of Saint-Médard, later appointed by the king as bishop of Soissons without abandoning his status as abbot. In this case, however, the problem is different. Cf. Barbier 1997, 221.

cil held in Arles (a. 449–461) with the aim of mediating between Faustus, abbot of Lerins, and certain bishops, it was decreed that the monastery and those monks who had not been ordained priests depended exclusively on the abbot, while the bishop was only responsible for ensuring observance of the doctrine, including the approval of the rule that was to be followed at the monastery.[58] If a monastery was simultaneously a diocesan see, this implied that it could detach itself completely, not only in terms of property, from any other authority. The monastery's rule was now approved by its own bishop and, if such was his office in Braga at the same time, he would act simultaneously as bishop of the monastery and metropolitan. One would assume that this would not, in principle, involve any conflict, inasmuch as all the bishops abided in fellowship; however, there are signs that this was not exactly so.

At the First Council of Braga, held in 561, the metropolitan bishop was Lucretius, while Martin was that of Dumio, both attending as such. As mentioned, by 572 Martin had achieved the condition of metropolitan bishop and was probably still the holder of the see of Dumio, since it was not represented by anyone else. We do not know how the situation stood after Martin's death, but after the Visigothic conquest of the kingdom of the Suevi, the independence of the two sees prevailed for seven decades.[59] The accession of Fructuosus to the see of Dumio would have taken place shortly before 656 when he succeeded Richimirus. Fructuosus might have been summoned, because of his prestige as a monk and ascetic leader, to restore order in a structure that his predecessor's actions had endangered. He could himself have condemned his predecessor's will when he became aware of his exaggerated liberality with the see's property, although it is more likely that it would have been done by the monks themselves. If, as noted, the structure of the monastery in the seventh century entailed the coexistence of an abbot and a bishop, it is likely that one and the other did not have the same notion of common property. Moreover, it is difficult to know how the functions of one and the other could be defined in relation to the property of the monastery/bishopric. In any case, as far as we know, Fructuosus bore no previous relationship with Dumio, so that his appointment must have been an episcopal imposition to the monks under circumstances that his biographer prefers to overlook, and there is nothing to prove that he was simultaneously abbot of the monastery.[60]

---

[58] *Concilium Arelatense in causa Fausti abbatis insulae Lerinensis (449–461)*. The rule is included in *Hispania* already in the Council of Lérida of 546 (*Concilium Ilerdense*, c. 3).

[59] García Moreno 1974, 150–151. 158–159.

[60] See Díaz y Díaz 1974, 14, n. 4. Orlandis and Ramos-Lissón 1986, 343, also attribute this abbot-bishop condition to him. Mansilla Reoyo 1994, I: 209, believes that he was a monk at Dumio when he was chosen bishop of Braga, which seems contradictory.

This said, at the same conference held in 656, the bishops also addressed another matter: the bishop of Braga, Potamius, had sent a letter to the council declaring himself guilty of fornication. Summoned to attend, he confirmed everything he had laid down in writing and confessed that nine months since he had relinquished the government of the see, he had shut himself in a cell to do penance. At the hearing, the bishops scrutinized whether he had defamed himself willingly or under threat of some type of violence. Irrespective of that being the customary procedure, it seems that there was some suspicion that Potamius might have been under pressure to give up the see. Indeed, the prelates decided not to deprive him of his episcopal dignity, but being subjected to lifetime penance involved being deprived of his see. Immediately thereafter, they decreed that from then on Fructuosus, bishop of the Church of Dumio, would also rule over the Church of Braga, undertaking the care of all its properties and souls, thereby managing and preserving the entire metropolis of *Gallaecia*.[61] Such decision seemed aimed at establishing order both in Dumio and in Braga, but the bishops proceeded with exaggerated caution and added the sentence against Potamius to the decree of appointment in order to prevent any future disturbance.[62] Fructuosus' prestige, as had Martin's in the past, without excluding an unquestionable position of power, even personal ambition, would have promoted an extraordinary solution that required a council agreement, whose legitimacy, given the circumstances, appears to raise doubts among the bishops themselves. This could have been the same legal mechanism used in the previous century at a council, probably that of Lugo, whose minutes, as noted before, have only left a tenuous trace. In any case, a new and almost uninterrupted period lay ahead,[63] in which the sees of Dumio and Braga would form a unit whose implications require examination.

---

[61] *Concilium Toletanum X, Item decretum pro Potamio episcopo: Tunc uenerabilem Fructuosum ecclesiae Dumiensis episcopum communi omnium nostrorum electione constituimus ecclesiae Bracarensis gubernacula continere, ita ut omnem metropolim prouinciae Galleciae cunctosque episcopos populosque conuentus ipsius omnemque curam animarum et rerum Bracarensis ecclesiae gubernanda suscipiens ita componat atque conseruet, ut et Deum nostrum de rectitudine operis sui glorificet, et nobis de incolomitate ecclesiae eius gaudium praeste* (Martínez Díez and Rodríguez 1992, 540–541).

[62] Ibid: *Quia uero ad futurum prospicere conuenit, ne exoriri in statu pacis possit quaedam commotio litis, Patrum sententiam quae iam dictum Potamium episcopum rectitudine damnat, huic decreto conectere uigilantia nostra procurat.* In such sentence it is once again discussed that although Potamius deserved to be removed from office they chose to be benevolent in his punishment.

[63] As we shall see, there is only evidence of another bishop in Dumio between 688 and 693. Ferreiro 2017, 99, identifies one Beniamin as bishop of Dumio in the minutes of the Council of Toledo of 681, but the list is that of the bishops who signed the *Decretum Gundemari regis* in 610, whose text was provided as an annex to the minutes of the Twelfth Council of Toledo.

Fructuosus' consecration as metropolitan of Braga should not be regarded as something unconnected to his ambitions. His biographer insists that he had vehemently opposed his appointment,[64] but this is once again a figure of modesty in keeping with the hagiographic genre and the text's purpose of praising his ascetic condition over that of bishop.[65] If, albeit with caution, we consider that his accession to Dumio could have been based on his prestige as father of monks alone, his access to the upper echelons of the Church of *Gallaecia* has, nonetheless, a political reading. Shortly after Reccesvind's accession to power, perhaps also in 653, Fructuosus had written a letter to the king in an attempt to mediate for those who were victims of reprisal since the time of his father, Chindasvind.[66] The text is apparently marked by a fear of offending the king, whose generosity he praises, while justifying his request, accepting potential reprisals as the contribution to the greater good of concord in the kingdom. Fructuosus belonged to a prominent aristocratic family,[67] whether or not he had suffered repression under Chindasvind's rule, but his position as stated in the letter probably represents a large part of Gothic nobility in supporting Reccesvind with the hope of restoring the order before 643.[68] The text is addressed both to the king and to the bishops who met at the council, which was almost certainly held in Toledo in 653, where reconciliation with the punished and the search for balance in the exercise of power, including the anomalous mechanism that led to Reccesvind's accession to the throne, would be central. It must not have been an easy assembly, since any rectification of the immediate past was a condemnation of Reccesvind himself, who had ruled jointly with his father during the last four years of the latter's reign, and involved breaking the oath of allegiance made to Chindasvind in the preceding council,[69] even if it was now understood as an act of force demanded by need rather than a deliberate action.[70]

It is difficult to understand Fructuosus' initiative as an individual act. Although we can hardly use such a weak testimony as the two letters, full of mutual praise, that Fructuosus and Braulius would have exchanged a decade earlier,[71] they can be

---

64 *Vita Fructuosi* 18: *contra uoluntatem suam* [...] *perniciter resistendo*.
65 The clash between the image of the ascetic who leads an isolated life, in keeping with the Egyptian model, and his real integration as bishop and representative of a specific aristocratic group is brought to light by Henriet 2012.
66 A commentary and translation of the text in Martín-Iglesias, Díaz, and Vallejo Girvés 2020, 698–701 and 719–722. See Martin 2006; Díaz 2012, 102–108.
67 Kampers 2012 carries out a detailed prosopographical study of his family ties.
68 Martin 2008, 54–55.
69 *Concilium Toletanum VII*, c. 1. See García y García 1981.
70 *Concilium Toletanum VIII* (Martínez Díez and Rodríguez 1992, 390). See Díaz 2014, 1134–1140.
71 Braulius of Saragossa, *Epistolae* 43 y 44. See Martín-Iglesias, Díaz, and Vallejo Girvés 2020, 698–719.

used to conclude that they shared the same view on the kingdom's political and ecclesiastical problems.[72] Braulius had presided over the episcopal mediation with Chindasvind four years earlier so that the latter would associate his son with the throne;[73] Fructuosus' initiative was in a way a continuation of that. If Fructuosus was appointed because of his prestige and, probably, for being someone from outside the episcopal body, the final result of the council would not have been other than emphasizing his role as an effective mediator. We have noted that such prestige would have also made him an effective candidate to intervene in the matters of Dumio and would have, indeed, influenced his election as metropolitan. His appointment as bishop of Braga took place barely three years after this conflict, while its echoes still resounded. This was accomplished by means of a decree drawn up at a council marked by the influence of Eugenius (II), metropolitan of Toledo, with the attendance of only 17 bishops, including Fructuosus, and five represented by vicars. Eugenius, who had already taken part in the council of 653 – signing it third– came from Toledo but had associated himself with Braulius in Zaragoza,[74] where he had been his archdeacon and had been summoned by Chindasvind, against his will, to occupy the see of the *urbs regia*.[75] Eugenius is likely to have been behind both the appointment for Dumio and for Braga, and therefore respond to a demand from the same influential group that Braulius had headed until his death.[76] On the other hand, the search for a figure outside the Gallaecian diocesan church could have been justified by the perception that the Church of *Gallaecia* was undergoing a process of corruption. An earlier council of 647, also held in Toledo, in which Eugenius' signature appears in second place, had addressed the matter of answering the Gallaecian clergy's complaints *contra pontificum suorum rapacitates*, which condemned bishops' abuses against diocesan and also monasterial basilicas and, in generic terms, their mediocrity.[77] The capacity of the bishop of Toledo to, with the king's consent, consecrate prelates and replace

---

[72] Kampers 2012, 58, after reading the *Versiculi editi a beatissimo Fructuoso*, conveyed alongside the *Vita Fructuosi* (Díaz y Díaz 1974, 123), suggests a possible indirect kinship, or at least a framework involving a same setting of crossed family interests.

[73] Braulius of Saragossa, *Epistolae* 37 (*Suggerendum*).

[74] Ildefonsus of Toledo (De uir. ill. 13) mentions that some time he was devoted to monastic life in Zaragoza.

[75] Braulius of Saragossa, *Epistolae* 31, where he beseeches the king to seek another candidate (see also 32 and 33).

[76] Teja 1995 analyses how such influence could originally revolve around family clans that made the office of bishop a matter of inheritance; the evidence provided refers to the third to fifth century, but the phenomenon can be traced up to the seventh century. See Lynch and Galindo 1959, 3–13.

[77] *Concilium Toletanum VII*, c. 4.

deceased bishops in any see across the kingdom would not be formally recognized until 681,[78] but the draft of the canon took that prerogative for granted, even if not explicitly concluded.[79] Nonetheless, it was complex to use the rules of the Visigothic Church to argue for the simultaneity of jurisdiction over the sees of Dumio and Braga.

In a framework so deeply rooted in tradition as was the diocesan structure, any changes to the episcopal organization chart gave rise to an unquestionable feeling of legal uncertainty and, usually, rejection. An example of reactions against innovation can be observed a few years later when the Council of Toledo held in 681 addressed a complaint made by Stephanus, bishop of Mérida and metropolitan of Lusitania, who claimed to have been forced by King Wamba, who had died the previous year, to appoint a bishop for the monastery of the small town of Aquis.[80] In their decision to revoke such an appointment, the conciliar fathers did not argue that a monastery could not be an episcopal see, but resorted to a detailed conciliar tradition and legislation that assesses different casuistries among which such possibility is not mentioned. Wamba's decision was revoked, although Cuniuldus, who had been chosen for the new see, was not removed from office since it was decided that he had not acted deceitfully but had only waited for a vacant see. From then on, the monastery was left under the rule of an abbot without episcopal privilege. The Aquis episode is probably the culmination of an age-old conflict between monasteries and diocesan bishops: a struggle that was not new and had most likely begun in the early stages of the Hispanic Church. The Council of Seville held in 619 addressed the issue of establishing laws against bishops' assaults on monasteries, which, out of covetousness, were despoiled and even destroyed,[81] and at the great Council of Toledo held in 633, the bishops had to set a limit to the abuse of bishops who acquired the goods of the monasteries of their dioceses and turned them into private properties, reaffirming that monasteries had complete patrimonial autonomy and that their function was to safeguard the doctrine, appoint those who would be in charge and correct any violations of the rule.[82] By contrast, the council held in Merida in 666 warned against insolence shown to their bishops by presbyters and abbots who, considering that their churches and monasteries were exempted from them, ignored their duties.[83]

---

78 *Concilium Toletanum XII*, c. 6.
79 Díaz 2014, 1146, n. 225.
80 *Concilium Toletanum XII*, c. 4.
81 *Conciliun Spalense II*, c. 10.
82 *Concilium Toletanum IV*, c. 51.
83 *Concilium Emeritensem*, c. 11.

We do not know how things stood in the monastery of Aquis, but there is no question that at some point it claimed recognition before King Wamba, who agreed to grant it the condition of bishopric, thereby drastically limiting the possibility of interference by the bishop of the area, or even that of the metropolitan. The council also took the opportunity to tackle other initiatives taken by the same king, who would have attempted to turn a suburban church of Toledo into a bishopric, doing so in *aliis uicis uel uillulis*. It seems that the only appointment that was effectively resolved was that of Cuniuldus, although the occasion was used to recall a series of canon laws that bishops should establish themselves in cities, in no case *in uicis et uilluis*, therefore there could not be two bishops in a same city and that would be no bishop in a territory that had never had one. Likewise, changes in jurisdiction over a territory or community were also forbidden, as was the interference of bishops of one province in the affairs of another.[84]

Fructuosus was a monk who, years before his accession to the bishopric of Dumio, had founded numerous monasteries and had written a harsh monastic rule that we assume was followed by the monks of his monasteries.[85] Each diocese had to submit the rule for approval by the corresponding bishop. We do not know what rule they followed at Dumio, whether they followed a specific instruction or, more likely, were governed by instructions the superior deemed appropriate based on tradition and on a *codex regularum*, as did many monasteries of the time. Neither do we know whether his rule was integrated into Dumio's discipline, but what is unquestionable is that his condition as bishop and monastic policy maker would not cease to be part of the development of daily life. Nonetheless, being the bishop of Dumio did not authorize him to intervene outside his limited jurisdiction. He could not mediate in a monastic situation that sources related to *Gallaecia* defined as multiple and complex.[86] To be able to intercede in the monastic life of the entire province, Fructuosus required extraordinary powers. This is where his personal ambition played a role in his decision to stand as a candidate for the metropolitan see. His appointment, as mentioned, endorsed his authority over all the churches

---

84 *Concilium Toletanum XII*, c. 4.
85 Pettiau 2017.
86 The *Regula communis* (cc. 1–2) gathers negative references condemning patrimonial monasteries, urban or suburban experiences promoted by presbyters with eminently tax collection purposes. The same rule also seems to organize experiences of a family-based monasticism where the separation of cathedrals seems difficult to control. The individualistic trends led by Valerius of Bierzo or the accounts of monasticism in his surroundings that he presents with far from flattering overtones invoke more or less Orthodox forms. The existence of the *Regula Consensoria Monachorum* provides an approximation to pactual forms but far from those conveyed by the *Regula communis*. See Díaz 2020.

of *Gallaecia*. In fact, the drafting of the decree seems to imply greater authority than what traditionally corresponded to provincial metropolitans, which was limited to ensuring that there were no doctrinal differences among churches and to act as judges when disputes arose among their suffragans.[87] This is why some years later, when he was already the bishop of Dumio and Braga, a part of Galician monasticism would follow another rule, the *Regula communis* or abbots' rule, which, although not seen as drafted by Fructuosus, seems to have been inspired by him and endorsed by his authority. This rule of exceptional interest, though the specifics of which will not be examined here, was created to establish order in a monastic structure through which family groups, perhaps entire peasant communities, organized themselves in the form of monasteries. This was an instance of resistance against the voracity of local aristocrats, the Church itself and other rival forms of monasticism that accused them of heterodoxy.[88]

The *Regula communis* refers to an *episcopo qui per regulam uiuit* that presents itself in opposition to other *episcopi saecularibus*,[89] while an annex to it, the *Pactum*, utilized a comparable formula *episcopus que sub regula uiuit*,[90] to which monks of the monasteries governed by the *Regula communis* could resort if the abbot refused to hear their complaints. These references assume the hypothetical fact that monasteries regulated by it were subjected to the discipline of a bishop who was, in turn, subjected to a rule and would be the one to authorize the use of the *Regula communis*. While it is likely that there was a link between these heterodox communities and the monastery of Dumio,[91] the evidence available is indirect. At one time, the rule mentioned a see referred to as *nostra ecclesia*[92] The anonymous text that narrates Fructuosus' biography reports that after being elected bishop of Braga, he devoted the rest of his life to almsgiving and to the founding of monasteries.[93] Although the expression could have been a hagiographic commonplace in the monastic founders' *Vitae*,[94] that it could recall such activity should

---

87 Sotomayor Muro 2004, 294–295.
88 Díaz 2011b.
89 *Regula communis* 2.
90 *Pactum* ll. 793–794 (Dias 2001, 164).
91 Bishko 1984, 22.
92 *Regula communis* 20. There could be doubts as to whether their reference is the episcopal see or the community of monks who share the ecclesiastical office itself.
93 *Vita Fructuosi* 18: *elemosinarum dispensatione atque monasteriorum consummauit aedificatione*.
94 Díaz y Díaz 1974, 113, n. 9, believes that the sentence draws directly from *Vitas Sanctorum Patrum Emeretensium*, V, III.

not be disregarded.[95] From the reading of the *Regula communis* it may be deduced that his monasteries were scattered across a wide geographical space and located in economically marginal areas. It anticipated that the abbots of a certain area would gather once a month to discuss the coherence of their practices[96] in what would be a true monastic confederation, a precedent for future monastic systems, in this case under the auspices of a monastery whose condition as a bishopric granted it exceptional uniqueness. Nonetheless, as noted before, while the bishop of Dumio could not exercise jurisdiction outside his estate, he could do so if acting as metropolitan, especially when a general council of the Church of Hispania has granted him authority over all the bishops and communities of the province. It seems, therefore, reasonable that the bishop referred to in the *Regula communis* would be Fructuosus himself, metropolitan of Braga by extension, provided that he shared the monastic conditions that made possible such episcopal obedience.

The acceptance of the *Regula communis* and its annexed *Pactum* as a monastic model was not unanimous, as there were other perceptions of monasticism. The *Regula communis* alludes to conflicts with what it terms as secular bishops. The system is likely to have remained unaltered while Fructuosus held his preeminent position as head of the Church of *Gallaecia* and continued after his death shortly before 675. In the minutes of the Third Council of Braga, Leudigisus' signature appears first, probably because of his position as metropolitan, but Dumio is not mentioned.[97] Leudigisus was succeeded by Liuva, at least until 684 when, represented by an abbot who went by the name Reccesindus, he seems to continue as bishop of both dioceses.[98] The situation is interrupted after the disappearance of Liuva. At the Council of Toledo held in 688, Faustinus represents Braga and Vincentius does likewise for Dumio.[99] In principle, after more than thirty years of unifi-

---

95 Díaz y Díaz 1995, 40–41, believes that the *Regula communis* would represent his way of organizing monasteries when he becomes bishop of Braga. Although the only specifically recalled monastery is that built *inter Bracarensem urbem et Dumiensem cenobium in cacumine modici montis praecipuum aedificauit monasterium* (*Vita Fructuosi* 19), undoubtedly referring to Montelios, where he was buried. Council laws only allowed the bishop to build one monastery at the expense of the episcopal property, for which he could use up to one fiftieth of the see's assets; alternatively, he could order the building of a church, even one intended as his own burial place, circumstances under which the sum would be half (*Concilium Toletanum VIII*, c. 5). See Díaz 2017, 477.
96 *Regula communis* 10.
97 *Concilium Bracarense III* (Vives 1963, 378).
98 *Concilium Toletanum XIII: Ego Liuba Bracarensis et Dumiensis episcopus*; *Concilium Toletanum XIV: Reccesindus abba, agens Liubani episcopi Bracarensis*. On this occasion, only Braga is mentioned. Reccesindo could have reasonably been the abbot of Dumio, but it is merely a hypothesis.
99 *Concilium Toletanum XV*. Because of where Vincent's name stands on the signature list, 57th of the 61 attending bishops, it could be assumed that his promotion to bishop had been very recent.

cation, a return to this state of separation seems striking. There was probably a conflict. The primacy of the Church of *Gallaecia*, as confirmed in 656, lay with Braga; indeed, it was metropolitan authority that would have allowed a law applied by its bishop to be followed hypothetically in the territory of other dioceses, but the network of monasteries that made up the confederation of Fructuosus' followers would have technically depended on Dumio,[100] its bishop being the only one subject to a rule that could pose a threat to the balance of the entire provincial Church.

The situation unraveled five years later in a peculiar way. Faustinus was transferred to Seville, when the holder of the see of Seville, Felix, was summoned to Toledo where Sisibertus, the metropolitan, involved in a process of sedition, had been discharged.[101] Faustinus' position was then occupied by yet another Felix who had been the bishop of Oporto, whom the episcopal decree that formalized such transfers – in principle, against the canon – appoints bishop to the see of Braga.[102] The minutes read: *Felix in Dei nomine Bracarensis atque Dumiensis sedium episcopus*.[103] The decree does not mention any conflict involving the Galician Church; the reason claimed is, like the canon that punished him, to settle the conflict caused in the matter of governing the bishops by Sisibertus' discharge, since, as metropolitan of the *urbs regia*, he was the indisputable head of the entire Church of Hispania. It is likely that the obligation to intervene using an extraordinary measure, as was a conciliar decree, would have been taken advantage of to solve other conflicts, and, unquestionably, to compensate loyalties. One such conflict could have been the awkward situation brought about by the return of two elements in the Church of Braga, which surely had led to an embarrassing duality

---

100 Orlandis 1971, 103, considers that these foundations would be a kind of subsidiaries of a parent abbey.

101 The episode of Sisibertus' involvement in a plot to dethrone Egica is still a shadowy affair, at least as regards being able to provide a detailed explanation of its implications in the internal struggles among the power elites. In any case, once his involvement was discovered he was deposed and excommunicated by means of a canonical punishment ruled by his fellow-bishops, although the accusation was essentially political: *infidelitas* to the king which, as reported, entailed depriving him of all his possessions, which were transferred to the prince, and permanent exile (*Concilium Toletanum XVI*, c. 9). See García Moreno 1974, 121–122; Orlandis and Ramos-Lissón 1986, 491–496.

102 *Concilium Toletanum XVI, Decretum iudicii ab uniuersis editum* (Vives 1963, 513–515). The decree is included in the minutes between the canons and the council's confirmatory law, albeit such document also explains that the decision was taken before its formal conclusion: [...] *ideo non congruit nos prius concilium inchoare nisi illo prius canonica ac legali censura multato in loco eius alius fuerit subrogatus Toletanae sedis cathedram retenturus.*

103 *Concilium Toletanum XVI* (Vives 1963, 518).

of authority, at least as far as the monastic confederation was concerned. We must bear in mind that bishoprics' jurisdictions were in principle territorial;[104] as already mentioned, monasteries enjoyed autonomy over their properties, but were subject to the discipline of the bishops of the corresponding diocese in terms of doctrine. In a council held in Huesca in 589 it was decreed that the abbots of each diocese would be summoned on a yearly basis, alongside deacons and presbyters, to be instructed by their bishop;[105] there is no reason to believe that the rule no longer operated. A network of monasteries under the authority of the bishop of Dumio, whose jurisdiction exclusively applied to the monastery, its properties and its dependents, meant an intromission into the pastoral and doctrine surveillance functions of territorial bishops. This could be accepted if the bishop in charge was the metropolitan, but would produce an uncomfortable situation of interference if it was the bishop of the monastery of Dumio, whose theoretical jurisdiction only encompassed the properties and dependents of the monastery. The evident result was that the relations between these bishops (let us define them as 'secular') and the monastic communities within their diocesan communities became profoundly ambiguous.[106]

Fructuosus' accession to the unified see of Braga and Dumio afforded an exceptional opportunity for the development of monasticism in *Gallaecia* – Fructuosus being a staunch advocate of monastic life – but Dumio's role is likely to have become devalued over his long term as bishop, and during the subsequent bishoprics of Leudigisus and Liuva. The system created by Fructuosus necessarily sacrificed the prevalent independence of the see of Dumio. Such a breakdown between Faustinus and Vincentius might mark a point of contention, or perhaps the result of a demand for independence from Dumio as the result of confrontation with his predecessor. In any case, the appointment of Felix restored order to the unified system that prevailed once institutional and religious continuity was interrupted after the fall of the monarchy of Toledo. At such time, the future of the pactual monasticism supported by Dumio, or Dumio and Braga, becomes reduced to the continuity of the pactual and familiar formulas tested there, although as isolated communities since the confederation had disappeared and with it Dumio's prominence. When the restoration of sees in the northwest of Hispania takes place in the early medieval period, Dumio would reappear as a mere denomination, a sort of *ad honorem* bishopric held by the titular head of the see of Mondoñedo, to which Alphonse III allotted the former see and the monastery itself and

---

104 Lauwers 2008; Poveda Arias 2019.
105 *Concilium Oscense* (Vives 1963, 158).
106 Wood 2006, 191–199.

which, until the eleventh century, was known as *mindoniense, britoniense* or *dumiense* without distinction;[107] nothing suggests that the monastic see as such was restored at any time.[108] After a number of vicissitudes, including its transfer to Lugo, the see of Braga became one of the most outstanding in the peninsular west from the eleventh century onwards, after Bishop Pedro's restoration,[109] although its consolidation was not without conflicts that stemmed to a large extent from the Suevic-Gothic past, and clearly from competition with Lugo.[110]

Bibliography

Primary Sources

Beda, *Historia ecclesiastica gentis Anglorum:* Michael Lapidge. ed. 2008–2010. *Beda, Storia degli Inglesi (Historia ecclesiastica gentis Anglorum).* 2 Vols. Roma-Milano: Mondadori Editore.

Braulius of Saragossa, *Epistolae:* Ruth Miguel Franco and José C. Martín-Iglesias. eds. 2018. *Corpus Christianorum, Series Latina (CC SL).* 114B, *Braulionis Caesaraugustani Epistulae et Isidori Hispalensis Epistulae ad Braulionem. Braulionis Caesaraugustani Confessio uel professio Iudaeorum ciuitatis Toletanae.* Turnhout: Brepols.

Capitula Martini: Claude W. Barlow. ed. 1950. *Martini Episcopi Bracarensis. Opera Omnia,* 123–144. New Haven: Yale University Press.

Gregory of Tours, *Decem libri historiarum:* Bruno Krusch and Wilhelm Levison. eds. [1885] 1937. *Monumenta Germaniae Historica. Scriptores rerum Merovingicarum (MGH, SS rer. Merov.).* 1, 1. Hannover: Hahn.

Ildefonsus of Toledo, *De uirorum illustrium scriptis:* Carmen Codoñer Merino. ed. 1972. *El 'De viris illustribus' de Ildefonso de Toledo. Estudio y edición crítica.* Salamanca: Universidad de Salamanca.

Isidore, *De uiris illustribus:* Carmen Codoñer Merino. ed. 1964. *El 'De viris illustribus' de Isidoro de Sevilla. Estudio y edición crítica.* Salamanca: Consejo Superior de Investigaciones Científicas.

Isidore, *Etymologiarum:* Marc Reydellet. ed. 1984. *Isidore de Séville. Étymologies. Livre IX.* Paris: Les Belles Lettres.

---

107 David (1947, 62. 128. 162) suggests the possibility, based on the episcopal catalogue of the Chronicle of Albelda, of it being the episcopate of Dumio itself, whose bishop-abbot would have fled to the northern valleys in the late ninth century and whom Alfonso III would have granted permission to settle in Mondoñedo. See García y García 1986; López Alsina 2013, 106. 118. It is likely that the bishop of Dumio, who participated in the consecration of the church of San Pedro de Montes in 919, was that of Mondoñedo. See González Rodríguez 2017.

108 David (1947, 57) gathers the existence of documents from the tenth century that specify the boundaries of the diocese of Dumio, some of them authentic and others false.

109 Da Costa [1959–1960] 1997–2000; Mansilla Reoyo 1994, II: 47–90.

110 Mansilla Reoyo 1961; Vones 2019, 169–170; Bermúdez Veloso and Ibáñez Beltrán 2020.

Isidore, *Historiae:* Cristobal Rodríguez Alonso. ed. 1975. *Las historias de los godos, vándalos y suevos de Isidoro de Sevilla. Estudio, edición crítica y traducción.* León: Centro de Estudios e Investigación San Isidoro.

Martin of Braga, *De ira:* Chiara Torre. ed. 2008. *Martini Bracarensis De Ira. Introduzione, testo, traduzione e commento*, 102–135. Roma: Herder.

Martin of Braga, *Exhortatio humilitatis:* Claude W. Barlow. ed. 1950. *Martini Episcopi Bracarensis. Opera Omnia*, 74–79. New Haven: Yale University Press.

Martin of Braga, *Formula uitae honestae:* Claude W. Barlow. ed. 1950. *Martini Episcopi Bracarensis. Opera Omnia*, 204–250. New Haven: Yale University Press.

Martínez Díez, Gonzalo and Félix Rodríguez eds. 1992. *La colección canónica hispana, V. Concilios hispanos: segunda parte (CCH V).* Madrid: Consejo Superior de Investigaciones Científicas.

Parrochiale Suevum: Pierre David. ed. 1947. *Etudes historiques sur la Galice et le Portugal du VIe a XIIe siècles (CCSL 175)*, 413–420. Lisboa-Paris : Livraria Portugália Editora.

Regula communis: Paula C. B. Días. ed. 2001. *Regula Monastica Communis ou Exhortatio ad Monachos? (Séc. VII, Explicit). Problemática. Tradução. Comentário*, Coimbra: Universidade.

Vita Fructuosi: Manuel C. Díaz y Díaz. ed. 1974. *La vida de San Fructuoso de Braga. Estudio y edición crítica.* Braga: Diario do Minho.

Vives, Jose. ed. 1963. *Concilios visigóticos e hispano-romanos.* España cristiana 1. Barcelona/Madrid: Consejo Superior de Investigaciones Científicas.

Secondary Sources

Alberro, Manuel. 2003 "Viajes marítimos de celtas britones a Gallaecia en el siglo V." *Lucensia* 13:239–260.

Andrés, Adelaida. 2010. "Martín de Braga." In *La Hispania visigótica y mozárabe. Dos épocas en su literatura*, edited by Carmen Codoñer Merino, 71–81. Salamanca: Universidad.

Barbier, Josiane. 1997. "Les actes mérovingiens pour Saint-Médard de Soissons : une révision." In *Saint-Médard : trésors d'une abbaye royale. Textes et iconographie reunís par Denis Defente*, 181–241. Paris-Soissons: Musé de Soissons.

Barlow, Claude W. 1952. "Prosopography of Martin of Braga." *Folia* 6,1: 5–15.

Bermúdez Veloso, Mariña, and Luis M. Ibáñez Beltrán. 2020. "Una cartografía para los once condados de la diócesis de Lugo: hacia una nueva aproximación al *Parrochiale Suevum*." *Vínculos de Historia* 9:181–201.

Bickel, Ernst. 1905. "Die Schrift des Martinus von Bracara Formula vitae honestae." *Rheinisches Museum* 60:505–551.

Bishko, Charles J. 1984. "The Pactual Tradition in Hispanic Monasticism." In *Spanish and Portuguese Monastic History, 600–1300*, 1–43. London: Variorum.

Branco, Maria J. V. 1999. "St. Martin of Braga, The Sueves, and Gallaecia." In *The Visigoths: Studies in Culture and Society*, edited by Alberto Ferreiro, 63–97. Leiden: Brill.

Buenacasa, Carles. 2004. "Espiritualidad vs racionalidad económica: los dependientes eclesiásticos y el perjuicio económico a la iglesia de Dumio en el testamento de Ricimiro (656)." *Polis* 16:7–32.

Castellanos García, Santiago. 1998. "El testamento de Ricimiro de Dumio en el contexto de la consolidación episcopal en la Hispania tardoantigua." *Hispania Antiqua* 22:427–437

Castillo Maldonado, Pedro. 2012. "*In hora mortis:* deceso, duelo, rapiña y legado en la muerte del obispo visigótico." *Hispania Sacra* 44.1:7–28.

Castillo Maldonado, Pedro. 2017. "Martín de Braga. Doctor de la Hispania sueva." In *Autoridad y autoridades de la iglesia antigua. Homenaje al profesor José Fernández Ubiña*, edited by Francisco Salvador Ventura, Pedro Castillo Maldonado, and Purificación Ubric Rabaneda, 475–489. Granada: Universidad.

Codoñer Merino, Carmen. 1972. *El "De viris illvstribus" de Ildefonso de Toledo*. Salamanca: Universidad.

Da Costa, Avelino J. [1959–1960] 1997–2000. *O bispo D. Pedro e a organizaçao da diocese da Braga*. 2 Vols. Coimbra: Universidade.

David, Pierre. 1947. *Études historiques sur le Galice et le Portugal du VIe au XIIe siècles*. Lisboa-Paris : Portugalia.

De Juan, María T. 1998. "La gestión de los bienes en la Iglesia hispana tardoantigua: confusión patrimonial y sus consecuencias." *Polis* 10:167–180.

Dias, Paula C. B. 2001. *Regula monástica commvnis ou exhortatio ad monachos? (Séc. VII, Explicit). Problemática. Tradução. Comentario*, Coimbra: Edições Colibri.

Díaz, Pablo C. 1987. *Formas económicas y sociales en el monacato visigodo*. Salamanca: Universidad.

Díaz, Pablo C. 1995. "Propiedad y poder: La Iglesia de Lusitania en el siglo VII." In *Los últimos romanos en Lusitania*, Cuadernos Emeritenses 10, edited by Agustín Velázquez Jimenez, 49–72. Mérida: Museo Nacional de Arte Romano.

Díaz, Pablo C. 1998. "El *Parrochiale Sueuum*: organización eclesiástica, poder político y poblamiento en la *Gallaecia* tardoantigua." In *Homenaje a José M° Blázquez*. Vol. VI, edited by Jaime Alvar, 35–47. Madrid: Ediciones Clásicas.

Díaz, Pablo C. 2011a. *El reino suevo (411–585)*. Madrid: Akal.

Díaz, Pablo C. 2011b. "*Regula communis*. Monastic space and social context." In *Western Monasticism ante litteram. The spaces of monastic observance in Late Antiquity and the Early Middle Ages*, edited by Hendrik Dey and Elizabeth Fentress, 117–135. Turnhout: Brepols.

Díaz, Pablo C. 2012. "Confiscations in the Visigothic Reign of Toledo: A Political Instrument." In *Expropiations et confiscations dans les royaumes barbares. Une approche régionale*, Collection de l'École Française de Rome 470, edited by Pierfrancesco Porena, and Yan Rivière, 93–112. Roma: École Française.

Díaz, Pablo C. 2014. "Concilios y obispos en la Península Ibérica (siglos VI–VIII)." In *Chiese locali e chiese regionali nell'alto medioevo*, Settimane di Studio dell Fondazione centro di Studi sull'Alto Medioevo. LXI, 1095–1158. Spoleto: Centro italiano di studi sull'alto Medioevo.

Díaz, Pablo C. 2017. "Las fundaciones monásticas en la península ibérica (siglos VI–VIII)." In *Monachesimo d'Oriente e d'Occidente nell'Alto Medioevo*. Settimane di studio della Fondazione Centro Italiano di Studi sull'Alto Medioevo LXIV, 463–497. Spoleto: Centro italiano di studi sull'alto Medioevo.

Díaz, Pablo C. 2020. "Social Plurality and Monastic Diversity in Late Antique Hispania (Sixth to Eighth Century)." In *The Cambridge History of Medieval Monasticism in the Latin West. 1. Origins to the Eleventh Century*, edited by Alison Beach, and Isabelle Cochelin, 195–211. Cambridge: University Press.

Díaz y Díaz, Manuel C. 1995. "El monacato fructuosiano y su desarrollo." In *El monacato en la diócesis de Astorga durante la Edad Media*, 33–48. Astorga: Ayuntamiento.

Fernandez Alonso, Justo. 1955. *La cura pastoral en la España romanovisigoda*. Roma: Iglesia Española en Roma.

Fernández Calo, Manuel. 2016. "Os Synodi suevo-católicos: implicacións político-administrativas dunha bipartición metropolitana." *Cuadernos de Estudios Gallegos* 63:125–162.

Ferreiro, Alberto. 1980. "The westward journey of St. Martin of Braga." *Studia monástica* 22,2:243–251.
Ferreiro, Alberto. 1981. "The missionary labors of St. Martin of Braga in 6th century Galicia." *Studia Monastica* 23,1:11–26.
Ferreiro, Alberto. 1988. "Early medieval missionary tactics: the example of Martin and Caesarius." *Studia Historica. Historia Antigua* 6:225–238.
Ferreiro, Alberto. 2017. "The see of Dumium/Braga before and under Visigothic rule." *Euphrosyne* 45:97–115.
Fontán, Antonio. 1974. "Martín de Braga: Proyección histórica de su persona y su obra." In *Humanismo romano (clásicos – medievales – modernos)*, 191–217. Barcelona: Planeta.
Fontes, Luis A. de O. 1991. "Salvamento Arqueológico de Dume (Braga). Resultados das Campanhas de 1989-90 e 1991-92." *Cadernos de Arqueología.* Série II, 8–9:199–230.
Fontes, Luis A. de O. 1992. "O norte de Portugal no periodo suevo-visigotico. Elementos para o seu estudo." In *XXXIX Corso di Cultura sull'Arte Ravennate e Bizantina: Aspetti e problemi di archeologia e storia dell'arte della Lusitania, Galizia, e Asturie tra tardoantico e medioevo*, 217–248. Ravenna: Girasole.
Fontes, Luis A. de O. 2006. *A basílica sueva de Dume e o túmulo dito de Sao Martinho.* Braga: Universidade do Minho.
García Gallo, Alfonso. 1956. "El testamento de San Martín de Dumio." *Anuario de Historia del Derecho Español* 26:369–385.
García y García, Antonio. 1981. "El juramento de fidelidad en los concilios visigóticos." In *Innovación y continuidad en la España visigótica*, edited by Ramón Gonzálvez Ruíz, 105–123. Toledo: UPSA.
García y García, Antonio. 1986. "Ecclesia Britonensis." *Estudios Mindonienses* 2:121–134.
García Moreno, Luis A. 1974. *Prosopografía del reino visigodo de Toledo.* Salamanca: Universidad.
González Rodríguez, Rafael. 2017. "El epígrafe de consagración de la iglesia del monasterio de san Pedro de Montes. En torno a sus fuentes literarias y sus fundamentos ideológicos y políticos." *Estudios bercianos* 40:15–26.
Gonzálvez Ruíz, Ramón. 2007. "Agali. Historia del monasterio de san Ildefonso." *Toletum: boletín de la Real Academia de Bellas Artes y Ciencias Históricas de Toledo* 54: 99–145.
Henriet, Patrick 2012. "Un horizon hagiographique d'opposition au pouvoir. Les milieux monastiques et ascétiques de l'Espagne septentrionale au VIIe siècle." In *Hagiographie, idéologie et politique au Moyen Âge en Occident*, Hagiologia 8, edited by Edina Bozoky, 93–110. Turnhout: Brepols.
Hernández Lobato, Jesús. 2012-2013. "El poema In refectorio de Martín de Braga: ¿Un *ready-made* literario?" *Voces* 23–34:75–92.
Kampers, Gerd. 2012. "Annäherung an ein wisigotisches Primatengeschlecht (I), Beobachtungen zu den sog. Versiculi editi a beatissimo Fructuoso." *Millennium. Jahrbuch zu Kultur und Geschichte des ersten Jahrtausends n. Chr.* 9:255–259.
Kampers, Gerd. 2012. "Annäherung an ein wisigotisches Primatengeschlecht (II), Beobachtungen zu den Nachrichten der Vita Fructuosi über den Heiligen und seine Familie." *Millennium. Jahrbuch zu Kultur und Geschichte des ersten Jahrtausends n. Chr.* 9:261–276.
Kreiner, Jamie. 2011. "About the Bishop: The Episcopal Entourage and the Economy of Government in Post-Roman Gaul." *Speculum* 86:321–360.
Lauwers, Michel. 2008. "*Territorium non facere diocesim*. Conflits, limites et représentation territoriale du diocèse (V[e]–XIIIe siècle)." In *L'espace du diocèse dans l'occidente médiéval (Ve-XVIIIe siècle)*, edited by Florian Mazel, 23–65. Rennes : Presses universitaires.
Livermore, Harold V. 1987. "The Britones of Galicia." *Estudios Mindonienses* 3: 355–364.

López Alsina, Fernando. 2013. "El *Parrochiale Suevum* y su presencia en las cartas pontificias del siglo XII." In *Das begrenzte Papsttum: Spielräume päpstlichen Handelns. Legaten – delegierte Richter – Grenzen*, edited by Klaus Herbers, Fernando López Alsina, and Frank Engel, 105–131. Berlin-Boston: De Gruyter.

López Pereira, José E. 2014. "Martín de Braga, de la Galia a Gallaecia." In *Estudios de filología e historia en honor del profesor Vitalino Valcárcel*. Vol. 1, edited by Íñigo Ruíz Arzalluz, 543–556. Vitoria/Gasteiz: UPV.

Lynch, Carlos H., and Pascual Galindo. 1959. *San Braulio obispo de Zaragoza (631–651). Su vida y sus obras*. Madrid: Consejo Superior de Investigaciones Científicas.

Mansilla, Demetrio. 1961. "Formación de la Provincia Bracarense después de la invasión árabe." *Hiapania Sacra* 14:5–25.

Mansilla, Demetrio. 1968. "Obispados y metrópolis del Occidente peninsular hasta el s. X." *Bracara Augusta* 22:11–40.

Mansilla, Demetrio. 1994. *Geografía eclesiástica de España. Estudio histórico-geográfico de las diócesis*. 2 Vols. Roma: Instituto Español de Historia Eclesiástica.

Martin, Céline. 2006. "Des fins de règne incertaines: répression et amnistie des groupes aristocratiques dans le royaume de Tolède (deuxième moitié du VIIe siècle)." In *Les élites au haut Moyen Âge. Crises et renouvellements*, edited by François Bougard, 207–223. Turnhout: Brepols.

Martin, Céline. 2008. "La réforme visigothique de la justice : les années Recceswinth." In *Derecho y justicia: el poder en la Europa medieval*, edited by Nilda Guglielmi, and Adeline Rucquoi, 37–59. Buenos Aires: IMHICIHU – CONICET.

Martín-Iglesias, José C., Pablo C. Díaz, and Margarita Vallejo Girvés. 2020. *La Hispania tardoantigua y visigoda en las fuentes epistolares*, Nueva Roma 51. Madrid: Consejo Superior de Investigaciones Científicas.

Martínez Díez, Gonzalo. 1967. "La colección canónica de la iglesia sueva los *capitula Martini*." *Bracara Augusta* 21:224–243.

Merêa, Manuel P. 1953. "Sobre o testamento de S. Martinho de Dume." In *Estudos de Direito Hispânico Medieval*. II, 50–53. Coimbra: Universidade.

Miguel Franco, Ruth. 2011. "Braulio de Zaragoza, el rey Chindasvinto y Eugenio de Toledo: imagen y opinión en el *Epistolarium* de Braulio de Zaragoza." *Emerita* 79:155–176.

Norton, Peter. 2007. *Episcopal Elections 250–600. Hierarchy and Popular Will in Late Antiquity*. Oxford: Oxford University Press.

Oliger, Paul R. 1958. *Les Èvêques reguliers. Recherche sur leur condition juridique depuis les origines du monachisme jusqu'a la fin du Moyen-Áge*. Paris-Louvain: Desclée de Brouwer.

Orlandis, José. 1971. "Las congregaciones monásticas en la tradición suevo-visigótica." In *Estudios sobre instituciones monásticas medievales*, 95–123. Pamplona: EUNSA.

Orlandis, José and Ramos-Lissón, Domingo. 1986. *Historia de los concilios de la España romana y visigoda*. Pamplona: EUNSA.

Orselli, Alba M. 1999. "Eredità senecane nel Tardo Antico: l'esempio di Martino di Braga." In *Seneca nella coscienza dell'Europa*, edited by Ivano Dionigi, 81–110. Milano: Mondadori Bruno.

Panzram, Sabine. 2018. "La formación del orden metropolitano en la Península Ibérica (siglos IV a VI)." *Pyrenae* 49,1:125–54.

Pérez de Benavides, Manuel M. 1975. *El testamento visigótico. Una contribución al estudio del derecho romano vulgar*. Granada: Universidad.

Pettiau, Herold. 2017. "La Vie de saint Fructueux de Braga quelques aspects de la relation entre l'ascète et la société en Espagne wisigothique." In *Corona Monastica: Moines bretons de Landévennec : histoire et mémoire celtiques. Mélanges offerts au père Marc Simon,* edited by Luis Lemoine, and Bernard Merdrignac, 51–63. Rennes : Presses universitaires.

Poveda Arias, Pablo. 2019. "La diócesis episcopal en la Hispania visigoda: concepción, construcción y disputas por su territorio." *Hispania Sacra* 71,1: 9–24.

Roedel, Leila R. 1997. "A Cristianização e a tradição clássica na transição da Antigüidade para a Idade Media: o caso do reino Suevo." *Boletim do CPA (Sao Paulo, Brasil)* 2,4: 111–127.

Sánchez-Pardo, José C. 2014. "Organización eclesiástica y social en la Galicia tardoantigua. Una perspectiva geográfico-arqueologica." *Hispania Sacra* 66:439–480.

Sánchez Salor, Eustaquio. 1976. *Jerarquías eclesiásticas y monacales en época visigótica.* Salamanca: Universidad.

Soares, Luis R. 1996. *Linhagem cultural de S. Martinho de Dume e outros etudos dumienses.* Lisboa: Casa da Moeda.

Sotomayor, Manuel. 2004. "Términos de la organización territorial eclesiástica en los concilios hispano-romanos y visigodos." In *Mélanges d'Antiquité Tardive. Stvdiola in honorem Noël Duval,* edited by Catherine Balmelle, 283–297. Turnhout: Brepols.

Sterk, Andrea. 2004. *Renouncing the World Yet Leading the Church. The Monk-Bishop in Late Antiquity.* Cambridge (Ma)-London: Harvard University Press.

Silva, Leila R. Da. 2008. *Monarquia e Igreja na Galiza na segunda metade do século VI. O modelo de monarca nas obras de Martinho de Braga dedicados ao rei suevo.* Niteroi/RJ: Editora da Universidade Federal Fluminense.

Teja, Ramón. 1995. "Las dinastías episcopales en la Hispania tardo-romana." *Cassiodorus* 1:29–39.

Thompson, Edward A. 1980. "The Conversion of the Spanish Suevi to Catholicism." In *Visigothic Spain: New Approaches,* ed. Edward James, 77–92. Oxford: Clarendon Press.

Vallejo Girvés, Margarita. 2012. *Hispania y Bizancio. Una relación desconocida.* Madrid: Akal.

Vones, Ludwig. 2019. "Restauration ou bouleversement ? La reconstitution des espaces diocésains dans la péninsule Ibérique au Haut Moyen Âge." *Mélanges de la Casa de Velázquez* 49,2:165–194.

Wood, Susan. 2006. *The Proprietary Church in the Medieval West.* Oxford: University Press.

List of Contributors

Marco Cristini
obtained his PhD in Classics at Scuola Normale Superiore (Pisa, Italy) in 2020 with a dissertation about the foreign policy of Theoderic's successors under the supervision of Andrea Giardina. He subsequently held a fellowship at the Center for Advanced Studies "Migration and Mobility in Late Antiquity and the Early Middle Ages" at the Eberhard Karls Universität Tübingen, and is currently research fellow at the Istituto Italiano di Storia Antica in Rome. His main research interests are Ostrogothic Italy, diplomacy in Late Antiquity, Procopius of Caesarea, Cassiodorus and Jordanes. He published two monographs (*Teoderico e i regni romano-germanici [489–526]: rapporti politico-diplomatici e conflitti*, and *Baduila: Politics and Warfare at the End of Ostrogothic Italy*), both in 2022, and several papers in international highranking journals. He also authored the BBKL entries on Cassiodorus and Procopius. He is now working on a critical edition of the fragments of Cassiodorus' panegyrics.

Katy Cubitt
is Professor of Medieval History at the University of East Anglia, UK. She specialises in the history of the early medieval church, particularly in England where she is interested in the history of councils and bishops. Her work brings together continental connections and influences on the English Church. Another strand in her research concerns the seventh-century Mediterranean world and the role of the papacy and church councils in the formation of Christian culture. She has published widely on the Anglo-Saxon and religious history, including her first book, *Anglo-Saxon Church Councils c. 650–c. 850* (1995). She is just completing a monograph on the practice of penance and confession in tenth- and eleventh-century England: *Sin and Society in Tenth- and Eleventh-Century England* to be published by Cambridge University Press in 2022/23. She is President Elect of the Ecclesiastical History Society.

Pablo C. Díaz
obtained a PhD in History from the University of Salamanca under the supervision of Marcelo Vigil, dealing with the study of the economic and social relations generated by the Visigothic monasticism in Hispania. Since 1982 he is professor of Ancient History at the University of Salamanca. His most recent research focused on the Late Antique period, especially assessing the impact that the invasions of the Suevi and Visigoths had on the preceding Hispano-Roman structures. He has a particular interest in the processes of institutional adaptability of the Suevi and Visigoths, the continuity or rupture in the forms of exploitation of the territory and the response of peasant communities to the dominant forms in the environment. The result of this research is some 160 contributions to congresses, courses, seminars, conferences or round tables and about 130 publications (books, book chapters, articles), including (with José C. Martín-Iglesias and M. Vallejo Girvés) *La Hispania tardoantigua y visigoda en las fuentes epistolares* (Madrid 2020).

Bruno Dumézil
is professor of Medieval History at Sorbonne University. His work focuses on the Early Middle Ages in the West, through the history of migration, social networks and leadership. He organized archaeological exhibitions: *Nos ancêtres les barbares* (2008) and *L'Austrasie, le royaume mérovingien oublié* (2016) in collaboration with the National Museum of Archeology of Saint-Germain-en-Laye. He has published several books including *Les racines chrétiennes de l'Europe. Conversion et liberté dans les*

royaumes barbares V–VIIIe siècle (Paris 2005), *La reine Brunehaut* (Paris 2008), *Les royaumes barbares d'Occident* (Paris 2010), *Servir l'État dans la Gaule franque* (Paris 2013), *Les Barbares* (Paris 2016) and *Le baptême de Clovis* (Paris 2019). Currently, his work focuses on political epistolography.

Julio Escalona
received his doctorate in 1996 by the Universidad Complutense de Madrid. He is currently research professor at the *Consejo Superior de Investigaciones* Científicas (CSIC) in Madrid and belongs to the Research Group Redes de Poder en las Sociedades Medievales. He is Honorary Senior Research Associate of the Institute of Archaeology (University College London, UK) and full member of the Spanish Society of Agrarian History (SEHA). His primary research field is the historical and archaeological study of territory, society and power in early medieval Europe. Furthermore, he is interested in the analysis of medieval written sources from the point of view of historical memory, political discourse and document forgery, as well as in the application of Information Technologies to research in Medieval History and Archaeology (especially database design and e-mapping). He has participated in numerous national and international projects and is co-editor, for example, of (with Orri Vésteinsson and Stuart Brookes) *Polity and Neighbourhood in Early Medieval Europe* (Turnhout 2019).

Kevin Grotherr
is a research assistant at the "RomanIslam – Center for Comparative Empire and Transcultural Studies" and a PhD student in Ancient History at the University of Hamburg. He studied History and Archaeology and Cultural History of the Ancient Mediterranean at the University of Hamburg and the Universidad de Salamanca (Spain). Since 2022 he is a holder of a doctoral scholarship of the Konrad-Adenauer-Stiftung. His main research interest is the history of Christianity in the 'Long Late Antiquity', in particular the history of ecclesiastical offices as well as ancient military history. In his PhD project *Herrschaft qua Amt oder Charisma? 'Bischofsherrschaft' zwischen Lusitania und Levante im 6. und 7. Jahrhundert*, he is taking a supra-regional look at the phenomenon of 'Bischofsherrschaft' in Late Antiquity.

Martin Horst
is currently a research associate at the "RomanIslam – Center for Comparative Empire and Transcultural Studies" at the University of Hamburg, about to depart for a research stay at the DHI Paris in order to collate further data for his PhD thesis. In the course of his studies of history and classical archaeology, the focus has settled on the areas of late antiquity and the reception of antique heritage in the Middle Ages. The thesis aims to provide a database concerning aristocratic and episcopal networks in late- and post-Roman Gaul of sufficient density to allow an algorithmic analysis of their structures. Ideally, this would clarify any changes therein during the transformations of the fifth century AD.

Charles Mériaux
obtained his PhD by the Université de Lille in 2002 with a study about *La formation des diocèses septentrionaux de la Gaule du VIe au Xe siècle (Arras/Cambrai, Tournai et Thérouanne). Mission, topographie chrétienne et culte des saints*. After research stays, for instance, in Göttingen, and positions in Reims and Paris, he currently is professor of Medieval History at the Université de Lille. His research focuses on the history of the High Middle Ages in general and more particularly on hagiography and the cult of saints, the rural clergy in the Latin West, with a strong interest in the documentary files issued of the ecclesiastical province of Reims. Among his recent publications is a monograph dedicated to *La naissance de la France. Les royaumes des Francs (V^e–VIIe siècle)* (Paris 2014).

Isabelle Mossong,

after completing a Master's degree in Ancient History at the University of Strasbourg in 2007, started her doctoral research on the epigraphy of the Christian clergy throughout the Italian Peninsula in a German-French cotutelle at the Freie Universität Berlin and the University of Strasbourg. From 2012 to 2014 she was a foreign member of the l'École française de Rome, funded by the Research Fund of Luxembourg. Since 2016 she has been based in Munich, as a research officer for Latin epigraphy at the Commission for Ancient History and Epigraphy of the German Archaeological Institute. Besides being the editor in charge of the monographic series *Vestigia*, she regularly teaches at the Universities of Augsburg and Munich. Her research activities now concentrate mainly on the North-Western territory of the Iberian Peninsula, both by contributing to the new CIL-volume on the *Conventus Asturum* and by preparing a habilitation thesis on this contact zone located at the extreme occidental border of the Roman Empire. Her recent publications include *Der Klerus des spätantiken Italiens im Spiegel epigraphischer Zeugnisse: eine soziohistorische Studie* (Berlin 2022).

Sabine Panzram

is Professor of Ancient History at Hamburg University. She obtained her PhD at Münster University (2001) after completing her studies in Freiburg and Barcelona. She has been a research fellow (DFG) at the German Archaeological Institute in Berlin (2010–2012) and has held a Marie Curie Senior Fellowship at the École des Hautes Études Hispaniques et Ibériques – Casa de Velázquez in Madrid (2018–2019). She focuses on social history of power in the Western Mediterranean, and in particular on urban history in the Iberian Peninsula. Since 2010 coordinator of Toletum, an interdisciplinary network for early career researchers focusing on the Iberian Peninsula in Antiquity (DFG), since 2020 director (with S. Heidemann) of the Center for Advanced Studies "RomanIslam – Center for Compared Empire and Transcultural Studies" (DFG) and since 2021 principal investigator (with L. Brassous) of ATLAS, an atlas of Late Antique cities in the South of the Iberian Peninsula and North Africa (3rd–8th centuries) (ANR-DFG). Among her latest publications stands out (with L. Livorsi et al.) *Regesta Pontificum Romanorum. Iberia Pontificia. Vol. VII: Hispania Romana et Visigothica* (Göttingen 2022).

Pablo Poveda Arias

holds a PhD by the University of Salamanca. After holding two postdoctoral positions in Hamburg University, one funded by the Fritz Thyssen Stiftung (*Bishops and Competitiveness in the Post-Imperial West: Gaul and Hispania [5th–8th Centuries]*) and another as research assistant at the Center for Advanced Studies "RomanIslam – Center for Comparative Empire and Transcultural Studies", he is currently assistant professor at the University of Valladolid. His research is focused on dynamics of power in the Visigothic and Merovingian kingdoms, in particular those concerning the kingship and the Church. He has published several articles in journals of recognized impact such as *Reti Medievali, European Review of History, Hispania Sacra, Gladius* and *Studia Historica. Historia Medieval*, among others, all of them in the framework of national and international funded research projects.

Margarita Vallejo Girvés

is Professor of Ancient History at the University of Alcalá de Henares. She is particularly interested, within the field of Late Antiquity, in the relations between the Eastern Roman or Byzantine Empire and Visigothic Hispania, as well as in the evolution of exile as a legal public penalty and in the history of the 5th century in the eastern Mediterranean area. Currently she is also interested in Byzantine empresses of the 6th and 7th centuries and is leading a research project on this topic. She has been a researcher on three research projects with national public funding and is the author or editor of several Spanish and foreign monographs on these subjects, as well as numerous articles and book chapters, including (with Pablo C. Díaz and José C. Martín-Iglesias) *La Hispania tardoantigua y visigoda en las fuentes epistolares* (Madrid 2020).

Francesco Veronese
obtained his PhD in History of Medieval Christianity in 2012 at the Universities of Padua (Italy) and Paris 8 – Vincenne-Saint-Denis (France). Later he was granted with post-doc fellowships at the University of Padua (2013–2016), in the context of the research project on *Social Conflicts, Kinship Structures and Local Communities in Early Medieval Italy (8th–11th centuries)*; and at the Istituto Storico Italiano per il Medioevo (ISIME), Rome (2017–2019). He was assigned with teaching duties in Medieval History and Gender History at the University of Padua. His research interests span from saints and relics' cults, mobility, and hagiography to marriage, family and gender issues in Carolingian times (8th–10th centuries). He is currently editing, together with Annamaria Pazienza (Ca' Foscari University, Venice – University of Tübingen), a special issue of the *Mélanges de l'École Française de Rome – Moyen Âge* on the mobility of the living and the dead in the Early Middle Ages (forthcoming).

Katharina Winckler
is working as researcher at the *Institute for Medieval History* in Vienna. Since her PhD, published as *Die Alpen im Frühmittelalter. Die Geschichte eines Raumes in den Jahren 500 bis 800* (Wien 2012), she has focused on spatial history, the economic and social history of the alpine region and Agilolfingian and Carolingian Bavaria. For the project *Digitising Patterns of Power* (2015–2018) she worked with an interdisciplinary team on the digitization and visualisation of power in space with a case study on the territory of the Bavarian bishops. Currently she works on her habilitation project – *Migration als Thema gelehrten Denkens. Eine Untersuchung vormoderner und frühneuzeitlicher Ansätze einer Migrationstheorie* – investigating and visualising ideas of territory in the southeast part of the Carolingian empire.

Ian Wood
obtained a PhD. at Corpus Christi College Oxford. He is currently Professor Emeritus at the University of Leeds where he has been since 1976, since 1995 as Professor of Early Medieval History. He has held guest professorships at the universities of Vienna (1994–1995, 2000) and Rhus (1997), and fellowships at the Netherlands Institute for Advanced Study (1995–1996), the British School at Rome (2006) and the Collegium Budapest (2009). Since 2019 Wood is member of the British Academy. Wood's research focuses on the history of the Early Middle Ages, the history of missions in Europe, early medieval historiography and the transition from Late Antiquity to the Middle Ages. After co-ordinating the European Science Foundation's scientific program on the Transformation of the Roman World (1992–1998), he was one of the principal investigators of the HERA-funded project *Cultural memory and the resources of the past, 400–1000 AD*. Among his most recent publications are (with A. O'Hara) *Jonas of Bobbio, Life of Columbanus, Life of John of Réomé, and Life of Vedast* (Liverpool 2017) and *The Transformation of the Roman West* (Leeds 2018).

Index of Places, Names and Subjects

Rulers (emperors, kings; caliphs, emirs) and their relatives have been formatted in small caps; both they and the antique authors appear under the names with which they are commonly referred to in Anglo-American bibliography. Other Roman personal names are sorted by *gentilicia*.

Aachen 219
abbot-bishop 125–126, 132, 304, 312, 322
ABD-AL-RAHMĀN II OF CÓRDOBA 144
ABD-AL-RAHMĀN III OF CÓRDOBA 145
Acacian Schism 184, 188
admonitio generalis 218
admonitio synodalis 86
Adoptionist controversy 142
AGAPETUS, BISHOP OF ROME 185, 187, 190–193, 199–200
Agaune 175, 178
Agericus, bishop of Verdun 207–208
Agobard, archbishop of Lyon 88
Aix-en-Provence/Aquae Sextiae 33, 41, 43–44, 48–49
Al-Andalus 143–144, 148, 154
Álava 146, 148
Alemannia 124, 127
ALFONSO II OF ASTURIAS 144
ALFONSO III OF ASTURIAS 145–147, 322
ALFONSO IV OF LEÓN 152
ALFONSO VI OF LEÓN 155
AMALASUINTHA 190, 195
Ambrose, bishop of Milan 222, 226, 228–235, 269, 274, 277, 279
Ammianus Marcellinus 252, 255, 258
Andelot 207
Andreas of Bergamo 229–230, 235
Angilbert, archbishop of Milan 229–235
Anselm, archbishop of Milan 219, 229
Anthimus, patriarch of Constantinople 183, 191–192, 194–195, 197
apocrisiary 295–296
Aprunculus, bishop of Langres/bishop of Auvergne 167, 171, 173–175
Aquis 316–317
Aquitaine 85, 118, 171–172, 228, 273, 275
Arab conquest of 711 142–143

Arbeo/Aribo, bishop of Freising 118, 121–122, 128
Arianism/Homoean 14, 58–60, 62, 64–68, 167, 170, 173, 175, 178, 184, 186–187, 189–190, 193, 200, 286, 290, 292–293
Arles/Arelate 6, 8, 14, 27, 31–33, 35–36, 38–40, 42–44, 48–49, 170, 172, 275, 279, 312
Arn, archbishop of Salzburg 124, 129, 131–132
Assidona/Medina Sidonia 285–288, 296
Astorga/Asturica Augusta 142, 144
ATHALARIC/ATHALARICUS 186–187, 189–190, 196
ATHANAGILD 286–287, 292, 295, 303
Athanasius, bishop of Alexandria 252–253, 255, 258, 260
Austrasia 207–208, 211
Auvergne 171
Auxerre/Autessiodurum 127
Ávila/Abula 142
Avitus, bishop of Vienne 49–50, 167–170, 173, 175–178

Baetica 141–142, 270, 285–286, 293
Bagauda, bishop 289–290, 293
Balearic Islands 286–287
Basilio, bishop of Muñó 150–151
Bavaria 117–119, 121–127, 129–130, 132, 156, 219, 225–226
Belisarius 193–196, 198, 200
Benedict of Aniane 223–224
BERNARD OF ITALY 219, 227, 229
Bertchram/Bertram, bishop of Le Mans 211–212
Besançon/Vesontio 37, 39
Bischofshofen 123–125, 130
Boethius 185–187, 189, 199
Boniface, archbishop of Mainz 99, 108–109, 115, 119–120, 122, 132
BONIFATIUS, BISHOP OF ROME 35, 252–253

Bordeaux/Burdigala   16, 28, 267, 269, 273, 275–277
Braga/Bracara Augusta   16, 145–146, 302, 304, 311–313, 315–316, 318–321
Braulius, bishop of Zaragoza   314–315
Brescia   88, 235
Breves Notitiae   115, 123–124
Breviarium (Liberatus)   185, 191
Britonia   301, 304
BRUNHILD OF AUSTRASIA   205–206, 208–209
Burgundia   48–49, 127, 167, 171, 174, 178, 211, 219
Byzantine court   302
Byzantine Hispania   16, 58, 140, 285, 289–296
Byzantium   15, 183, 185, 199, 303

calendae   87
caliphate   148
canones   70, 83–84, 89–91, 96, 116, 131, 140, 154–155, 169, 171, 176–178, 214, 268, 270–272, 279–280, 304–307, 310–311, 316, 320
Cardeña   150–153
caritas   1, 3, 55, 57, 84, 310
CARLOMAN   85, 228
Carolingian *correctio*   218, 222–224, 227, 234
Carolingian court   116
Carolingian reforms   15, 82, 224, 234
Cartagena/Carthago Spartaria   285–287, 291–292, 294, 296
Carthaginiensis   286, 292–293
Castile   139, 146–152, 154–155
Catholicism   59–60, 64–66, 68, 125, 168, 170, 173–175, 285, 289–290, 293, 301–302, 309
Celidonius, bishop of Besançon   37, 41
CHARLEMAGNE   123, 126–127, 131, 144, 217–218, 228–229
CHARLES THE BALD   81, 88
CHILDEBERT II OF AUSTRASIA   207–208
CHILDERIC   171, 208–209, 211
CHILPERIC OF NEUSTRIA   83, 169–170, 173, 206, 208
CHINDASVIND/FLAVIUS CHINDASVINDUS REX   314–315
Chronicle of Alfonso III   145, 147–148
CHROTECHILDIS/CLOTILDE   168, 174
church councils
 – Gaul
  – Agde (506)   171, 302

 – Arles (449–461)   311–312
 – Auxerre (585)   82
 – Bordeaux (384)   16, 267
 – Douzy (871)   89
 – Lyon (518/23)   169, 176–177
 – Orange (441)   5, 9, 36, 39–40
 – Orleans (538)   84
 – Riez (439)   5, 9, 36, 39
 – Trier (386)   269
 – Tusey (860)   89
 – Vaison (529)   9, 82
 – Italy
 – Milan (355)   255
 – Rome (417)   32, 34
 – Turin (398/399)   28, 31, 33, 267, 279
 – Iberian Peninsula
 – Braga (561)   312
 – Braga (572)   70, 305
 – Braga (675)   319
 – Coyanza (1055)   155–156
 – Huesca (589)   16, 321
 – Merida (666)   310, 316
 – Saragossa (380)   267–268, 270, 272–273
 – Seville (619)   316
 – Toldeo (589)   57, 65, 142, 287, 290
 – Toledo (400)   267
 – Toledo (633)   8, 316
 – Toledo (653)   290, 306, 314–315
 – Toledo (656)   302, 309
 – Toledo (681)   313, 316
 – Toledo (688)   319
 – others
  – Chalcedon (451)   83
  – Epaon (517)   169, 171, 176
Claudius, *dux* of Lusitania   66–67
Clermont/Arvernis   44, 49, 82, 167, 170–172, 174, 210
CLOTAR/CLOTHAR II   206, 211–213
CLOVIS   48, 174
Codex Carolinus   130
Codex of San Millán   153
Codex regularum/codices regularum   154, 317
coemeterium Maximi   253
Columbanus   118, 120, 125
Comenciolus   285, 294, 296
comes   66

Index of Places, Names and Subjects — 335

Constantinople   15-16, 183, 185-200, 253, 259, 291, 294-296
Constantius, bishop of Uzès   37, 41-42
conversion   8, 59-60, 64-66, 68, 99-100, 117, 122, 142, 144, 175, 211, 285, 289-290, 293-294, 296, 301-306
Corbie   91
Corbinian, bishop of Freising   121-123, 126, 132
Córdoba/Corduba   144-145
Coucy   90
Crónica Albeldense   145-146
cult of saints   10, 15, 61-62, 72-73, 117, 120, 217, 220-221, 225-228, 230-233, 235-236, 290

Damasian epigrams   258, 262
DAMASUS, BISHOP OF ROME   256-257, 262, 269, 272, 274, 278
dean   84-85, 87-88, 153
Delphinus, bishop of Bordeaux   270, 273-275
Denia/Dianium   286, 287
Desiderius, bishop of Vienne   15, 205, 207, 212-213
diocesan clergy   3, 6-7, 14, 16, 34, 56, 69-71, 75, 81-91, 107, 153, 210-213, 220, 222-224, 229, 315
dioecesis Hispaniarum   285, 287
Dionysius, bishop of Milan   255
disputatio   43-44, 62
Divisio regnorum   218
Dobdagrecus, abbot-bishop   125-126
Dume/Dumio   146, 302-306, 309, 311-315, 317, 319-321
dux   66-67

ecclesiastical primacy   31, 34, 36, 39, 217
Edict of Milan   253
Egidius, bishop of Reims   15, 205, 207-209,
Egino, bishop of Verona   222-227
Egyptian monasticism   306, 314
Elche/Illici   286-287
Embrun/Ebrodunum   37, 43-44, 48
Emmeram, bishop of Regensburg   118, 121-123, 127, 132
Episcopal
– abbey   303-304

– authority   14, 55, 68-69, 71, 73, 76, 83-84, 100-101, 105, 107, 149, 155, 219
– domus   310-311
– exile   28, 48, 249, 256, 261-263
– residence   62, 66, 125
Ercavica/Arcavica   291
Eugenius II, metropolitan of Toledo   315
Eulalia of Mérida   12, 61, 65, 73
Eulogio of Córdoba   144
EUSEBIUS, BISHOP OF ROME   250, 253, 256-258, 262
Eutropius   168, 291-293
Evodius   82, 276
excommunication   32, 34, 70, 90, 104, 176-177, 209-210, 214, 248, 272-273, 320
exhortatio humilitatis   308
exile   11, 15, 28, 50, 55-56, 59, 63-68, 73, 76, 100, 167-168, 171-175, 177, 184-185, 192, 194, 197-198, 200, 209, 212, 214, 247-263, 274, 276, 285, 296, 320

Faustinus, bishop of Braga   319-321
Faustus, bishop of Riez   47, 49, 171-173
Favars   86
FELIX II., BISHOP OF ROME   258-259
Felix, bishop of Dumio   320-321
Felix, bishop of Trier   278-280
Felmiro, bishop of Valpuesta   152
Fernán González, count of Castile   148, 151-152
Fidelis, bishop of Merida   55, 57, 69-74
Flodoard of Reims   88
Florentius, bishop of Orange (?)   176-178
Formula vitae honestae   307-309
Fredegar   205-206, 212
FREDEGUND OF NEUSTRIA   209, 211
Freising   115-116, 119, 124, 126, 128-129
Fructuosus, bishop of Braga-Dumio   311-321
funerary inscriptions   258, 262

Gallaecia   141, 302-303, 306, 315, 317, 321
Goths
– Visigoths   15-16, 47-50, 56, 59, 64, 139, 142, 150, 167, 170, 172, 286-289, 290, 292, 294, 296, 303, 312
– Ostrogoths   178, 184-185, 190-196, 198-199
governor   285, 294
GRATIANUS   273, 275

Gregorianum-Hadrianum 223–224
GREGORY I (THE GREAT), BISHOP OF ROME 98–99, 102, 205, 211, 213, 287–289, 294–296
Gregory, bishop of Tours 59, 64, 83, 167, 169–171, 174–175, 205, 208–209, 211, 232–233, 303
Guisando, Abbot 149, 152
GUNDOBAD 168–171, 173–175, 178
GUNTRAM OF ORLÉANS 206, 209–211

HADRIAN/ADRIANUS/ADRIAN II., POPE 81, 88, 90
Hedenulf, bishop of Loan 86
Henotikon 184
heresy 16, 35, 59, 62, 116, 118, 120–121, 123, 126, 187, 252, 267, 275–276, 278, 293–294
HERMENEGILD 59, 64, 286–287, 290–292
herovalliana collection 89
heterodoxy 29, 184, 318
Hilarius/Hilary, bishop of Arles 1, 2, 4–6, 8–9, 27, 36–42, 44, 46
Hilarius/Hilary, bishop of Narbonne 32–35
HILARIUS/HILARY, POPE 6, 7, 15, 17, 142
Hincmar, archbishop of Reims 81, 84–91
Hincmar, bishop of Loan 81, 88–91
Historia Apostolica 194, 196
Hydatius, bishop of Mérida 269–270, 272–273, 276–277

Ianuarius, bishop of Malaca 16, 285, 287–288, 296
Iberian Peninsula 13–16, 55–56, 64–65, 70, 267–270, 273, 275, 285–287, 292–293, 295
Ibiza/Ebussus 285–287
imitatio Imperii 58, 197
imperial court 197, 269, 273, 276, 279, 295
Ingenuus, bishop of Embrun 37, 40–41, 43–44,
Irish christianity 120, 123, 125, 156
Irish mission 118, 120–121, 126, 303
Isidore of Seville/Isidorus Hispalensis, bishop of Seville 8, 58–61, 64, 155, 269, 287–290, 292–295, 302, 304, 308
Ithacius, bishop of Ossonoba 268–269, 271, 273–279
ius possessionis 311

Jimeno 153

JOHN I, POPE 15, 183, 185–186, 188, 190, 192, 199–200, 250
JUSTIN 183, 187–190, 200
JUSTINIAN 15, 183, 185–200, 253, 259, 286, 292–293, 295

Langres/Langres-Passau/Civitas Lingonum 127–128, 171
Laon 45, 87, 90
lapsi 256
Le Mans/Suindinum 211–212
Leander, bishop of Seville 291, 293, 295
LEO I., BISHOP OF ROME 5–6, 9, 36–38, 40, 42–43, 45, 183
Leodegarius, bishop of Autun 83
León 141, 144–146, 155
LEOVIGILD/LIUVIGILD 14, 55, 57–65, 67, 73, 286, 290–293
Leudigisus, bishop of Braga 319, 321
Liber Commicus 154
Liber confraternitatum 119, 124–125
Liber Constitutionum 169
Liber Iudicum 154
Liber pontificalis 119, 185–189, 192, 194–195, 197, 255, 257–258
Liber scintillarum 218
Liber Vitae Patrum 169, 174
LIBERIUS, BISHOP OF ROME 196, 250–252, 255–256, 258–260, 262
Licinianus, bishop of Carthago Spartaria 16, 286–296
Life of Ambrose 231, 233
Life of Apollinaris of Valence 168
Life of Avitus of Vienne 168
Life of Caesarius of Arles 173
Life of Coronatus 226
Life of Marcellus of Die 168
Life of saint Zeno 225
Limoges 86
Lindisfarne 98–100, 311
Lisieux/Noviomagus Lexoviorum 209–210
Liuti/Liudi/Liudinus, bishop 123–125
Liuva, bishop of Braga 319, 321
Liviana 171
Lodève/Luteva 35, 48
Lorch/Lauriacum 117
LOTHAR 227, 229–230, 233

Louis the Pious   114, 227–229, 233
Lucifer, bishop of Cagliari   254–256
Lugo/Lucus Augusti   146, 305, 322
Lusitania   57, 74, 270
Lycia   183, 185, 253
Lyon/Lugdunum   168, 176–177

Macedonius   274
magister militum   6, 28, 38, 45–46, 170
Magnus Maximus   16, 267, 269, 275, 277
Málaga/Malaca   285, 287
maleficium   276
Mamertus, bishop of Vienne   45–47, 170
manichaeism   173
Manno, bishop of Neuburg   128
Marcellus, bishop of Rome   250–251, 253, 256–257, 262
Marcianus, bishop of Augusta Vindelicorum (?)   255–256, 261–262
Mareas   259–260, 262
Marseille/Massilia   33–34, 41, 44, 172, 211
Martin, abbot/bishop of Dumio   16, 302–309, 311–313,
Martin, bishop of Tours   16, 232–233, 267–269, 276–279
martyrs   10, 62, 64, 68, 72, 123, 144, 210, 213, 221, 226–227, 231–232, 234, 252, 277
Masona, bishop of Merida   2, 14, 55, 57–58, 60–63, 65–68, 73–75
Maurice/Mauricius Tiberius   285, 289, 292–296
Maximus, bishop of Neaples   169, 254–256
Merida/Mérida/Augusta Emerita   55–57, 60–61, 63, 65–67, 69, 71, 73–74, 145
Merovingians   48, 50, 82–83, 122, 171, 178, 205–207, 210, 214, 233
metropolitan bishop   5–7, 14, 16, 27–51, 57–58, 63, 82, 98, 102, 140, 142, 144, 170, 228, 301, 305–306, 312, 314–321
Milan/Mediolanum   15, 196, 217, 226, 228–229, 231–236, 252, 255, 269, 274, 279
monastery   2, 116, 123–124, 126–130, 152, 169, 171, 175, 177–178, 212, 225, 230, 233, 234
monastery Agali   301, 304
– monastery of Aquis   316–317
– monastery of Asán   16, 285, 288, 290, 293
– monastery of Dumio   16, 301–302, 306, 309, 311–312, 318

– monastery of Lérins   8, 38
– monastery of Saint Bénigne   127
– monastery of San Victorián
– (San Martín de Asán)   289
– monastery of Servitanus   291–292
– *monasterium Maximi*   303
monastic bishop   14, 110, 116, 120, 125–127
Mondoñedo   146, 321–322
Monophysitism   191, 194, 259, 293–294
Mouzon   90
Muñó   150–151

Narbonne/Narbo Martius   37, 43, 47–48
neophyte   258–259
Nepopis, bishop of Merida   55, 73–75
nepotism   71
nestorianism   197
Neuburg/Nova Civitate   128
Neustria   83, 208, 212
Nicene-Calcedonians   293
Noricum   115
Notitia Arnonis   123–124

Odilo, duke of Bavaria   120, 124–125, 128
Orange/Arausio   5, 9, 36, 39, 49
Ordoño I of Asturias   144
Osma   142, 146, 150

papal authority   6, 29–29, 31, 33–34, 41–42, 45–47, 50, 98–99, 101, 106, 110–111, 183–184, 193, 196
papal travels   30, 183, 185, 188, 191, 199–200, 295
parroquiale suevum   309
Passau   115, 119, 123, 126, 128–131
Passio et translatio Firmi et Rustici   226
passio   83, 121, 212–213, 225–227
patriarch   120, 130, 188, 191–192, 194, 200, 247, 295–296
Patroclus, bishop of Arles   5, 28, 31–35
patronage   10, 61, 72, 74, 76, 279
Paulus, bishop of Merida   57, 69–71
Pavia/Ticinum   168, 218, 228
Pechina/Urci   286–287
persecution   15, 59, 167–168, 171, 173–175, 177–178, 183–184, 186–187, 189, 226, 250–251, 253, 278

Phoebadius, bishop of Agen   270, 274
PIPPIN OF ITALY   217–218, 225, 229
PLACIDUS VALENTINIANUS III.   35, 38, 42
plot   59, 67, 174, 184, 194, 208–209, 320
Potamius, bishop of Braga   313
Praetextatus, bishop of Rouen   83, 207–209
praetorian prefecture   2, 9, 196, 199
Priscillian, bishop of Ávila   16, 267–278
Priscillianism   16, 29, 34, 267–281
Proculus, bishop of Marseille   32–34
Proculus, bishop of Tours   167, 174
pseudoepiscopus   68, 273

Raetia   115–116, 227
RAMIRO II OF LEÓN   148
Ratold, bishop of Verona   222–223, 225–228
Ravenius, bishop of Arles   36, 38, 42–44
Ravenna   183–186, 193, 195, 250
Rebellion of Bernhard of Italy   219, 229
Rebellion of Byzantine bishops   296
Rebellion of Hermenegild   59, 64, 286–287, 290, 292
RECCARED   57, 60, 65–68, 142, 285–286, 289–291, 293–295
RECCESWINTH   309
Regensburg/Castra Regina   115–116, 119, 121, 129
Regino of Prüm   86
Regna
– Gaul
  – Burgundian Kingdom   48–49
  – Carolingian Kingdom   230
  – Frankish Kingdom   83, 167, 175
  – Visigothic Kingdom   28, 178
– Iberian Peninsula
  – Kingdom of Asturias   143–144, 147–148, 207
  – Kingdom of León   139, 145, 154–155
  – Kingdom of Pamplona   148
  – Kingdom of Toledo   145
  – Visigothic Kingdom   15, 48–49, 58–59, 141, 167, 286
  – Suevic Kingdom   140, 302, 309, 312
– Italy
  – Lombard Kingdom   217, 219, 226, 228
  – Ostrogothic Kingdom   192
Regula communis   318–319

Reichenau   222–224, 226
Reims/Civitas Remorum   14, 28, 81, 87, 89, 207
Remigius, bishop of Reims   45, 48, 122
Richimirus, bishop of Dumio   306, 309–312
Riculfus   83
Riez/Colonia Julia Augusta Apollinarium Reiorum   5, 37, 171
Rimini/Ariminum   184
Rodez/Ruthena Civitas   174
Rome   5–7, 12, 14–15, 29–31, 35–36, 38, 41–47, 50, 88, 90–91, 97, 106, 111, 116, 118, 120, 122, 141–142, 183–185, 191, 193–200, 223, 228, 247, 249–253, 255–260, 262, 269, 274
Rothad, bishop of Soissons   81, 88
Rouen/Rotomagus   29
royal *diploma*   96
Rupert, bishop of Salzburg   119, 121–123, 132

Säben/Sabiona   115, 117, 122, 129, 261
Saint Gall   217–218, 222, 227
Salamanca   146
Salzburg   115–116, 119, 123–126, 129–132
San Millán de la Cogolla   150, 153
Santiago   145–146
Saragossa/Zaragoza/Caesaraugusta   64, 270, 272–273, 315
schism   118, 120, 184, 188, 252–253, 259
scriptoria   149, 153
secular authorities   3, 10, 14, 42, 55, 57–58, 66, 81, 140, 149, 156, 168, 184, 198–199, 206, 248, 265, 267, 273–274, 288, 294, 307
Sendgericht   85
Septimania   66, 141
Severus, bishop of Malaca   286–288, 296
Sidonius Apollinaris, bishop of Clermont   44, 49, 167, 169–173, 303
SIGEBERT I   205–208, 210
SIGISMUND   169–170, 175–178
Silvanus, bishop of Calahorra   7, 142
SILVERIUS, BISHOP OF ROME   183, 185, 193–196, 200, 253, 258
Simplicius, bishop of Vienne   32–34
Sintpert, bishop   128–129
Sisibertus, metropolitan of Toledo   320
Sisteron/Segustero   171
Smaragdus of Saint Mihiel   155

social networks   10, 16, 28, 38–43, 50, 88, 127, 143, 146–148, 155–156, 178, 220, 234, 279–280
Soissons   45, 88
Spaniae   58
Stephanus of Assidona, bishop   285, 287, 296
Stephanus, bishop of Merida   56, 316
Stephanus, treasurer of Sigismund   176–178
suffragan bishop/bishoprics   27, 29–31, 40–41, 43–45, 50, 87–90, 102, 228, 235–236, 318
Sunna, arian bishop of Merida   55, 60–62, 66–68, 73, 76
SYMMACHUS, BISHOP OF ROME   49, 184–185
Symposius, bishop of Astorga   271–273, 277, 280
Syracuse/Syracusae   185, 253

THEODAHAD   185–187, 190–193, 195,
THEODERIC   184–190, 193, 197–200
THEODERIC/THEODORIC II   61, 212
Theodo, duke of Bavaria   118–119, 121–122, 133
Theodore, bishop of Tours   168, 174
THEODOSIUS I.   233, 270, 275
Theodulf, bishop of Orléans   85, 223–224
THEUDELINDA/THEUDELINDE   117, 120–122
Thomas, *archbishop* of Milan   228, 232
Tituli Fuldenses   226
Toledo/Toletum   8, 63, 142, 144–145, 267, 280, 290, 311, 314–315, 320
TOTILA/BADUILA   195, 198–199
Toulouse/Tolosa   48, 172
Tours/Civitas Turonorum   30, 44–45, 83, 168, 171, 233
Trisingus   81, 90–91
Turin/Augusta Taurinorum   32–33, 279
tyrannus   257, 262, 308

Umayyads   13, 16

usurpation   33, 210, 275, 294
Uzès/Eutica   37, 48

Valencia/Valentia   291
VALENTINIANUS II.   275
Valeránica   152–154
Valpuesta   149–153
Vandals   177, 183–184, 286
Vaudreuil   209
Verona   15, 217, 221–229
via salaria   252–253, 259
Victricius, bishop of Rouen   29–30
Vienne/Vienna   31, 40, 42–43, 48, 212–213
VIGILIUS, BISHOP OF ROME   15, 183, 185, 194, 196–200
Vincentius, bishop of Caesaraugusta   59
Vincentius, bishop of Ibiza   287–288
Virgil, bishop of Salzburg   119–122, 124, 126, 128, 130–131
viris illustribus   292
Vita Abbatum Acaunensium   169
Vita Apollinaris   176–178
Vita Bonifatii   119, 128
Vita Columbani   118
Vita Corbiniani   121
Vita Epiphanii   168
Vita Eptadii   169
Vita Marcelli   168, 172
Vita Ruperti   121
Vitas Sanctorum Patrum Emeritensium   3, 55–58, 65–66, 68, 70, 75, 318
Viventiolus, archbishop of Lyon   176–178

WAMBA   309, 316–317
WITTERIC   66–67
Würzburg tractates   268–269

Zeno, bishop of Verona   222, 225–226
ZOSIMUS, BISHOP OF ROME   5, 31–34

www.ingramcontent.com/pod-product-compliance
Lightning Source LLC
Chambersburg PA
CBHW020220170426
43201CB00007B/270